Advances in Spatial Science

Springer

Berlin
Heidelberg
New York
Barcelona
Hong Kong
London
Milan
Paris
Tokyo

Titles in the Series

C. S. Bertuglia, M. M. Fischer and *G. Preto* (Eds.)
Technological Change, Economic Development and Space
XVI, 354 pages. 1995. ISBN 3-540-59288-1
(out of print)

H. Coccossis and *P. Nijkamp* (Eds.)
Overcoming Isolation
VII, 272 pages. 1995. ISBN 3-540-59423-X

L. Anselin and *R. J. G. M. Florax* (Eds.)
New Directions in Spatial Econometrics
XVX, 420 pages. 1995. ISBN 3-540-60020-5

H. Eskelinen and *F. Snickars* (Eds.)
Competitive European Peripheries
VIII, 271 pages. 1995. ISBN 3-540-60211-9

J. C. J. M. van den Bergh, P. Nijkamp and *P. Rietveld* (Eds.)
Recent Advances in Spatial Equilibrium Modelling
VIII, 392 pages. 1996. ISBN 3-540-60708-0
(out of print)

P. Nijkamp, G. Pepping and *D. Banister* (Eds.)
Telematics and Transport Behaviour
XII, 227 pages. 1996. ISBN 3-540-60919-9

D. F. Batten and *C. Karlsson* (Eds.)
Infrastructure and the Complexity of Economic Development
VIII, 298 pages. 1996. ISBN 3-540-61333-1

T. Puu
Mathematical Location and Land Use Theory
IX, 294 pages. 1997. ISBN 3-540-61819-8

Y. Leung
Intelligent Spatial Decision Support Systems
XV, 470 pages. 1997. ISBN 3-540-62518-6

C. S. Bertuglia, S. Lombardo and *P. Nijkamp* (Eds.)
Innovative Behaviour in Space and Time
X, 437 pages. 1997. ISBN 3-540-62542-9

A. Nagurney and *S. Siokos*
Financial Networks
XVI, 492 pages. 1997. ISBN 3-540-63116-X

M. M. Fischer and *A. Getis* (Eds.)
Recent Developments in Spatial Analysis
X, 434 pages. 1997. ISBN 3-540-63180-1

R. H. M. Emmerink
Information and Pricing in Road Transportation
XVI, 294 pages. 1998. ISBN 3-540-64088-6

P. Rietveld and *F. Bruinsma*
Is Transport Infrastructure Effective?
XVI, 384 pages. 1998. ISBN 3-540-64542-X

P. McCann
The Economics of Industrial Location
XII, 228 pages. 1998. ISBN 3-540-64586-1

L. Lundqvist, L.-G. Mattsson and *T. J. Kim* (Eds.)
Network Infrastructure and the Urban Environment
IX, 414 pages. 1998. ISBN 3-540-64585-3

R. Capello, P. Nijkamp and *G. Pepping* (Eds.)
Sustainable Cities and Energy Policies
XI, 282 pages. 1999. ISBN 3-540-64805-4

M. M. Fischer and *P. Nijkamp* (Eds.)
Spatial Dynamics of European integration
XII, 367 pages. 1999. ISBN 3-540-65817-3

M. M. Fischer, L. Suarez-Villa and *M. Steiner* (Eds.)
Innovation, Networks and Localities
XI, 336 pages. 1999. ISBN 3-540-65853-X

J. Stillwell, S. Geertman and *S. Openshaw* (Eds.)
Geographical Information and Planning
X, 454 pages. 1999. ISBN 3-540-65902-1

G. J. D. Hewings, M. Sonis, M. Madden and *Y. Kimura* (Eds.)
Understanding and Interpreting Economic Structure
X, 365 pages. 1999. ISBN 3-540-66045-3

A. Reggiani (Ed.)
Spatial Economic Science
XII, 457 pages. 2000. ISBN 3-540-67493-4

D. G. Janelle and *GD. C. Hodge* (Eds.)
Information, Place, and Cyberspace
XII, 381 pages. 2000. ISBN 3-540-67492-6

P. W. J. Batey and *P. Freidrich* (Eds.)
Regional Competition
VIII, 290 pages. 2000. ISBN 3-540-67548-5

B. Johansson, Ch. Karlsson and *R. R. Stough* (Eds.)
Theories of Endogenous Regional Growth
IX, 428 pages. 2001. ISBN 3-540-&7988-X

G. Clarke and *M. Madden* (Eds.)
Regional Science in Business
VIII, 363 pages. 2001. ISBN 3-540-41780-X

M. M. Fischer and *Y. Leung* (Eds.)
GeoComputational Modelling
XII, 279 pages. 2001. ISBN 3-540-41968-3

M. M. Fischer and *J. Fröhlich* (Eds.)
Knowledge, Complexity and Innovation Systems
XII, 477 pages. 2001. ISBN 3-540-41969-1

M. M. Fischer, J. Revilla Diez and *F. Snickars*
Metropolitan Innovation Systems
VIII, 270 pages. 2001. ISBN 3-540-41967-5

L. Lundqvist and *L.-G. Mattson* (Eds.)
National Transport Models
VIII, 202 pages. 2002. ISBN 3-540-42486-1

J. R. Cuadrado-Roura and *M. Parellada*
Regional Convergence in the European Union
VIII, 368 pages. 2002. ISBN 3-540-43242-6

Geoffrey J. D. Hewings
Michael Sonis
David Boyce
Editors

Trade, Networks and Hierarchies

Modeling Regional and Interregional Economies

With 100 Figures
and 111 Tables

Springer

Prof. Geoffrey J. D. Hewings
University of Illinois
Regional Economics Applications Laboratory
607 S. Mathews,
Urbana, IL 61801-3671, USA

Prof. Michael Sonis
Bar Ilan University
Department of Geography, Faculty of Social Sciences
52900 Ramat-Gan, Israel

Prof. David Boyce
University of Illinois at Chicago
Department of Civil and Materials Engineering,
Transport Laboratory (TransLab)
842 W. Taylor Street (M/C 246)
Chicago, IL 60607-7023, USA

Library of Congress Cataloging-in-Publication Data applied for
Die Deutsche Bibliothek – CIP-Einheitsaufnahme
Trade, Networks and Hierarchies: Modeling, Regional and Interregional Economies;
with 111 Tables / Geoffrey J. D. Hewings ... (Ed.). –
Berlin; Heidelberg; New York; Barcelona; Hong Kong; London; Milan; Paris; Tokyo: Springer, 2002
(Advances in Spatial Science)

ISBN 978-3-642-07712-8

Springer-Verlag Berlin Heidelberg New York
a member of BertelsmannSpringer Science + Business Media GmbH

http://www.springer.de

Printed in Germany

Cover design: Erich Kirchner, Heidelberg

For Philip Israilevich, 1948-1997

A REAL mensch

Preface

In 1989, after several years of discussion and negotiation, the Regional Economics Applications Laboratory (REAL) was formed. This unique relationship between the Federal Reserve Bank of Chicago and the University of Illinois at Urbana-Champaign has been a significant source of intellectual inspiration for many students, visiting colleagues and members of the participating institutions for the past decade.

The idea for REAL was hatched by Philip Israilevich and Geoffrey Hewings in typical Chicago style – in the back room of a local bar. In early December 1997, their collaboration came to an untimely end when Philip died after a three-year battle with cancer.

The challenge of moving across a spectrum from theory to model development to implementation and interpretation provided the underlying motivation for REAL's formation together with an equally important component, namely the translation of many of these efforts into a form that could be understood and implemented by policy-makers. For Philip, REAL and the Regional Science Association International provided the forums for his intellectual endeavors, although he also contributed many papers in banking. In recognition of his contributions and to provide a sense of the current research in the fields in which he published, many of the authors of these chapters assembled in Chicago in November, 1998 to participate in a small seminar in his honor. Several others who were not able to come nevertheless contributed chapters to this volume. Subsequently, all of the papers have been revised and updated.

The authors would like to thank the Federal Reserve Bank of Chicago for hosting the seminar and particularly for the support provided by Dr. Curt Hunter, Senior Vice President and Director of Research and his assistant, Shirley Harris as well as the encouragement generated by Dr. Douglas Evanoff. Gerry Gallagher of REAL also helped with the logistics as well as facilitating many of the interactions between the authors. The economics' editorial staff of Springer has been incredibly helpful and patient and they are to be thanked for their continuing support of this field.

Finally, we hope that Philip's wife Sue and his children, Rebecca and Isaac, will take pride in the fact that so many colleagues took the time to honor an individual who had touched their lives in so many ways. While this book is dedicated to Philip, you helped create an environment that enabled him to succeed academically, and for that we thank you.

Geoffrey J.D. Hewings
Michael Sonis
David Boyce

Chicago, January, 2002

Preface

Table of Contents

Part II Structure and Structural Change

Part III Methodological Issues

1 Introduction

Geoffrey J.D. Hewings,[1] Michael Sonis[2] and David Boyce[3]

[1] Regional Economics Applications Laboratory, University of Illinois at Urbana-Champaign, USA
e-mail: hewings@uiuc.edu
[2] Regional Economics Applications Laboratory, University of Illinois at Urbana-Champaign, USA and Bar Ilan University, Israel
e-mail: sonism@mail.biu.ac.il
[3] Department of Civil and Materials Engineering, University of Illinois at Chicago, USA
e-mail: dboyce@uic.edu

1.1 Overview

There was a time, in the rather recent past, where it was relatively easy to classify contributions to regional science in terms of contributions to specific sub-fields, such as location theory, transportation systems analysis, regional economic modeling and so forth. In the interim, enormous strides have been taken to combine many of the prevailing modeling paradigms into more comprehensive, integrated systems. As a result of these processes, considerable progress has been made in solving problems at the "edge" of the sub-fields; the intellectual spillover from these challenges has been considerable and is reflected in many of the contributions in this volume.

This integration is best reflected in the emerging area of what may be referred to as spatial trade modeling. While the myriad contributions in spatial interaction modeling that have explored gravity, entropy, intervening opportunities and the major problems of allocation and distribution across networks, these ideas were largely absent from the more classical trade models in economic trade theory. As regional scientists embraced the opportunities presented by the new computable general equilibrium models, economists began to re-discover space, the role of geographical separation and the extensive insights that could be gleaned from an approach now characterized as a combination of new economic geography and new trade theory.

However, there are many other areas of integration that have challenged the field – linking environmental and economic systems, addressing issues of innovation diffusion, economic restructuring and model specification. Several of the chapters in this volume have been motivated by these challenges. What is emerging, then, is a field in which trade, networks and hierarchies characterize the new integrated models – hence the choice of the title for the contributions.

1.2 Trade and Transportation

One of the areas in which the blurring of distinctions between models and spatial specification has been most apparent is in trade impact analysis. The term region has been used to specify trading relationships among blocks of countries, interregionally within countries or even within metropolitan area. The recent publication of Fujita *et al.* (1999) has served to stimulate the notion of the spatial economy as an important organizing principle in understanding how economies function, interact and develop varying degrees of direct and indirect dependence on each other.

The first two chapters explore linkages between trade and transportation. While it has long been argued theoretically that transportation networks play an important role in facilitating interaction and conditioning the volume and direction of trade (in goods as well as people), measurement of these impacts has proven to be more elusive. Bröcker has had a long interest in trade modeling; in the present chapter, the focus is directed towards an assessment of the impacts of transportation investment on interregional income inequality in the EU. Using the masterplan for the European road network, he explores the impacts of changes in transportation costs. The methodology draws on a number of familiar traditions in regional science, including Alonso's theory of movement now incorporated into a spatial computable general equilibrium model. In fact, one of the major contributions of this chapter is the consistent formalism that ties spatial interaction, regional allocation and regional welfare measurements to the same, consistent theoretical framework. To this base, the CGE model handles monopolistic competition and links gravity-type models into the framework – again using a new, consistent theoretical underpinning.

The chapter by Boyce focuses on the US economy; in similar fashion to Bröcker, a transportation network appears prominently in the analysis. However, the major contribution is the integration of commodity flow models with transportation network analysis – something proposed many years ago, yet never realized empirically. The integration involves merging input-output and an interregional transportation network; the motivation derives in large part from the increased importance that interregional commodity flows play in the US economy on the one hand and the potential vulnerability of the system to disruptions generated by nature (such as earthquakes or floods). The model was successfully implemented for 24 region and 11 commodities, after some initial problems related to the existence of regions of varying size; the parameter values appeared reasonable and one attractive feature of the model, in contrast to other attempts to model similar systems, was the relatively rapid convergence of the solution.

Kouparitsas returns attention to regional trade at the level of nation states; he asked a deceptively simple question – why do countries pursue reciprocal trade agreements? Of course, generating the answer is not so simple and recourse to a CGE model for NAFTA enables a variety of approaches, drawing on recent, received trade theory, to be tested. The key issue is whether countries are better off liberalizing trade unilaterally or engaging in reciprocal trade agreements; compounding the problem is the small country-large country issue, manifested in the NAFTA context with Mexico-US interactions. One of the important findings from this analysis is that, irrespective of country size, unilateral liberalization always makes the liberalizing country worse off. This result is in apparent conflict with trade theory but only because Kouparitsas shows that for a wide range of estimates of the elasticity of substitution between domestic and foreign goods, small countries can influence their terms of trade. An interesting challenge would be to see whether this escape from the terms of-trade driven prisoners' dilemma would also apply to countries joining the expanding EU.

One of the more important aspects of globalization is the changing ownership of enterprises; there has been relatively little work on this issue, especially in terms of economic impact on specific economies. Drawing on well over a decade of experience with CGE models of the Scottish economy, Gillespie *et al.*, seek new insights into the employment impacts of foreign direct investment, but with the manufacturing sector disaggregated by ownership. A second innovation is the way in which inward FDI is assumed to impact the regional economy; in contrast to input-output-alone based modeling, the authors assume that in the short-run capacity constraints may exist and, in addition, they explore the role of local wage bargaining. Two further developments should be highlight – the time path of the region's response and the degree to which there might exist a distinct structure for the FDI sectors (for example, in the purchases and sales relationships). It turns out that the issue of structure is an important one in assessing FDI impacts at the regional level.

From Scotland, the focus of attention moves south of the equator to Brazil and to an examination of the trading patterns of a very important agricultural sector in that nation's economy, sugar cane. Guilhoto *et al.*, explore the national and regional impact of this sector and its associated economic complex, with the regional attention directed to the Northeast. This region enjoys an asymmetric relationship with the rest of Brazil – it is much more dependent on the latter than the rest of Brazil is on the Northeast. In the sugar cane industry, this dependency is further compounded by significant differences in production structure, reflecting differences in the age of technology that is used in this sector. These differences are visually highlighted through their presentation in a set of economic landscapes; the next task would be to incorporate these findings into one of the several multiregional CGE models of Brazil to explore some of the issues identified in the previous chapter by Gillespie *et al.*.

One of the major impediments to economic integration in Brazil is the transportation network; In contrast to the US and the countries of the EU, interregional trade is a much smaller portion of total trade. Hence, one would speculate that transportation investment would have significant spillover effects in one of the EU countries, the Netherlands. However, Oosterhaven and Stelder propose that *net* not gross multiplier effects should be considered and they seek to estimate the impacts on the rest of the economy from major transportation investments in Schiphol airport in Amsterdam or in the port of Rotterdam. In this way, it will be possible for some sectors in some regions to exhibit negative impacts – dependence on the rest of the country is higher than the rest of the country is dependent on the region (sector) in question.

Higano *et al.* construct a dynamic multi-region, multi-industry optimal programming model to estimate the economic development in each area, and then analyze what kind of economic change will occur in Taiwan by expanding and changing the transportation system by computer simulation and tracing the impacts on the environment. One of the main findings from these simulations is the suggestion that the drastic curtailment of emissions that has been proposed should not be performed at once, but phased in as a gradual curtailment of pollutant emissions. In this fashion, the impact on the economy would be minimized while attaining reasonable levels of environmental quality.

In contrast to the previous chapters that explored various aspects of trade at the macro or sectoral levels, the Giarratani *et al.* contribution models an intermediate good producing industry, ferrous scrap, that is characterized by significant changes in geographical location and technology over the past two decades. Why is this sector important? Essentially because scrap is a major input into the steel industry and can account for up to one-third of the sales price of a finished steel product. Further, the price of scarp varies across space and over time. Even though, as noted earlier, the interregional linkages within the US are well developed, elements of imperfect competition enter the scrap market, creating distortions that present a major challenge to modelers. In regional science, modeling individual sectors in this form has fallen out of favor in recent decades; the results presented in Giarratani *et al.* show just how valuable such an exercise can be in helping explain the behavior of "downstream" industrial sectors, especially ones such as the steel industry that enter into the production functions of almost every goods' producing activity.

1.3 Structure and Structural Change

The next set of chapters approaches economic structure from a variety of perspectives. Dietzenbacher and Hoekstra extend a growing literature in decomposition analysis; the importance stems from a need to generate insights into the nature of change in economic structure over time, to isolate the main contributors and to provide the basis for some assessment of the likely changes anticipated in the near term. For example, while many theorists challenged the utility of input-output based analyses as a result of assumptions surrounding the absence of coefficient change, empirical analysis revealed that, in many countries, changes in the structure of demand were far more important than changes in the structure of production. Employing an RAS-based approach, Dietzenbacher and Hoekstra decompose output growth in the Netherlands between 1975 and 1985 with an explicit focus on both coefficient change and changes in trading patterns with selected EU countries and the rest of the world. They find some important technological effects, most probably related to energy prices changes, and some more significant changes in demand, with changes in exports to some EU countries increasing and others decreasing output in the Netherlands.

A similar exploration, this time focusing on the Chicago economy, is provided by Okuyama *et al.*. Using a set of input-output tables generated for the period 1980-1997, analysis centers on application of the field of influence notion to explore the economy-wide impacts of changes in individual coefficients. At the macro level, the changes in the structure of the economy appear minimal; however, when attention is directed to more detailed, sector-by-sector evaluations, there is evidence of some important changes in, for example, the hierarchy of backward and forward linkages. The results confirm some earlier analyses that revealed a process of hollowing out, whereby intra-regional interdependence was replaced by inter-regional dependence. In contrast to this region-specific analysis, West's chapter is more general in scope and examines the role of assumptions in building spatial models. The challenge here is to be sure that when comparative analysis is undertaken, analysts are aware of the role of different assumptions and the implications that these differences will have for interpreting findings about, inter alia, the role of structural change. West's review encompasses input-output, CGE and the family of econometric and input-output systems that often serve as an intermediate modeling system between the relative simplicity of input-output and the economy-wide perspectives embraced by CGE models. As he notes, it would be difficult to propound arguments in favor of a single model; on the other hand, the modeling "market" seems to be converging on systems that are adapting to the perceived advantages of competitive models such that a more general system may eventuate.

One such set of models, the integration of econometric and input-output analysis, is the focus of attention in the chapter by Lesage and Rey. The explore forecasting differences for a variety of competing approaches that include interindustry demand variables and various Bayesian approaches as a way of addressing interindustry linkages. While the Bayesian approaches seemed to dominate, the results were not clear-cut; for example, the forecast horizon was an important component of the choice of approach, with over one third of the non-Bayesian estimators providing more accurate forecasts. While the absence of a clear "winner" might be seen as disappointing, the results provide some obvious challenge for additional work and reinforce West's findings that there are important trade-off issues that need to be considered in the construction of a models and in the evaluation of the results generated by competing models.

The Leontief-Strout gravity model is one of the most well known regional models in the literature. It has appeared in various guises in a variety of modeling systems. Roy approaches a similar problem to the one discussed in the Boyce chapter, but approaches it from a different perspective – introducing uncertainty, the role of capacity constraints and reflects on the way in which regional pricing information, were it to be available, could help shape the model. In this journey, Roy moves this modeling tradition much closer in spirit to the CGE framework and thus establishes a basis for a more extensive (and imaginative) interregional CGE system. By working with movements in quantity rather than monetary terms, he is able to reveal some additional modeling flexibility; most importantly, he shows the significant benefits to be gained from casting the system in a probabilistic rather than a deterministic framework. In the process, he has uncovered an apparent error in the input-output balance relations of the classical multi-regional model.

Testa, reflecting on the results of over a decade monitoring and interpreting the impressive restructuring of the Midwest economy over the period 1970-2000, reveals how many of the modeling systems described in earlier chapters can be used to aid in interpreting and explaining changes. Here, the effects of restructuring are presented in ways that justify the enormous investment in regional modeling – the insights could not have been generated from published data alone, but were garnered from explicit analysis. One of the important lessons to be learned from this exercise is the importance of translating model results into communicable language that can inform policy debates. In the same spirit, Kilkenny and Nalbarte, promote some new vision of what is important in an economy. Whereas Testa is examining large metropolitan and multistate economies, Kilkenny and Nalbarte focus their attention on smaller, rural economies. They promote the notion of a keystone sector, drawing on a rich literature that examines not just economic linkages but social contact spaces. The formalism, drawing on graph theoretic concepts will be familiar to many regional scientists; however, the procedures have been significantly modified and enhanced to produce a view of an economy that is very different. For example, regional scientists have rarely considered churches, clubs and other social organizations in their formal models; in the empirical example, it turned out that financial intermediators played a key role, but not exclusively in a classical input-output type of relationship. The one obvious challenge from this work is the forging of a link between economic and social networks – are their mutually reinforcing and to what extent do these intersections play a role in the economic development not only of rural communities but metropolitan ones as well.

Jackson and Dzikowski return attention to the Midwest, employing a spatial decomposition method to examine changes in economic structure in this region. The focus on this region may seem parochial, yet, as they remind us, it generates almost one fifth of the US personal income and almost a quarter of the nation's population. Some of their findings are surprising in view of the literature reviewed in Testa's chapter; it would appear that the states comprising the Midwest are still somewhat differentiated, even though trading relationships are increasing and are being dominated by intra-industry rather than interindustry trade. Their findings confirm some earlier analysis, using the economic landscape methodology described in the Guilhoto *et al.* chapter, that showed that while the macro structure (percentage allocation of output by sector) of these state economies was becoming more similar, the internal (input-output) structures remained rather diverse.

In seeking explanation for the diminution of the differences of the economic structures of different spatial regimes, reliance of the role of innovation would appear to be essential. Reggiani *et al.* provide a valuable account of the role of innovation and the various success factors associated with this process. Employing a variety of techniques, including neural network analysis, they explore ways of "forecasting" innovative industries. The policy implications are far-reaching and communities, states and countries vie with each other to create an environment conducive to the successful attraction of innovative industries and, equally importantly, to their launch into the productive system.

An essential feature of any economic system is the role of feedback processes; Sonis *at al.*, introduce the idea of a spatial production cycle and use this to examine integration within the Midwest economy of the US. These production cycles are explored using feedback loop analysis and an explicit hierarchy of trade flows is extracted. The impact of the methodology will be enriched when additional years of trade data are available so that explorations of the changes in the structure, intensity and spatial arrangements of these cycles can be documented. The limited evidence available from the EU and the US suggest that interregional trade intensity is increasing but the nature and direction of the trends, the identification of winners and losers in this competition remains unclear. Further, the integration of international and interregional spatial production cycles provides an obvious complement to the type of analysis revealed by Kouparitsas in his chapter of trade agreements.

The final section of this volume introduces some new perspectives on familiar and unfamiliar themes in regional science. Kimura *et al.*, propose a way to integrate the models of Sraffa, Leontief and Miyazawa. These various approaches have been viewed as separate systems with little or no formal linkage, although the Miyazawa-Leontief linkage is much better known and evaluated. In the spirit of West's chapter, the analysis described here attempts to forge a general umbrella under which each model can be nested and the explicit linkages identified. The resulting system provides for a richer array of possibilities for further analysis and, pedagogically, offers insights into the communality of thinking among three great contributors to the economic structure literature.

1.4 Methodological Issues

The next two chapters, by Israilevich and Haddad et al., address a problem that has not bee given much attention – just how important is the input-output accounting in the construction and application of CGE models? Israilevich's thinking, in progress at the time of his death, reflects concerns about the assumptions employed and the degree to which CGE models address issues of consistency in input-output relations as the model moves away from the calibration period. Haddad *et al.*, provide a comparative assessment, drawing on experiences with two different CGE systems, one grounded in the more familiar Walrasian system and the other in what may be referred to a Marshallian tradition. However, the problem is compounded by exactly the sort of comparative analysis problems articulated by West; for example, different closure rules may result in entirely different impacts from the role of input-output specification. This chapter adds one more set of issues to the list of those needing attention as model integration proceeds.

Changes in economic structure affect many other economic factors within a regional economy, as the chapters by Dietzenbacher and Hoekstra and Jackson and Dzikowksi revealed. One further set of factors, the environment, is explored by Fritz *et al.* The findings here reveal that the complex processes of interdependence characterizing the economic transactions serve to generate some unexpected results on pollution generation. Even with no changes in pollution generation coefficients, the direct and indirect impact on an economy undergoing structural change reveals a not intuitively obvious set of results. Further, the notion of indirect pollution generation highlights the role that demand plays in an economy; changes in the demand for products serves to change the needs within the regional economy and, indirectly, the type and quantity of pollutants. From a policy perspective, the analysis reveals the important need to consider structural change in formulating environmental regulations.

The final chapter addresses a problem familiar to all regional modelers – trying to construct sophisticated systems with limited data. Madsen and Jensen-Butler have labored for many years to improve the quality of regional and interregional economic models in Denmark. The present chapter reports some of their recent initiatives in the development of an interregional social accounting system. They reflect on these challenges under conditions of limited information and exploit some of the methodology that has been developed over the last two decades to fill in major gaps in ways that are theoretically and empirically supportable.

1.5 Final Thoughts

One of the major themes that emerges from this collection is the progress towards commonality in modeling perspectives and the enormous strides that have been taken in the development of integrated models. Of course, it is too early to claim that a common modeling platform has been achieved but the evidence is mounting that, little by little, apparently disparate modeling paradigms are yielding to more expansive views of the way the economy functions.

A collection such as this ten or twenty years ago would have exhibited sharp differences in perspectives between trade modelers and transportation modelers, between the input-output and the CGE folks and between those operating at one spatial scale and those at another. Whether the process of globalization has permeated the thinking of academics and practitioners is unclear, yet there is a remarkable degree of openness in thinking evident in the chapters in this volume and in presentations in professional meetings and in the published literature. What was formerly regarded as exogenous to one group of modelers is now being embraced endogenously and mergers of paradigms appear on the horizon.

Of course, it would be naïve to think that the process will be smooth, without difficulties and without some sharp conflicts. However, as Boyce noted in his chapter, the visionary thinking of Isard (1960) in his first comprehensive review of methods of regional science under the rubric "channels of synthesis" seems to resonate much more in current regional science work than in times past. While there are many, major challenges within specific modeling paradigms, scholars are increasingly coming to realize that the challenges of integration are even more exciting and it is hoped that this collection will encourage the next generation to continue to explore these issues.

Reference

Isard, W. 1960. *Methods of Regional Analysis*, MIT Press, Cambridge, MA.

Part I Trade and Transportation

2 Spatial Effects of European Transport Policy: a CGE Approach[1]

Johannes Bröcker

University of Kiel, Institute of Regional Research, D-24098 Kiel, Germany
e-mail: Broecker@economics.uni-kiel.de

2.1 Introduction

While transport policy had no high priority on the agenda of the European Community until the mid eighties, an increasing activity in this field has been witnessed during the last 15 years. After the European Court had sentenced the commission of having failed in promoting the common market in transport, the commission started to develop a common transport policy (CTP). The most important milestones are:

- Deregulation of trucking.
- Railway deregulation by separating infrastructure management and operation and guaranteeing non-discriminatory access to infrastructure.
- Deregulation of civil aviation, though still incomplete: fair competition in airport charging, slot regulation and computer reservation is yet to be brought about.
- Promoting interconnection and interoperability between nationally fragmented systems as well as between different modes.
- Applying progressively the principle of charging for marginal social costs not yet fully reflected in private transport costs.
- Developing Trans-European Transport-Networks (TEN-T). In the Maastricht treaty which became effective in 1993[2] a new title has been introduced, with Article 129b (now Article 154) assigning the obligation to the union administration to contribute to the establishment of trans-European networks in transport, telecommunication and energy. Following this prescription, a master-plan for transport infrastructure has been set up including a priority list of projects in the present community area as well as a system of corridors and priority areas for central and eastern Europe.

The CTP aims at supporting the expansion of the European Union, the deepening of integration between its members and at protecting the environment. It shall enhance efficiency and competitiveness as well as the so-called "social and economic

[1] I thank Frank Richter for his excellent support in data gathering and computing. Financial support by the Deutsche Forschungsgemeinschaft for the project "Wie wirken sich neue Verkehrstechnologien und die Entwicklung Transeuropäischer Netze auf die Europäische Standortverteilung aus?" is gratefully acknowledged·

[2] Treaty Establishing the European Community, *Official Journal of the European Communities* C 340, 1997, November 10.

cohesion". The latter phrase constantly reappearing in EU documents includes the goal of reducing income inequality between regions. Obviously it is hard to achieve these objectives with one instrument all at the same time. It is likely that there are trade-offs between efficiency and equity objectives.

This paper concentrates on the economic cohesion objective by trying to answer whether certain policy measures in the above list increase or reduce interregional income inequality in the EU. To this end we carry out two simulation experiments within a multiregional computable general equilibrium (CGE) model for Europe: First, we add the new roads of the TEN-T master-plan to the European road network and compare the spatial allocations with and without these TEN-T road projects (section 2.6.1). Second, we reduce the overall level of transport costs and compare the spatial allocations with lower and higher levels of transport costs (section 2.6.2). This is to find out whether lower transport costs due to increased competition in a deregulated transport market and due to increased technical efficiency is relatively more or less beneficial for relatively poor regions in the Community. At the same time, the experiment shows the spatial implications of higher transport costs that could result from marginal social cost pricing, given the efficiency of transport operating.

2.2 Evaluation Methods

Though extensive research is already under way for assessing the infrastructural needs as well as costs and benefits of individual projects, very little is still known about the spatial distribution of the benefits. Traditional approaches to cost benefit and regional impact analysis are not really capable of taking account of the complex mechanisms by which transport cost changes affect the spatial allocation. This holds true already in a static framework, not to speak about the even more complex channels through which the transport system affects economic dynamics. The critical issue is to assign the benefits from using the transport links to regions. Assigning costs and benefits from construction and maintenance to regions is less of a problem, and traditional techniques like multiplier analysis are acceptable. Assessing the benefits from newly installed capacities and answering to the question where they accrue, however, is much more difficult. Four types of methods are used in practice.

The *first* is to assign benefits as measured by direct cost reductions or consumer surpluses gained on the links under study, to the place of investment itself. This method is applied in the official German manual for transport infrastructure evaluation (see Bundesminister für Verkehr, 1993 for example). Its shortcomings are so obvious, that a further discussion is not worth the effort.

The *second* method is to measure benefits by estimating rates of return on infrastructure investments in a production function approach, using cross section, time series, or panel data (see Pfähler *et al.*, 1996 for an excellent survey of this approach). Intricate econometric problems have to be solved for this type of analysis that, however, are not the subject of this paper. As far as the regional distribution of effects is concerned, however, the shortcomings of this approach are similar to those of the first one. While accessibility changes may affect many regions – possibly in a different way, depending on the pattern of interregional flows – all output effects are exclusively attributed to the region, where the investment is done.

The *third* method is to distribute benefits to regions according to accessibility changes, which are quantified by a potential type or any other kind of indicator. A well-made example of this approach is (Vickerman *et al.*, 1999; see also Rietveld and Bruinsma, 1998 for an extensive survey and application of this method). This is more convincing than the first two approaches, but still lacks a theoretical foundation. The way in which accessibility changes are measured as well as the way that they are linked to regional benefits are arbitrary (for accessibility measurement see Bröcker, 1989, 1998b).

The *fourth* method is to establish an interregional demand driven input-output model with trade coefficients depending on transportation costs. The STREAMS model (Leitham *et al.*, 1999) is a good recent example of a study making extensive use of input-output techniques. Though this seems attractive because a lot of sectoral detail can be taken account of, it gives a theoretically unconvincing picture of the effects of changing transport costs, because price and quantity changes are not treated simultaneously in a consistent way.

The up to date alternative to the before mentioned approaches is to set up a multiregional computable general equilibrium, in which transport costs explicitly appear as an impediment to interregional trade. This is what we are going to do in this paper. It confines to the regional welfare effects resulting from a change in transaction costs for trading goods and services. Effects from the construction phase, from financing and maintenance are not considered. Use of the links for other than trade purposes, such as commuting, tourism, leisure trips etc., is not considered either. We model a static equilibrium for two sectors (local goods and tradables) and many regions. Firms in the tradables sector supply a large number of symmetrical product varieties under monopolistic competition. Trade between regions is costly, with costs depending on transport distances through a given transport network as well as on national trade impediments.

Section 2.3 of the paper explains the formal structure of the model by describing the household sector, the production sector and the specification of transport cost and by deriving the equilibrium equations for the entire model. This section largely coincides with Bröcker (1998a), where the same type of model is applied to estimating welfare effects of economic integration. Section 2.4 shows how the system is empirically implemented, section 2.5 briefly describes the data basis, section 2.6 presents comparative static simulations, and a final section draws conclusions regarding methodology as well as regarding the policy question posed in the title.

2.3 A Spatial CGE Analysis

In the following we set up a computable equilibrium model for Europe, subdivided into a large number of regions. The model is large, as far as the number of regions is concerned (more than 800), but small in terms of sectoral detail. There is a single factor of production (with a fixed supply in each region) and two types of goods, tradables and non tradables. Households consume both types of goods, and firms use both types of goods plus the single production factor for producing a non tradable local good and a regional subset of tradables. Regions only interact through trading tradables among each other.[3] Transferring goods between regions is costly, the costs depending on transport distance, inter alia. The model is static. Welfare effects of new road links are obtained from introducing the new links into the network and calculating new counterfactual equilibria with reduced distances. The model is like the one applied to the integration issue in Bröcker (1998a), with a few minor modifications.

2.3.1 Final Demand

Consider a closed system of n regions, each covering a representative household and a production sector. The household in region r owns the fixed regional factor stock F_r giving him a factor income $Y_r = w_r F_r$ with factor price w_r. The households' total disposable income N_r is Y_r plus a net income flow from other regions, G_r (possibly negative), that is exogenous for the sake of simplicity.[4] The households spend this income totally for local non-tradable goods and for a composite of tradables. Their preferences have a Cobb-Douglas form, such that fixed shares εN_r and $(1-\varepsilon)N_r$ are spent for non-tradables and tradables, respectively. This demand represents all kinds of final demand of the real world, including public consumption and private and public investment. The composite tradable is composed of a large number of tradables stemming from all regions of the system. The composition index is a symmetrical CES index with elasticity of substitution σ.

2.3.2 Production

The same composite of tradables, which households consume, is used as an input by firms. This input is combined with the service of the regional factor stock and with the local non-tradable good, which they produce themselves. They produce an intermediate good by a constant returns (Cobb-Douglas) technology with cost shares α, β, and γ, $\alpha+\beta+\gamma=1$, for factor service, local goods and tradables, respectively. This homogeneous intermediate serves a double purpose: first, it is one-to-one transformed to the local good, and secondly it is transformed to different brands of tradables. Tradable brands are produced with a certain amount of fixed costs per brand and with constant marginal costs. Costs are measured in terms of the intermediate good.

Firms are price taking on the input markets and on the market for the local good, and act under monopolistic competition with free entry on the market for tradable outputs. Here the Spence/Dixit/Stiglitz formalism applies, which implies (1) that the price of a tradable output p_r equals[5] the costs per unit of the intermediate good (i.e., it equals the price of a non-tradable good) and (2) the number (or more precisely the

---

[3] For technical reasons, a further form of interaction, namely interregional income flows, are introduced. They are exogenous, however, and need not concern us here.

[4] Strictly speaking, it is not G_r but the real flow $\tilde{G}_r$, that is exogenous. G_r is defined as $G_r = \tilde{G}_r \overline{p}$, with a price index $\overline{p}$. This price index is a linear-homogeneous function of prices.

[5] Equality here means equality up to a constant factor depending on the arbitrary choice of units.

measure) of brands equals[6] the real output of tradables, S_r / p_r. S_r is the output value of tradables.

These assumptions allow the derivation of the supply and demand of tradables as functions of regional prices p_r and q_r where q_r is the price per unit of a composite tradable. From the cost share, α, we infer that the output value of firms is Y_r / α. It is used for final demand of local goods $\varepsilon(Y_r + G_r)$ and for local goods used as input $\beta Y_r / \alpha$. The rest is the value of tradables supplied, which is

$$\begin{aligned} S_r &= \left(\frac{1-\beta}{\alpha}\right) Y_r - \varepsilon(G_r + Y_r) \\ &= (\nu - \varepsilon) Y_r - \varepsilon G_r \end{aligned} \tag{2.1}$$

with $\nu = (1-\beta)/\alpha$. Demand for tradables equals demand of households $[(1-\varepsilon)(Y_r + G_r)]$ plus demand of firms $\gamma Y_r / \alpha$, which yields:

$$\begin{aligned} D_r &= \left(1 - \varepsilon + \frac{\gamma}{\alpha}\right) Y_r + (1-\varepsilon) G_r = \\ &= (\nu - \varepsilon) Y_r + (1-\varepsilon) G_r = \\ &= S_r + G_r \end{aligned} \tag{2.2}$$

Hence, S_r and D_r are linear in Y_r and G_r. Y_r is log-linear in the prices p_r and q_r, because:

$$p_r = \frac{1}{\mu_r} w_r^{\alpha} p_r^{\beta} q_r^{\gamma}$$

due to the Cobb-Douglas technology. Solving for w_r and inserting into $Y_r = w_r F_r$ yields:

$$Y_r = L_r p_r^{\nu} q_r^{1-\nu} \tag{2.3}$$

with elasticity $\nu > 1$. L_r is a constant depending on regional factor stock and productivity. It is calibrated such that Y_r equals observed regional GDP in the benchmark equilibrium.

2.3.3 Transport Cost and Equilibrium

The final step is to introduce transport costs in interregional trade. Assume that transferring a good, worth of one \$, from *r* to *s* requires a transport service worth of $\$(\tau_{rs} - 1)$. The transport service is performed by using up composite tradables in the region of destination. Then $p_r \tau_{rs}$ is the price to be paid in *s* for a brand from *r*, and the trade flow from *r* to *s* (in value terms) is (see Bröcker, 1998a):

---

[6] See footnote 5.

$$t_{rs} = \frac{p_r l_r (p_r \tau_{rs})^{-\sigma}}{\sum_r p_r l_r (p_r \tau_{rs})^{-\sigma}} D_s \tag{2.4}$$

with elasticity of substitution $\sigma > 1$. l_r is the measure of brands in *r*, defined as $l_r = S_r / p_r$. Hence, we obtain:

$$t_{rs} = \frac{S_r (p_r \tau_{rs})^{-\sigma}}{\sum_r S_r (p_r \tau_{rs})^{-\sigma}} D_s \tag{2.5}$$

According to the CES index, the price of a composite tradable is:

$$q_s = \psi \left[\sum_r l_r (p_r \tau_{rs})^{1-\sigma} \right]^{\frac{1}{1-\sigma}} \tag{2.6}$$

with an arbitrary constant ψ fixing units. With $l_r = S_r / p_r$, this becomes:

$$q_s = \psi \left[\sum_r S_r p_r^{-\sigma} \tau_{rs}^{1-\sigma} \right]^{\frac{1}{1-\sigma}} \tag{2.7}$$

Finally, the equilibrium condition:

$$S_r = \sum_s t_{rs} \tag{2.8}$$

closes the system.

We introduce two kinds of trade costs: costs related to geographic distance, and costs for overcoming impediments to international trade. If region *r* belongs to country *k* and region *s* to country *l*, then the mark-up factor is:

$$\tau_{rs} = f(g_{rs}) \delta_{kl} \tag{2.9}$$

where g_{rs} denotes transport distance and *f* is the transport cost function with *f*(0)=1. A plausible assumption is that *f* increases with increasing distance, but at a diminishing rate. An obvious specification would be:

$$\tilde{f}(g_{rs}) = 1 + \varsigma g_{rs}^{\omega}$$

with parameters $\varsigma > 0$ and $0 < \omega < 1$. The problem with this specification, however, is the following. The parameters of the transport cost function will be estimated using observations on international trade. It turns out that the cost function appears in a gravity formula for interregional trade in the equilibrium solution. The gravity equation has the distance function, $\left[\tilde{f}(g_{rs})\right]^{-\sigma}$, that has to be fitted to observed trade patterns. Unfortunately, it is impossible to estimate the three parameters, σ, ς, and ω, appearing in this function, because the effects of two of them, σ and ς, are not separable from one another. Technically speaking, the level sets of the likelihood function are close to degeneration in (σ, ς)-space. The reason is easy to see. If $\tilde{f}$ is sufficiently close to one (in the order 1.2, say), then:

$$\tilde{f}(g_{rs}) \approx \exp\left(\varsigma g_{rs}^{\omega}\right)$$

and

$$\left[\tilde{f}(g_{rs})\right]^{-\sigma} \approx \exp\left(-\sigma\varsigma g_{rs}^{\omega}\right)$$

Here ς and σ merge to a single parameter $\sigma\ \varsigma$. Hence, we prefer the specification

$$f(g_{rs}) = \exp\left(\varsigma g_{rs}^{\omega}\right) \tag{2.10}$$

implying that the gravity distance function becomes exactly:

$$\left[f(g_{rs})\right]^{-\sigma} = \exp\left(-\sigma\varsigma g_{rs}^{\omega}\right) \tag{2.11}$$

Now ω and the merged parameter $\sigma\varsigma$ are well estimable, and we need other sources of information to separate the estimates for ς and σ. (See section 2.4 for more on this).

f is not globally concave; the second derivative is negative for small g_{rs}, but changes sign for a sufficiently large g_{rs}. For the specific parameters we are working with, however, f remains concave even for the longest distance in our system, and f and $\tilde{f}$ do not differ much.

$(\delta_{kl} - 1) \geq 0$ is a tariff equivalent of all costs stemming from the fact, that a good has to be exported from country k to country l. These include tariffs, but also, and more important, all costs stemming from non-tariff barriers, like costs due to language differences, costs for bureaucratic impediments, time costs spent at border controls and so forth. $\delta_{kl} = 1$ for $k = l$, of course, but it is suggested to be strictly larger than unity for $k \neq l$, even if countries k and l are both members of the EU (for a recent survey on international trade barriers see Helliwell, 1998).

Equations (2.1), (2.2), (2.3), (2.5), (2.7) and (2.8) give us supply S_r, demand D_r, factor income Y_r, trade flows t_{rs}, and prices q_r and p_r as functions of exogenous variables L_r, G_r, τ_{rs} and parameters ν, ε, and σ.

2.3.4 A Gravity Interpretation

It is interesting to observe, that the equilibrium has some similarities with Alonso's (1978) theory of movement that is not based on microeconomic assumptions, but on gravity analogies. Alonso proposed to make constraints in a doubly constrained gravity model depend on balancing factors, whose inverses have an accessibility interpretation. To detect this similarity, write (2.5) and (2.8) as:

$$t_{rs} = S_r a_r \tau_{rs}^{-\sigma} D_s b_s \tag{2.12}$$

$$\sum_s t_{rs} = S_r \tag{2.13}$$

$$\sum_r t_{rs} = D_s \tag{2.14}$$

which is obviously a doubly constrained gravity form. The supply side balancing factor is inversely related to the supply price: $p_r = a_r^{-1/\sigma}$. Note that a high price p_r (a low a_r) implies good accessibility to sales markets. The demand side balancing factor b_s is not quite a monotonous transformation of q_s, but something very close to that:

$$b_s = \left[\sum_r S_r p_r^{-\sigma} \tau_{rs}^{-\sigma}\right]^{-1}$$

Compare this with:

$$\left(\frac{q_s}{\psi}\right)^{\sigma-1} = \left[\sum_r S_r p_r^{-\sigma} \tau_{rs}^{1-\sigma}\right]^{-1} \tag{2.15}$$

The only difference is the exponent for τ_{rs}. Note that a high price q_s and a high balancing factor b_s mean poor accessibility to markets supplying tradables.

Alonso (1978) allows supply and demand to be decreasing functions of their respective balancing factors. An analogous property holds in our case. Due to equation (2.3), supply is increasing in the supply price p_r (i.e., decreasing in a_r). Demand is decreasing in the demand price q_s (i.e., decreasing in the indicator on the RHS of (2.15), that is close to the balancing factor b_s).

2.4 Calibration

Calibrating the model means to assign concrete numbers to each parameter and exogenous variable such that the equilibrium solution exactly reproduces the observed data. Numbers have to be assigned to the following parameters:

- the share parameters α, β, γ, and ε;
- the exogenous variable, L_r, representing a combination of the regional factor stock and its level of productivity (see equation 2.3);
- the parameters ζ, ω, and δ_{kl} of the distance cost function and
- the elasticity of substitution σ.

We deal with them in turn.[7]

The share parameter α can be read in the national accounts. It would be no problem to introduce a specific parameter for each country, but it is not worth the effort to do so. We used the German figure for all countries. β, γ, and ε are fixed by guessing that local goods have a 60% share in inputs as well as final demand. We found results not to be affected substantially by varying this share within a plausible range.

[7] A further exogenous variable is the net real transfer $\tilde{G}_r$. It is obtained from the national trade deficit and distributed by region. It has to be introduced for making the regional budgets balance and has virtually no impact on the results.

If we know σ and the parameters of the transport cost function that we address in the next paragraph, then the exogenous variable L_r is obtained jointly with the benchmark price system by solving the doubly constrained gravity system (2.12) to (2.14), with observed data inserted for S_r and D_s.

Assuming σ for a moment to be given, we obtain the parameters of the distance cost function from a regression estimate of the gravity equation (2.12). After some manipulation this equation is written:

$$t_{rs} = \exp\left(\tilde{a}_r + \tilde{b}_s - \rho g_{rs}^{(\omega)} - \tilde{\delta}_{kl}\right), \tag{2.16}$$

with

$\tilde{a}_r = \log(S_r a_r)$, $\tilde{b}_s = \log(D_s b_s - \sigma\varsigma)$, $\tilde{\delta}_{kl} = \sigma \log \delta_{kl}$ and $\rho = \sigma\varsigma\omega$ and $g_{rs}^{(\omega)}$ denotes the Box-Cox-Transform:

$$g_{rs}^{\omega} = \frac{g_{rs}^{\omega} - 1}{\omega}$$

According to (2.16), the logs of observed flows are linear in a set of explanatory variables, among them row and column dummies (with parameters $\tilde{a}_r$ and $\tilde{b}_s$) and one Box-Cox-transformed variable. Note that, with $\omega = 0$ and $\omega = 1$, we obtain the power form and the exponential form of the distance function as special cases. We expect decreasing costs per kilometer with increasing distance, implying $0 < \omega < 1$. If we specify the log impediment $\tilde{\delta}_{kl}$ to be linear in observed variables explaining the level of international trade impediments, this implies that $\tilde{\delta}_{kl} = \pi z_{kl}$ with appropriate observable vector z_{kl} and parameter vector π, we can add a random disturbance to the RHS of (2.16) and fit the regression by maximizing the likelihood.

As we in fact do not have the required data on a regional scale, we use international trade flows instead, assuming that (2.16) is also valid for aggregated flows crossing the border. The regression then reads:

$$X_{kl} = \exp\left(\tilde{a}_r + \tilde{b}_s - \rho \bar{g}_{rs}^{(\omega)} - \pi z_{kl}\right) + u_{kl}$$

where X_{kl} is the value of trade from country k to country l; $\tilde{a}_k$ and $\tilde{b}_l$ represent fixed effects of the export and import country, respectively; u_{kl} is a random disturbance and $\bar{g}_{kl}$ is the weighted average distance from regions in country k to regions in country l, with regional GDPs taken as weights. Regarding z_{kl}, we tried dummies for existence/non-existence of a common border (CB), existence/non-existence of a common language (LA), a dummy taking on a value of one if the respective flow crosses the former iron curtain (IC) and zero otherwise, and a few more dummies. It turns out that the estimates for ρ and ω are stable. A typical result is given in table 2.1, obtained from 1995 trade between 37 European countries. The estimate is based on the assumption that the errors are independent and have a variance proportional to the conditional expectation of the trade flows (see Bröcker and Rohweder, 1990 for details). The values of the standard errors are White's (1980) heteroskedastic-consistent estimates.

Table 2.1 Regression results, international trade

	ω	ρ	IC	LA
Coefficient	0.582	0.021	-0.659	0.696
Standard error	0.056	0.008	0.067	0.072

All parameter estimates are as expected. The former iron curtain roughly halves, a common language roughly doubles trade, *ceteris paribus*; both effects are highly significant. The distance impact is highly significant with the expected sign as well. The Box-Cox-parameter ω is significantly larger than zero and significantly smaller than one, as required. In other words, the power as well as the exponential form of the gravity distance function can be rejected with high certainty.
Now we can take $\hat{\rho}/\hat{\omega} \approx 0.036$ as an estimate of $\sigma\zeta$. Hence, our transport cost function (2.10) reads:

$$\tau_{rs} = \exp\left(\frac{0.036}{\sigma} g_{rs}^{\omega}\right)\delta_{kl} \qquad (2.17)$$

How to calibrate σ? We use two pieces of information, empirical observations on monopolisitic price mark-ups and evidence about the share of transport cost in the value of traded goods. The monopolistic competition approach implies that $\sigma/(\sigma - 1)$ is the price mark-up, i.e., the ratio of average to marginal costs. Recent OECD estimates (Martins *et al.*, 1996) render mark-ups in the order of 1.2, averaged over industries. There are strong variations over sectors, of course, but minor ones over countries. This estimate corresponds to a σ-estimate around 6.

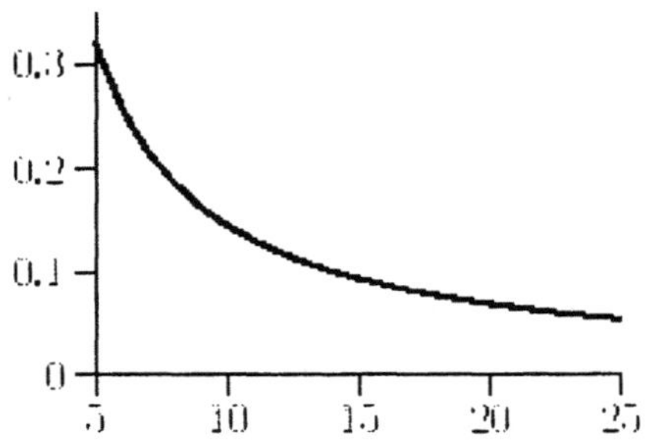

Figure 2.1 Transport cost intensity

There is another independent piece of information, however, that makes this estimate of σ appear rather low. Holding other parameters constant in equation (17), we can calculate transport costs from (17) as a function of σ. Given the estimated impact of distance on interregional trade, represented by the parameters ρ and ω, transport cost estimates are lower, the higher the value of σ.

Figure 2.1 plots the transport cost intensity C over different values of σ. C is defined as the ratio of total transport costs (only the distance related part, not international trade impediments) to the value of interregional trade:[8]

$$C = \frac{\sum_{rs} \hat{t}_{rs} \exp\left(\frac{0.036}{\sigma} g_{rs}^{\omega}\right)}{\sum_{rs} \hat{t}_{rs}} - 1$$

$\hat{t}_{rs}$ is the calibrated trade flow, which only depends on estimates of ρ and ω, not on σ.

Following the literature, this ratio should be smaller than 0.1 (see Weber, 1987 for a survey), implying a σ larger than 13. The following simulations are calculated with $\sigma = 16$. Lower estimates imply implausibly high transport costs and, hence, implausibly high welfare gains generated by transport distance reductions. Sensitivity studies show that varying σ, while holding ρ and ω constant, has a negligible impact on the spatial distribution of the welfare effects, whereas it has a considerable impact on the level of effects. Note that holding ρ and ω constant while varying σ implies that an increasing σ is compensated by a decreasing ζ and vice versa. This is responsible for an approximate inverse proportional relation between levels of welfare effects and the parameter σ (see Bröcker, 1998c for results of the sensitivity analysis).

2.5 Data

For solving the calibration equations, given the parameters u, ε, σ, ω, and ζ, we need data on transport distances g_{rs}, international trade X_{kl}, and regional GDP, Y_r. All data refer to 1995.

Transport distances are shortest routes through a road network with 3606 nodes and 6213 non-directed arcs. There are 6 types of links: (1) motorways, (2) roads with four or more lanes, (3) main roads, (4) car ferries, (5) border crossings, and (6) shipping lines (only for connections to the rest of the world). Distances along each type of link are translated to travel times (in minutes), taking average speeds, waiting times etc., into account. Introducing border crossings as special links allows for modeling the time costs spent for border formalities. Link lengths are taken from auto atlases and additional information for ferries. Modes of transport other than road are neglected (except overseas shipping). Each region is assigned to a node of the network, which is usually its administrative center.

Regional GDP is estimated by distributing national GDP among regions of the respective country. National figures are from the World Bank (Weltbank, 1996) and EUROSTAT (1997). They are given in purchasing power parity dollars. They are broken down by region using regional GDP data from Europäische Kommission, (1995) and various national statistics (Statistisches Bundesamt (nd); Glowny Urzad Statystyczny. 1996; Bundesamt für Statistik der Schweiz, (nd); Statistisk Sentralbyrå

[8] Only trade within and between the 37 countries mentioned before is included for calculating C in figure 2.1.

Norwegen. (nd); Hungarian Central Statistical Office, 1999; Hallett, 1997). Regional GDP data are not available for some eastern European countries (Russia, Ukraine, Belarus, Turkey). For these countries, national figures are distributed among regions according to the index $Q_r = P_r V_r^{0.07}$. P_r is regional population and V_r is regional population density. The same procedure is used in the cases of Italy and Romania, where regional data are available only on a higher agglomerated level. The density factor takes the fact into account, that GDP per capita is higher in more agglomerated regions. The exponent .07 is obtained from a regression analysis for countries with available regional GDP information.

Finally, data on international trade are from IMF (1997), given in US dollars. For trade between reporting countries in the IMF statistic there is a double-entry information, namely the import figure from the importing country and the export figure from the exporting country. Theoretically, both should only differ by the valuation. Exports are valued in f.o.b., imports in c.i.f. prices. As a consequence, import values should always exceed export values (though only slightly). Unfortunately, this is by no means true in practice. Both figures deviate from each other, more or less randomly in both directions. Comparing deviations for different countries shows that the statistics of these countries seem to be reliable in varying degrees. Rather than just averaging export and import figures, it is preferable to give higher weights to the figures stemming from more reliable statistics. For that end, however, we need an estimate of the reliability of the statistics of the respective countries.

We solve this problem by assuming that export as well as import figures are randomly disturbed observations of the same, though unknown trade flow. The variance of the random disturbance is assumed to vary between countries. Formally, let H_{kl} denote the true (but unknown) trade flow from country k to country l, and let X_{kl} and M_{kl} be the corresponding observations from the export and import statistics of countries k and l, respectively. Then we make the following assumption:

$$X_{kl} = H_{kl} + H_{kl}^{\lambda} \xi_k \varepsilon_{kl}$$
$$M_{kl} = H_{kl} + H_{kl}^{\lambda} \chi_l e_{kl}$$

ε_{kl} and e_{kl} are iid random variables. The factor H_{kl}^{λ}, $\lambda > 0$, implies larger errors for larger flows. The factor ξ_k scales the errors in the export statistic of country k. The factor χ_l scales the errors in the import statistic of country l. A statistic is the less reliable, the larger these factors.
The statistical problem is to estimate the flows H_{kl} and the parameters λ, ξ_k and χ_l, given the observations X_{kl} and M_{kl}. We use a procedure iterating between the MLE for the flows, given the parameters, and the MLE for the parameters, given the flows. With Gaussian errors, the MLE for the flows solves the equations

$$\frac{X_{kl}}{\xi_k^2} + \frac{M_{kl}}{\chi_l^2} = \left(\frac{1}{\xi_k^2} + \frac{1}{\chi_l^2} \right) H_{kl}$$

This is intuitively clear: The estimated flow is the weighted average of the export and import figure, with lower weights put on less reliable statistics. The parameters are estimated by regressing logs of squared estimated errors in the export and import statistics, as obtained in the forgoing iteration, against logs of trade flows and country dummies (see Judge *et al.*, 1988, pp. 366-369, for a similar approach to estimating multiplicative heteroscedasticity). Stable and plausible estimates are obtained in a few iterations.

2.6 EU Transport Policy and Economic Cohesion: Simulation Experiments

2.6.1 Experiment 1: Spatial Effects of New Roads

As noted earlier, our first experiment is to study the spatial impact of new road links in Europe, which are planned or already under construction in the framework of the TEN initiative. There are two sets of projects to be studied, those within the present European Union and those in the countries of central and eastern Europe.

For the area of the present Community, an expert group appointed by the European Council in December 1993 in Brussels (the Christophersen-Group) suggested a list of projects of common interest. Based on this report a decision has then been made by the European Council in Essen, December 1994, about 14 high priority projects and 21 further important projects. Among the 14 high priority projects there are 8 rail projects (5 of which are high speed train projects), one airport, 3 road projects and 2 combined road-rail projects, namely the Öresund fixed link and the so-called Nordic Triangle. (see figure 2.2 for the road projects in this list). The cost estimate of the high priority projects is more than 300 billion Euro. By 1999, three projects are finished and the others are either under construction or in a mature planning phase. Up to now, Union institutions were involved in 30% of the financing (TEN-T, 1997).

In parallel with these activities, a dialogue with the countries of central and eastern Europe was launched aiming at an extension of the network to the east. It started at the European Conference of Ministers of Transport 1995 in Crete. A set of transport corridors was suggested, and a final decision was then made by the 3rd Pan-European Transport Conference in Helsinki, June 1997. The conference declaration defined 9 combined rail/road corridors and the Danube inland water way as the 10th transport corridor in central and eastern Europe.

A third activity, closely connected with the two before mentioned processes, referred to as TINA (Transport Infrastructure Needs Assessment) started in September 1995, when the European Transport Council and the ministers of transport of the ten countries in central and eastern Europe, which are now candidates for EU membership, decided to coordinate the transport network planning for these countries and the EU. A TINA secretariat is now installed in Vienna coordinating the assessment process. The Pan-European corridors are the backbone of the network that is going to be specified in detail and to be extended by local links in the TINA process. The costs for the projects specified by now are estimated to be around 90 billion Euro. The EU is going to co-finance 1 billion Euro per year in the framework of the so-called ISPA fund (Instrument for Structural Policies for Pre-Accession), starting in 2000. As it turned out that there are transport needs in the candidate countries not fitting into the corridor concept, 4 so-called PETrAs (Pan-European Transport Areas) have been added to the corridors in the TINA master plan (European Commission and TINA Secretariat. 1999).

The experiment reported here is confined to road projects. For the EU area, we study the impact of the road projects within the high priority list of the Christophersen-Group. For central and eastern Europe, we assume that freeways are built or completed along each Helsinki-corridor (except the Danube inland water way, of course). Figure 2.2 shows the annual spatial welfare changes brought about by these projects as shares in regional GDP (relative equivalent variations). The measure of welfare change is based on the utility changes of the regional households, generated by installing the respective links and thereby reducing the costs for transferring goods between regions. Utility changes of household come from the production side and the consumption side. On the production side, a better access of firms to input and output markets for tradables increases the factor return, thus bringing a higher income to the household. On the consumption side, a better access to the supply of tradables reduces prices and increases the available product diversity. The utility need not increase everywhere, however; a region making only little use of a new link but trading intensively with those regions making much use of it could suffer from the fact, that demand for its output will shift away to other, more accessible, places. Our empirical results confirm that these effects do exist, but they are generally small.

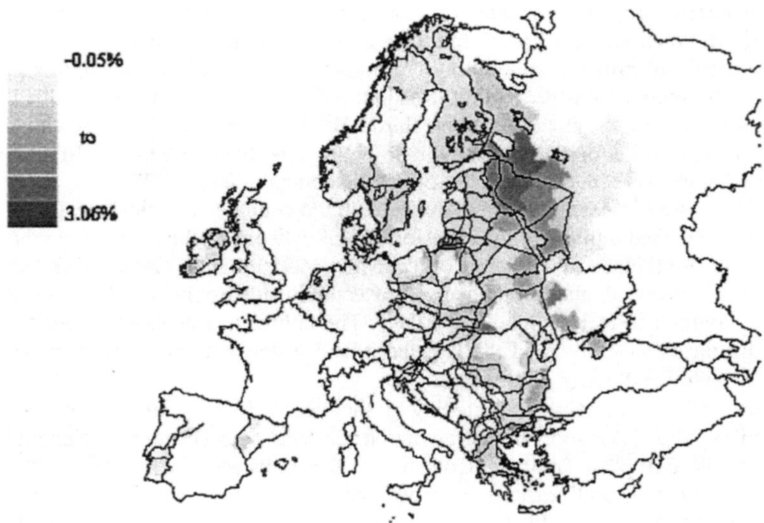

Figure 2.2 Welfare effects of TEN road projects in the EU, percent of GDP

Utility changes of households are translated to monetary measures of welfare change by the concept of Hicksian equivalent variations. If building the road makes a household better off, then the equivalent variation is the amount of money one would have to give to the household if the road was not built, in order to make the household as well off as it would be with the road. The figures show ratios of the annual additional welfare to regional GDP (relative equivalent variations).

Typically, a new road link generates welfare gains in a band-like area along the link as well as in cone-like areas pointing to the ends of the respective link. As expected, welfare gains decrease according to a gravity law with increasing distance from the link. A new link can also make regions worse off, namely those that have no advantages from using the new links for selling or buying goods. Generally, however, these losses are small.

As already mentioned, reducing income inequality between regions is an objective of building and improving the TEN, and thus has a high priority. If this policy were effective, welfare gains should be relatively high in relatively poor regions. Regarding the projects in the list of the Christophersen-Group, this should be particularly true for the road projects, which explicitly have been concentrated in the geographical periphery in order to improve its accessibility, while the rail projects are mainly in the highly congested central areas.

It turns out that the evidence in favor of the conclusion that the TEN projects support cohesion is weak. Generally, gains are somewhat higher in poorer regions, if we measure them in relative terms, but not, if we measure them in absolute per capita terms. Relative equivalent variations of the projects within the EU are weakly negatively correlated (r = -0.13) with per capita incomes over the EU regions, while per capita welfare gains are virtually uncorrelated (r = -0.02) with per capita incomes. A similar observation holds for central and eastern Europe: within the group of the ten candidate countries of the EU, relative equivalent variations correlate weakly negatively (r= -0.21) with incomes per capita, while per capita welfare gains even correlate weakly positively (r=0.16) with incomes per capita. Incomes are measured in real terms, valued at purchasing power parities. Taking both sets of projects together, relative gains more strongly correlate negatively (r = -0.46) with per capita incomes in the whole prospective area of the enlarged Community, because in central and eastern Europe the relative gains are much higher than in western Europe. They are not so in per capita terms, however, because eastern Europe is so poor. Hence, for absolute gains in per capita terms, the respective correlation is almost zero.

2.6.2 Experiment 2: Spatial Effects of a General Reduction of Transport Costs

In this experiment we reduce all transport distances within the prospective area of the enlarged EU (plus Switzerland and Norway) by 25 percent. Figure 2.3 shows the spatial effects, measured by relative equivalent variations. The map reveals an obvious center-periphery pattern. Regions in the periphery of Europe like Sicily, Galicia in north-west Spain, Ireland, the north of Scotland and of Scandinavia gain most. There is also a center-periphery pattern within countries, with national agglomeration centers gaining less than national peripheries.

Do lower transport costs favor poorer regions more than richer ones? The answer again depends on whether gains are measured in absolute or relative terms. Within the EU, relative gains are negatively correlated with income per capita (r = -0.41). The same holds true for the group of candidate countries (r = -0.50). Hence, reducing transport costs generally is in favor of cohesion within both areas, as long as relative effects are considered. For the whole area of the prospective enlarged EU, the correlation is smaller (r = -0.10), because the relative gain in the candidate countries is smaller than in the EU. In terms of absolute gains per capita, however, the opposite is true; they correlate with $r = 0.34$, $r = 0.69$ and $r = 0.72$ with income per capita in the EU, in the candidate countries and the whole area, respectively.

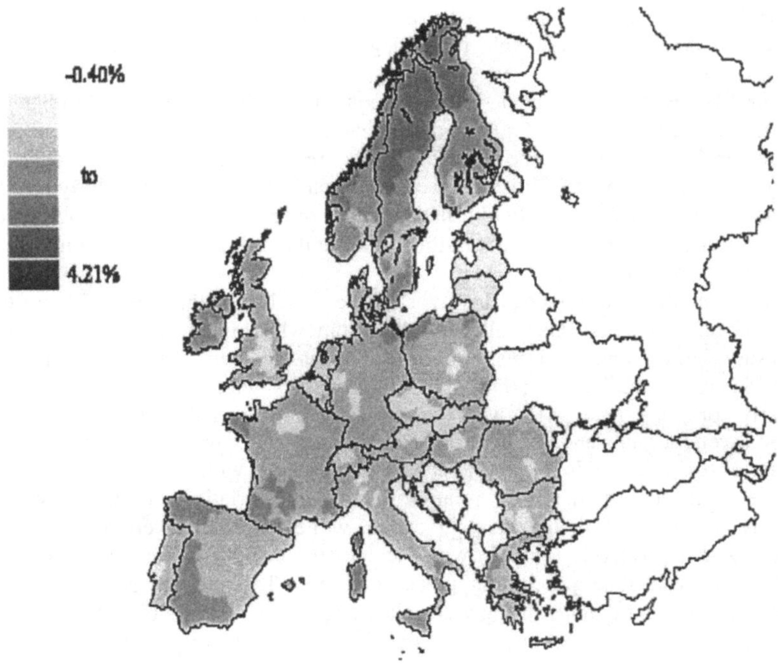

Figure 2.3 Welfare effects of a general reduction of transport costs, percent of GDP

2.7 Concluding Remarks

The approach presented in this paper has several advantages over traditional methods applied to transport project evaluation. Most importantly, it is well founded in microeconomic theory. Spatial interaction, regional allocation and regional welfare measurement are all derived from the same consistent theoretical framework. Furthermore, economies of scale at the firm level and economies of agglomeration at the regional level, which have always been regarded as vital to transport project evaluation, are well integrated into the CGE analysis by the monopolistic competition assumption. A nice by-product of the model is that familiar concepts in empirical regional science like gravity models and potential measures reappear in our system, though in a modified form and with a new theoretical underpinning.

The shortcomings of our approach, however, are also obvious. Two of them are the most important, namely the high level of sectoral aggregation and the lack of dynamics. Industries in the real world differ in many respects, which are all averaged out by merging them into just two sectors (tradables and non-tradables). Three main dimensions of sectoral differentiation are vital to transport project evaluation: (1) factor intensity, (2) transport cost intensity, and (3) degree of monopoly. Varying factor intensities of industries and varying factor abundance over regions give rise to comparative advantage effects of integration, which are excluded from our aggregated approach by assumption. Furthermore, regions might also be differently affected due to differing transport cost intensities and degrees of monopoly of their industries. These spatial differentials are also excluded from our analysis by assumption. The other important drawback is neglecting dynamics. Decreasing transport costs could affect regional rates of growth through their impact on factor flows and, more importantly, on knowledge flows and rates of innovation. The theoretical study of these aspects in the context of new growth theory is still in its infancy, and there is a long way to go, until they can be implemented into an operational empirical analysis. Here is the most challenging field of future research in transport project evaluation.

Regarding the policy issue under study in this paper, we conclude that transport cost reductions and new transport links, which are a result of the Common Transport Policy of the EU, may reduce relative income differences in Europe to a limited extent, but not absolute income differences. Hence, whether the CTP can achieve a better cohesion in the Community is at least questionable. A better transport system is good for efficiency, but regarding it as an effective regional policy instrument at the same time is requiring too much.

References

Alonso, W. 1978. "A Theory of Movement." In N.M. Hansen, ed. *Human Settlement Systems*. Cambridge, MA., Ballinger. pp. 195-212.

Bröcker, J. 1989. "How to eliminate certain defects of the potential formula." *Environment and Planning A*, 21, 817-830.

Bröcker, J. 1998a. "How would an EU-membership of the Visgrád countries affect Europe's economic geography." *Annals of Regional Science*, 32, 91-114. Erratum, 34, 469-471.

Bröcker, J. 1998b. "Measuring Accessibility in a General Equilibrium Framework." In A. Reggiani, ed. *Accessibility, Trade and Locational Behaviour*. Aldershot, Ashgate. pp. 41-59.

Bröcker, J. 1998c. "Spatial effects of new transport links: preliminary results from a spatial computable general equilibrium analysis. *Diskussionsbeiträge aus dem Institut für Wirtschaft und Verkehr*, Technische Universität Dresden, Nr. 4/98.

Bröcker, J. and H. Rohweder. 1990. "Barriers to International Trade: Methods of Measurement and Empirical Evidence." *The Annals of Regional Science*, 4, 289-305.

Bundesamt für Statistik der Schweiz. (nd). http://www.admin.ch/bfs.

Bundesminister für Verkehr. 1993. Gesamtwirtschaftliche Bewertung von Verkehrswegeinvestitionen. Schriftenreihe des BMV, Heft 72, Bonn.

Europäische Kommission. 1995. *REGIO-Regionaldatenbank, Beschreibung des Inhalts*. Luxemburg, Amt für amtliche Veröffentlichungen der Europäischen Gemeinschaft.

European Commission and TINA Secretariat. 1999. *Draft Final Report*. CD-ROM, Vienna, TINA Secretariat.

EUROSTAT. 1997. *Europa ohne Grenzen*. Nr. 10. Beilage: Schlüsselzahlen.

Glowny Urzad Statystyczny. 1996. *Rocznyk Statystyczny 1996*. Warszawa.

Hallet, M. 1997. "National and Regional Development in Central and Eastern Europe: Implications for EU Structural Assistance European Commission." *Economic Papers*, 120. Directorate-General for Economic and Financial Affairs, Brussels.

Helliwell, J.F. 1998. *How Much Do National Borders Matter?* Washington, D.C., Brookings Institution Press.
Hungarian Central Statistical Office. 1999. *Gross Domestic Product.* Unpublished data, Library and Documentation Service, Budapest.
International Monetary Fund. 1997. *Direction of Trade Statistics Yearbook 1997.* Washington, D.C., IMF.
Judge, G.G., R.C. Hill, W.E. Griffiths, H. Lütkepohl and T.-C. Lee. 1988. *Introduction to the Theory and Practice of Econometrics.* New York, Wiley.
Leitham, S., J. Downing, A. Martino and D. Fiorello. 1999. "European Transport Forecasts for 2020: The STREAMS Model Results." http://fpiv.meap.co.uk/fpiv/streams3.htm.
Martins, J.O., S. Scarpetta and D. Pilat. 1996. "Mark-up ratios in manufacturing industries: estimates for 14 OECD countries." *OECD Working Papers*, Vol. IV, Economic Department Working Papers. No. 162, Paris, OECD.
Pfähler, W., U. Hofmann and W. Bönte. 1996. "Does extra public infrastructure capital matter?" *Finanzarchiv, N.F.*, 53, 68-112.
Rietveld, P. and F. Bruinsma. 1998. *Is Transport Infrastructure Effective? Transport Infrastructure and Accessibility: Impacts on the Space Economy*, Advances in Spatial Science, Heidelberg, Springer-Verlag.
Statistisches Bundesamt (nd). Länderbericht, several editions. Metzler und Poeschel, Stuttgart.
Statistisk Sentralbyrå Norwegen. (nd). http://www.ssb.no.
TEN-T Progress Report. 1997. www.europa.eu.int/en/comm/dg07/tentpp9807/index.htm.
Vickerman, R., K. Spiekermann and M. Wegener. 1999. "Accessibility and economic development in Europe. *Regional Studies*," 33, 1-15.
Weber, J. 1987. Logistikkostenrechnung. Heidelberg, Springer-Verlag.
Weltbank. 1996. *Vom Plan zum Markt: Weltentwicklungsbericht 1996*. UNO-Verlag, Bonn.
White, H. 1980. "A heteroskedastic-consistent covariance matrix estimator and a direct test of heteroskedasticity." *Econometrica*, 48, 817-838.

3 Combined Model of Interregional Commodity Flows on a Transportation Network*

David Boyce

Department of Civil and Materials Engineering, University of Illinois at Chicago, Chicago, IL 60607 USA
e-mail: dboyce@uic.edu

3.1 Introduction

This chapter is motivated by two ongoing research objectives of the author. The first concerns models of flows on transportation networks. Whether the subject is personal travel or freight transportation, representation of the transportation network is necessary to determine realistically interzonal/interregional travel/transportation costs. The methodological effort required to achieve such results is nontrivial, but the issues raised by such an attempt are enlightening and worthwhile. This insight is demonstrated once more by the models considered here.

The second objective concerns integrating, or combining, models that are conventionally regarded as separate entities. Traditionally, individual models were connected in flowcharts. Perhaps the most widely known early example is Isard's Channels of Synthesis in his *Methods of Regional Analysis* (Isard, 1960, Ch. 9). The problems with this approach are numerous. First, individual models are often inconsistent in terms of their inputs, outputs and internal assumptions. Second, the solution of an integrated model, which combines the purposes of two or more individual models, is generally different, and more efficiently found, than with an ad hoc sequential approach. The most prominent example of this difficulty is the widely discussed problem of solving the four-step urban travel forecasting procedure with feedback. See Boyce and Daskin (1997) for further details.

In this chapter, the author returns to the problem of interregional commodity flow analysis, a fascinating modeling problem in which he was engaged during the 1980s, but put aside to focus his attention on urban transportation modeling research and practice. See Boyce and Hewings (1981) and Batten and Boyce (1986). In this case the problem is to integrate input-output models representing each region of a system of regions with an interregional commodity flow and transportation network model.

There appears to be a real demand for such a model. Regions (states, metropolitan regions, counties, etc.) are faced with allocating scarce capital budgets to infrastructure

* The support of the National Science Foundation through the National Institute of Statistical Sciences is gratefully acknowledged. Advice and comments by Jerome Sacks, Geoffrey Hewings, T. J. Kim and Hillel Bar-Gera are gratefully acknowledged. ASM M. Morshed performed the computer programming activities with skill and dedication. The opinions expressed herein are those of the author alone.

improvements. They need forecasts to determine which links of the interregional highway network are likely to be subjected to increasing flows in the future. Private transportation companies (railroads, motor carriers, etc.) are also faced with long-term capital decisions, and will benefit from better forecasts. Seismic events in California and floods in the Mississippi Valley during the past decade illustrate that Nature also can have a devastating effect on the operations of transportation networks. To answer questions about the priority of structural and other enhancements to the network requires that we have better insights into its redundancy.

In this chapter, I explore the formulation of models suited to addressing these and similar questions. In the next section, I begin with some assumptions about the size and complexity of the problem being addressed and the data available. Then I formulate two models of increasing complexity in an attempt to explore these requirements. Finally, I present our preliminary model implementation including some parameter estimates. I conclude with some thoughts about future prospects for this line of inquiry.

3.2 Requirements and Data

The model formulations described below are motivated by the following scenario. A large region or nation is divided into several (say 5-10) economic/political regions. Each region comprises one or more urban regions as well as rural agricultural, forestry or mining activities. We presume that regional economic models encompassing both input-output and econometric relationships exist for each region which describe the relation over time between regional production by sector for regional consumption, investment and government, as well as exports to other regions. We wish to augment the descriptions and forecasts provided by these regional models with a forecast of the interregional commodity flows by sector and mode, and the associated vehicle flows placed on the interregional transportation system. Depicting these interregional relationships not only help to understand the implications of regional growth for transportation investment, but also improve the validity of the regional models themselves.

In the following, we assume that each sector produces one aggregate commodity. Therefore, we use the terms *sector* and *commodity* interchangeably. Our initial level of aggregation is 11 sectors/commodities plus the construction and service sectors which produce only for local intermediate and final demand. Hence these sectors have no shipments out of their region of production.

Because each region consists of perhaps several urban areas, as well as rural areas, a reasonable representation of interregional commodity flows requires that the regions be divided into several subregions connected by road and rail transportation networks. We presume that the regional production and final demands can be allocated to these subregions. Assuming three to five subregions per region, we might have 15-50 subregions in the entire interregional system.

Commodity flow data for the United States are collected periodically by the U.S. Bureau of the Census in cooperation with the Bureau of Transportation Statistics of the U.S. Department of Transportation. Flow data are available by commodity between the 50 states and between somewhat smaller regional economic units called National

Transportation Analysis Regions (NTAR). Interregional flows by mode are also available, but not by commodity. Finally, flows by commodity and mode are only provided by state of origin. Working within these data limitations presents another challenge to the research.

Network representations are also available for the National Highway System, which consists of Interstate and other primary roads, from Oak Ridge National Laboratory (1996). Similarly, railroad networks are available indicating main and secondary lines for the principal railroad companies.

3.3 Interregional Commodity Flow Models

We begin with the formulation of an interregional commodity flow model for flows between the subregions described above. This formulation provides a starting point for and integrated input-output and commodity flow model, and also may be regarded as integrating the standard interregional flow model with a transportation network model. We assume that exports and imports by commodity for each subregion are given by regional models, and allocated to the subregional level for the period of analysis, which we may take as one year. Our problem is to estimate the flows by sector/commodity between each pair of subregions, and allocate these flows to the transportation network.

To begin the formulation, consider a model for one mode, which we will regard as motor carriers operating on highways. This mode can transport any commodity. Let x_{ij}^m be the annual economic flow of commodity *m* (dollars) from subregion *i* to subregion *j*. The total economic flow of commodity *m* leaving subregion *i* per year is X_i^m. Likewise, the total economic flow of commodity *m* arriving at subregion *j* is Y_j^m. Even though the transportation network representation may be rather abstract, we wish to consider routes through this network. Let h_{ijr}^m denote the annual physical flow of commodity *m* (tons) from subregion *i* to *j* by route *r*, D_{ijr} be the length of that route (miles), and f_a denote the total annual physical flow on link *a* of the network over distance of d_a. Finally, let g^m denote the ratio of the total interregional economic flow to total annual physical flow (dollars/ton). This ratio is the basis for converting specific interregional economic flows to physical flows for determining route and link flows.

Now we are ready to define the relationships among these variables and other quantities. First, consider the two following definitions:

1. Link flow (tons) equals the sum of the route flows on all routes between all subregions using link *a*.

$$f_a \equiv \sum_m \sum_{ijr} h_{ijr}^m \delta_{ijr}^a \tag{3.1}$$

where $\delta_{ijr}^a = 1$, if route *r* from *i* to *j* uses link *a*, and 0 otherwise.

2. Interregional length of route r (miles) equals the sum of the link distances along route r.

$$D_{ijr} \equiv \sum_a d_a \delta_{ijr}^a \tag{3.2}$$

Next we require three sets of flow conservation equations by origin and destination subregion and between subregions:

3. The sum of the annual interregional flows of commodity m from subregion i equals the total flow of commodity m leaving subregion i.

$$\sum_j x_{ij}^m = X_i^m, \text{ for all commodities } m \text{ and subregions } i \tag{3.3}$$

4. The sum of the annual interregional flows of commodity m to subregion j equals the total flow of commodity m entering subregion j.

$$\sum_i x_{ij}^m = Y_j^m, \text{ for all commodities } m \text{ and subregions} \tag{3.4}$$

5. The sum of the annual physical flows of commodity m on all routes r between subregions i and j equals the annual economic flow of commodity m from i to j.

$$\sum_r h_{ijr}^m = \frac{x_{ij}^m}{g^m}, \text{ for all commodities } m \text{ and pairs of subregions } i \text{ and } j \tag{3.5}$$

To obtain a model that has economic flows similar to reality, we assume, in principle, that the dispersion of flows between all pairs of subregions, as measured by the entropy function, is equal to the actual dispersion of flows:

$$-\sum_{ij} x_{ij}^m \ln x_{ij}^m = S^m, \text{ for all commodities } m \tag{3.6}$$

where S^m is the dispersion of actual flows of commodity m, as defined by the same entropy function. As will be seen in the resulting model below, invoking this dispersion constraint in the formulation results in a model that exhibits the cross-hauling phenomena observed in reality. That is, flows of the same *aggregate* commodity occur in both directions. Since the opposing flows may be quite different detailed commodities, such cross-hauling may be regarded as an aggregation effect, rather than as inefficiency of the transportation system. In defining this constraint we recognize that the actual flows cannot be fully observed. Therefore, we do not propose to utilize this concept as a formal constraint, but rather to apply the dispersion principle in formulating the model.

Finally, all route flows must be nonnegative, implying that all links flows are also nonnegative.

$$h_{ijr}^m \geq 0, \text{ for all commodities } m, \text{ and all routes } r \text{ connecting subregions } i \text{ and } j. \tag{3.7}$$

Having defined the constraints on interregional and route flows, we are ready to consider the objective function. On the assumption that shippers prefer to hold their transportation costs as low as possible, subject to the dispersion of flows represented by the entropy constraint, we define the interregional part of the objective function as follows:

$$\min \sum_a d_a f_a \equiv \sum_a d_a \left(\sum_m \sum_{ijr} h_{ijr}^m \delta_{ijr}^a \right) \equiv \sum_m \sum_{ijr} h_{ijr}^m \left(\sum_a d_a \delta_{ijr}^a \right) \equiv \sum \sum D_{ijr} h_{ijr}^m \tag{3.8}$$

Shown in function (3.8) are two different forms of the objective function derived by using Definitions (1, 2). Using network concepts, total shipment distance can be stated either in terms of links or routes.

3.3.1 Model 1

Model 1 can now be derived by minimizing function (3.8) with regard to link flows, or in the case of the route flow definition, with regard to route flows, plus a term related to intraregional flows, subject to Constraints (3.3), (3.4), (3.5), (3.6) and (3.7). The Lagrangian function is:

$$L = \sum_m \sum_{i \neq j} \sum_{r \in R_{ij}} D_{ijr} h_{ijr}^m + \sum_m \sum_i D_{ii}^m x_{ii}^m + \sum_m \sum_i \rho_i^m \left(X_i^m - \sum_j x_{ij}^m \right) +$$

$$+ \sum_m \sum_j \sigma_j^m \left(Y_j^m - \sum_i x_{ij}^m \right) + \sum_m \sum_{ij} u_{ij}^m \left(\frac{x_{ij}^m}{g^m} - \sum_r h_{ijr}^m \right) + \sum_m \frac{1}{\beta^m g^m} \left(\sum_{ij} x_{ij}^m \ln x_{ij}^m + S^m \right)$$

where:

D_{ii}^m = is the mean intraregional shipment distance for sector m within region i,

β^m = the reciprocals of the Lagrange multipliers of Constraints (3.6),

ρ_i^m = the multipliers of Constraints (3.3),

σ_j^m = the multipliers of Constraints (3.4),

u_{ij}^m = the multipliers of Constraints (3.5).

The resulting optimality conditions are:

$\sum_a d_a \delta_{ijr}^a - u_{ij}^m \geq 0$, for all commodities m, routes r, and subregions i and j;

$h_{ijr}^m \left(\sum_a d_a \delta_{ijr}^a - u_{ij}^m \right) = 0$, for all commodities m, routes r, and subregions i and j;

$-\rho_i^m - \sigma_j^m + \left(\frac{1}{\beta^m g^m} \right) \left(\ln x_{ij}^m + 1 \right) + \left(\frac{u_{ij}^m}{g^m} \right) = 0$, for all commodities m and subregions i and j;

Constraints (3.3), (3.4), (3.5), (3.6) and (3.7).

Since the third condition involves the natural logarithm of x_{ij}^m, all economic flows of each commodity must be positive, although they may be very small. Solving the third condition for x_{ij}^m, we obtain:

$$x_{ij}^m = A_i^m X_i^m B_j^m Y_j^m \exp\left(-\beta^m u_{ij}^m\right), \text{ for all commodities } m \text{ and subregions } i, j \qquad (3.9)$$

where A_i^m and B_j^m are balancing factors that assure that constraints (3.3 and 3.4) are satisfied, and $u_{ii}^m \equiv D_{ii}^m$. Equation (3.9) is a doubly-constrained spatial interaction model for each commodity m.

The deterrence parameter, β^m, is related to the dispersion of shipments of commodity m. The multipliers, u_{ij}^m, may be interpreted as the minimum travel distance from subregion i to subregion j for commodity m. Since there is no representation of congestion in the above formulation, all shipments from i to j occur on a single minimum distance route, and the models for each commodity are independent. The equivalence of u_{ij}^m to the minimum distance interregional route is demonstrated by the first two optimality conditions.

Now, let us try to make Model 1 slightly more realistic by adding a new constraint set defining link capacities:

$$f_a \le k_a, \text{ for all links } a \qquad (3.10)$$

where k_a is the capacity of link a. If we minimize function (3.8), plus intraregional shipment distances, subject to constraints (3.3) to (3.7) and (10), we obtain a slightly different form of the above optimality conditions:

$$\sum_a (d_a + \lambda_a)\delta_{ijr}^a - u_{ij}^m \ge 0, \text{ for all commodities } m, \text{ routes } r, \text{ and subregions } i, j.$$

$$h_{ijr}^m\left(\sum_a (d_a + \lambda_a)\delta_{ijr}^a - u_{ij}^m\right) = 0, \text{ for all commodities } m, \text{ routes } r, \text{ and subregions } i, j.$$

$$-\rho_i^m - \sigma_j^m + \left(\frac{1}{\beta^m g^m}\right)\left(\ln x_{ij}^m + 1\right) + \left(\frac{u_{ij}^m}{g^m}\right) = 0, \text{ for all commodities } m \text{ and subregions } i$$

and j.

$$f_a \le k_a, \text{ for all links } a$$

$$\lambda_a\left(f_a - k_a\right) = 0, \text{ for all links } a$$

Constraints (3.3) to (3.7)

The effect of adding the link capacity constraint (3.10), with its Lagrange multiplier λ_a, is to add a distance-like penalty to the length of link a. The effect of the penalty λ_a is to restrict the link flow to its capacity, and to introduce additional routes into the solution. Of course, the value of λ_a is zero if the link flow is less than capacity. If some values of λ_a are positive, then these values are also reflected in the values of the equilibrium distance u_{ij}^m. Constraints (3.10) on link flows has another far-reaching effect: the models for each commodity are no longer independent of each other, as they were before this constraint set was introduced.

The disadvantage of adding link capacity constraints is that the problem is now harder to solve computationally, since the values of the multipliers λa must be determined for each link. This problem has been solved by Chang *et al.* (2000) by applying the Danzig-Wolfe decomposition method. See also Patriksson (1994) for discussion of related solution methods.

An alternative approach, following the experience of urban travel forecasting models is to define a link congestion function that increases sharply as link flow approaches capacity. The function, however, should be unconstrained; that is, its value approaches infinity as flow approaches infinity, not as it approaches some upper limit. Nevertheless, the slope of the function may be very steep. A piecewise linear function with a break-point near capacity is also possible. If $d_a(f_a)$ is the effective distance at flow f_a, then function (3.8) may be revised as follows, and minimized together with intraregional shipment distances with respect to constraints (3.3), to (3.7).

$$\min \sum_a \int_0^{f_a} d_a(x)dx \tag{3.11}$$

The resulting optimality conditions are as follows:

$\sum_a d_a(f_a)\delta_{ijr}^a - u_{ij}^m \geq 0$, for all commodities m, routes r, and subregions i, j.

$h_{ijr}^m\left(\sum_a d_a(f_a)\delta_{ijr}^a - u_{ij}^m\right) = 0$, for all commodities m, routes r, and subregions i and j.

$-\rho_i^m - \sigma_j^m + \left(\frac{1}{\beta^m g^m}\right)(\ln x_{ij}^m + 1) + \left(\frac{u_{ij}^m}{g^m}\right) = 0$, for all commodities m, subregions i and j.

Constraints (3.3) to (3.7)

In this result, the equilibrium distance u_{ij}^m is determined by the link distance functions $d_a(f_a)$. As with the link capacity constraint set, the commodity flow models are interrelated through the distance functions defined for each link.

3.3.2 Model 2

Next we explore an approach to integrating the models across sectors of production and consumption, as well as across the transportation network. This approach is based on the concepts of Leontief and Strout (1963), as extended by Wilson (1970). We assume that subregions are indifferent regarding the source of the supply of commodities, either locally or from another subregion. On this basis we define the following *commodity balance* constraint, which states that the flow of commodity m into subregion j equals the use of that commodity for producing other commodities (intermediate demand) plus subregional consumption, investment, government expenditures and exports out of the system of regions (final demand).

$$\sum_i x_{ij}^m = \sum_n a^{mn}\left(\sum_k x_{jk}^n\right) + y_j^m, \text{ for all sectors } m \text{ and subregions } j \tag{3.12}$$

where a^{mn} is the quantity of inputs from sector m required to produce one unit of output of sector n in the system of regions, the quantities being measured in dollars; y_j^m is the final demand for output of sector m in subregion j. By using this constraint in place of origin and destination constraints (3.3) and (3.4), we link together the intermediate and final demand of all sectors.

If we minimize function (3.11), plus intraregional shipment distances, subject to constraints (3.5), (3.6), (3.7), and (3.12), we obtain the following new optimality conditions for x_{ij}^m and x_{jj}^m.

$$\left(\frac{1}{\beta^m g^m}\right)\left(\ln x_{ij}^m + 1\right) + \sum_l \gamma_i^l a_i^{lm} - \gamma_j^m + \frac{u_{ij}^m}{g^m} \geq 0,$$ for all commodities m and subregions i and j; (3.13a)

$$\left(\frac{1}{\beta^m g^m}\right)\left(\ln x_{jj}^m + 1\right) + \sum_l \gamma_j^l a_j^{lm} - \gamma_j^m + \frac{D_{jj}}{g^m} \geq 0,$$ for all commodities m and subregions i. (3.13b)

Here, γ_i^l and γ_j^m are Lagrange multipliers for constraints (3.12) for subregion i and commodity l, and subregion j and commodity m, respectively. Solving for x_{ij}^m, we obtain:

$$x_{ij}^m = \exp(-\beta^m g^m \sum_l \gamma_i^l a_i^{lm} - 1) \cdot \exp\left(\beta^m g^m \gamma_j^m\right) \cdot \exp\left(-\beta^m u_{ij}^m\right),$$ for all commodities m and pairs of subregions i and j.

By defining δ_i^m and ε_j^m in an obvious manner, we obtain the following spatial interaction model:

$$x_{ij}^m = \delta_i^m \quad \varepsilon_j^m \exp\left(-\beta^m u_{ij}^m\right),$$ for all commodities m and pairs of subregions i and j.

Here, δ_i^m is associated with the flows of commodities l required to make the exports from subregion i, and ε_j^m concerns the requirements for commodity m at subregion j. Note that the final demands y_j^m do not appear directly in the model, but are represented implicitly by the Lagrange multipliers. Clearly, the two other versions of link functions could also be employed in Model 2.

3.4 An Initial Implementation

Model 2 served as the basis for an implementation effort for an interregional commodity flow model of the Midwestern United States, which consists of the states of Illinois, Indiana, Michigan, Ohio and Wisconsin. This region is also designated as the East North Central Region, one of the nine U. S. Census regions. In order that the commodity flows could be represented on the transportation network, each state was divided into three subregions, except for Ohio which was divided into four subregions because of its shape and location of major metropolitan areas. Because related modeling objectives required that the subregions be defined on states, we could not use the National Transportation Analysis Regions defined as functional economic regions. The eight Census regions outside the Midwest were utilized to represent interregional trading regions between the 16 Midwest subregions and the remainder of the United States. Hence, the entire model consisted of 24 regions, 16 substate areas and 8 Census regions.

Two input-output models were implemented by the Regional Economic Applications Laboratory for the Midwest Region and the Remainder of the U. S. in order that the interindustry structure of the Midwest could be represented separately from the rest of the country. Final demands for the five Midwest states and the Remainder of the U.S. were estimated for the 1993 base year, and disaggregated to the 16 substate areas and eight Census regions on the basis of population and employment.

Initially, the model was solved without reference to route and link flows by using fixed interregional distances using trial values of the distance sensitivity parameters β^m. Inspection of the resulting commodity flow matrices for the nine Census regions including the Midwest as one region showed that a undue level of trade flows (about 80%) were occurring between the Midwest and the remaining Census regions. The reason for these excessive flows was the large number of subregions within the Midwest as compared with the smaller number of Census regions representing the remainder of the U. S. In effect, the model was treating each region as an equal alternative destination. Hence, this specification of regions is an example of the well-known Independence of Irrelevant Alternatives (IIR) Property of the logit model.

A standard way to treat the IIR condition is to restructure the decision tree and to apply a nested logit model. In this case, the structure would consist of an interregional model for the Census regions coupled with a subregional model for the Midwest. A problem with this construct is that the Midwest region would need to be represented as one centroid on the interregional transportation network for the purpose of computing distances at the regional level; then subregional distances would be based on this single centroid. Since the principal interest was in modeling Midwest states and their trading relationships with each other as well as the remainder of the U. S., this approach seemed counter-productive.

Instead, a different approach was defined on the basis of two concepts. First, we recognized that the relative size of Census regions and state subregions could be represented by the historical output level of each region. In effect, the prior probability of a shipment from subregion to subregion is proportional to its historical output level. Thus, these output levels could be included in the entropy functions as prior probabilities $\overline{X_i^m}$ for region i and commodity m. Second, because of the vast differences in shipment distances within the Midwest and among the Census regions and the Midwest, we realized that two sets of distance sensitivity parameters were needed. One set was defined for shipments within the Midwest; a second set pertains to shipments between the Midwest and the Census regions, and between the Census regions outside the Midwest.

The resulting model structure incorporating these two features is shown in equations (3.14).

$$x_{ij}^m = \overline{X_i^m}\,\delta_i^m \varepsilon_j^m \exp\left(-\beta_M^m u_{ij}^m\right),\ \forall \text{ commodities } m, \text{ substate regions } i, j \in M \qquad (3.14a)$$

$$x_{IJ}^m = \overline{X_I^m}\,\delta_I^m \varepsilon_J^m \exp\left(-\beta_R^m u_{IJ}^m\right),\ \forall \text{ commodities } m, \text{ Census regions } I, J \in R \qquad (3.14b)$$

$$x_{Ij}^m = \overline{X}_I^m \delta_I^m \varepsilon_j^m \exp\left(-\beta_R^m u_{Ij}^m\right), \ \forall \text{ commodities } m, \ I \in R, j \in M \quad (3.14c)$$

$$x_{iJ}^m = \overline{X}_i^m \delta_i^m \varepsilon_J^m \exp\left(-\beta_R^m u_{iJ}^m\right), \ \forall \text{ commodities } m, \ i \in M, J \in R \quad (3.14d)$$

$$x_{jj}^m = \overline{X}_j^m \delta_j^m \varepsilon_j^m \exp\left(-\beta_M^m d_{jj}^m\right), \ \forall \text{ commodities } m, \text{ substate regions } j \in M \quad (3.14e)$$

$$x_{JJ}^m = \overline{X}_J^m \delta_J^m \varepsilon_J^m \exp\left(-\beta_R^m d_{JJ}^m\right), \ \forall \text{ commodities } m, \text{ Census regions } J \in R \quad (3.14f)$$

Note that $i, j \in M$ represent the 16 Midwest substate regions and $I, J \in R$ represent the 8 Census regions outside the Midwest. Likewise, β_M^m and β_R^m represent the distance sensitivities of commodity *m* for the Midwest and Remainder of the U. S., respectively. The balancing factors

$$\delta_i^m = \exp(-\beta_M^m g^m \sum_l \gamma_i^l a_M^{lm} - 1), \quad \text{for commodity } m, \text{ substate region } i \in M$$

$$\varepsilon_j^m = \exp\left(\beta_M^m g^m \gamma_j^m\right), \quad \text{for commodity } m, \text{ substate region } j \in M$$

and similarly for the balancing factors for the other regions.

This model was initially estimated as an interregional commodity flow model by setting the value per ton parameters g^m equal to 1. The parameter values were estimated using an experiment method developed by Sacks *et al.* (1989). The best parameter values found to date are shown in table 3.1.

Table 3.1 Estimated Parameter Values and ρ_m^2 Values

Commodity	Midwest β_M^m	Midwest ρ_m^2	Remainder of the US β_R^m	Remainder of the US ρ_m^2
1 Agriculture, Forestry, and Fisheries	0.0120	87.8	0.0040	53.4
2 Mining	0.0150	79.0	0.0040	52.0
4 Food and Kindred Products	0.0072	73.2	0.0030	74.4
5 Chemicals and Allied Products	0.0045	48.1	0.0020	75.4
6 Primary Metals Industries	0.0050	57.1	0.0022	69.0
7 Fabricated Metals Industries	0.0060	80.1	0.0023	63.3
8 Industrial Machinery and Equipment	0.0048	57.5	0.0014	13.6
9 Electric and Other Electric Equipment	0.0050	22.6	0.0009	29.9
10 Transportation Equipment	0.0040	17.9	0.0017	71.0
11 Other Non-Durable Manufacturing	0.0080	75.6	0.0030	67.9
12 Other Durable Manufacturing	0.0060	72.8	0.0015	56.4

The goodness-of-fit measure used in estimated the parameters is ρ^2, which is defined on three likelihood measures as follows:

$$\rho_m^2 = \frac{L_{\text{model}}^m - L_{\text{null}}^m}{L_{\text{perfect}}^m - L_{\text{null}}^m}$$

$$L^m_{\text{model}} = \sum_{ij} \left(\frac{N^m_{ij}}{N^m_{..}} \right) \ln \left(\frac{x^m_{ij}}{x^m_{..}} \right), \text{ the model likelihood for commodity } m;$$

$$L^m_{\text{perfect}} = \sum_{ij} \left(\frac{N^m_{ij}}{N^m_{..}} \right) \ln \left(\frac{N^m_{ij}}{N^m_{..}} \right), \text{ the perfect likelihood for commodity } m;$$

$$L^m_{\text{null}} = \sum_{ij} \left(\frac{N^m_{ij}}{N^m_{..}} \right) \ln \left(\frac{\bar{x}^m_{ij}}{\bar{x}^m_{..}} \right), \text{ the null likelihood for commodity } m;$$

where:

N^m_{ij} is the annual flow of commodity *m* from region *i* to region *j* observed in the 1993 Commodity Flow Survey of the U. S. Census

x^m_{ij} is the flow of commodity *m* from region *i* to region *j* predicted by equations (3.14)

$\bar{x}^m_{ij}$ is the predicted flow of commodity *m* from region *i* to *j* if $\beta^m = 0$.

$N^m_{..}$ is the sum of the annual flow of commodity *m* over all regions

$x^m_{..}$ is the sum of the predicted flow of commodity *m* over all regions

$\bar{x}^m_{..}$ is the sum of the predicted flow of commodity *m* over all regions if $\beta^m = 0$.

These measures were computed separately for two cases: a) the five Midwest states; b) the nine Census regions, including the Midwest or East North Central region as one region.

3.5 Conclusions

To our knowledge, only one attempt to solve the model formulation proposed by Wilson (1970) has been reported. Rho *et al.* (1989) found that the iteration scheme proposed by Wilson converged very slowly for the case of four sectors and about 80 regions. However, their model included several other components that may have retarded the convergence. They were able to solve the model successfully using Powell's hybrid method. In the models described above, a similar approach may be necessary.

In contrast to that experience, the solution of this 13 sector, 24 region model has been relatively straightforward, once the issue of large vs. small regions was addressed. The balancing factors are solved quickly, typically in about 50 iterations to fine convergence. Future activities concern solving the model in conjunction with the transportation network, and adding a mode choice model to the formulation.

References

Batten, D.F. and D.E. Boyce. 1986. "Spatial Interaction, Transportation, and Interregional Commodity Flow Models." In P. Nijkamp, ed. *Handbook of Regional and Urban Economics, Volume 1*. Amsterdam, North-Holland, pp. 357-406.

Boyce, D.E. and G.J.D. Hewings. 1981. "Interregional Commodity Flow, Input-Output and Transportation Modeling: An Entropy Formulation." Prepared for the Conference on Interregional Models, First World Regional Science Congress, Cambridge, MA, 1980.

Boyce, D.E. and M.S. Daskin. 1997. "Urban Transportation." In C. ReVelle and A. McGarity, eds. *Design and Operation of Civil and Environmental Engineering Systems.* New York, John Wiley and Sons, pp. 277-341.

Chang, E., A. Ziliaskopoulos, S.T. Waller and D.E. Boyce. 2000. "Solution Algorithm for the Combined Interregional Commodity Flow and Transportation Network Model with Link Capacity Constraints." *Working Paper*, Transportation Center, Northwestern University, Evanston.

Evans, S.P. 1976. "Derivation and Analysis of Some Models for Combining Trip Distribution and Assignment." *Transportation Research*, 10, 37-57.

Isard, W. 1960. *Methods of Regional Analysis*. Cambridge, MA., MIT Press.

Leontief, W.W. and A. Strout. 1963. "Multiregional Input-Output Analysis." In T. Barna, ed. *Structural Interdependence and Economic Development*. London, Macmillan.

Oak Ridge National Laboratory. 1996. Description of the Oak Ridge National Highway Network, Version 1.3 (C), Center for Transportation Analysis., Oak Ridge, TN.

Patriksson, M. 1994. *The Traffic Assignment Problem, Models and Methods*. Utrecht, VSP.

Rho, J. H., D.E. Boyce and T.J. Kim. 1987. "Comparison of Solution Methods for Wilson's Interregional Commodity Flow Model." *Geographical Analysis*, 21, 259-267.

Sacks, J., W. Welch, T. Mitchell, and H. Wynn, 1989. "Design and Analysis of Computer Experiments." ***Statistical Science***, 4, 409-435.

Wilson, A.G. 1970. "Interregional Commodity Flows: Entropy Maximizing Procedures." *Geographical Analysis*, 2, 255-282.

4 Why Do Countries Pursue Reciprocal Trade Agreements? A Case Study of North America

Michael A. Kouparitsas*

Federal Reserve Bank of Chicago, P.O. Box 834, Chicago IL 60690-0834
e-mail: mkoup@frbchi.org

4.1 Introduction

Despite the considerable effort that has been directed to global trade agreements, such as the General Agreement on Tariffs and Trade, much of the trade liberalization achieved in the postwar era has in fact come from far-reaching reciprocal regional trade agreements that have involved just a few players. Early regional trade pacts, such as the European Union (EU), involved countries of roughly equal size, while the trend over the last decade has been for regional agreements that bring together one or more small countries and a large country or an established free-trade zone.[1,2] This trend has captured the attention of trade theorists because while trade theory argues that the best course of action for large countries may be reciprocal trade agreements, it also argues that the best course of action for a small country is always unilateral trade liberalization.[3]

The theory underlying reciprocal trade liberalization agreements evolved from the optimal tariff literature, which dates back to Scitovsky (1942) and Johnson (1953-54). The basic idea is that governments maximize their nations' welfare by unilaterally setting trade barriers so as to exploit their country's monopoly and monopsony power in world markets. A well-known implication of this theory is that countries that set their trade barriers optimally are made worse off by unilateral trade liberalization,

* This is a substantially revised version of the paper titled "Would free trade have emerged in North American without NAFTA?" I would like to thank seminar participants at the Board of Governors, Federal Reserve Bank of Chicago, Southern Methodist University, University of Virginia, and Michigan State University for useful comments on an earlier draft and Roger Thryselius for help in creating figure 4.1. All errors and omissions are mine. The views expressed herein are those of the author and not necessarily those of the Federal Reserve Bank of Chicago or the Federal Reserve System.

[1] Prominent examples of this type of agreement are: the Canada-United States Free Trade Agreement (CFTA) involving the United States (U.S.) and Canada; the North American Free Trade Agreement (NAFTA) involving the CFTA and Mexico; and the European Union (EU) expansion involving the EU, Austria, Finland, and Sweden.

[2] Some small countries, such as Mexico undertook some unilateral liberalization before negotiating a regional free trade agreement with a large trading partner. These unilateral programs were limited to the partial reduction of import taxes on goods. This pales in comparison to the trade liberalization undertaken in the regional agreements, which is designed to eliminate all tariff and non-tariff barriers to not only goods trade, but also services trade and international capital flows. Adding to this is empirical work by Roland-Host, Reinert and Sheills (1994) which found the pre-liberalization levels of North American import protection provided by actual import tariffs in 1988 were extremely low when compared with the protection levels implied by tariff-equivalent estimates of non-tariff barriers.

[3] See, for example, the discussion on unilateralism vs. regional trade liberalization in Krugman (1991, p. 26)

while binding reciprocal trade agreements between countries makes them better off. Many trade theorists have gone on to argue that the cooperative and non-cooperative payoffs from trade liberalization implied by the optimal tariff literature take on the form of a classic prisoner's dilemma. In that setting, the dominant strategy of countries acting unilaterally is to pick the inefficient outcome of maintaining their trade barriers, while the efficient outcome of jointly eliminating trade barriers can only be achieved through a binding reciprocal trade agreement between countries.

Fluctuations in the terms of trade drive the prisoners' dilemma theory of reciprocal trade liberalization. Unilateral liberalization creates an excess supply of the country's exportable and an excess demand for the country's importable, which leads to a deterioration of their terms of trade and a fall in their real income. The loss of real income typically outweighs the gains from removing the deadweight losses associated with trade barriers, so the liberalizing country is made worse off. At the same time the trading partners of the liberalizing country are made better off because their terms of trade improve. In contrast, reciprocal agreements have a negligible impact on the terms of trade of all trading partners, so all countries gain by the size of the deadweight losses associated with trade barriers. This comes about because one country's excess supply of exportables satisfies another country's excess demand for importables. It is easy to see this in the simple case of symmetric trading partners where a reciprocal trade agreement would leave the terms of trade of all countries unchanged.

A key assumption supporting this theory is that countries can influence their terms of trade through their trade policies. This has led economists, such as Krugman (1991), to question the relevance of the prisoners' dilemma theory in explaining the recent shift to reciprocal agreements involving small and large countries/regions, since the actions of small countries are assumed to have little influence on their own terms of trade. Others have responded to this by arguing that the process of reciprocal liberalization is purely motivated by political considerations, such as regional defense. Bagwell and Staiger (1998) evaluate these competing views within the context of a theoretical model in which governments are motivated by political and terms-of-trade considerations. Within their framework, they show that more general government objectives do not change the view that reciprocal trade agreements provide an escape from a terms-of-trade driven prisoner's dilemma, and that this is all that reciprocal agreements do.

This chapter examines the issue in another way by directly estimating the cooperative and non-cooperative payoffs implicit in actual free trade agreements negotiated between small and large countries to see if they take the form of the prisoners' dilemma. My analysis lends support to the terms-of-trade driven prisoners' dilemma theory of reciprocal trade liberalization. Using simulation results from a quantitative trade model calibrated to North American data, I show that the Canadian-US Free Trade Agreement (CFTA) and North American Free Trade Agreement (NAFTA) take on the two essential elements of the terms-of-trade driven prisoners' dilemma. First, I show that if the countries/regions involved in these agreements had unilaterally liberalized their trade by the same amount specified by the CFTA and NAFTA they would have been made worse off, while their regional trading partners would have been made better off. Next, I show that the countries/regions involved in these agreements are indeed better off by pursuing reciprocal trade liberalization along the lines specified by the CFTA and NAFTA.

The method used in this paper to measure welfare gains from trade liberalization is quite different from earlier quantitative analyses of the CFTA and NAFTA. Previous analysis relied on static computable general equilibrium (SCGE).[4] Despite their complexity, these models ignore three important dynamic consequences of trade liberalization that causes them to incorrectly estimate the welfare gains from trade liberalization.

First, static models limit the world supply of capital to that available in the pre-liberalized steady state. Therefore, static welfare and output gains associated with liberalization come from a reallocation of capital across sectors and countries. This ignores the fact that capital accumulation is generally more efficient under liberalized trade, because trade barriers on durable goods are essentially a tax on investment, and therefore understates the potential welfare and output gains that accrue from liberalization.

Some researchers working within a static framework have attempted to rectify this weakness by incorporating exogenous increases in the supply of capital and/or total factor productivity in their quantitative analysis (see, for example, the NAFTA studies of Brown, *et al.*, 1992; and Sorbazo, 1994). In the absence of a fully specified dynamic model, it is impossible to quantify the appropriate size of the capital accumulation and its likely effect on consumption, labor effort and ultimately welfare; hence, despite claims to contrary, these studies offer no guide to the dynamic consequences of trade liberalization.

Secondly, static trade models also potentially underestimate the gains from liberalization by not allowing for trade in financial assets, which is a by-product of restricting national current accounts to zero. This comes about because capital flows serve three basic (although not mutually exclusive) purposes that directly raise national and international welfare. By trading international assets, agents can achieve a higher level of welfare by maintaining smooth consumption paths while undertaking major capital investment and sectoral reallocation of factors following liberalization. In addition, international capital flows raise welfare by allowing for a more rapid adjustment to the new policy environment. Finally, by trading international assets, agents can achieve a more efficient allocation of resources across countries.

Thirdly, the appropriate measure of the change in welfare from liberalization is the permanent change in pre-liberalization steady state consumption that has the same present value as the consumption path that agents experience along the transition path to the post-liberalization steady state. There is no transition path in static models because they explicitly assume that trade liberalization agreements are fully implemented at the date they are signed and that factors of production are perfectly mobile. In other words, static models assume that the economy jumps from the pre-liberalized to the post-liberalized steady state at the time the agreement is signed. In this setting, the change in welfare from liberalization is simply measured as the difference between the post- and pre-liberalized consumption. This approach potentially overstates the welfare gains from liberalization if there are significant costs associated with reallocating factors of production or if trade policies are phased-in over a long period of time.

I overcome these limitations and in the process more accurately measure the welfare effects of trade liberalization by utilizing a dynamic computable general

[4] See, for examples, conference volumes by Waverman (1992), Lustig, *et al.* (1992), Francois and Shiells (1994), Kehoe and Kehoe (1995), and Francois and Reinert (1997).

equilibrium model (DCGE). The model developed in this paper incorporates, capital accumulation, trade in financial assets, costs of reallocating factors of production and a slow phase-in of trade policy changes. In a companion paper, (Kouparitsas, 1998), I analyze the dynamic gains from trade and show that ignoring capital accumulation and trade in financial assets reduces the welfare gains of trade liberalization, while ignoring the costs of reallocating factors of production and the slow phase-in of policies overstates the welfare gains of trade liberalization.

The remainder of the chapter is organized as follows. The North American trade model is described in detail in section 4.2. Model parameterization and the method used to generate the model's transitional dynamics are discussed in section 4.3. Section 4.4 reports the chapter's main results on unilateral vs. reciprocal liberalization. The chapter concludes in section 4.5 by way of a brief summary of the main results and suggestions for future empirical research.

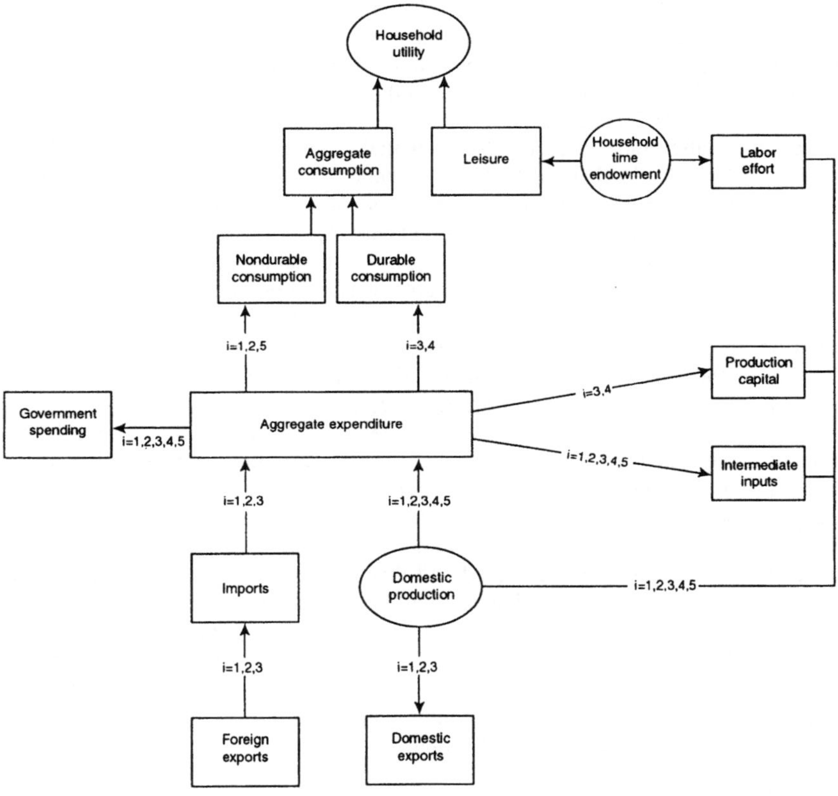

Notes: i denotes industry—primary, i=1; nondurable manufacturing, i=2; durable manufacturing, i=3; construction, i=4; services, i=5.

Figure 4.1 Model Flow Diagram for a Representative Country

4.2 A Model of North American Trade

The model developed in this paper is similar to earlier DCGE studies of U.S. unilateral trade liberalization by Goulder and Eichengreen (1992) and multilateral liberalization of the Asia Pacific region by McKibbin and Wilcoxen (1996). The main difference between the present paper and these earlier studies is that I am interested in the consequences of unilateral and reciprocal liberalization across North American countries. I follow these earlier studies by modeling the countries/regions of interest individually (U.S. and Canada in the case of the CFTA analysis, and the CFTA region and Mexico in the case of the NAFTA analysis), while consigning the remaining countries to a residual rest of the world (ROW). All countries/regions, including the ROW, are fully specified in the sense that production, consumption, investment, work effort and trade decisions are the result of explicit optimization decisions.

The inclusion of a fully specified ROW ensures that all quantities and prices are determined within the model. This avoids the need for ad hoc residual ROW supply and demand equations and constant import prices that are used in partial equilibrium dynamic studies, such as, Keuschnigg and Kohler (1997) and Jorgenson and Ho (1994). This feature of the model is an important part of the present study, and arguably all trade liberalization analysis, since I am interested in the effects of unilateral and reciprocal trade liberalization on the liberalizing countries' terms of trade.

Figure 4.1 provides a summary of the domestic and international goods and factor flows in the model. Each country/region has five production industries: primary raw materials, non-durable manufactures, durable manufactures, construction, and services. Primary raw materials, non-durable manufactures and durable manufactures are traded goods, while construction and services are non-traded goods. Primary goods include agriculture and mining; these goods are largely used as intermediate inputs in the production of non-durable and durable manufactured goods. Non-durable manufactures include food processing, beverages, chemicals, textiles, paper and apparel used as intermediate inputs in the production of other goods and a non-durable consumption good. Durable goods include basic metal and non-metal products, wood and furniture products, machinery and transportation equipment. Construction includes residential and non-residential structures. The production and household capital stocks are made up from investment of durable manufactures, construction goods and service sector inputs. Services cover utilities, finance, insurance, real estate, transportation, and retail and wholesale activities. Services are largely used as a non-durable consumption good. In the following discussion industries are indexed by i or j, while countries/regions are indexed by h or ℓ.

4.2.1 Preferences

Each country, ℓ, has a single infinitely lived representative household that maximizes its lifetime utility, U_ℓ, at time t=0, from consuming a composite consumption good $c_{\ell t}$ and leisure $L_{\ell t}$:

$$U_\ell = \sum_{t=0}^{\infty} \beta^t \frac{\left(c_{\ell t}^{\theta_{c\ell}} L_{\ell t}^{1-\theta_{c\ell}}\right)^{1-\sigma}}{1-\sigma} \text{ for } \sigma > 0 \text{ and } \sigma \neq 1,$$

and (4.1)

$$U_\ell = \sum_{t=0}^{\infty} \beta^t \left[\theta_{c\ell} \ln(c_{\ell t}) + (1-\theta_{c\ell}) \ln(L_{\ell t})\right] \text{ for } \sigma = 1,$$

where $0 < \beta < 1$, $0 < \theta_{c\ell} < 1$ for all ℓ. β denotes the household's subjective rate of time discount and $1/\sigma$ is the household's intertemporal elasticity of substitution.

Consumption is an aggregate of non-durable consumption goods, $nd_{\ell t}$, and the service flow from the household durable goods, which is assumed to be proportional to the stock of household durable goods, $d_{\ell t}$. Non-durable goods and the flow of services from household durable goods are aggregated according to a constant elasticity of substitution (CES) function:

$$c_{\ell t} = \left(\omega_{c\ell} nd_{\ell t}^{1-\eta} + (1-\omega_{c\ell}) d_{\ell t}^{1-\eta}\right)^{\frac{1}{1-\eta}}, \tag{4.2}$$

where $0 \leq \omega_{c\ell} \leq 1$ and $\eta > 0$ for all ℓ. The elasticity of substitution between non-durable consumption goods and durable services is $1/\eta$. Different varieties of non-durable consumption goods, $c_{j\ell t}$, are also aggregated by a CES function:

$$nd_{\ell t} = \sum_j \left(\omega_{cj\ell} c_{j\ell t}^{1-\kappa}\right)^{\frac{1}{1-\kappa}}, \tag{4.3}$$

where $0 \leq \omega_{cj\ell} \leq 1, \sum_j \omega_{cj\ell} \leq 1$ and $\kappa > 0$ for all ℓ. The elasticity of substitution between different varieties of non-durable consumption goods is $1/\kappa$.

4.2.2 Production Technology

Following the static CGE literature, I make the standard multi-sector assumption that sector j's gross production, $y_{j\ell t}$, is described by a two-level CES function (see, for example, Shoven and Whalley, 1992):

$$y_{j\ell t} = \left(\omega_{yj\ell} va_{j\ell t}^{1-\varepsilon_j} + (1-\omega_{yj\ell}) m_{j\ell t}^{1-\varepsilon_j}\right)^{\frac{1}{1-\varepsilon_j}}, \tag{4.4}$$

where $0 \leq \omega_{yj\ell} \leq 1$ and $\varepsilon > 0$ for all j, ℓ. The first level of production involves a "value-added" term, $va_{j\ell t}$, and an "intermediate goods" term, $m_{j\ell t}$. The elasticity of substitution between the value-added and intermediate inputs in sector j is $1/\varepsilon_j$.
The value-added term is described by Cobb-Douglas technology, which uses capital $k_{j\ell t}^s$ and labor services $N_{j\ell t}^s$:

$$va_{j\ell t} = k_{j\ell t}^{s\theta_{j\ell}} N_{j\ell t}^{s1-\theta_{j\ell}}, \tag{4.5}$$

where $0 < \theta_{j\ell} \leq 1$ for all j, ℓ.

The other factor of production is the intermediate goods term, which is a composite of intermediate inputs from all five sectors. In the following discussion, $m_{ij\ell t}$ denotes the flow of intermediate goods from sector i to sector j in country ℓ. These different types of intermediate inputs are aggregated according to the following CES function:

$$m_{j\ell t} = \sum_i \left(\alpha_{ij\ell} m_{ij\ell t}^{1-\psi_j}\right)^{\frac{1}{1-\psi_j}} , \tag{4.6}$$

where $0 \le \alpha_{ij\ell} \le 1$, $\sum_i \alpha_{ij\ell} = 1$ and $\psi > 0$ for all i, j, ℓ. The elasticity of substitution between different types of intermediate inputs in sector j is $1/\psi_j$.

4.2.3 Investment Behavior

There are two types of physical investment in this model. First, firms and households invest in physical capital goods that are either used as inputs in the production of goods or household services. Production capital, $x_{\ell t}$, and household durable investment, $s_{\ell t}$, is a composite of durable manufactures, $z_{3\ell t}$, construction, $z_{4\ell t}$, and service goods, $z_{5\ell t}$. The three types of investment goods are aggregated according to a CES function:

$$x_{\ell t} + s_{\ell t} = \sum_j \left(\omega_{zj\ell} z_{j\ell t}^{1-\upsilon}\right)^{\frac{1}{1-\upsilon}} , \tag{4.7}$$

where $0 \le \omega_{zj\ell} \le 1, \sum_j \omega_{zj\ell} = 1$ and $\upsilon > 0$ for all j, ℓ. The elasticity of substitution between different varieties of investment goods is $1/\upsilon$.
I assume that production and household capital goods depreciate at a rate δ. Another feature of the dynamic model is that it allows for costs of adjusting sectoral and aggregate capital stocks. I use a quadratic aggregate cost of adjustment function in which the size of the adjustment costs is determined by the parameter, ξ. Higher values of ξ imply greater adjustment costs. Using this notation, I can describe the accumulation of production capital, $k_{j\ell t}$, and household durable goods, $d_{j\ell t}$, in country ℓ by the following:

$$k_{\ell t+1} = x_{\ell t} - \frac{\xi}{2}\left(\frac{x_{\ell t}}{k_{\ell t}} - \frac{x_\ell}{k_\ell}\right)^2 k_{\ell t} + (1-\delta)k_{\ell t}, \tag{4.8}$$

$$d_{\ell t+1} = s_{\ell t} - \frac{\xi}{2}\left(\frac{s_{\ell t}}{d_{\ell t}} - \frac{s_\ell}{d_\ell}\right)^2 d_{\ell t} + (1-\delta)d_{\ell t}, \tag{4.9}$$

where $0 < \delta \le 1, \xi > 0$ and x_ℓ / k_ℓ and s_ℓ / d_ℓ denote the steady state investment to capital stock and household durable investment to durable stock ratios, for all ℓ.

I also allow for costs of adjusting sectoral capital stocks using a similar convex sectoral cost of adjustment function. Sector j's service flow from capital is described by the following:

$$k_{j\ell t}^s = k_{j\ell t} - \frac{\xi_j}{2}\left(\frac{k_{j\ell t}}{k_{\ell t}} - \frac{k_{j\ell}}{k_\ell}\right)^2 k_{\ell t}, \tag{4.10}$$

$$k_{\ell t} = \sum_j k_{j\ell t} \tag{4.11}$$

where $\xi_j > 0$ and $k_{j\ell} / k_\ell$ denotes the steady state ratio of sector j to aggregate capital for all j, ℓ.

Secondly, firms store goods for later use as intermediate inputs in the production of future goods. The time period in the model is a quarter, drawing on the empirical evidence from Ramey (1989) who suggests that intermediate goods require one quarter to put in place. Based on this finding, I assume that period $t+1$ intermediate inputs, $m_{ij\ell t+1}$, are produced in period t.

4.2.4 Trade Flows

The model allows for trade between the North American countries of interest and the ROW. Where the ROW is a composite of Canadian and U.S. (CFTA area and Mexican) trading partners in the case of the CFTA (NAFTA). Let $f_{jh\ell t}$ denote country ℓ 's private use of good j produced in country h. For $h \neq \ell$, $f_{jh\ell t}$ denotes country ℓ 's private imports of good j from country h. Private final expenditure for good j is described by the following, using a CES aggregation function for foreign and home goods:

$$c_{j\ell t} + z_{j\ell t} + \sum_i m_{ji\ell t+1} = \sum_k \left(\omega_{jh\ell} f_{jk\ell t}^{1-\mu_j} \right)^{\frac{1}{1-\mu_j}}, \tag{4.12}$$

where $0 \leq \omega_{jh\ell} \leq 1$, $\sum_h \omega_{jh\ell} = 1$ and $\mu_j > 0$ for all j, ℓ.[5] Recall that $c_{j\ell t}$ describes non-durable consumption of good j, $z_{j\ell t}$ describes investment using good j, and $m_{ij\ell t}$ denotes the flow of intermediate goods from sector i to sector j at time t. The elasticity of substitution between home produced and all imported varieties of good j is $1/\mu_j$.

4.2.5 Government

Each country has a government that imposes tariffs and non-tariff barriers on imported goods. The tariff rate in country ℓ for good j imported from country h is $\tau_{jh\ell t}$. It is difficult to model non-tariff barriers (NTBs) directly so I take the standard approach of using so-called tariff equivalent NTBs. A tariff equivalent NTB is simply the level of tariff protection that would yield the same allocation of output, expenditure and factors of production as the NTB in the pre-liberalized steady state. The country ℓ tariff equivalent NTB for good j imported from country h is $\rho_{jh\ell t}$. The revenue from the tariff and the quota rents from the NTBs are rebated by lump-sum payments, denoted by $TR_{\ell t}$ and $QR_{\ell t}$ respectively. The government also levies a lump-sum tax, $LT_{\ell t}$, to finance its current spending. The price of country h's good j in terms of the numeraire

[5] Differentiating goods by location is necessary to rule out complete specialization. See Baxter (1992) for a discussion of how complete specialization, along the lines of Ricardian comparative advantage, emerges in a dynamic Heckscher-Ohlin-Samuleson model where goods are not differentiated by production location.

good is denoted by p_{jht}.[6] Using this notation, country ℓ's government budget constraint is given by the following:

$$\sum_h \sum_j p_{jht} g_{jh\ell t} + TR_{\ell t} + QR_{\ell t} = \sum_{h \neq \ell} \sum_j \left(\tau_{jh\ell t} + \tau_{jh\ell t} \right) p_{jht} f_{jh\ell t} + LT_{\ell t}, \tag{4.13}$$

$$TR_{\ell t} = \sum_{h \neq \ell} \sum_j \tau_{jh\ell t} p_{jht} f_{jh\ell t}, \tag{4.14}$$

$$QR_{\ell t} = \sum_{h \neq \ell} \sum_j \rho_{jh\ell t} p_{jht} f_{jh\ell t}, \tag{4.15}$$

where $g_{jh\ell t}$ is the country ℓ's government consumption of good j from country h. Combining these results implies $LT_{\ell t} = \sum_h \sum_i p_{iht} g_{ih\ell t}$. For simplicity, I assume that the public sector and the private sector have the same aggregation function for all goods, so real government spending on good j is:[7]

$$g_{j\ell t} = \sum_h \left(\omega_{jh\ell} g_{jh\ell t}^{1-\mu_j} \right)^{\frac{1}{1-\mu_j}}, \tag{4.16}$$

Real government spending is held constant in the trade policy simulations.

4.2.6 Resource Constraints

Labor, $N_{\ell t}$, is a non-reproducible factor of production and is mobile between sectors $N_{j\ell t}$ within a country, subject to small adjustment costs. Following my approach to sectoral capital adjustment costs, I employ a quadratic cost of adjustment function where the costs of adjusting labor in sector j are governed by a parameter φ_j, where higher levels imply higher adjustment costs. Using this notation, sector j's effective input of labor is:

$$N_{j\ell t}^s = N_{j\ell t} - \frac{\varphi_j}{2} \left(\frac{N_{j\ell t}}{N_{\ell t}} - \frac{N_{j\ell}}{N_\ell} \right)^2 N_{\ell t}, \tag{4.17}$$

$$N_{\ell t} = \sum_j N_{j\ell t}, \tag{4.18}$$

where $\varphi_j > 0$ for all j, ℓ. The household's endowment of total hours is normalized to unity, which imposes the following constraint on labor and leisure:

$$1 - L_{\ell t} - N_{\ell t} = 0 \text{ for all } \ell. \tag{4.19}$$

Households trade one period bonds $b_{\ell t}$ and the price of these assets in terms of the numeraire good is p_{bt}. With this notation in hand, in each country, a representative household's intertemporal budget constraint is:

$$\sum_j p_{j\ell t} y_{j\ell t} + b_{\ell t} + QR_{\ell t} + TR_{\ell t} = \sum_h \sum_j \left(1 + \tau_{jh\ell t} + \rho_{jh\ell t} \right) p_{jht} f_{jh\ell t} + LT_{\ell t} \text{ for all } \ell. \tag{4.20}$$

[6] I maintain ROW non-durable manufactured goods as the numeraire throughout the analysis.

[7] Backus, Kehoe and Kydland (1995) make a similar assumption in their dynamic one-sector model of international trade.

Each regional economy is also subject to the following sectoral resource constraints:

$$y_{j\ell t} = \sum_h x_{jh\ell t} + g_{jh\ell t} \text{ for all } \ell . \tag{4.21}$$

Finally, regional economies are subject to an international bond market constraint:

$$\sum_\ell b_{\ell t} = 0 . \tag{4.22}$$

4.2.7 Equilibrium and Model Solution

The representative household in each country/region owns all productive inputs. Each period, households maximize their utility by selling their capital services, labor services and intermediate goods to firms in the same country on the competitive market, taking prices as given, and buying goods from domestic and foreign firms on the competitive market, taking prices as given. Households also trade assets internationally with foreign residents on the competitive market, taking the price as given. Firms maximize profits by selling their goods on the competitive market, taking prices as given, to both domestic and foreign residents and buying capital services, labor inputs and intermediate goods from households in the same economy on the competitive market, taking prices as given. The competitive equilibrium is described by the sequences of capital, labor, consumption, investment, bonds and their associated prices that satisfy the regional representative household's and firm's optimization problems and the market clearing conditions.

Since I assume that the agents have perfect foresight, this allows me to follow Mendoza and Tesar (1998) in solving for the model's post-liberalization steady state and transitional dynamics using a linearized version of the shooting algorithm proposed by Lipton, *et al.*, (1982). This approach is necessary because the solution of the transitional dynamics of trade liberalization requires the simultaneous solution of the paths of foreign debt accumulation and the net foreign asset positions in the post-liberalization steady state.

Following Mendoza and Tesar (1998), I take an initial guess of the long-run bond positions to which countries converge after trade liberalization and solve for the post-liberalization steady state. I then use the linear approximation algorithm of King, *et al.*, (1988) to generate the transitional dynamics around this new steady state. Using this approximation, I simulate the transitional dynamics for 2,500 periods by setting the initial conditions to the pre-liberalization values of the state variables. The simulations produce a path of foreign debt dynamics that converges to some long-run position; if this long-run position differs from the initial guess, the post-liberalization debt positions are updated and the process is repeated. The number of iterations it takes to converge depends on the non-linearity of the model. For example, this method converges in just a few iterations if household preferences and production functions are assumed to be Cobb-Douglas.

4.3 Benchmark Parameters

The model must be parameterized before I can apply numerical solution methods. Direct estimation of all the model's parameters is ruled out by the fact that there are insufficient international data to estimate all preference, production, and trade parameters. Researchers working with SCGE models have overcome this problem by using model calibration (see, for example, Shoven and Whalley 1992). More recently, this approach has been extended to DCGE models of international trade (see, for example, Backus, *et al.*, 1995). Calibration essentially involves two steps. First, the researcher chooses a set of elasticities that describe the degree of substitution in consumption, production, and trade. Secondly, given this set of elasticities, the researcher chooses shares in preference, production, and trade aggregation functions so that the model's steady state matches actual expenditure, output, production, and trade shares estimated from data at a specific point in time (or the base year).

In my case, I draw on the SCGE and DCGE literatures whenever possible. Multi-sector features of the dynamic model are calibrated using elasticities from well-known static studies such as Roland-Holst, *et al.*, (1994); Brown, *et al.*, (1992); Sorbazo (1994) and Whalley (1985). Similarly, dynamic features of the model are calibrated by drawing on the parameter set used in the international DCGE literature. I follow most SCGE studies of the CFTA and NAFTA in calibrating the model's base years or pre-liberalization steady states to data from 1988. Table 4.1 summarizes the model's parameters.

4.3.1 Reference Parameters

I follow the DCGE literature in specifying that the intertemporal elasticity of substitution $1/\sigma$ is 0.5 and that the consumption/leisure share parameter $\theta_{c\ell}$ is consistent with 20 percent of the agent's total time being devoted to market activity. This assumption is more general than the utility functions used in Goulder and Eichengreen (1992) and McKibbin and Wilcoxen (1996) where a fixed supply of labor was assumed by imposing that $\theta_{c\ell} = 1$. The subjective discount factor, β, is set to 0.9852, implying an annual interest rate of about 5 percent. My benchmark elasticities of substitution for household durable, $1/\eta$, and non-durable, $1/\kappa$, goods are set to unity (that is, nested household preferences are Cobb-Douglas), which is typical in SCGE studies. Finally, $\omega_{c\ell}$ and $\omega_{cj\ell}$ are calibrated so that they match national accounts estimates of household non-durable and durable expenditure shares for 1988.

4.3.2 Production and Investment Parameters

The description of production in the previous section follows the static CGE literature by assuming a two level CES structure, with a Cobb-Douglas value-added component and intermediate goods aggregated by a CES function. I rely on Bruno's (1984) estimate of the elasticity of substitution between the value-added component and the intermediate goods aggregate. He finds that across industrial countries this elasticity is 0.5, suggesting that there are greater substitution possibilities in my dynamic model than is typical in static CGE studies that assume production is Leontief by imposing zero elasticities of substitution. I follow the static literature in assuming that the elasticity of substitution between different types of intermediate goods is the same as the elasticity of substitution between value-added and intermediate inputs. All other production parameters are derived from cost shares estimated from the input-output tables of Canada, Mexico and the U.S. The ROW is largely made up of large industrial countries, so I model their production functions using U.S. input-output data.

Table 4.1 Benchmark Parameters

	CFTA			NAFTA			All
	Canada	US	ROW	Mexico	CFTA	ROW	
Preferences							
β							0.98
$1/\sigma$							0.50
θ_c							0.18
$1/\eta$							1
ω_c							0.80
$1/\kappa$							1
ω_{c1}	0.01	0.01	0.01	0.08	0.01	0.01	
ω_{c2}	0.17	0.17	0.17	0.24	0.17	0.17	
ω_{c5}	0.82	0.82	0.82	0.68	0.82	0.82	
Investment							
δ							0.03
$1/\upsilon$							1
ω_{i3}	0.52	0.52	0.52	0.41	0.52	0.52	
ω_{i4}	0.39	0.39	0.39	0.47	0.39	0.39	
ω_{i5}	0.09	0.09	0.09	0.12	0.09	0.09	
ξ							10
Production							
$1/\varepsilon$							0.5
$1/\psi$							0.5
Primary							
θ_1	0.35	0.35	0.35	0.35	0.35	0.35	
ω_{y1}	0.70	0.43	0.34	0.96	0.35	0.27	
α_{11}	0.29	0.32	0.36	0.31	0.31	0.35	
α_{21}	0.05	0.06	0.07	0.38	0.07	0.07	
α_{31}	0.01	0.01	0.01	0.04	0.01	0.01	
α_{41}	0.00	0.00	0.00	0.00	0.00	0.00	
α_{51}	0.64	0.61	0.56	0.27	0.61	0.57	
ξ_1							100
φ_1							100
Non-Durable Man.							
θ_2	0.48	0.48	0.48	0.63	0.48	0.48	
ω_{y2}	0.64	0.36	0.32	0.74	0.33	0.27	
α_{12}	0.13	0.13	0.13	0.36	0.12	0.13	
α_{22}	0.51	0.56	0.59	0.44	0.57	0.58	
α_{32}	0.01	0.01	0.01	0.00	0.01	0.01	
α_{42}	0.00	0.00	0.00	0.00	0.00	0.00	
α_{52}	0.36	0.30	0.27	0.19	0.30	0.28	
ξ_2							10
φ_2							10
Durable Man.							
θ_3	0.32	0.32	0.32	0.57	0.32	0.32	

Table 4.1 (continued)

	CFTA			NAFTA			All
	Canada	US	ROW	Mexico	CFTA	ROW	
ω_{y3}	0.63	0.32	0.22	0.78	0.23	0.16	
α_{13}	0.00	0.00	0.00	0.03	0.00	0.00	
α_{23}	0.03	0.03	0.03	0.03	0.03	0.03	
α_{33}	0.55	0.60	0.68	0.51	0.63	0.68	
α_{43}	0.00	0.00	0.00	0.00	0.00	0.00	
α_{53}	0.42	0.37	0.29	0.42	0.34	0.29	
ξ_3							10
φ_3							10
Construction							
θ_4	0.34	0.34	0.34	0.30	0.34	0.34	
ω_{y4}	0.65	0.37	0.27	0.75	0.27	0.21	
α_{14}	0.00	0.00	0.00	0.00	0.00	0.00	
α_{24}	0.01	0.02	0.02	0.02	0.02	0.02	
α_{34}	0.30	0.35	0.44	0.60	0.37	0.43	
α_{44}	0.00	0.00	0.00	0.00	0.00	0.00	
α_{54}	0.68	0.63	0.54	0.37	0.61	0.55	
ξ_4							10
φ_4							10
Services							
θ_5	0.33	0.33	0.33	0.60	0.33	0.33	
ω_{y5}	0.81	0.58	0.51	0.98	0.49	0.42	
α_{15}	0.00	0.00	0.00	0.00	0.00	0.00	
α_{25}	0.01	0.02	0.02	0.04	0.02	0.02	
α_{35}	0.00	0.00	0.00	0.00	0.00	0.00	
α_{45}	0.01	0.01	0.01	0.02	0.01	0.01	
α_{55}	0.97	0.97	0.97	0.93	0.97	0.97	
ξ_5							10
φ_5							10
Trade							
Primary							
$1/\mu_1$							1.5
ω_{1can}	0.62	0.11	0.06				
ω_{1usa}	0.23	0.66	0.18				
ω_{1mex}				0.72	0.12	0.05	
ω_{1cfta}				0.17	0.66	0.22	
ω_{1row}	0.15	0.22	0.76	0.10	0.22	0.72	
Non-Durable Man.							
$1/\mu_2$							1.5
ω_{2can}	0.66	0.08	0.02				
ω_{2usa}	0.25	0.78	0.12				
ω_{2mex}				0.73	0.04	0.02	
ω_{2cfta}				0.18	0.79	0.15	
ω_{2row}	0.09	0.15	0.86	0.09	0.17	0.84	
Durable Man.							
$1/\mu_3$							1.5
ω_{3can}	0.44	0.14	0.02				
ω_{3usa}	0.41	0.62	0.18				
ω_{3mex}				0.52	0.06	0.01	
ω_{3cfta}				0.32	0.65	0.20	
ω_{3row}	0.15	0.24	0.80	0.17	0.29	0.78	

The quarterly depreciation rate, δ, is set at 3 percent and the aggregate capital adjustment parameter, ξ, is set to 10, which is consistent with most quarterly DCGE studies. My estimates of the sectoral labor and capital adjustment costs function parameters are based on the multi-sector international real business cycle analysis of Kouparitsas (1996). I show in that paper that the observed volatility of U.S. sectoral investment and labor hours implies relatively higher adjustment costs in the primary sector, which is consistent with the view that primary sector factors of production are more industry specific.

There is a dearth of empirical literature on the degree of substitution between different types of household and industrial durable goods. In light of this, I follow the SCGE literature's approach to non-durable aggregation by setting the elasticity of substitution between different types of durable goods to unity. The ω_{xjt}'s are calibrated so that they match estimates of expenditure shares for investment goods from national account data for 1988.

Table 4.2 Levels of Protection in North America Prior to Implementation of CFTA and NAFTA

Tariff

Primary products

	Exporter			
Importer	Canada	Mexico	U.S.	ROW
Canada		0.01	0.01	0.00
Mexico	0.00		0.02	0.00
U.S.	0.01	0.01		0.01

Non-durable manufactured goods

	Exporter			
Importer	Canada	Mexico	U.S.	ROW
Canada		0.18	0.07	0.14
Mexico	0.04		0.05	0.10
U.S.	0.04	0.05		0.10

Durable manufactured goods

	Exporter			
Importer	Canada	Mexico	U.S.	ROW
Canada		0.04	0.02	0.04
Mexico	0.01		0.03	0.02
U.S.	0.01	0.03		0.03

Composite protection rates (tariffs and NTBs)

Primary products

	Exporter			
Importer	Canada	Mexico	U.S.	ROW
Canada		0.20	0.61	0.27
Mexico	0.80		0.81	0.72
U.S.	0.61	0.88		0.77

Non-durable manufactured goods

	Exporter			
Importer	Canada	Mexico	U.S.	ROW
Canada		0.68	0.34	0.44
Mexico	0.78		0.41	0.47
U.S.	0.16	0.22		0.20

Durable manufactured goods

	Exporter			
Importer	Canada	Mexico	U.S.	ROW
Canada		0.25	0.26	0.31
Mexico	0.01		0.13	0.22
U.S.	0.39	0.07		0.28

Notes: Roland-Holst, *et al.* (1994) report estimates for 26 sectors. Sectoral aggregates reported in this article are weighted by 1988 import shares. ROW is rest of the world.

Source: Roland-Holst, *et al.* (1994)

4.3.3 Trade Flow and Policy Parameters

Explicit tariff rates are readily available from various national and international trade organizations and previous static studies. In contrast, it is difficult to incorporate NTBs, such as quotas and other non-price restrictions, in SCGE models, so researchers use so-called tariff equivalent measures of NTBs in their quantitative analysis. A tariff equivalent NTB is simply the tariff that would be necessary to generate the same sectoral and international distribution of output, expenditure and factors of production as the NTB in the pre-liberalized steady state. Table 4.2 provides an overview of the Roland-Host, *et al.* (1994) comprehensive estimates of the levels of tariff and tariff equivalent NTB protection that existed prior to the signing of the CFTA and NAFTA in 1988. For comparability with earlier static analyses, I set the pre-CFTA and NAFTA levels of protection in my model to match Roland-Holst *et al.*'s estimates. The resulting sectoral and international distribution of output, expenditure and factors of production are close to the base year data. This suggests that the alternative strategy of estimating the tariff equivalent NTB's directly from the dynamic model using the actual sectoral and international distribution of output, expenditure and factors of production would yield values similar to those estimated by Roland-Holst, *et al.* (1994).

The CFTA was signed in 1988 and was designed to eliminate all trade barriers between Canada and the U.S., as described in table 4.2. The majority of the tariff reductions were to be phased in over a 10 to 15 year period, starting the first quarter of 1989 and ending in 2004. NAFTA followed the signing of the CFTA in 1992, so I model NAFTA as the joint free trade agreement between the CFTA area and Mexico. In practical terms, NAFTA involves the removal of barriers to Mexican exports to CFTA area, and CFTA area exports to Mexico. In similar fashion to the CFTA, the majority of tariff reductions are expected to be phased-in over 10 to 15 years, starting in the first quarter of 1994 and ending in 2009. All policy simulations begin in the period following the signing of the initial trade agreement (first quarter of 1988 for CFTA and first quarter of 1993 for NAFTA). I conduct the simulations as if agents in the world economy perfectly anticipated the path of trade liberalization described above. This assumes that agents knew at the date of the initial signing that the CFTA and NAFTA would be implemented one year after the signing and phased-in over a 15 year period.

There is a wide range of values for the elasticity of substitution between home and foreign goods, $1/\mu_j$, used in the quantitative trade literature. I consider a range of values; my benchmark model adopts an elasticity of 1.5 for all goods, a value that is widely used in the international DCGE literature (see, for example, Backus, *et al.*, 1995) and multi-country static CGE studies of trade liberation, such as Whalley (1985). My lower bound estimates are based on the empirical studies of Shiells and Reinert (1993) for Canada and the U.S., and Sobarzo (1994) for Mexico, which were used by Roland-Host, *et al.*, (1994) in their analysis of the CFTA and NAFTA. They find the elasticity of substitution is closer to unity. My upper bound is based on the Brown, *et al.*, (1992) trade liberalization analysis that uses an elasticity of substitution of 3. My sensitivity analysis suggests that the welfare gains depend critically on these elasticities of substitution; trade liberalization generates significantly lower welfare effects if there is a low degree of substitution between home and foreign goods. However, my sensitivity analysis shows that the main results reported in this paper are robust to the range of parameters used in quantitative trade liberalization analyses. Note that I adjust the $\omega_{jk\ell}$'s across these experiments so that the models' trade shares match the pattern found in trade flow data for the North American countries/regions in 1988.

4.4 Unilateral vs. Reciprocal Liberalization

Below, I report the results of simulations of the quantitative North American trade model under various unilateral and reciprocal trade liberalization scenarios. Before turning to those findings I describe the welfare measure used in this paper.

4.4.1 Welfare Analysis

I calculate the welfare effects of liberalization by measuring the effect on country ℓ 's representative households' lifetime utility U_ℓ. For example, let λ_ℓ represent the permanent percentage change in the level of pre-liberalization consumption in country ℓ that would make households in country ℓ as well off as the path of consumption and leisure enjoyed under trade liberalization $\{\tilde{c}_{\ell t}, \tilde{L}_{\ell t}\}_{t=0}^{\infty}$, that is:

$$\sum_{t=0}^{\infty} \beta^t u\left(\bar{c}_\ell (1+\lambda_\ell), \bar{L}_\ell\right) = \sum_{t=0}^{\infty} \beta^t u\left(\tilde{c}_{\ell t}, \tilde{L}_{\ell t}\right), \tag{4.23}$$

where u is the representative household's momentary utility function and $\left(\bar{c}_\ell, \bar{L}_\ell\right)$ is country ℓ 's representative household's respective steady state levels of consumption and leisure in the pre-liberalization environment. In other words, $\bar{c}_\ell \lambda_\ell$ measures the amount by which one would have to change consumption in the pre-liberalized environment to make households as well off as under trade liberalization (λ_ℓ is typically referred to as the compensating variation). If $\lambda_\ell > 0$ households in country ℓ are better off than they were in the pre-liberalization steady state.

4.4.2 Welfare Effects of Reciprocal Liberalization

The top row of table 4.3 reports the welfare calculations from the CFTA and NAFTA experiments. The first three columns of table 4.3 show that the compensating variation in consumption required to leave households indifferent between the initial steady state and the CFTA is 2.07 percent for Canada and 0.21 percent for the U.S. Based on these results, the CFTA leads to welfare improvements for Canada and the U.S. The last three columns of table 4.3 report the same calculations for the NAFTA experiments. My estimates suggest that NAFTA will improve welfare of the CFTA area and Mexico. The compensating variation in consumption is 0.08 percent for the CFTA area and 1.12 percent for Mexico. In each case, the welfare improvements are greater for the small country. Note also that the ROW also gains from the CFTA and NAFTA.

4.4.3 Aggregate Effects of Reciprocal Liberalization

The middle panel of table 4.3 reports the aggregate steady state effects of the CFTA in the first three columns and NAFTA in the last three columns. The CFTA is estimated to have had a larger effect on North America than NAFTA; apart from this finding, the response to the CFTA and NAFTA policies are quite similar. My estimates suggest that the reciprocal agreements will or have led to an expansion of output, investment, consumption, labor hours and trade for both liberalizing partners. The smaller countries are expected to enjoy a much larger gain in their steady state output. Under the CFTA, U.S. steady state gross domestic product (GDP) is estimated to have risen by 2.04 percent, which is considerably smaller than the estimated 11.09 percent increase in Canadian steady state GDP. Similarly, under NAFTA, Mexico's steady state GDP is predicted to rise by 6.87 percent, while the CFTA area's steady state GDP is expected to rise by 0.55 percent.

Table 4.3 Long-run effects of North American Bilateral Trade Agreements *(percentage deviation from pre-liberalization steady state)*

	CFTA			**NAFTA**		
Variable	**Canada**	**U.S.**	**ROW**	**Mexico**	**CFTA**	**ROW**
Welfare effects	2.07	0.21	0.06	1.12	0.08	0.03
Aggregate effects						
Real GDP	11.09	2.04	-0.02	6.87	0.55	-0.01
Real consumption	8.45	1.67	0.17	5.36	0.45	0.06
Labor hours	3.42	0.50	-0.11	3.28	0.17	-0.03
Real wage	8.28	1.67	0.13	5.08	0.48	0.04
Capital stock	19.17	3.68	0.13	8.40	0.66	0.02
Real rental rate	-6.31	-1.42	-0.10	-1.38	0.01	-0.01
Total imports	42.57	11.95	1.98	26.07	3.44	0.62
Exports to World	47.39	12.93	-0.68	29.64	3.71	-0.12
to Canada		60.93	2.51			
to U.S.	56.50		1.94			
to Mexico					41.08	1.29
to CFTA				38.38		0.60
to ROW	3.36	-1.05		2.27	-0.24	
Terms of trade	-0.90	-0.74	1.39	-0.78	-0.29	0.45
Net foreign assets/GDP	-5.43	-0.15	0.64	-3.84	0.04	0.19
Sectoral effects						
Primary						
Output	17.33	2.32	-0.22	19.39	-0.50	-0.56
Labor hours	9.43	0.77	-0.34	15.74	-1.17	-0.60
Capital stock	26.47	3.92	-0.11	23.32	-0.71	-0.55
Exports	46.51	9.96	-0.83	73.22	5.70	-3.29
Nondurable mfg.						
Output	9.62	3.28	0.02	7.10	1.43	-0.04
Labor hours	0.28	1.39	-0.12	1.48	0.73	-0.10
Capital stock	15.89	4.56	0.11	8.12	1.21	-0.04
Exports	23.27	13.99	0.24	25.43	5.32	-0.25
Durable mfg.						
Output	27.79	3.64	-0.23	7.13	1.00	0.05
Labor hours	18.48	1.95	-0.35	2.14	0.70	0.02
Capital stock	36.92	5.14	-0.12	8.82	1.17	0.08
Exports	56.55	13.16	-0.92	12.13	2.66	0.37
Construction						
Output	9.80	1.65	0.06	6.10	0.37	0.01
Labor hours	2.20	0.29	-0.06	2.62	0.12	-0.02
Capital stock	18.11	3.43	0.17	9.33	0.59	0.03
Services						
Output	6.23	1.21	0.05	3.98	0.28	0.01
Labor hours	0.60	0.06	-0.04	-0.08	0.05	-0.01
Capital stock	16.26	3.19	0.19	6.45	0.52	0.04

As predicted, liberalization leads to greater capital accumulation in the liberalizing countries. The fall in the real rental rate implies that the supply of capital increases by more than the demand for capital. Labor effort rises despite the increase in wealth, driven by the significant rise in the real wage. As expected, bilateral trade flows increase following trade liberalization. The CFTA is estimated to have increased the level of U.S.-Canada trade flows by 60 percent. The impact of NAFTA is smaller, with CFTA-Mexico trade flows expected to rise by 40 percent.

Another feature of these simulation results is the prediction that trade liberalization between a large and small country leads to a large capital inflow to the latter country. In the case of the CFTA, inflows to Canada are estimated to have increased by 5.43 percent of annual GDP, while the inflows to Mexico under NAFTA are expected to rise by 3.84 percent of annual GDP. Looking across the row (table 4.3), it is clear that the Canadian (and Mexican) capital inflows are jointly driven by capital flows from the U.S. (CFTA) and ROW.

Finally, these reciprocal agreements are also expected to have an asymmetric impact on the terms of trade of the large and small country, with the terms of trade of the small country deteriorating by more than those of the larger liberalizing partner.

4.4.4 Sectoral Effects of Reciprocal Liberalization

The lower panel of table 4.3 describes in detail the sectoral steady state effects of the CFTA in the first three columns and NAFTA in the last three columns. The CFTA is estimated to have expanded the steady state output of all U.S. and Canadian industries. Underlying this sectoral response is a large increase in the volume of U.S.-Canada trade in durable manufactured goods. Under NAFTA, all non-primary sectors are predicted to expand in the CFTA area and Mexico in the long run. In contrast to its North American partners, Mexico's primary sector is also expected to expand under NAFTA. Sectoral changes in labor hours and capital investment tend to mimic changes in sectoral GDP.

4.4.5 Welfare Effects of Unilateral Liberalization

Table 4.4 describes in detail the results of Canada and the U.S. (CFTA area and Mexico) unilaterally liberalizing their trade by the same level agreed to in the CFTA (NAFTA). In the upper panel, I report the results of the CFTA experiments involving Canada and the U.S while in the lower panel, I report the findings of the NAFTA experiments involving the CFTA area and Mexico. This table is organized the same way as table 4.3, but I limit the results to the welfare and aggregate effects of unilateral liberalization. The first three columns report the results of the smaller partner's unilateral liberalization (Canada in the upper panel and Mexico in the lower panel). The middle three columns report the results of the larger partner's unilateral liberalization (U.S. in the upper panel and CFTA area in the lower panel). The final three columns repeat the reciprocal liberalization results previously reported in table 4.3.

Three basic results emerge from these experiments. First, unilateral liberalization makes the liberalizing country worse off and its regional trading partner better off. Secondly, the liberalizing country's terms of trade deteriorate following liberalization, while its trading partner's terms of trade improve. Finally, the trade flows between the liberalizing country and its regional trading partner rise, while trade flows between the liberalizing country and the ROW fall.

Table 4.4 Long-run effects of unilateral and bilateral liberalization
(percentage deviation from pre-liberalization steady state)

	CFTA								
	Removal of barriers to U.S. exports in Canada			Removal of barriers to Canadian exports in U.S.			Removal of barriers to Canadian and U.S.		
Variable	Canada	U.S	ROW	Canada	U.S	ROW	Canada	U.S	ROW
Welfare effects	-5.48	1.33	0.00	7.56	-1.09	0.07	2.07	0.21	0.06
Aggregate effects									
Real GDP	6.15	0.54	-0.02	4.44	1.35	0.02	11.09	2.04	-0.02
Real consumption	-0.28	1.42	0.04	8.69	0.18	0.15	8.45	1.67	0.17
Labor hours	4.58	-0.37	-0.04	-1.23	0.81	-0.07	3.42	0.50	-0.11
Real wage	0.72	1.18	0.03	7.35	0.40	0.12	8.28	1.67	0.13
Capital stock	5.60	1.79	-0.01	12.66	1.65	0.17	19.17	3.68	0.13
Real rental rate	-0.13	-0.97	0.01	-6.23	-0.38	-0.12	-6.31	-1.42	-0.10
Total imports	8.85	7.87	0.77	30.31	2.46	1.95	42.57	11.95	1.98
Exports to World	32.28	2.46	-0.37	11.43	9.40	-0.13	47.39	12.93	-0.68
to U.S.		32.65	31.02		21.39	-21.58		60.93	2.51
to Canada	18.65		-1.63	31.57		3.81	56.50		1.94
to ROW	-18.73	1.29		26.75	-2.57		3.36	-1.05	
Terms of trade	-17.16	5.54	0.62	19.33	-6.45	1.38	-0.90	-0.74	1.39
Net foreign assets/GDP	-1.43	-0.26	0.26	-3.64	0.13	0.35	-5.43	-0.15	0.64
	NAFTA								
	Removal of barriers to CFTA exports in Mexico			Removal of barriers to Mexican exports in CFTA			Removal of barriers to Mexican and CFTA exports		
Variable	Mexico	CFTA	ROW	Mexico	CFTA	ROW	Mexico	CFTA	ROW
Welfare effects	-2.65	0.37	0.00	3.83	-0.29	0.04	1.12	0.08	0.03
Aggregate effects									
Real GDP	3.11	0.16	-0.01	3.61	0.36	0.01	6.87	0.55	-0.01
Real consumption	-0.32	0.39	0.01	5.66	0.04	0.06	5.36	0.45	0.06
Labor hours	2.94	-0.10	-0.01	0.19	0.25	-0.02	3.28	0.17	-0.03
Real wage	-0.07	0.33	0.01	5.09	0.12	0.04	5.08	0.48	0.04
Capital stock	1.81	0.47	-0.02	6.47	0.15	0.05	8.40	0.66	0.02
Real rental rate	0.81	-0.22	0.02	-2.21	0.23	-0.04	-1.38	0.01	-0.01
Total imports	5.80	2.25	0.16	18.88	0.80	0.65	26.07	3.44	0.62
Exports to World	20.00	0.74	-0.11	7.97	2.75	0.03	29.64	3.71	-0.12
to CFTA		20.05	19.90		17.43	-15.48		41.08	1.29
to Mexico	15.78		-0.61	19.17		1.28	38.38		0.60
to ROW	-13.48	0.51		18.32	-0.82		2.27	-0.24	
Terms of trade	-11.51	1.58	0.14	12.08	-2.01	0.46	-0.78	-0.29	0.45
Net foreign assets/GDP	-0.67	-0.09	0.08	-2.93	0.13	0.10	-3.84	0.04	0.19

4.4.6 Basic Intuition

Table 4.4 provides insight into the way that trade liberalization affects the liberalizing country and its trading partners. The intuition is essentially a dynamic analogue of the well-known static unilateral liberalization analysis presented in textbook discussions of optimal tariffs (see, for example, Caves and Jones, 1973, ch. 12). Trade liberalization creates an excess demand for the liberalizing country's imported goods and an excess supply of the liberalizing country's exported goods, lowering the relative price of the liberalizing country goods in terms of foreign goods. In other words, it leads to a worsening of the liberalizing country's terms of trade. This lowers the income/wealth of the liberalizing country and raises the income/wealth of its trading partners.

Liberalization lowers the cost of capital (that is, it shifts the supply curve of capital to the right) for all countries/regions, leading to greater capital accumulation, that in turn raises the demand for labor for both the liberalizing country and its trading partners. Real wages rise by relatively more in the non-liberalizing country because, in the liberalizing country, the increased demand for labor is offset by an increased supply of labor that comes from the fall in wealth due to the deterioration of the terms of trade. Real wages rise in the non-liberalizing country because greater wealth decreases the supply of labor. In fact, the wealth effect dominates the increased demand from labor coming from cheaper capital inputs, so labor effort is reduced in the non-liberalizing country.

The asymmetric wealth effects of unilateral trade liberalization are also evident in consumption. Lower wealth in the liberalizing country lowers consumption, this is only partially offset by higher real wages that raise consumption. In contrast, the wealth and real wage effects work in the same direction in the non-liberalizing country, thus generating a sizeable increase in consumption.

Table 4.5 Welfare payoffs from unilateral and bilateral liberalization

CFTA

U.S. \ Canada	Liberalize trade	Maintain barriers
Liberalize trade	0.21, 2.07	-1.09, 7.56
Maintain barriers	1.33, -5.48	0.00, 0.00

NAFTA

CFTA \ Mexico	Liberalize trade	Maintain barriers
Liberalize trade	0.08, 1.12	-0.29, 3.83
Maintain barriers	0.37, -2.65	0.00, 0.00

4.4.7 Prisoners' Dilemma

Table 4.5 summarizes the welfare data from table 4.4 in the form of a standard two agent, non-cooperative game in which the choices are to unilaterally liberalize trade or maintain trade barriers. The upper panel describes the game underlying the CFTA and the lower panel describes the game underlying NAFTA. The lower left element in each cell is the payoff to the large country while the upper right element is the payoff to the small country. Both games take on the form of the classic prisoners' dilemma. In each case liberalization is strictly dominated, so that in the absence of cooperation the outcome is the inefficient maintenance of barriers. In other words, the model predicts that in the absence of enforceable reciprocal agreements, such as the CFTA and NAFTA, the North American countries would maintain their trade barriers.

Table 4.6 Welfare payoffs from unilateral and bilateral liberalization (different trade elasticity estimates)

CFTA

	Low elasticity model		Benchmark model		High elasticity model	
Canada / U.S.	Liberalize trade	Maintain barriers	Liberalize trade	Maintain barriers	Liberalize trade	Maintain barriers
Liberalize	0.10	7.72	2.07	7.56	5.57	8.85
trade	0.10	-1.40	0.21	-1.09	0.47	-0.81
Maintain	-7.89	0.00	-5.48	0.00	-3.11	0.00
barriers	1.43	0.00	1.33	0.00	1.42	0.00

NAFTA

	Low elasticity model		Benchmark model		High elasticity model	
Mexico / CFTA	Liberalize trade	Maintain barriers	Liberalize trade	Maintain barriers	Liberalize trade	Maintain barriers
Liberalize	0.11	3.77	1.12	3.83	3.50	5.11
trade	0.02	-0.40	0.08	-0.29	0.26	-0.16
Maintain	-3.67	0.00	-2.65	0.00	-1.49	0.00
barriers	0.40	0.00	0.37	0.00	0.42	0.00

4.4.8 Sensitivity Analysis

There is a wide range of estimates of the elasticity of substitution between home and foreign goods used in the quantitative trade literature. Table 4.6 adds to the analysis of table 4.5 by revealing the payoff structure using different trade elasticity estimates from two well-known static CGE studies of the CFTA and NAFTA. The low elasticity panel refers to payoffs when the model is simulated with the elasticities used by Roland-Host, *et al.*, (1994). The high elasticity panel refers to the payoffs when the model is simulated with the elasticities used by Brown, *et al.*, (1992). They estimate the elasticity of substitution between home and foreign goods to be 3, which compares with the benchmark model elasticity of 1.5, and Roland-Host, *et al.*, (1994) estimate of around 1.

Although the magnitudes are different, the results of these experiments are qualitatively identical to those from the benchmark model. The most obvious quantitative difference is that the welfare gain (loss) from reciprocal (unilateral) liberalization is much greater (smaller) with higher elasticities of substitution. This comes about because relative prices are less responsive under higher elasticities of substitution, so the negative wealth effects of unilateral trade liberalization are reduced as elasticities rise. In addition, the deadweight losses associated with trade barriers rise as demand curves become more elastic.

4.5 Conclusion

Trade theory has long argued that while it may be in the best interests of a large country to pursue reciprocal trade agreements to escape from a terms-of-trade driven prisoners' dilemma, the best course of action for a small country is always unilateral trade liberalization. This prediction is inconsistent with the growing trend toward reciprocal trade agreements involving a small country and large country/region. Using simulation results from a quantitative trade model, I am able to shed light on why small and large countries pursue reciprocal trade agreements. I show that the payoffs from unilateral and reciprocal trade liberalization implicit in recent North American trade agreements between a small country and a large country/region take on the form of the well-known prisoners' dilemma. In particular, I find that, irrespective of country size, unilateral liberalization makes the liberalizing country worse off, while making its regional trading partner better off, and that cooperative agreements make all liberalizing partners better off. These estimates run counter to the prediction of trade theory because my model violates the key assumption that small countries cannot influence their terms of trade. In fact, I show that trade liberalization can have a significant impact on a small country's terms of trade for a wide range of estimates of the elasticity of substitution between domestic and foreign goods.

My quantitative analysis is limited to two recent North American trade agreements. An interesting extension of this paper, and a further test of the prisoners' dilemma theory of reciprocal trade liberalization, would be to estimate the payoffs implicit in other regional trade agreements involving small and large countries, such as the recent expansion of the European Community.

References

Backus, D.K., P.J. Kehoe and F.E. Kydland. 1995. "International business cycles: Theory and evidence." In: T.F. Cooley, ed. *Frontiers of Business Cycle Research.* Princeton, N.J., Princeton University Press.

Bagwell, K., and R.W. Staiger. 1998. "Will preferential agreements undermine the multilateral trading system?" *The Economic Journal*, 108, 1162-1182.

Baxter, M. 1992. "Fiscal policy, specialization and trade in the two-sector model: The return of Ricardo?" *Journal of Political Economy*, 100, 713-744.

Brown, D.K., A.V. Deardorff, and R.M. Stern. 1992. "A North American Free Trade Agreement: Analytical issues and a computational assessment." *The World Economy,* 15, 11-30.

Bruno, M. 1984. "Raw materials, profits and the productivity slowdown." *Quarterly Journal of Economics*, 99, 1-29.

Caves, R.E. and R.W. Jones. 1973. *World Trade and Payments.* Boston, Little, Brown and Company.

Feenstra, R.C. 1995. "Estimating the effects of trade policy." In: G.M. Grossman and K. Rogoff, eds. *Handbook of International Economics*, Volume III. Amsterdam, North Holland.

Francois, J.F., and K.A. Reinert. 1997. *Applied Methods for Trade Policy Analysis.* Cambridge, U.K., Cambridge University Press.

Francois, J.F., and C.R. Shiells. 1994. *Modeling Trade Policy: Applied General Equilibrium Assessments of North American Free Trade.* Cambridge, U.K., Cambridge University Press.

Goulder, L.M. and B. Eichengreen. 1992. "Trade liberalization in general equilibrium: intertemporal and interindustry effects." *Canadian Journal of Economics*, 25, 253-280.

Ho, M.S., and D.W. Jorgenson. 1994. "Trade policy and U.S. economic growth." *Journal of Policy Modeling*, 16, 119-146.

Johnson, H.G. 1953-54. "Optimum tariffs and retaliation." *Review of Economic Studies*, 21, 142-153.

Kehoe, P.J., and T.J. Kehoe. 1995. *Modeling North American Economic Integration.* Dordrecht, Kluwer Academic Publishers.

Keuschnigg, C., and W. Kohler. 1997. "Dynamics of trade liberalization." In J.F. Francois and C.R. Shiells, eds. *Modeling Trade Policy: Applied General Equilibrium Assessments of North American Free Trade.* Cambridge, U.K., Cambridge University Press.

King, R.G., C.I. Plosser, and S.T. Rebelo. 1988. "Production, growth and business cycles I: The basic neoclassical model." *Journal of Monetary Economics*, 21, 195-232.

Kouparitsas, M.A. 1996. "North-South business cycles." *Working Paper 96-9.* Chicago, Federal Reserve Bank of Chicago.

Kouparitsas, M.A. 1998. "Dynamic trade liberalization analysis: Steady state, transitional and inter-industry effects." *Working Paper 98-15.* Chicago, Federal Reserve Bank of Chicago.

Krugman, P. 1991. "The move toward free trade zones." In Federal Reserve Bank of Kansas City, Symposium.

Lipton, D, J. Poterba, J. Sachs, and L. Summers. 1982. "Multiple shooting in rational expectations models." *Econometrica*, 50, 1329-1333.

Lustig, N., B.P., Bosworth, and R.Z. Lawrence. 1992. *North American Free Trade: Assessing the Impact.* Washington, D.C., The Brookings Institution.

McKibbin, W.J., and P.J. Wilcoxen. 1996. "The theoretical and empirical structure of the G-cubed model." *Brookings Discussion Papers in International Economics*, No. 118, Brookings Institution, Washington, D.C.

Mendoza, E.G., and L.L. Tesar. 1998. "The international ramifications of tax reform: Supply-side economics in a global economy." *American Economic Review*, 88, 226-245.

Ramey, V.A. 1989. "Inventories as factors of production and economic fluctuations." *American Economic Review*, 79, 338-354.

Roland-Holst, D.W., K.A. Reinert, and C.R. Shiells. 1994. "A general equilibrium analysis of North American economic integration." In J.F. Francois and C.R. Shiells, eds. *Modeling Trade Policy: Applied General Equilibrium Assessments of North American Free Trade.* Cambridge, U.K., Cambridge University Press.

Scitovsky, T. 1942. "A reconsideration of the theory of tariffs." *Review of Economic Studies*, 9, 89-110.

Sobarzo, H.E. 1994. "The gains for Mexico from a North American Free trade Agreement: An applied general equilibrium assessment." In J.F. Francois and C.R. Shiells, eds. *Modeling Trade Policy: Applied General Equilibrium Assessments of North American Free Trade.* Cambridge, U.K., Cambridge University Press.

Shiells, C.R., and K.A. Reinert. 1993. "Armington models and terms-of-trade effects: Some econometric evidence for North America." *Canadian Journal of Economics*, 26, 299-316.

Shoven, J.B., and J. Whalley. 1992. *Applying General Equilibrium.* Cambridge, UK, Cambridge University Press.

Waverman, L. 1992. "Mini Symposium: Modeling North American Free Trade." *The World Economy*, 15, 1-10.

Whalley, J. 1985. *Trade Liberalization Among Major Trading Areas.* Cambridge, MA., MIT Press.

5 The Regional Impact of Foreign Direct Investment: Structure and Behavior in an Ownership-Disaggregated Computable General Equilibrium Model[1]

Gary Gillespie[1], Peter G. McGregor[1], J. Kim Swales[1], Ya Ping Yin[2]

[1] Fraser of Allander Institute and International Centre for Macroeconomic Modelling, Department of Economics, University of Strathclyde, Glasgow, Scotland.
e-mail: gary@gillespieg.freeserve.co.uk, p.mcgregor@strath.ac.uk, j.k.swales@strath.ac.uk
[2] Department of Economics, Social Sciences and Tourism, University of Hertfordshire, Hatfield, AL10 9AB, England
e-mail: y.p.yin@herts.ac.uk

5.1 Introduction

Despite government rhetoric in support of indigenous regional development, in practice the attraction of foreign-owned inward investment remains a key plank of regional policy. Just under half of all expenditure on UK Regional Selective Assistance (RSA) is awarded to foreign-owned firms (PA Cambridge Economic Consultants, 1993) and individual regional development agencies vie for the attraction of incoming plants, often offering an extensive package of incentives.[2] In Gillespie *et al* (2001a) we assess the impact of RSA-assisted investment on the Scottish economy using a computable general equilibrium (CGE) approach. Our earlier analysis makes no distinction between the foreign- and UK-owned manufacturing sectors, yet the former accounted for 39% and 23% of Scottish Manufacturing gross output and employment, respectively, during 1996 (Scottish Office, 1999). There is, therefore, a substantial foreign-owned component of Scottish manufacturing, and this may have a significant impact on the behavior of the regional economy of Scotland. Accordingly, in this chapter we refine our earlier approach to focus directly on the employment effects of export-oriented Foreign Direct Investment (FDI).

The case for further model disaggregation, to allow separate identification of

---

[1] We are grateful for comments from participants: in the Seminars on Regional Economic Modeling in Honor of Philip Israilevich, Federal Reserve Bank of Chicago, November 1998; the North American Regional Science Association, Santa Fe, November 1998; the NIESR Conference on Inward Investment, Technological Change And Growth: The Impact of Multinational Corporations on the UK Economy, September 1999; and The Network of Industrial Economists Meeting: Industrial Policy In A Devolved Economy, December 1999. We are also indebted to Scottish Enterprise National for funding related research.

[2] This was evident with the regional rivalry demonstrated during efforts to win the £1.7bn LG. Electronics plant, which located in Newport, South Wales. The Public Accounts Committee Report No 2 (1996) documents the extent and form that public assistance took in the case of Health Care International, located in Clydebank Scotland, which received substantial assistance over and above the standard incentive package.

foreign- and UK-owned components of the manufacturing sector, is compelling, in terms of both modeling accuracy and policy relevance. First, the distinctive "structure" of foreign-owned manufacturing firms, in terms of higher capital intensities, greater import propensities and higher wages, for example, has been well documented (see e.g., Barry and Bradley, 1997; Davies and Lyons, 1991; Gillespie, 1998, 2000). These differences can only be captured by a model that separates out the foreign-owned sub-sector of manufacturing. Secondly, a number of theories of FDI imply that foreign-owned firms may behave differently from indigenous firms and this can only be captured through ownership-disaggregation. Thirdly, the scale of the assistance to inward investment relative to UK-owned firms is itself controversial. Complaints from the UK-owned sector that the funds would be better employed to foster indigenous development are commonplace, and cannot reasonably be dismissed out of hand. Furthermore, policy-makers themselves clearly have an interest in assessing whether they have the balance between foreign-owned and UK sector incentives correct. An ownership-disaggregated model is essential if such issues are ultimately to be addressed. Finally, the current proposals for UK devolution have stimulated concern over the possibility of heightened regional "fiscal competition" among UK regions to attract inward investments. However, tackling this issue would necessitate development of an ownership-disaggregated model that is explicitly multi-regional in nature, which is beyond the scope of the present chapter.

The approach we develop in this chapter is complementary to, and supportive of, existing work in this area. Our approach continues to concentrate on the system-wide demand-induced effects of FDI,[3] but extends the previous official evaluations (H M Treasury, 1995, 1997; PA Cambridge Economic Consultants; 1995), which employ input-output and Keynesian multiplier approaches, in a number of important respects. First and most importantly, we address the issue using a modeling framework that explicitly disaggregates the manufacturing sector by ownership. To our knowledge this is the first application of an ownership-disaggregated regional computable general equilibrium model. Secondly, we examine the impact of the demand stimulus afforded by export-oriented inward investment under a much wider range of visions of the host regional economy. In particular, we allow for the fact that the short-run may be characterized by the presence of capacity constraints and for the possibility of local wage bargaining, so capturing the labor market displacement effects that are identified in the existing FDI literature (see, for example, English Unit, 1992; PA Cambridge Economic Consultants, 1993, 1995; Driffield, 1995). Thirdly, we identify the time path of the host region's response to the inward investment, whereas past official studies have tended to neglect this issue (except in terms of the build up of the initial investment itself). Fourthly, we adapt the analysis of Haddad *et al* (2002) and Israilevich *et al* (1996) to allow us to isolate the effects of the distinctive "structure" of the foreign-owned sector, including its input-output linkages and factor intensities, on the regional impact of inward investment.

The remainder of the chapter is structured as follows. In Section 5.2 we explain

[3] The limited number of existing empirical, system-wide studies of FDI impacts have been mostly econometric or Input-Output (I-O) based, with the manufacturing sector wholly foreign-owned or disaggregated on the basis of ownership (Foster and Malley, 1988; Bradley *et al.*, 1993, 1995; Hill and Roberts, 1995). These models often have traditional Keynesian roots with typically passive supply sides (Foster and Malley, 1988; Alexander and Whyte, 1995; Hill and Roberts, 1995). Bradley *et al.*, (1993, 1995) is an exception in presenting a model with an econometrically parameterized and well-specified supply side.

our approach to measuring the impact of FDI, including our attempt to separate out the influences of "structure" and "behavior" in governing the regional impact of FDI. We then discuss, in Section 5.3, how we specify and calibrate our ownership-disaggregated CGE system. Next, in Section 5.4, we report the simulation results. Finally, brief conclusions are presented in Section 5.5.

5.2 Measuring the Regional Economic Impact of FDI, and Identifying the Contributions of Structure and Behavior in Regional CGEs

We begin by considering the precise nature of the "disturbance" to the host economy that FDI represents. Then we discuss the factors that are likely to determine the importance of structure and behavior in regional CGEs.

5.2.1 The Nature of the FDI Shock to the Host Region

In this chapter, we seek to measure the demand-induced employment effects of export-oriented inward investment on the regional economy. As in our evaluation of RSA (Gillespie *et al,* 2001a), we take the investment to be exogenous. We motivate this exogeneity assumption through our interest in the impact of a substantial, policy-induced inward investment on the host region. The policy-making process itself is not, however, transparent and is often shrouded in confidentiality restrictions, so that it is not readily amenable to modeling. Our emphasis on the employment effects of the investment shock reflects the main concern of UK regional policy, but our analysis in fact identifies the effect on a whole range of key economic variables within the region. Nonetheless, we do not seek to provide a complete welfare analysis of the regional impact of FDI.

Furthermore, we follow the standard evaluation procedures and concentrate primarily on the demand-induced effects of FDI. The traditional focus of applied studies, including the past official UK evaluations tends to ignore the literature on FDI that identifies the possibility of a major supply shock associated with inward investment, namely efficiency spillovers to the indigenous sector. The key problem in capturing such effects is the comparative lack of evidence on their probable scale (although see e.g. Barrell and Pain, 1997a; Pain, 2001). Accordingly, while the framework that we develop in this chapter can accommodate such effects (in contrast to input-output which cannot generally be used to analyze supply shocks) we abstract from them here although, of course, we recognize the need to include them in any overall evaluation of the impact of FDI on the host region (Gillespie *et al.*, 2001b).

The focus on export-oriented FDI is less restrictive than it may seem. In our case the host region is Scotland (which accounts for under 9% of UK economic activity), and so firms locating there to sell to the "domestic" UK and European markets would be considered export-oriented. However, we do simplify the present analysis by assuming that the inward investment is 100% export-oriented, so that there is no displacement in the domestic goods market.[4] In this chapter, therefore, we take the inward investment shock to consist of an initial stimulus to regional investment combined with a permanent boost to regional exports. (The scale of the changes is discussed in Section 5.3 below). Both disturbances constitute shocks to the demand side, although each, of course, generally induces a range of supply-side responses.

Our analysis throughout this chapter concentrates on the single region case. Extension to the interregional context would be necessary to capture aspects of the fiscal competition that is likely to characterize the behavior of the devolved UK regions. While we have developed an interregional CGE (McGregor *et al*, 1999), we have not yet been able to disaggregate it by ownership. Clearly, however, relaxation of the restrictions of our present analysis constitutes a major program for future research.

5.2.2 The Importance of Structure and Behavior in Regional CGEs

Haddad *et al* (2002), drawing on related ideas in Israilevich *et al* (1997) and Gazel *et al* (1996)[5], explore the comparative importance of what they term "structural coefficients" and "behavioral parameters" in computable general equilibrium models (CGEs).[6] The former essentially reflect the base year social accounting matrix (SAM), and the latter refer to the functional forms and key parameters of the CGE. For example, in the production functions, the factor-intensity parameters are calibrated using the SAM data, and are therefore taken to be structural, whilst the elasticity of substitution parameters are imposed, and, consequently, are taken to be behavioral. In this chapter we seek to explore this distinction further. We begin by considering *a priori* what factors are likely to govern the contribution of structure and behavior, in the sense these terms are used by Haddad *et al* (2002), to the regional impact of any demand shock.

The "short-run" of many regional CGEs, including the model we employ in this chapter, is often characterized by sectorally fixed capital stocks and geographically immobile labor. In this context any final demand stimulus will cause the price of both labor and capital services to rise, and this in turn will generate various relative price changes and induce supply-side responses. In such a context sectoral responses are extremely unlikely to be uniform because sectors will be affected to different extents because of factor intensities and may be subject, for example, to different price-elasticities of demand In these circumstances behavior (price elasticities) differs among sectors, and structure (factor intensities) is insufficient to pre-determine the systems' responses to demand disturbances. Indeed, because of this the economic structure is itself endogenous, evolving in response to the various incentives provided by relative price changes. Thus demand stimuli in the presence of any regional-specific factor would typically imply a different input-output table and SAM after the disturbance from that used to calibrate the model initially. This, of course, does not imply that initial structure "does not matter" in these circumstances. Rather the implication is that not only structure matters: behavior influences the system's

---

[4] On average, the foreign-owned manufacturing sector in Scotland exported 76% of its output in 1989.

[5] These in turn build on earlier work by Hewings (1977,1985).

[6] The analysis of Haddad *et al.* (2002) explores these ideas in Marshallian CGEs (e.g. Israilevich *et al.*, 1997), as well as the better known Walrasian CGEs, such as that employed here.

response to disturbances as well as the factors that underlie differences in initial structure.

The long-run effects of a demand stimulus in the context of a small open region may be quite different, however. McGregor, *et al.* (1996) show that, while local wage bargaining and capacity constraints may characterize the short run behavior of a small, open region, in the long run capital accumulation/ decumulation and net migration flows may ultimately ensure the absence of any regional-specific factor. In the short run, different assumptions about the behavior of sectors can generate radically different responses to demand disturbances, but in the long run these differences tend to disappear, as the solutions for a wide range of models all converge on the input-output solution. In the long run it is "as if" factors are in infinitely elastic supply: demand disturbances therefore do not have any impact on relative prices, so that there is no incentive for substitution in consumption or production. The fact that behavior may differ radically among sectors in the face of relative price changes becomes irrelevant when conditions ensure the absence of such changes. Here behavior, as captured by the key parameters and behavioral relations of CGE, may matter a great deal in the short run (in addition to structure), but does not matter at all in the long run. In the long run, for demand disturbances in the absence of regional-specific factors, only structure matters and the model results are pre-determined by the nature of the initial input-output table and model.

In this chapter, we explore the contributions of structure and behavior in influencing the overall impact of a specific demand shock, namely inward investment, on the host region. This particular application is of special interest given the emphasis that many have placed on the distinctiveness of the structure of the foreign-owned sub-sector. Naturally, the higher capital intensity, lower linkages with the domestic sector, and higher wages are, for example, all captured in the base year, ownership-disaggregated SAM. Here we seek to measure the extent to which this distinctiveness in structure governs the regional impact of FDI, and to what extent differences in behavior prove important in this context. We achieve this by comparing the simulation properties of a hypothetical model, which is predicated upon an assumption of identical structure and behavior of foreign- and UK-owned sub-sectors of manufacturing, with models that incorporate actual differences in structure and in behavior. We explain precisely how we proceed in the next section's discussion of our simulation strategy.

5.3 The Simulation Framework and Models

We begin by presenting an overview of the CGE framework that we use in this chapter, AMOSFDI. We then outline the simulation strategy that we adopt in this chapter, which involves comparative simulations of three specific model configurations of AMOSFDI. We finally explain the precise specification and calibration of these three models. This includes a discussion of differences: in behavior among the three models as reflected in different functional forms and key parameters, and differences in structure, as reflected in the SAMs to which the models are calibrated.

5.3.1 AMOSFDI General Simulation Framework

AMOSFDI is a CGE modeling framework parameterized on data from a UK region, Scotland.[7] A very brief description is presented in this section: more detail is available in Appendix 5.1 and a full listing of the model is provided in Harrigan *et al* (1991). AMOSFDI has: four transactor groups, namely households, foreign-owned and UK-owned corporations, and government;[8] four commodities and activities, viz. foreign owned and UK manufactures, non-manufacturing traded and sheltered,[9] and two exogenous external transactors (the rest of the UK, RUK; and the rest of the world, ROW). Throughout this chapter commodity markets are taken to be competitive. We do not explicitly model financial flows, our assumption being that Scotland is a price-taker in competitive UK financial markets.

The AMOSFDI framework allows a high degree of flexibility in the choice of key parameter values, model closures and even aggregative structure. However, a crucial characteristic of the model is that, no matter how it is configured, we impose cost minimization in production with multi-level production functions, generally of a CES form but with Leontief and Cobb-Douglas being available as special cases (Leontief is used here in Model 3 below). There are four major components of final demand: consumption, investment, government expenditure and exports. Of these, real government expenditure is exogenous. Consumption is a linear homogeneous function of real disposable income. Exports (and imports) are generally determined via an Armington link (Armington, 1969) and are therefore relative-price sensitive (though in Model 3, the treatment of the exports of the foreign-owned manufacturing sector is exceptional in that we impose a Leontief functional form). Investment is a little more complex, as we discuss below, although the initial inward investment is treated as exogenous throughout.

In all the simulations in this chapter we impose a single Scottish labor market characterized by perfect sectoral mobility. However, we consider two alternative hypotheses about the determination of regional wages. First, we investigate a national bargaining labor market closure under which the regional nominal wage is exogenous. This is the assumption that characterizes most conventional analyses of regional economic behavior, of both a theoretical (e.g. Harris, 1989; Holden and Swales, 1995) and empirical (e.g., Roper and O'Shea, 1991) nature. This is most often motivated by appeal to the nominal-wage-taking behavior implied for a small open region that is part of a spatially integrated wage-bargaining system. However, a number of authors have recently argued in favor of a regional bargained real wage function (BRW) in

---

[7] AMOS is an acronym for a macro-micro model of Scotland. AMOSFDI is the ownership-disaggregated variant of the model, developed specifically to allow us to investigate the impact of FDI. For a good survey of CGE models see Dervis *et al.* (1982) and Shoven and Whalley (1984, 1992): for good examples of previous applications in a regional context, see Harrigan and McGregor (1988), Higgs *et al.* (1988), Jones and Whalley (1988), Kimbell and Harrison (1984), Kraybill *et al.*, (1992), Morgan *et al.* (1989), and Rickman (1992). Partridge and Rickman (1998) provide a critical review of regional CGE modeling.

[8] In AMOSFDI, Scotland is treated as a self-governing economy, in the sense that there is only one consolidated government sector. Central government activity is partitioned to Scotland and combined with local government activity.

[9] Manufacturing comprises sectors 12-89, non-manufacturing traded sectors 1-10, 91-97, 99-102 and 109-111 and non-traded sectors 11, 90 and 98, 103-108, 112 and 114 in the 1989 Scottish Input-Output Tables (Scottish Office Industry Department, 1994).

which the regional real consumption wage is directly related to workers bargaining power, and therefore inversely to the regional unemployment rate (Minford *et al*, 1994). Here we take the bargaining function from the regional econometric work reported by Layard, Nickell and Jackman (LNJ, 1991):

$$w_{s,t} = \alpha - 0.068 u_s + 0.40 w_{s,t-1} \tag{5.1}$$

where: w_s and u_s are the natural logarithms of the Scottish real consumption wage and the unemployment rate respectively, t is the time subscript and α is a calibrated parameter. Empirical support for this "wage curve" specification is now widespread, even in a regional context (Blanchflower and Oswald, 1994).

Within each period of the multi-period simulations we report here, both the total capital stock and its sectoral composition are fixed, and commodity markets clear continuously. The exogenous inward investment stimulus in the manufacturing sector occurs in the first period. Each sector's capital stock is then updated between periods via a simple capital stock adjustment procedure, according to which, investment equals depreciation plus some fraction of the gap between the desired level of the capital stock and its actual level. This process of capital accumulation is compatible with a simple theory of optimal firm behavior given the assumption of quadratic adjustment costs. Desired capital stocks are determined on cost-minimization criteria and actual stocks reflect last period's stocks adjusted for depreciation and gross investment. The economy is assumed initially to be in long-run equilibrium, where desired and actual capital stocks are equal[10]. Where migration is incorporated in the model, population is also updated "between" periods. We take net migration to be positively related to the real wage differential and negatively to the unemployment rate differential in accordance with the econometrically estimated model reported in LNJ (1991). This model is based on that in Harris and Todaro (1970), and is commonly employed in studies of US migration (e.g. Greenwood *et al*, 1991; Treyz *et al* , 1993). The migration function we adopt is therefore of the form.

$$m = \beta - 0.08(u_s - u_r) + 0.06(w_s - w_r) \tag{5.2}$$

where: m is the net in-migration rate (as a proportion of the indigenous population); w_r and u_r are the natural logarithms of the real consumption wage and unemployment rates, respectively, in the rest of the UK, and β is a calibrated parameter. In the multi-period simulations reported below the net migration flows in any period are used to update population stocks at the beginning of the next period, in a manner analogous to the updating of the capital stocks. The regional economy is initially assumed to have zero net migration, and ultimately, net migration flows re-establish this population equilibrium.

---

[10] Our treatment is wholly consistent with sectoral investment being determined by the relationship between the capital rental rate and the user cost of capital. The capital rental rate is the rental that would have to be paid in a competitive market for the (sector specific) physical capital: the user cost is the total cost to the firm of employing a unit of capital. Given that we take the interest, capital depreciation and tax rates to be exogenous, the capital price index is the only endogenous component of the user cost. If the rental rate exceeds the user cost, desired capital stock is greater than the actual capital stock and there is therefore an incentive to increase capital stock. The resultant capital accumulation puts downward pressure on rental rates and so tends to restore equilibrium. In the long run, the capital rental rate equals the user cost in each sector, and the risk-adjusted rate of return is equalized between sectors.

Unless otherwise specified (see below) all sectors use a CES technology with "best guess" elasticities of substitution of 0.3 (Harris, 1989) and Armington trade substitution elasticities of 2.0 (Gibson, 1990). The capital stock adjustment parameter (λ) is taken to be 0.5 in each sector.[11] Throughout, we typically discuss results by interpreting the conceptual "periods" of our model as "years". We believe this to be reasonable in that all of the data we have employed in the calibration (and, where applicable, estimation) of the model are annual. However, since the model is not (and cannot be) entirely econometrically estimated on annual data, this interpretation is suggestive, rather than definitive.

5.3.2 Simulation Strategy: Identifying the Influence of the Structure and Behavior of the Foreign-Owned Sector

Starting from a model in which there is no distinction between the UK- and foreign-owned manufacturing sectors, we wish to disaggregate by ownership in a way that allows us to identify the separate contributions of differences in initial structure and in behavior. Our approach involves a slight adaptation of the approach developed by Haddad *et al* (2002) and by Israilevich *et al* (1997) and Gazel *et al* (1996). We begin by generating a model that, in effect, allows us to abstract from the distinctive structure and behavior of the foreign-owned sector. Model 1 assumes that the foreign-owned sector is identical to the domestically owned sector, in every respect except scale. The underlying input-output table and SAM for this model are, of course, hypothetical, derived on the assumption that all that we know about the foreign-owned sector is its share in total output. This captures a naïve "neoclassical" perspective that maintains that location and ownership are irrelevant. Such a model would also represent our "best guess" about FDI impacts in the absence of an appropriate ownership-disaggregated database.[12] This is an assumption that, in fact, characterizes a number of applied studies of the impact of FDI in Scotland (e.g. Alexander and Whyte, 1995; Gillespie *et al,* 1997), because published Scottish input-output tables do not separately identify the foreign-owned manufacturing sector. However, Gillespie (1998) has constructed an ownership-disaggregated version of the 1989 Scottish input-output tables (from a variety of disparate data sources), so that it is now feasible to implement an ownership-disaggregated modeling approach.

The purpose of Model 1 is, of course, to provide us with a useful benchmark that assists in the identification of the structural and behavioral influences of inward investment on the host region. In fact, in a world where the conditions assumed by Model 1 actually prevailed FDI would be rather less prevalent than it is, since many ownership and location advantages are thereby ruled out. Model 2, in contrast, acknowledges the true differences in the structures of the domestic and foreign-owned sectors, but maintains the hypothesis of identical behavior. Here the behavioral

[11] This default value of the adjustment parameters is based on investment equations estimated for the Scottish manufacturing sector. This is, in fact, the only sector in AMOSFDI for which a time series of investment data exists. For other sectors information is available only for the years in which a Scottish input-output table has been constructed.

[12] Our approach is similar in some respects to the hypothetical extraction methods that have traditionally been used to measure the importance of various sectors (or sub-sectors) for the relevant economy through simulating the consequences of suppressing some input-output linkages. (See e.g. Lahr and Miller, 1997, for a review.)

equations of each sector are identical in terms of specification and the values of key parameters. However, the differences in structure are embodied in the ownership-disaggregated input-output table, and wider SAM, which constitutes the database of Model 2. Comparative simulation of Models 1 and 2 thus allows us to determine the impact that differences in structure have on the impact of the FDI shock to the system, and to gauge the contribution to modeling accuracy of developing ownership-disaggregated databases.

Model 3 allows for the possibility that the behavior of the foreign-owned sector is distinctive and accommodates the structural differences embodied in the SAM used to calibrate Model 2. Model 3 reflects one theory of the behavior of the foreign-owned sector, namely that it is very much less sensitive to local price changes than is the indigenous sector. The motivation for this specification is in terms of FDI for "domestic" production (PA Cambridge Economic Consultants, 1995).[13] The representative firm here is taken to be a foreign-owned multi-plant/ multi-regional firm, which allocates production across space. The regional plant's output is determined by the parent's decision and so becomes exogenous to the region. The production structure is also inflexible, reflecting, for example, the adoption of an internationally adopted standard of production. Accordingly, we characterize Model 3 in terms of quite widespread Leontief functional forms, for trade demands as well as production systems. Comparative simulations of Models 1 and 3 allow us to infer the impact of structure and behavior combined, and comparisons with Model 2 allow us to separate out the impact of each influence on overall system behavior.

For simplicity of exposition we do not investigate alternative specifications of "behavior" differences here. Inclusion of alternative model types increases the number of results to be handled multiplicatively. Instead we confine our attention to Models 1 through 3, although the exercise should be thought of as illustrative of the general approach. The specifics of the assumptions about the behavior of inward investors can, of course, be varied and will be in future work (Gillespie, *et al.*, 2001b).

5.3.3 The Specification and Calibration of the Simulation Models

We begin by discussing differences in the behavioral parameters among the three models and then consider structural differences. Together, these determine the calibrated form of each of the simulation models.

Differences in behavior: functional forms and key parameter values for each of the AMOSFDI models. Models 1 and 2 assume that foreign- and UK-owned manufacturing sectors exhibit identical behavior, and so possess identical functional forms and key parameter values, specifically those of the general default specification presented in section 5.3.1. Many of the behavioral equations and key parameters used in Models 1 and 2 remain unchanged in Model 3, namely all equations other than those for the two manufacturing sectors. Table 5.1 summarizes the major alterations to specification and to key parameter values. Note that the specification of the non-

[13] PA Cambridge Economic Consultants (1995) report that the main reasons for inward investors locating in the UK are market led. They identify that of those inward investors (some 70%) seeking to establish new markets, 70% were targeting the UK. The average share of total sales in the UK, by inward investors, average 49%.

manufacturing traded and sheltered sectors is exactly as in the general framework. For Models 1 and 2 the entries in the first two columns of Table 5.1 would, of course, be identical to those in the last column.

The major distinguishing feature of Model 3 is its assumption of universal Leontief functional forms for production and trade relationships for the foreign-owned manufacturing sector. However, the key parameter values for the UK-owned manufacturing sector have also been changed, so as to maintain the overall sensitivity of the manufacturing sector to price changes. (Adjustments were made using the foreign sector's output share.) The basic idea here is that the performance of manufacturing as a whole may be accurately captured in an aggregate model and this is retained in the disaggregated version. In terms of the compact form of the general model summarized in Appendix 5.1, these changes impact on the manufacturing sectors' equations for: price determination (equation A1 of Appendix 5.1); labor and capital demands (equations A7 and A8) and consumption, desired capital stock and export demands (equations A13, A15, and A18). (These sectors' intermediate demands, while not identified in the compact form are, of course, also altered). Naturally, the impact of the Model 3 specification is to make the foreign-owned sector much less price-sensitive in all respects, while making the UK-owned sector rather more price-sensitive.

Table 5.1 Functional forms and key parameter values for Model 3

Functional Forms	UK-owned Manufacturing	Foreign-owned Manufacturing	Non-Manufacturing Traded & Sheltered Sectors
Technology:	CES (0.45)	Leontief	CES (0.3)
Trade Demands:	CES (2.97)	Leontief	CES (2.0)

Table 5.2 Type I and II output multipliers associated with the hypothetical (identical structure) and actual SAMs

	Type I Output Multiplier:		Type II Output Multiplier:	
	Identical Structure	Actual Structure	Identical Structure	Actual Structure
UK-Owned Manufacturing	1.45	1.54	1.77	1.90
Foreign-owned Manufacturing	1.45	1.29	1.77	1.50
Non-Manufacturing Traded	1.35	1.35	1.76	1.76
Sheltered Sector	1.14	1.14	1.73	1.73

Differences in structure: the SAMs. Model 1 assumes that the structure of the UK and foreign-owned manufacturing sectors is identical. The SAM for this model (Appendix 5.2) is constructed on the assumption that we have no prior information about either manufacturing sector apart from the scale of each sector in terms of gross output. We divide the manufacturing row and column into their UK- and foreign-owned components in accordance with the ratio of outputs. This generates two technically identical sectors that differ only in terms of scale. The other two models embody the actual differences in structure as between the UK- and foreign-owned manufacturing sectors as estimated by Gillespie (1998). (See Appendix 5.1). Some indication of the significance of the differences in structure can be seen by inspection of Table 5.2 which presents the type I and II output multipliers implied by the input-output components of both the hypothetical (identical structure) and actual SAMs.

By construction the multipliers for the UK- and foreign-owned manufacturing sectors reported in Table 5.2 are the same for the hypothetical SAM that imposes identical structure. The actual structure implies quite different multiplier values, with significantly larger (smaller) values for the output multipliers of the UK-owned (foreign-owned) manufacturing sector. This reflects the fact that the UK manufacturing sector has stronger intermediate linkages with the other sectors in the model and is more labor intensive. Note that the multipliers for the non-manufacturing traded and sheltered sectors are the same for both models, a feature that reflects the way the input-output table was disaggregated.

5.4 Simulation of the AMOSFDI Models

In each model we take the inward investment to generate a 3% increase in capacity and output. In each model this is associated with an increase in output of £248 million, all of which is exported, as the second and third rows of table 5.3 indicate. (Recall that we assume 100% export FDI). The output and capacity effects can be thought of as reflecting all the knowledge that the policy-maker interested in assessing FDI impacts possesses. Because the foreign-owned sector is in fact more export-intensive than UK-owned manufacturing (which is captured by Models 2 and 3, but not Model 1), the percentage stimulus to exports is smaller in Models 2 and 3 as compared to Model 1. Furthermore, the assumed 3% stimulus to capacity in the foreign-owned sector (required to meet the new demand) necessitates a higher investment stimulus in Models 2 and 3 since this sector is in fact more capital intensive than it is assumed to be in Model 1. Table 5.3 summarizes the nature of the disturbances applied to each model.

Table 5.3 The impact of the export-FDI shock in terms of capital stock, exports, output and direct employment across Models 1, 2 and 3

	Model 1		Models 2 & 3	
	%	Value	%	Value
Capital Stock	3.0	£151m	3.0	£182m
Exports	4.43	£248m	3.97	£248m
Output	3.0	£248m	3.0	£248m
Employment	3.0	5,162	3.0	3,392

In the simulations we report below, therefore, inward investment is modeled as a combination of two shocks: a first period investment shock (associated with construction), and a permanent export stimulus which begins in period 2 when the new plant is assumed to commence production.

Since we simulate the export-FDI shock for four labor market closures and for each of the three models, we cannot discuss the simulation results of each case in detail. We begin by providing a brief summary of the impact of the FDI shock in Model 1 under two of the labor market closures, to illustrate the kinds of reactions that are stimulated in the host economy. We then proceed to a comparison of the long-run results across all model types and labor market closures. Finally, we discuss the adjustment paths to long-run equilibrium.

5.4.1 The Impact of the Inward Investment in Model 1 Under Regional Wage Bargaining with and without Migration

Limitations of space preclude a detailed account of all the results here. In any case, the qualitative results of the policy-induced FDI stimulus are similar to those reported in Gillespie *et al* (2001a) for RSA-assisted investment as a whole. Accordingly, we simply illustrate the general forces at work in the host region by focusing on two illustrative simulation results, namely those for Model 1 under regional bargaining with and without migration

Table 5.4 summarizes the detailed simulation results for Model 1. (The results for national bargaining with migration differ little from those without, though the endogenous population effects are associated with a slightly greater stimulus to the host region, and so they are not reported in table 5.4.) Columns 4-6 of table 5.4 report the results of the inward investment shock where population is fixed, but there is regional bargaining. Column 4 reports the period-one simulations for this case. These results reflect only the initial demand impact of the investment associated with the policy-induced FDI, since we assume it takes a year to expand capacity in anticipation of producing to export. Total output and employment rise in this period, mainly in the sheltered sector which includes construction, although employment and value-added fall in both foreign- and UK-owned manufacturing.

Because of fixed capacity in this interval, the proportionate change in employment in each sector is greater than that in value added. The demand stimulus increases capital rentals and, because of regional bargaining, wages also rise. Value-added prices therefore rise and there is a loss of competitiveness, reflected in export crowding out. The additional labor market displacement effect that occurs under regional bargaining explains why the impact effects are so much less than under national bargaining (reported in column 1 of Table 5.4).

Column 5 of Table 5.4 presents the results for period 2, in which the capacity effects generated by the inward investment are first felt and the impact of the increase in export demand is first experienced. The combined impact of the expansion in foreign-owned manufacturing export demand and the increase in its capacity has a larger effect than the first-period investment shock. However, the beneficial effects are now concentrated in foreign-owned manufacturing, and the further pressure on the wage because of the fall in the unemployment rate is such as to lead to a greater contraction of the UK-owned manufacturing sector.

Table 5.4 Detailed simulation results for Model 1

	NATIONAL BARGAINING			REGIONAL BARGAINING				
	POPULATION FIXED			POPULATION FIXED			POPULATION ENDOGENOUS	
Model 1	Period 1	Period 2	Long Run	Period 1	Period 2	Long Run	Period 2	Long Run
GDP (income measure)	0.11	0.37	0.56	0.05	0.21	0.25	0.22	0.58
Consumption	0.13	0.36	0.48	0.13	0.34	0.37	0.34	0.58
Investment	1.79	0.62	0.60	1.79	0.35	0.35	0.36	0.62
Nominal before-tax wage	0.00	0.00	0.00	0.11	0.31	0.32	0.30	0.00
Real bef. tax cons. wage	-0.04	-0.08	0.00	0.05	0.18	0.21	0.17	0.00
Total employment	0.13	0.42	0.57	0.06	0.21	0.25	0.22	0.59
UK Manufacturing:	0.03	0.15	0.26	-0.05	-0.08	-0.07	-0.07	0.26
Foreign Manufacturing:	0.03	3.17	3.29	-0.05	2.95	2.96	2.96	3.30
Non-Manu Traded:	0.08	0.24	0.48	0.00	0.02	0.09	0.03	0.51
Sheltered	0.25	0.17	0.25	0.19	-0.03	-0.01	-0.02	0.27
Total unempl.	-0.97	-3.12	-4.20	-0.46	-1.57	-1.81	-1.46	0.57
Labor particip. rate	0.03	0.10	0.13	0.01	0.05	0.06	0.05	0.00
Total population	0.00	0.00	0.00	0.00	0.00	0.00	0.02	0.59
Price of value added								
UK Manufacturing	0.02	0.11	0.00	0.08	0.26	0.27	0.25	0.00
Foreign Manufacturing	0.02	0.12	0.00	0.08	0.27	0.27	0.27	0.00
Non-Manuf. Traded	0.08	0.24	0.00	0.12	0.34	0.25	0.33	0.00
Sheltered	0.16	0.11	0.00	0.24	0.29	0.27	0.29	0.00
Capital rental rates								
UK Manufacturing	0.09	0.48	0.00	-0.06	0.06	0.08	0.07	0.00
Foreign Manufacturing	0.09	0.55	0.00	-0.06	0.14	0.08	0.15	0.00
Non-Manu traded	0.26	0.81	0.00	0.12	0.39	0.09	0.41	0.00
Sheltered	0.82	0.56	0.00	0.73	0.22	0.08	0.24	0.00
Consumer price index	0.04	0.08	0.00	0.06	0.13	0.10	0.13	0.00
Value-added								
UK Manufacturing	0.02	0.11	0.26	-0.04	-0.06	-0.06	-0.05	0.26
Foreign Manufacturing	0.02	3.13	3.29	-0.04	2.96	2.97	2.97	3.30
Non-Manu Traded	0.05	0.17	0.48	0.00	0.02	0.11	0.02	0.51
Sheltered	0.20	0.14	0.25	0.15	-0.02	0.00	-0.02	0.27
Sectoral Output								
UK Manufacturing	0.03	0.13	0.26	-0.03	-0.02	-0.01	-0.01	0.26
Foreign Manufacturing	0.03	3.15	3.29	-0.03	3.01	3.02	3.01	3.30
Non-Manu Traded	0.06	0.19	0.48	0.01	0.04	0.13	0.05	0.51
Sheltered	0.20	0.14	0.25	0.16	-0.01	0.01	-0.01	0.27
Capital stocks:								
UK Manufacturing	0.00	0.00	0.26	0.00	0.00	-0.00	0.00	0.26
Foreign Manufacturing	0.00	3.00	3.29	0.00	3.00	3.03	3.00	3.30
Non-Manu Traded	0.00	0.00	0.48	0.00	0.00	0.16	0.00	0.51
Sheltered	0.00	0.00	0.25	0.00	0.00	0.06	0.00	0.27
Exports								
UK Manufacturing	-0.02	-0.10	0.00	-0.07	-0.23	-0.24	-0.22	-0.00
Foreign Manufacturing	-0.02	4.32	4.43	-0.07	4.18	4.19	4.18	4.43
Non-Manu Traded	-0.11	-0.35	0.00	-0.17	-0.48	-0.36	-0.48	-0.01
Sheltered	-0.29	-0.20	0.00	-0.43	-0.53	-0.50	-0.52	-0.01
Nominal income								
Households disposable	0.17	0.44	0.48	0.19	0.47	0.48	0.47	0.58
Firms disposable	0.34	0.75	0.57	0.26	0.49	0.44	0.50	0.60

Employment in the sheltered sector peaks in period 1, following the construction of the FDI plant, and then returns to just below its base value. While the capital stock of foreign-owned manufacturing has increased by 3%, the rental rate in this sector is still increased slightly in period 2, reflecting the scale of the stimulus to demand that this sector enjoys, and the increased wage.

By period 2, employment is close to its long-run equilibrium value in contrast to the national bargaining case, although the effects of the higher intermediate demand and consumption generated by the export FDI shock continue to stimulate all sectors slightly relative to period 2. However, in the long run, as inspection of column 6 of Table 5.4 confirms, the rise in the real wage remains above base, which leads to permanently higher prices across all sectors and a permanent deterioration in the region's competitiveness. Accordingly, exports by the foreign-owned sector increase by less (4.19%) than the initial export shock (4.43%), indicating displacement of foreign-owned manufacturing exports. Moreover, there is long-run labor market displacement in both UK-owned manufacturing and the sheltered sector.

In UK-owned manufacturing, value added falls in the long-run as a result of the permanent increase in its value-added prices. Moreover, UK-owned manufacturing capacity also remains unchanged despite the export FDI shock, although capital stocks increase in the non-manufacturing traded and sheltered sectors due to the their lower export intensities. The loss of regional competitiveness through local wage pressures limits the expansion in the host region. Even in the long run there remains labor market displacement in three of the four sectors in the model. (See Table 5.5, which confirms net displacement of 76 jobs in foreign-owned manufacturing, where the initial direct increase in employment is 5,162.)

Table 5.5 The long-run impact of an incoming 100% export FDI plant generating 5,162 direct jobs, with Model 1, regional bargaining, fixed population

Model 1:	Long-Run Impact:	
Gross Domestic Product	£83m	
Household Disposable Income	£136m	
	Employment	
	Totals	Multiplier
Total Employment	5,517	1.07
UK-Owned Manufacturing	-256	-0.05
Foreign-owned Manufacturing	5,086	0.99
Non-Manufacturing Traded	761	0.15
Sheltered Sector	-79	-0.02

Figure 5.1 plots the period-by-period changes in the levels of aggregate and sectoral employment. The most striking feature of these results is that employment in foreign-owned manufacturing adjusts almost immediately to its long-run value. Indeed in this case, total employment approaches its long-run equilibrium level very rapidly, though in non-manufactured traded it takes some time for capacity to fully adjust.

When population is endogenous, the increased activity in the host region stimulated by the inward investment generates in-migration. This in-migration further stimulates activity in two ways. First, the increase in population is associated with higher welfare transfers from government. Secondly, in-migration limits the regional unemployment rate, and so moderates the upward pressure on the wage under regional bargaining. The overall impact of the first effect is small and does not qualitatively change the nature of the region's response. However, the role of in-migration in reducing labor market pressure has a big effect on the regional impact of inward investment.

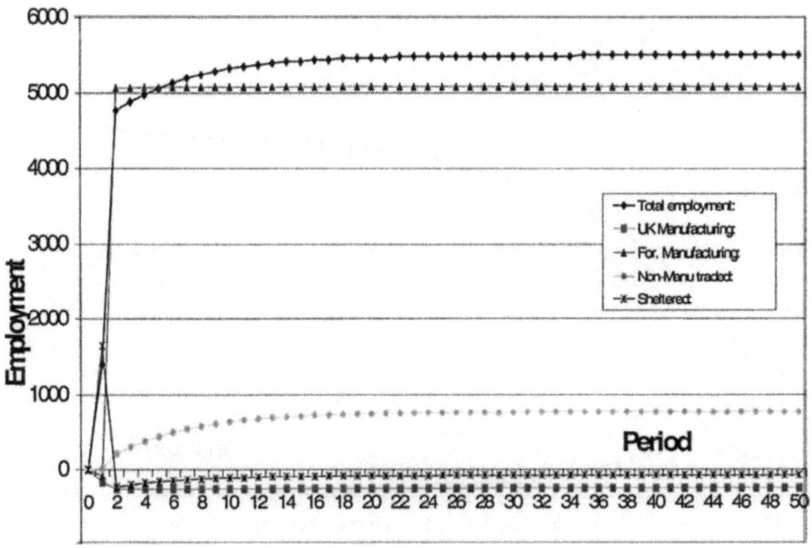

Figure 5.1 Changes in employment broken down by sector for an export-FDI shock in Model 1 with regional bargaining

Since migration has no effect until period 2 the impact effects of the FDI shock in the presence of migration are identical to those without, as reported in column 4 of table 5.4. In period 2, in-migration begins in response to the period-1 rise in both the real wage and employment rates (column 7 of table 5.4). Population increases slightly in period 2 and so restrains the rise in the nominal wage and reduces the loss of competitiveness as compared to the fixed population case, thereby stimulating exports and employment. However, more importantly, with the flow equilibrium specification used in AMOSFDI, migration continues until the real wage, unemployment and participation rates return to their original level. Accordingly, even where there is regional bargaining, migration ensures input-output results in the long run (McGregor *et al,* 1995,1996), and so the scale of effects here is ultimately much greater than if population is fixed. While the production function in each sector allows factor substitution, the ultimately unchanged input prices and the linear homogeneity assumptions imply that there is no incentive to change technique. The system behaves as if there were fixed technical coefficients. The result is illustrated in column 8 of Table 5.4. Note that all prices have returned to their initial values and that in every sector employment, capital and output all rise by the same percentage amount

Figure 5.2 plots the period-by-period percentage change in total employment, the real wage and population as a result of the 100% export FDI shock with regional bargaining and migration. As explained earlier, the results for period 1 are exactly the same as for the fixed population case. However, in subsequent periods employment here evolves in a quite different way to the fixed population case. In particular, total employment only gradually approaches its long-run equilibrium level as in-migration gradually pushes down the real wage towards its original level, and capital accumulation proceeds.

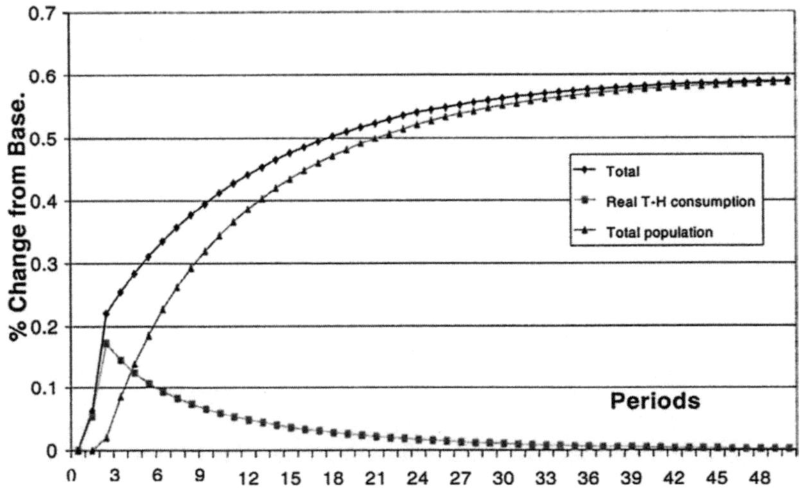

Figure 5.2 Proportionate change in total employment, real wage, and population following an FDI export shock in Model 1 with regional bargaining and migration

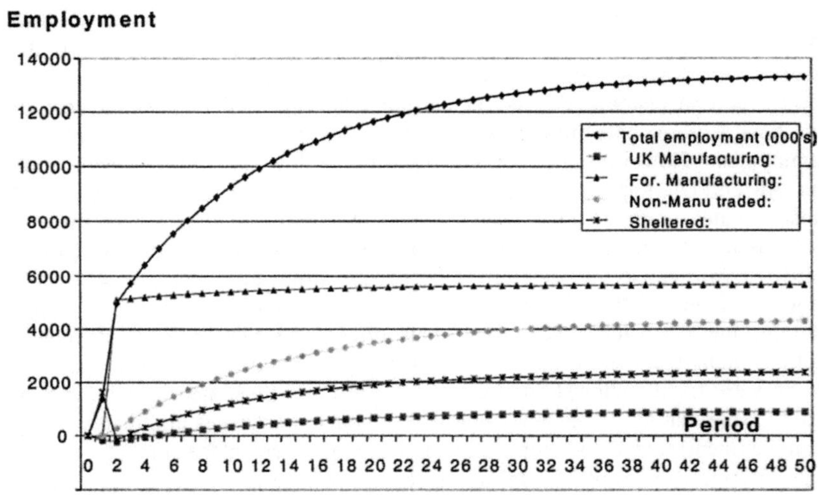

Figure 5.3 Change in total employment and employment by sector for an FDI-export shock in Model 1 with regional bargaining and migration

Figure 5.3 plots the changes in the levels of employment by sector as a result of the export-FDI shock. The immediate expansion in the capacity of foreign manufacturing facilitates its very rapid adjustment to long-run equilibrium. In the other sectors capital can only be adjusted gradually, and this, together with adjustment of the population, delays overall achievement of long-run equilibrium. Recall that the inward investment is associated with 5,162 direct jobs. Note that there is net aggregate labor market displacement until period 3. Labor market crowding-out persists in the UK-owned manufacturing sector until period 5 and the sheltered sector experiences a one period fall (period 2) in employment due to the effects of the higher regional wage. (Table 5.6 summarizes the long-run employment effects and associated multipliers.)

Table 5.6 The long-run impact of an incoming 100% export-FDI plant generating 5,162 direct jobs with Model 1, regional bargaining and migration

Model 1:	Long Run Impact:	
Gross Domestic Product	£192m	
Household Disposable Income	£167m	
	Employment	
	Totals	Multiplier
Total Employment	13,422	2.60
UK-Owned Manufacturing	948	0.18
Foreign-owned Manufacturing	5,686	1.10
Non-Manufacturing Traded	4,369	0.85
Sheltered Sector	2,420	0.47

However, with migration the adjustment towards long-run equilibrium is more protracted than it otherwise would be. By periods 2 and 10, total employment is 37% and 70% of its long-run total compared with 71% and 92%, respectively, for the same export FDI shock with national bargaining and migration. Under the regional bargaining closure with endogenous population, the long run is not achieved until period 78.

Clearly, the scale of the demand-side effect is determined by the structural characteristics of the foreign-owned sector, and is the same for each model closure. The very substantial differences are clearly attributable to the nature of the induced supply-side reaction, which is governed by the nature of regional wage determination and the net migration response.

This discussion suffices to clarify the nature of the system's response to the FDI-export shock. We do not discuss the other multi-period simulation results in detail. However, the detailed results for Models 2 and 3 are presented Appendices 5.4 and 5.5.

5.4.2 The Long-Run Results

Table 5.7 summarizes the long-run impact of the FDI stimulus on employment for each model and for the four labor market closures. Recall that these are the solutions obtained when all sectoral capital stocks are fully adjusted to their desired levels and, for those cases in which migration occurs at all, where population adjustments are also complete.

Table 5.7. The long-run employment impact of the export-oriented FDI

	National Bargaining	Regional Bargaining	National & Regional Bargaining + Migration
Model 1	12,791	5,517	13,422
Model 2	8,760	3,761	9,256
Model 3	8,760	3,626	9,256

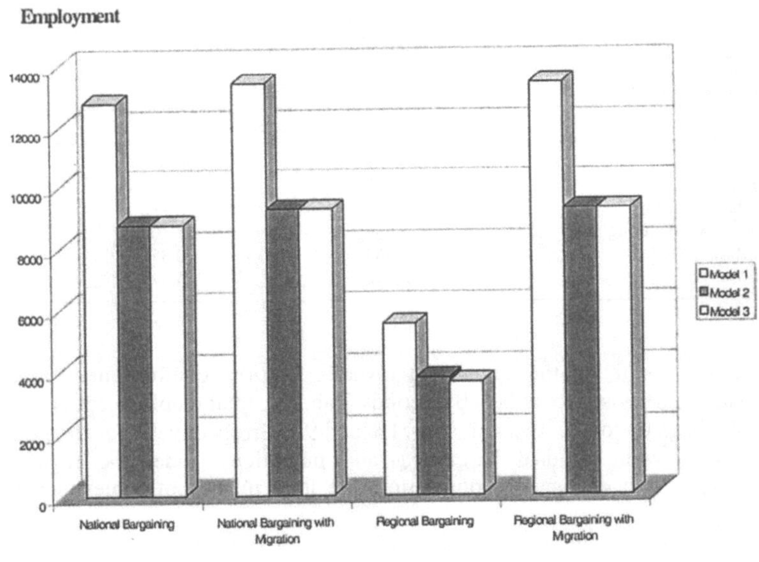

Figure 5.4 The long-run employment effects of export oriented inward investment (£248 million stimulus to exports)

We begin by considering differences in results across labor market closures. First, the results of the national and regional bargaining closures are identical when population is endogenous. In the presence of migration, as we have seen, the regional bargaining model converges on an input-output solution. Although regional wages initially rise in response to the FDI-export shock, in-migration eventually pushes the wage back to its original level. Under these circumstances differences in wage bargaining ultimately do not matter: in the long run it is as if labor is in infinitely elastic supply to the region. The national bargaining closure in fact also eventually converges on an input-output solution even in the absence of migration (as inspection of column 3 of table 5.4 confirms). The reason is simply that in this closure, with the nominal wage fixed, and capital accumulation ultimately pushing rental rates back to

their initial values, prices do not change across long-run equilibria. However, since population is fixed the employment effects are a little less in this model than in the presence of migration. The differences between columns 1 and 3 of table 5.7 simply reflect the impact of the higher welfare payments associated with the larger populations implied by the presence of endogenous migration. The really distinctive results here are those for the regional bargaining case with no migration. We know that the much smaller employment effects associated with this model arise because the demand stimulus results in a permanent increase in the real wage and in prices, so making labor market displacement permanent. Under these conditions labor remains a regional-specific factor even in the long run.

Next consider how the results vary across the different models. Inspection of table 5.7 and figure 5.4 reveals that the most striking feature of these results are the much higher employment estimates associated with Model 1 than the other two models, a feature of all the labor market closures. However, recall that this model is associated with a higher direct employment impact. In fact, Models 2 and 3 yield identical results within each labor market closure except regional bargaining. This is, of course, the only case that does not converge on an input-output solution in the long run. Recall that Model 1 is the hypothetical model predicated upon an assumption that UK-owned manufacturing sectors are identical in both structure and behavior. Model 2 assumes identical behavior but the "true" structure while Model 3 also captures both "true" behavior and "true" structure.

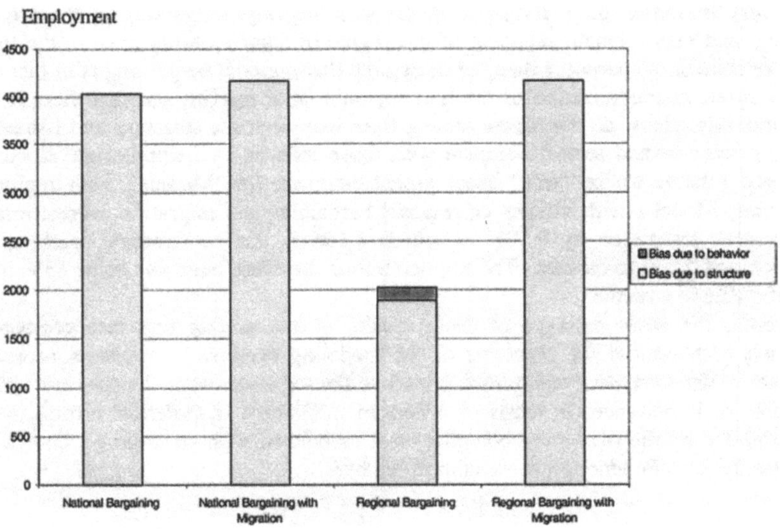

Figure 5.5 Overestimation of long-run employment due to inappropriate assumptions of identical structure and behavior

It appears from these results that for a demand shock originating in the foreign-owned manufacturing sector, over the long run at least, structure matters a great deal (Model 2 compared to Model 1) whereas behavioral differences do not (Model 3 compared to Model 2). Inspection of figure 5.5 makes the main points emphatically.

If, as researchers are forced to do in the absence of ownership-disaggregated input-output tables, identical behavior and structure are inappropriately assumed, then the employment impacts of export-oriented FDI are very substantially overestimated. In fact, the estimated employment impacts exceed the actual impact by 46%, 45% and 56% respectively for the national bargaining, both endogenous population and the regional bargaining cases respectively. Secondly, the contribution of structure to this bias totally dominates the influence of behavior. The latter has no impact in three of the four cases, and a small influence in the regional bargaining case. These results are in line with our earlier discussion of the likely determinants of the influence of structure and behavior. Where input-output results are generated by a regional CGE in the long run we expect that only structure matters: the initial input-output table is sufficient, given input-output model assumptions, to completely pre-determine the results. However, where this is not so, due here to labor being regional-specific even in the long run in the regional bargaining case, behavior will matter too. In our particular example, even in this case behavior does not seem to matter a great deal. Here getting structure wrong leads to an overestimate in employment of 1891, whereas getting behavior wrong results in an additional underestimate of only 135, or some 6.7% of the total error in the regional bargaining case.

Recall that a number of applied studies have, in fact, made use of Model 1 since ownership-disaggregated input-output tables have not previously been available for Scotland. It seems clear that this approach would generate very serious over-estimates of the likely long-run employment effects of the export-FDI shock, and should be avoided. However, it is also apparent that the chosen labor market closure may prove to be very important too. Evidence in favor of regional bargaining in the UK is growing, and many remain skeptical of the degree of labor mobility even in the long run. For illustrative purposes then, let us assume that regional bargaining is in fact the most accurate characterization of the host region's labor market, and that there is no labor mobility. How do the biases arising from inappropriate structure and behavior (of the foreign-owned sector) compare with those induced by inappropriate closure? Measured relative to the "true" employment estimate, i.e., Model 3 with regional bargaining, Model 1 with national or regional bargaining and migration overestimates employment generation by 9,796, of which 4,166 is due to structure, nothing to behavior, and 5,630 to closure. The implied bias is therefore huge and some 43% of it is attributable to structure.

Overall, the main message of these results is that getting structure correct is extremely important if the objective of the modeling exercise is to obtain accurate estimates of the long-run employment impact of inward investment. Furthermore, this compares in importance (in terms of orders of magnitude of potential errors), with those implied by the maximum potential error associated with an incorrect choice of labor market closure amongst those considered here.

5.4.3 The Time Paths of Employment Adjustment

We know that, in general, policy makers are concerned about the time path of adjustment as well as long-run equilibria. Indeed, in a UK context, the Treasury typically does not look at effects extending beyond a 10-year horizon, implying that where adjustment is extended, long-run equilibrium values of employment become irrelevant to policy-making. Accordingly, we now consider the time paths of

adjustment of employment. We already know from our consideration of the export-FDI shock on the regional bargaining closures of Model 1, that adjustment may be very extended and that the time paths of adjustment to long-run equilibrium may differ radically, as may the long-run equilibrium itself. Figure 5.6 plots the time paths of total employment associated with each of the models for the regional bargaining closures, with and without migration. A number of points are immediately apparent. First, as we already know, Models 2 and 3 converge on the same long-run employment solution and this lies below that for Model 1, but these models do have slightly different adjustment paths. Furthermore, each of the models is associated with a different long-run solution in the absence of migration, and again Model 1 overestimates the employment impact substantially (and Model 2 does slightly) if Model 3 is taken as the "true" model.

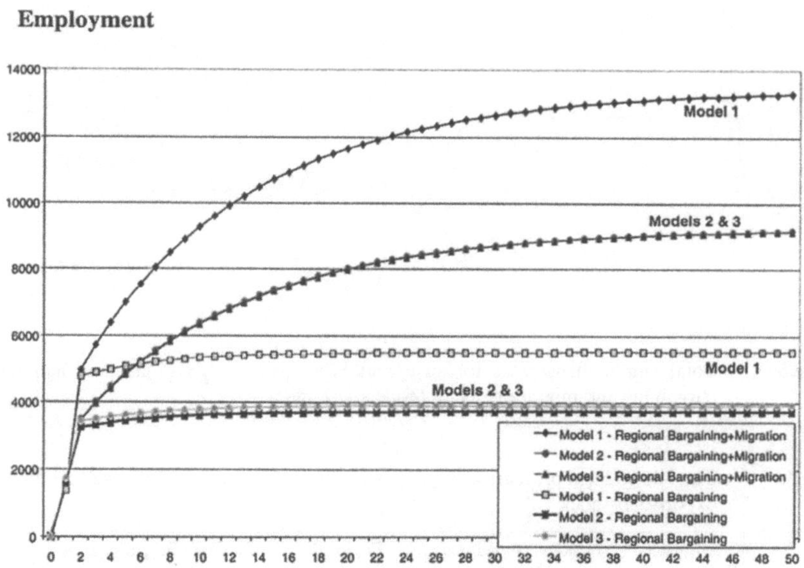

Figure 5.6 Total employment generated by an export FDI shock with regional bargaining with and without migration, using Models 1, 2 and 3

Figure 5.7 repeats the total employment paths for regional bargaining with migration and contrasts this with the solutions for the national bargaining model with migration. While Models 2 and 3 converge on the same long-run solution under local and national bargaining their adjustment paths are different. An important implication of these observed differences in adjustment paths across model types and labor market closures is that behavior differences are much more influential in the short-run, and this may be important in practice because of policy makers' time horizons. The UK Treasury, for example, typically assesses the employment impact of a project by computing the discounted sum of employment over a 10-year period (HM Treasury,

1995; 1997), to yield total "present value job years" (PVJYs). In Table 5.8, we report the total PVJYs for each model and labor market closure, using the 6% discount rate recommended by the Treasury.[14]

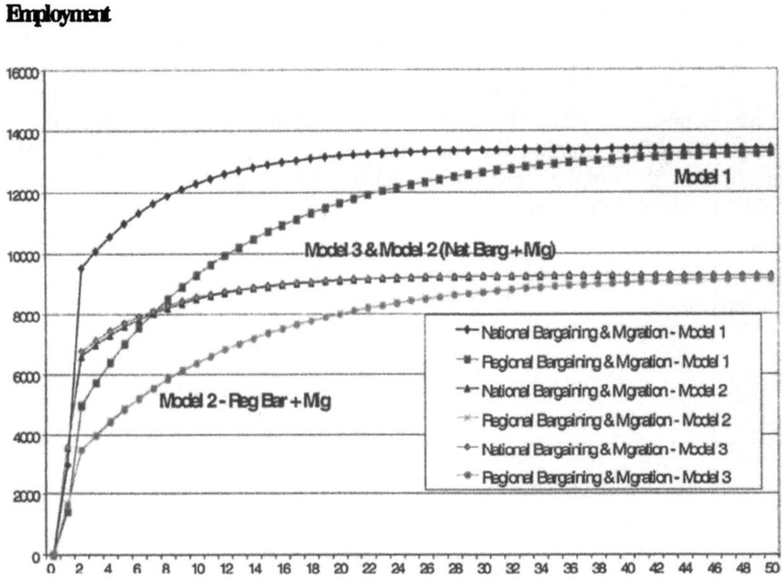

Figure 5.7 Total employment paths for an export FDI shock with regional and national bargaining and migration, using Models 1, 2 and 3

Table 5.8 Total discounted present value job years (PVJYs) for periods 1 through 10 for an export-FDI shock

	National Bargaining	National Bargaining + Migration	Regional Bargaining	Regional Bargaining + Migration
Model 1	72,029	73,516	33,882	47,267
Model 2	51,148	52,226	23,850	33,471
Model 3	51,795	52,951	23,352	33,159

Each model and closure is associated with a unique estimate of PVJYs. While the national and regional bargaining closures converge on the same long-run equilibrium value in the presence of migration, the much more rapid adjustment apparent under the national bargaining closure implies that PVJYs are systematically significantly greater

[14] These total PVJYs estimates include period 1 employment. In official evaluations of regional policy, the period 1 employment impact is usually excluded as this is viewed as temporary employment that is typically associated with the construction of the plant (HM Treasury, 1995; 1997).

under this closure. Indeed, the estimate of PVJYs under regional bargaining with migration is only an average of some 64% of the corresponding estimates for the national bargaining closure. Notice that the use of PVJYs results in the national bargaining with no migration closure enjoying a substantial differential over regional bargaining with migration, despite that fact that the latter exhibits higher long-run equilibrium employment levels. Again, this reflects the very extended adjustment process that we observe under regional bargaining with endogenous population. This is also the source of the dramatic change in the comparison between this case and regional bargaining with a fixed population. Although the former still ranks above the latter, the differential is much reduced because of the relatively very rapid speed of adjustment under regional bargaining with no migration.

Consider next differences in PVJYs across models. First, the results for Models 2 and 3 now differ within each closure (whereas long-run equilibria only differed within the regional bargaining closure with fixed population). Furthermore, the results now differ between the regional and national bargaining closures under endogenous population. Under the national bargaining closures adjustment is more rapid in Model 3 than Model 2, whereas relative adjustment speeds are reversed under regional bargaining.

Focusing on PVJYs has the effect of generating a wider variety of results across both closures and models. Neither result is surprising. The PVJYs measure ignores everything that happens to employment after year 10, and weights initial effects much more highly than delayed effects. The short-run therefore matters a great deal in the computation of PVJYs. Furthermore, we know that some labor market closures, notably regional and national bargaining under endogenous population, may generate radically different short-run behavior even though they ultimately converge on the input-output solution. Similarly, we know that structure tends to increase in importance through time, at least for those models that ultimately converge on input-output solutions. In the short-run in such models behavior differences bite on relative price changes, but in the long-run these become less and less important. However, while using PVJYs opens up additional significant differentials among some closures as compared to focusing on long-run equilibrium levels of employment, the additional differences among models tends to be small. Thus, again, the overriding message, even from inspection of PVJYs that attribute substantial weight to the short-run, is that structure matters much more than behavior in influencing the employment effects of FDI.

Inspection of Figures 5.8 and 5.9 confirms these observations. Thus inappropriate use of a model that takes structure and behavior to be identical leads to large overestimation of the likely employment effects, although the percentage errors are less and more uniform across models for PVJYs than for equilibrium employment levels. Thus the smallest over-estimate is 27.9% for the national bargaining with migration case, and the highest is 34% for the regional bargaining closure.

Secondly, behavior now matters across all closures and, for national bargaining closures, it actually counteracts, to a degree, the overestimation of employment effects attributable to structure (reflecting the change in adjustment speeds across closures noted above). However, while, as we would expect, the shorter-run focus of PVJYs does result in behavior increasing in importance, the influence of structure continues to completely dominate. (The percentages of total errors attributable to behavior are 3.1, 3.5, 4.7 and 2.2 for the national bargaining and regional bargaining cases respectively.)

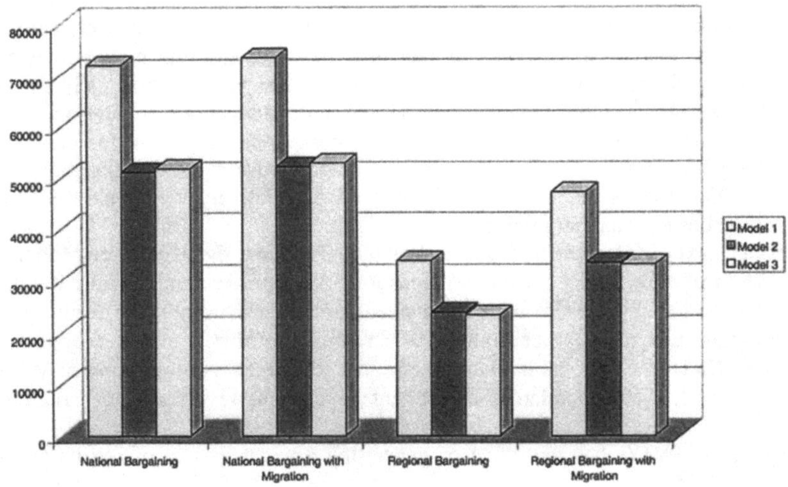

Figure 5.8 Total Present Value Job Years (PVJYs), years 1 through 10 (£248 million stimulus to exports)

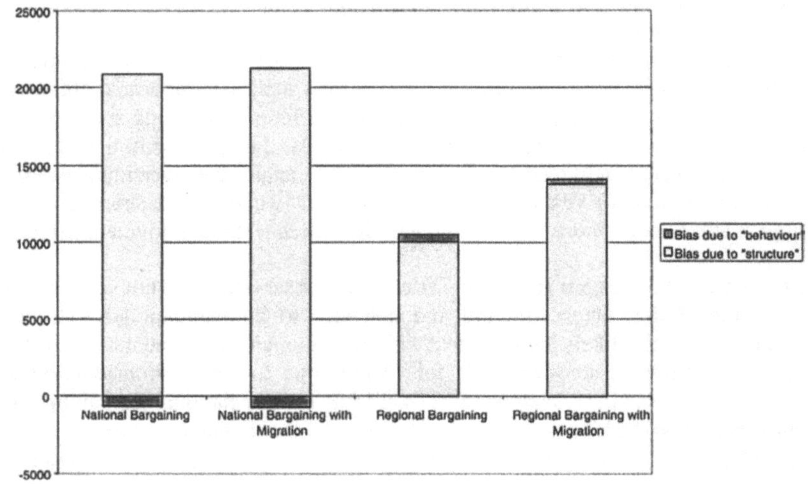

Figure 5.9 Errors in estimates of Present Value Job Years (PVJY) due to inappropriate assumptions of identical structure and behavior

We should perhaps end on a note of caution concerning the generality of our results. First, our finding that structure is substantially more important than behavior in governing employment outcomes, even when these are measured in terms of PVJYs, may be specific to the models that we examine here, and also depend, of course, on how distinctive the foreign-owned sector is in fact. Furthermore, the importance of structure will in general depend also on the precise way in which PVJYs are measured. Clearly, the shorter the time horizon over which PVJYs are summed and the higher the discount rate, the greater the weight that would attach to the short run and the greater would be the potential for behavior to become more important in influencing the demand-induced employment impact of any inward investment. Thirdly, our model employs a high level of sectoral aggregation. Further disaggregation could radically alter results. For example, the electronics industry in Scotland is dominated by foreign-owned firms, so that their characteristics are closer to those of the entire sector. Finally, we deal only with demand shocks. Convergence on input-output results is not a feature of the system's response to supply shocks, and we have already noted that these may well accompany the demand stimuli in the case of FDI (Gillespie *et al.*, 2001b). In such circumstances structure need not be dominant, even in the long-run.

5.5 Conclusions

In this chapter we provide an analysis of the likely demand-induced employment impact of a policy-generated inward investment on the host region, using what is, to our knowledge, the first ownership-disaggregated, regional CGE model. This work extends our earlier analysis which focused on the impact of all RSA-assisted investment, not just its FDI component, using a CGE model that did not differentiate between foreign- and UK-owned manufacturing sectors (Gillespie *et al,* 2001a). We adapt the contributions of Gazel *et al.* (1996), Haddad *et al.* (2002) and Israilevich *et al.* (1997) to provide a means of separately identifying the influence of structure and behavior in the overall regional employment impact of inward investment. We find that structure is very important in this respect, and much more important than behavior. This is to be expected in terms of long-term equilibrium employment levels, given that many labor market closures converge on input-output solutions in the long run. It is perhaps less expected under closures that do not converge on input-output, or when employment impacts are measured in terms of present value job years, which attach considerable weight to the short run. Indeed, overall we find that structure generates errors in the measurement of employment effects that are of a similarly large order of magnitude to those generated by the maximum possible error in the choice of labor market closure used here. However, the generality of the results that we obtain is not assured and merits further investigation.

Possible extensions of our analysis include: further disaggregation of both domestically owned and foreign-owned sub-sectors of manufacturing; consideration of the sensitivity of our findings to alternative models of foreign-ownership; allowance for product market displacement; accommodation of "efficiency spillovers";[15] incorporation of the possible impact of FDI on trade flows (e.g. Barrell and Pain, 1997); provision of a more complete welfare evaluation; rendering the FDI decision

[15] We have illustrated the possible effects in the context of a CGE model that does disaggregate by ownership. (Gillespie *et al,* 2001b.)

endogenous; generalization to the interregional context to capture aspects of fiscal competition that are likely to characterize the behavior of devolved UK regions. While these extensions undoubtedly constitute a major research challenge, the framework developed in this chapter will, we believe, ultimately prove capable of accommodating them all.

References

Alexander, J.M. and T.R. Whyte. 1995. "Output, Income and Employment Multipliers for Scotland." *Scottish Economic Bulletin*, 50, Winter 1994/95.

Armington, P. 1969. "A Theory of Demand for Products Distinguished by Place of Production." *IMF Staff Papers*, 16, 157-178.

Barry, F and J. Bradley. 1997. "FDI and Trade: The Irish Host-Country Experience." *Economic Journal*, 107, 1798-1811.

Barrell, R. and N. Pain. 1997. "Foreign Direct Investment, Technological Change, and Economic Growth within Europe." *Economic Journal*, 107, 1770-1786.

Blanchflower, D.G. and A.J. Oswald. 1994. *The Wage Curve*. Cambridge, MA., M.I.T. Press.

Bradley, J., J.F. Gerald, and I. Kearney, I. 1993. "Modelling Supply in an Open Economy Using a Restricted Cost Function." *Economic Modelling*, 11-21.

Bradley, J., K. Whelan, and J. Wright. 1995. "Hermin Ireland." *Economic Modelling*, 12, 249-274.

Davies, S.W., and B.R. Lyons. 1991. "Characterising relative performance: the productivity advantages of foreign owned firms in the UK." *Oxford Economic Papers*, 43, 584-595.

Dervis, K., J. De Melo, and S. Robinson. 1982. *General Equilibrium Models for Development Policy*. Cambridge, Cambridge University Press.

Driffield, N. 1995. "The Indirect Employment Effects of FDI into the UK." Paper presented at the Regional Science Association, British and Irish Section, Annual Conference 13-15 September 1995, Cardiff Business School.

English Unit. 1992. *The Knock-On Effects of Inward Investment – English Overview*. London, HMSO.

Foster J. and J. Malley. 1988. "The Domestic and Foreign-Owned Sectors of Scottish Manufacturing: A Macroeconomic Approach to their Relative Performance and Prospects." *Scottish Journal of Political Economy*, 35, 250-265.

Gazel, R, G.J.D. Hewings, and M. Sonis. 1996. "Trade, sensitivity and feedbacks: interregional impacts of the US-Canada Free Trade Agreement", in J.C.J.M. van den Bergh, P. Nijkamp and P. Rietveld (eds.) *Recent Advances in Spatial Equilibrium Modelling* Heidelberg, Springer Verlag.

Gibson, H. 1990. "Export Competitiveness and UK Sales of Scottish Manufactures", Paper delivered to the Scottish Economists' Conference, The Burn, 1990.

Gillespie G., P.G. McGregor, J.K. Swales, and Y.P. Yin. 1997. "The Regional Impact of Inward Investment: Product Market Displacement, Labour Market Effects and Efficiency Spillovers." *Strathclyde Papers in Economics* 97/2. Department of Economics, University of Strathclyde, Glasgow.

Gillespie G. 1998. "Foreign-Owned Multipliers: Evidence From A Scottish Input-Output Model." *Strathclyde Papers In Economics* 98/1, Department of Economics, University of Strathclyde, Glasgow.

Gillespie, G. 2000. "Modelling the System-Wide Impact of Foreign Direct Investment (FDI): An Ownership-Disaggregated Regional Computable General Equilibrium (CGE) Analysis." Unpublished Ph.D. Thesis, Department of Economics, University of Strathclyde, Glasgow.

Gillespie G, P.G. McGregor, J.K. Swales and Y.P. Yin. 2001a. "The Displacement and Multiplier Effects of Regional Selective Assistance: A Computable General Equilibrium Analysis." *Regional Studies*, 35, 125-139.

Gillespie G., P.G. McGregor, J.K. Swales, and Y.P. Yin. 2001b. "A Regional Computable General Equilibrium Analysis of the Demand and "Efficiency Spillover" Effects of Foreign Direct Investment." in N. Pain ed. *Inward Investment, Technological Change and Growth: The Impact of Multinational Corporations on the UK Economy*. Basingstoke, Palgrave.

Greenwood, M.J, G. Hunt, D.S. Rickman, and G.I. Treyz. 1991. "Migration, Regional Equilibrium, and the Estimation of Compensating Differentials." *American Economic Review*, 81, 1382-90.

Haddad, E., G.J.D. Hewings, and M. Peter. 2002. "Input-Output Systems in Regional and Interregional CGE Modeling." This volume, chapter 13.

Harrigan, F. and P.G. McGregor. 1988. "Price and Quantity Interaction in Regional Economic Models: The Importance of Openness and Closures." In F. Harrigan and P.G McGregor, eds. *Recent Advances in Regional Economic Modelling*. London, Pion.

Harrigan, F., P.G, McGregor, N. Dourmashkin, R. Perman, J.K. Swales, and Y.P. Yin. 1991. "AMOS: A Macro-Micro Model of Scotland." *Economic Modeling*, 10, 424-479.

Harris, J.R. and M.P. Todaro. 1970. "Migration, Unemployment and Development: A Two-Sector Analysis." *American Economic Review*, 60, 126-142.

Harris, R.I.D. 1989. *The Growth and Structure of the UK Regional Economy 1963-85*. Aldershot, Avebury.

Hewings, G.J.D. 1977. "Evaluating the Possibilities for Exchanging Regional Input-Output Coefficients." *Environment and Planning A*, vol. 9, 927-944.

Hewings, G.J.D. 1985. "The Role of Prior Information in Updating Regional Input-Output Models." *Socio-Economic Planning Sciences*, 18, 319-336.

Higgs, P.J., B.R. Paramenter, and R.J. Rimmer. 1988. "A Hybrid Top-Down, Bottom-Up Regional Computable General Equilibrium Model." *International Regional Science Review*, 11, 317-28.

Hill, S. and A. Roberts. 1995. "Inward investment, Local Linkages and Regional Development." Paper presented at the Regional Science Association, British and Irish Section, Annual Conference, 13-15 September 1995, Cardiff Business School.

H M Treasury. 1995. *A Framework for the Evaluation of Regeneration Projects and Programmes*. London, HMSO.

H M Treasury. 1997. *Appraisal and Evaluation in Central Government: Treasury Guidance*. London, The Stationary Office.

Holden, D.R. and J.K. Swales. 1995. "The Additionality, Displacement and Substitution Effects of a Factor Subsidy." *Scottish Journal of Political Economy*, 42, 113-126.

Israilevich, P.R., G.J.D. Hewings, G.R. Schindler, and R. Mahidhara. 1996. "The choice of input-output table embedded in regional econometric input-output models." *Papers in Regional Science*, 75, 103-119.

Israilevich, P.R., G.J.D. Hewings, M. Sonis, and G.R. Schindler. 1997. "Forecasting Structural Change with a Regional Econometric Input-Output Model." *Journal of Regional Science*, 37, 565-90.

Jones, R. and J. Whalley. 1988. "Regional Effects of Taxes in Canada, an Applied General Equilibrium Approach." *Journal of Public Economics*, 37, 1-28.

Kimbell, L.J. and G.W. Harrison. 1984. "General Equilibrium Analysis of Regional Fiscal Incidence." In H.E. Scarf and J.B. Shoven eds. *Applied General Equilibrium Analysis*. Cambridge, Cambridge University Press.

Kraybill, D.S., T.G. Johnson, and D. Orden. 1992. "Macroeconomic Imbalances: A Multiregional General Equilibrium Analysis." *American Journal of Agricultural Economics*, 74, 726-736.

Lahr, M.L. and R.E. Miller. 1997. "A Taxonomy of Extractions: A Framework for Understanding the Various Approaches Used to Measure the Importance of an Industry." *Working Paper* No. 131, Centre for Urban Policy Research, Rutgers, The State University, New Brunswick, NJ.

Layard, R., S. Nickell, and R. Jackman. 1991. *Unemployment: Macroeconomic Performance and the Labor Market*. Oxford, Oxford University Press.

McGregor, P.G., J.K. Swales, Y.P. Yin. 1995. "Migration Equilibria /Disequilibria and the Natural Rate of Unemployment in a Regional Context." *International Journal of Manpower*, 16, 66-72.

McGregor, P.G., J.K. Swales, Y.P. Yin. 1996. "A Long-Run Interpretation of Regional Input-Output Analyses." *Journal of Regional Science*, 36, 479-501.

McGregor, P.G., J.K. Swales, Y.P. Yin. 1999. "Spillover and Feedback Effects in General Equilibrium Interregional Models of the National Economy: A Requiem for Interregional Input-Output?" In G. J. D. Hewings, M. Sonis, M Madden and Y Kimura eds. *Understanding and Interpreting Economic Structure.* Springer, Heidelberg.

Minford, P., P. Stoney, J. Riley, and B. Webb. 1994. "An Econometric Model of Merseyside: Validation and Policy Simulations." *Regional Studies*, 28, 563-575.

Morgan, W., J. Mutti, and M. Partridge. 1989. "A Regional General Equilibrium Model of the United States: Tax Effects of Factor Movement and Regional Production." *Review of Economics and Statistics*, 71, 626-35.

PA Cambridge Economic Consultants Limited. 1993. *Regional Selective Assistance 1985 – 88.* London, HMSO.

PA Cambridge Economic Consultants Limited. 1995. *Assessment of the Wider Effects of Foreign Direct Investment in Manufacturing in the UK.* London, HMSO.

Pain, N. 2001. *Inward Investment, Technological Change and Growth: The Impact of Multinational Corporations on the UK Economy.* Basingstoke, Palgrave.

Partridge, M.D. and D.S. Rickman, D.S. 1998. "Regional Computable General Equilibrium Modeling: A Survey and Critical Appraisal." *International Regional Science Review*, 21, 205-248.

Rickman, D.S. 1992. "Estimating the Impact of Regional Business Assistance Programmes: Alternative Closures in a General Computable Equilibrium Model." *Papers in Regional Science*, 71, 421-435.

Roper, S. and G. O'Shea. 1991. "The Effects of Labor Subsidies in Northern Ireland 1967-79: A Simulation Exercise." *Scottish Journal of Political Economy*, 38, 273-292.

Scottish Office. 1999. "The Manufacturing Sector in Scotland 1996." *Statistical Bulletin: Industry Series,* no. IND/1999/J1.5.

Scottish Office Industry Department. 1994. *Scottish Input-Output Tables for 1989.* Edinburgh, HMSO.

Shoven, J.B. and J. Whalley. 1984. "Applying General Equilibrium Models of Taxation and Trade: An Introduction and Survey." *Journal of Economic Literature*, 22, 1007-51.

Shoven, J.B. and J. Whalley. 1992. *Applying General Equilibrium.* Cambridge University Press, Cambridge.

Treyz, G.I., D.S. Rickman, and M.I. Greenwood. 1993. "The Dynamics of U.S. Internal Migration." *Review of Economic and Statistics*, 75, 209-214.

Appendix 5.1 A Condensed Version of AMOSFDI

Equations	**Short-run**
(A1) Price determination	$p_i = p_i\left(w_n, w_k\right)$
(A2) Wage setting	$w_n = w\left(N / L, cpi, t_n\right)$
(A3) Labor force	$L = \overline{L}$
(A4) Consumer price index	$cpi = \sum_i \theta_i p_i + \sum_i \theta_i^{RUK} \overline{p}_i^{RUK} + \sum_i \theta_i^{ROW} \overline{P}_i^{ROW}$
(A5) Capital supply	$K_i^s = \overline{K}_i^s$
(A6) Capital price index	$kpi = \sum_i \gamma_i p_i + \sum_i \gamma_i^{RUK} \overline{p}_i^{RUK} + \sum_i \gamma_i^{ROW} \overline{P}_i^{ROW}$
(A7) Labor demand	$N_i^d = N_i^d\left(Q_i, w_n, w_k\right)$
(A8) Capital demand	$K_i^d = K_i^d\left(Q_i, w_n, w_k\right)$
(A9) Labor market clearing	$\sum_i N_i^d = N$
(A10) Capital market clearing	$K_i^s = K_i^d$
(A11) Household income	$Y = \Psi_t N w_n \left(1 - t_n\right) + \Psi_k \sum_i K_i w_{ki} \left(1 - t_k\right) + \overline{T}$
(A12) Commodity demand	$Q_i = C_i + I_i + G_i + X_i$
(A13) Consumption demand	$C_i = C_i\left(p_i, \overline{p}_i^{RUK}, \overline{P}_i^{ROW}, Y, cpi\right)$
(A14) User cost of capital	$uck = uck\left(kpi\right)$
(A15) Desired capital stock	$K_i^* = K_i^d\left(Q_i, w_n, uck\right)$
(A16) Investment demand	$I_i = I_i\left(p_i, \overline{p}_i^{RUK}, \overline{p}_i^{ROW}, \sum_i b_{ij} I_j^d\right);$ $I_j^d = \lambda_j\left(K_j^* - K_j\right)$
(A17) Government demand	$G_i = \overline{G}_i$
(A18) Export demand	$X_i = X_i\left(p_i, \overline{p}_i^{RUK}, \overline{p}_i^{ROW}, \overline{D}^{RUK}, \overline{D}^{ROW}\right)$
Multi-period model	**Stock up-dating equations**
(A19) Labor force	$L_t = L_{t-1} + nmg_{t-1}$
(A20) Migration	$\frac{nmg}{L} = nmg\left(w_n / cpi, w_n^{RUK} / cpi^{RUK}, N / L, N^{RUK} / L^{RL}\right.$
(A21) Capital stock	$K_{i,t} = \left(1 - d_i\right) K_{i,t-1} + I_{i,t-1}^d$

Notation

Activity-Commodities

i, *j* are activity/commodity subscripts (There are four of each in AMOSFDI: UK-owned manufacturing, foreign-owned manufacturing, non-manufacturing traded and sheltered.)

Transactors

RUK = Rest of the UK, *ROW* = Rest of the World

Functions

Nmg(.)	net migration function
p (.)	CES cost function
uck(.)	user cost of capital function
$K^S(.)$, $W(.)$	Factor supply or wage-setting equations
$K^d(.)$, $N^d(.)$	CES factor demand functions
$C(.)$, $I(.)$, $X(.)$	Armington consumption, investment and export demand functions, homogenous of degree zero in prices and one in quantities

Variables

C	consumption
D	exogenous export demand
G	government demand for local goods
I	investment demand for local goods
I^d	investment demand by activity
K^d, K^S, K	capital demand, capital supply and capital employment
L	labor force
N^d, N	labor demand and total employment
Q	commodity/activity output
T	nominal transfers from outside the region
X	exports
Y	household nominal income
b	elements of capital matrix
cpi, *kpi*	consumer and capital price indices
d	physical depreciation
nmg	net migration
p	price of commodity/activity output
t_n, t_k	average direct tax on labor and capital income
u	unemployment rate
uck	user cost of capital
w_n, w_k	price of labor to the firm, capital rental
Ψ	share of factor income retained in region
θ	consumption weights
γ	capital weights
λ	capital stock adjustment parameter

Appendix 5.2 The Social Accounting Matrix for Model 1 (SAM1)

	UK Manuf.	For Manuf.	Non-manuf	Sheltered	Households	Corporate	Government.	Capital	Stocks	Tourist Expend	RUK	ROW	Skilled Labor	Unskilled Labor	Value Added	Tax	Total
UK Manuft.	1718	833	785	398	1178	0	226	176	57	146	6024	5547	0	0	0	0	17088
For Manuft.	833	404	380	193	571	0	110	86	27	71	2920	2689	0	0	0	0	8283
Non-manu.t	2713	1315	3296	426	7016	0	670	608	106	964	3897	1107	0	0	0	0	22117
Sheltered	320	155	1346	913	2983	0	7936	2309	11	28	1031	172	0	0	0	0	17204
RUK	3898	1890	2448	965	5513	1173	2552	3135	52	268	0	0	0	0	0	0	21894
G&S	3898	1890	2448	965	5513	0	2552	3135	52	268	0	0	0	0	0	0	20721
Transfers	0	0	0	0	0	1173	0	0	0	0	0	0	0	0	0	0	1173
ROW	2570	1246	1625	270	4043	1202	1323	1860	19	213	0	0	0	0	0	0	14371
G&S	2570	1246	1625	270	4043	0	1323	1860	19	213	0	0	0	0	0	0	13169
Transfers	0	0	0	0	0	1202	0	0	0	0	0	0	0	0	0	0	1202
Taxes on expen.	242	117	969	131	3853	0	190	159	1	80	248	462	0	0	0	0	6452
Subsidies	-356	-173	-286	-11	-1005	0	0	0	0	-10	0	0	0	0	0	0	-1840
Skilled labor	1234	598	6054	6450	0	0	0	0	0	0	0	0	0	0	0	0	14337
Unskilled labor	2722	1319	1943	4677	0	0	0	0	0	0	0	0	0	0	0	0	10662
OVA	1130	548	3457	2724	0	0	0	0	0	0	0	0	0	0	0	0	7858
Sales by FD	65	31	100	67	523	0	-563	-397	-36	53	22	135	0	0	0	0	0
Households	0	0	0	0	0	4060	3395	0	0	0	0	0	14337	10662	1179	0	33632
UK Corporate	0	0	0	0	1925	0	1247	0	0	0	0	34	0	0	6365	0	9571
Government	0	0	0	0	5111	2518	0	0	0	0	5252	320	0	0	314	4612	18127
Capital	0	0	0	0	1921	619	1042	0	0	0	2500	2093	0	0	0	0	8173
Total	17088	8283	22117	17204	33632	9571	18127	7937	237	1813	21894	12558	14337	10662	7858	4612	207929

Note: G&S Goods and Services; OVA Other Value Added; FD Final demand

Appendix 5.3 The Social Accounting Matrix for Model 2

	UK Manuf.	For Manuf.	Non-manuf	Sheltered	Households	Corporate	Government.	Capital	Stocks	Tourist Expend	RUK	ROW	Skilled Labor	Unskilled Labor	Value Added	Tax	Total
UK Manuft.	2214	590	893	478	1379	0	229	188	32	170	6504	4410	0	0	0	0	17088
For Manuft.	670	313	272	114	370	0	106	74	52	47	2440	3826	0	0	0	0	8283
Non-manu.t	3345	682	3296	426	7016	0	670	608	106	964	3897	1107	0	0	0	0	22117
Sheltered	357	118	1346	913	2983	0	7936	2309	11	28	1031	172	0	0	0	0	17204
RUK	2991	2797	2448	965	5513	1173	2552	3135	52	268	0	0	0	0	0	0	21894
G&S	2991	2797	2448	965	5513	0	2552	3135	52	268	0	0	0	0	0	0	20721
Transfers	0	0	0	0	0	1173	0	0	0	0	0	0	0	0	0	0	1173
ROW	1972	1844	1625	270	4043	1202	1323	1860	19	213	0	0	0	0	0	0	14371
G&S	1972	1844	1625	270	4043	0	1323	1860	19	213	0	0	0	0	0	0	13169
Transfers	0	0	0	0	0	1202	0	0	0	0	0	0	0	0	0	0	1202
Taxes on expen.	270	90	969	131	3853	0	190	159	1	80	248	462	0	0	0	0	6452
Subsidies	-364	-164	-286	-11	-1005	0	0	0	0	-10	0	0	0	0	0	0	-1840
Skilled labor	1389	444	6054	6450	0	0	0	0	0	0	0	0	0	0	0	0	14337
Unskilled labor	3062	979	1943	4677	0	0	0	0	0	0	0	0	0	0	0	0	10662
OVA	1111	566	3457	2724	0	0	0	0	0	0	0	0	0	0	0	0	7858
Sales by FD	71	25	100	67	523	0	-563	-397	-36	53	22	135	0	0	0	0	0
Households	0	0	0	0	0	4060	3395	0	0	0	0	0	14337	10662	1179	0	33632
UK Corporate	0	0	0	0	1925	0	1247	0	0	0	0	34	0	0	6365	0	9571
Government	0	0	0	0	5111	2518	0	0	0	0	5252	320	0	0	314	4612	18127
Capital	0	0	0	0	1921	619	1042	0	0	0	2500	2093	0	0	0	0	8173
Total	17088	8283	22117	17204	33632	9571	18127	7937	237	1813	21894	12558	14337	10662	7858	4612	207929

Note: G&S Goods and Services; OVA Other Value Added; FD Final demand

Appendix 5.4 Detailed Simulation Results for Model 2

	NATIONAL BARGAINING			REGIONAL BARGAINING				
	POPULATION FIXED			POPULATION FIXED			POPULATION ENDOGENOUS	
Model 1	Period 1	Period 2	Long Run	Period 1	Period 2	Long Run	Period 2	Long Run
GDP (income measure)	0.13	0.29	0.42	0.07	0.18	0.21	0.19	0.43
Consumption	0.15	0.28	0.37	0.15	0.27	0.29	0.27	0.43
Investment	2.15	0.58	0.56	2.15	0.40	0.39	0.41	0.57
Nominal before-tax wage	0.00	0.00	0.00	0.14	0.21	0.22	0.20	0.00
Real ef. tax cons. wage	-0.05	-0.05	0.00	0.06	0.13	0.15	0.11	0.00
Total employment	0.16	0.29	0.39	0.07	0.15	0.17	0.16	0.41
UK Manufacturing:	0.04	0.11	0.19	-0.07	-0.06	-0.05	-0.04	0.20
Foreign Manufacturing:	0.03	3.13	3.20	-0.05	2.99	3.01	3.00	3.20
Non-Manu traded:	0.09	0.16	0.31	0.00	0.01	0.05	0.02	0.34
Sheltered	0.30	0.14	0.20	0.22	0.01	0.02	0.02	0.21
Total unempl.	-1.21	-2.22	-2.99	-0.56	-1.11	-1.27	-1.01	0.00
Labor particip. rate	0.04	0.07	0.09	0.02	0.03	0.04	0.03	0.00
Total population	0.00	0.00	0.00	0.00	0.00	0.00	0.02	0.41
Price of value added								
UK Manufacturing:	0.02	0.07	0.00	0.09	0.18	0.19	0.17	0.00
Foreign Manufacturing:	0.03	0.12	0.00	0.09	0.21	0.17	0.20	0.00
Non-Manu traded:	0.09	0.16	0.00	0.14	0.22	0.17	0.22	0.00
Sheltered	0.19	0.09	0.00	0.28	0.22	0.19	0.21	0.00
Capital rental rates								
UK Manufacturing:	0.12	0.36	0.00	-0.09	0.03	0.06	0.05	0.00
Foreign Manufacturing:	0.11	0.41	0.00	-0.02	0.19	0.06	0.20	0.00
Non-Manu traded:	0.31	0.52	0.00	0.14	0.23	0.06	0.26	0.00
Sheltered	0.98	0.47	0.00	0.88	0.24	0.06	0.25	0.00
Consumer price index	0.05	0.05	0.00	0.07	0.09	0.07	0.09	0.00
Value-added								
UK Manufacturing:	0.03	0.09	0.19	-0.05	-0.04	-0.04	-0.04	0.20
Foreign Manufacturing:	0.02	3.09	3.20	-0.03	3.00	3.03	3.00	3.20
Non-Manu traded:	0.06	0.11	0.31	0.00	0.00	0.06	0.01	0.34
Sheltered	0.24	0.12	0.20	0.18	0.01	0.03	0.01	0.21
Sectoral Output								
UK Manufacturing:	0.03	0.10	0.19	-0.04	-0.02	-0.02	-0.01	0.20
Foreign Manufacturing:	0.03	3.11	3.20	-0.01	3.04	3.06	3.05	3.20
Non-Manu traded:	0.07	0.12	0.31	0.01	0.02	0.07	0.03	0.34
Sheltered	0.24	0.12	0.20	0.19	0.01	0.04	0.02	0.21
Capital stocks:								
UK Manufacturing:	0.00	0.00	0.19	0.00	0.00	-0.01	0.00	0.20
Foreign Manufacturing:	0.00	3.00	3.20	0.00	3.00	3.06	3.00	3.20
Non-Manu traded:	0.00	0.00	0.31	0.00	0.00	0.09	0.00	0.33
Sheltered	0.00	0.00	0.20	0.00	0.00	0.07	0.00	0.21
Exports								
UK Manufacturing:	-0.03	-0.08	0.00	-0.10	-0.19	-0.20	-0.18	-0.00
Foreign Manufacturing:	-0.02	3.90	3.97	-0.06	3.84	3.86	3.84	3.97
Non-Manu traded:	-0.13	-0.23	0.00	-0.20	-0.32	-0.25	-0.31	0.00
Sheltered	-0.35	-0.17	0.00	-0.52	-0.40	-0.34	-0.39	0.00
Nominal income								
Households disposable	0.20	0.34	0.37	0.22	0.35	0.36	0.36	0.43
Firms disposable	0.41	0.59	0.45	0.31	0.41	0.36	0.42	0.47

Appendix 5.5 Detailed Simulation Results for Model 3

	NATIONAL BARGAINING			REGIONAL BARGAINING				
	POPULATION FIXED			POPULATION FIXED			POPULATION ENDOGENOUS	
Model 1	Period 1	Period 2	Long Run	Period 1	Period 2	Long Run	Period 2	Long Run
GDP (income measure)	0.13	0.30	0.42	0.06	0.18	0.21	0.19	0.43
Consumption	0.16	0.29	0.37	0.15	0.27	0.28	0.27	0.43
Investment	2.15	0.60	0.56	2.15	0.41	0.39	0.43	0.57
Nominal before-tax wage	0.00	0.00	0.00	0.13	0.21	0.21	0.20	0.00
Real bef. tax cons. wage	-0.05	-0.05	0.00	0.06	0.13	0.14	0.11	0.00
Total employment	0.16	0.30	0.39	0.07	0.14	0.16	0.15	0.41
UK Manufacturing:	0.04	0.11	0.19	-0.11	-0.12	-0.13	-0.10	0.20
Foreign Manufacturing:	0.05	3.18	3.20	0.03	3.15	3.15	3.15	3.20
Non-Manu traded:	0.09	0.16	0.31	0.00	0.01	0.05	0.02	0.34
Sheltered	0.30	0.15	0.20	0.23	0.01	0.02	0.02	0.21
Total unempl.	-1.22	-2.28	-2.99	-0.54	-1.10	-1.23	-1.00	0.00
Labor particip. rate	0.04	0.07	0.09	0.02	0.03	0.04	0.03	0.00
Total population	0.00	0.00	0.00	0.00	0.00	0.00	0.02	0.41
Price of value added								
UK Manufacturing:	0.02	0.05	0.00	0.09	0.16	0.18	0.15	0.00
Foreign Manufacturing:	0.00	0.01	0.00	0.10	0.17	0.17	0.16	0.00
Non-Manu traded:	0.09	0.16	0.00	0.14	0.22	0.16	0.22	0.00
Sheltered	0.19	0.10	0.00	0.28	0.22	0.18	0.21	0.00
Capital rental rates								
UK Manufacturing:	0.08	0.25	0.00	-0.10	-0.04	0.06	-0.03	0.00
Foreign Manufacturing:	0.00	0.03	0.00	0.00	0.08	0.05	0.06	0.00
Non-Manu traded:	0.31	0.54	0.00	0.14	0.24	0.06	0.26	0.00
Sheltered	0.98	0.49	0.00	0.88	0.24	0.06	0.26	0.00
Consumer price index	0.05	0.05	0.00	0.07	0.09	0.07	0.09	0.00
Value-added								
UK Manufacturing:	0.03	0.09	0.19	-0.08	-0.09	-0.11	-0.08	0.20
Foreign Manufacturing:	0.05	3.18	3.20	0.03	3.15	3.15	3.15	3.20
Non-Manu traded:	0.07	0.11	0.31	0.00	0.01	0.06	0.01	0.33
Sheltered	0.24	0.12	0.20	0.18	0.01	0.03	0.02	0.21
Sectoral Output								
UK Manufacturing:	0.03	0.10	0.19	-0.07	-0.06	-0.08	-0.05	0.20
Foreign Manufacturing:	0.05	3.18	3.20	0.03	3.15	3.15	3.15	3.20
Non-Manu traded:	0.07	0.13	0.31	0.01	0.02	0.07	0.03	0.34
Sheltered	0.24	0.12	0.20	0.19	0.01	0.04	0.02	0.21
Capital stocks:								
UK Manufacturing:	0.00	0.00	0.19	0.00	0.00	-0.06	0.00	0.20
Foreign Manufacturing:	0.00	3.00	3.20	0.00	3.00	3.15	3.00	3.20
Non-Manu traded:	0.00	0.00	0.31	0.00	0.00	0.09	0.00	0.33
Sheltered	0.00	0.00	0.20	0.00	0.00	0.07	0.00	0.21
Exports								
UK Manufacturing:	-0.03	-0.08	0.00	-0.14	-0.25	-0.28	-0.24	-0.01
Foreign Manufacturing:	0.00	3.97	3.97	0.00	3.97	3.97	3.97	3.97
Non-Manu traded:	-0.14	-0.24	0.00	-0.20	-0.32	-0.24	-0.31	-0.01
Sheltered	-0.35	-0.18	0.00	-0.51	-0.40	-0.33	-0.39	-0.01
Nominal income								
Households disposable	0.20	0.34	0.37	0.22	0.35	0.35	0.36	0.43
Firms disposable	0.40	0.58	0.45	0.31	0.41	0.36	0.42	0.47

6 Economic Landscapes: An Application to the Brazilian Economy and to the Sugar Cane Complex*

Joaquim J.M. Guilhoto,[1] Marta C. Marjotta-Maistro,[2] and Geoffrey J.D. Hewings[3]

[1] ESALQ, University of São Paulo, Brazil and Regional Economics Applications Laboratory, University of Illinois, USA
e-mail: guilhoto@usp.br
[2] ESALQ, University of São Paulo, Brazil
e-mail: mcmarjot@carpa.ciagri.usp.br
[3] Regional Economics Applications Laboratory, University of Illinois, 607 S. Mathews, Urbana, Illinois, 61801 U.S.A
e-mail: hewings@uiuc.edu

6.1 Introduction

In this chapter, some new perspectives are provided on the problem of presenting, in a compact way, the vast amount of information contained in input-output tables, while, at the same time, making it possible to understand what is going on. These perspectives are developed through the use of *economic landscapes*; this concept is not a new one (see for example, Sonis, *et al.*, 2000), but it is given a new meaning in this chapter. Economic landscapes provide a way of viewing the economy; this three-dimensional representation of the economy has *x-y* axes that are the sectors or the agents involved in the productive process, while the vertical (*z*) axis provide the values that resulted from the transactions and interactions, directly and indirectly. These heights can be values of production, value added, imports, number of people employed, differences in structural changes, and so forth.

An application is made considering: a) the Brazilian economy as a whole, and b) the sugar cane complex in the Northeast and in the Rest of Brazil regions. To undertake the analysis, use is made of an interregional input-output system for the Brazilian economy, constructed for 2 regions (Northeast and Rest of Brazil), for the years of 1985, 1992, and 1995.

In the next section, a brief overview of the Brazilian economy is provided as well as the role that the sugar cane complex has played in the Brazilian economy and in the 2 regions used in the chapter. The third section will make a brief presentation of the methodology while in the fourth section, the landscapes are presented. Some final comments complete the chapter.

* Guilhoto would like to acknowledge the grant received from the Hewlett Foundation through the Center for Latin American and Caribbean Studies at the University of Illinois.

6.2 The Brazilian Economy and the Sugar Cane Complex, 1985/1995

This section is divided into three parts; first, a brief overview of the Brazilian economy is provided, followed by some general characteristics of the Brazilian macro regions. The final part will focus on the sugar cane complex in the Brazilian economy and in the two regions being considered here, the Northeast and the Rest of Brazil regions.

6.2.1 A Brief Overview of the Brazilian Economy in the 1980s and 1990s

In the 1980s, the Brazilian economy experienced a very low growth rate, especially when compared to its long run history. In the 1980s, the national GDP grew at a yearly average rate of only 1.56 % (Bonelli and Gonçalves, 1998). In contrast, the 1990s can be divided into two periods; from 1990 to 1993, the economy went through a period of recession, with the GDP growing at a yearly average rate of 1.6 %, while industry and agriculture grew at yearly rates of 0.3% and 2.3% respectively. In the second period, from 1993 to 1997, the yearly average GDP growth rate was 4.4%, while industry, agriculture, and services grew, respectively, 3.8%, 6%, and 3.1% (Bonelli and Gonçalves, 1998).

In 1994, investment accounted for 16.3% of Brazilian GDP; in 1995 this share grew to 19.2% (Baer, 1996 and Conjuntura Econômica, 1997). The quality of the investment also improved and at the same time there was growth in the share of imported capital goods. Together, these changes contributed to an increase in productivity; with a consequent increase in wages (5.7% in 1993, and 6.2% in 1995) there was also a decrease in the unemployment rates from 5.3% in 1993 to 4.6% in 1995 (IBGE, 1997a and Conjuntura Econômica, 1997).

The strong performance of the industrial sector in the 1990 was followed by the growth in importance of the service sector, mainly due to increased subcontracting by the industrial sector after the economy was opened up, a process that started in 1990 (Bonelli and Gonçalves, 1998). While the 1980s are characterized by a closed economy, the 1990s can be said to be a decade of openness and modernization in Brazil.

Finally, some remarks should be made about the tendencies and the sectoral progress in the Brazilian economy in the last decade. The share of the industrial sector in the economy declined from 48% in 1985 to 42% in 1990 and to 34% in 1995, while the service sector's shares grew respectively from 40%, to 47% and to 54%. The shares of the agricultural sector were maintained, 12% for 1985, 11% for 1990, and 12% for 1995 (Melo *et al.*, 1998).

6.2.2 The Brazilian Macro Regions

As shown in figure 6.1, Brazil is normally divided into five macro regions (IBGE 1997a,b); some summary characteristics are show in table 6.1. Note, in particular, the strong concentration of the national GDP in the Southeast region, with a share of

56.97%. The Northeast on the other hand, has a much smaller share in the GDP, 13.62%. The Northeast region has serious problems of drought and in the beginning of the formation of the Brazilian State it used to be it most important region, this region has 18.28% of the Brazilian territory and 28.50% of its population.

Figure 6.1 Brazilian Macro Regions

Table 6.1 Main Economical and Geographical Characteristics of the Brazilian Macro Regions

	Size		Population (1996)		Urban Population	GDP 1995
	km^2	Share (%)	Number (1,000)	Share	%	Share (%)
North	3,851,560	45.25	11,288	7.19	62.36	5.27
Northeast	1,556,001	18.28	44,767	28.50	65.21	13.62
Central West	1,604,852	18.85	10,501	6.69	84.42	7.25
Southeast	924,266	10.85	67,001	42.66	89.29	56.97
South	575,316	6.76	23,514	14.97	77.22	16.89
Brazil	8,511,996	100.00	157,070	100.00	78.36	100.00

Source: IBGE (1997a and 1997b); Considera and Medina (1998).

6.2.3 The Sugar Cane Complex

During the last decade, the sugar cane complex has experienced a restructuring process prompted in large part by the government removing its authority to control the trade emanating from the sugar cane complex. This complex is defined as the production of sugar cane, sugar and alcohol in the economy. Until 1990, the sugar cane complex was under the strict control of the federal government, through the Sugar and Alcohol Institute (created in 1933), which was responsible for the control of production, price, exports, and market share of the producing Brazilian regions. In 1990, the sugar sector was the first one to be released from government control, followed by the alcohol sector in 1997, and the sugar cane sector in 1999. In the new context of a free market economy, the agents in the process have to learn to survive in a market free from the government rules and subsidies. Producers have had to learn how to be efficient and how to gain market share by attending to consumer demands, a process tracked by Marjotta-Maistro (1998).

It is important to put this problem in a historic perspective, especially in view that, since the colonial period, the Northeast region has always been a traditional producer of sugar, and it has always been under the government control. At the same time, the other producing regions use more advanced technology and have adopted a more market-oriented view. This has had an impact on how the market has reacted to the opening of this sector.

Table 6.2 Sugar Cane Production (1,000 Ton of Kg) and Share (%) Northeast and Rest of Brazil Regions, 1985/86 to 1998/99

Year	Northeast	NE Share	Rest of Brazil	RB Share	Total
1985/86	67,645	27.36	179,556	72.64	247,201
1986/87	65,949	27.57	173,230	72.43	239,179
1987/88	80,008	29.80	188,495	70.20	268,503
1988/89	62,851	24.32	195,561	75.68	258,412
1989/90	69,762	27.61	182,881	72.39	252,643
1990/91	71,689	27.29	190,984	72.71	262,673
1991/92	68,730	26.32	192,389	73.68	261,119
1992/93	68,723	25.31	202,752	74.69	271,475
1993/94	39,609	16.20	204,817	83.80	244,426
1994/95	57,328	19.63	234,775	80.37	292,103
1995/96	60,688	19.99	242,869	80.01	303,557
1996/97*	60,652	18.64	264,809	81.36	325,461
1997/98*	65,861	19.52	271,477	80.48	337,338
1998/99*	57,753	17.04	281,219	82.96	338,972

* Includes the production of the North region
Source: Agrianual (Various Issues).

One of the main programs implement by the government was the Proálcool in 1975. The literature divides the implementation of the Proálcool into two stages: a) the first one was directed to the increase in the production of alcohol to be mixed with the gasoline; and b) the second stage, after 1980, created a goal to have alcohol as the only source of power for automobiles. In the second stage the goals of production were much higher, i.e., the alcohol production should increase by 10.7 billion of liters in four years against an expected increase of 2.5 billion of liters in five years during the first stage.

Notwithstanding the deregulation of the main activities in the sector, the presence of Federal government is still felt, through the formation of regulatory stocks and their sale through auctions; and in terms of regulations determining how much alcohol should be mixed with gasoline.

In the 1990s the Brazilian production of sugar cane increased from around 262.7 thousand ton of kg in 1991-92 to around 339.0 thousand ton of kg in 1998-99 (table 6.2). Brazilian sugar production reached 19 million ton of kg in 1999-00, with an increase of 3.8% over the production in the 1998/99 period. The alcohol production reached 12.8 million of m^3 in 1999-00 (tables 6.4 and 6.5). These results put Brazil as one of the main sugar and alcohol producers in the world. While the exports of sugar are important for the sector and the economy, the same is not true for the alcohol, a product mainly directed to the Brazilian market to be used as either the sole energy source for automobiles or in combination with gasoline.

Table 6.3 Land of Sugar Cane Harvested (Hectares), Share (%), and Productivity (Ton of Kg per Hectare)
Northeast and Rest of Brazil Regions, 1985/86 to 1998/99

Year	Northeast	NE Share	NE Productivity	Rest of Brazil	RB Productivity	RB Share	Total
1985/86	1,330,122	34.00	50.86	2,581,943	66.00	69.54	3,912,065
1986/87	1,287,228	32.57	51.23	2,664,614	67.43	65.01	3,951,842
1987/88	1,556,454	36.12	51.40	2,752,221	63.88	68.49	4,308,675
1988/89	1,312,427	31.88	47.89	2,804,948	68.12	69.72	4,117,375
1989/90	1,378,723	33.83	50.60	2,697,116	66.17	67.81	4,075,839
1990/91	1,476,795	34.44	48.54	2,810,830	65.56	67.95	4,287,625
1991/92	1,402,388	33.30	49.01	2,808,503	66.70	68.50	4,210,891
1992/93	1,363,932	32.46	50.39	2,838,572	67.54	71.43	4,202,504
1993/94	1,022,653	27.91	38.73	2,641,069	72.09	77.55	3,663,722
1994/95	1,188,843	27.35	48.22	3,157,141	72.65	74.36	4,345,984
1995/96	1,255,966	27.51	48.32	3,309,695	72.49	73.38	4,565,661
1996/97*	1,229,812	25.43	49.32	3,606,365	74.57	73.43	4,836,177
1997/98*	1,276,329	26.16	51.60	3,603,081	73.84	75.35	4,879,410
1998/99*	1,181,888	23.77	48.87	3,790,125	76.23	74.20	4,972,013

* Includes the production of the North region
Source: Agrianual (Various Issues)

Table 6.4 Sugar Production (1,000 Ton of Kg) and Share (%)
Northeast and Rest of Brazil Regions, 1985/86 to 1999/00

Year	Northeast*	NE Share*	Rest of Brazil	RB Share	Total
1985/86	3,199	40.91	4,620	59.09	7,819
1986/87	3,348	41.04	4,809	58.96	8,157
1987/88	3,158	39.56	4,825	60.44	7,983
1988/89	2,817	34.91	5,253	65.09	8,070
1989/90	3,096	42.79	4,140	57.21	7,236
1990/91	2,857	38.77	4,512	61.23	7,369
1991/92	2,831	32.53	5,873	67.47	8,704
1992/93	3,146	33.40	6,274	66.60	9,420
1993/94	2,318	24.70	7,067	75.30	9,385
1994/95	3,398	28.48	8,535	71.52	11,933
1995/96	3,085	24.88	9,315	75.12	12,400
1996/97	3,950	28.21	10,050	71.79	14,000
1997/98	4,435	27.72	11,565	72.28	16,000
1998/99	3,099	16.93	15,201	83.07	18,300
1999/00	2,115	11.12	16,899	88.88	19,014

* Includes the production of the North region
Source: Associação das Indústrias de Açúcar e Álcool do Estado de São Paulo, USDA, União da Agroindústria Canavieira do Estado de São Paulo.

As can be seen in tables 6.2 and 6.3, since 1989-90 the share of the Northeast region in the sugar cane production has decreased from around 27% to 17%, while the share of land harvested has decreased from around 34% to 24%, with almost no change in productivity. On the other hand, the share of the Rest of Brazil has increased as well as it productivity, revealing it to be a more dynamic region than the Northeast region. If one looks at the share of the Rest of Brazil region in the production of sugar (table 6.4), alcohol (table 6.5), and sugar exports (table 6.6), one can see that the share of this region has increase to around 90% in all of the three markets. Understanding and interpreting these changes will provide the focus of this chapter. The next section will present the theoretical background, with the following section providing the empirical relation.

Table 6.5 Alcohol Production (Millions of m^3) and Share (%) Northeast and Rest of Brazil Regions, 1985/86 to 1999/00

Year	Northeast*	NE Share*	Rest of Brazil	RB Share	Total
1985/86	2,021	17.10	9,799	82.90	11,820
1986/87	2,215	21.06	8,301	78.94	10,516
1987/88	1,787	15.60	9,667	84.40	11,454
1988/89	1,754	14.97	9,959	85.03	11,713
1989/90	1,980	16.67	9,901	83.33	11,881
1990/91	1,807	15.34	9,976	84.66	11,783
1991/92	1,776	14.01	10,905	85.99	12,681
1992/93	1,672	14.25	10,064	85.75	11,736
1993/94	909	8.06	10,369	91.94	11,278
1994/95	1,579	12.41	11,147	87.59	12,726
1995/96	1,833	14.45	10,856	85.55	12,689
1996/97	1,900	13.54	12,130	86.46	14,030
1997/98	1,700	11.33	13,300	88.67	15,000
1998/99	1,200	8.96	12,200	91.04	13,400
1999/00	1,146	8.97	11,624	91.03	12,770

* Includes the production of the North region
Source: Associação das Indústrias de Açúcar e Álcool do Estado de São Paulo, USDA, União da Agroindústria Canavieira do Estado de São Paulo.

Table 6.6 Sugar Exports (Ton of Kg) and Share (%) Northeast and Rest of Brazil Regions, 1985/86 to 1998/99

Year	Northeast*	NE Share*	Rest of Brazil	RB Share	Total
1988/89	1,363,921	88.22	182,111	11.78	1,546,032
1989/90	1,250,524	81.39	285,844	18.61	1,536,368
1990/91	1,197,013	85.18	208,269	14.82	1,405,282
1991/92	1,302,528	76.42	401,919	23.58	1,704,447
1992/93	1,312,807	61.21	831,837	38.79	2,144,644
1993/94	862,535	33.76	1,692,454	66.24	2,554,989
1994/95	1,815,924	43.95	2,315,457	56.05	4,131,381
1995/96	1,639,355	36.29	2,877,492	63.71	4,516,847
1996/97	1,484,044	30.90	3,319,430	69.10	4,803,474
1997/98	2,060,711	33.65	4,062,442	66.35	6,123,153
1998/99	819,828	12.76	5,603,272	87.24	6,423,100

* Includes the exports of the North region
Source: Moraes (2000)

6.3 Theoretical Background

Define a standard Leontief system:

$$X = AX + Y \tag{6.1}$$

where X is a vector $(n \times 1)$ of total production by sector; Y $(n \times 1)$ is the final demand; and A is a $(n \times n)$ matrix of technical coefficients. The usual solution is:

$$X = BY \tag{6.2}$$

with:

$$B = (I - A)^{-1} \tag{6.3}$$

where B $(n \times n)$ is the Leontief inverse matrix.

To construct an economic landscape, in production values, to reveal how the economic system will work directly and indirectly to produce one unit of the jth sector for the final demand, the A matrix of direct coefficients is post multiplied by the diagonal of the jth column of matrix B $\left(\hat{B}_{\bullet j}\right)$, i.e.:

$$L_j = A\left(\hat{B}_{\bullet j}\right) \tag{6.4}$$

where L_j is the economic landscape for sector j.

To estimate the economic landscape for a given sector in the economy, in terms of value added, employment, imports, etc. this can be done by first estimating the coefficient of the value added, for example, as:

$$w_k = VA_k / X_k \tag{6.5}$$

where w_k is the coefficient of the value added for sector k, VA_k is the value added of sector k, and X_k is the production level of sector k. Now it is possible to obtain the value added generated, directly and indirectly, in each sector by the sale of one unit of sector j to the final demand v_{kj}, i.e.,

$$v_{kj} = w_k b_{kj} \tag{6.6}$$

where b_{kj} is an element of the matrix B defined above.

To obtain the value added matrix of sector j that will be used to construct the value added economic landscape for this sector $\left(L_j^w\right)$, one must first obtain the share of each direct coefficient in a given row e_{ij}, then the resulting matrix is post multiplied by the diagonal matrix of vector v, as follows:

$$e_{ij} = a_{ij} / \sum_{i=1}^{n} a_{ij} \tag{6.7}$$

$$L_j^w = E\left(\hat{V}_j\right) \tag{6.8}$$

The next section will present the economic landscapes for the two Brazilian regions considered in this chapter with a particular focus on the sugar cane complex.

6.4 Economic Landscapes and Structural Changes

In this section, an analysis will be made of the structural changes that took place in the Brazilian economy, and in the two-region system, from 1985 to 1995. To better understand the impact of the openness process on the productive structures, the analysis will focus on three points in time, 1985, 1992, and 1995. After this macro perspective, attention will be directed to how the sugar cane complex changed in the same time period in these regions, and how these changes can be related to the changes that occurred in the economy as a whole.

6.4.1 The Brazilian Economy

The information for the analysis of the structural changes in the Brazilian economy are shown in tables 6.7 and 6.8 and displayed in economic landscapes presented in figures 6.2 to 6.5. The economic landscapes are shown in four blocks: in the upper left corner are the transactions within the Northeast while in the upper right corner one has the sales from the Northeast region to the Rest of Brazil. In the bottom part, one has first, the sales from the Rest of Brazil to the Northeast while the final part reveals the transactions inside the Rest of Brazil region. The heights in this case are the values of the Leontief inverse less the unit diagonal element, i.e., they are the direct and indirect requirements used in the productive process to produce one unit of a given product to the final demand.

Table 6.7 Sum of the Landscapes Heights from the Leontief Inverse Northeast and Rest of Brazil Regions: 1985, 1992, 1995

Quadrant	1985	1992	1995
Northeast to Northeast	20.78	20.71	18.65
Northeast to Rest of Brazil	1.64	1.62	1.36
Rest of Brazil to Northeast	10.33	9.97	6.85
Rest of Brazil to Rest of Brazil	34.16	33.92	29.96
Total	66.91	66.22	56.82

When comparing the differences among the regions, for 1995, notice that the total height of the Rest of Brazil region (29.96) is larger than the one for the Northeast region (18.65) implying that the Rest of Brazil region has a more linked productive process, an indication of a higher level of development, confirmed by the data presented in section 6.2. Concerning the interregional transactions, one can see that there is a greater dependence of the Northeast region on the Rest of Brazil (total height value of 6.85) than the Rest of Brazil on the Northeast region (total height value of 1.36).

Table 6.8 Changes and Growth Rates (%) of the Sum of the Landscapes Heights from the Leontief Inverse
Northeast and Rest of Brazil Regions: 1985, 1992, 1995

Quadrant	Changes			Growth Rates (%)		
	1992 – 1985	1995 – 1992	1995 – 1985	1992 – 1985	1995– 1992	1995– 1985
Northeast to Northeast	-0.07	-2.06	-2.12	-0.33	-9.93	-10.23
Northeast to Rest of Brazil	-0.02	-0.26	-0.28	-1.26	-16.00	-17.06
Rest of Brazil to Northeast	-0.36	-3.12	-3.48	-3.45	-31.33	-33.70
Rest of Brazil to Rest of Brazil	-0.24	-3.96	-4.20	-0.71	-11.68	-12.31
Total	-0.69	-9.40	-10.09	-1.03	-14.20	-15.08

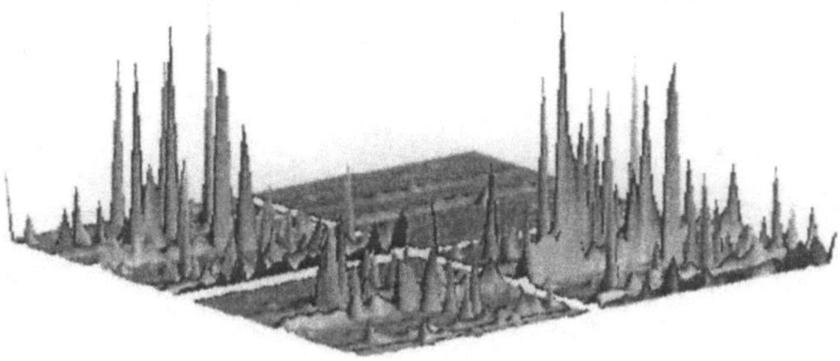

Figure 6.2 Economic Landscape of the Leontief Inverse
Northeast and Rest of Brazil Regions: 1985

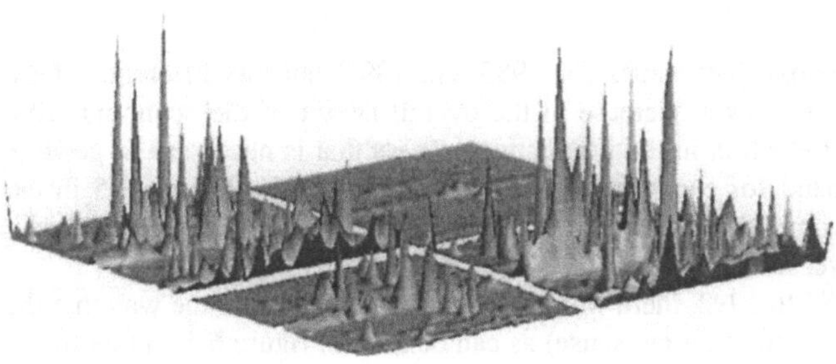

Figure 6.3 Economic Landscape of the Leontief Inverse
Northeast and Rest of Brazil Regions: 1995

Figure 6.4 Economic Landscape of the Changes in the Leontief Inverse Northeast and Rest of Brazil Regions: 1995 Less 1985

Figure 6.5 Economic Landscape of the Changes in the Leontief Inverse Northeast and Rest of Brazil Regions: 1992 Less 1985

The economic landscapes for 1985 and 1995 and the differences between them show that there was a decrease in the overall height of the economy, given that the amount of production in the productive process that is necessary to generate one unit of final demand for each one of the 70 sectors in the economy (35 in each region) decreased from 66.91 to 56.82. However, this change has not uniform across all sectors or over time.

From 1985 to 1992, there were practically no changes in the way that the economy behaved (in an input-output sense) as can be seen in figure 6.5 and by the fact that the total value of the heights decreased only from 66.91 to 66.21. The major change occurred from 1992 to 1995 when this value decreased by 14.20% to 56.82. This can be explained, in part, by the opening of the economy, begun in the 1990's, that probably has increased the dependence on imported goods and, as a consequence, probably decreased the value of the transactions inside the productive process of the

Brazilian economy. This may be an indication of "hollowing out" (see Hewings *et al.* 1998), whereby an economy becomes more dependent on external markets for inputs and sales.

Also, this change was not homogenous throughout the two regions; the overall decrease in the heights between 1985 to 1995 was 15.08%, but the larger decreases are found in the transactions among the regions with the heights of the sales from the Northeast to the Rest of Brazil decreasing by 17.06%, while those from the Rest of Brazil to the Northeast region decreasing by 33.70%. The opening up of the economy has probably enabled the Northeast region to increase its transactions with external-to-the-country markets in place of transactions with the Rest of Brazil.

Now attention will be directed to the analysis of the sugar cane complex in the Brazilian economy and on its regions.

6.4.2 The Sugar Cane Complex

Information for the sugar cane complex, consisting of the sugar cane, alcohol, and sugar sectors is revealed into tables 6.9 to 6.12, in figures 6.6 to 6.11 for the Northeast, and in tables 6.13 to 6.16 and figures 6.12 to 6.17 for the Rest of Brazil.

Figures 6.6, 6.8, and 6.10 for the Northeast region, and figures 6.12, 6.14, and 6.16 for the Rest of Brazil are the graphical representation of equation (6.4), i.e., they show the direct and indirect requirements of inputs to produce one unit of a given sector to the final demand. At the same time, Figures 6.7, 6.9, and 6.11 for the Northeast region, and figures 6.13, 6.15, and 6.17 for the Rest of Brazil are the graphical representation of equation (6.8), i.e., they show how each cell of the matrix contributed to the value added generated in the production of one unit of a given sector to the final demand. While figures 6.6 to 6.17 only present the result for 1995, tables 6.9 to 6.16 present the results for 1985, 1992 and 1995.

Tables 6.9 and 6.13 show, respectively, for the Northeast and Rest of Brazil regions, the use of inputs and how much is generated in value added in the productive process of sugar cane, alcohol, and sugar; these values are thus the sum of the landscape heights for inputs and value added.

Tables 6.10 and 6.14, respectively, for the Northeast and Rest of Brazil show how the direct and indirect inputs used in the productive process of a given sector are distributed among the quadrants. For example, in table 6.10, for 1985, it can be seen that from the total inputs used to produce one unit of sugar cane in the Northeast region, 57.20% originated in the Northeast region and are used in this region, 0.70% originated in the Northeast and are sold to the Rest of Brazil, 22.92% originated in the Rest of Brazil and are sold to the Northeast, and finally, 19.19% originated and are used in the Rest of Brazil.

The interpretation applies to tables 6.12 and 6.16, the difference being that in these tables the attention in on the dependence on each quadrant of the value added generated in the productive process of a given sector. In the case of tables 6.11 and 6.15, they show, respectively, for the Northeast and Rest of Brazil regions, how the value added generated in the productive process of a given sector is allocated between the two regions.

Table 6.9 Sum of the Landscapes Heights for Inputs and Value Added: Sugar Cane, Alcohol, and Sugar Sectors – Northeast: 1985, 1992, 1995

Landscape	Year	Sugar Cane	Alcohol	Sugar
Inputs	1985	0.33	0.95	1.00
Inputs	1992	0.37	0.95	1.01
Inputs	1995	0.22	0.77	0.87
Value Added	1985	0.97	0.97	0.97
Value Added	1992	0.94	0.95	0.95
Value Added	1995	0.95	0.98	0.98

Table 6.10 Share (%) of the Sum of the Landscapes Heights for Inputs in each Quadrant: Sugar Cane, Alcohol, and Sugar Sectors
Northeast: 1985, 1992, 1995

Year	Quadrant	Sugar Cane	Alcohol	Sugar
1985	Northeast to Northeast	57.20	86.01	85.74
1985	Northeast to Rest of Brazil	0.70	0.23	0.25
1985	Rest of Brazil to Northeast	22.92	7.18	7.32
1985	Rest of Brazil to Rest of Brazil	19.19	6.58	6.69
1992	Northeast to Northeast	57.22	83.88	85.35
1992	Northeast to Rest of Brazil	0.65	0.25	0.23
1992	Rest of Brazil to Northeast	23.06	8.43	7.62
1992	Rest of Brazil to Rest of Brazil	19.07	7.44	6.80
1995	Northeast to Northeast	71.50	94.29	94.00
1995	Northeast to Rest of Brazil	0.48	0.10	0.10
1995	Rest of Brazil to Northeast	16.11	3.19	3.32
1995	Rest of Brazil to Rest of Brazil	11.90	2.42	2.58

For the Northeast (tables 6.9 to 6.11), it is possible to see that the largest changes in the way that the sugar cane complex behaved from 1985 to 1995 occurred in the 1992 to 1995 period, following the overall trend observed for the economy as a whole. The same happened for the Rest of Brazil (tables 6.13 to 6.16). However, if one looks at tables 6.2 to 6.6, it is clear that the changes that occurred in the sugar cane complex of the Northeast were negative, given that the complex has continuously been loosing market share in the economy, while the sugar cane complex in the Rest of Brazil region gained market share. This can be explained in part by the fact that the overall heights of the Sugar Cane complex in the Rest of Brazil are higher than the ones at the Northeast region, implying a more modern and integrated complex with the rest of the economy. In addition, the sugar cane complex in the Northeast decreased its transactions with the Rest of Brazil region, isolating itself from the modernization process that had occurred in the Rest of Brazil.

Looking at figures 6.6 to 6.11 for the Northeast, it is clear that the one sector more dependent than others on inputs from the Rest of Brazil is the sugar cane sector, probably due to the necessity that this sector has of modern inputs used in the productive process, inputs that have not become locally available. On the other hand, the production of alcohol and sugar depend mainly on the inputs of the sugar cane sector that are available locally. Also, the overall height of the alcohol and sugar sectors are larger than the ones of the sugar cane sector meaning that these sectors have a larger multiplier effect in the economy than the one revealed by the sugar cane sector alone.

Table 6.11 Share (%) of the Value Added in each Region:
Sugar Cane, Alcohol, and Sugar Sectors – Northeast: 1985, 1992, 1995

Year	Region	Sugar Cane	Alcohol	Sugar
1985	Northeast	94.49	94.96	94.67
1985	Rest of Brazil	5.51	5.04	5.33
1992	Northeast	92.95	93.45	93.75
1992	Rest of Brazil	7.05	6.55	6.25
1995	Northeast	97.09	98.04	97.70
1995	Rest of Brazil	2.91	1.96	2.30

Table 6.12 Share (%) of the Sum of the Landscapes Heights for Value Added in each Quadrant: Sugar Cane, Alcohol, and Sugar Sectors
Northeast: 1985, 1992, 1995

Year	Quadrant	Sugar Cane	Alcohol	Sugar
1985	Northeast to Northeast	64.09	76.98	76.56
1985	Northeast to Rest of Brazil	0.15	0.14	0.15
1985	Rest of Brazil to Northeast	30.40	17.98	18.11
1985	Rest of Brazil to Rest of Brazil	5.36	4.90	5.18
1992	Northeast to Northeast	63.77	77.17	76.86
1992	Northeast to Rest of Brazil	0.21	0.20	0.19
1992	Rest of Brazil to Northeast	29.18	16.28	16.90
1992	Rest of Brazil to Rest of Brazil	6.83	6.36	6.05
1995	Northeast to Northeast	78.26	87.70	86.30
1995	Northeast to Rest of Brazil	0.11	0.07	0.08
1995	Rest of Brazil to Northeast	18.83	10.33	11.40
1995	Rest of Brazil to Rest of Brazil	2.81	1.89	2.22

It is also possible to see that the economic landscapes for the relation of inputs inside the productive process is different from the ones generated when the value added is used. This is clear when comparing figures 6.6, 6.8, and 6.10 (inputs) with, respectively, figures 6.7, 6.9, and 6.11 (value added) for the Northeast region. The share of the value added generated in each region is shown in table 6.11, while table 6.12 shows the dependence of the total value added on the transactions that occur in the productive process. Table 6.12 can also be seen as a combination of the information provided in tables 6.10 and 6.11. From figures 6.9 and 6.11, the dependence of the value added generated in the alcohol and sugar sectors on the sugar cane sector is clearly revealed.

For the Rest of Brazil, from figures 6.11 to 6.17, it is possible to see that there are more links among the sectors than in the Northeast region; for the inputs used in the productive process (figures 6.12, 6.14, and 6.16), the total sum of the heights are larger in the Rest of Brazil region (tables 6.9 and 6.13). Considering the dependence of the sectors between the regions (tables 6.10, 6.12, 6.14, and 6.16), the sectors in the Northeast region are more dependent on the sectors of the Rest of Brazil than vice-versa.

As a general conclusion, it is possible to say that the sugar cane complex in the Rest of Brazil economy reveals itself to be a more modern and dynamic complex when compared to the one in the Northeast region, and as a result of that it has gained an increased share in the market, especially since 1992 when the openness process started in the economy and the government stepped aside from the sector.

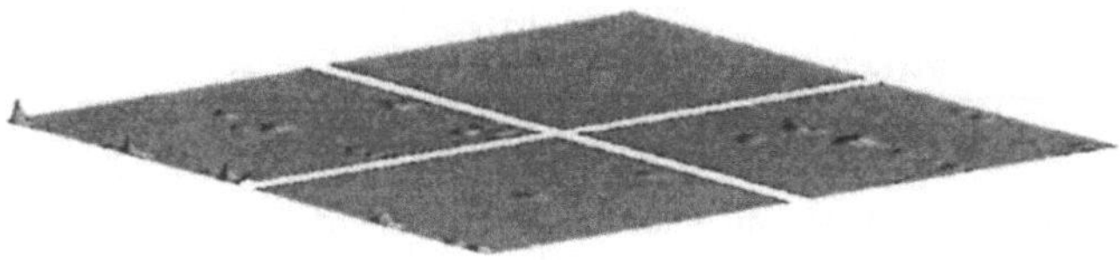

Figure 6.6 Economic Landscape for Inputs of the Sugar Cane Sector in the Northeast Region: 1995

Figure 6.7 Economic Landscape for Value Added of the Sugar Cane Sector in the Northeast Region: 1995

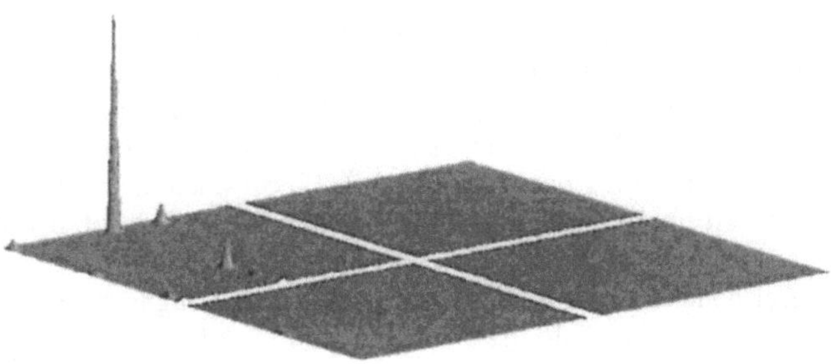

Figure 6.8 Economic Landscape for Inputs of the Alcohol Sector in the Northeast Region: 1995

Figure 6.9 Economic Landscape for Value Added of the Alcohol Sector in the Northeast Region: 1995

Figure 6.10 Economic Landscape for Inputs of the Sugar Sector in the Northeast Region: 1995

Figure 6.11 Economic Landscape for Value Added of the Sugar Sector in the Northeast Region: 1995

Table 6.13 Sum of the Landscapes Heights for Inputs and Value Added: Sugar Cane, Alcohol, and Sugar – Rest of Brazil: 1985, 1992, 1995

Landscape	Year	Sugar Cane	Alcohol	Sugar
Inputs	1985	0.46	1.15	1.62
Inputs	1992	0.51	1.11	1.58
Inputs	1995	0.38	0.97	1.50
Value Added	1985	0.93	0.95	0.91
Value Added	1992	0.91	0.92	0.88
Value Added	1995	0.92	0.93	0.87

Table 6.14 Share (%) of the Sum of the Landscapes Heights for Inputs in each Quadrant: Sugar Cane, Alcohol, and Sugar - Rest of Brazil: 1985, 1992, 1995

Year	Quadrant	Sugar Cane	Alcohol	Sugar
1985	Northeast to Northeast	3.54	1.19	1.48
1985	Northeast to Rest of Brazil	3.88	1.43	1.76
1985	Rest of Brazil to Northeast	0.75	0.25	0.31
1985	Rest of Brazil to Rest of Brazil	91.83	97.12	96.46
1992	Northeast to Northeast	3.39	1.64	1.47
1992	Northeast to Rest of Brazil	3.67	1.78	1.70
1992	Rest of Brazil to Northeast	0.78	0.38	0.33
1992	Rest of Brazil to Rest of Brazil	92.15	96.20	96.50
1995	Northeast to Northeast	1.90	0.94	1.34
1995	Northeast to Rest of Brazil	3.55	1.59	2.16
1995	Rest of Brazil to Northeast	0.27	0.13	0.18
1995	Rest of Brazil to Rest of Brazil	94.27	97.33	96.32

Table 6.15 Share (%) of the Value Added in each Region: Sugar Cane, Alcohol, and Sugar - Rest of Brazil: 1985, 1992, 1995

Year	Region	Sugar Cane	Alcohol	Sugar
1985	Northeast	1.43	1.34	2.43
1985	Rest of Brazil	98.57	98.66	97.57
1992	Northeast	1.51	1.58	2.32
1992	Rest of Brazil	98.49	98.42	97.68
1995	Northeast	1.28	1.41	3.17
1995	Rest of Brazil	98.72	98.59	96.83

Table 6.16 Share (%) of the Sum of the Landscapes Heights for Value Added in each Quadrant: Sugar Cane, Alcohol, and Sugar - Rest of Brazil: 1985, 1992, 1995

Year	Quadrant	Sugar Cane	Alcohol	Sugar
1985	Northeast to Northeast	1.22	1.13	2.03
1985	Northeast to Rest of Brazil	4.22	2.52	2.83
1985	Rest of Brazil to Northeast	0.21	0.22	0.41
1985	Rest of Brazil to Rest of Brazil	94.35	96.13	94.74
1992	Northeast to Northeast	1.27	1.31	1.91
1992	Northeast to Rest of Brazil	3.94	2.45	2.64
1992	Rest of Brazil to Northeast	0.24	0.27	0.4
1992	Rest of Brazil to Rest of Brazil	94.55	95.97	95.04
1995	Northeast to Northeast	1.16	1.26	2.84
1995	Northeast to Rest of Brazil	3.52	2.16	2.72
1995	Rest of Brazil to Northeast	0.12	0.14	0.33
1995	Rest of Brazil to Rest of Brazil	95.20	96.43	94.11

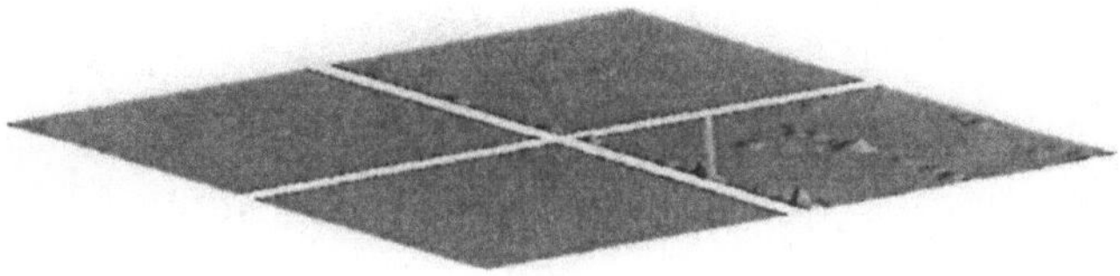

Figure 6.12 Economic Landscape for Inputs of the Sugar Cane Sector in the Rest of Brazil Region: 1995

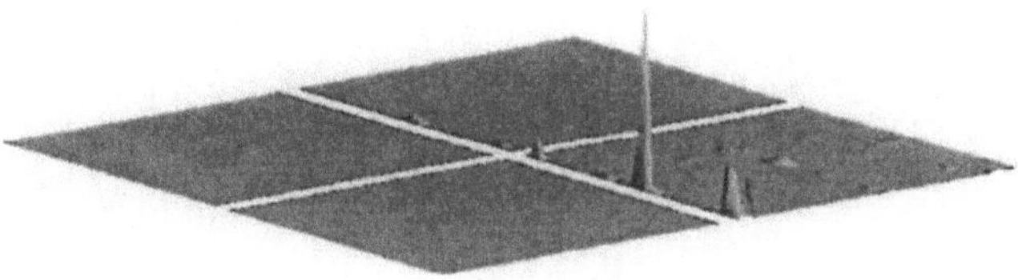

Figure 6.13 Economic Landscape for Value Added of the Sugar Cane Sector in the Rest of Brazil Region: 1995

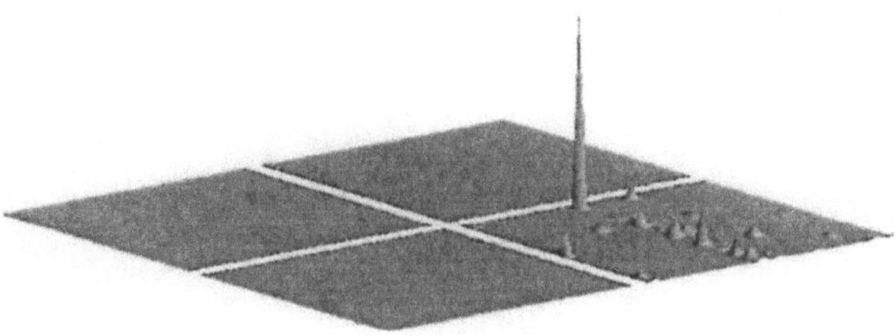

Figure 6.14 Economic Landscape for Inputs of the Alcohol Sector in the Rest of Brazil Region: 1995

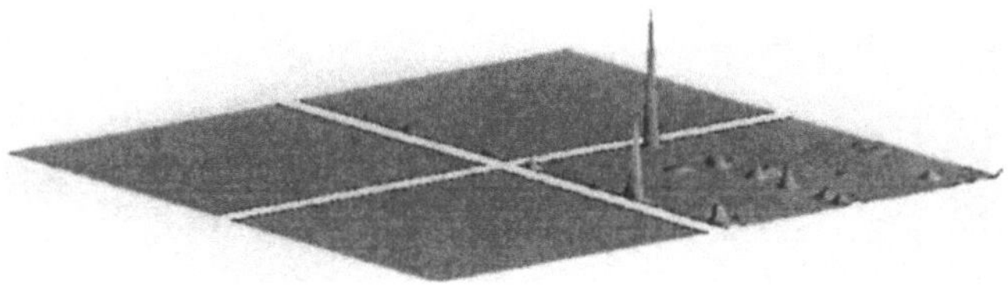

Figure 6.15 Economic Landscape for Value Added of the Alcohol Sector in the Rest of Brazil Region: 1995

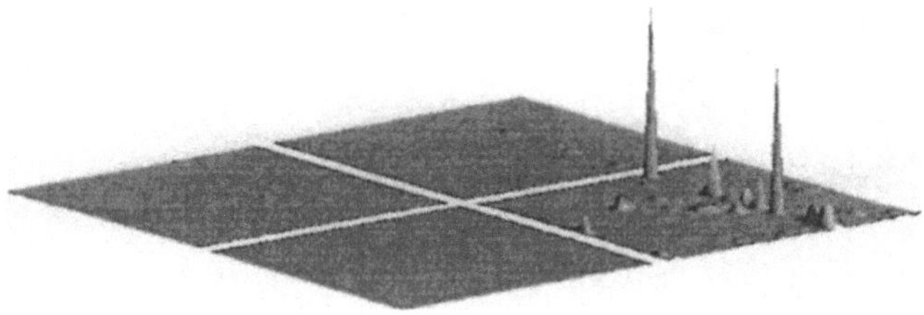

Figure 6.16 Economic Landscape for Inputs of the Sugar Sector in the Rest of Brazil Region: 1995

Figure 6.17 Economic Landscape for Value Added of the Sugar Sector in the Rest of Brazil Region: 1995

6.5 Final Comments

This chapter enhanced the application of the use of economic landscapes in the interpretation of structural changes in a national economy as a whole, and in terms of the interdependence between a two-region division of the national economy. These economic landscapes can also prove useful in identification of the relations of a given sector with other sectors and regions.

However, the use of economic landscapes does not replace previous methods of analysis used with input-output systems; it complements other techniques by providing a visual assessment of major structural changes that might not be revealed by other methods. Of course, the methodology provides no casual or behavioral interpretations but may be seen as providing an opportunity to conduct exploratory analysis. For example, the revealed differences in structure of the sugar cane complex between the Northeast and the Rest of Brazil sets the stage for more interpretive analysis that would seek to provide reasons for these differences. The asymmetrical dependencies between the Northeast and the Rest of Brazil highlighted in this chapter also raise questions about economic development strategies focusing on industrial complex analysis; the issues have become more complex since the Brazilian economy has been opened to increased penetration from imports. Will Brazil's participation in MERCOSUR and eventually an Americas Free Trade Area provide welfare gains to Northeast industries that now have greater choice in the spatial selection of inputs. At the same time, Northeast industries will face increasing competition (from foreign goods penetration) in the Rest of Brazil and in the world market. To answer these questions, more extensive, general equilibrium models would be appropriate, such as those developed for Brazil by Guilhoto (1995), Haddad (1999), and Casimiro Filho *et al.* (2000) (see also Rocha *et al.*, 2000 and Guilhoto and Hewings, 2001).

References

Agrianual. Various Issues. São Paulo: FNP.

Associação das Indústrias de Açúcar e Álcool do Estado de São Paulo. *Boletim Informativo.* Various Issues.

Baer W. 1996. *A Economia Brasileira.* São Paulo: Nobel.

Bonelli, R., and R.R. Gonçalves. 1998. "Para Onde Vai a Estrutura Industrial Brasileira?" In IPEA (1998). *A Economia Brasileira em Perspectiva – 1998.* Rio de Janeiro: IPEA. Vol. 2, Chapter 16, pp. 617-664.

Casimiro Filho, F., M.T. Rocha, P.V.P.S. Lima, S.H.G. Miranda, and J.J.M. Guilhoto. 2000. "MIBRA-USP, An Interregional Applied General Equilibrium Model for the Brazilian Economy." Paper presented to the 6th World Congress of the Regional Science Association International, Lugano, Switzerland, May 16 to 20.

Conjuntura Econômica. 1997. "Indicadores Econômicos," 51, no. 8.

Considera, C.M. and M.H. Medina. 1998. "PIB por Unidade da Federação: Valores Correntes e Constantes – 1985/96". Rio de Janeiro: IPEA, *Texto para Discussão*, 610.

Guilhoto, J.J.M. 1995. *Um Modelo Computável de Equilíbrio Geral para Planejamento e Análise de Políticas Agrícolas (PAPA) na Economia Brasileira.* Tese de Livre Docência. Universidade de São Paulo.

Guilhoto, J.J.M. and G.J.D. Hewings eds. 2001. *Structure and Structral Change in the Brazilian Economy.* Aldershot, Ashgate.

Haddad, E.A. 1999. *Regional Inequality and Structural Changes: Lessons from the Brazilian Experience*. Aldershot, Ashgate.

Hewings, G.J.D., M. Sonis, J. Guo, P.R. Israilevich and G.R. Schindler. 1998. "The hollowing out process in the Chicago economy, 1975-2015." *Geographical Analysis*, 30, 217-233.

IBGE. 1997a. *Anuário Estatístico do Brasil 1996*. 56. Rio de Janeiro.

IBGE. 1997b. *Contagem da População 1996*. Rio de Janeiro.

Marjotta-Maistro, M. C. 1998. *Análise do Consumo Industrial de Açúcar no Estado de São Paulo*. Master Dissertation, Departamento de Economia, Administração e Sociologia. ESALQ. University of São Paulo. 100 p. 1998

Melo, H.P., F. Rocha, G Ferraz, G. di Sabbato, R. Dweck. 1998. "O Setor Serviços no Brasil: uma Visão Global – 1985/95." In IPEA (1998). *A Economia Brasileira em Perspectiva*. Rio de Janeiro:IPEA. Vol. 2, Chapter 17, pp. 665-712.

Moraes, M.F.D. 2000. *A Desregulamentação do Setor Sucroalcooleiro do Brasil*. São Paulo: Editora Caminho.

Rocha M.T., J.J.M. Guilhoto. P.V.P.S. Lima, F. Casimiro Filho, and S.H.G. Miranda. 2000. "Exchange Rate Versus Tariff Policies in Brazil: Results from MIBRA-USP, an Interregional Applied General Equilibrium Model of the Brazilian Economy." Paper presented to the 47th North American Meetings of the Regional Science Association International. Chicago, Illinois, USA, November 9 to 11.

Sonis, M., G.J.D. Hewings, and J. Guo. 2000. "A New Image of Classical Key Sectors Analysis: Minimum Information Decomposition of the Leontief Inverse." *Economic Systems Research*, 12, 401-423.

União da Agroindústria Canavieira do Estado de São Paulo. *Boletim Informativo*. Various Issues.

USDA. Information from the site www.fas.usda.gov.

7 On the Economic Impact of the Transport Sector: A Critical Review with Dutch Bi-Regional Input-Output Data*

Jan Oosterhaven and Dirk Stelder

Department of Economics, University of Groningen, P.O. Box, 800, 9700 AV Groningen, The Netherlands
e-mail: oosterhaven@eco.rug.nl; stelder@eco.rug.nl

7.1 Introduction: the Problem of Exaggerated Impacts

Arguments for state aid and state intervention in favor of certain sectors of industry are often based on their assumed economic importance for the region or nation at hand. The same argument is used, especially in small open economies, when decisions about large infrastructure projects have to be taken. In the Netherlands, both lines of reasoning are combined by special interest groups that argue in favor of state support in the case of extensions of the port of Rotterdam and of Schiphol airport, which are considered to function as the motors of the Dutch economy. But also in the case of more peripheral regions, such as the northern Netherlands, transport and distribution activities and infrastructure investments are considered to be of great importance for the economic development of such regions (see Henstra, *et al.*, 1999). Mostly, the arguments are not primarily based on the own size and the direct impact of the sector or project at hand, but on its assumed indirect importance for the regional or national economy.

To substantiate such claims consultants, but also academics, traditionally multiply direct employment or some other kind of size indicator with a sector- or project-specific employment or other multiplier. The result is an estimate of the total direct plus indirect plus induced plus whatever other impacts one can think of (see in the case of plant closedowns, Cole, 1988, discussed in Jackson, *et al.*, 1997, and Oosterhaven, 2000). Basically, this traditional approach is wrong. This can easily be shown empirically, since applying the same approach to all sectors of a certain economy will result in an (implicit) estimate of the size of that economy that is many times larger than its actual size.

In section 7.2, we will discuss the theoretical delusion that is responsible for this outcome and we will present a new concept, the *net multiplier*, that results in a correct estimate of the size of the whole economy. In section 7.3, we will present empirical results for the Dutch transportation sector based on the new Dutch bi-regional input-output tables (see Eding *et al.* 1999). And, we will compare the outcomes of using the

*This contribution is a translation and revision of Stelder, Oosterhaven and Eding (1999). The authors thank Gerard J. Eding, Jaap B. Polak and Annette S. Zeilstra for helping with earlier versions of this article, and they thank the participants of the International Input-Output Conference in Macerata, August 2000, for some additional improvements.

traditional (gross) multiplier approach with those of using our new *net* multiplier concept for four different subsectors of the transportation industry and for both the northern Netherlands and the Netherlands as a whole.

Besides the importance of a sector or a project for the gross national product, policy-makers in small open economies are often also interested in the importance of that sector or project for the national balance of trade. In that case, the gross versus net multiplier distinction, though theoretically still important, does not play such an important role in an empirical sense. Instead it is important whether or not an equal-handed treatment of exports and imports is followed. This is especially true when indirect exports and imports are included in the comparison. Section 7.4 shows how this indirect trade impact issue can be treated in a fair way by means of using a non-biased combination of the supply-driven and the demand-driven input-output model, provided that one does not interpret the results in a causal way.

Finally, section 7.5 summarizes the theoretical and empirical results, and extrapolates the discussion from the present static framework into the dynamic issue of the importance of investments in transport infrastructure for the growth of a regional or national economy.

7.2 Gross Versus Net Multiplier Effects: the Theory

For the moment, we will forget about infrastructure projects and concentrate on the economic importance of a certain sector. The *direct* economic importance of a certain sector can, seemingly easily, be measured by some kind of size indicator, preferably by its direct contribution to GRP or GNP, or else by its direct contribution to total regional of national employment. There are, however, pitfalls that will become clear when the question of the indirect economic importance is posed.

The line of reasoning and the calculation of the *indirect* economic importance of a sector normally starts with its relations with other actors in the economy. Here we will concentrate mainly on its relations with other sectors. It is of importance to make a sharp distinction between the concept of relation or linkage, on the one hand, and the concept of effect or impact, on the other hand. The difference being that the first concept is causally neutral and essentially static, whereas the second concept implies causality and is essentially dynamic. Clearly, when the issue of the indirect economic importance of a certain sector is concerned one is, or at least one should be interested in causality.

As regards relations with other sectors, traditionally a distinction is made between *forward linkages* with downstream, processing industries and *backward linkages* with upstream, supplying industries. These two causally neutral concepts find their origin in theories of unbalanced sectoral development (Hirschman, 1958) and unbalanced regional development (Myrdal, 1957). In those theories, however, linkages are already interpreted in a very causal way, in the sense that they are viewed as important channels through which growth impulses are passed on; starting from companies, industries or regions that are considered to function as the (causal) growth engines of the economies at hand. With these authors the causality issue is solved externally by means of labeling certain sectors as exogenous and others as endogenous.

This does not mean, however, that a causal interpretation may be given to the concept of linkages itself, because one and the same linkage between a supplying sector i and a processing sector j may be the vehicle of both a causal forward effect and a causal backward effect. A *forward effect* occurs when, *e.g.*, productivity increases of industry i, through lower output prices, are passed on to industry j. A *backward effect* occurs when, *e.g.*, output increases of industry j, through increases in the demand for inputs, are passed on to industry i. Hence, the existence of large forward or backward linkages, as such, does not tell anything about the direction of causality. The industry at hand may either be (passively) receiving impulses from other sectors or it may (actively) be sending impulses to other sectors. Moreover, when the impulses are negative, having large linkages actually does not represent a merit but a vice, either for the (receiving) industry at hand or for the (receiving) rest of the economy.

Consequently, the existence of large forward and backward linkages, without further information, does not imply that the sector at hand can be considered a key sector for regional of national development, despite the fact that this is regularly done in empirical development economics (see e.g. Schultz, 1977). To be labeled a *key sector*, a second criterion has to be satisfied. The sector at hand, besides having large linkages to pass on growth impulses, also needs to generate these growth impulses itself; *i.e.* the growth in this sector needs to be considered as (largely) exogenous from the rest of the economy (see Beyers, 1976, and Oosterhaven, 1981, ch. 5, for a further discussion).

The practical upshot of the above discussion is that, in order to get a clear interpretation, forward and backward *linkages* are best measured by means of the *direct size* of those linkages themselves, without relying on any (implicit) model of the economy. This leads to using:

the shares of intermediate sales in total sales as a measure of the *direct forward* linkages per sector (*i.e.* the row sums of the matrix of intermediate output coefficients, Bi), and

the share of intermediate purchases in total costs as a measure of the *direct backward* linkages per sector (*i.e.* the column sums of the matrix with intermediate input coefficients, $i'A$).

Both measures and their underlying matrices, A and B can be derived from regional or national input-output tables in the usual manner (see Oosterhaven, 1981, or Miller and Blair, 1985).

Instead of direct linkages, the standard approach mostly uses measures for the *total* of direct and indirect linkages, *i.e.*

the row sums of the Ghosh-inverse as a measure of the *cumulative forward* linkages per sector [*i.e,* . $Gi = (I-B)^{-1}i$], and

the column sums of the Leontief-inverse as a measure of the *cumulative backward* linkages per sector [*i.e.,* $i'L = i'(I-A)^{\prime}$].

Unfortunately, these last two measures are equal to the *multipliers* of, respectively, the supply-driven input-output model (Ghosh, 1958) and the traditional demand-driven input-output model. Hence, they do not represent causally neutral linkages, but forward and backward *causal effects* that are based on specific causal relationships and a specific designation of model variables as being either exogenous or endogenous. Since the underlying models represent two mutually contradictory extremes, wrong interpretations of these so-called cumulative linkages are almost unavoidable (see Oosterhaven, 1988, 1996, for details).

To illustrate the double counting of impacts and the over-estimation of the economic importance of a certain sector that is the consequence of this confusion, we will first summarize the causality and the exogenous/endogenous distinction in the standard demand-driven Leontief model. In this model, the final demand f for sectoral outputs is exogenous. Any change in whatever part of total demand for sectoral outputs is matched, without supply constraints, by endogenous sectoral production x. Sectoral production, in its turn, determines the endogenous intermediate demand for sectoral outputs Ax as well as the endogenous demand for primary inputs, such as value added v and imports m. The model solution for value added is the following:

$$v = v_c' x = v_c' (I - A)^{-1} f = v_c' Lf \tag{7.1}$$

where v_c' represents the row with value added coefficients (see Oosterhaven, 1981, or Miller & Blair, 1985, for details).

From (7.1), it is clear that the value added multipliers $v_c'L$ may only be multiplied with exogenous final demand, f, and not with endogenous total output, x. When the latter is done, this unavoidably leads to an over-estimation of the importance of the sector at hand. The reason being that (7.1) assumes that the intermediate part of total output (Ax) is endogenously determined by the size of (mainly the other sectors') total output. Multiplying the total of x with the value added multipliers, $v_c'L$, results in double-counting the endogenous part (x - f). When calculating the importance of Schiphol airport for national employment BCI/NEI (1997, table 5.1), for instance, forget that part of the backward employment effect actually occurs in the aviation industry that was already included in the direct (platform-tied) employment at Schiphol that was assumed exogenous.

Things get even more wrong when ad hoc estimates of causal forward effects are added to the so-called direct effect, which total is then multiplied by standard employment or value added multipliers in order to estimate the so-called backward effects of a certain sector of project. This procedure easily leads to triple counting of effects. Besides the above-mentioned double counting of part of the direct effect with part of the backward effects, this will also lead to double counting of part of both the direct and the backward effects with the forward effects. When evaluating the economic impact of a rail freight line from the port of Rotterdam to the Ruhr-area, Knight Wendling (1992), for instance, added the backward effects of the Rotterdam port industries on inland freight transport to the forward effects of the freight line on the Rotterdam port industries.

The principal reason for all this over-estimation and double-~~counting~~ is simple: multipliers are used outside the context of the model from which they are derived. The simple remedy "don't do it", however, is too naive. Practitioners will continue to need simple devices like multipliers, which they will unavoidably want to simply multiply with total output, total employment or total value added. Therefore, we propose to label the old, standard multipliers as *gross* multipliers, which may only be multiplied with (exogenous) final demand. Next to this, a new so-called net multiplier is needed that can simply be multiplied with the total of a certain sector in order to get the impact of that sector on the economy.

In the case of total output, the *net total output multipliers* will be equal to the old (gross) output multipliers $i'L$ multiplied by $\hat{f}_c$, the diagonal matrix with the fractions of total sectoral output that may be considered exogenous (*i.e.* f_j / x_j). In the case of value added and employment multipliers, the corresponding net multipliers need of course to be multiplied with total sectoral value added or total sectoral employment. This means that, just as with the old (gross) multipliers, the new net value added and employment multipliers need to be standardized. This leads to the following definition of the *Type I standardized net value added multipliers*:

$$\text{SNVAM-I}' = v_c' (I - A)^{-1} \hat{v}_c^{-1} \hat{f}_c \tag{7.2}$$

where $\hat{f}_c$ is the matrix with the sectoral final output ratios that secures the *net* character of the multipliers, and $\hat{v}_c^{-1}$ represents the diagonal inverse of the sectoral value added ratios that secures the standardization with respect to sectoral value added. The above net multipliers represented the so-called Type I net multipliers that are derived from the basic Leontief model.

In the next empirical section, however, we will use so-called *Type II standardized net* employment and net value added *multipliers*:

$$\text{SNVAM-II}' = v_c' (I - A - Q)^{-1} \hat{v}_c^{-1} \hat{f}_c^{ex} \tag{7.3}$$

where $q_{ij} \in Q$ indicates the endogenous consumption expenditures on products from sector i paid from labor incomes in sector j per unit of output in sector j, and where $\hat{f}_c^{ex}$ represents the exogenous final output ratios. These Type II multipliers are derived from the following extended input-output model (see Oosterhaven, 1981, for its interregional generalization used in the next section):

$$v = v_c' (I - A - Q)^{-1} f^{ex} = v_c' L^{ext} f^{ex} \tag{7.4}$$

where $f^{ex} = f - Qx$, and where L^{ext} stands for the extended Leontief-inverse.

Comparing (7.1) with (7.4) shows that the Type II gross multipliers are larger than the Type I gross multipliers, whereas Type II final output is smaller than Type I exogenous final output (provided of course that $Q > \mathbf{0}$). In case of the net multipliers, however, no such systematic relation can be found. In fact, the output-weighted average of both the Type I and the Type II *net* multipliers equals unity. With the output-weighting vector $x_c = x(i'x)^{-1}$, this follows from:

$$\text{SNVAM-I}'(x_c) = \left[v_c' L \hat{v}_c^{-1} \hat{f}_c\right] x_c = \left[v_c' L \hat{f} \hat{v}^{-1}\right] x_c = \left[v' \hat{v}^{-1}\right] x_c = 1 \tag{7.5}$$

The proof for the Type II net multipliers runs analogous with L^{ext} and f^{ex}.

The above property is, of course, precisely the reason for developing the concept of the net multiplier. It also avoids the double counting of impacts. This means that when each sectoral *net* multiplier is multiplied with its appropriate sectoral total (output, employment, whatever), the total for the whole economy will result, instead of some multiple of it. For the Type II net value added multipliers this follows from:

$$\text{SNVAM-II}' v = v_c' L^{ext} \hat{v}_c^{-1} \hat{f}_c^{ex} v = v_c' L^{ext} \hat{f}^{ex} \hat{v}^{-1} v = v' \hat{v}^{-1} v = v' i = v \tag{7.6}$$

The proof for the Type I net multipliers again runs parallel.

7.3 Application to the Northern and the National Dutch Transport Sectors

Before discussing these net multipliers empirically, first, the traditional way of 'showing' the direct economic importance of a sector is presented graphically in figures 7.1 to 7.4. These figures relate to, respectively, the total of the three northern provinces and the Netherlands as a whole. They show results for the following subdivision of the transportation sector: public passenger transport (National Account sectors 71-72.2); road freight transportation (National Account sectors 72.3/4); air, sea and inland shipping ("A&W"; NA-sectors 73-75); travel agencies & auxiliary freight services ("other transport services"; NA-sector 76).

Figure 7.1 shows, on the horizontal axis, the employment share of total transportation in the North to be 4.2% (1.2% + 1.9% + 0.5% +0.5%), with road freight transport being the largest subsector. The vertical axis shows that the value added per transportation worker is close to the national average, except for the capital-intensive water and air transport services, where it is far higher, and except for the more intensive-intensive "other transport services", where it is lower than average. Multiplying the horizontal and vertical axis yields the rectangular surfaces, which represent the value added shares of the subsectors. Thus, for example, in terms of employment, northern air and water transport is of the same size as "other transport services" but in terms of value added it contributes more than twice as much to the regional economy.

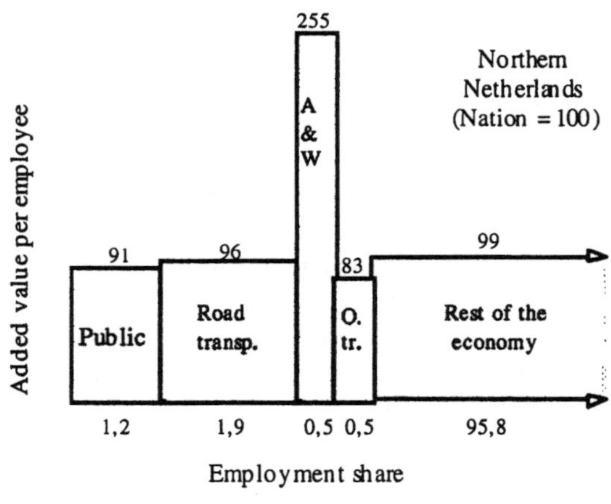

Figure 7.1 The direct regional importance of the regional transport sector

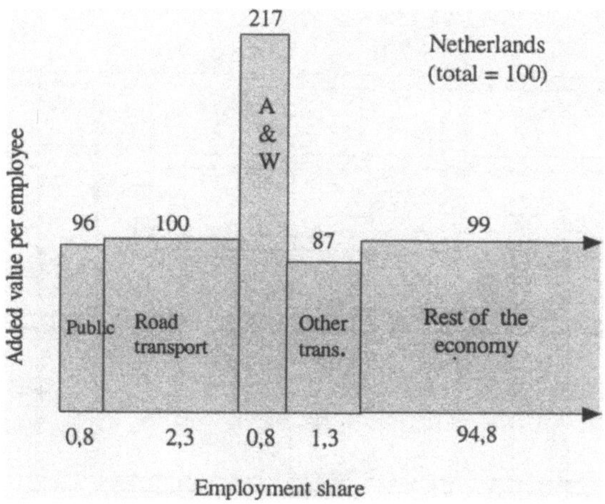

Figure 7.2 The direct national importance of the national transport sector

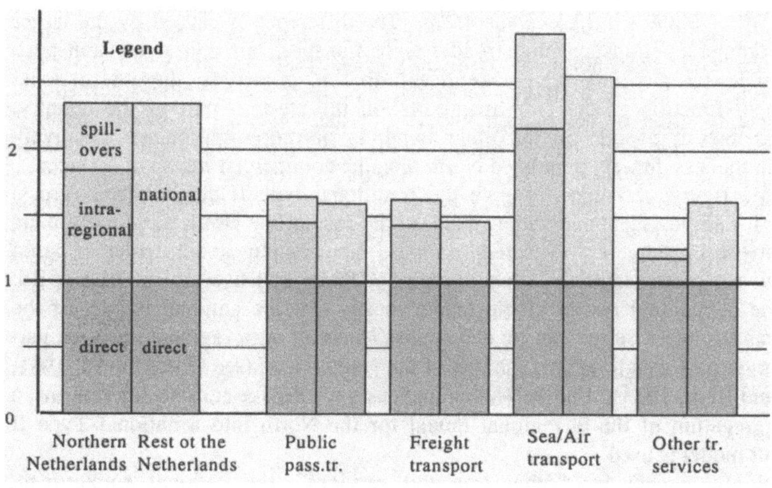

Figure 7.3 Type II regional and national employment multipliers

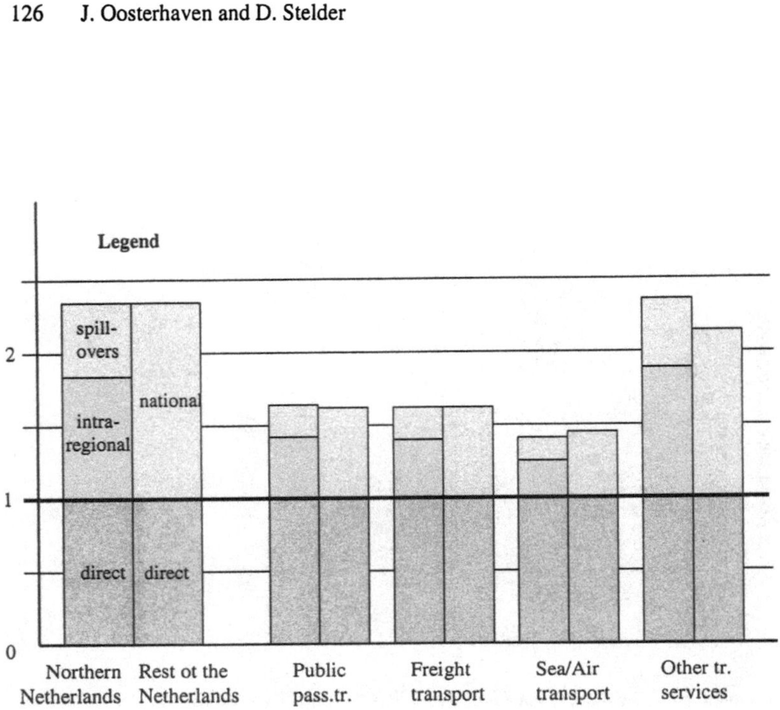

Figure 7.4 Type II regional and national *value added* multipliers

Comparing figures 7.1 and 7.2, it appears that the direct national importance of the transportation sector in terms of employment is larger than in the North, namely 5.2% (0.8% + 2.3% + 0.8% + 1.3%) versus 4.2%. The difference is caused by the larger share of commercial transportation (road freight transport, air and water transport, travel agencies & auxiliary freight services), that is related to the international transshipment function of the two 'mainports' in the western part of the country. Public passenger transport, on the other hand, is of more importance, relatively speaking, in the less densely populated North than the commercial transport services.

Next, the figures 7.3 and 7.4 give the traditional type II standardized (gross) multipliers for employment and value added. In the case of the North these multipliers are calculated by means of a Type II *bi-regional* input-output model, which is based on the new set of rectangular Dutch bi-regional make and use tables (RUG/CBS, 1999). The bi-regional nature of the model means that the national impact of the northern transportation sector can be decomposed into an intra-regional northern part and a spillover part which regards the rest of the Netherlands (see Oosterhaven, 1981, or Miller and Blair, 1985). For the Netherlands as a whole, for consistency reasons, a straight aggregation of the bi-regional model for the North into a national Type II input-output model is used.

Interestingly, except for "other transport services", the national employment multipliers for the northern subsectors are larger than those for the corresponding national subsectors. In the case of air and water transport, this is understandable in view of the much higher value added per worker in the North (compare figures 7.1 and 7.2). This also shows up in the very large intra-regional employment multiplier of 2.29, which is caused by the very small direct employment coefficient of air and water transport (that is by the large $\hat{v}_c^{-1}$ in the multiplier formula). In the case of the remaining two northern subsectors (public passenger transport and road freight transport) smaller foreign import leakages explain part of the larger size of the northern multipliers. In the case of the smaller northern employment multiplier for the "other transport services", the larger cluster linkages within the rest of the Netherlands are the main explanation.

Table 7.1 summarizes the traditional (gross) approach to measuring the economic importance of a certain sector for the national or regional economy. The upper part summarizes the information on the direct economic impact from figures 7.1 and 7.2. The middle part summarizes the traditional type II standardized (gross) multipliers from the figures 7.3 and 7.4. The lower, concluding part of table 7.1 shows the result of multiplying the upper part, with the direct economic importance of the transportation subsectors, with the regional and national multipliers from the middle part.

The direct, indirect and induced *regional importance* is found to be almost systematically smaller than the corresponding national importance. The only exception is the direct, indirect and induced employment importance of 1.8% of public transportation in the North, which is significantly larger than the corresponding national importance of 1.4%. The systematic difference is explained by the interregional spillovers to the rest of the country, which are neglected when the importance of a regional sector for the regional economy is calculated. The systematic differences are, especially, large in the case of air and water transport and "other transport services". In both cases, the intra-regional multipliers of the northern subsectors are considerably below the national multipliers of the national subsectors.

Table 7.1 The traditional, gross view on the importance of the transport sector

Type of importance	Public transport		Road freight transport		Air/sea/inland shipping		Other transport serv.		Total	
	North	Nation	North	Nation	North	Nation	North	Nation	North	Nation
Direct EM (%)	1.2	0.8	1.9	2.3	0.5	0.8	0.5	1.3	**4.2**	**5.2**
Direct VA (%)	1.0	1.2	2.0	1.9	1.3	2.9	0.2	0.6	**4.5**	**6.7**
Regional SG EM M	1.54		1.51		2.29		1.22			
National SG EM M	1.88	1.70	1.86	1.56	3.36	2.88	1.32	1.72		
Regional SG VA M	1.48		1.49		1.41		2.00			
National SG VA M	1.76	1.65	1.80	1.68	1.74	1.76	2.52	2.19		
EM importance (%)	1.8	1.4	2.9	3.7	1.2	2.3	0.6	2.2	**6.6**	**9.5**
VA importance (%)	1.5	2.0	3.1	3.3	1.8	5.1	0.3	1.4	**6.7**	**11.8**

Notes: EM= employment, VA= value added, SG = standardized gross, M = multiplier.

Next, note that in terms of value added, the *national importance* of the transportation sector is above the psychologically important threshold of 10%. Thus, the lobbyist will use that number to claim that *at least* 12% of the Dutch economy is dependent on the transport sector. At least, because the above calculations still exclude the forward economic impact of the transportation sector on, especially, the location decisions of international industrial and service activities. Such activities, the lobbyist will claim, will especially locate in the Netherlands because of the presence of its "excellent cluster" of international transport and distribution services. This way of thinking is popularized in the public debate by using the phrase "without transportation, everything stands still".

Other lobbyists, however, will use the same type of reasoning to underscore the importance of their sectors. And indeed, in our modern age "without energy, everything stands still" too, while Marxists rightfully claim that "without the mighty arm of labor" everything also stands still. What is left out of the equation is the fact that *dependence* (mostly) is a *two-sided phenomenon*. Not only are all other sectors dependent upon transportation services; also, the transportation sector is dependent upon the demand and demand growth of all these other sectors. The way to quantify this other side of the coin, this "depending upon", is to use net multipliers instead of the traditional (gross) multipliers, as was argued in section 7.2.

Table 7.2 shows the values of these *net multipliers* in case of the northern and the national Dutch transportation sectors. Not surprisingly, the net multipliers of public transportation are found to be smaller than 1.00. The reason is that only little of the output of public transport goes to exogenous final demand (see $\hat{f}_c^{ex}$ in the Type II net multiplier formula). Most of the outputs of public transport go to household consumption demand that is (mostly) endogenous in the Type II input-output model that is used in the calculations behind table 7.2. In fact, only the public transportation by the elderly and other economically non-active parts of the population is exogenous, as our Type II model only reckons with endogenous *labor* incomes. The net employment multipliers of the northern "other transport services" are smaller than 1.00 too, as opposed to the net national multiplier that is exactly equal to 1.00. The reason is that the northern "other transport services" mainly cater for local households and businesses, whereas the national "other transport services" also serve international customers, whose demand is exogenous.

These empirical numbers underscore two theoretical properties. First, net multipliers are model-specific as are gross multipliers. Secondly, as opposed to gross multipliers, net multipliers actually reduce the "importance" of certain sectors. Consequently, one does not easily "forget" that multipliers are model-specific and may not be used outside that context.

Table 7.2 The alternative, net view on the importance of the transport sector

	Public transport		Road freight transport		Air/sea/inland shipping		Other transport serv.		Total	
Type of importance	North	Nation	North	Nation	North	Nation	North	Nation	North	Nation
Regional SN EM M	0.74		1.36		2.02		0.76			
National SN EM M	0.79	0.76	1.57	1.18	2.74	2.25	0.62	1.00		
Regional SN VA M	0.71		1.34		1.25		1.16			
National SN VA M	0.74	0.74	1.52	1.28	1.42	1.38	1.18	1.27		
EM importance (%)	0.9	0.6	2.6	2.8	1.1	1.8	0.4	1.3	**4.9**	**6.5**
VA importance (%)	0.7	0.9	2.8	2.5	1.6	4.0	0.2	0.8	**5.3**	**8.2**

Notes: EM= employment, VA= value added, SN = standardized net, M = multiplier.

When the upper, direct importance part of table 7.1 is multiplied with the upper, *net* multiplier part of table 7.2, the concluding, lower part of table 2 results. The basic feature of the lower part of table 7.1 remains. The regional importance of the transport sector for the North is much smaller than the national importance of the national transport sector. In terms of value added the difference was as large as that between 6.7% and 11.8% in table 7.1. Now it is as large as that between 5.3% and 8.2%. Interesting, however, is the fact that the *weighted average net/gross correction* for the North is smaller than that for the whole of the Netherlands, both for employment and for value added (see table 7.3). A consideration of the properties (7.5) and (7.6), and the fact that the intra-regional gross multipliers are smaller than the corresponding national gross multipliers, explains this phenomenon. Being smaller, gross intra-regional multipliers exaggerate the (one-sided dependency) measurement of importance less. Hence, they need to be corrected less too. At the national level, however, the correction is larger.

Table 7.3 Net and gross impacts compared (% shares)

	Employment		Value added	
	North	Nation	North	Nation
Gross impacts	6.6	9.5	6.7	11.8
Net/gross correction	74%	68%	79%	69%
Net impacts	4.9	6.5	5.3	8.2

7.4 Direct Versus Cumulative Contribution to the Balance of Trade

The measurement of the importance of a certain sector for the national balance of trade is not without difficulties either. The problem here is simpler, as it most often comes down to an unbalanced use of information on exports as compared to imports. Examples are the statements of a sector's (relatively) large contribution to total national exports, without a correction for the sometimes also large use of foreign imports. An example for The Netherlands is the chemical industry, which indeed has a large share in total Dutch exports, but also has a rather large share in total foreign imports. The only fair way to compare the direct contributions of sectors to the national balance of trade balance is to compare the *direct net contributions*. This can be done in essentially two different ways:

1. One can subtract the *own direct imports* of a certain sector from its own direct exports. Depending on the accounting conventions used, this most often leads to an (implicit) estimate of total imports that falls short to the actual imports of the economy at hand. The reason is that government and households (statistically) also take part in foreign imports, whereas they (mostly) do not take part in foreign exports. The result is a systematic over-estimation of each sectors' contribution to the balance of trade. When commodity data are absent, the only refuge is to correct for the (implicitly estimated) export surplus. This will of course be 'forgotten', because of the theoretical and empirical complexities involved.
2. A better alternative is, therefore, to subtract *all competitive imports* of products of the sector at hand from its direct exports. This may best be done at the commodity level that is present in all make and use tables. When summed over all commodities using a make-use

accounting framework, the total contribution to the national balance of trade will (almost) equal the size of the national balance of trade. The difference, of course, being the non-competitive imports that cannot be allocated to a domestic industry. In the case of an industry-by-industry framework, the same procedure can be used, but then a full matrix of foreign imports by sector of origin is needed.

Direct information from the recent Dutch bi-regional input-output tables (RUG/CBS, 1999) gives the net direct contributions of the transport sectors' products to the national balance of trade in table 7.4. The difference with the earlier tables is that table 7.4 compares the North with the rest of the Netherlands and not with the whole of the Netherlands[1]. Except for public transport, whose services are neither imported nor exported except through foreign visitors to the Netherlands and vice versa, all transport subsectors show a considerable *net direct contribution*. Given the strong international position of the Dutch transportation sector this is not surprising.

Other sectors often complain about such numbers, as they do not reckon with the *indirect exports* of *e.g.* agricultural outputs through the food industry. Several ad hoc approaches are used to remedy this neglect; the most direct, but incorrect approach is to simply attribute the exports of other (forwardly linked) sectors to the exports of the sector at hand and show how large the contribution of this combined export is. This procedure neglects that the exports of that the other sector are only possible thanks to numerous other inputs besides those of the sector at hand. In the case of agriculture, this applies to all non-agricultural inputs (including labor) that are also needed to produce the export of the food industry. Furthermore, such simply procedures (mostly) also neglect the fact that correcting for indirect exports logically implies that a fair and balanced comparison also requires a comparable correction for *indirect imports*.

Despite several theoretical drawbacks, we believe that only the combined use of the supply-driven input-output model (to measure indirect exports) and the demand-driven model (to measure indirect imports) will produce a fair and equal-handed comparison between sectors. As long as the result is not interpreted in any causal sense, but is used mainly as a descriptive device, the drawback will not be too severe (see Oosterhaven, 1988, 1996).

To measure cumulative (*i.e.* direct and indirect) imports the following *standardized gross (backward) import multipliers* may be used:

$$\text{SGIM}' = m_c' (I - A)^1 \hat{m}_c^{-1} \tag{7.7}$$

where $\hat{m}_c^{-1}$ indicates the diagonal inverse of the sectoral import ratios that secures the standardization of the regular backward import multipliers $\hat{m}_c' L$.

The cumulative (i.e. direct and direct) exports of a certain sector are measured analogously by means of *standardized gross (forward) export multipliers*:

$$\text{SGEM} = \hat{e}_c^{-1} (I - B)^{-1} e_c \tag{7.8}$$

where $\hat{e}_c^{-1}$ indicates the diagonal inverse of the sectoral export ratios that secures the standardization of the regular forward export multipliers Ge_{ek}.

---

[1] This is done for consistency reasons, as the import data detail on a regional level is not comparable to that on the national level (see RUG/CBS, 1999).

It can be shown that the combined use of both multipliers will *almost* reproduce the aggregate national balance of trade to which the individual sectors' contributions are to be determined. This follows from:

$$e'\text{SGEM-SGIM}'m = e'\hat{e}_c^{-1}Ge_c - m_c'L\hat{m}_c^{-1}m = x'Ge_c - m_c'Lx \tag{7.9}$$

The over-estimation on both sides of the balance of trade is comparable, since the Leontief-inverse, *L*, and the Ghosh-inverse, *G*, are both derived from the same matrix of intermediate transactions, and have the same weighted average value $x^{tot} / f^{tot} = x^{tot} / k^{tot}$, with k = total primary and *tot* stands for the aggregate macro total; see Oosterhaven, 1996).

An exact fit is reached if the standardized *net import* and *net export multipliers* are used instead of the gross multipliers. The proof for imports runs analogous to that for value added in (7.6), with $i'm = m$. Standardized net export multipliers are defined analogously, using $\hat{k}_c$ for the primary input ratios that secure the net character of the multipliers. The proof for the *exact reproduction of the balance of trade* then runs as follows:

$$e'\text{SNEIM-SNIM}'m = e'\hat{k}_c\hat{e}_c^{-1}Ge_c - m = k'Ge_c - m = x'e_c - m = e - m \tag{7.10}$$

Hence, using net multipliers as in (7.10) is again better than using gross multipliers as in (7.9), but here using gross multipliers is empirically acceptable as the over-estimation occurs on both sides of the balance of trade in the same way.

Table 7.4 The net contribution of the transport sector to the national balance of trade

In %-points of total sectoral output	Public transport	Road freight transport	Air/sea/inland shipping	Other transport s.	Total
Northern Netherlands					
Direct net contribution	1	36	71	23	**37**
Cumulative net contribution	- 12	23	69	12	**27**
Rest of the Netherlands					
Direct net contribution	2	35	66	28	**42**
Cumulative net contribution	- 8	26	63	20	**35**

The "cumulative contribution" rows of table 7.4 show the result of using gross import and gross export multipliers in the case of the Dutch transport sectors. Clearly, the contribution of public transport is now negative, as no indirect exports of any significance are present, whereas a considerable amount of indirect imports is now reckoned with. For the other transport sectors, indirect imports are also more important than indirect exports, but the net contribution is still positive. The lower numbers, however, give a more balanced evaluation of the contribution of the transportation sectors to the Dutch balance of trade. Only for air and water transport, when correcting for indirect exports and imports, we hardly see a reduction of its contribution to the foreign balance of trade. In view of the strong transshipment function of the port of Rotterdam and Schiphol airport, which dominate this sector, this is not surprising either.

7.5 Conclusion: How About Infrastructure Impacts?

Both the theoretical discussion and the empirical illustration show that claims of economic importance are often misleadingly high. The chapter introduces the concept of the *net multiplier* to remedy this systematic upward bias. The most appealing aspect of this new multiplier is that it can be smaller than 1.00, which gives a numerical expression to the notion that certain sectors may be more dependent on the rest of the economy than the rest of the economy is on them.

Nevertheless, the input-output models behind the net multiplier concept developed in this chapter are the same as the models behind the traditional (gross) multipliers. This means that they are equally (comparatively) static, while they also neglect price-volume interactions. Especially when the discussion centers on the evaluation of new infrastructure proposals, and not around the importance of sectors as such, input-output models are inadequate even when net multipliers are used. In those cases, computable spatial general equilibrium models are needed (see e.g. Bröcker, 1995, 1998). Such models need to have an inter-industry character in order to capture forward effects, which mostly start with transport cost reductions, and to capture backward effects, which mostly start with transport demand effects. Moreover, such models need to have an interregional character, as the same type of infrastructure will have a very different effect depending upon the regions where it is installed. Finally, for small open economies such models also need to incorporate the relevant neighboring countries in order to capture international (re)location decisions to and from the country at hand.

For the time being, however, we will need net multipliers to give a more balanced evaluation of the regional and national economic importance of transportation and other economic sectors as such.

References

BCI/NEI. 1997. *Ruimtelijke-economische verkenning van de Toekomstige Nederlandse Luchtvaart Infrastructuur*. Nijmegen/Rotterdam, Buck Consultants International/Nederlands Economisch Instituut.

Beyers, W.B. 1976. "Empirical identification of key sectors: some further evidence." *Environment and Planning A*, 8, 231-6.

Bröcker, J. 1995. "Chamberlinian Spatial Computable General Equilibrium Modelling: A Theoretical Framework." *Economic Systems Research*, 7,137-149.

Bröcker, J. 1998. "Operational Spatial Computable General Equilibrium Modelling." *The Annals of Regional Science*, 32,367-387.

Cole, S. 1988. "The delayed impacts of plant closures in a reformulated Leontief model." *Papers of the Regional Science Association*, 65, 135-149.

Eding, G.J., J. Oosterhaven J, B. de Vet, H. Nijmeijer. 1999. "Constructing Regional Supply and Use Tables: Dutch Experiences." In: G.J.D. Hewings, M. Sonis, M. Madden and Y. Kimura, eds. *Understanding and Interpreting Economic Structure*. Heidelberg, Springer Verlag. pp. 237-63.

Ghosh, A. 1958. "Input-output Approach in an Allocation System." *Economica*, 25, 58-64.

Henstra, D.A., H.P. Krolis and J. Oosterhaven. 1999. *Noord-Nederland op de logistieke kaart gezet*. Delft, TNO Inro.

Hirschman, A.O. 1958. *The Strategy of Economic Development*. New Haven, Yale University Press.

Jackson, R.W., M. Madden and H.A. Bowman. 1997. "Closure in Cole's Reformulated Leontief Model." *Papers in Regional Science*, 76, 21-28

Knight Wendling Consulting. 1992. *Macro-economische en maatschappelijke kosten-baten analyse van de Betuweroute*. Amsterdam, Rapport voor het Ministerie van V&W.

Miller, R.E. and P.D. Blair. 1985. *Input-Output Analysis: Foundations and Extensions*. Englewood Cliffs, NJ, Prentice-Hall.

Myrdal, G. 1957. *Economic Theory and Underdeveloped Regions*. London, Duckworth.

Oosterhaven, J. 1981. *Interregional Input-Output Analysis and Dutch Regional Policy Problems*. Aldershot, Gower.

Oosterhaven, J. 1988. "On the plausibility of the supply-driven input-output model." *Journal of Regional Science*, 28, 203-17.

Oosterhaven, J. 1996. "Leontief versus Ghoshian price and quantity models." *Southern Economic Journal*, 62, 750-9.

RUG/CBS. 1999. *Regionale Samenhang in Nederland. Bi-regionale input-output tabellen en aanbod- en gebruiktabellen voor de 12 provincies en de twee mainport regio's*. Rijksuniversiteit Groningen/Centraal Bureau voor de Statisitiek, REG-publicatie 20, Stichting Ruimtelijke Economie Groningen.

Schultz, S. 1977. "Approaches to identifying key sectors empirically by means of input-output analysis." *Journal of Development Studies* 14, 77-96.

Stelder, T.M., J. Oosterhaven and G.J. Eding. 1999. "Het huidige belang van de vervoerssector voor de nationale en de noordelijke economie." In: J.P. Elhorst and D. Strijker, eds. *Het economisch belang van het vervoer, verleden, heden en toekomst*. Groningen, REG-publicatie 18, Stichting Ruimtelijke Economie, pp. 37-49.

8 The Influence of Transport Investments on Economy and Environment: An Analysis from the Perspective of Taiwan

Yoshiro Higano,[1] Takeshi Mizunoya,[2] Cheol-Ho Shin[3] and Hsin-Lung Lo[4]

[1] Institute of Agricultural and Forest Engineering, University of Tsukuba, 1-1-1 Ten-Nodai, Tsukuba Science City, Ibaraki, 305-8572, Japan
e-mail: higan@jsrsai.envr.tsukuba.ac.jp
[2] Graduate School of Life and Environmental Sciences, University of Tsukuba, 1-1-1 Ten-Nodai, Tsukuba Science City, Ibaraki, 305-8572, Japan
e-mail: mizu@jsrsai.envr.tsukuba.ac.jp
[3] Doctoral Program in Agricultural Sciences, University of Tsukuba, 1-1-1 Ten-Nodai, Tsukuba Science City, Ibaraki, 305-8572, Japan
e-mail: shin@jsrsai.envr.tsukuba.ac.jp
[4] Product Planning Department, AOpen Japan Inc., 3-6-5 Tozuka, Kawaguchi City, Saitama, 333-0811, Japan
e-mail: kinrin@mub.biglobe.ne.jp

8.1 Introduction

In this chapter, we first construct a dynamic multi-region, multi-industry optimal programming model to estimate the economic development in each area, and then analyze what kind of economic change will occur in Taiwan by expanding and changing the transportation system by computer simulation. Finally we make a comprehensive economic-environment analysis of how much impact the improvement of the transportation network would have on the economy and the environment in Taiwan.

We propose some improvement measures after objectively grasping the present conditions and problems of the traffic network system in Taiwan. We have divided Taiwan into five zones on the basis of population, industry, amount of natural resources, location, and the degree of development in order to compare and analyze the flow of the traffic network system and its physical distribution among these five areas. In addition, the influence of these development plans on the environment, especially on the atmosphere has been analyzed.

8.2 Dynamic Multi-Regions, Multi-Industries Optimal Programming Model

Nowadays, our most important problem is how to minimize the impact on the environment, while maximizing economic growth. In this research, by adding constraints on the emission of pollutants to cover the environmental problem that accompanies economic activity, we will get an optimal solution that maximizes economic welfare with minimum emission of pollutants. Further, we also estimate the patterns of transportation activity and consider regional development in Taiwan.

8.2.1 Construction of the Model

We divided the study area into 5 zones with major cities as the primary connecting nodes of a traffic-based system. We determined the nodes of each region, network links and traffic routes based on the real traffic data for Taiwan. Detailed node numbers for each region are summarized in table 8.1 and the 11 industrial sectors are defined in table 8.2.

Table 8.1 Outlines of the Zones

Zone number	Zone node	Important city	Area (km^2)	Population
1 Taipei	Taipei	Taipei, Taoyuan, Xinzhu	4,973	7,799,500
2 Taizhong	Taizhong	Miaoli, Taizhong, Zhanghua, Nantou	9,026	3,766,600
3 Tainan	Tainan	Jialin, Jiayi, Tainan	5,209	2,387,500
4 Gaoxiong	Gaoxiong	Gaoxiong, Pingdong, Taidong	9,084	3,759,700
5 Hualian	Hualian	Hualian, Yilan	6,766	822,600
6 Foreign Country	(SanFrancisco)			

Table 8.2 Industrial Classifications

1	Agriculture (Forest, Fishing industry, Stock Farming are included)
2	Mining
3	Manufacturing Industry
4	Electricity/Energy
5	Other Service Industry
6	Truck Transport Service Industry
7	Railway Transport Service Industry
8	Waterway & Seaway Transport Service Industry
9	Transport Service Industry in and around the Port
10	Airway Transport Service Industry
11	Transport Service Industry in and around the Airport

This study concentrates on a planning horizon of 20 years (1991-2010); these 20 years have been divided into four 5-year planning periods, as shown in table 8.3.

Table 8.3 Planning Periods

Period	t	Year
1st	1	1991-1995
2nd	2	1996-2000
3rd	3	2001-2005
4th	4	2006-2010

We have considered three kinds of pollutants in the model, as shown in table 8.4

Table 8.4 Pollutants

	Pollutants
1	CO_2
2	SOx
3	NOx

8.2.2 Sets of (Classification) Indices and Index Functions

$I \equiv$ indices of the industry
$Q \equiv$ indices of the housing stock type
$J \equiv$ indices of the Taiwan zone; $\hat{J} \equiv$ indices of the foreign zone
$J \equiv JJ \equiv J \cup \hat{J}$
$I_s \equiv$ indices of the service industry
$I_o \equiv$ indices of the other service industry
$I_l \equiv$ indices of the non-service industry
$I_v \equiv$ indices of the transport-physical distribution industry $\equiv v_1 \cup v_2 \cup v_3 \cup v_4 \cup v_5$
$v_1 \equiv$ indices of the truck transport industry
$v_2 \equiv$ indices of the railway transport industry
$v_3 \equiv$ indices of the seaway & waterway transport industry
$v_4 \equiv$ indices of the inter-harbor distribution industry
$v_5 \equiv$ indices of the airway transport industry
$v_6 \equiv$ indices of the airports distribution industry
$I \equiv I_l \cup I_o \cup I_v \equiv I_l \cup I_s$, $I_s \equiv I_o \cup I_v$
$MT(i,j,r) \equiv$ indices of the transport route from zone i to zone j, to the extent of the rank $(i,j \in JJ, 1 \le r \le 3)$
$ML \equiv$ indices of the links of the transport facilities
101-199 Expressway; 201-299 Railway; 301-399 Highway; 401-499 Seaway & Waterway; 41-49 Harbors; 501-599 Air Corridor; 51-59; Airports
$MM \equiv$ indices of transport facilities
$JCT(j) \equiv$ indices of the link of transport facilities, belonging to zone j
$MS(j)$ = 1 (links 101-199); 2 (links 201-299); 3 (links 301-299); 4 (links 401-499); 5 (links 41-49); 6 (links 501-599); 7 (links 51-59)
$NR(t)$: Use the transport route to the extent of the rank $NR(t)$ in period t $(0 \le t \le N_h)$
$JH(k,r) \equiv (i,j,l)$ The transport route l to the extent of the rank r from zone i to zone j goes through the transport facilities of 'Expressway' in zone k in period t $(k \in J, 1 \le r \le 4)$
$JRL(k,r) \equiv (i,j,l)$ Similar to $JH(k,r)$ but using Railway facilities
$JS(k,r) \equiv (i,j,l)$ Similar to $JH(k,r)$ but using Seaway and Waterway facilities
$JR(k,r) \equiv (i,j,l)$ Similar to $JH(k,r)$ but using Highway facilities
$JA(k,r) \equiv (i,j,l)$ Similar to $JH(k,r)$ but using Air Corridor facilities
$JP(j) \equiv$ indices of the inter-harbor link belonging to zone j
$JA(j) \equiv$ indices of the airports link belonging to zone j

$MOOD(k,r) \equiv (p,q,l)$ The transport route l to the extent of the rank r from zone p to zone q uses the link of transport facilities k $\left[l \in MT(p,q,r), p,q \in JJ\right]$ $(k \in ML, 1 \le r \le 4)$
$MLC \equiv$ indices of the link of transport facilities, all or part of which belongs to Taiwan
$P \equiv$ indices of the air pollutant

8.2.3 Variables

$Y_{ij}(t)$: output of industry i in zone j in period t, $(i \in I, j \in J, 0 \le t \le N_h)$
$\Delta K_{ij}(t)$: capital formation of i in zone j in period t $(i \in I, j \in J, 0 \le t \le N_h)$
$\Delta H_{ij}(t)$: housing stock formation of i in zone j in period t $(i \in Q, j \in J, 0 \le t \le N_h)$
$\Delta SK_{ij}(t)$: social overhead capital formation from i in zone j in period t
$(j \in J, 0 \le t \le N_h)$
$DW_{ij}(t)$: number of workers living in zone j, employed in i in period t
$(i \in I, j \in J, 0 \le t \le N_h)$
$CF_{ij}^{kl}(t)$: shipment of commodity k from zone i to j by route l
$(i, j \in JJ, k \in I_t, l \in MT(i, j, NR(t)), 0 \le t \le N_h)$
$C_{kj}(t)$: consumption of commodity k exceeding the minimum permissible level in zone j in period t $(j \in J, k \in I_l \cup I_o, 0 \le t \le N_h)$
$\Delta R_p(t)$: capital formation of the transportation infrastructure of the link p
$(j \in J, k \in I_l \cup I_o, 0 \le t \le N_h)$
$EX_i^k(t)$: export of commodity k from Taiwan to zone i in period t
$(k \in I_t, i \in \hat{J}, 0 \le t \le N_h)$
$IM_i^k(t)$: import of commodity k into Taiwan to zone i in period t
$(k \in I_t, i \in \hat{J}, 0 \le t \le N_h)$
$BEX(t)$: accumulated amount of the excess imports into Taiwan from period 0 to period t $(0 \le t \le N_h)$
$K_{ij}(t)$: capital stock of the industry i in zone j in period t $(i \in I, j \in J, 0 \le t \le N_h)$
$H_{ij}(t)$: housing capital stock of type i in zone j in period t $(i \in I, j \in J, 0 \le t \le N_h)$
$R_p(t)$: capital stock of the transportation infrastructure of link p in period t
$(j \in J, k \in I_l \cup I_o, 0 \le t \le N_h)$
$SK_j(t)$: social overhead capital of commodities in zone j in period t $(j \in J, 0 \le t \le N_h)$
$GH_{ij}(t)$: natural increase in the number of workers of industry i in zone j in period $(t+1)$ $(i \in I, j \in J, 0 \le t \le N_h - 1)$
$ISH_{ij}(t)$: social increase in the number of workers of industry i in zone j in period $(t+1)$ $(i \in I, j \in J, 0 \le t \le N_h - 1)$

$OSH_{ij}(t)$: social decrease in the number of workers of industry i in zone j in period $(t+1)$ $(i \in I, j \in J, 0 \le t \le N_h - 1)$

$GNP(t)$: gross national product in period t ($0 \le t \le N_h - 1$)

$NNP(t)$: net national product in period t ($0 \le t \le N_h - 1$)

$INV(t)$: gross investment in period t ($0 \le t \le N_h - 1$)

$NI(t)$: net investment in period t ($0 \le t \le N_h - 1$)

$CC(t)$: gross consumption in period t ($0 \le t \le N_h - 1$)

$CFF_{ij}^k(t)$: shipment of commodity k from zone i to j in period t $(i, j \in JJ, k \in I_l, 0 \le t \le N_h)$

$RP_{pi}(t)$: air pollutant emission from industry i in period t $(i \in I, p \in P, 0 \le t \le N_h)$

$IP_{pj}(t)$: air pollutant emissions in zone j in period t $(j \in J, p \in P, 0 \le t \le N_h)$

$TP_p(t)$: air pollutant emissions in period t $(p \in P, 0 \le t \le N_h)$

8.2.4 Parameters

a_{ki}^j : matrix of input-output coefficients, from industry k to i in zone j $(j \in J, k \in I_l \cup I_{\bar{o}}, i \in I)$

μ_{ki} : coefficient matrix of industrial formation $(k \in I_l \cup I_{\bar{o}}, i \in I)$

λ_{ki} : coefficient matrix of housing capital formation $(k \in I_l \cup I_{\bar{o}}, i \in Q)$

ψ_k : coefficient matrix of social overhead capital formation $(k \in I_l \cup I_{\bar{o}})$

$\sigma_k(t)$: minimum permissible level of consumption of commodity k per households corresponding to one worker $(k \in I_l \cup I_{\bar{o}}, 0 \le t \le N_h)$

$\tau_{MS(s)}^k$: coefficient matrix of the transport capital (infrastructure) formation $(i \in MM, k \in I_l \cup I_O)$

$\omega_s(j)$: ratio of the transportation infrastructure link s that belongs to zone j $(s \in ML, j \in JJ)$

$DDR(s)$: geographical distance of the transportation infrastructure of link s $(s \in ML)$

$v_{MS(s)}^R$: coefficient that converts the magnitude of 'section capacity multiplied by km' of the transportation infrastructure i to monetary value terms $(i \in MM)$

Y_d : conversion coefficient of 'day' variable to 'period' variable (here, five calendar years)

a_k^s : output of the transport industry k per one unit operation of the commodity k $(s \in I_l, k \in v_1)$

$DH(p, q, j, l)$: economic distance that the expressway link belonging to transport route l from zone p to q goes through zone j $(j \in J, p, q \in JJ, l \in MT(p, q, 4))$

$DR(p, q, j, l)$: as above for highway links

$DRL(p, q, j, l)$: as above for railway links

$DS(p,q,j,l)$: as above for waterway and seaway links
$DA(p,q,j,l)$: as above for airway links
ρ : social discount rate per period
$\hat{\rho}$: interest rate on the borrowed money
$\tilde{\rho}$: growth rate of the amount of consumption of the minimum permissible rate
ρ^s : growth rate of the social overhead capital stock of the minimum permissible level
$\overline{UEX_i(t)}$: upper limit of exports from Taiwan to zone i in period t $(i \in \hat{J}, 0 \le t \le N_h)$
$\overline{LEX_i(t)}$: lower limit of exports from Taiwan to zone i in period t $(i \in \hat{J}, 0 \le t \le N_h)$
$\overline{UIM_i(t)}$: upper limit of imports from zone i to Taiwan in period t $(i \in \hat{J}, 0 \le t \le N_h)$
$\overline{LIM_i(t)}$: lower limit of imports from zone i to Taiwan in period t $(i \in \hat{J}, 0 \le t \le N_h)$
$\overline{LBEX(t)}$: upper limit of the amount of accumulated excess import in period t $(0 \le t \le N_h)$
α_{ij} : output-capital ratio of industry i in zone j $(i \in I, j \in J)$
β_{ij} : output-labor ratio of industry i in zone j $(i \in I, j \in J)$
d^H : reciprocal if the number of workers is one per household
g_i^k : conversion coefficient that converts one unit of commodity k to the load of the transportation infrastructure $(k \in I_l, i \in MM)$
$d^s(t)$: minimum permissible level of the social overhead capital per workers $(0 \le t \le N_h)$
$\delta_i^{\hat{K}}$: rate of depreciation of the capital stock of industry i $(i \in I)$
$\delta_i^{\hat{H}}$: rate of depreciation of the housing capital stock of type i $(i \in Q)$
$\delta^{\hat{S}}$: rate of depreciation of the social overhead capital
$\delta_i^{\hat{R}}$: rate of depreciation of the transportation infrastructure $(i \in MM)$
$\hat{n}$: natural growth rate of the number of workers
r^{IS} : upper limit ratio of the number of workers transferring among the industries to the total one
N_h : planning horizon
b_{pi} : emission coefficient matrix of the industries $(i \in I, p \in P)$

8.2.5 Structural Equations and Objective Functions

Flow balance equation, non-service industry:

$$\sum_{i \in I} a_{ki}^j Y_{ij}(t) + \sum_{i \in I} \mu_{ki} \Delta K_{ij}(t) + \sum_{i \in Q} \lambda_{ki} \Delta H_{ij}(t) + \psi_k \Delta SK_j(t) + \sum_{i \in I} \sigma_k(t) DW_{ij}(t)$$
$$+ C_{kj}(t) + \sum_{s \in JCT(j)} \tau_{MS(s)}^k w_s(j) DDR(s) v_{MS(s)}^R \Delta R_s(t) - \sum_{i \in JJ} \sum_{l \in MT(i, jNR(t))} CF_{ij}^{kl}(t) \le 0 \quad (8.1)$$

$(k \in I_l, j \in J, 0 \le t \le N_h)$

2) Flow balance equation, other service industry:

$$\sum_{i\in I} a_{ki}^{j} Y_{ij}(t) + \sum_{i\in I} \mu_{ki} \Delta K_{ij}(t) + \sum_{i\in Q} \lambda_{ki} \Delta H_{ij}(t) + \psi_{k} \Delta SK_{j}(t) +$$
$$\sum_{i\in I} \sigma_{k}(t) DW_{ij}(t) + C_{kj}(t) +$$
$$+ \sum_{s\in JCT(j)} \tau_{MS(s)}^{k} \omega_{s}(j) DDR(s) v_{MS(s)}^{R} \Delta R_{s}(t) - Y_{kj}(t) \le 0 \tag{8.2}$$
$$(k\in I_0, j\in J, 0\le t\le N_h)$$

Flow balance equation, transportation physical distribution industry:
truck transport service industry

$$\sum_{s\in I_l} a_k^s \left\{ \sum_{(p,q,l)\in JH(j,NR(t))} DH(p,q,j,l) CF_{pq}^{sl}(t) + \sum_{(p,q,l)\in JR(j,NR(t))} DR(p,q,j,l) CF_{pq}^{sl}(t) \right\}$$
$$-Y_{kj}(t) \le 0$$
$$(k\in v_1, j\in J, 0\le t\le N_h) \tag{8.3}$$

railway transport service industry

$$\sum_{s\in I_l} \sum_{(p,q,l)\in JRL(j,NR(t))} a_k^s DRL(p,q,j,l) CF_{pq}^{sl}(t) - Y_{kj(t)} \le 0 \tag{8.4}$$
$$(k\in v_2, j\in J, 0\le t\le N_h)$$

waterway & seaway transport service industry

$$\sum_{s\in I_l} \sum_{(p,q,l)\in JS(j,NR(t))} a_k^s DS(p,q,j,l) CF_{pq}^{sl}(t) - Y_{kj}(t) \le 0 \tag{8.5}$$
$$(k\in v_3, j\in J, 0\le t\le N_h)$$

transport service industry in and around the port

$$\sum_{s\in I_l} \sum_{i\in JP(j)} \sum_{(p,q,l)\in MOOD(i,NR(t))} a_k^s CF_{pq}^{sl}(t) - Y_{kj}(t) \le 0 \tag{8.6}$$
$$(k\in v_4, j\in J, 0\le t\le N_h)$$

air transport service industry

$$\sum_{s\in I_l} \sum_{(p,q,l)\in JA(j,NR(t))} a_k^s DA(p,q,j,l) CF_{pq}^{sl}(t) \le 0 \tag{8.7}$$
$$(k\in v_5, j\in J, 0\le t\le N_h)$$

transport service industry in and around the airport

$$\sum_{s\in I_l} \sum_{i\in JA(j)} \sum_{(p,q,l)\in MOOD(i,NR(t))} a_k^s CF_{pq}^{sl}(t) - Y_{kj}(t) \le 0 \tag{8.8}$$
$$(k\in v_6, j\in J, 0\le t\le N_h)$$

Shipment balance equation, shipment from each zone in Taiwan (including exports):

$$\sum_{j\in JJ} \sum_{l\in MT(i,j,NR(t))} CF_{ij}^{kl} - Y_{ki}(t) \le 0 \quad (k\in I_l, i\in J, 0\le t\le N_h) \tag{8.9}$$

Shipment balance equations:
exports

$$\sum_{k\in I_l}\sum_{j\in J}\sum_{l\in MT(j,i,NR(t))} CF_{j,i}^{kl}(t)-EX_i(t)=0 \quad (i\in \hat{J},0\le t\le N_h) \tag{8.10}$$

$$\overline{LEX_i(t)}\le \overline{EX_i(t)}\le \overline{UEX_i(t)} \quad (i\in \hat{J},0\le t\ge N_h) \tag{8.11}$$

imports

$$\sum_{k\in I_l}\sum_{j\in J}\sum_{l\in MT(i,j,NR(t))} CF_{ij}^{kl}-IM_i(t)=0 \quad (i\in \hat{J},0\le t\le N_h) \tag{8.12}$$

$$\overline{LIM_i(t)}\le IM_i(t)\le \overline{UIM_i(t)}\ (i\in \hat{J},0\le t\le N_h) \tag{8.13}$$

export-import balance equation

$$\sum_{\gamma=1}^{t+1}(1+\hat{\rho})^{r-1}\left\{\sum_{k\in I_l}\sum_{i\in \hat{J}}\sum_{j\in J}\sum_{l\in MT(i,j,NR(\gamma-1))} CF_{ij}^{kl}(\gamma-1)-\sum_{k\in I_l}\sum_{i\in J}\sum_{i\in \hat{J}}\sum_{l\in MT(i,jNR(r-1))} CF_{ij}^{kl}(r-1)\right\}- \tag{8.14}$$
$$-BEX(t)=0 \qquad (0\le t\le N_h)$$

$$BEX(t)\le \overline{LBEX(t)} \quad (0\le t\le N_h) \tag{8.15}$$

Demand-Supply balance equations:
demand-supply balance equation of the industrial capital

$$Y_{ij}(t)-\alpha_{ij}K_{ij}(t)\le 0(j\in J,i\in I,0\le t\le N_h) \tag{8.16}$$

demand-supply balance equation of the workers

$$Y_{ij}(t)-\beta_{ij}DW_{ij}(t)\le 0(j\in J,i\in I,0\le t\le N_h) \tag{8.17}$$

demand-supply balance equation of the housing capital

$$d^H\sum_{i\in I}DW_{ij}(t)-\sum_{i\in Q}H_{ij}(t)\le 0(j\in J,0\le t\le N_h) \tag{8.18}$$

demand-supply balance equation of the transportation infrastructual facilities

$$\sum_{k\in I_l}\sum_{(i,j,l)\in MOOD(p,NR(t))} g_{MS(p)}^{k}CF_{ij}^{kl}(t)-Y^dR_p(t)\le 0(p\in ML,0\le t\le N_h) \tag{8.19}$$

demand-supply balance equation of the social overhead capital

$$d^s(t)\sum_{i\in I}DW_{ij}(t)-SK_j(t)+SSK_j(t)=0 \tag{8.20}$$

Capital formation:
industrial capital

$$K_{ij}(t+1)-\left\{1-\hat{\delta}_i^K\right\}K_{ij}(t)-\Delta K_{ij}(t)=0 \quad (i\in I,j\in J,0\le t\le N_h-1) \tag{8.21}$$

housing capital

$$H_{ij}(t+1)-\left\{1-\hat{\delta}_i^H\right\}H_{ij}(t)-\Delta H_{ij}(t)=0 \quad (i\in Q, j\in J, 0\le t\le N_h-1) \tag{8.22}$$

social overhead capital

$$SK_j(t+1)-\left\{1-\hat{\delta}^S\right\}SK_j(t)-\Delta SK_j(t)=0 \quad (j\in J, 0\le t\le N_h-1) \tag{8.23}$$

transportation infrastructure facilities

$$R_j(t+1)-1-\left\{1-\hat{\delta}^R_{MS(j)}\right\}R_j(t)-\Delta R_f(t)=0 \quad (j\in MLC, 0\le t\le N_h-1) \tag{8.24}$$

Population movement and growth:
natural growth

$$\sum_{i\in I}\sum_{j\in J}GH_{ij}(t)-\sum_{i\in I}\sum_{j\in J}\hat{n}^h DW_{ij}(t)=0 \quad (0\le t\le N_h-1) \tag{8.25}$$

social population movement

$$\sum_{i\in I}\sum_{j\in J}ISH_{ij}(t)-\sum_{i\in I}\sum_{j\in J}OSH_{ij}(t)=0(0\le t\le N_h-1) \tag{8.26}$$

$$\sum_{i\in I}\sum_{j\in J}OSH_{ij}(t)-r^{IS}\sum_{i\in I}\sum_{j\in J}DW_{ij}(t)\le 0(0\le t\le N_h) \tag{8.27}$$

growth of population

$$\begin{aligned}&DW_{ij}(t+1)-DW_{ij}(t)-GH_{ij}(t)-ISH_{ij}(t)+OSH_{ij}(t)=0\\&(i\in I, j\in J, 0\le t\le N_h)\end{aligned} \tag{8.28}$$

National income accounts
gross national product (GNP)

$$\begin{aligned}&\sum_{j\in J}\sum_{i\in I}Y_{ij}(t)-\sum_{j\in J}\sum_{i\in I}\sum_{k\in I_I\cup I_{\bar{O}}}a^j_{ki}Y_{ij}(t)+\sum_{p\in J}\sum_{k\in I_I}\sum_{ij\in JTH}\sum_{l\in MT(i,j,NR(t))}m^k\cdot a^k_i DH(i,j,p,l)CF^{kl}_{ij}(t)\\
&-\sum_{j\in J}\sum_{i\in I}\left(\sum_{k\in I_I\cup I_{\bar{O}}}\mu_{ki}-1\right)\Delta K_{ij}(t)-\sum_{j\in J}\sum_{i\in I}\left(\sum_{k\in I_I\cup I_{\bar{O}}}\lambda_{ki}-1\right)\Delta H_{ij}(t)-\sum_{j\in J}\left(\sum_{k\in I_I\cup I_{\bar{O}}}\psi_k-1\right)\Delta SK_j(t)\\
&-\sum_{s\in MLC}\left(\sum_{k\in I_I\cup I_{\bar{O}}}\tau^k_{MS(s)}-1\right)wc(s)DDR(s)v^R_{MS(s)}\Delta R_s(t)-GNP(t)=0 \qquad (0\le t\le N_h)\end{aligned} \tag{8.29}$$

net national product (NNP)

$$\begin{aligned}&GNP(t)-\sum_{j\in J}\sum_{i\in I}\hat{\delta}^k_i K_{ij}(t)-\sum_{j\in J}\sum_{i\in Q}\hat{\delta}^H H_{ij}(t)-\sum_{j\in J}\hat{\delta}^s SK_j(t)-\\
&-\sum_{j\in MLC}\hat{\delta}^R_{MS(j)}DDR(j)v^R_{MS(j)}R_j(t)-NNP(t)=0 \qquad (0\le t\le N_h)\end{aligned} \tag{8.30}$$

gross investment

$$\sum_{j\in J}\sum_{i\in I}\left(\sum_{k\in I_I\cup I_{\bar{O}}}\mu_{ki}\right)\Delta K_{ij}(t)+\sum_{j\in J}\sum_{i\in Q}\left(\sum_{k\in I_I\cup I_{\bar{O}}}\lambda_{ki}(t)\right)\Delta H_{ij}(t)+\sum_{j\in J}\left(\sum_{k\in I_I\cup I_{\bar{O}}}\psi_k\right)\Delta SK_j(t)$$
$$+\sum_{s\in MLC}\left(\sum_{k\in I_I\cup I_{\bar{O}}}\tau^k_{MS(s)}\right)wc(s)DDR(s)v^R_{MS(s)}\Delta R_s(t)-INV(t)=0 \quad (0\le t\le N_h-1) \tag{8.31}$$

net investment

$$\sum_{i\in I}\sum_{j\in J}\{K_{ij}(t+1)-K_{ij}(t)\}+\sum_{i\in Q}\sum_{j\in J}\{H_{ij}(t+1)-H_{ij}(t)\}+\sum_{j\in J}\{SK_j(t+1)-SK_j(t)\}$$
$$+\sum_{s\in MLC}wc(s)DDR(s)v^k_{MS(s)}\{R_s(t+1)-R_s(t)\}-NT(t)=0 \quad (0\le t\le N_h-1) \tag{8.32}$$

consumption

$$\sum_{i\in I}\sum_{j\in J}\sum_{k\in I_I\cup I_{\bar{O}}}\sigma_k(t)DW_{ij}(t)+\sum_{j\in J}\sum_{k\in I_I\cup I_{\bar{O}}}C_{kj}(t)-CC(t)=0 \quad (0\le t\le N_h) \tag{8.33}$$

Air pollutants

$$\sum_{j\in J}b_{pi}Y_{ij}(t)-RP_{pi}(t)=0\ (i\in I, p\in P, 0\le t\le N_h) \tag{8.34}$$

$$\sum_{i\in I}b_{pi}Y_{ij}(t)-IP_{pi}(t)=0\ (j\in J, p\in P, 0\le t\le N_h) \tag{8.35}$$

$$\sum_{j\in J}\sum_{i\in I}b_{pi}Y_{ij}(t)-TP_p(t)=0\ (p\in P, 0\le t\le N_h) \tag{8.36}$$

Other amounts:

physical distribution O-D flows

$$\sum_{l\in MT(i,j,NR(t))}CF^{kl}_{ij}(t)-CFF^k_{ij}(t)=0 \quad (i,j\in JJ, k\in I_I, 0\le t\le N_h) \tag{8.37}$$

Objective functions:

maximization of GNP

$$\max.FV_1=\sum_{t=0}^{N_h}\left(\frac{1}{1+\rho}\right)^t GNP(t)$$
$$s.t.\ eqs.\ (8.1)-(8.37) \tag{8.38}$$

maximization of N.N.P

$$\max.FV_2=\sum_{t=0}^{N^h}\left(\frac{1}{1+\rho}\right)^t NNP(t)$$
$$s.t.\ eqs.\ (8.1)-(8.37) \tag{8.39}$$

maximization of welfare subject to the constraints on the amount of terminal capital stock

$$\max.FV_3 = \sum_{j\in J}\sum_{k\in I_I \cup I_O} \alpha_{kj}^C(t)C_{kj}(t) + \sum_{j\in J}\alpha_j^C(t)SSK_j(t) + \sum_{i\in Q}\sum_{j\in J}\alpha_{ij}^H(t)H_{ij}(t) \tag{8.40}$$

$s.t.$ $\quad eqs.$ (8.1) – (8.37)

$$\sum_{i\in I}\sum_{j\in J} K_{ij}(N_h) \geq \overline{K} \tag{8.41}$$

maximization of welfare subject to the constraints on the air pollutants emissions

$$\max.FV_4 = \sum_{j\in J}\sum_{k\in I_I \cup I_O} \alpha_{kj}^C(t)C_{kj}(t) + \sum_{j\in J}\alpha_j^C(t)SSK_j(t) + \sum_{i\in Q}\sum_{j\in J}\alpha_{ij}^H(t)H_{ij}(t)$$

$s.t.$ $\quad eqs.$ (8.1) – (8.37). (8.42)

$$TP_p(t) \leq \overline{TP_p(t)} \ (p \in P, 0 \leq t \leq N_h)$$

8.3 Results of the Simulation

8.3.1 The Base Case

In the base case, we carried out a computer simulation, attempting to determine the maximum GNP levels for each period, keeping the level of pollutant emissions for all of Taiwan for the year 1991 as the upper constraint. In 1991, total emissions were: CO_2 600million tons; SOx 600 thousand tons; and NOx 450 thousand tons. Under these conditions with 1991 levels set as upper constraints, GNP levels for each period are illustrated in figure 8.1.

The upper constraint and emission of pollutants for respective periods are as illustrated in figures 8.2 to 8.4.

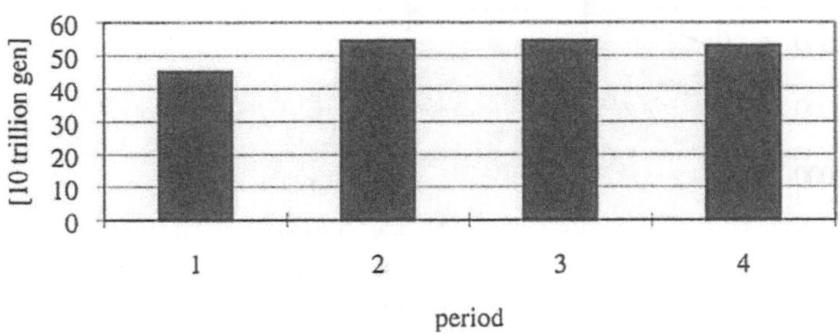

Figure 8.1 Case 1 (Base case): Comparison of GNP in Each Period

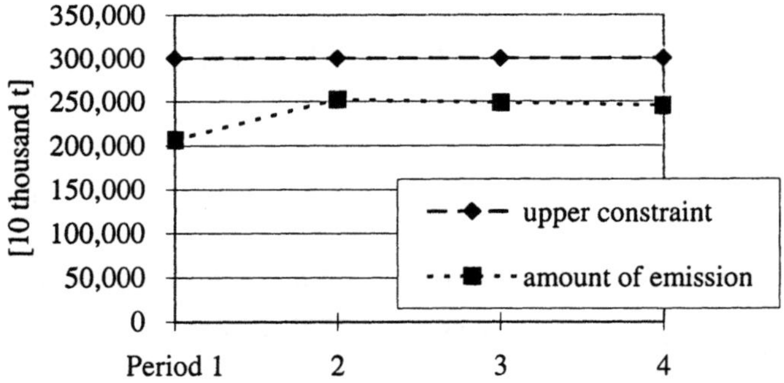

Figure 8.2 Base Case: Comparison of CO2 Emission Amounts in Respective Periods vs. Upper Constraint Level

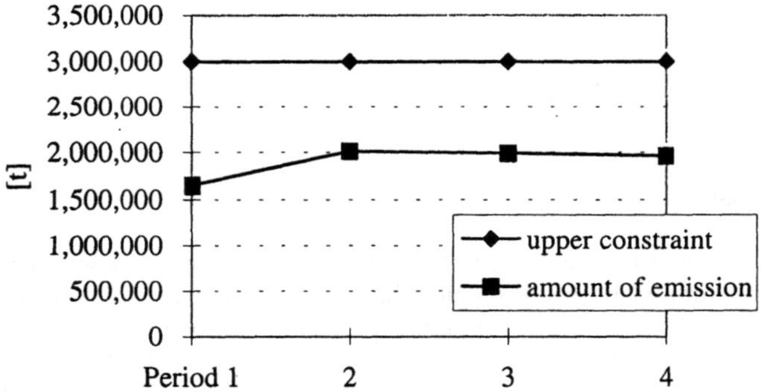

Figure 8.3 Base Case: Comparison of SOx Emission Amounts in Respective Periods vs. Upper Constraint Level

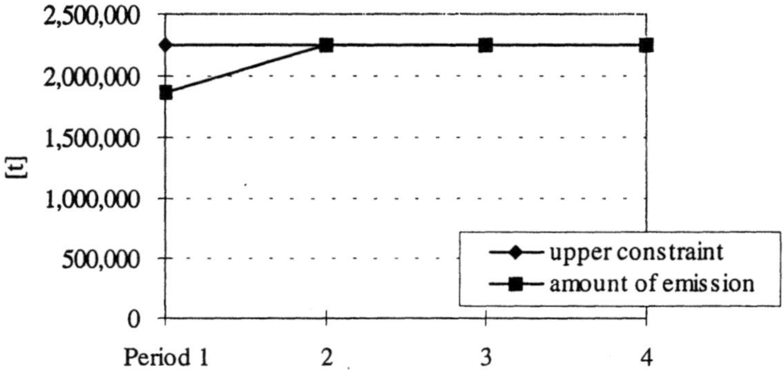

Figure 8.4 Base Case: Comparison of NOx Emission Amounts in Respective Periods vs. Upper Constraint Level

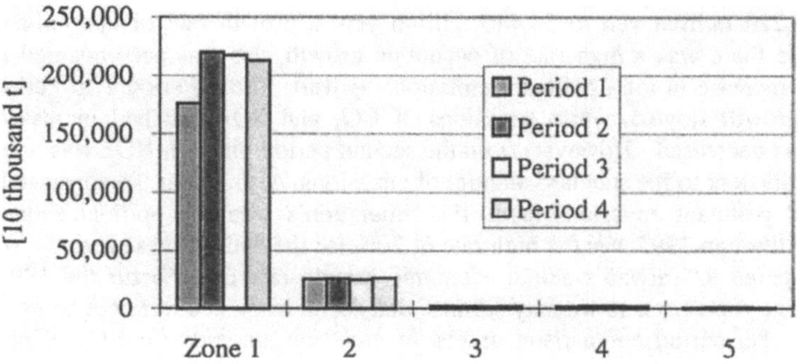

Figure 8.5 Base Case: Per-Period Comparison Graph of Emission Amounts for CO2 in Each Zone

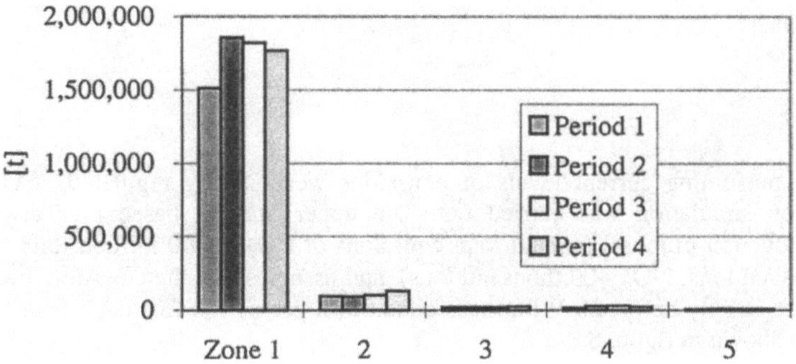

Figure 8.6 Base Case. Per-Period Comparison Graph of Emission Amounts for SOx in Each Zone

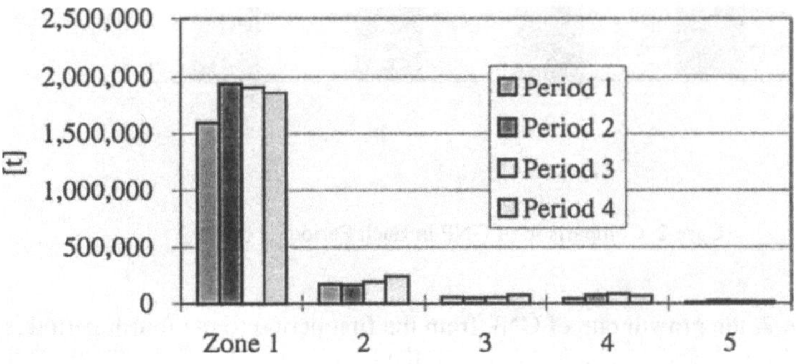

Figure 8.7 Base Case Per-Period Comparison Graph of Emission Amounts for NOx in Each Zone

From Period 1 to Period 2, a trend in GNP growth was determined, growing from a level of 45,220 million yen to 54,440 million yen, a growth rate of approximately 20%. While there was a high rate of economic growth, this was accompanied by a remarkable increase in total pollutant emissions as well. From Period 2 to Period 4, economic growth slowed, while emissions of CO_2 and SOx that had increased in period 2 then decreased. However, from the second period onward, NOx was emitted at levels equivalent to the standard amount of emissions. Also, under the constraints of 1991 actual pollutant emissions level, the simulation's resulting optimal economic growth rate through 1995 was the high rate of 20% for the entire 5-year period. When this is compared to Taiwan's actual economic growth rate of 10% for the 1991-95 period, a large gap exists, so we may surmise that social resources were not being used effectively. Per-period comparison graphs of emission amounts for CO_2, SOx and NOx in each zone are illustrated in figures 8.5 through 8.7.

In Zone 1, where each industry is actively producing, the emission amounts are by far the largest, followed by Zone 2. In Zone 3, which is dominated by the manufacturing industry, and in Zone 4 and 5, in which the agriculture industry is developing, the rise in NOx emissions stands out, when compared to the increases in CO_2 and SOx.

8.3.2 Case 2

In Case 2, presuming current levels of emissions were strictly regulated, a GNP-maximization simulation was carried out. The upper limit is based on Taiwan's pollution reduction proposal (annual total emissions of CO_2 at 400 million tons; SOx at 500 thousand tons; NOx 400 thousand tons), and assumes that the emission amount standards are strictly enforced. With these conditions, per-period fluctuations in GNP totals are as shown in figure 8.8.

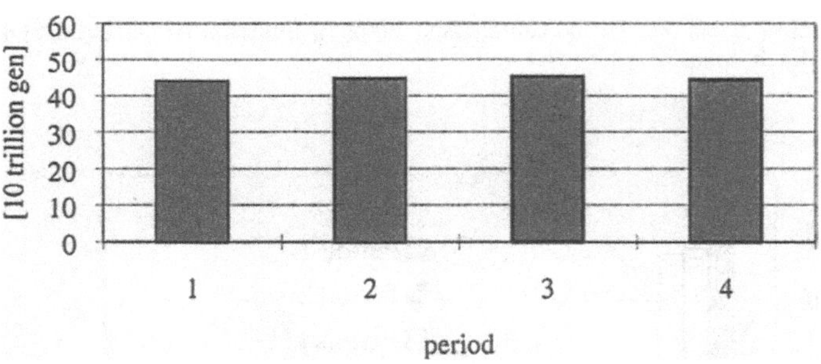

Figure 8.8 Case 2. Comparison of GNP in Each Period

In Case 2, the growth rate of GNP from the first period to the fourth period is not high as in Case 1 and is about 2% lower than base growth. This shows that the emission restrictions are fairly large to be accepted generally. The standard and emitted amounts of pollutants in each period are shown in figures 8.9 through 8.11.

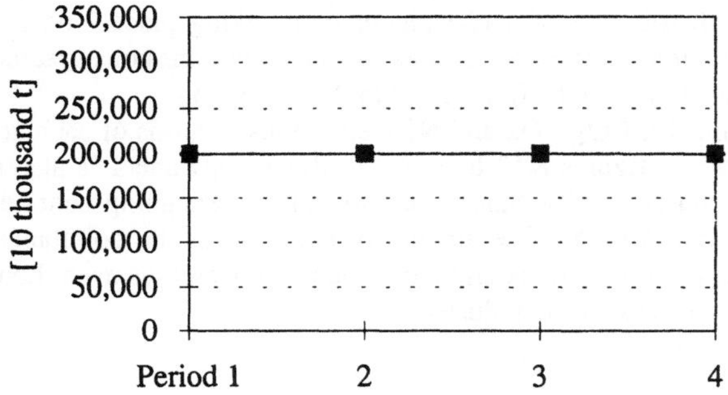

Figure 8.9 Case 2. Comparison of CO2 Emission Amounts in Respective Periods vs. Upper Constraint Level

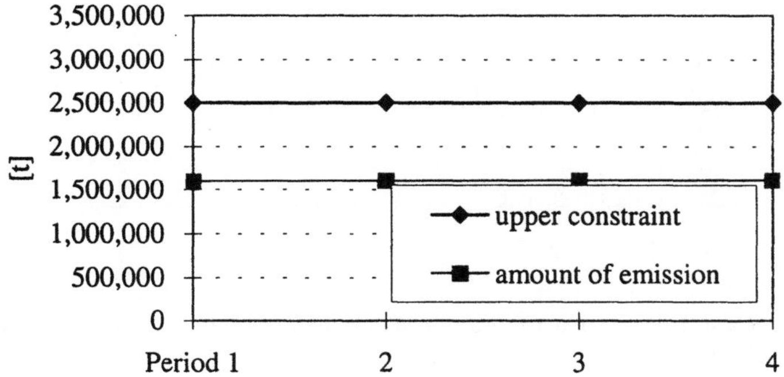

Figure 8.10 Case 2. Comparison of SOx Emission Amounts in Respective Periods vs. Upper Constraint Level

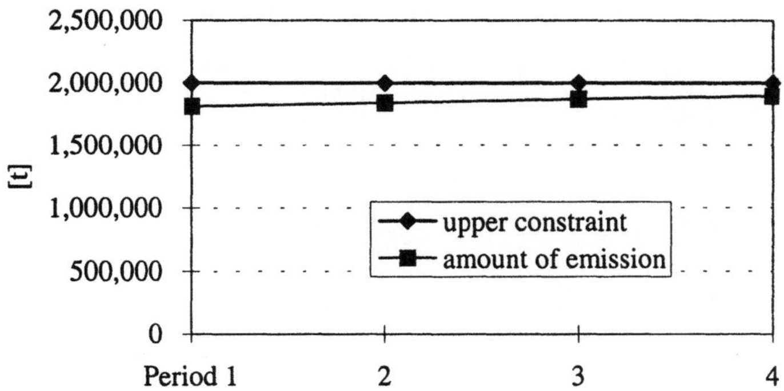

Figure 8.11 Case 2. Comparison of NOx Emission Amounts in Respective Periods vs. Upper Constraint Level

In contrast to the base case (Case 1), in this simulation, the amount of CO_2 emitted is equivalent to the emission constraints over all periods. Therefore it is clear that the most appropriate distribution of social recourses is taking place, under the restrictions of the CO_2 emission constraints. In Case 2, the NOx emissions gradually approach the emission standards from the first period to the 4th period.

The comparative figures for CO_2, SOx and NOx emissions in terms of each zone in each period are as shown in figures 8.12 to 8.14. In this case, Zone 1 is also the area that emits the most pollutants in Taiwan. The ranks of the remaining zones are: Zone 2, Zone 3, Zone 4, and Zone 5. The amount of emission of the pollutants in Zone 2 increases while that in Zone 1 in the 2nd period actually decreases even though it is a region dominated by manufacturing industry.

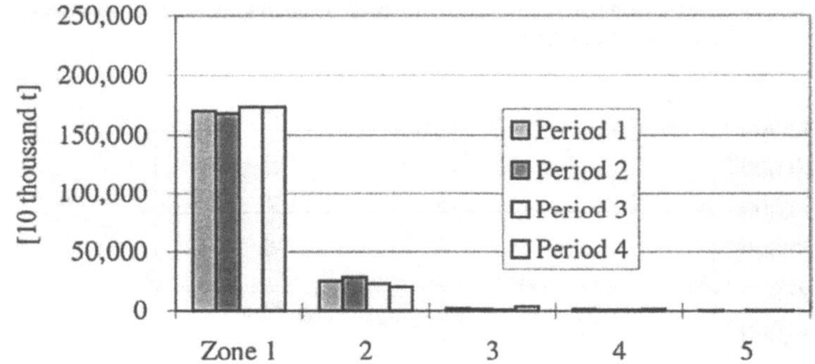

Figure 8.12 Case 2. Per-Period Comparison Graph of Emission Amounts for CO_2 in Each Zone

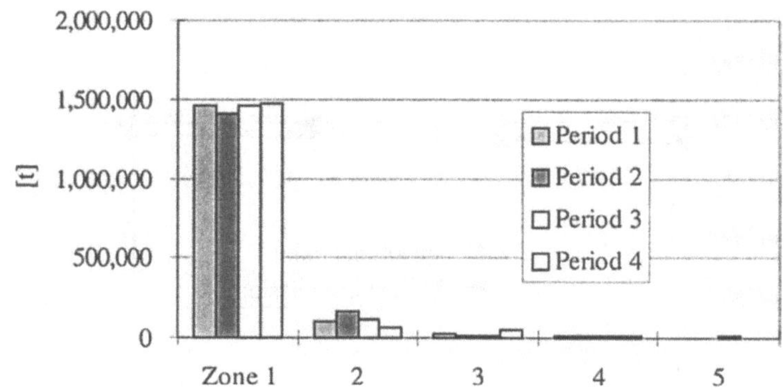

Figure 8.13 Case 2. Per-Period Comparison Graph of Emission Amounts for SO_x in Each Zone

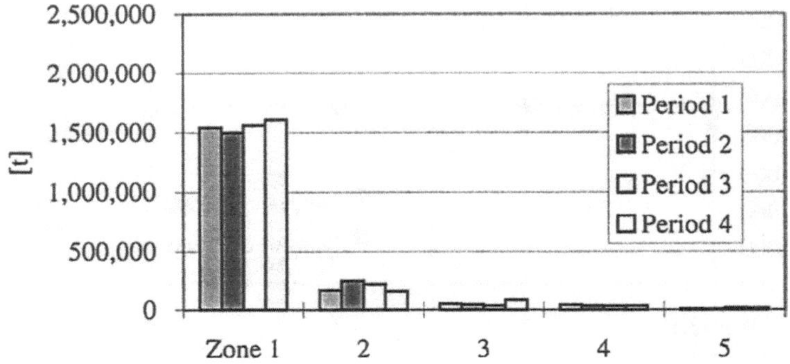

Figure 8.14 Case 2. Per-Period Comparison Graph of Emission Amounts for SO_x in Each Zone

8.3.3 Case 3

In this case, the NOx emission overlaps with the emission standards in Case 1 while CO_2 emissions overlap with the standard in Case 2. The GNP in each period of Case 3 occupies a middle position between that of Case 1 and Case 2. It grows in the 1st period of this case is almost equal to the same period of Case 1. And it grows at about 10% from the 1st period to the 2nd period, and then gradual with a more growth rate from the 2nd period to the 4th period.

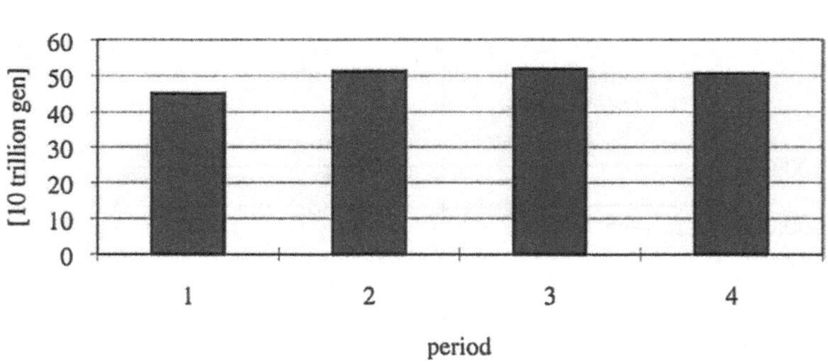

Figure 8.15 Case 3. Comparison of GNP in Each Period

The standards and emissions of pollutants in each period of this case are shown in figures 8.16 through 8.18.

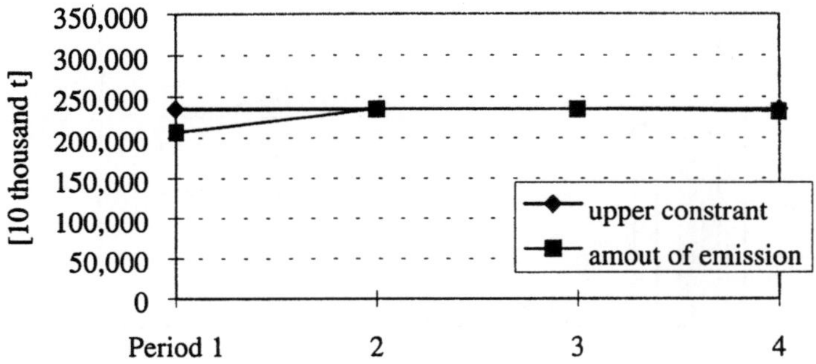

Figure 8.16 Case 3. Comparison of CO2 Emission Amounts in Respective Periods vs. Upper Constraint Level

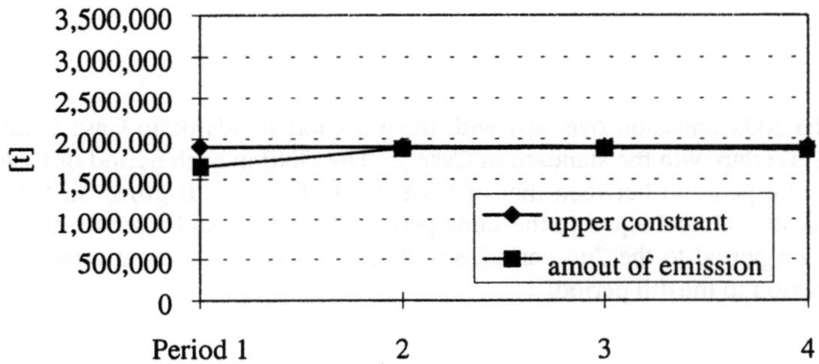

Figure 8.17 Case 3. Comparison of SOx Emission Amounts in Respective Periods vs. Upper Constraint Level

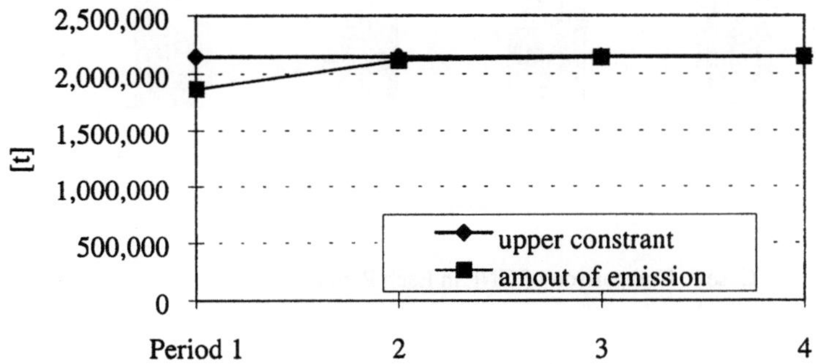

Figure 8.18 Case 3. Comparison of NOx Emission Amounts in Respective Periods vs. Upper Constraint Level

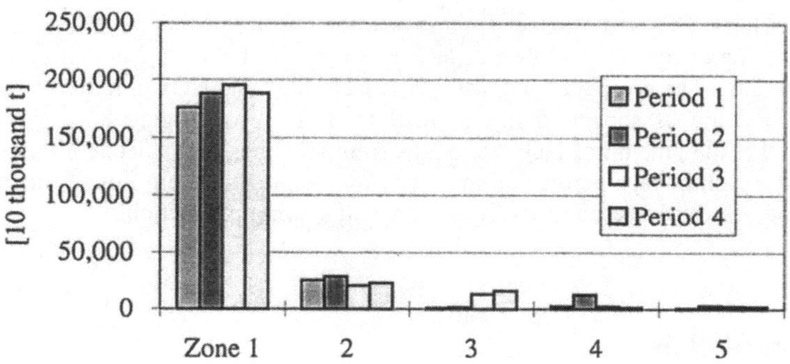

Figure 8.19 Case 3. Per-Period Comparison Graph of Emission Amounts for CO2 in Each Zone

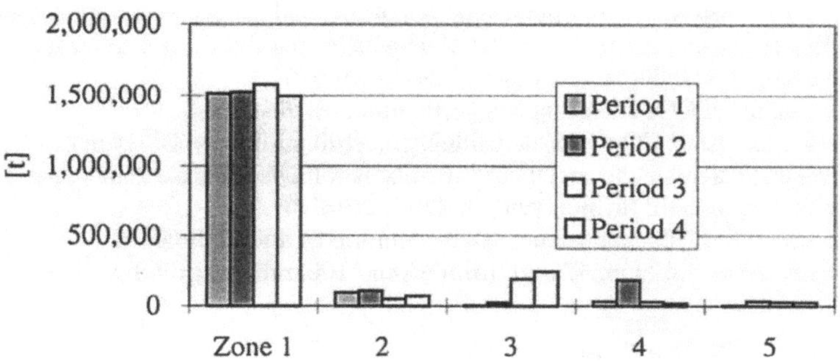

Figure 8.20 Case 3. Per-Period Comparison Graph of Emission Amounts for SOx in Each Zone

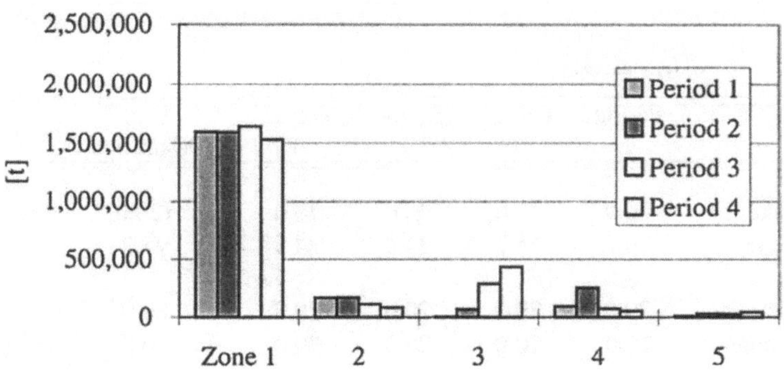

Figure 8.21 Case 3. Per-Period Comparison Graph of Emission Amounts for NOx in Each Zone

In this case, NOx is emitted at the upper constraint from the 2nd period to the 4th period. Similarly, CO_2 and SOx are emitted near the upper constraints. Therefore, in this case, we can understand that the production is optimized at the upper constraint of all air pollutants. The comparative emissions of CO_2, SOx and NOx in terms of zones in each period are as shown in figures 8.19 to 8.21. From figure 8.21, we can understand that the amount of NOx emissions from all zones except Zone 3 does not change very much in each period. In this case, NOx emissions from Zone 3 increase as the period passes as a result of increases in manufacturing production.

8.4 Evaluation

8.4.1 The Estimation of the Social Cost

GNP and CO_2, SOx and NOx total emissions for Case 1 to Case 3 are summarized in tables 8.5 to 8.8. The discounted present prices of the GNP of each case are shown in table 8.9. We can calculate the social cost of CO_2 as follows by Case 2 and Case 3.

The change in GNP (trillion yen): 4,729-4,153=576
The amount of CO_2 emission cuts (100 million t): 94-80=14
The social cost of CO_2: 576/14 (trillion yen / 100 million t)=411 (yen / t)

Similarly, we can calculate the social cost of NOx as follows for Case 2 and Case 3.

The change in GNP (trillion yen): 4,729-4,153=576
The amount of NOx emission cuts (100 million t): 860-800=60
The social cost of NOx: 576/60 (trillion yen / 100 million t)=960 (yen / t)

Table 8.5 GNP in All Cases

Case	Period 1	Period 2	Period 3	Period 4	Total (10 billion yen)
1	4,522	5,454	5,451	5,306	20,733
2	4,394	4,471	4,539	4,457	17,861
3	4,522	5,131	5,199	5,065	19,917

Table 8.6 CO_2 Emissions

	Period 1	Period 2	Period 3	Period 4	Total (100 million t)
Case 1					
upper constraint	30.0	30.0	30.0	30.0	120.0
emission amount	20.7	25.2	24.8	24.5	95.2
Case 2					
upper constraint	20.0	20.0	20.0	20.0	80.0
emission amount	20.0	20.0	20.0	20.0	80.0
Case 3					
upper constraint	23.5	23.5	23.5	23.5	94.0
emission amount	20.7	23.5	23.5	23.2	90.9

Table 8.7 SOx Emissions

	Period 1	Period 2	Period 3	Period 4	Total (10 thousand t)
Case 1					
upper constraint	300.0	300.0	300.0	300.0	1200.0
emission amount	165.4	201.1	198.8	196.2	761.5
Case 2					
upper constraint	250.0	250.0	250.0	250.0	1000.0
emission amount	160.1	160.7	161.3	161.2	643.3
Case 3					
upper constraint	190.0	190.0	190.0	190.0	760.0
emission amount	166.0	188.0	188.0	186.0	728.0

Table 8.8 NOx Emissions

	Period 1	Period 2	Period 3	Period 4	Total (10 thousand t)
Case 1					
upper constraint	225.0	225.0	225.0	225.0	900.0
emission amount	186.7	225	225	225	861.7
Case 2					
upper constraint	200.0	200.0	200.0	200.0	800.0
emission amount	181.3	184.1	187.0	189.7	742.1
Case 3					
upper constraint	215.0	215.0	215.0	215.0	860.0
emission amount	187.0	211.0	214.0	215.0	827.0

Table 8.9 The Discounted Present Prices of GNP

Case	GNP (trillion yen)
1	4,955
2	4,153
3	4,729

We cannot calculate the social cost of SOx with the method described earlier since the amount of SOx emission was always below a standard value in all three cases. However, if the upper constraint of SOx emission in Case 3 is made more severe, the social cost of SOx can also be calculated.

The change of GNP (trillion yen): 4,729-4,712=17

The amount of SOx emission cuts (100 million t): 760-748=12

The social cost of SOx: 17 / 12 (trillion yen / 100 million t)=1,417 (yen / t)

8.4.2 The Influence on the Physical Distribution

The total physical distribution amount of each industry for all periods (20 years) changed as shown in table 8.10, if the upper constraints of CO_2 emission are made more severe by only ten million tons compared to Case 3.

Table 8.10 Changes in Production (10 billion yen)

Sector	Change in production
Primary Industry (Agriculture)	134.4
Secondary Industry (Mining)	14.2
Tertiary Industry (Manufacturing)	575.3
Quaternary Industry (Energy)	125.0
The Total Change Amount	533.9

The fall in total physical distribution in the energy industry, which emits large pollutant volumes overall, was substantial. Total physical distribution fell 5.35 trillion yen (overall). This is equivalent to approximately 50% of Taiwan's 1991 GNP.

8.4.3 The Validity of Emission Standards

We compare the GNP and the emissions of pollutants from Case 1 to Case 3. If the GNP in Case 1is now set to 1, we will get the following results.

The GNP in Case 2 = 0.83
The amount of CO_2 emission curtailment in Case 2 = 4 billion [t]
The amount of SOx emission curtailment in Case 2 = 2 million [t]
The amount of NOx emission curtailment in Case 2 = 1 million [t]

The GNP in Case 3 = 0.95
The amount of CO_2 emission curtailment in Case 2 = 2.6 billion [t]
The amount of SOx emission curtailment in Case 2 = 4.4 million [t]
The amount of NOx emission curtailment in Case 2 = 1.6 million [t]

There are fewer reductions in pollutants in Case 3 compared to the Case 2. However, there was a large difference (12%) in the GNP between Case 1 and Case 2. This finding may indicate that the curtailment policy that is being carried out at present in Taiwan is too severe to be accepted generally. Therefore, in order to make policy more amenable, the government should slightly reduce the amounts of the target curtailment.

8.5 Conclusions

The findings suggest a need to reconsider the current contaminant policy. According to the simulation results of this research, the restrictions for pollution emissions that were set up as part of the present policy turn out to reduce the present value of GNP by about 17% from its base value. However, when the restrictions of pollution emission were targeted for the future, the emission restrictions in this curtailment policy result in a future GNP that is only 5% smaller than one that might be expected in the absence of constraints.

Therefore, one of the main findings from these simulations is that the drastic curtailment of emissions should not be performed at once, as proposed in the present curtailment policy, but phased in as a gradual curtailment of pollutant emissions. In this fashion, the impact on the economy would be minimized while attaining reasonable levels of environmental quality.

References

Budget Bureau of Public Administration Agency of Taiwan 1991. *Editorial Report of Input-Output Table of Taiwan,*. Taipei.

Budget Bureau of Public Administration Agency of Taiwan 1991. *Input-Output Table of Taiwan (150 industry detail).* Taipei.

Budget Bureau of Public Administration Agency of Taiwan. 1990. *Agriculture and Fishery General Survey Summery in Taiwan Area.* Taipei.

Budget Bureau of Public Administration Agency of Taiwan. 1991. *Input-Output Table of Taiwan (569 industry detail).* Taipei.

Budget Bureau of Public Administration Agency of Taiwan. 1991. *Industry and Commerce and Service General Survey Summery in Taiwan Area.* Taipei.

Budget Bureau of Public Administration Agency of Taiwan. 1995. *The statistical yearbook of Taiwan.* Taipei.

Council for Economic Planning and Development of Taiwan 1991. *Six Year's Planning of Country Construct.* Taipei.

Council for Economic Planning and Development of Taiwan. 1993. *Taiwan Statistical Data Book.* Taipei.

Ishi, H. 1993. *Public Policy for Transportation Network,* Chuo Keizai-Sha. Kakumoto, K. 1976. *Contemporary Transportation Policy - Theory and Economy for Traveling.* Tokyo, Toyo Keizai.

Japan Association for Statistics. 1995. *Input-Output Table of Japan in 1990* Tokyo, Management and Coordination Agency of Japan.

Kohno, H., Y. Higano, and Y. Matsumura. 1994. "Dynamic Takeoff-Accelerating Effects and the Feasibility of the Asian Expressway Network on China." Paper presented at the *International Academic Symposium on Economic Development Strategies for the North Asian Area,* Social Science Academy of Jilin Province, China.

Kohno, H., Y. Higano, Y. Matsumura and H. Mitomo. 1987. "Dynamic Appraisal of the Asian Expressway Network Benefits on China." Paper presented at the 10th Pacific Regional Science Conference of the Regional Association, Pusan, Korea.

Ministry of Transport of Taiwan. 1995. *Transportation Policy White Paper.* Taipei.

Morisugi, H. and T. Miyagi. 1993. *Appraisal of Urban Transportation.* Tokyo, Corona Publishing Co.

Nagao, S. 1970 *The Guide to Input-Output Analysis.* Tokyo, JUSE Press Ltd..

Nakanishi, K. 1971. *Contemporary Transportation Policy,* Tokyo, Seizando.

Nishida, K. 1971. *The Analysis of Exhaust Gas from Automobile,* Tokyo, Kodansha.

Statistics Bureau Ministry of Transport of Taiwan. 1995. *The Transportation Statistical Data of Taiwan in 1983.* Taipei.

Transportation Institute of Transport Ministry of Taiwan. 1996 *Transportation analysis data.* Taipei.

Yoshioka, K., A. Ikeda, M. Shinozaki, M. Kan, H. Hayami and K. Fujiwara. 1992. "Input-Output Table for Environmental Analysis," *Keio Economic Observatory Occasional Paper J.No.26.*

Zhang, K. N. 1975. *The Model Make Use of the Programs.* Taipei, Shan-Shan Publishing Company

9 The US Regional Ferrous Scrap Model*

Frank Giarratani,[1] Gene Gruver,[1] and Craig Richmond[2]

[1] Department of Economics, University of Pittsburgh, Pittsburgh, PA 15260
e-mail: frankg+@pitt.edu; gruver@pitt.edu
[2] Im Tobelacker 7,8044 Gockhausen, Switzerland
e-mail:CMLR_Richmond@compuserve.com

9.1 Introduction

The U.S. regional ferrous scrap model developed at the University of Pittsburgh is capable of simulating price interactions at a significant degree of geographic detail. In this model, estimates of the supply and demand for ferrous scrap in hundreds of local markets are used to estimate a set of equilibrium prices. The model can be used to simulate the impact of market changes such as new plant locations or transport rate adjustments on regional scrap prices. The analysis involved is based on realistic modeling of regional price interactions as well as careful attention to metallurgical relationships. The capability of the model provides a linkage between basic supply and demand conditions and an extensive network of regional scrap prices. Modeling simulations can be used to map price gradients across the United States based on very small county-based regions, providing useful information on spatial price differences.

The investment of effort in a highly disaggregated and data-intensive regional model for ferrous scrap is justified by the fact that scrap prices play a central role in the competitive dynamics of the steel industry. Ferrous scrap constitutes an important component of cost in modern steel production, and scrap prices vary significantly over space and time. The need for spatial disaggregation is obvious because the cost of transporting scrap results in relatively large regional price differentials. For example, in January 2000, No. 1 Heavy Melting, a particular grade of ferrous scrap, could be obtained at a delivered price of \$64 per gross ton in Portland, Oregon or \$69 in the Carolinas, while the same product would cost 60 - 85 percent more when delivered to Chicago or Pittsburgh. At the same time, export brokers in San Francisco and Los Angeles were reported to pay only \$37 per gross ton for this product. The cost of scrap also represents a significant proportion of the selling price of steel products shipped. As an example, in Chicago in January 2000, scrap cost represented approximately one-third of the sales price of reinforcing rods if produced in electric furnaces. As with most commodities, the price of scrap varies significantly over time as well as over space. For example, the composite price for shredded scrap began

* This research is supported by the Alfred P. Sloan Foundation through the Alfred P. Sloan Steel Industry Center (http://steel.ucsur.pitt.edu/steel/index.htm), which is organized jointly by faculty members at the University of Pittsburgh and Carnegie Mellon University. Craig Richmond developed the prototype for this model as his doctoral dissertation at the University of Pittsburgh. Dilek Aykut, Carey Treado and Yulonda Woods have served as graduate student research assistants on this project.

1998 at nearly $150, it dropped to $90 at the beginning of 1999, and had risen back to over $130 by the beginning of 2000 (*American Metal Market*, Feb. 4, 2000, p. 24).

Our model is designed to analyze the underlying causes of these variations in ferrous scrap prices and their implications, but its focus is decidedly on variations in prices over geographical regions. As such, its application can bring evidence to bear on a wide range of economic problems. In this chapter, we present the formal structure of the model, explain the solution algorithm, and present the model's equilibrium solution for two generic types of ferrous scrap.

9.2 Characteristics of the Market for Ferrous Scrap

9.2.1 Demand

The improvement and wide adoption of electric arc furnaces (EAFs) and continuous casters over the last quarter century have dramatically increased the demand for purchased scrap. EAF operators can, and typically do, use 100 percent scrap for their metal input or furnace "charge". This compares to the basic oxygen furnace (BOF), the alternative technology for converting iron into steel, for which operators face a metallurgical maximum proportion of scrap to pig iron. The proportion of metallic charge in BOF furnaces averages thirty-five percent. Electric furnace capacity has increased, not only in the U.S., but also in many countries around the world. In many countries, the resulting demand for scrap exceeds domestic supply and the U.S. has been a significant exporter to satisfy that excess demand. Recently, the Asian financial crisis coupled with increased new export supply from the former Soviet Union have had a significant impact on the U.S. ferrous scrap market (Marley 2000c).

9.2.2 Supply

In addition to imports, ferrous scrap is supplied by three distinct domestic sources. Home scrap, prompt scrap, and obsolete scrap are the common names given to three sources. Scrap quality considerations and scrap price responsiveness are closely related to the scrap source.

Home scrap is the byproduct of foundry and steel mill operations. It is the loss of product due to spillage, cutting, and quality problems experienced during the iron and steel production and casting operations. Another term used to describe home scrap production is “yield loss”. The introduction of continuous casting as a replacement for ingot casting has decreased yield loss from about 30 percent to 15 percent of steel produced (Richmond, 1997, p. 54).

The second source of scrap, prompt scrap, is the result of cutting, milling, drilling, and other processes that produce scrap as a byproduct of manufacturing products from iron and steel. Since both home and prompt scrap come from new products, the metallurgical characteristics of the resulting material is known. Typically, scrap from these sources has a low level of "residual" elements such as copper and other non-ferrous metals, and residuals can affect the properties of steel in use. As a result, most purchased low-residual scrap comes from these sources. Unlike home scrap, which is produced at mills or foundries that use scrap, prompt scrap typically is produced at other locations and must be purchased and transported.

The third source, obsolete scrap, comes from products and structures that are obsolete in the sense of having been used and discarded. This "post-consumer" product has metallurgical characteristics that tend not to be uniform or well known, and most obsolete scrap has a high-residuals content. Furthermore, the costs related to the collection and processing of obsolete scrap tend to make the supply of this source of scrap much more dependent on the price of scrap than is the case for home and prompt scrap, which result as the byproduct of other production activities.

Ferrous scrap is a heterogeneous input and an important feature of the model specification is to account for this characteristic. Important factors contributing to this heterogeneity include distance between supplier and consumer, type and quality of scrap, and timing of demand over the year. Competitive small-scale suppliers and large-scale consumers have traditionally characterized the market structure; however, significant consolidation on the supply side has occurred in recent years. There is no organized futures market for scrap, but some analysts have speculated that the introduction of business-to-business Internet exchanges may dramatically alter that characteristic of the market (Worden 2000, Marley 2000a; 2000b).

9.3 An Overview of the Model's Structure and Methodology

The U.S. regional ferrous scrap model is based on seven classes of market participants (each represented by an economic behavioral function). Participants on opposing sides of the market are assumed to face each other in a pricing game. Four classes supply scrap to the market and three classes demand scrap from the market. A key behavioral function is the supply function for obsolete scrap. Sensitivity tests with the model indicate that the supply of obsolete scrap is especially important in determining the absolute level of equilibrium prices. Point estimates of demand at 240 locations and supply at 1212 locations provide initial modeling conditions. Locations are linked by specified cost/distance relationships. Supply is allocated to plant demand locations based on relative delivered prices, and a logistic function underpins the allocation process.

A solution to the model is found when supply equals demand for every participant at current prices, using a numerical algorithm. Finally, solution values from the model are linked to a Geographic Information System to facilitate the presentation of results in the form of geographic maps that focus on major steel markets. The model has been programmed in GAUSS to provide an efficient numerical solution.

9.3.1 Related Literature

The roots of the spatial pricing literature go back, at least, to the well-known model of Hotelling (1929). As noted by d'Aspremont, *et al.*, (1979), the existence of an equilibrium solution in formal spatial models is problematic. Discontinuities in the demand functions result when customers are overly sensitive to price or when there are discrete distributions of customers. These discontinuities often imply that solutions to spatial pricing problems do not exist. Yet, in applied modeling, it is often difficult to avoid discrete distributions of demand and discrete choices: To buy or not to buy. de Palma, *et al.* (1985) argue that many of the existence problems in spatial competition models like Hotelling's model may be solved by introducing heterogeneity into the model specification. dePalma and his colleagues argue that actual markets are characterized by heterogeneity as a rule, and that heterogeneity extends to consumers, suppliers and products. Even if economic agents or goods were homogeneous, the data we employ in modeling would inevitably mix "apples" and "oranges" and call the resulting composite "fruit". Thus, participants may be modeled as heterogeneous either on grounds of the empirical accuracy or because of technical tractability. In the case of the ferrous scrap industry, both arguments may be invoked. Consumers, suppliers, and the scrap itself are all heterogeneous, while the published data aggregates over time as well as products and consumers of various types.

de Palma, *et. al.* introduce heterogeneity to the behavior of agents by making choice a probabilistic function of underlying characteristics, and the logistic function is the means by which this is accomplished. The reader is referred to de Palma, *et al.* (1985), de Palma, *et al.* (1994), Sheppard, *et al.*, (1992), and Anderson and de Palma (1992a; 1992b) for a discussion of the theoretical issues involved in this strategy.

Use of the logistic function has two primary advantages in our model. First, by using the logistic function (which is presented below in equations 9.8 and 9.9) a wide range of substitution behaviors may be replicated by varying the substitution parameter (B) between infinity and zero. As this parameter approaches infinity, choice is highly substitutable and completely dependent on relative prices, which means that a merchant can capture the whole market by a small advantage over the competitors' offers. For instance, increasing the offer price by some very small amount may cause a supplier to switch from supplying none to supplying all of the quantity available at a given location. As B approaches zero, the allocation shares are much less responsive to price differentials. With this parameter value the model form captures complete non-substitution behavior. A second strength of this model is its concise first derivative with respect to the merchant's strategic variables. The chief advantage of the form of this derivative is that it facilitates the calculation of numerical solutions.

9.3.2 Formulating a Tractable Model

Sheppard, *et al.*, (1992) and de Palma, *et al.* (1994) have no economic behavior on the side of the market that evaluates the apportionment function (demand in their models) beyond the apportionment itself. Total demand is fixed. Supply at each location accommodates demand under the assumption of fixed marginal costs. The U.S. regional ferrous scrap model differs from this construction in important ways. For high-residual scrap the regional supply functions are upward sloping and non-linear, and the supply side of the market apportions the quantities as specified by the logistic function. In effect, each scrap supplier faces a set of customers and allocates supply to those customers in a probabilistic way. In our model, the demand side of the market has an input substitution function, but total demand is fixed. Switching the side of the market that evaluates the apportionment function is an important difference between the ferrous scrap model and previous models.

9.3.3 Formal Structure

Let the P_{ik}^L, P_{ik}^H identify the C.I.F. prices and p_{ik}^L, p_{ik}^H the F.O.B. prices for scrap sold by region of supply i to region of demand k. The superscripts L and H identify low-residual and high-residual scrap quality. Then the following equations hold for $i = 1 \ldots I$; $k = 1 \ldots K$:

$$p_{ik}^L = P_{ik}^L - t_{ik} \tag{9.1}$$

$$p_{ik}^H = P_{ik}^H - t_{ik} \tag{9.2}$$

The transportation and other cost of transfer t_{ik} over the distance d_{ik} from i to k is specified as,

$$t_{ik} = \alpha + \beta d_{ik} \tag{9.3}$$

where, $\alpha = \alpha_1$, $\beta = \beta_1$, if $d_{ik} \le \hat{d}$, otherwise $\alpha = \alpha_2$, $\beta = \beta_2$.
Trucks are assumed to be the mode for shipments less than the fixed distance parameter $\hat{d}$ and rail otherwise, each mode has different cost parameters.

The quantities of low-residual and high-residual scrap sold by region of supply i to region of demand k are represented by q_{ik}^L and q_{ik}^H. These quantities are shares ρ_{ik}^L and ρ_{ik}^H of the total quantities Q_i^{LS} and Q_i^{HS} supplied by region i to all K demand regions. That is,

$$q_{ik}^L = \rho_{ik}^L Q_i^{LS} \tag{9.4}$$

$$q_{ik}^H = \rho_{ik}^H Q_i^{HS} \tag{9.5}$$

Total low-residual scrap Q_i^{LS} is estimated and fixed exogenous to the model. Total high-residual scrap Q_i^{HS} is assumed proportional to population Pop_i and the proportion is an endogenous increasing function of the weighted average F.O.B. price,

$$Q_i^{LS} = \hat{Q}_i^{LS} \tag{9.6}$$

$$Q_i^{HS} = f\left(\sum_{k=1}^{K} \rho_{ik}^H p_{ik}^H\right) \bullet Pop_i \tag{9.7}$$

The shares[1] ρ_{ik}^L and ρ_{ik}^H supplied by region i to demand region k are specified as logistic functions of relative F.O.B. prices:

$$\rho_{ik}^L = \frac{e^{B\tilde{p}_{ik}^L}}{\sum_{k=1}^{K} e^{B\tilde{p}_{jk}^L}} \tag{9.8}$$

[1] Note that the functional form insures that the sum of ρ_{ik}^L and ρ_{ik}^H over k will always equal 1 implying the ρ_{ik}^L and ρ_{ik}^H values can be interpreted as shares.

$$\rho_{ik}^{H} = \frac{e^{B\tilde{p}_{ik}^{H}}}{\sum_{k=1}^{K} e^{B\tilde{p}_{jk}^{H}}}. \tag{9.9}$$

The larger the parameter B the greater the sensitivity of the share to differentials in relative prices. Equilibrium solutions to the model have been obtained for values of B ranging from 30-60. A value for B of approximately 60 produces solutions consistent with the degree of regional price variation observed in published sources. The share is made a function of relative but not absolute prices by dividing each price by the average price so the normalized prices are distributed around unity. This normalization allows the parameter value of B to be independent of absolute price levels. That is,

$$\tilde{p}_{ik}^{L} = \frac{p_{ik}^{L}}{\sum_{k=1}^{K} p_{jk}^{L}/m} \tag{9.10}$$

$$\tilde{p}_{ik}^{H} = \frac{p_{ik}^{H}}{\sum_{k=1}^{K} p_{jk}^{H}/m} \tag{9.11}$$

Combining the above specifications we can write,

$$q_{ik}^{H} = \frac{e^{B\tilde{p}_{ik}^{H}}}{\sum_{k=1}^{K} e^{B\tilde{p}_{jk}^{H}}} Q_{i}^{HS} \tag{9.12}$$

$$q_{ik}^{L} = \frac{e^{B\tilde{p}_{ik}^{L}}}{\sum_{k=1}^{K} e^{B\tilde{p}_{jk}^{L}}} Q_{i}^{LS} \tag{9.13}$$

9.3.4 Characterizing Equilibrium

The equilibrium conditions that supply equal demand for each demanding region and each type of scrap are:

$$\sum_{i=1}^{I} q_{ik}^{L} = Q_{k}^{LD} \tag{9.14}$$

and

$$\sum_{i=1}^{I} q_{ik}^{H} = Q_{k}^{HD} \tag{9.15}$$

The proportion of low-residual scrap demanded, is regulated by a technical minimum requirement of low-residual and the substitution of low-residual for high-residual as the price of low approaches that of high-residual from above as follows,

$$\frac{Q_k^{LD}}{Q_k^{TD}} = \min\left\{1, \frac{a}{\left(\frac{P_k^L}{P_k^H} - 1\right)} + \frac{Q_k^{LMin}}{Q_k^{TD}}\right\} \tag{9.16}$$

where Q_k^{LMin} is the technical minimum quantity of low-residual scrap and,

$$Q_k^{TD} = Q_k^{LD} + Q_k^{HD}. \tag{9.17}$$

The larger the value of parameter a, the greater the substitution of low-residual for high-residual scrap for any ratio of low-residual to high-residual prices up to the point at which 100% low-residual scrap is used. A value of $a = .004$ was used in the solution reported here. Issues related to choice of parameter values are discussed below.

The absolute level of prices is driven by the price of high-residual scrap. The input substitution function insures that the price for high-residual scrap represents a lower limit for the price of low-residual scrap. Adjustments in the high-residual price are responsible for the changes in the quantity of scrap supplied and necessary to bring total supply into equality with total demand.

The assumption that the buyers do not discriminate with respect to price implies that the C.I.F. price at each demand region k is independent of the region of supply i,

$$P_{ik}^L = P_k^L \text{ and } P_{ik}^H = P_k^H \, \forall i,k. \tag{9.18}$$

9.4 A Description of the Solution Algorithm

The model is driven by the C.I.F. prices and the solution algorithm follows a process of adjusting these prices until the equilibrium conditions are satisfied. The process iterates through the following steps:

1. Pick an initial values of $P_{ik}^L = P_k^L$ and $P_{ik}^H = P_k^H \, \forall i,k$
2. Use P_k^L and $P_k^H \, \forall k$ to calculate Q_k^{LD} and Q_k^{HD} .
3. Use $P_{ik}^L = P_k^L$ and $P_{ik}^H = P_k^H \, \forall i,k$ to calculate p_{ik}^L, p_{ik}^H .
4. Use p_{ik}^L, p_{ik}^H to calculate ρ_{ik}^L and ρ_{ik}^H .
5. Use p_{ik}^L, p_{ik}^H , ρ_{ik}^L and ρ_{ik}^H to calculate Q_i^{HS} .
6. Use p_{ik}^L, p_{ik}^H , ρ_{ik}^L , ρ_{ik}^H , and Q_i^{HS} to calculate q_{ik}^L and q_{ik}^H .
7. Use q_{ik}^L and q_{ik}^H to check for equilibrium with Q_k^{LD} and Q_k^{HD} .
   a. If equilibrium is satisfied, stop.

b. If equilibrium not satisfied use excess demand values to adjust $P_{ik}^{L} = P_{k}^{L}$ and $P_{ik}^{H} = P_{k}^{H} \forall i, k$ and return to step 2.

This process may be described in words as follows. For C.I.F. mill bid prices at each demand location, the algorithm works through each supply region. Transport costs are subtracted from 240 mill bid prices (customers) resulting in a matrix of 240 x 1,212 local F.O.B. bid prices. For each supply region primary and secondary supply functions are calculated to determine first, how much total supply to bring to the market, and second, what portion of that supply will go to each customer. A running sum is made of the quantity supplied to each customer. When the algorithm has passed through every supplying location, the total supply going to each customer is then known. This total is compared to the customer's demand target that is a price independent fixed quantity. The customer may have been supplied with too little or too much. If the quantity supplied is close enough to the target in every case, then the algorithm ends. Otherwise each customer updates her price; adapting it so as to acquire a quantity closer to her target. The algorithm begins again. Efficient convergence to a market solution is attained by adaptations of the Newtonian algorithm.

9.5 Data

The U.S. regional ferrous scrap model is data intensive. The basic units that constitute the supply and demand data sets are counties and plants respectively. Some aggregating is done to both. This process reduces the number of consumers from over 500 to 240 demand regions and the number of supplying locations from over 3000 to 1212.

Consumers represent steel mills, foundries, and exporters. An extensive independent database on U.S. steel plants has been developed for use with the model. This database is used in conjunction with data from *County Business Patterns* (Various years) and export data from the Department of Commerce to determine levels of demand and input substitution parameters for each individual consuming agent. Similarly, the 1212 supplying agents for high-residual scarp are parameterized by using population data at the county level from the U.S. Department of Commerce, Bureau of the Census and a per capita obsolete scrap supply function. The supply function is estimated using scrap prices from the *American Metal Market* and consumption data obtained electronically from the United States Geological Survey. Low-residual scrap supply is estimated as prompt scrap by applying industry specific scrap generating coefficients to steel shipment data from the *Annual Statistical Report* of the American Iron and Steel Institute. Employment data related to steel consuming manufacturing sectors from the *Regional Economic Information System* (Various years) is used to allocate low-residual scarp supply to geographical regions. *Carload Waybill Statistics* are used to help estimate transport costs parameters.

There are two sources of published ferrous scrap prices: *American Metal Market* and *Iron Age: New Steel*. Both journals publish prices on nearly identical locations and collect their data in a similar manner. Some differences exist in the scrap qualities that are covered. In addition to numerous quality grades, three types of prices are cited: broker buying prices, consumer buying prices, and export yard buying prices.

Broker buying prices are quoted F.O.B., on rail cars, at the seller's location. The latter two price types are both C.I.F. prices and include transport costs and the brokerage fee. The distinction between export yards and domestic consumers reflects a difference in quality standards.

9.5.1 Choosing Parameter Values

A wide range of economic behaviors are captured in the possible values that can be assigned to the substitution parameter in the logistic function, and there is little experience to guide parameterization, because use of the logistic function in an empirical spatial pricing model is relatively novel. de Palma, *et al.* (1994) set the parameter corresponding to *B* by first determining the lowest levels where solutions still exist and then picking a higher value. Selection of the parameter levels investigated for the present model began with an intuitive determination of a reasonable range for the parameter.

Table 9.1 Hypothetical example of allocation shares based on the logistic function

F.O.B. Prices	Prices Normalized by Mean = 104.9	Allocation Shares B = 30	Allocation Shares B = 60
80	0.763	0.000	0.000
90	0.858	0.000	0.000
100	0.954	0.002	0.000
105	1.001	0.007	0.000
110	1.049	0.028	0.002
115	1.097	0.116	0.035
119	1.135	0.364	0.347
120	1.144	0.484	0.615

For purposes of illustration, table 9.1 presents a hypothetical example whereby a single seller confronts 8 possible consumers. The offer price of the first consumer translates back to an F.O.B price of 80 for the seller; whereas, the offer price of the eighth consumer translates back to an F.O.B. price of 120. The remaining consumers are distributed within this range. Dividing by the mean of 104.9 normalizes the prices. The two columns on the right are associated with two different values of the substitution parameter *B*, and for each parameter value the table shows the shares allocated to each consumer based on its offer price. At $B = 30$, a consumer that represents an F.O.B price of 120 to the seller would be allocated 48.4 percent of the seller's supply. For $\boldsymbol{B} = 60$, the same consumer would be allocated 61.5 percent of the seller's supply. Moreover, at the higher value for the substitution parameter, 96.2 percent of the total supply would go to only two consumers; whereas, significant supply amounts would be allocated to three or four consumers at a value of $\boldsymbol{B} = 30$.

The speed with which the apportionment shifts is dependent on both the parameter in the logistic function and on how rapidly relative prices change as a function of variable transport costs. Given transport costs, the proximity of a supply region can be translated directly into a level of price advantage. Assuming a rail freight charge of

2.2 cents per mile, having a location that is 45 miles closer to a supplier is roughly equivalent to a $1 price advantage for a consumer.

For our analysis, a small number of scrap dealers were asked how long they would withhold supply for an expected increase in price of a given size. Dealers seemed only marginally sensitive to a $1 price difference, but very sensitive to a $10 difference. Translating dollars into miles, sharing should happen at a 45-mile proximity advantage but would be unlikely at a 450-mile advantage. In the simulations reported here a value of 60 is used for the parameter $\boldsymbol{B}$. This implies that for this example a consumer with a $1 offer price disadvantage ($119 versus $120 and equivalent to 45 miles further distant) will still receive a 35 percent allocation of the supply. The consumer with a $5 disadvantage ($115 versus $120 and equivalent to 225 miles) will receive a 3.5 percent allocation.

The substitution parameter (a) also is important in determining the equilibrium solution. Specifically, the rate at which low-residual scrap is substituted for high-residual scrap as the price of the former approaches the price of the latter is determined by the value of this parameter. Figure 9.1 illustrates this point. For the model solutions reported in this chapter the value for the substitution parameter is $a = .004$. As shown in figure 9.1, when a is set at this value, very little substitution of will occur until the price premium for low-residual scrap is less than 10 percent. For example, when the price premium for low-residual scrap is 20 percent only about 2 percent more low-residual scrap will be used than the minimum assumed in the example (i.e., 22 percent rather than 20 percent). If the substitution parameter had been set at $a = .04$ the rate of substitution would have been much more rapid. Thus, even at a 20 percent premium the use of low-residual scrap would have been doubled relative to the minimum requirement. The choices of both parameters, a and $\boldsymbol{B}$, have been calibrated to help the model replicate known characteristics of markets.

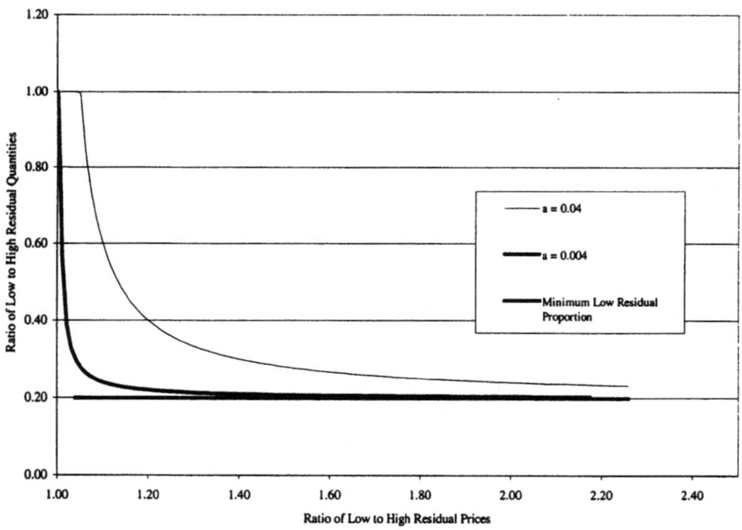

Figure 9.1 Substitution of low-residual for high-residual ferrous scrap

9.6 Solution Values for Equilibrium Prices

The base-case solutions presented here are approximate representations for the 1994 ferrous scrap market in the United States in that the data upon which the model depends most critically have been compiled for that year. In evaluating the modeling outcomes, we focus on three market attributes: (1) price levels in specific regions, (2) geographic price gradients between key markets, and (3) price differences between grades of ferrous scrap.

The first two of these attributes are presented most effectively by observing the "macro" view of modeling results in terms of geographic price surfaces. We present two maps: One for low-residual ferrous scrap prices and one for high-residual ferrous scrap prices. In both maps, we present the average F.O.B price in each of 1212 supply locations, by representing the absolute price level in each supply region as map shading.

Figure 9.2 Spatial distribution of equilibrium prices for low-residual ferrous scrap, 1994

Figure 9.2 shows the modeling solution for equilibrium low-residual ferrous scrap prices in 1994 in terms of U.S. dollars per gross ton. As indicated by the map, scrap pricing in the United States is focused on a geographic core surrounding the Great Lakes extending eastward to encompass the Pittsburgh region. Prices in the core region range from 130-150 dollars per gross ton, and prices decrease monotonically from the core in radial regions. Similarly, figure 9.3 shows the modeling solution for equilibrium high-residual ferrous scrap prices in 1994. Here, the pattern also is clearly that of core and periphery. However, the core is much more narrowly focused on the Chicago region. Notice also that the price gradient in high-residual scrap is less steep than that in low-residual scrap. This is most evident if one focuses on radial band that represents a 20-dollar decrease from the price band in the core region; that is, the band immediately adjacent to the core. For the high-residual solution (figure 9.3) this band extend southward all the way to the Gulf of Mexico, eastward to much of the coast surrounding the Philadelphia region, and westward well into Texas and the band of states immediately to its north.

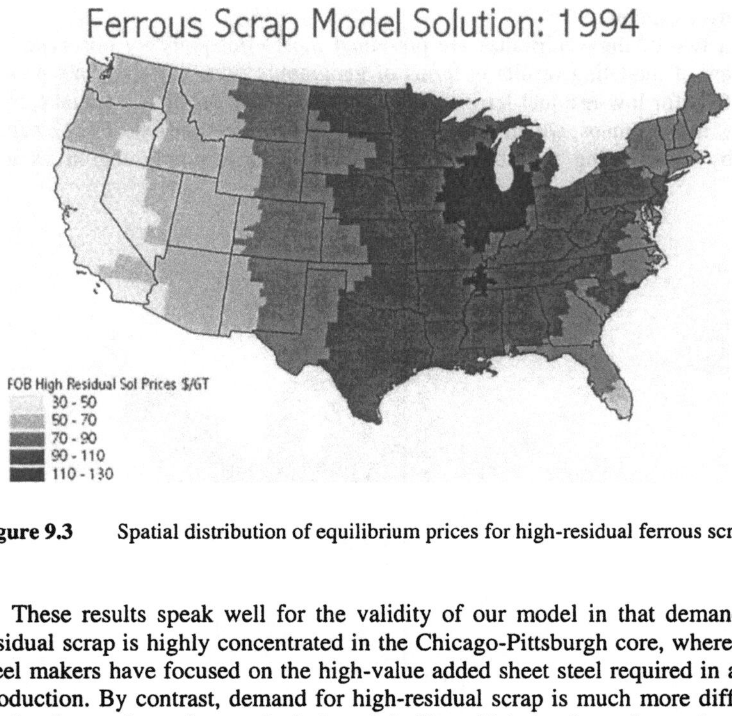

Figure 9.3 Spatial distribution of equilibrium prices for high-residual ferrous scrap, 1994

These results speak well for the validity of our model in that demand for low-residual scrap is highly concentrated in the Chicago-Pittsburgh core, where integrated steel makers have focused on the high-value added sheet steel required in automobile production. By contrast, demand for high-residual scrap is much more diffused. This grade of scrap is used extensively by minimills, which dominate the market for "long" products and the locational pattern for minimills also is very diffused. These patterns also reflect the importance of the geographic distribution of the supply of ferrous scrap. A key source of low-residual scrap is steel-using manufacturing activity as compared to the source of high-residual scrap, which is comprised primarily of post-consumer steel products. Because manufacturing activity is more highly concentrated in space than the consumer population, the supply of high-residual scrap is more diffused than that of low-residual scrap. The plant location patterns described here result from intense intra-industry competition between integrated steel makers and minimills, as explained by Ahlbrandt, *et al.*, (1996).

With caution, modeling results also may be compared to published prices for ferrous scrap in particular markets. Caution is in order for several reasons. First, region-specific price data for ferrous scrap are available for only a very small set of city-based regions. Second, modeling results are based on "generic" types of high-residual and low-residual scrap, but published data are for very specific types that do not necessary map to the model's generic counterparts. Finally, ferrous scrap prices are highly variable over time, so any single published price in a given year (or the yearly average published price) may not represent the market in that year very well.

Figure 9.4 compares solution values from the model for the delivered equilibrium prices of high-residual ferrous scrap to published prices for two specific types of high-residual scrap, No. 1 Heavy Melting (No. 1 Melt) and No. 2 Heavy Melting (No. 2 Melt). It may be helpful to think of the model's solution values for this variable as a composite of all obsolete scrap for which the average level of residual elements is approximately 0.55 percent. This is greater than the 0.50 percent residual level assumed for No. 1 Melt and less than the 1.01 percent level assumed for No. 2 Melt. But, the composite is clearly closer to No. 1 Melt. (See Richmond, 1997 p. 78; and Whipp, 1993, for a technical discussion.)

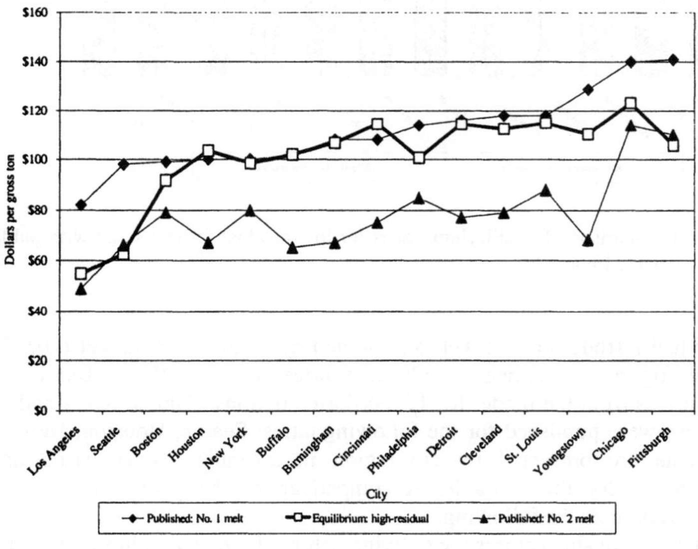

Figure 9.4 Comparison of equilibrium prices for high-residual ferrous scrap with published prices, 1994

The observations in Figure 9.4 are for fifteen city-based regions, as represented on the horizontal axis. Data are presented in ascending order based on the equilibrium prices from the model. Several attributes of the solution are evident from this figure. First, model solutions are much closer to No. 1 melt than they are for No. 2 Melt, which one might predict based on the residual concentrations of the model's composite as compared to the actual market types, No. 1 Melt and No. 2 Melt. Second, in the published data the price in Los Angeles is a clear outlier (i.e., extreme low value) for both market types, and the model's solution values clearly capture the outlying nature of published prices on the Pacific Coast. Finally, with only one exception, modeling solution equilibrium prices are bounded by the published data in the city-regions.

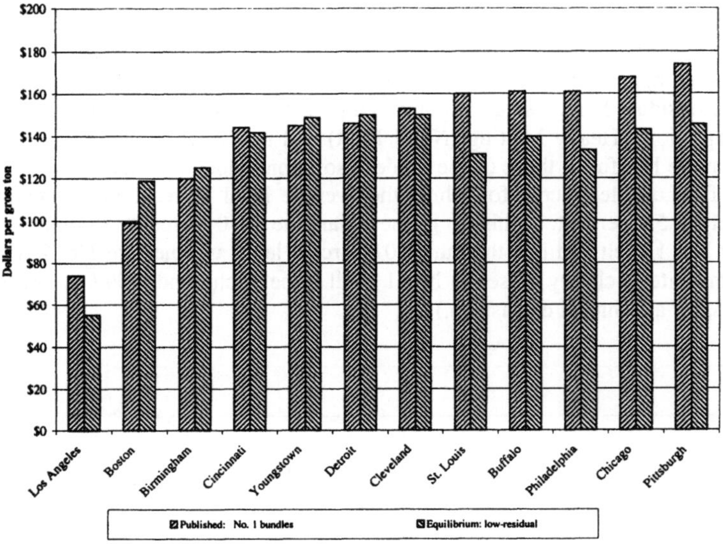

Figure 9.5 Comparison of equilibrium prices for low-residual ferrous scrap with published prices, 1994]

Low-residual ferrous scrap is well-represented by a particular market type, No. 1 Bundles, and figure 9.5 compares published price data for No. 1 Bundles with equilibrium prices from the model for 12 city-based regions. Unlike No. 1 and No. 2 Melt, no prices were published for the following cities: Seattle, Houston, New York. Again the data are presented by city-region in ascending order based on the equilibrium prices for this variable. A comparison of the published data to the equilibrium prices finds the following:

(1) The model once again captures the outlying nature of the market in Los Angeles.

(2) Model solution equilibrium prices are extremely close to the published data in approximately one-half of the remaining city-regions.

(3) In regions where the equilibrium price differs substantially from the published price, one still observes a positive correlation between equilibrium prices and the published data. That is, most often, higher or lower published prices between any two city-regions correspond with higher or lower solution values between similar pairs of city-regions.

In assessing the validity of the model's solution values, our final point of comparison is the market premium for low-residual scrap as compared to high-residual scrap. Data on this variable are available from published sources for 12 city-regions, and table 9.2 presents a comparison between data from these sources and equilibrium solution values from the model. For six of the twelve city-regions, the difference in the price premium is equal to or less than 10 percentage points and in four of these, the difference is five percentage points or less. Two of the remaining six regions (Boston and Los Angeles) are international ports with anomalous characteristics: the Boston data show no premium for low-residual ferrous scrap and the Los Angeles data report a "negative" premium for the same grade. Four city-regions (Buffalo, St. Louis,

Pittsburgh, and Youngstown) show differences ranging from 14 percentage points to 23 percentage points.

Table 9.2 The price premium for low-residual scrap in selected cities: A comparison based on published prices and equilibrium prices from the model

City-based regions	Premium for No. 1 Bundles over No. 1 Melt based on published prices	Premium for low-residual scrap over high-residual scrap based on equilibrium prices from the model	Difference in percent premium: Published prices – equilibrium prices from the model
Buffalo	58 %	37 %	21 %
Philadelphia	41 %	33 %	9 %
St. Louis	36 %	14 %	21 %
Cincinnati	33 %	24 %	10 %
Cleveland	30 %	33 %	-3 %
Detroit	26 %	31 %	-5 %
Pittsburgh	23 %	38 %	-14 %
Chicago	20 %	16 %	4 %
Youngstown	12 %	35 %	-23 %
Birmingham	11 %	17 %	-6 %
Boston	0 %	29 %	-29 %
Los Angeles	-10 %	1 %	-11 %

Note: Published prices are from American Metals Market for the first quarter 1994. The Los Angeles price is for export yards; The others are not specified. No. 1 Bundles are reported as dealer prices. When a price range is published, the high end of the range is reported.

9.7 Conclusions

Our objective in this modeling exercise is to represent the behavior of economic agents sufficiently well so as to capture essential characteristics of actual market outcomes. The tasks involved are immense in that data requirements on both sides of the market (supply and demand) are substantial. It is commonly acknowledged that the market for ferrous scrap in the United States is highly competitive, and this competition is furthered by the fact that interregional trade links the hundreds of individual scrap markets we model. Nevertheless, in some of those markets elements of imperfect competition may exist in that a dominant scrap supplier or a dominant steel mill could conceivable exercise some degree of market control because of its size vis-à-vis the local market or an advantage in terms of information about the local market. Transport networks also are complex and some regional scrap markets are better "connected" with other markets because of network differences.

For all of these reasons, and more, we acknowledge that the model we have developed departs from the real markets in which ferrous scrap is transacted, where the fortunes of individual entrepreneurs are won and lost. The empirical evidence presented in this chapter, however, lend credence to the validity of the model's structure and its ability to capture some of the most important aggregate features and micro features of the market. Compared to real markets, a "simple" behavioral mechanism underlies the allocation of scrap supply to competing uses in this model, and that mechanism certainly is not completely descriptive of the complex bargaining that is involved in many market transactions. Nevertheless, if one's judgment is guided by the ways in which the model's solution links to real-world outcomes, the validity of the model is well supported. In the prior literature, the logistic model of consumer choice had been shown --- in theory --- to offer regional scientists a way to circumvent many of the existence and specification problems associated with the spatial pricing problem. The results presented here demonstrate the power of this modeling specification in practice for large-scale applications.

The validity of this model in application rests on the ability of its structure to capture the essence of market behavior, and the empirical findings presented here lay the basis for claiming such validity. The application potential of this model is immense in that solutions can be obtained for market scenarios bearing on a variety of major investment decisions, including expansions in steel making capacity at existing plants and new plant locations. Strategic decisions related to the use of various iron-ore substitutes for ferrous scrap also can be evaluated. The impact of changes in the transport structure or transport rates can be assessed on individual markets or on the connectedness of all markets. The model has been designed to take full advantage of privately held information on individual steel making plants or on transport alternatives between local markets, whenever such information may be available to supplement or replace related parts in the model's basic design.

The model's output is detailed, including information on quantities of supply and demand, on the direction and volume of material transport, and on the prices paid for each transaction. The output could be aggregated to represents average prices, market areas, or the degree of market sharing. The extraction and aggregation of predictions makes it possible to match observable data with less measurement and specification error. The model output may be combined to represent relative prices or comparative advantage of some locations over others. The output may be used as an input to construct a more encompassing model of optimal location. For instance, one might construct a profit surface by combining layers representing both costs and revenues. Finally, the output can be used as a descriptive tool to discuss the large geographic features of a market and how those features are likely to adapt to trends in supply and demand. We expect that the structure of this model will apply equally well in academic and business analysis related to ferrous scrap markets and closely related markets for steel.

References

Ahlbrandt, R.S., R. Fruehan and F. Giarratani. 1996. *The Renaissance of American Steel*. Oxford University Press, Oxford.

American Iron and Steel Institute (Various years). *Annual Statistical Report*, American Iron and Steel Institute, Washington DC:

American Metal Market (Various issues). American Metal Market, New York.

Anderson, S. and A. de Palma. 1992a. "The Logit as a Model of Product Differentiation." *Oxford Economic Papers*, 44, 51-67.

Anderson, S. and A. de Palma. 1992b. *Discrete choice theory of product differentiation*. Cambridge, Massachusetts Institute of Technology Press.

Carload Waybill Statistics. 1989. U.S. Department of Transportation, Federal Railway Administration. Washington, Government Printing Office.

County Business Patterns. Various years. U.S. Department of Commerce, Bureau of the Census. CD ROM and computer tape. Washington: Administrative and Customer Services Division.

d'Aspremont C., J.J. Gabszewitz, and J-F. Thisse. 1979. "On Hotelling's Stability in Competition." *Econometrica,* 17, 1145-1151.

de Palma, A., V. Ginsburgh, Y.Y. Papagiorgiou, and J-F. Thisse. 1985. "The Principle of Minimum Differentiation Holds under Sufficient Heterogeneity." *Econometrica,* 53, 767-781.

de Palma, A., R. Lindsey, B. von Hohenbalken and D.S. West. 1994. "Spatial price and variety competition in an urban retail market, A nested logit analysis." *International Journal of Industrial Organization,* 12, 331-357.

Greenhut, M.L., G. Norman, and C-S. Hung. 1987. *The Economics of Imperfect Competition A Spatial Approach.* Cambridge University Press, Cambridge.

Hotelling, H. 1929. "Stability in Competition." *Economic Journal,* 39, 41-57.

Iron Age: New Steel. (Various issues). Cahners Business Information, Oak Brook, Il

James W. Brown Associates. 1994. *U.S. Mini-Mill Feedstock Availability, Quality, and Cost Through the Year 2000.* New York: Chilton Publications.

Marley, M. 2000a. "Aluminum.com will unveil global online marketplace at ISRI." *American Metal Market,* 108, No. 49, 1.

Marley, M. 2000b. "Scrap execs differ on e-commerce." *American Metal Market,* 108, No. 51, 1.

Marley, M. 2000c. "US ferrous Exports, Role as 'world's largest scrap yard' changing." *American Metal Market,* Special Report: Metals Recycling, March 14, 2000, p. 2a.

Regional Economic Information System. (Various years). CD ROM, U.S. Department of Commerce, Bureau of the Economic Analysis. Washington: Administrative and Customer Services Division.

Richmond, C. 1997. "Simulating differences in ferrous scrap prices over geographic space using the logistic model of choice for differentiated products." Unpublished doctoral dissertation, University of Pittsburgh.

Sheppard E., R. Haining, and P. Plummer. 1992. "Spatial Pricing in Interdependent Markets." *Journal of Regional Science,* 32, 55-75.

Whipp, R. 1993. "A spreadsheet model for Optimizing the Scrap Mix in Electric Furnace Shops." *Iron and Steel Maker,* July, 31-34.

Worden, E. 2000. "MetalSite, other interests preparing to start up new Internet site." *American Metal Market,* 108, No. 49, 1.

Part II Structure and Structural Change

10 The RAS Structural Decomposition Approach[1]

Erik Dietzenbacher[1] and Rutger Hoekstra[2]

[1] University of Groningen, Faculty of Economics/SOM Research Institute, P.O. Box 800, NL-9700 AV Groningen, The Netherlands
e-mail: e.dietzenbacher@eco.rug.nl
[2] Department of Spatial Economics, Faculty of Economics and Econometrics, Vrije Universiteit Amsterdam, De Boelelaan 1105, NL-1081 HV Amsterdam, The Netherlands
e-mail: rhoekstra@econ.vu.nl

10.1 Introduction

Technology and trade are widely considered to be significant driving forces of economic growth and have been subject to numerous studies. The input-output framework is a useful tool in this respect, because it coherently integrates information on the production technologies of the sectors and on the import and export relations. Input-output tables for different years, therefore may provide insight into how these economic processes have affected the economic structure and growth.

Technological change may be divided into a number of separate components. First, substitution of one intermediate input for another may occur. One might think of the general tendency in the past to replace metals by plastics in many production processes. Another phenomenon that has been widely observed is that less goods are used as intermediate inputs, while the use of services (and service-related products such as office machines) increases. Although it is, in general, not the case that goods are actually replaced by services, also these sort of changes will be referred to as substitution effects. Secondly, another type of technological improvement that may occur is the substitution of intermediate inputs for primary inputs. A rise in the share of intermediate inputs relative to the primary inputs, implies a productivity increase with respect to the primary inputs because a smaller quantity of primary input is used per unit of output. Due to the ambiguity of the primary inputs in the data we have used,[2] this effect will be referred to as the intermediate input intensity effect, rather than using the term productivity effect. That is, per unit of output more intermediate inputs are used.

Van der Linden and Dietzenbacher (1995, 2000) developed a method for decomposing the change in the input coefficients into these two types of technological changes and an additional cell-specific effect, using the RAS approach. This chapter utilizes this method in the setting of a structural decomposition analysis to assess the

[1] We would like to thank Jeroen van den Bergh, Alex Hoen, Jan van der Linden, Bart Los and Jan Oosterhaven for their comments, suggestions and help with the data.

[2] Primary inputs refer to all cost categories, except for intermediate goods and services. Next to payments for labor and capital, they also include indirect taxes minus subsidies, the operating surplus and non-competitive imports. Our data set only allows to distinguish between non-competitive imports and other primary inputs.

influence of technological change on the output of the Netherlands for the period 1975-1985. Its empirical application is characterized by large technological shifts due to the price shocks induced by the oil crises of the mid- and late 1970s.

The Netherlands is a small and very open economy with a longstanding tradition as a trading nation. They have been a member of the European Union (EU) and its predecessor, the EEC, since the foundation in 1958. Together with Belgium, the Netherlands have the largest degree of integration in the EU, in terms of their dependence on imports from and exports to the other member states (see e.g. Dietzenbacher *et al.*, 1993, and Dietzenbacher and Van der Linden, 1997). It is clear that changes in the exports may crucially affect the Dutch production levels. The structural decomposition analysis above, is therefore also used to examine how the sectoral outputs in the Netherlands have been affected by changes in the final demands, which includes the effects of the changing trade relationships (see Oosterhaven and Van der Linden, 1997, and Oosterhaven and Hoen, 1998, for decomposition analyses at the EU level). Factors that are distinguished in this part of the decomposition analysis are the following. Changes in the overall level of the final demands. Changes in the destination of the final demands (or the distribution over the final demand categories), covering for example the substitution of exports to Germany for exports to Belgium. Changes in the composition (or product mix) of the final demands, such as the substitution of energy for food products in the exports to Germany. The way in which each of these three factors affect the outputs is termed the level effect, the category effect, and the product mix effect, respectively.

The availability of input-output tables and detailed trade data enable us to get some insight into the effects of changes in both technology and trading relationships on output growth. The plan of this chapter is as follows. Section 10.2 introduces structural decomposition analyses. In section 10.3, the method proposed by Van der Linden and Dietzenbacher (1995, 2000) is illustrated, while in Section 10.4 the decomposition of the final demand categories is set out. This chapter uses constant price interregional data that will be discussed in section 10.5. In section 10.6, the empirical results are presented which are followed by some concluding remarks in section 10.7.

10.2 Structural Decomposition Analysis

Structural decomposition analysis (SDA) is a comparative static method to assess the structural changes in an economy using input-output data. Based on the idea that the change over time in some variable is decomposed into the changes in its determinants, it is widely used as a tool to quantify the underlying sources of the change. For recent applications see Oosterhaven and Van der Linden (1997), Cabrer *et al.* (1998), Cronin and Gold (1998), Oosterhaven and Hoen (1998), Wier (1998), Albala-Bertrand (1999), Alcala *et al.* (1999), Mukhopadyay and Chakraborty (1999), Wier and Hasler (1999), Dietzenbacher *et al.* (2000), Hitomi *et al.* (2000), Jacobsen (2000), Casler (2001), Dietzenbacher (2001), and Milana (2001), while Rose and Casler (1996) give a detailed overview.

In this chapter, we analyze the changes in the outputs. The standard Leontief model is given by $x = Ax + f$, where x denotes the vector of sectoral outputs, A the $n \times n$ matrix of input coefficients and f the vector of final demands. The input coefficients are obtained from the matrix Z of intermediate deliveries. They denote the input of good i per unit of output of good j, that is, $a_{ij} = z_{ij} / x_j$ or $A = Z\hat{x}^{-1}$ in matrix notation, where $\hat{x}$ denotes the diagonal matrix with the outputs on its main diagonal and all other entries equal to zero. The solution for the Leontief model is given by $x = (I - A)^{-1} f = Lf$, where $L \equiv (I - A)^{-1}$ denotes the Leontief inverse. For the decomposition of the changes in the outputs, several equivalent forms may be used. Examples are:

$$\Delta x = (\Delta L) f_1 + L_0 (\Delta f) \tag{10.1}$$

$$\Delta x = (\Delta L) f_0 + L_1 (\Delta f) \tag{10.2}$$

$$\Delta x = (\Delta L) f_1 + L_1 (\Delta f) - (\Delta L)(\Delta f) \tag{10.3}$$

$$\Delta x = (\Delta L) f_0 + L_0 (\Delta f) + (\Delta L)(\Delta f) \tag{10.4}$$

Each of the forms (10.1) and (10.2) adopts different weights for the changes, while each of the forms (10.3) and (10.4) uses the same weights but includes a so-called interaction term. It is clear that the decomposition form is not unique and the number of equivalent forms increases rapidly when the number of determinants exceeds two (as in the present case). Dietzenbacher and Los (1997, 1998) have analyzed the sensitivity across decomposition forms and found that the average of all the forms they considered could be approximated very well by the average of the so-called polar forms. In the present case this means taking the average of the forms (10.1) and (10.2) (which equals the average of (10.3) and (10.4) only in the two determinant case). This results in the following decomposition formula:

$$\Delta x = \tfrac{1}{2}(\Delta L)(f_0 + f_1) + \tfrac{1}{2}(L_0 + L_1)(\Delta f) \tag{10.5}$$

The first term on the right hand side gives the changes in the outputs if the input coefficients had changed (implying a change ΔL in the Leontief inverse) while the final demands had been unchanged. In the same way, the second term reflects the contribution of changes in the final demands by measuring what the output changes would have been if final demands had changed while technology (reflected by the input matrix A) had remained constant.

As was indicated in the introduction, the aim of this chapter is twofold. First, to analyze how the changes in the input matrix A have affected the outputs (the methodology for which is explained in section 10.3). Secondly, to provide some insight in the importance of export relations and the changes therein for a small, open economy like the Netherlands (see section 10.4 for the methodological aspects).

10.3 Applying the RAS Technique

The decomposition form in (10.5) will be further developed into a nested form. That is, in this section the first term will be further decomposed into the underlying sources of the changes in the input coefficients. Note that $\Delta L = L_0(\Delta A)L_1 = L_1(\Delta A)L_0$ and thus:

$$\Delta L = \tfrac{1}{2} L_0(\Delta A)L_1 + \tfrac{1}{2} L_1(\Delta A)L_0 \tag{10.6}$$

Next the changes ΔA in the input coefficients are further decomposed. For this purpose we follow the approach developed in Van der Linden and Dietzenbacher (1995, 2000). Changes in the input coefficients are decomposed into column-specific changes indicating the change in a sector's intermediate input intensity (or productivity as discussed in the introduction), row-specific changes reflecting the average substitution of intermediate inputs between sectors, and cell-specific changes (i.e. the changes that are not explained by the row and column changes).

Column-specific changes imply that the entire column in A_0 for sector j is multiplied by s_j. It is thus assumed that structural changes of this type leave the mix of intermediate inputs unaffected. Due to a process innovation or economies of scale, for example, a unit of output is now produced using the same percentage less of each intermediate input.

It is clear that at the aggregation level of most datasets (including our own), many different forms of structural changes take place simultaneously within a single sector j. The multipliers s_j should therefore be viewed as reflecting average column-specific effects. Yet, it may not be expected that such multipliers can provide an adequate description of all the structural changes that have occurred.

Due to the row-specific changes, the entire row i in A_0 is multiplied by r_i. For example, a product innovation may imply that each sector uses the same percentage less of intermediate input i. In the same way, some other input may be used more in each sector. Again, the effects described by the multipliers r_i are average substitution effects and it is not to be expected that all types of substitution follow such a simple pattern. All changes that are not captured by the uniform row and column multiplications are accounted for by the cell-specific changes, as we will see shortly.

Since the changes in the intermediate input intensities and the average substitution effects occur simultaneously, the matrix A_0 is affected as follows:

$$\tilde{a}_{ij}^1 = r_i a_{ij}^0 s_j \text{ or } \tilde{A}_1 = \hat{r} A_0 \hat{s} \tag{10.7}$$

where $\hat{r}$ and $\hat{s}$ are the diagonal matrices with the multipliers r_i and s_j.

As mentioned before, it may not be expected that the column-specific and the row-specific changes alone are able to provide a full description of all the changes that have taken place. In other words, A_1 will differ from $\tilde{A}_1$. These differences are the cell-specific changes that cannot be captured by column-specific and row-specific changes alone. Hence, the cell-specific changes are defined as:

$$\varepsilon_{ij} = a_{ij}^1 - \tilde{a}_{ij}^1 = a_{ij}^1 - r_i a_{ij}^0 s_j \text{ or } \varepsilon = A_1 - \tilde{A}_1 = A_1 - \hat{r} A_0 \hat{s} \tag{10.8}$$

Next we have to find the multipliers r_i and s_j. Since both the column-specific and the row-specific changes are average effects, it is required that they yield the correct result on average. That is, it is required that the matrix of intermediate deliveries corresponding to $\tilde{A}_1$ (i.e. $\tilde{A}_1\hat{x}_1$) has the correct column and row sums. Let e denote the n-element summation vector, i.e. $e' = (1,\ldots,1)$ where a prime is used to indicate transposition. The correct row sums are given by $Z_1 e = A_1 x_1 \equiv u_1$ and the correct column sums by $e'Z_1 = e'A_1\hat{x}_1 \equiv v_1'$. The requirements to be fulfilled by the multipliers r_i and s_j are then as follows:

$$\tilde{A}_1 x_1 = \hat{r}A_0\hat{s}x_1 = u_1 \text{ and } e'\tilde{A}_1\hat{x}_1 = e'\hat{r}A_0\hat{s}\hat{x}_1 = v_1' \tag{10.9}$$

The problem of finding the multipliers r_i and s_j under the restrictions in (10.9) may be solved iteratively by the well-known RAS method as developed in Stone (1961). This method was developed for updating matrices of intermediate deliveries (or input matrices) given their row and column totals. A detailed description is given in Miller and Blair (1985), while more technical aspects are dealt with in Bacharach (1970) and MacGill (1977). It should be mentioned that the economic background of the RAS technique, i.e. interpreting the column multipliers as intermediate input intensity effects and the row multipliers as substitution effects, has been criticized in e.g. Lecomber (1975) and Miernyk (1977). Also the performance of the RAS method for purposes of updating has been questioned, e.g. by Allen and Gossling (1975) and Lynch (1986). Van der Linden and Dietzenbacher (2000), however, refute this critique by arguing that the row-specific and the column-specific multipliers should not be considered as the sole determinants of the changes. Once the cell-specific changes are taken into account, the RAS method may well be used for descriptive purposes. The results then indicate how much of the actual changes that have taken place can be explained from (column-specific) changes in intermediate intensities and (row-specific) average substitution effects alone. For other recent contributions see Golan *et al.* (1994), de Mesnard (1994, 1997), Polenske (1997), Dietzenbacher and Hoen (1998), Toh (1998), Gilchrist and St. Louis (1999), Andréosso-O'Callaghan and Yue (2000), and Jalili (2000).

Finally, it should be noted that the solution of (10.9) is not unique. That is, if the multipliers r_i and s_j satisfy (10.9), also the multipliers λr_i and s_j/λ do, for any arbitrary value λ. To overcome this problem the results are scaled such that the sum of all average substitution effects r_i is zero. In other words, the total use of intermediate inputs is the same with substitution as it would have been without substitution. This yields:

$$(r'A_0\hat{s}x_1)/(e'A_0\hat{s}x_1) = 1 \tag{10.10}$$

From (10.8) we may now write $\Delta A = \hat{r}A_0\hat{s} + \varepsilon - A_0$. Using the same averaging procedure that led to (10.5), we may now decompose ΔA. Note that A_0 may be written as $\hat{r}_0 A_0 \hat{s}_0$ with $\hat{r}_0 = \hat{s}_0 = I$. This yields:

$$\Delta A = \tfrac{1}{2}(\hat{r} - I)A_0(\hat{s} + I) + \tfrac{1}{2}(\hat{r} + I)A_0(\hat{s} - I) + \varepsilon \tag{10.11}$$

Substituting (10.11) into (10.6), and substituting the resulting expression for ΔL into (10.5) implies that its term $\tfrac{1}{2}(\Delta L)(f_0 + f_1)$ can be decomposed into the following three terms:

$$\tfrac{1}{8}[L_0(\hat{r}-I)A_0(\hat{s}+I)L_1 + L_1(\hat{r}-I)A_0(\hat{s}+I)L_0](f_0+f_1) \tag{10.12a}$$

$$\tfrac{1}{8}[L_0(\hat{r}+I)A_0(\hat{s}-I)L_1 + L_1(\hat{r}+I)A_0(\hat{s}-I)L_0](f_0+f_1) \tag{10.12b}$$

$$\tfrac{1}{4}[L_0\varepsilon L_1 + L_1\varepsilon L_0](f_0+f_1) \tag{10.12c}$$

Equation (10.12a) gives the changes in the outputs due to the changes in the intermediate input intensities (i.e. column-specific changes). Expression (10.12b) describes the consequences of the average substitution effects (i.e. row-specific changes), and equation (10.12c) indicates the effects due to cell-specific changes.

10.4 Decomposing the Final Demands

In this section we further decompose the second term in equation (10.5). We distinguish between changes in the level of final demands, changes in the categorical distribution and changes in the product mix of final demands (see also Lin and Polenske, 1995). The level of final demands is given by the scalar g which measures the total amount of all expenditures for final demands. The empirical application in Section 10.6 is based on an input-output table that records 24 sectors and that allows to distinguish the following nine final demand categories. Exports to Germany, Belgium, France, Italy and Denmark, exports to other members of European Union, exports to the rest of the world, consumption by households, and other final demands. The categorical distribution is given by the vector d and its element d_k denotes the part of the total final demand expenditures that is spent by category k (=1,...,9), with $\Sigma_k d_k = 1$. The product mix within the final demand categories is given by the 24×9 bridge matrix B. Its element b_{ik} gives the part of the final demands in category k that is spent on products of sector i. Note that the column sums of the bridge matrix add to one. The final demand vector f can now be written as gBd. Note that the separate final demand categories can be singled out by using $gB\hat{d}$ instead, in which case the final demand vector is obtained as $f = gB\hat{d}e$. Following Dietzenbacher and Los (1998) the two polar decompositions of Δf are as follows

$$\Delta f = (\Delta g)B_0\hat{d}_0e + g_1(\Delta B)\hat{d}_0e + g_1B_1(\Delta\hat{d})e \quad \Delta f = (\Delta g)B_1\hat{d}_1e + g_0(\Delta B)\hat{d}_1e + g_0B_0(\Delta\hat{d})e$$

Substituting the average of these two expressions into equation (10.5) implies that its second term $\tfrac{1}{2}(L_0+L_1)(\Delta f)$ can be decomposed further into the following three components:

$$\tfrac{1}{4}(L_0+L_1)(\Delta g)(B_0\hat{d}_0 + B_1\hat{d}_1)e \tag{10.13a}$$

$$\tfrac{1}{4}(L_0+L_1)[g_1(\Delta B)\hat{d}_0 + g_0(\Delta B)\hat{d}_1]e \tag{10.13b}$$

$$\tfrac{1}{4}(L_0+L_1)(g_1B_1 + g_0B_0)(\Delta\hat{d})e \tag{10.13c}$$

Equation (10.13a) gives the level effect, i.e. the change in the outputs due to the change in the level of the final demands. The category effect in expression (10.13b) shows how changes in the categorical distribution of the final demands affect the outputs. The product mix effect in equation (10.13c) indicates the effects of changes in the product mix of the final demands on the outputs.

It should be mentioned that the RAS method could have been applied also for the decomposition of the final demands. In that case, let F denote the 24×9 final demand matrix, with $f = Fe$. The RAS technique then yields $\tilde{F}_1 = \hat{\rho} F_0 \hat{\sigma}$. The row-specific multiplier ρ_i again reflects the average substitution between products and the column-specific multiplier σ_j covers the category effect, assuming that the product mix within this category remains constant. Cell-specific changes are obtained from $F_1 = \tilde{F}_1 + \delta$ and Δf in (10.5) is given by $\hat{\rho} F_0 \sigma + \delta e - F_0 e$. The typical constraints in (10.9) are for the present case given by $\hat{\rho} F_0 \sigma = F_1 e$ and $\rho' F_0 \hat{\sigma} = e' F_1$, respectively. The scaling similar to (10.10) yields $(\rho' F_0 \sigma)/(e' F_0 \sigma) = 1$.

The reason we have not adopted the RAS approach in decomposing the final demands, is that the assumption underlying the interpretation of the row-specific multipliers ρ_i is questionable. It means that, on average, each category changes the use of good i by the same percentage. In other words, this change is assumed to hold for consumption by Dutch households, for exports to each destination,[3] and for other purposes (including government consumption, domestic investments and inventory stock changes). Given the large diversity of these categories, we feel that assuming a uniform change in the entire row of F is much less plausible than it is for the input matrix A. It is unlikely that Dutch consumers, investors, the government and importers in each of the distinguished destinations, all have a similar pattern of average substitution between products.

10.5 Description of the Data

The empirical application in the next section is a decomposition of output growth in the Netherlands between 1975 and 1985. Since we want to focus on two aspects, *viz.* a further breakdown of the changes in the input coefficients and the effects of a changing trade pattern, the data need to satisfy certain criteria. For the decomposition of the input matrix it is required that the data are in constant prices because otherwise changes in input coefficients reflect price changes as well as technical changes. To analyze the effects of changes in the trade pattern it is important to have sufficiently detailed information on the exports. To this end we have adapted the intercountry input-output tables for the European Union (EU).

These intercountry input-output tables have been constructed at the University of Groningen on the basis of the Eurostat harmonized national input-output tables (see Eurostat, 1979) and harmonized international trade data (Eurostat, 1990). Details on the construction are given in Van der Linden and Oosterhaven (1995), Van der Linden (1998) and Hoen (1999). We have used the tables for 1985 and for 1975 in constant

[3] Note that exports are used for various purposes, such as foreign consumption, investments and as intermediate inputs in foreign production processes.

prices (in ECUs) of 1985. The tables give all trade flows within and between six members of the European Union (The Netherlands, Germany, France, Belgium, Italy and Denmark) for a 25-sector classification scheme (see Appendix 10.A). Final demands consist of "household consumption", "government consumption", "capital stock formation", "inventory stock changes", "exports to non-included EU members" and "exports to other countries".

In this analysis we will only be focussing on the Netherlands and we therefore have to adapt the data accordingly. The matrix Z gives the domestic intermediate deliveries (i.e. within the Netherlands). The final demands consist of domestic household consumption, exports to each of the five included EU members (covering the deliveries to production sectors and to final demand categories), total exports to non-included EU members, total exports to other countries, and other domestic final demands (i.e. government consumption, capital stock formation and inventory stock changes in the Netherlands). The above setup is also known as the input-output table *without* imports (see Konijn, 1994). By constructing the data in this way we are in fact assuming that all imports are non-competitive, i.e. that the imported goods have been produced in a different way than the domestic goods.

As a check of the results we also ran the decomposition using the input-output table *with* imports. In this case, all imports are assumed to be competitive and are added to the intermediate input matrix Z. To keep the table balanced the imports have to be subtracted from the final demand and we therefore get *net* exports (export minus imports) for all the trading partners specified. The results of the decomposition for this so-called competitive imports case are given in Appendix 10.B.

Due to data problems, we had to aggregate the sectors 8 ("office and data processing machines") and 9 ("electrical goods") into a single sector for the calculations in the text. The calculations displayed in Appendix 10.B for the competitive imports case did not require this additional aggregation.

A remarkable entry in the data, is the negative diagonal element (-3057) in the matrix of intermediate deliveries for the Netherlands in 1985, for sector 17 ("recovery, repair services, wholesale and retail trade"). Negative elements do occur sporadically in the final demand categories of the official input-output statistics, in which case they are attributable to the accounting of (transport or trade) margins. Also the row of indirect taxes minus subsidies in input-output tables occasionally records negative entries when sectors are highly subsidized. Inclusion of negative elements in the intermediate deliveries, however, is economically nonsense because it implies that a negative amount of an input is required in the production technology of the sector. To overcome this problem, we have compared the column elements of the sector in question to those in other countries. It turned out that the production technology (excluding the negative diagonal element) used in the Netherlands was very similar to that of Denmark and France. An estimate of the Dutch diagonal element (1300) was then obtained on the basis of the French and Danish technologies in 1985 and was inserted into the Dutch table. Although no adaptation would be entirely satisfactory, it should be noted that adjustments of this figure influence the outcomes only marginally, as was indicated by a sensitivity analysis. It is obvious that, as a consequence of this adaptation, any specific result for this sector should be interpreted only with great care.

10.6 Empirical Results

The implementation of the decomposition described in Sections 10.3 and 10.4, was applied to the Dutch part of the intercountry input-output tables for the EU for the period 1975-1985. Table 10.1 provides an overview of the final demand categories in both years. The first two columns give the absolute amounts of the exports of Dutch goods and services to each of the other five member countries, to the rest of the EU, and to the rest of the world (ROW), and the Dutch expenditures for household consumption and for other final demand purposes (government consumption, domestic capital stock formation and inventory stock changes). In order to get an impression of the Dutch trade relationships, the last four columns give the corresponding import figures.

Table 10.1 Summary of final demand and import changes in the period 1975-1985 for the Netherlands

	Total final demands (1000 million ECU)		Relative share in final demands		Relative share in exports		Imports (1000 million ECU)		Relative share of imports	
	1975	1985	1975	1985	1975	1985	1975	1985	1975	1985
Germany	22409	22629	13%	11%	33%	25%	6566	8921	15%	15%
France	5643	7392	3%	3%	8%	8%	2516	2884	6%	5%
Italy	2858	4676	2%	2%	4%	5%	964	1122	2%	2%
Belgium	7307	12423	4%	6%	11%	14%	2874	4544	7%	8%
Denmark	1624	1212	1%	1%	2%	1%	206	368	0%	1%
Rest EU	7580	20831	5%	10%	11%	23%	5177	6255	12%	11%
ROW	21099	20825	13%	10%	31%	23%	24093	33845	57%	58%
Consumption	58513	77875	35%	36%						
Other FD	40284	46336	24%	22%						
Total	167316	214197	100%	100%	100%	100%	42397	57938	100%	100%

The table clearly shows the Dutch economy's dependence on exports (particularly with Germany) which comprise over 40% of the total final demand in both years. The single most important final demand category in table 10.1, however, is the delivery of products to consumers, which accounts for over a third of the total. Taking a closer look at the exports over the 1975-1985 period, we note two opposite shifts. First, the share of exports going to other EU countries has substantially increased, which is consistent with the increasing economic integration in this period. The second change is the decreasing importance of Germany and of the ROW as destinations for the exports. Despite the fact that in absolute terms the exports remain approximately constant, their share in the total has diminished significantly. Another remarkable feature in table 10.1 is the regional spread of the imports. Whereas the ROW plays a relatively modest role as far as Dutch exports are concerned, it is by far the most important origin of Dutch imports (almost 60%). Also note that, in contrast to the export figures, the import shares are remarkably stable over time. The table shows that the Netherlands have had very large trade surpluses with all European trading partners (amounting to 29117 in 1975 and 45068 in 1985), but run a trade deficit with the rest of the world (2994 and 13020, respectively).

The results of the decomposition of technical changes using the RAS technique are presented together with the total effect of final demand changes in table 10.2. The total technology effects and the total final demand effects are obtained by applying equation (10.5). The further decomposition of the total technology effects follows equations (10.12). That is, the substitution effects are given in equation (10.12b), the intermediate input intensity effects in (10.12a), and the effects of cell-specific changes in (10.12c). The percentages in brackets are the shares of the effects relative to the row total. Note that a positive (negative) percentage indicates that the corresponding effect has the same (respectively the opposite) sign as the total output change, be it an increase or decrease. The complete sector classification is given in Appendix 10.A.

Table 10.2 Specific technology and total final demand effects at sector level for the Netherlands (1975-1985)

	TECHNOLOGY EFFECTS								FINAL DEMAND EFFECTS		TOTAL
	Total		Substitution		Intermediate input intensity		Cell-specific Substitution				
1 Agri	1947	27%	3872	53%	-1964	-27%	38	1%	5393	73%	7340
2 Ener	-7225	134%	-12178	225%	4931	-91%	22	0%	1816	-34%	-5409
3 Meta	262	48%	-185	-34%	440	81%	7	1%	283	52%	545
4 Mine	-266	-201%	-1221	-925%	938	710%	18	14%	398	301%	132
5 Chem	826	12%	540	8%	448	6%	-162	-2%	6342	88%	7168
6 MetP	-99	-13%	-1130	-149%	1024	135%	8	1%	858	113%	760
7 AlMa	-63	-50%	-460	-369%	386	310%	12	9%	187	150%	125
8 ODMa + 9 ElGo	1297	47%	1006	37%	409	15%	-118	-4%	1456	53%	2754
10 TrEq	357	95%	182	48%	144	38%	31	8%	19	5%	376
11 Food	3897	29%	6047	46%	-2215	-17%	65	0%	9390	71%	13286
12 Text	108	-27%	-11	3%	129	-32%	-9	2%	-516	127%	-408
13 Pape	359	12%	-309	-11%	809	28%	-141	-5%	2562	88%	2921
14 Rubb	128	16%	-144	-18%	292	35%	-19	-2%	695	84%	823
15 Oman	-34	86%	-486	1217%	498	-1246%	-46	115%	-6	14%	-40
16 Buil	1827	135%	-1170	-86%	2446	181%	551	41%	-473	-35%	1354
17 ReTr	4605	34%	3277	24%	1396	10%	-67	0%	8840	66%	13445
18 Lodg	824	28%	671	23%	219	7%	-66	-2%	2135	72%	2959
19 InTr	-655	-138%	-2170	-458%	1482	313%	33	7%	1129	238%	474
20 MATr	-26	-2%	-154	-12%	116	9%	12	1%	1303	102%	1277
21 Auxi	203	20%	-376	-38%	539	54%	39	4%	799	80%	1001
22 Comm	27	3%	-684	-79%	718	83%	-6	-1%	835	97%	862
23 Cred	-473	-20%	-4530	-190%	4083	171%	-27	-1%	2862	120%	2389
24 Omse	6823	43%	5122	32%	1790	11%	-89	-1%	9020	57%	15843
25 PSer	4315	22%	3590	18%	703	4%	22	0%	15357	78%	19672
Total	18965	21%	-901	-1%	19760	22%	106	0%	70685	79%	89651

The results in table 10.2 show that, consistent with most SDA literature, the total final demand effects (79%) are far greater than the total influence of changes in the technology (21%). Nevertheless, the influence of changes in technology is still quite sizeable when compared to SDA literature over similar time periods. Note that 82% of all output changes due to the technology effects, takes place in the services sectors (17-25).

Looking at the column totals, the overall substitution effect is negligible, as might have been expected. Due to the scaling in equation (10.10), the average input coefficient is not affected by substitution. As a consequence, it is likely that the corresponding effect on total output is negligible. Also the total effect of the cell-specific changes is extremely small, which even holds for almost all sectors separately. This implies that the decomposition of input coefficient changes, into row-specific substitution effects and column-specific intermediate input intensity effects, provides a most adequate description of the actual changes. This reinforces the conclusion in Van der Linden and Dietzenbacher (1995, 2000) that the RAS method may be a useful tool for descriptive purposes.

Table 10.3 Row and column multipliers and input coefficient totals

	Multipliers		Column totals		Row totals	
	r	S	1975	1985	1975	1985
1 Agri	1.25	0.72	0.46	0.52	0.38	0.44
2 Ener	0.60	1.23	0.27	0.23	1.53	1.00
3 Meta	0.93	1.27	0.25	0.26	0.17	0.20
4 Mine	0.59	1.14	0.36	0.37	0.20	0.15
5 Chem	1.15	1.09	0.39	0.37	0.29	0.36
6 MetP	0.71	1.22	0.28	0.34	0.33	0.34
7 AIMa	0.69	1.35	0.25	0.34	0.16	0.14
8 ODMa +9 ElGo	2.29	1.50	0.15	0.24	0.08	0.18
10 TrEq	1.27	1.33	0.32	0.41	0.07	0.13
11 Food	2.10	0.88	0.49	0.55	0.46	0.60
12 Text	0.97	1.26	0.21	0.29	0.11	0.11
13 Pape	0.90	0.88	0.42	0.40	0.47	0.42
14 Rubb	0.86	1.01	0.27	0.30	0.10	0.13
15 Oman	0.71	1.06	0.26	0.30	0.15	0.13
16 Buil	0.81	1.50	0.38	0.49	0.44	0.44
17 ReTr	1.57	1.63	0.27	0.37	0.57	0.96
18 Lodg	2.42	0.65	0.43	0.43	0.04	0.10
19 InTr	0.46	1.13	0.28	0.33	0.17	0.13
20 MATr	0.62	0.83	0.20	0.17	0.03	0.05
21 Auxi	0.71	1.23	0.19	0.29	0.09	0.14
22 Comm	0.76	1.03	0.10	0.13	0.19	0.18
23 Cred	0.82	1.17	0.78	0.80	0.79	0.73
24 Omse	2.19	1.56	0.13	0.20	0.37	0.90
25 Pser	2.43	1.11	0.18	0.25	0.15	0.43

The changes in the intermediate input intensities have led to a considerable increase of the total output. At the overall macro level, it appears that the use of domestic intermediate deliveries per unit of output has increased by 15% from 0.307

in 1975 to 0.353 in 1985. A quick calculation in which the economy is assumed to be made up of only a single sector, yields an increase in the (scalar) Leontief inverse $(1/1-a)$ from 1.443 in 1975 to 1.546 in 1985. Multiplying the difference by the average of the total final demands (which are 167,316 in 1975 and 214,197 in 1985) gives an output increase due to the intermediate input intensity change of 19570, which is extremely close to the result in table 10.2. In answering the question what has caused this change in the intermediate input intensity, it turns out that the gross value added per unit of output fell by 9% from 0.517 in 1975 to 0.472 in 1985. This implies that the imports per unit of output have been more or less constant (i.e. 0.176 and 0.175, respectively). So, at least at the overall level, it is not the case that the intermediate input intensity has increased because domestic intermediate goods have been substituted for imported intermediate goods.

At the sectoral level, the picture is much more varied of course. The substitution effects can easily be traced back to the row-specific multipliers r_i, which are listed in table 10.3. The substitution effect is positive whenever $r_i > 1$, and negative if $r_i < 1$. It should be noted that the figures in table 10.2 present absolute changes. When these changes are taken as a percentage of the sector's total output, their pattern appears to be much in line with the pattern of the r_i's.

Explaining the intermediate input intensity effects at the sectoral level is much more complex. For a single sector j, it certainly is insufficient to consider just the multiplier s_j. Only when the sector's diagonal element is very dominant, this may provide an adequate explanation. Most sectors, however, require a much more intricate explanation. For example, for agriculture (sector 1) it turns out that the diagonal element of the matrix A is only 0.06 in 1975, while the input into the food industry (sector 11) yields an input coefficient of 0.29. Since the food industry reduces its intermediate input intensity itself and since it delivers a large amount to final demand categories, this certainly contributes substantially to the large negative effect found for agriculture. In the same way, the small s_j for agriculture is important for the negative intermediate input intensity effects on the food industry, because the inputs from the food industry into agriculture yield an input coefficient of 0.21. Another interesting sector in this respect is lodging (sector 18), which had the smallest s_j. Still, the effects of changing intermediate input intensities on its output are positive and even amount to 10% of its 1975 output. It turns out that this sector's diagonal element is zero and all the other input coefficients in its row are positive, although fairly small. When considering the intermediate input intensity effects, however, almost all of these input coefficients increase, which explains why the resulting output change for lodging is positive.

A particularly interesting sector to examine in the period under consideration is the energy sector (2 – "fuel and power products"). The price shocks that accompanied the oil crises of the 1970's are the most likely reasons for the shifts in production technologies over this period. The influence of the oil shocks is clearly visible in the results at sector level, the decrease in the output of the energy sector (by 12% from 45722 in 1975 to 40313 in 1985) is most striking. The results show that the substitution effect is very large, *i.e.* the overall substitution trends in the economy have resulted in a large decrease in the use of energy as an input. Clearly the energy price increases and price changes in the sectors that are highly dependent on energy inputs (such as metals, 3; minerals, 4; and inland transport, 19) are consistent with these substitution effects. The large intermediate input intensity effects on the output of the energy sector, reflect that almost each sector depends on energy at least to some extent (the average input coefficient in row 2 was 0.06 in 1975 and 0.04 in 1985). Since 19 out of 24 sectors use more intermediate inputs, this affects the output of the energy sector considerably.

In explaining the results of table 10.2, we have used the multipliers r_i and s_j which are presented in table 10.3. For most of the sectors it is found, at least to some extent, that s_j is larger than one if the input coefficients in column j have increased. Using the column sums of the matrix A of input coefficients for this purpose, this relationship is observed for 19 out of 24 sectors (exceptions are the sectors 1, 2, 5, 11, and 18). In the same way, if the input coefficients in row i increase, one might expect r_i to be larger than one. On the basis of the row sums of A, this holds for 18 sectors (exceptions are the sectors 6, 12, 14, 16, 20, and 21). Clearly, these relationships are far too simple to give a full explanation, because they neglect the fact that row and column changes occur simultaneously. The RAS method takes full account of this simultaneous nature of the changes. As a consequence, however, explaining the observed outcomes for the multipliers r_i and s_j often requires the cumbersome task to consider the (changes in the) entire rows and columns, instead of just focusing on summary statistics such as the row and column totals.

The column-specific multipliers s_j in table 10.3 show that five sectors (1, 11, 13, 18, and 20) have decreased their (domestic) intermediate input intensity between 1975 and 1985. For "paper and printing products" (sector 13) and "maritime and air transport services" (sector 20), this involves a substitution towards the use of imported intermediate inputs. The import coefficients of these two sectors increase from 0.18 to 0.22 and from 0.38 to 0.52, respectively. The row-specific multipliers r_i indicate the substitution patterns amongst the intermediate inputs. It should be borne in mind that we have applied a scaling such that the overall substitution effect for the entire economy is zero. Table 10.3 shows substitution away from energy (sector 2) and minerals (4), away from heavy manufacturing such as metal products (6) and heavy machinery (7), away from all three transport sectors (19-21), and away from some of the services sectors (22, 23). This is counterbalanced by substitution towards the "computer" sector (8+9), towards the food industry (11), towards lodging (18), and towards two of the largest service sectors (24, 25).

The results for the decomposition of the final demands are presented in table 10.4. The level effects are obtained from equation (10.13a), the category effects from (10.13b), and the product mix effects from (10.13c). Since the final demand block consists of seven export vectors, one household consumption vector and a vector with other final demands, the full representation of results would be given by 27 vectors of sectoral output changes. The figures in table 10.4 provide the total output changes obtained from summing the sectoral outcomes.

Looking at the column totals in table 10.4, it turns out that the level effects explain almost the entire output changes that are due to final demand changes. Note that both the category effects and the product mix effects describe the consequences of reshuffling the total final demand, between categories and between products respectively. Therefore, one might have expected the contribution of these two effects to be relatively close to zero, at the overall level.

Table 10.4 Results of the final demand decomposition

	LEVEL EFFECT		CATEGORY EFFECT		PRODUCT MIX EFFECT		TOTAL
Germany	8386	648%	-8086	-625%	993	77%	1294
France	2454	86%	230	8%	176	6%	2860
Italy	1487	50%	1477	50%	-15	0%	2950
Belgium	3590	48%	4117	55%	-223	-3%	7485
Denmark	526	-118%	-1144	257%	173	-39%	-446
Rest EU	5010	24%	14764	71%	1017	5%	20791
ROW	7836	2458%	-8269	-2594%	752	236%	319
Consumption	25358	91%	4004	14%	-1527	-5%	27835
Other FD	15361	202%	-6675	-88%	-1088	-14%	7598
Total	70008	99%	418	1%	258	0%	70685

The results for the category effects clearly reflect the observations we made on the basis of table 10.1. The final demand share of the exports to Germany and to the rest of the world, and the share for other final demand purposes all declined. In contrast, the share of the exports to the rest of the EU and to Belgium, and the share of household consumption increased. The findings for the product mix effects indicate to what extent the total output has been affected by the change in the products supplied to the nine final demand categories. At first sight, it seems as if this product substitution is particularly strong for the products that households consume. Closer inspection, however, shows that the product mix effect of household consumption is only very moderate when the size of this consumption (see table 10.1) is taken into account. When the figures are corrected for size, it appears that the product mix effect of the exports to Denmark and to the rest of the EU are the largest.

10.6.1 A Comparison with the Competitive Imports Case

When the results above for the non-competitive imports case are contrasted with those in Appendix 10.B for the competitive imports case (i.e. where all imports are considered to be competitive), a number of clear-cut differences arise. The most important is the increase of the intermediate input intensity effects, the total of which nearly doubles due to the shift of imports from the primary inputs to the intermediate inputs. The total technology effect also increases significantly, from 21% to 35%, which is largely due to the fact that the imports have been subtracted from the final demand categories and have therefore reduced the final demand effects. Note that the input coefficients matrix A becomes larger and therefore also the Leontief inverse L. Although the final demands decline, the increase in L more than compensates this, due to the non-linear nature of inversion.

To give an impression, we carry out some "notepad calculations" again for the case where all sectors are aggregated into one. The input coefficient was 0.307 in 1975 and 0.353 in 1985, under the non-competitive imports assumption. When all imports are assumed to be competitive, the single input coefficient a raises to 0.483 in 1975 and 0.528 in 1985. The corresponding scalar Leontief inverses become 1.934 and 2.119, respectively. The increase in the Leontief inverse between 1975 and 1985 was 0.103

under the non-competitive imports assumption and amounts to 0.185 under the competitive imports assumption. As a consequence, the total final demand effect yields 63,509 and the total technology effect[4] amounts to 25,926. For the non-competitive imports case, the total effects in table 10.2 were fairly close to the calculations for the single-sectored economy. In the competitive imports case this no longer holds. The explanation is that for some products the final demands have become negative now that exports are net exports. These negative final demands have a considerable impact on the sectoral results, while the outcome of the "notepad calculation" is comparable to sectoral calculations with average, and thus positive, final demands.

At the sector level, one of the more surprising results is the change in sign of the substitution effect for the sectors 8 ("office and data processing machines") and 9 ("electrical goods") when the results in table 10.2 are compared with those in table B.1 in Appendix 10.B. A negative substitution effect seems counterintuitive for these "computer" sectors which one would have expected to be expanding already in that period.

The final demand effects in table B.2 cannot be directly compared to the effects in table 10.4 because of the adjustment for imports. This means that the export effects of all the trading partners are now the effects of changes in the *net* exports (i.e. the difference between the exports and the imports). Some of the final demand changes are therefore negative (notably the net exports to Germany and to the rest of the world). The outcomes for the category effects in table B.2 are in line with the observations in table 10.1 whenever net exports (and in particular the contribution of each category to the total net exports) are considered.

The assumption of all imports being either competitive or non-competitive is unrealistic. Unfortunately the present data set does not distinguish between the two types of import. What would be necessary for a satisfactory decomposition of the technology and trade would be knowledge of the actual competitive and non-competitive imports of the Netherlands.

10.7 Conclusions

In this chapter, we have demonstrated that the RAS decomposition of technology (as suggested in Van der Linden and Dietzenbacher, 1995, 2000) can be implemented in a structural decomposition analysis and have applied it to the technological changes over the period 1975-1985 for the Netherlands. The results show that the total technological effect is quite significant particularly for the results of the input-output table *with* imports. The oil crises and energy price shocks are likely explanations for these large shifts in production technologies and the substitution effect away from energy is particularly large. The cell-specific effects are generally very minor which indicates that, in a period of such extreme technological change, the average substitution and average intermediate input intensity effects provide an adequate description of the technological effects.

[4] For a single-sectored economy, the substitution effect and the effect of a cell-specific change are both zero.

The decomposition of the final demand effects showed that the changes in the exports to Germany and to the countries outside the EU have decreased output, while the growth in exports to other EU nations has spurred output.

Improvement of the data is required to distinguish between competitive and non-competitive imports. This would allow for a more appropriate decomposition of the *technical* coefficients instead of decomposing the (domestic) *input* coefficients as was done in this study. If such data were available, the intermediate input intensity effect could in fact be directly related to the productivity effect (with respect to the primary inputs).

References

Albala-Bertrand, J.M. 1999. "Structural change in Chile: 1960-90." *Economic Systems Research*, 11, 301-319.

Alcala, R., G. Antille, and E. Fontela. 1999. "Technical change in the private consumption converter." *Economic Systems Research*, 11, 389-400.

Allen, R.I.G. and W.F. Gossling. (eds) 1975. *Estimating and Projecting Input-Output Coefficients*. London, Input-Output Publishing Company.

Andréosso-O'Callaghan, B. and G. Yue. 2000. "An analysis of structural change in China using biproportional methods." *Economic Systems Research*, 12, 99-111.

Bacharach, M. 1970. *Biproportional Matrices and Input-Output Change*. Cambridge, Cambridge University Press.

Cabrer, B., D. Contreras, and A. Sancho. 1998. "Prices revisited: their effects on industrial structure." *Economic Systems Research*, 10, 31-43.

Casler, S.D. 2001. "Interaction terms and structural decomposition: an application to the defense cost of oil." In M.L. Lahr and E. Dietzenbacher (eds). *Input-Output Analysis: Frontiers and Extensions*. London, Palgrave (forthcoming).

Cronin, F.J. and M. Gold. 1998. "Analytical problems in decomposing the system-wide effects of sectoral technical change."*Economic Systems Research*, 10, 325-336.

Dietzenbacher, E. 2001. "An intercountry decomposition of output growth in EC countries." In M.L. Lahr and E. Dietzenbacher (eds). *Input-Output Analysis: Frontiers and Extensions*. London, Palgrave (forthcoming).

Dietzenbacher, E. and A.R. Hoen. 1998. "Deflation of input-output tables from the user's point of view: a heuristic approach." *Review of Income and Wealth*, 44, 111-122.

Dietzenbacher, E., A.R. Hoen, and B. Los. 2000. "Labor productivity in Western Europe 1975-1985: an intercountry, interindustry analysis." *Journal of Regional Science*, 40, 425-452.

Dietzenbacher, E. and J.A. van der Linden. 1997. "Sectoral and spatial linkages in the EC production structure." *Journal of Regional Science*, 37, 235-257.

Dietzenbacher, E., J.A. van der Linden, and A.E. Steenge. 1993. "The regional extraction method: applications to the European Community," *Economic Systems Research*, 5, 185-206.

Dietzenbacher, E. and B. Los. 1997. "Analyzing decomposition analyses." In A. Simonovits and A.E. Steenge (eds). *Prices, Growth and Cycles*. London, MacMillan, pp. 108-131.

Dietzenbacher, E. and B. Los. 1998. "Structural decomposition techniques: sense and sensitivity." *Economic Systems Research*, 10, 307-323.

Eurostat (1979) *European System of Integrated Economic Accounts, ESA*. 2nd edition. Luxembourg, Eurostat.

Eurostat (1990) *External Trade Statistics: User's Guide*. Luxembourg, Eurostat.

Gilchrist, D.A. and L.V. St Louis. 1999. "Completing input-output tables using partial information, with an application to Canadian data." *Economic Systems Research*, 11, 185-193.

Golan, A., G. Judge, and S. Robinson. 1994. "Recovering information from incomplete or partial multisectoral economic data." *Review of Economics and Statistics*, 76, 541-549.

Hitomi, K., Y. Okuyama, G.J.D. Hewings, and M. Sonis. 2000. "The role of interregional trade in generating change in the regional economies of Japan, 1980-1990." *Economic Systems Research*, 12, 515-536.

Hoen, A.R. 1999. *An Input-Output Analysis of European Integration*. Capelle a/d IJssel, Labyrint Publication, Ph.D. thesis.

Jacobsen, H.K. 2000. "Energy demand, structural change and trade: a decomposition analysis of the Danish manufacturing industry." *Economic Systems Research*, 12, 319-343.

Jalili, A.R. 2000. "Comparison of two methods of identifying input-output coefficients for exogenous estimation." *Economic Systems Research*, 12, 113-129.

Konijn, P.J.A. 1994. *The make and use of commodities by industries: On the compilation of input-output data form the national statistics*. Faculteit Bestuurskunde, Universiteit Twente, Enschede, the Netherlands, Ph.D. thesis.

Lecomber, J.R.C. 1975. "A critique of methods of adjusting, updating and projecting matrices." In R.I.G. Allen and W.F. Gossling (eds). *Estimating and Projecting Input-Output Coefficients*. London, Input-Output Publishing Company, pp. 43-56.

Lin, X. and K.R. Polenske. 1995. "Input-output anatomy of China's energy-demand change." *Economic Systems Research*, 7, 67-84.

Linden, J.A. van der. 1998. *Interdependence and Specialisation in the European Union*. Capelle a/d IJssel, Labyrint Publication, Ph.D. thesis.

Linden, J.A. van der and E. Dietzenbacher, E. 1995. "The nature of changes in the EU cost structure of production 1965-1985: an RAS approach." In H. Armstrong and R. Vickerman (eds). *Convergence and Divergence among European Regions*. London, Pion, pp. 124-139.

Linden, J.A. van der and E. Dietzenbacher. 2000. "The determinants of structural change in the European Union: a new application of RAS." *Environment and Planning A*, 32, 2205-2229.

Linden, J.A. Van der and J. Oosterhaven. 1995. "Intercountry EC input-output relations: construction method and main results for 1965-1985." *Economic Systems Research*, 7, 249-269.

Lynch, R.G. 1986. "An assessment of the RAS method for updating input-output tables." In I. Sohn (ed.). *Readings in Input-Output Analysis: Theory and Applications*. New York, Oxford University Press, pp. 271-284.

MacGill, S.M. 1977 "Theoretical properties of biproportional matrix adjustments." *Environment and Planning A*, 9, 687-701.

Mesnard, L. de. 1994. "Unicity of biproportion." *SIAM Journal on Matrix Analysis and Applications*, 15, 490-495.

Mesnard, L. de. 1997. "A biproportional filter to compare technical and allocation coefficient variations." *Journal of Regional Science*, 37, 541-564.

Miernyk, W.H. 1977. "The projection of technical coefficients for medium-term forecasting." In W.F. Gossling (ed.). *Medium-Term Dynamic Forecasting, The 1975 London Input-Output Conference*. London, Input-Output Publishing Company, pp. 29-42.

Milana, C. 2001. "The input-output structural decomposition analysis of 'flexible' production systems." In M.L. Lahr and E. Dietzenbacher (eds). *Input-Output Analysis: Frontiers and Extensions*. London, Palgrave (forthcoming).

Miller, R.E. and P.D. Blair. 1985. *Input-Output Analysis: Foundations and Extensions*. Englewood Cliffs, NJ, Prentice-Hall.

Mukhopadhyay, K. and D. Chakraborty. 1999. "India's energy consumption changes during 1973-74 to 1991-92." *Economic Systems Research*, 11, 423-438.

Oosterhaven, J. and A.R. Hoen. 1998. "Preferences, technology, trade and real income changes in the European Union: an intercountry decomposition analysis for 1975-1985." *Annals of Regional Science*, 32, 505-524.

Oosterhaven, J. and J.A. Van der Linden. 1997. "European technology, trade and income changes for 1975-85: an intercountry input-output decomposition." *Economic Systems Research*, 9, 393-411.

Polenske, K.R. 1997. "Current uses of the RAS technique: a critical review." In A. Simonovits and A.E. Steenge (eds). *Prices, Growth and Cycles*. London, MacMillan, pp. 58-88.
Rose, A. and S. Casler. 1996. "Input-output structural decomposition analysis: a critical appraisal." *Economic Systems Research*, 8, 33-62.
Stone, R. 1961. *Input-Output and National Accounts*. Paris, OECD.
Toh, M.-H. 1998. "The RAS approach in updating input-output matrices: an instrumental variable interpretation and analysis of structural change." *Economic Systems Research*, 10, 63-78.
Wier, M. 1998. "Sources of changes in emissions from energy: a structural decomposition analysis." *Economic Systems Research*, 10, 99-112.
Wier, M. and B. Hasler. 1999. "Accounting for nitrogen in Denmark – a structural decomposition analysis." *Ecological Economics*, 30, 317-333.

Appendix 10.A Sector Classification

1.	Agri	Agriculture, forestry and fishery products
2.	Ener	Fuel and power products
3.	Meta	Ferrous and non-ferrous ores and metals
4.	Mine	Non-metallic mineral products
5.	Chem	Chemical products
6.	MetP	Metal products except machinery and transport equipment
7.	AIMa	Agriculture and industrial machinery
8.	ODMa	Office and data processing machines
9.	ElGo	Electrical goods
10.	TrEq	Transportation equipment
11.	Food	Food, beverages and tobacco
12.	Text	Textiles and clothing, leather, footwear
13.	Pape	Paper and printing products
14.	Rubb	Rubber and plastic products
15.	Oman	Other manufacturing products
16.	Buil	Building and constructing
17.	ReTr	Recovery, repair services, wholesale and retail trade
18.	Lodg	Lodging and catering services
19.	InTr	Inland transport services
20.	MATr	Maritime and air transport services
21.	Auxi	Auxiliary transport services
22.	Comm	Communication services
23.	Cred	Credit and insurance
24.	Omse	Other market services
25.	Pser	Non-market services

Appendix 10.B Results for the Competitive Imports Case

In tables 10.2 and 10.4 (in the main text), the decomposition is performed on the input-output table without imports, which means that only domestic inputs are included in the intermediate deliveries. Implicitly it is assumed that all imports are non-competitive, i.e. they are assumed to have a different production technology than the domestic products. In tables B.1 and B.2 we present the equivalent results of tables 10.2 and 10.4 under the assumption that all imports are in fact competitive and are included in the intermediate input matrix. To balance the table, the import quantities have to be subtracted from the final demand. When we decompose this new final demand vector, the result is an analysis of changes in the net exports (i.e. exports minus imports) to the trading partners on the sectoral outputs.

Table 10.B.1 Specific technology and total final demand effects in the competitive imports case.

	TECHNOLOGY EFFECTS								FINAL DEMAND EFFECTS		TOTAL
	Total		Substitution		Intermediate input intensity		Cell Specific Substitution				
1 Agri	3311	45%	3611	49%	-268	-4%	-32	0%	4029	55%	7340
2 Ener	-3863	71%	-18560	343%	14460	-267%	237	-4%	-1546	29%	-5409
3 Meta	2211	405%	412	76%	1850	339%	-51	-9%	-1666	-305%	545
4 Mine	-165	-125%	-1315	-996%	1120	848%	30	23%	297	225%	132
5 Chem	1397	19%	-1316	-18%	3095	43%	-382	-5%	5771	81%	7168
6 MetP	501	66%	-832	-110%	1357	179%	-23	-3%	259	34%	760
7 AlMa	112	90%	-970	-778%	1107	888%	-25	-20%	13	10%	125
8 ODMa	-172	-1445%	-318	-2672%	175	1470%	-29	-243%	184	1545%	12
9 ElGo	190	7%	-899	-33%	1084	40%	4	0%	2552	93%	2742
10 TrEq	433	115%	-280	-75%	677	180%	37	10%	-58	-15%	376
11 Food	5420	41%	5799	44%	-372	-3%	-8	0%	7866	59%	13286
12 Text	-283	69%	-802	197%	575	-141%	-55	14%	-125	31%	-408
13 Pape	1249	43%	136	5%	1329	46%	-216	-7%	1672	57%	2921
14 Rubb	639	78%	52	6%	581	71%	5	1%	185	22%	823
15 Oman	-246	616%	-1083	2712%	907	-2272%	-71	177%	206	-516%	-40
16 Buil	2116	156%	244	18%	1439	106%	433	32%	-762	-56%	1354
17 ReTr	5103	38%	2383	18%	2655	20%	65	0%	8342	62%	13445
18 Lodg	769	26%	576	19%	272	9%	-78	-3%	2190	74%	2959
19 InTr	-969	-204%	-2223	-469%	1249	264%	5	1%	1443	304%	474
20 MATr	-1021	-80%	-1481	-116%	463	36%	-3	0%	2299	180%	1277
21 Auxi	195	19%	-379	-38%	541	54%	32	3%	806	81%	1001
22 Comm	680	79%	89	10%	571	66%	20	2%	183	21%	862
23 Cred	403	17%	226	9%	256	11%	-79	-3%	1986	83%	2389
24 Omse	10521	66%	8094	51%	2473	16%	-46	0%	5322	34%	15843
25 PSer	2837	14%	1698	9%	1140	6%	-1	0%	16834	86%	19672
Total	31369	35%	-7136	-8%	38737	43%	-232	0%	58282	65%	89651

Table 10.B.2 Results of the final demand decomposition in the competitive imports case

	LEVEL EFFECT		CATEGORY EFFECT		PRODUCT MIX EFFECT		TOTAL
Germany	7801	-173%	-12780	283%	468	-10%	-4511
France	1994	56%	1270	36%	294	8%	3558
Italy	1501	35%	2692	62%	143	3%	4336
Belgium	3034	42%	4739	66%	-565	-8%	7208
Denmark	608	-51%	-1962	166%	172	-15%	-1182
Rest EU	4013	15%	23920	87%	-585	-2%	27348
ROW	-3015	16%	-14733	79%	-876	5%	-18625
Consumption	30021	96%	8329	27%	-6982	-22%	31368
Other FD	17379	198%	-6524	-74%	-2073	-24%	8783
Total	63335	109%	4951	8%	-10004	-17%	58282

*Note that the final demand effects of the 7 trading partners are in fact *net* export (export minus import) effects and therefore have a different interpretation than the results in table 10.2.

11 Structural Changes in the Chicago Economy: A Field of Influence Analysis

Yasuhide Okuyama,[1] Geoffrey J.D. Hewings,[2] Michael Sonis,[3] and Philip Israilevich[4]

[1] Department of Planning, State University of New York at Buffalo, Hayes Hall, 3435 Main St., Buffalo, NY 14214-3087, USA
e-mail: yokuyama@ap.buffalo.edu

[2] Regional Economics Applications Laboratory, University of Illinois, 607 S. Mathews, Urbana, Illinois 61801-3671, USA
e-mail: hewings@uiuc.edu

[3] Bar Ilan University, Ramat Gan, Israel and Regional Economics Applications Laboratory, University of Illinois, 607 S. Mathews, Urbana, Illinois 61801-3671, USA
e-mail: sonism@mail.biu.ac.il

[4] Deceased; formerly, Regional Economics Applications Laboratory, Federal Reserve Bank of Chicago, P.O. Box 834, Chicago IL 60690-0834

11.1 Introduction

The analysis of economic structure has created a demand for techniques that could provide insights into both the nature and changes of the structure over time. Renowned proposed techniques include the familiar multiplicative decomposition associated with the work of Pyatt and Round (1979) and of Round (1985, 1988) and interpretations using structural path analysis as in Defourny and Thorbecke (1984). These approaches were directed towards the evaluation of economies based on the structure of social accounting matrices. Narrowing to the changes of the structure over time, analysis of the evolution of interindustry relations has become a major topic for economic analysis. The traditional approach, introduced by Chenery (1953; Chenery and Watanabe, 1958) was further extended in various studies (for example, Carter, 1970; Harrigan *et al.*, 1980; Deutsch and Syrquin, 1989, among others).

Recent studies (Israilevich and Mahidhara, 1991, and Hewings *et al.*, 1998) have indicated that the Chicago metropolitan economy has experienced a *hollowing-out* phenomenon, in which the level of dependence on local purchases and sales is declining, especially in manufacturing sectors. While these studies employed the aggregated industrial sectors (7 and 9 sectors, respectively), further explorations using more detailed sector aggregation may reveal not only the nature and extent of internal changes under the hollowing-out effect but also the different changes in interindustrial relationships across sectors.

The main purpose of this chapter is to utilize some new approaches for investigating the economic structural changes, especially the hollowing-out effect, in the Chicago economy over the period of 1980–1997. The main analytical tool for this task is the *field of influence*, developed by Sonis and Hewings (1992). One of the advantages of the field of influence is the ability to handle all types of changes--single elements, multiple elements, or all elements in the matrix. One other important feature of this technique is its ability to provide a very simple basis for the comparison of the structures of different economies or the same economy over time. Employing this tool, impacts and differences of the hollowing-out effect across sectors are displayed and analyzed.

In the next section, the concept of field of influence is presented and reviewed. The third section presents an analysis of the Chicago economy over the period of 1980–1997. Thereafter, a summary of the findings is provided and the chapter concludes with some final remarks.

11.2 Analytical Framework: Fields of Influence

The concept of *fields of influence* was developed by Sonis and Hewings (1992) to provide a methodology that is general enough to handle all types of changes--single elements, all elements in a row or column, or all elements in the matrix. Interest in the problem of coefficient change is not new (see Sohn (1986), and Sonis and Hewings (1991) for the review of earlier works); the major theoretical developments that enabled the present initiatives were those of Sherman and Morrison (1949, 1950), Bullard and Sebald (1977, 1988), and Hewings and Romanos (1981), among others.

11.2.1 The Concept

Consider an $n \times n$ matrix of direct input coefficients, $A = \|a_{ij}\|$, and a matrix of the incremental changes in the direct input coefficients, $E = \|e_{ij}\|$. Also, let $B = (I - A)^{-1} = \|b_{ij}\|$, and $B(E) = (I - A - E)^{-1} = \|b_{ij}(E)\|$ be the Leontief inverses before and after changes, and let $\det B$, and $\det B(E)$ be the determinants of the corresponding inverses. Then, the following propositions hold (Sonis and Hewings, 1992).

Proposition 1. The ratio $Q(E)$ is the polynomial of the incremental changes, e_{ij}, of the following form:

$$Q(E) = \frac{\det B}{\det B(E)} = 1 - \sum_{i_1 j_1} b_{j_1 i_1} e_{i_1 j_1} + \sum_{k=2}^{n} (-1)^k \sum_{\substack{i_r \neq i_s \\ j_r \neq j_s}} {}' B_{or} \begin{pmatrix} j_1 j_2 \cdots j_k \\ i_1 i_2 \ldots i_k \end{pmatrix} e_{i_1 j_1} e_{i_2 j_2} \ldots e_{i_k j_k} \tag{11.1}$$

where $B_{or}\begin{pmatrix} j_1 j_2 \cdots j_k \\ i_1 i_2 \ldots i_k \end{pmatrix}$ is the $k \times k$ determinant that includes the components of the matrix *B* from the ordered set of columns $i_1, i_2, \ldots, i_k$ and rows $j_1, j_2, \ldots, j_k$.

Proposition 2. With *B* and *B(E)*, the following decomposition holds:

$$B(E) = B + \frac{1}{Q(E)} \left[\sum_{k=1}^{n} \sum_{\substack{i_r \neq i_s \\ j_r \neq j_s}} F \begin{pmatrix} i_1 \ldots i_k \\ j_1 \ldots j_k \end{pmatrix} e_{j_1 i_1} \ldots e_{j_k i_k} \right] \tag{11.2}$$

where the fields of influence, $F\begin{pmatrix} i_1 \dots i_k \\ j_1 \dots j_k \end{pmatrix}$, of order k of changes, $e_{j_1 i_1}, \dots, e_{j_k i_k}$ are $n \times n$ matrices with elements:

$$f_{ij}\begin{pmatrix} i_1 \dots i_k \\ j_1 \dots j_k \end{pmatrix} = (-1)^k \left[B_{or}\begin{pmatrix} i_1 \dots i_k i \\ j_1 \dots j_k j \end{pmatrix} - b_{ij} B_{or}\begin{pmatrix} i_1 \dots i_k \\ j_1 \dots j_k \end{pmatrix} \right] \tag{11.3}$$

where $i, j = 1, 2, \dots, n$.

Proposition 3. The structure of the fields of influence can be ascertained in the following form. The first order field of influence, $F[(i_1, j_1)]$, of the incremental change, $e_{i_1 j_1}$, is the $n \times n$ matrix generated by a multiplication of the jth. column of the matrix B with the ith row:

$$F[(i_1, j_1)] = \begin{pmatrix} b_{1i_1} \\ b_{2i_1} \\ \vdots \\ b_{ni_1} \end{pmatrix} \cdot \begin{pmatrix} b_{j_1 1} & b_{j_1 2} & \cdots & b_{j_1 n} \end{pmatrix} \tag{11.4}$$

This implies that if the change, e, occurs only in one place, (i_1, j_1), then the Leontief inverse $B(E)$ has the following form:

$$B(E) = B + \frac{e}{1 - b_{j_1 i_1} e} F(i_1, j_1) \tag{11.5}$$

or, in the original Sherman-Morrison (1950) coordinate form:

$$b_{ij}(e) = b_{ij} + \frac{b_{ij_1} b_{i_1 j} e}{1 - b_{j_1 i_1} e} \tag{11.6}$$

In the case when the changes occur in the ith row of the matrix A, $\begin{pmatrix} e_{i_1 1} & e_{i_1 2} & \dots & e_{i_1 n} \end{pmatrix}$, then the first order of field of influence would be:

$$B(E) = B + \frac{\sum_{s=1}^{n} e_{i_1 s} F[(i_1, s)]}{1 - \sum_{s=1}^{n} b_{si_1} e_{i_1 s}} \tag{11.7}$$

or, in the Sherman-Morrison (1949) coordinate form:

$$b_{ij}(e) = b_{ij} + \frac{b_{ii_1} \sum_{s=1}^{n} b_{sj} e_{i_1 s}}{1 - \sum_{s=1}^{n} b_{si_1} e_{i_1 s}} \tag{11.8}$$

11.2.2 Intensity of Direct Field of Influence and the Total First Order Intensity Matrix

Since the elements of the Leontief inverse and of each first order field of influence are positive (non-negative) numbers, the intensity of the first order field of influence, $F\left[(i_1, j_1)\right] = \left\| f_{ij}(i_1, j_1) \right\|$, can be defined as follows:

$$INT\left\{F\left[(i_1, j_1)\right]\right\} = \sum_{i,j} f_{ij}\left[(i_1, j_1)\right] = B_{\bullet i_1} B_{j_1 \bullet} \tag{11.9}$$

where

$$B_{\bullet i_1} = \sum_{i=1}^{n} b_{ii_1} \; ; \; B_{j_1 \bullet} = \sum_{j=1}^{n} b_{j_1 j} \tag{11.10}$$

are the column and row multipliers of the i_1th column and j_1th row of the Leontief inverse.

The first order *total intensity* matrix, whose components are the normalized intensities of the first order (direct) fields of influence, can be constructed as:

$$INT_1 = \frac{1}{M} \left\| INT\left\{F\left[(i, j)\right]\right\} \right\| \tag{11.11}$$

From equations (11.9) and (11.10):

$$INT_1 = \frac{1}{M} \left\| B_{\bullet i} B_{j \bullet} \right\| = \frac{1}{M} \begin{pmatrix} B_{1\bullet} \\ B_{2\bullet} \\ \vdots \\ B_{n\bullet} \end{pmatrix} \cdot \begin{pmatrix} B_{\bullet 1} & B_{\bullet 2} & \cdots & B_{\bullet n} \end{pmatrix} \tag{11.12}$$

where

$$M = \sum_{i,j} b_{ij} \tag{11.13}$$

is the intensity of the Leontief inverse *per se*. Furthermore, the expression for these first order fields of influence is equivalent to the *multiplier product matrix* (MPM), introduced by Sonis *et al.* (1997), by which the interactions between sectors are presented in terms of a hierarchy of backward and forward linkages.

$$MPM = \frac{1}{M} \left\| B_{j \bullet} B_{\bullet i} \right\| = \frac{1}{M} \begin{pmatrix} B_{1\bullet} \\ B_{2\bullet} \\ \vdots \\ B_{n\bullet} \end{pmatrix} \cdot \begin{pmatrix} B_{\bullet 1} & B_{\bullet 2} & \cdots & B_{\bullet n} \end{pmatrix} = \left\| m_{ji} \right\| = INT_1 \tag{11.14}$$

Consequently, the structure of the first order total intensity matrix, INT_1, is analogous to the cross-structure of each individual direct field of influence; thus, INT_1 can be decomposed into a hierarchy of crosses. The location of the first cross is defined as the location of the maximum intensity value, measured as the product of the largest row and column multipliers. The elements of rows and columns of INT_1 are proportional (but smaller) to those of the first cross.

Equation (11.5) displays that the direct field of influence, $F\left[(i,j)\right]$, enters the Leontief inverse, $B(E)$, in a form $F\left[(i,j)\right]e_{ij}$. Hence, each $F\left[(i,j)\right]$ and the first order total intensity matrix, INT_1, correspond only to the unit changes, $e_{ij}=1$. If it is necessary to reflect actual increments, the weighted first order (direct) total intensity matrix can be derived as follows:

$$WINT_1 = INT_1 * abs(E^T) \tag{11.15}$$

where the matrix $abs(E^T)$ includes absolute values of the components of the transposed increment matrix, E^T, and the sign $*$ implies the element-by-element multiplication of the matrices INT_1 and $abs(E^T)$. The matrix $WINT_1$ does not preserve the hierarchical cross-structure of INT_1; nevertheless, $WINT_1$ evaluates the superposition of the cross-structure of *homogenous changes* and the structure of *actual changes*.

11.2.3 Second Order Fields of Influence and Their Intensities

If the changes $e_{j_1 i_1}$ and $e_{j_2 i_2}$ occur simultaneously in the matrix of direct input coefficients, then the second order (synergetic) field of influence can be defined as the following linear combination of four first order (direct) fields of influence:

$$\begin{aligned} F\left[(j_1,i_1),(j_2,i_2)\right] = &-b_{i_1 j_1} F\left[(j_2,i_2)\right] + b_{i_1 j_2} F\left[(j_1,i_2)\right] \\ &+ b_{i_2 j_1} F\left[(j_2,i_1)\right] - b_{i_2 j_2} F\left[(j_1,i_1)\right] \end{aligned} \tag{11.16}$$

Using (11.16), the following holds for the components of the matrix of the second order field of influence:

$$F\left[(i_1,j_1),(i_2,j_2)\right] = \left\| f_{ij}\left[(i_1,j_1),(i_2,j_2)\right] \right\|;$$

$$f_{ij}\left[(i_1,j_1),(i_2,j_2)\right] = \begin{vmatrix} b_{i_1 j_1} & b_{i_1 j_2} & b_{i_1 j} \\ b_{i_2 j_1} & b_{i_2 j_2} & b_{i_2 j} \\ b_{i j_1} & b_{i j_2} & 0 \end{vmatrix} \tag{11.17}$$

With (11.17), the following can be shown:

$$F\left[(i_1,j_1),(i_2,j_2)\right] = -F\left[(i_1,j_2),(i_2,j_1)\right] \tag{11.18}$$

The intensity of the individual second order field of influence can be defined as a sum of all components of the matrix $F\left[(i_1,j_1),(i_2,j_2)\right]$:

$$INT\left\{F\left[(i_1,j_1),(i_2,j_2)\right]\right\} = \sum_{i,j} f_{ij}\left[(i_1,j_1),(i_2,j_2)\right] \tag{11.19}$$

Using (11.17) and rules for the summation of determinants, the following relationship may be obtained:

$$INT\left\{F\left[\left(i_1,j_1\right),\left(i_2,j_2\right)\right]\right\}=\begin{vmatrix} b_{i_1j_1} & b_{i_1j_2} & B_{i_1\bullet} \\ b_{i_2j_1} & b_{i_2j_2} & B_{i_2\bullet} \\ B_{\bullet j_1} & B_{\bullet j_2} & 0 \end{vmatrix} \tag{11.20}$$

where $B_{i_1\bullet}$, $B_{i_2\bullet}$, $B_{\bullet j_1}$, $B_{\bullet j_2}$ are the corresponding row and column multipliers of the Leontief inverse, B. Thus,

$$\begin{aligned} INT\left\{F\left[\left(i_1,j_1\right),\left(i_2,j_2\right)\right]\right\} &= b_{i_1j_2}B_{i_2\bullet}B_{\bullet j_1}+b_{i_2j_1}B_{i_1\bullet}B_{\bullet j_2}-\left(b_{i_1j_1}B_{i_2\bullet}B_{\bullet j_2}+b_{i_2j_2}B_{i_1\bullet}B_{\bullet j_1}\right)= \\ &= INT^{+}\left\{F\left[\left(i_1,j_1\right),\left(i_2,j_2\right)\right]\right\}-INT^{-}\left\{F\left[\left(i_1,j_1\right),\left(i_2,j_2\right)\right]\right\} \end{aligned} \tag{11.21}$$

where $INT^{+}\left\{F\left[\left(i_1,j_1\right),\left(i_2,j_2\right)\right]\right\}$ and $INT^{-}\left\{F\left[\left(i_1,j_1\right),\left(i_2,j_2\right)\right]\right\}$ are the positive and negative parts of the intensity $INT\left\{F\left[\left(i_1,j_1\right),\left(i_2,j_2\right)\right]\right\}$.

Consider, moreover, for each cell $\left(i_1,j_1\right)$ the following sums:

$$\begin{aligned} INT\left\{F\left[\left(i_1,j_1\right),(\bullet,\bullet)\right]\right\} &= \sum_{i,j} INT\left\{F\left[\left(i_1,j_1\right),(i,j)\right]\right\} \\ INT^{+}\left\{F\left[\left(i_1,j_1\right),(\bullet,\bullet)\right]\right\} &= \sum_{i,j} INT^{+}\left\{F\left[\left(i_1,j_1\right),(i,j)\right]\right\} \\ INT^{-}\left\{F\left[\left(i_1,j_1\right),(\bullet,\bullet)\right]\right\} &= \sum_{i,j} INT^{-}\left\{F\left[\left(i_1,j_1\right),(i,j)\right]\right\} \end{aligned} \tag{11.22}$$

Given the formula (11.20):

$$\begin{aligned} INT\left\{F\left[\left(i_1,j_1\right),(\bullet,\bullet)\right]\right\} &= \begin{vmatrix} b_{i_1j_1} & B_{i_1\bullet} & B_{i_1\bullet} \\ B_{\bullet j_1} & M & M \\ B_{\bullet j_1} & M & 0 \end{vmatrix} = \\ &= 2MB_{i_1\bullet}B_{\bullet j_1}-\left(M^2+MB_{i_1\bullet}B_{\bullet j_1}\right) \end{aligned} \tag{11.23}$$

Then, using (11.22):

$$\begin{aligned} INT^{+}\left\{F\left[\left(i_1,j_1\right),(\bullet,\bullet)\right]\right\} &= 2MB_{i_1\bullet}B_{\bullet j_1} \\ INT^{-}\left\{F\left[\left(i_1,j_1\right),(\bullet,\bullet)\right]\right\} &= M^2 b_{i_1j_1}+MB_{i_1\bullet}B_{\bullet j_1} \end{aligned} \tag{11.24}$$

Furthermore:

$$INT\left\{F\left[\left(i_1,j_1\right),(\bullet,\bullet)\right]\right\}=INT^{+}\left\{F\left[\left(i_1,j_1\right),(\bullet,\bullet)\right]\right\}-INT^{-}\left\{F\left[\left(i_1,j_1\right),(\bullet,\bullet)\right]\right\} \tag{11.25}$$

The following total second order intensity matrix can be defined:

$$INT_2=\frac{1}{M^2}\left\|INT\left\{F\left[(i,j),(\bullet,\bullet)\right]\right\}\right\| \tag{11.26}$$

Its positive and negative parts can be also defined as follows:

$$INT_2^+ = \frac{1}{M^2}\left\| INT^+\left\{F\left[(i,j),(\bullet,\bullet)\right]\right\}\right\|$$
$$INT_2^- = \frac{1}{M^2}\left\| INT^-\left\{F\left[(i,j),(\bullet,\bullet)\right]\right\}\right\| \quad (11.27)$$

Using the above relationships,

$$INT_2^+ = 2INT_1 \,;\; INT_2^- = B + INT_1 \quad (11.28)$$

Then,

$$INT_2 = INT_2^+ - INT_2^- = INT_1 - B \quad (11.29)$$

Or, the Leontief inverse matrix can be characterized as follows:

$$B = INT_1 - INT_2 \quad (11.30)$$

Since the sums of the elements of columns and rows in the Leontief inverse and in INT_1 are the same, the sums of the elements of INT_2 are zero. The analysis of the structure of INT_2 should include the scaling effects of the intra-sectoral economic activities and linkages. Hence, the diagonal of INT_2 will include negative entries. The scaling effect can be accommodated by the diagonal matrix, D:

$$-D = \begin{pmatrix} d_{11} & & & \\ & d_{22} & & \\ & & \ddots & \\ & & & d_{nn} \end{pmatrix}, \; d_{ii} > 0 \,, \; i = 1,2,\ldots,n \quad (11.31)$$

Consequently, the following residual matrix, $R = \left\| r_{ij} \right\|$, can be introduced:

$$R = -D + INT_2 \quad (11.32)$$

The matrix R has a zero main diagonal and, usually, the elements r_{ij} are positive. Moreover, since the sums of the column and row elements of INT_2 are zeros, the following relationships hold:

$$d_{ii} = \sum_{j \neq i} r_{ij} = \sum_{j \neq i} r_{ji} \,, \; i = 1,2,\ldots,n \quad (11.33)$$

Also,

$$B = INT_1 - INT_2 = INT_1 - (D + R) \quad (11.34)$$

INT_2 represents the synergetic interactions between different sectors; hence, it may have a structure that reflects the bilateral balances and imbalances through the push-pull backward and forward linkages. These balances and imbalances can be presented by symmetric and antisymmetric parts of R:

$$R = \frac{1}{2}\left(R + R^T\right) + \frac{1}{2}\left(R - R^T\right) = S + S_a \tag{11.35}$$

where $R^T = \left\| r_{ji} \right\|$ is the transposed matrix of R. The column and row sums of R and S are identical. Therefore, the column and row sums of the antisymmetric part, S_a, are zero. The matrices, S and S_a, indicate the complicated compensating relationships between the different sectors. As a result, the following decomposition of the Leontief inverse matrix may be presented:

$$B = INT_1 - (D + S + S_a) \tag{11.36}$$

where D represents the additional sectoral scale effects, whereas the remaining matrices, S and S_a, account for the symmetric and antisymmetric tendencies.

Using this field of influence technique, the structural change of the Chicago economy can be analyzed based on a time series of input-output tables. This analysis is the focus of the next section.

11.3 Structural Changes of the Chicago Economy: 1980–1997

The Chicago input-output tables are extracted from the Chicago Region Econometric Input-Output Model (CREIM). Table A.1 (appendix) shows the industrial sectors in CREIM. This system of 250 equations includes both exogenous and endogenous variables. Endogenous coefficient change serves as the mechanism to clear markets in the quantity-adjustment process (see Israilevich *et al.*, 1997, for more details). The input-output coefficient matrix is not observed directly; however, it is possible to derive analytically a Leontief inverse matrix and, through inversion, the estimated direct coefficient matrix. In this section, an empirical application of the concept of the field of influence will be illustrated using the 36-sector version of Chicago input-output tables during the period of 1980 to 1997, derived from CREIM.

11.3.1 Hierarchical Cross-Structure of the First Order Field of Influence

From equation (11.12), the first order total intensity matrices are constructed based on the Leontief inverse matrices during 1980 and 1997. Recall from equation (11.14) that the first order total intensity matrix is equivalent to the Multiplier Product Matrix (MPM). The properties of the MPM, and hence of INT_1, are such that the interactions between sectors are presented in terms of a hierarchy of backward and forward linkages (Sonis *et al.*, 2000). By preserving the rankings (hierarchies) of one time period, it is possible to visually evaluate the changes in structure that occur over time. A selection of MPMs (1980, 1985, 1990, and 1995) are provided for Chicago in figures 11.1 through 11.4. In the MPMs, the sectors are arranged in such a way that the northwest quadrant provides the highest elevation and the economic landscape slopes towards the southeast. In 1980, at the apex of the hierarchy is the intersection of sector 27 (Wholesale and Retail Trade) and sector 2 (Agriculture, Forestry, and Fisheries).

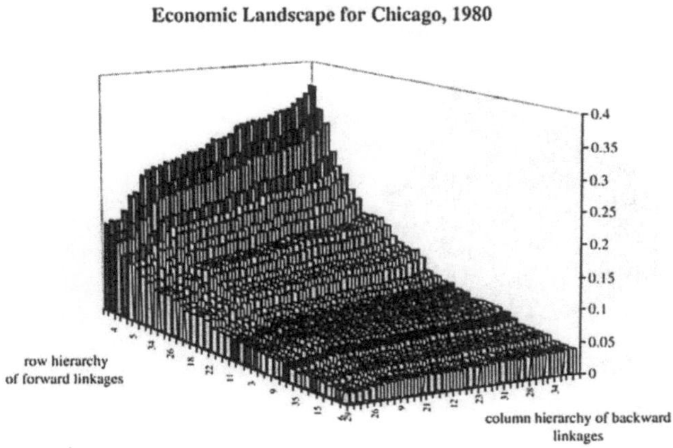

Figure 11.1 Structure of Chicago Economy (1980): Multiplier Product Matrix

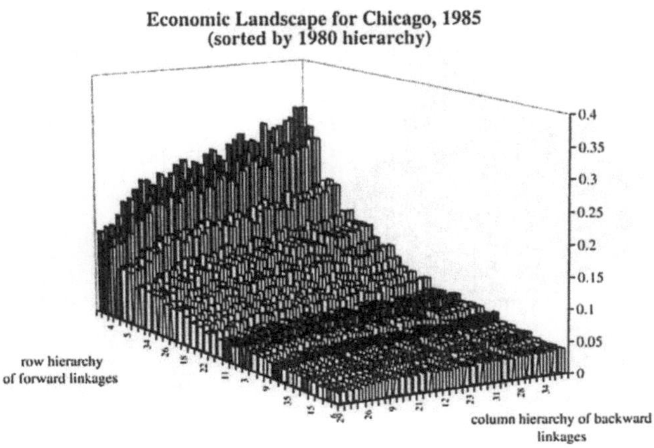

Figure 11.2 Structure of Chicago Economy (1985): Multiplier Product Matrix

Using this hierarchical system, a set of key sectors can be identified. The sectors that are characterized by well-developed backward and forward linkages include: 4 (Construction), 20 (Electronic and Electric Equipment), 24 (Railroad Transportation and Transportation Services), 27 (Wholesale and Retail Trades), 28 (Finance and Insurance), 30 (Lodging, Business, Engineering, Management, and Legal Services), 31 (Eating and Drinking Places), and 34 (Other Services).

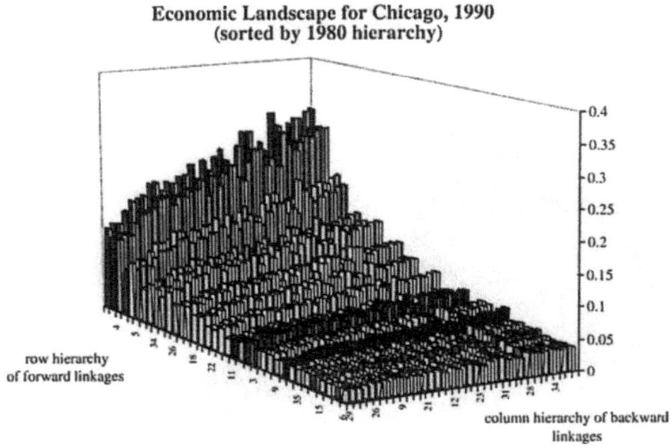

Figure 11.3 Structure of Chicago Economy (1990): Multiplier Product Matrix

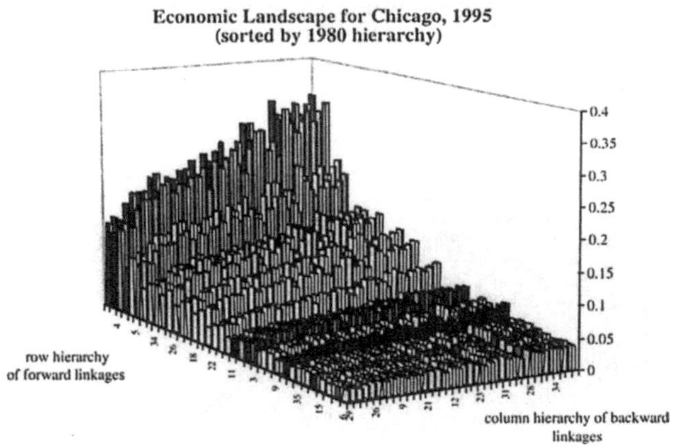

Figure 11.4 Structure of Chicago Economy (1995): Multiplier Product Matrix

The resultant hierarchy also reveals two other groups of important sectors: those with strong forward linkages--5 (Food and Kindred Products), 12 (Chemicals and Allied Products), 13 (Petroleum and Coal Products), 19 (Industrial Machinery and Equipment), and 29 (Real Estate); and those with strong backward linkages--2 (Agriculture, Forestry, and Fisheries), 15 (Leather and Leather Products), 33 (Motion Pictures, and Amusement and Recreation Services), 35 (Federal Government Enterprises), and 36 (State and Local Government Enterprises).

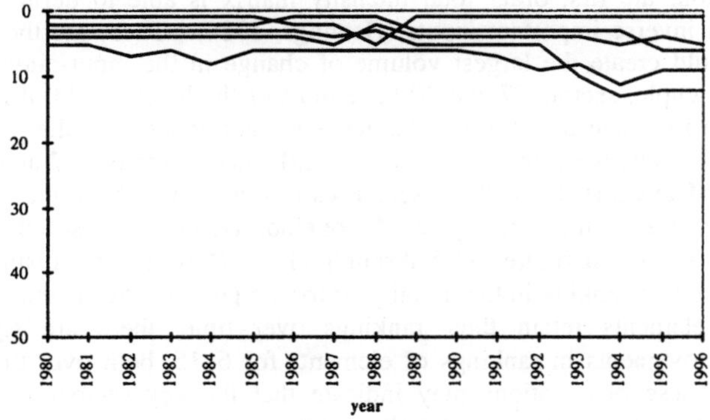

Figure 11.5 Fields of Influence in the Chicago Economy: Changes in Rank, 1980–1996 (Ranks 1–5)

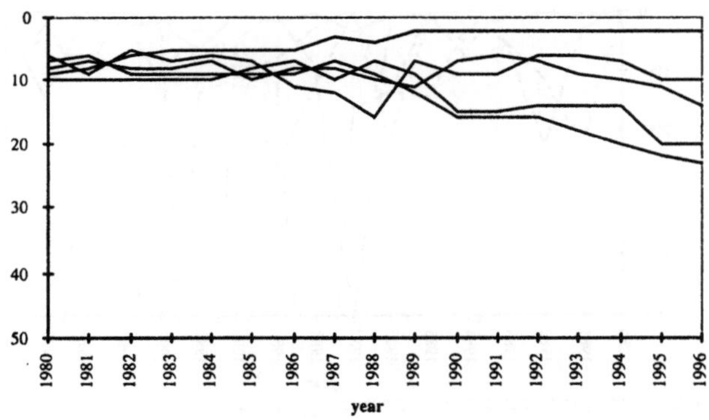

Figure 11.6 Fields of Influence in the Chicago Economy: Changes in Rank, 1980–1996 (Ranks 6–10)

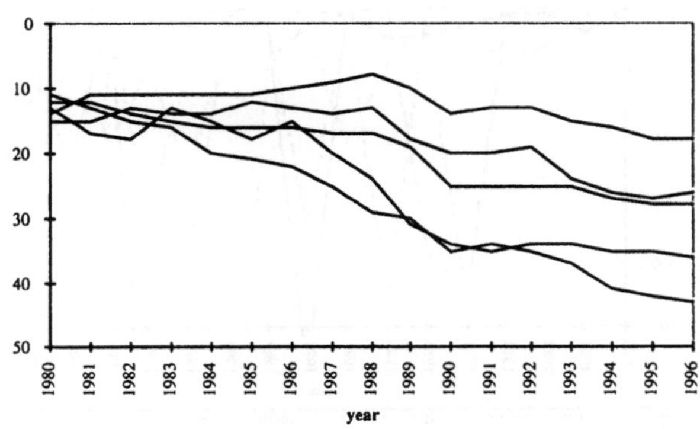

Figure 11.7 Fields of Influence in the Chicago Economy: Changes in Rank, 1980–1996 (Ranks 11–15)

In addition, the first order total intensity matrix is able to define the rank-size hierarchy of inverse important inputs (Hewings, 1984). These are the inputs whose changes would create the largest volume of change in the input-output system. In 1980, for example, sectors 27 and 30 have most of the largest field of influence row-wise (forward linkage direction). This tendency continues over the years; however, the number of cells with the largest field of influence in sectors 27 and 30 decreases gradually. Meanwhile, the cells in sector 4's row appear to have the largest field of influence, and their number increases. More elaborate details of structural change for Chicago are shown in figures 11.5 through 11.7. These figures display the top 15 elements based on ranking in the initial year for the period 1980–1996. While the five top-ranked elements retain their rankings over time, there are significant and increasing movements in rankings of elements for 6–15, both over time and across rankings. These observations may indicate that the key sectors for the Chicago economy remain the same, whereas the second and third groups of sectors change their rankings over time.

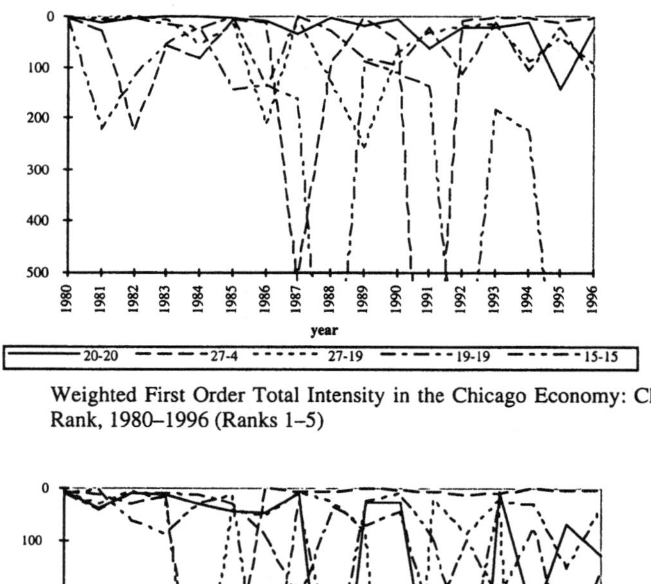

Figure 11.8 Weighted First Order Total Intensity in the Chicago Economy: Changes in Rank, 1980–1996 (Ranks 1–5)

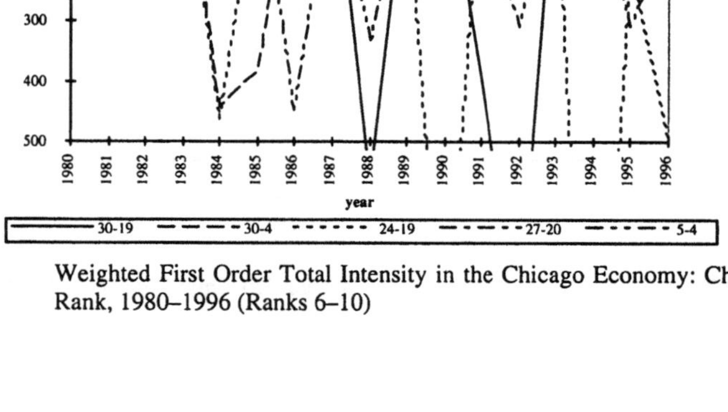

Figure 11.9 Weighted First Order Total Intensity in the Chicago Economy: Changes in Rank, 1980–1996 (Ranks 6–10)

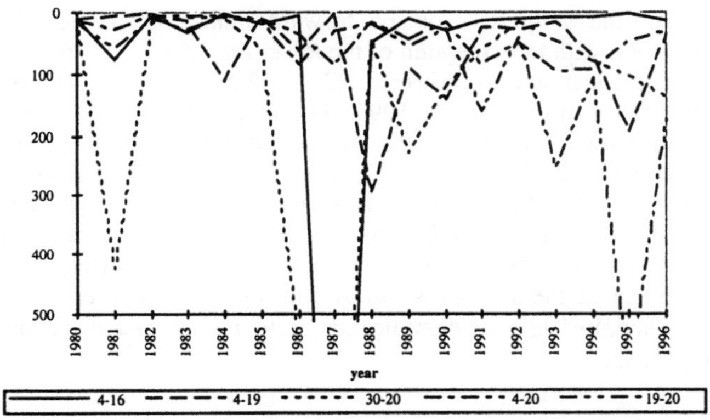

Figure 11.10 Weighted First Order Total Intensity in the Chicago Economy: Changes in Rank, 1980–1996 (Ranks 11–15)

11.3.2 Changes in the Weighted First Order Total Intensity Matrix

As noted in the earlier section, the first order total intensity matrix, INT_1, corresponds only to the unit change. In order to evaluate the impacts from the actual increments, the weighted first order total intensity matrices, $WINT_1$, for the period 1980–1996 are derived. Compared to the tendency observed in INT_1, $WINT_1$ has only some weak concentrations of cells; for example, sector 4 constantly has several cells in both rows and columns; Sectors 27 and 30 also have several cells each year in rows. However, these tendencies do not appear to be consistent over the years. Figures 11.8 through 11.10 indicate the ranking trends of the top 15 elements. In contrast to INT_1, the elements with the largest weighted total intensity move significantly, and apparently randomly, over time. Among the rankings, no specific patterns may be found; a possible common tendency might be that during 1980–1982, the movements of rankings seem smaller than in the later period, although they are still larger than INT_1's (but note the difference in the unit of the rank axis between INT_1 and $WINT_1$).

Since the structure of the weighted first order total intensity matrix, $WINT_1$, may not preserve the cross-structure of the total intensity matrix, INT_1, another approach to analyze the structure of $WINT_1$ is called for. *Complication curves*, introduced by Atkins (1974, 1981) and utilized for input-output frameworks by Sonis *et al.* (1994), are employed to summarize the process of structural complication. Complication curves describe the sequential addition of sectors to the simplex[1] according to the rank-size step of structural complication. Figures 11.11 through 11.14 display the complication curves in the selected years (1980, 1985, 1990, and 1995) for the following four sectors: for forward linkages, Sectors 27 and 30; for backward linkages, Sectors 4 and 19.

[1] The simplex is a minimal convex polyhedron in n-dimensional space with $n+1$ vertices (for further detail, see Sonis *et al.*, 1994).

Figure 11.11 shows that sector 27 (Wholesale and Retail Trade) has a rapid enlargement of the simplexes for the forward linkage in 1980. This tendency continues to 1985, with the exception of the lower rankings (60th and later); however, in 1990, the complication curve of sector 27 significantly changes to a relatively slow enlargement of the simplexes. In 1995, the complication curve moves again to a different trend--slow in the higher ranks (up to 35th), but having a rapid enlargement between 35th and 60th. In figure 11.12, sector 30 (Lodging, Business, Engineering, Management, and Legal Services) for the forward linkages, on the other hand, has a different trends over time. In 1980, there is a moderate enlargement of the simplexes; a relatively similar trend of enlargement continues in 1985; however, in 1990, a very rapid enlargement of the simplexes (up to 40th rank) is observed that becomes flat afterwards. Then, in 1995, the complication curve returns to a shape similar to those for 1980 and 1995.

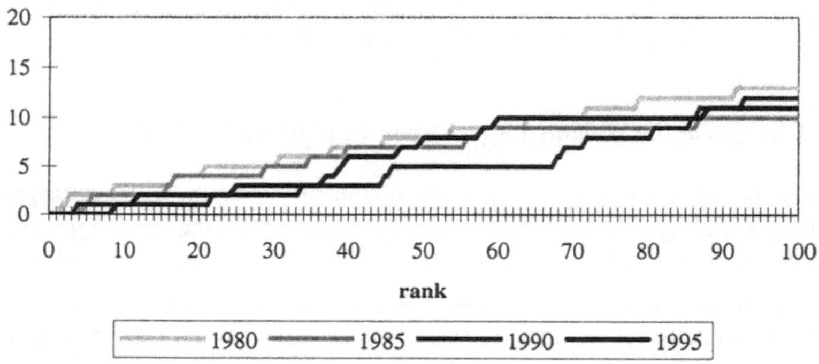

Figure 11.11 Structural Complications of the Forward Linkages Simplicial Family (Sector 27)

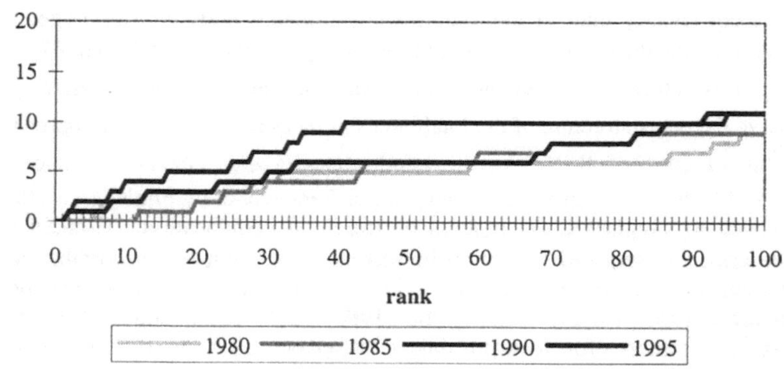

Figure 11.12 Structural Complications of the Forward Linkages Simplicial Family (Sector 30)

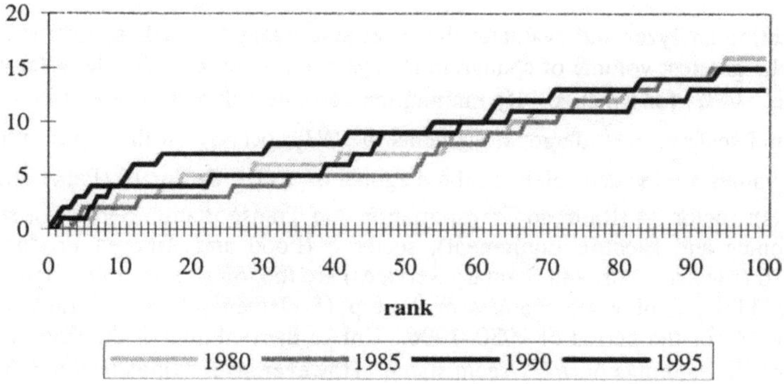

Figure 11.13 Structural Complications of the Backward Linkages Simplicial Family (Sector 4)

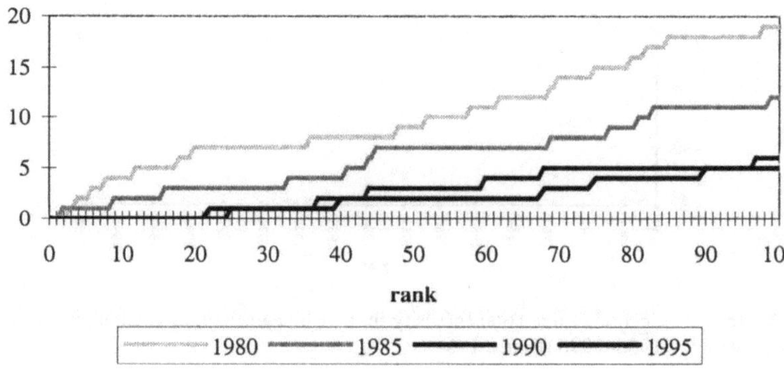

Figure 11.14 Structural Complications of the Backward Linkages Simplicial Family (Sector 19)

For backward linkages (figure 11.13), sector 4 (Construction) has a gradual enlargement of simplexes over the rankings, and has similar trends over the years; in 1990, the enlargement of the simplexes becomes a little rapid up to 40th rank, but is not significant. Figure 11.14 indicates that sector 19 (Industrial Machinery and Equipment) is considerably different from sector 4: 1980 shows a very rapid enlargement of simplexes throughout the rankings that significantly diminishes over the years; as a result, in 1995, only five cells (out of 36) are in the top 100 ranks. These observations clearly demonstrate that each sector changes in a different way over time, whether row-wise (backward linkage) or column-wise (forward linkage). Moreover, each coefficients changes in a different way over time. These observations are further analyzed in the next subsection utilizing the second order fields of influence.

11.3.3 Analysis of Second Order Total Intensity Matrices

This section analyzes and evaluates the synergetic interactions, those interactions that create the greatest volume of change in the system, by the second order total intensity matrices, INT_2, for Chicago. By ranking the absolute value of each cell in INT_2, the additional scale effects, diagonal elements of INT_2, occupy all the top 36 ranks--the largest values are located solely on the diagonal of INT_2. Sector 10 (Paper and Allied Products), sector 24 (Railroad Transportation and Transportation Services), sector 20 (Electronics and Electric Equipment), sector 5 (Food and Kindred Products), and sector 26 (Electric, Gas, and Sanitary Services) are the top five sectors. Figures 11.15 through 11.17 display the changes in the top 15 elements, based on ranking in the initial year, for the period of 1980–1996. Unlike the rankings of the first order total intensity, the rankings of INT_2 seem stable. However, as rankings become lower, the changes in the ranking become a little wider.

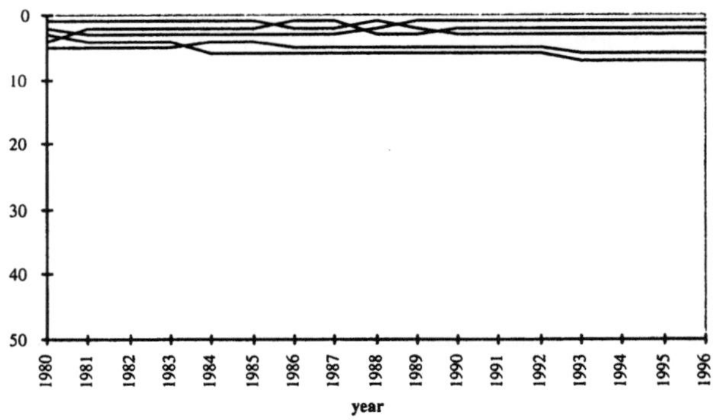

Figure 11.15 Second Order Total Intensity in the Chicago Economy: Changes in Rank, 1980–1996 (Ranks 1–5)

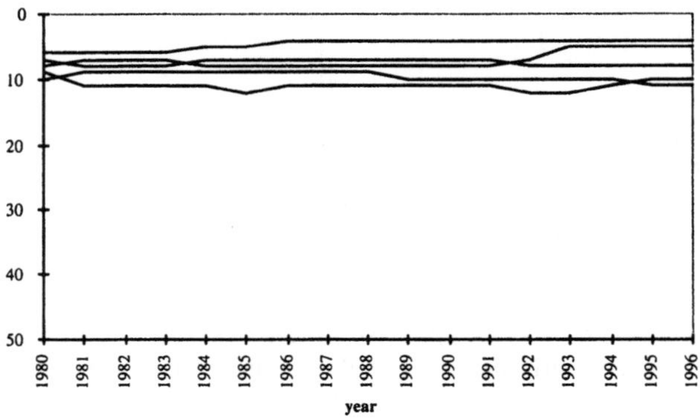

Figure 11.16 Second Order Total Intensity in the Chicago Economy: Changes in Rank, 1980–1996 (Ranks 6–10)

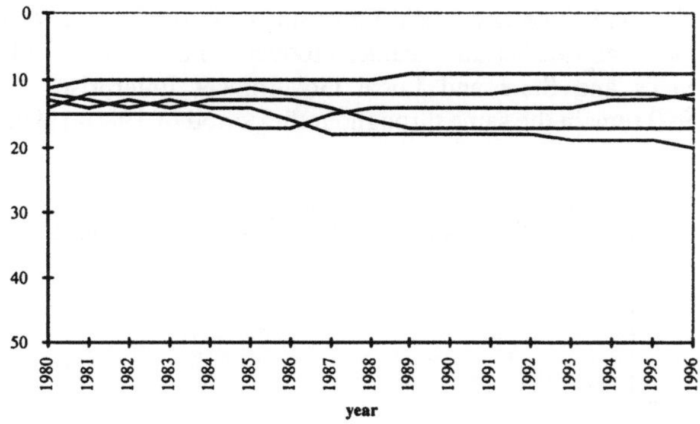

Figure 11.17 Second Order Total Intensity in the Chicago Economy: Changes in Rank, 1980–1996 (Ranks 11–15)

For the bilateral balances and imbalances (S and Sa in equation (36)), figure 11.18 reveals that the changes in the ranking of the largest positive bilateral balancing effects over the period of 1980–1996. The following pairs of sectors are the top five pairs in 1980: 26 and 30: Electric, Gas, and Sanitary Services and Lodging, Business, Engineering, Management, and Legal Services; 26 and 27: Electric, Gas, and Sanitary Services and Wholesales and Retail Trade; 4 and 5: Construction and Food and Kindred Products; 5 and 12: Food and Kindred Products and Chemicals and Allied Products; and 4 and 11: Construction and Printing and Publishing. The trends of rankings are relatively stable, although the top five rankings move over the years. The pair (26, 27) exhibits a significant decrease in rank.

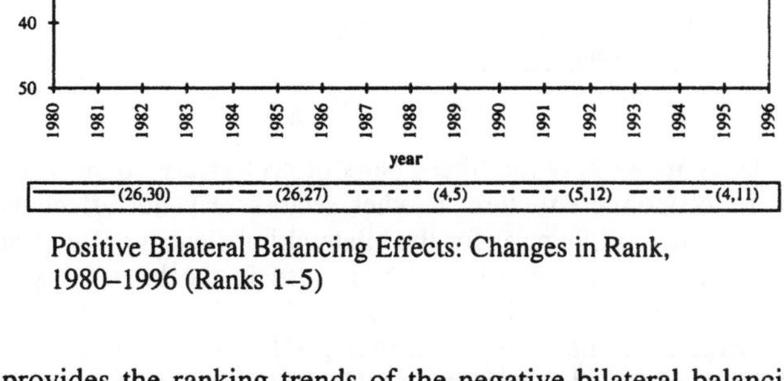

Figure 11.18 Positive Bilateral Balancing Effects: Changes in Rank, 1980–1996 (Ranks 1–5)

Figure 11.19 provides the ranking trends of the negative bilateral balancing effects. The largest cells (by absolute value) of the negative balances occur in the following pairs: 12 and 14: Chemicals and Allied Products and Rubber and Misc. Plastic

Products; 5 and 31: Food and Kindred Products and Eating and Drinking Places; 4 and 36: Construction and State and Local Government Enterprises; 5 and 15: Food and Kindred Products and Leather and Leather Products; and 26 and 36: Electric, Gas, and Sanitary Services and State and Local Government Enterprises. Strikingly, the rankings of 1980 remain the same throughout the period of 1980–1996.

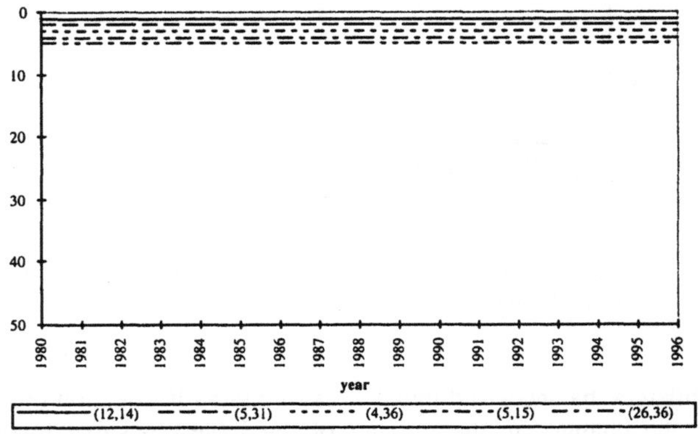

Figure 11.19 Negative Bilateral Balancing Effects: Changes in Rank, 1980–1996 (Ranks 1–5)

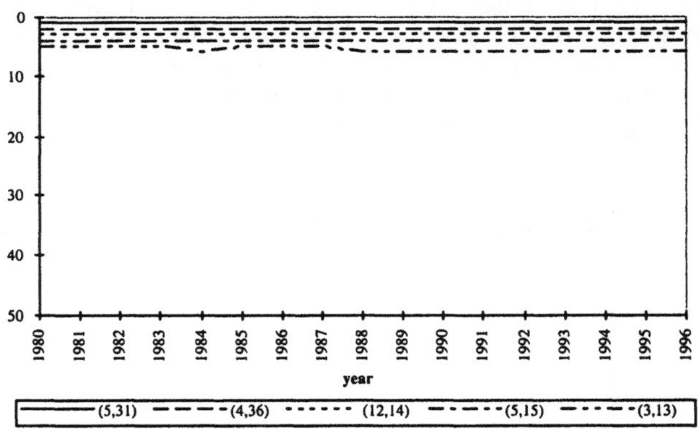

Figure 11.20 Bilateral Imbalancing Effects: Changes in Rank, 1980–1996 (Ranks 1–5)

This tendency may imply that these pairs of sectors are connected so tightly that changes in the economic structure in other sectors may not affect the relationship between them. The top five pairs for the bilateral imbalancing effects are provided in figure 11.20. Four of the top five pairs are also in the largest negative balancing effects as shown in figure 11.19. Furthermore, these four pairs' trends of ranks over time are the same as in the negative balancing effects--no change. The fifth ranked pair, 3 and 13: Mining and Petroleum and Coal Products, changes its rank by a very small amount over time. This observation further confirms the stability of those pairs in the largest negative balancing effects.

11.3.4 Comparative Analysis with the Weighted Second Order Total Intensity Matrices

The weighted second order total intensity matrix, $WINT_2$, can be introduced in a similar fashion to the weighted first order total intensity matrix, $WINT_1$. The distributions of the rank-size structure of INT_2 and of $WINT_2$, in absolute value, differ considerably, as observed in Sonis *et al.* (1994). Since, in both $abs|INT_2|$ and $abs|WINT_2|$, the cells on the main diagonal usually occupy the top 36 ranks, the analysis here focuses on these figures indicate the cells with the 25 largest $abs|INT_2|$ and $abs|WINT_2|$ in off-diagonal elements. For example, in 1985, the cells are weakly concentrated row-wise (forward linkage direction), especially in Sectors 4, 5, and 27. On the other hand, for $abs|WINT_2|$ in 1994, the cells are rather strongly concentrated column-wise (backward linkage direction) in Sectors 4 and 13. These tendencies in $abs|INT_2|$ and $abs|WINT_2|$ can be seen in other years.

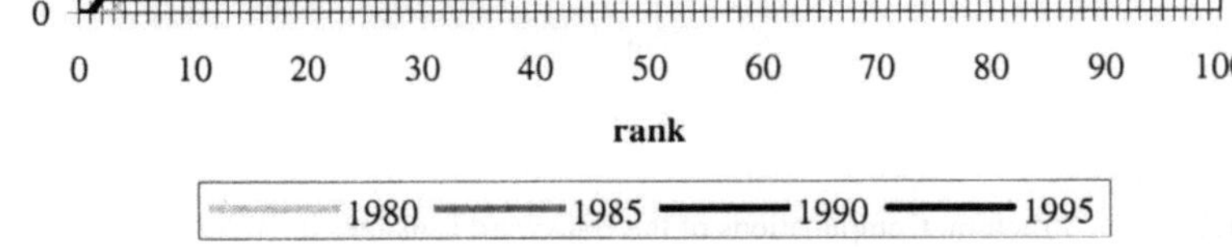

Figure 11.21 Structural Complications of the Forward Linkages in INT_2 (Sector 5)

Employing complication curves, more detailed analysis of qualitative structure of $abs|INT_2|$ and $abs|WINT_2|$ can be carried out. Figure 11.21 presents the complication curves of the forward linkage in sector 5 (Food and Kindred Products) for $abs|INT_2|$. Since the top 36 cells reside on the main diagonal (intraindustry connections), the complication curves are flat up to the 36th rank. Afterward, however, the complication curves exhibit a gradual enlargement of the simplexes, especially after the 70th rank or so. On the other hand, in Figure 11.22, the complication curves for sector 27 (Wholesale and Retail Trade) indicate the same tendency up to the 36th; between the 44th and 55th, they increase very rapidly; however, after the 60th rank, the complication curves become flat. In both sectors, furthermore, the differences over the years are very narrow, indicating few structural changes in forward linkages for these sectors, in terms of second order fields of influence.

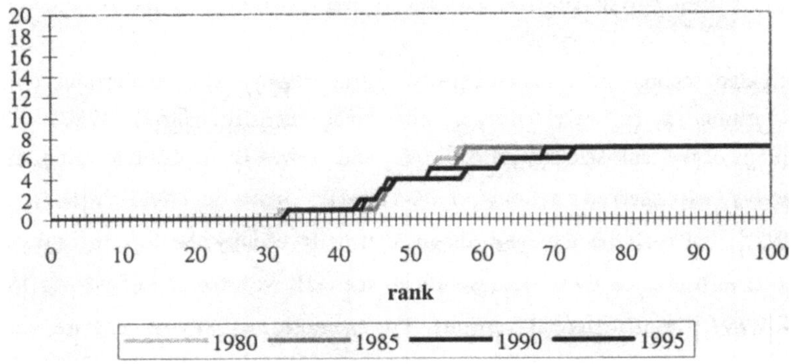

Figure 11.22 Structural Complications of the Forward Linkages in INT_2 (Sector 27)

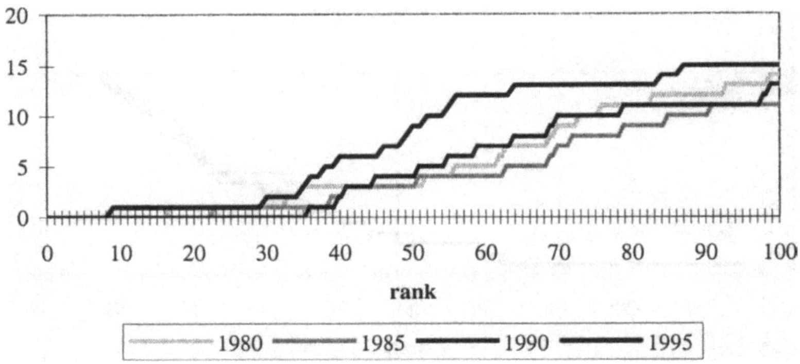

Figure 11.23 Structural Complications of the Backward Linkages in $WINT_2$ (Sector 4)

For $abs|WINT_2|$, the complication curves of Sectors 4 (Construction) and 13 (Petroleum and Coal Products) are exhibited in figures 11.23 and 11.24, respectively. For sector 4, a gradual enlargement of the simplexes can be seen during the period of 1980–1990; however, in 1995, the backward-linkage simplexes increase rapidly after the 30th rank. For sector 13, the changes of the complication curves over time are rather striking. In 1980, the complication curve is almost flat throughout the first 100 ranks. However, there is a considerably rapid enlargement of the simplexes in 1985; then, in 1990, the complication curve returns to a flat shape; and finally, it exhibits a gradual enlargement in 1995. The trends of the complication curves for sector 4 over time can be considered as due to structural change in the backward linkages; however, those for sector 13 may be seen as a result of the fluctuation of the economic structure.

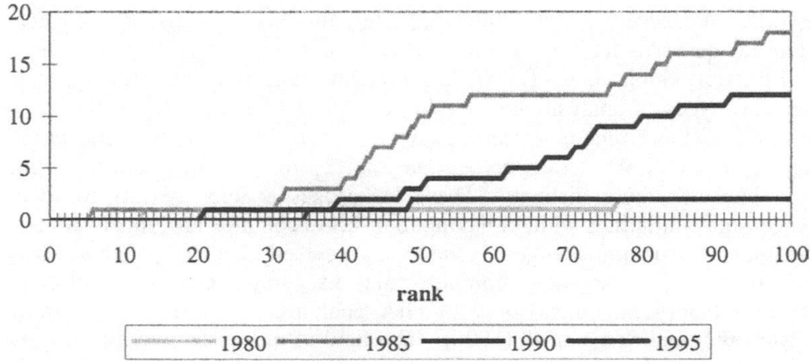

Figure 11.24 Structural Complications of the Backward Linkages in $WINT_2$ (Sector 13)

11.4 Summary: The Chicago Economy: 1980–1997

The period covered by this study suggests that the Chicago economy exhibits little change in appearance by the economic landscape (*multiplier product matrix*); however, changes in the hierarchy of forward and/or backward linkages obviously reflect some underlying changes in the structure of the Chicago economy. In fact, by the cross-structure of the direct (first order) fields of influence, the stability of some coefficients (interindustrial relationships) and the instability of some other coefficients are revealed. Using the weighted first order fields of influence, the actual changes in terms of fields of influence seem rather random; however, the introduction of *complication curves* enabled the assessment of the different behaviors of temporal change, especially between manufacturing sectors and service sectors.

Utilizing the second order (synergetic) fields of influence concept, the Chicago economy exhibits the stable trends of the scaling effects, bilateral balancing effects, and bilateral imbalancing effects over time. However, these observations need not lead to a conclusion of stable interindustry relationships. Rather, using *complication curves*, the trends and types of changes in forward and backward linkages differ considerably across sectors.

The above analysis clearly indicates the presence of a *hollowing-out* process in the Chicago economy. The manufacturing sectors have experienced significant structural changes in the last 17 years, while the service sectors have been rather stable in terms of field of influence. Further analysis of synergetic fields of influence for each pair of sectors may reveal more complicated trends in the Chicago economy.

11.5 Conclusions

The theoretical procedures utilized in this study provide significant opportunities for unique approaches to the interpretation of economic structure through input-output frameworks. As Jensen *et al.* (1988b) suggested, this field of influence concept may form one of the bases for a taxonomy across economies, and/or of a economy over time. However, Sonis *et al.* (2000) observed that this field of influence will not replace other types of analysis, but should be seen as offering a first or macro-level appreciation of the structure of an economy. Then, by the use of the *multiplier product matrix* (MPM) and *complication curves*, the visualization of economic structure becomes more distinct. These techniques enable analysts to focus on differences and similarities without having to resort to complex analytical detail.

The issue of structural change in general has received increasing attention over the years, and become ever more complex and disaggregated. A more complete evaluation of theory, in comparison with other techniques, may be found in Sonis and Hewings (1992) and Sonis *et al.* (1996). The field of influence concept may also be related to other methodologies; to reveal the structure of the propagation processes (Sonis and Hewings, 1993, 1995); and to uncover paths of influence (Sonis *et al.*, 2000). This concept can be easily utilized with social accounting, demographic, or other matrices.

While the field of influence is a useful tool to analyze each input-output table in a time series at a time, in the next chapter, temporal change in input coefficients is analyzed and evaluated using the bi-proportional or RAS technique to investigate the trends of structural change in the Chicago economy.

References

Atkins, R.H. 1974. *Mathematical Structures in Human Affairs*. London, Heineman Educational.

Atkins, R.H. 1981. *Multidimensional Man*. Harmondsworth, UK, Penguin.

Barker, T.S. 1985. "Endogenising Input-Output Coefficients by means of Industrial Submodels." In A. Smyshlyaev ed. *Input-Output Modeling*. Berlin, Springer-Verlag.

Bullard, C.W. and A.V. Sebald. 1977. "Effects of Parametric Uncertainty and Technological Change in Input-Output Models." *Review of Economics and Statistics* 59, 75-81.

Bullard, C.W. and A.V. Sebald. 1988. "Monte Carlo Sensitivity Analysis of Input-Output Models." *Review of Economics and Statistics* 70, 705-12.

Carter, A.P. 1980. "Changes in Input-Output Structure Since 1972." *Interindustry Review*, Summer.

Chenery, H.B. 1953. "Regional Analysis." In H.B. Chenery, P.G. Clark and V. Cao-Pinna eds. *The Structure and Growth of the Italian Economy*.

Chenery, H.B. and T. Watanabe. 1958. "International Comparisons of the Structure of Production." *Econometrica* 26, 487-521.

Conway, R. 1990. "The Washington Projection and Simulation Model, A Regional Interindustry Econometric Model." *International Regional Science Review* 13, 141-66.

Conway, R. 1991. "An Empirical Comparison of Regional Multipliers." In John J.Ll. Dewhurst, Geoffrey J.D. Hewings, and Rodney C. Jensen eds. *Regional Input-Output Modelling, New Developments and Interpretations*. Aldershot, Avebury.

Defourny, J. and E. Thorbecke. 1984. "Structural Path Analysis and Multiplier Decomposition within a Social Accounting Framework." *Economic Journal* 94, 111-36.

Deutsch, J. and M. Syrquin. 1989. "Economic Development and the Structure of Production." *Economic Systems Research* 1, 447-64.

Harrigan, F., J.W. McGilvay and I. McNicoll. 1980. "A Comparison of Regional and National Technical Structures." *Economic Journal* 90, 795-810.

Hewings, G.J.D. 1984. "The Role of Prior Information in Updating Regional Input-Output Models." *Socio-Economic Planning Sciences* 18, 319-36.

Hewings, G.J.D., and M.C. Romanos. 1981. "Simulating Less Developed Regional Economies under Conditions of Limited Information." *Geographical Analysis* 13, 373-90.

Hewings, G.J.D., M. Sonis, J. Guo, P. R. Israilevich, and G. R. Schindler. 1998. "The Hollowing-out Process in the Chicago Economy, 1975-2015." *Geographical Analysis* 30, 217-33.

Israilevich, P.R., and R. Mahidhara 1991. "Hog Butchers No Longer, Twenty Years of Employment Change in Metropolitan Chicago." *Economic Perspectives* 15, 2-13.

Israilevich, P.R., G.J.D. Hewings, G.R. Schindler, and R. Mahidhara. 1996. "The Choice of Input-Output Table Embedded in Regional Econometric Input-Output Models." *Papers in Regional Science* 75, 103-19.

Israilevich, P.R., G.J.D. Hewings, M. Sonis, and G.R, Schindler. 1997. "Forecasting Structural Change with a Regional Econometric Input-Output Model." *Journal of Regional Science* 37, 565-90.

Pyatt, G. and J.I. Round. 1979. "Accounting and Fixed Price Multipliers in a Social Accounting Matrix Framework." *Economic Journal* 89, 850-73.

Round, J.I. 1985. "Decomposing Multipliers for Economic Systems Involving Regional and World Trade." *Economic Journal* 95, 383-99.

Round, J.I. 1988. "Incorporating the International, Regional and Spatial Dimension into a SAM, Some Methods and Applications." In F.J. Harrigan and P.G. McGregor eds. *Recent Advances in Regional Economic Modeling*. London, Pion.

Schindler, G.R., P.R. Israilevich, and G.J.D. Hewings. 1994. "Chicago's Economic Transformation, Past and Future." *Economic Perspectives* 14, 2-9.

Sherman, J. and W.J. Morrison. 1949. "Adjustment of an Inverse Matrix Corresponding to Changes in the Elements of a Given Column or Given Row of the Original Matrix." *Annals of Mathematical Statistics* 20, 621.

Sherman, J. and W.J. Morrison. 1950. "Adjustment of an Inverse Matrix Corresponding to Changes in an Elements of a Given Matrix." *Annals of Mathematical Statistics* 21, 124-27.

Sohn, I. 1986. *Readings in Input-Output Analysis, Theory and Applications*. New York, Oxford University Press.

Sonis, M., and G.J.D. Hewings. 1991. "Fields of Influence and Extended Input-Output Analysis, A Theoretical Account." In John J.Ll. Dewhurst, Geoffrey J.D. Hewings, and Rodney C. Jensen eds. *Regional Input-Output Modelling, New Developments and Interpretations*. Aldershot, Avebury.

Sonis, M., and G.J.D. Hewings. 1992. "Coefficients Change in Input-Output Models, Theory and Applications." *Economic Systems Research* 4, 143-57.

Sonis, M., and G.J.D. Hewings. 1993. "Hierarchies of Regional Sub-Structures and Their Multipliers within Input-Output Systems, Miyazawa Revisited." *Hitotsubashi Journal of Economics* 34, 33-44.

Sonis, M., and G.J.D. Hewings. 1995. "Matrix Sensitivity, Error Analysis and Internal/External Multiregional Multipliers." *Hitotsubashi Journal of Economics* 36 1., 61-70.

Sonis, M., G.J.D. Hewings, and A. Bronstein. 1994. "Structure of Fields of Influence of Economic Changes, A Case Study of Changes in the Israeli Economy." *Discussion Paper* 94-T-10. Regional Economics Applications Laboratory, University of Illinois, Urbana.

Sonis, M., G.J.D. Hewings, and E. Hulu. 1997. "Interpreting Spatial Economic Structure, Feedback Loops in the Indonesian Interregional Economy, 1980, 1985." *Regional Science and Urban Economics* 27, 325-342.

Sonis, M., G.J.D. Hewings, and J. Guo. 1996. "Sources of Structural Change in Input-Output Systems, A Field of Influence Approach." *Economic Systems Research* 8, 15-32.

Sonis, M., G.J.D. Hewings, and J. Guo. 2000. "A New Image of Classical Key Sector Analysis, Minimum Information Decomposition of the Leontief Inverse." *Economic Systems Research* 12, 401-423.

Takayama, A. 1985. *Mathematical Economics, Second Edition*. New York, Cambridge University Press.
Wrigley, K.J. 1970. "Production Models and Time Trends of Input-Output Coefficients." In W.F. Gossling ed. *Input-Output in the United Kingdom*. 89-118. London, Cass.

Appendix

Table 11.A.1 Sectoring Scheme in the CREIM Model

Sector	Title	SIC
1	Livestock, Livestock Products, and Agricultural Products	01, 02
2	Agriculture, Forestry, and Fisheries	07, 08, 09
3	Mining	10, 12, 13, 14
4	Construction	15, 16, 17
5	Food and Kindred Products	20
6	Tobacco	21
7	Apparel and Textile Products	22, 23
8	Lumber and Wood Products	24
9	Furniture and Fixtures	25
10	Paper and Allied Products	26
11	Printing and Publishing	27
12	Chemicals and Allied Products	28
13	Petroleum and Coal Products	29
14	Rubber and Misc. Plastics Products	30
15	Leather and Leather Products	31
16	Stone, Clay, and Glass Products	32
17	Primary Metals Industries	33
18	Fabricated Metal Products	34
19	Industrial Machinery and Equipment	35
20	Electronic and Electric Equipment	36
21	Transportation Equipment	37
22	Instruments and Related Products	38
23	Miscellaneous Manufacturing Industries	39
24	Railroad Transportation and Transportation Services	40-47
25	Communications	48
26	Electric, Gas, and Sanitary Services	49
27	Wholesale and Retail Trade	50-57, 59
28	Finance and Insurance	60-64, 66, 67
29	Real Estate	65
30	Lodging, Business, Engineering, Management, & Legal Services	70, 73, 81, 87, 89
31	Eating and Drinking Places	58
32	Auto Repair, Services, and Parking	75
33	Motion Pictures, and Amusement and Recreation Services	78, 79
34	Other Services (Health, Education, Social, etc.)	
35	Federal Government Enterprises	
36	State and Local Government Enterprises	

12 Modeling Structural Linkages in Dynamic and Spatial Interindustry Systems

Guy R. West

Centre for Economic Policy Modeling, University of Queensland, Brisbane 4072, Queensland, Australia
e-mail: g.west@mailbox.uq.edu.au

12.1 Introduction

In economics, as in most other disciplines, we use models to illustrate complex relationships among economic variables and other related objects, such as the environment. A model is just a simplified characterization of reality. Like a road map, it highlights the main features of interest but treats as background those characteristics not crucial to the purpose at hand. Through simplification, less is held in view so that more can be understood of what is retained.

Many scientists (e.g. Friedman, 1953) have argued in favor of simplicity, because simple models are easier to understand, communicate and test empirically. However, this can lead to two criticisms: (a) the model is oversimplified, and (b) the assumptions are unrealistic. Oversimplification means that, through their selectivity, models can reach conclusions that are simply incorrect. What is omitted may turn out, in retrospect, to be crucial to the understanding of the underlying relationships. In answer to the criticism of oversimplification, one can argue that we can start with a simplified model then progressively build more complicated models as we learn more about the relationships. This is the idea expressed by Koopmans (1957). The question of unrealistic assumptions, on the other hand, is more uncertain. As Friedman (1953, pp.14-15) says: "The relevant question to ask about the 'assumptions' of a theory is not whether they are descriptively 'realistic' for they never are, but whether they are sufficiently good approximations for the purpose at hand. This question can be answered by only seeing whether the theory works, which means whether it yields sufficiently accurate predictions." A large part of this chapter is devoted to the question of selection of 'appropriate' assumptions, and the implications on the model building and application processes.

Unlike most people's views of the world, which are frequently based on models which are implicit (or subconscious) and reflect the individual's narrow interpretation of reality based on local experience, in economics the models need to be explicit, in which the objectives, relationships and assumptions are clearly specified so that the reader clearly understands how the conclusions are derived. Nevertheless, models are no more than useful abstractions that should always be viewed with some degree of skepticism.

This chapter attempts to provide an overview of the current position of regional modeling, and to provide a basis for discussion and comparison of the different modeling approaches currently on offer. It explores some issues relevant to model builders contemplating the construction and use of regional models for policy analysis and investigations into economic structure, dynamics and spatial systems in an interindustry framework.

12.2 What is Reality?

Economic models are only simple approximations to a very complex reality. But that begs the question: what is reality? Reality can vary with the eye of the beholder. Before considering the alternatives available and selecting an appropriate model, we need to have clear in our minds what 'reality' or part of reality we want to replicate. This is not a simple question, for it challenges our own perceptions of how we think the world operates, and will largely influence which modeling path to take.

We can identify two different types of reality. There is the *actual* reality of the real world in action, with all of its frictions, irrationalities and logical impurities, and there is *perceived* reality which is our perception of actual reality, based on our limited vision, personal biases and prejudices. There is also a *modeled* reality, which is that part of perceived reality that is represented in the operational model. Model validation, in essence, reflects these latter two aspects of reality: perceived validity in which a model can be considered to be more valid if it is based on a perceived reality which is closer to actual reality, and modeling validity which is a measure of how closely the model mirrors perceived reality, or that part of perceived reality it is intended to represent (Gass, 1983; McCarl, 1984).

This distinction between actual and perceived reality is quite important, since the ideological differences between models reflects, in the main, the different perceptions of reality in the minds of the model builders. For example, some would argue that a model based on neo-classical principles (or Keynesian principles, or whatever) has a high degree of perceptual validity, while others would vehemently disagree. This implies that one should be careful about accepting advice from modelers who may have a particular economic inclination (or, as is sometimes the case, commercial interests) without careful thought to the research question and the implications of that economic ideology on the results of the proposed modeling exercise.

This can lead to what is sometimes referred to as a Type III error, the hazard of using a good model in the wrong situation, leading to possible immense waste of time, money and effort and potentially catastrophic consequences (Carrier and Wallace, 1994). In other words, a model that is designed to provide useful insights into one aspect of the economy may not produce acceptable results from a different aspect. More generally, there is no implication that the selected model is generally valid or invalid across a range of applications. A major part of the cause of Type III errors is the communications gap that exists between the model builder and model user, and the fact that the perceived reality of the model builder is not necessarily the same as that of the model user.

12.3 Regional Interindustry Models: A Descriptive Background

Regional interindustry modeling has undergone substantial change over the last two to three decades. For many years, input-output was regarded as the workhorse of the regional modeler, and in some ways, this has not changed substantially; input-output still remains the core component of many regional models. What has changed is that the science of modeling has become more complex both in terms of trying to capture a wider subset of reality and in terms of its mathematical structure.

This evolution in regional modeling is aimed at one target: to describe and measure real world economic interdependencies in a dynamic, evolutionary and spatial environment. The paths taken, however, in attempts to capture this elusive goal vary quite substantially. The choice of model is always going to be controversial. When confronted with the task of deciding what type of model to build or use, the analyst has a number of choices. But the issues are not always clear. There are the obvious questions of cost, timeliness and availability of resources, but there are also other aspects. For example, potential users should ask the following questions:

What are the available model choices?
Can we meaningfully compare the available models?
How do the models differ in philosophy, scope, etc? When should we use one model in preference to another?
Given the huge cost involved in model development, what is the trade-off between complexity and simplicity (or transparency)?

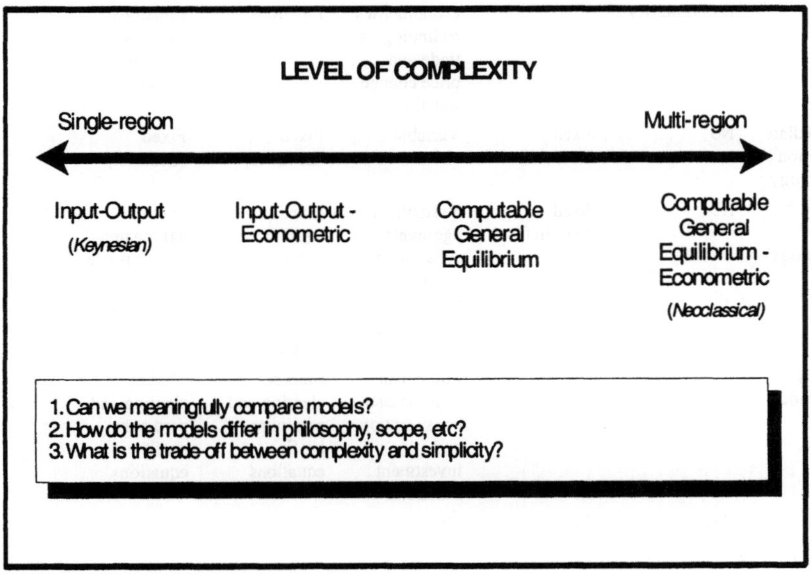

Figure 12.1 Generic Model Classes

Table 12.1 Generic Model Properties

Properties	Macro-Econometric	Input-Output	Input-Output - Econometric	Computable General Equilibrium	Computable General Equilibrium - Econometric
Philosophical Objective	Forecasting	Comparative static analysis	Track short-run and long-run dynamics	Measure optimal allocation of resources	Measure optimal allocation of resources
Main Use	Forecasting	Impact	Impact and forecasting	Impact	Impact
Level of Detail	Economic aggregates	Industry level	Industry level	Industry level	Industry level
Output	Long-run and short-run time path of aggregates	Output, income, employment multipliers and impacts	Long-run and short-run time path of aggregate and industry variables and impacts	Optimal long-run / short-run reallocation of resources	Optimal long-run / short-run reallocation of resources
Equilibrium	Long-run equilibrium Short-run non-equilibrium	Long-run partial equilibrium	Long-run equilibrium Short-run non-equilibrium	Long-run general equilibrium	Long-run general equilibrium
Dynamics	Long-run and short-run structural econometrics	No	Long-run and short-run structural econometrics; technological, trade and price change functions.	Mathematical growth / adjustment functions	Mathematical growth / adjustment functions; exogenous econometric forecasts
Intermediate Production Technology	No	Fixed (Leontief)	Variable	Fixed (Leontief)	Fixed (Leontief)
Primary Factor Technology	No	Fixed (Leontief)	Variable in aggregate; substitutable (econometric based functions)	Fixed in aggregate; substitutable (cost minimization, e.g. CES function)	Fixed in aggregate; substitutable (cost minimization, e.g. CES function)
Capacity Constraints	Partial	No	Full closure encompassing consumption and investment functions	Market clearing and zero pure profit equations	Market clearing and zero pure profit equations
Finance Sector	Yes	No	Yes	Yes	Yes

To answer these questions, we need to provide a brief descriptive outline of the main alternative modeling strategies currently on offer to the regional analyst.[1] For the purpose of this exercise, we can regard these different models as belonging to different generic model classes. The contenders are, roughly in order of increasing complexity (see figure 12.1), input-output (IO), input-output / econometric (IO/EC), computable general equilibrium (CGE) and computable general equilibrium / econometric (CGE/EC). The features of each model are summarized in table 12.1. There are also regional macro-econometric (EC) models but these are not considered here because they lack industry disaggregation, although they are listed in table 12.1 for comparative purposes

12.3.1 Input-Output

Input-output revolutionized the study of economic structure. The first empirical interindustry model[2] was developed by Leontief in the 1930's in his study of the American economy (Leontief, 1936; 1951), although the concept of interdependence among productive sectors can be traced back to Walras (1877) or even earlier to Quesnay's 1758 *Tableau Economique*.

The input-output table is a set of regional accounts that documents the production and disposal of the goods and services in an economic system over a given (annual) period and thus provides a very detailed picture of the structure of the economy.[3] It can be viewed as a simple equilibrium construct at a point in time, and the study of structural interdependence involves identifying how this equilibrium shifts over time and how this impacts on other regions through interregional trading relations.

The rationale behind the IO model (as distinct from the IO table) is the *multiplier*. The core equation of the IO model is the so-called 'open solution:'

$$\Delta X = A\Delta X + \Delta F = (I - A)^{-1}\Delta F = (I + A + A^2 + \cdots)\Delta F \tag{12.1}$$

that corresponds to the Type I model in figure 12.2, where X is the change in industry production levels as a result of a change to final demand F, and A represents the matrix of average input (purchase) coefficients by industry. The $(I - A)^{-1}$ matrix is a multiplier matrix representing the successive rounds of expenditure through the economy. Thus, for example, every $1 million increase in Government expenditure, F, results in an average increase in Gross Output X of some multiple $(I - A)^{-1}$ of the initial $1 million. This multiplier concept was popularized by Keynes during the economic depression of the 1930's, and has been progressively refined, disaggregated and adapted. For example, it is common practice to calculate value added, household income and employment multipliers, among others, which are simple extensions of the core output multipliers.

---

[1] It is impossible to give a detailed exposition of each model in this short section. Only an overview of each model is provided here. Readers are encouraged to source the references provided for more information.

[2] It should be noted that input-output is a special case of interindustry analysis. Interindustry economics encompasses any methodology that takes into account the interdependence among the productive units of the economy. Input-output is only one of several methods for analysing these interdependencies.

[3] There are many fine books that describe the 'classical' input-output model in detail. See, e.g. Miernyk (1965), Richardson (1972) or Miller and Blair (1985).

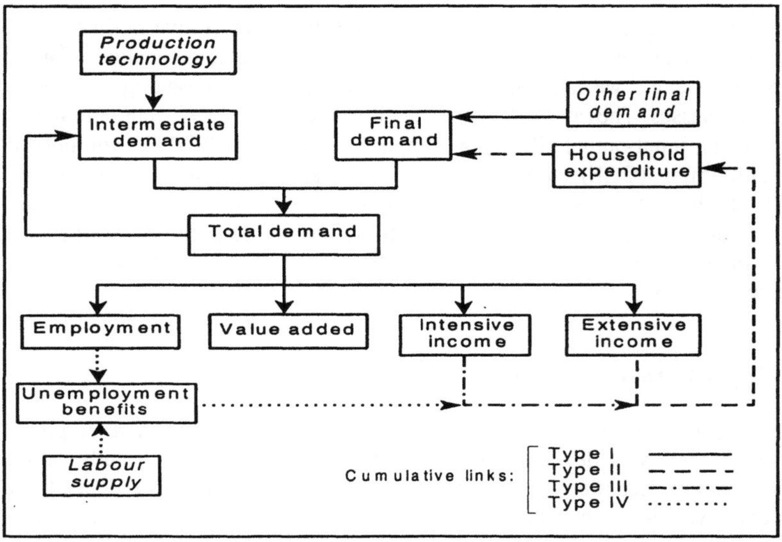

Figure 12.2 Type I – IV Input-Output Models

While the input-output table is simply an accounting statement, the transformation of the table into an operational model requires the use of a number of explicit assumptions. In terms of applied analysis, the focus of these assumptions comes down primarily to three main points: the static nature of the model, the linearity property, and unlimited supply and production capacity. It is for these reasons that more sophisticated models have been developed.

If the impacts involve substantial restructuring of local industries, input-output would not be appropriate. Being static in nature, it ignores the behavioral dynamics of change, including changing technology, investment and trade patterns.[4] The second assumption means that the input (production) coefficients are fixed average input propensities which implies that each dollar increase in output at the margin results in the same average proportional increase in inputs. This obviously rules out economies of scale. The final assumption means the model assumes full employment with no capacity constraints, and thus prices have no role to play through the supply and demand responses of the market mechanism.

One needs to view the application in the light of these restrictions. If the area under study is a small open economy relative to the rest of the nation, where factors of production (labor and capital) can easily move into and out of the region and local prices gravitate to external prices (subject to transport costs, etc.), then the IO model could be a reasonable choice. Conversely, if the economy is closed and there is likely to be 'crowding-out' of factors, then a more complex model is required.

There are a number of relatively simple extensions that can be made to the IO model, designed to move it closer to 'reality'. One common variation is the *extended* or *demo-economic* IO model. These are designed to capture part of the economic

[4] It has been suggested (e.g. Carter, 1970) that IO coefficients remain relatively stable in the face of technological change for several years. With globalisation and greater mobility of capital, both physical and intellectual, this time frame may be reduced.

activity associated with employed, unemployed and economically inactive households which is ignored in the Type I model in which only the productive industries are assumed endogenous.

If households are assumed to be an endogenous component of the economy selling labor and buying locally produced goods and services, the A matrix is extended (i.e. additional household rows and columns added) to include a 'household sector'. This is referred to as endogenizing 'extensive' income change (Type II model in figure 12.2). Here it is assumed that all consuming households are homogeneous and employed. Therefore if there is a stimulus to the economy, the only place where industries can draw additional labor is from outside the region. This is probably the most common IO model used in applied analyses.

Additional household induced effects that are sometimes added to the Type II model include 'intensive' income changes from the marginal changes in income of employed persons (e.g. due to economies of scale, etc.) (Type III model) and 'redistributive' income changes as local unemployed people (on unemployment benefits) become employed (Type IV model).

The simplest method of solving these extended models is in a commodity-activity framework. Early work in this area of modeling households came from Miernyk *et al.* (1967), Tiebout (1969), Blackwell (1978) and Miyazawa (1976). More recently, the procedure is commonly associated with the work of Batey and Madden (e.g. Batey and Madden, 1981; Batey, Madden and Weeks, 1987; Batey and Rose, 1990). Another variation by Oosterhaven and Folmer (1985) makes use of vacancy chains, using matrices of transition probabilities to determine how vacancies are filled. These procedures can also be applied to interregional migration flows (Batey and Weeks, 1987; Madden and Trigg, 1990; van Dijk and Oosterhaven, 1986; Oosterhaven and Dewhurst, 1990).

Unfortunately, while these extended or demo-economic models have the advantage of being parsimonious and perform well in certain situations, they retain the linear structure in which the household income coefficients are average propensities of marginal income groups and employment coefficients reflect average labor productivity rates. In impact studies, this leads to an overestimation of the flow-on (multiplier) effects, particularly if the initial impacts are relatively modest. For example, many industries can increase production in the short term without corresponding proportional increases in wage costs and employment, particularly if there is excess capacity. One variation, albeit more difficult to implement, which attempts to partly solve this problem is to replace some of the average input coefficients with marginal coefficients or elasticities of demand. This introduces a non-linear element into the model, i.e. non-constant returns to scale, with subsequent complications for finding a solution. In effect, the equation set becomes recursive; X depends on A and A depends on X in equation (12.1), necessitating an iterative solution procedure.

Evans (1954), later extended by Lahiri (1976), was one of the first to generalize the IO model to allow input coefficients to vary with the endogenous variables and utilized the power series expansion of equation (12.1) to obtain an iterative scheme for computing the solution to the non-linear model. Few empirical applications of marginal analysis have appeared, primarily due to data limitations (Tilanus, 1967; Bryden, 1973; Hamilton and Pongtanakron, 1983; West and Gamage, 1997).

However, in spite of these attempts to make the IO model more realistic, the majority of empirical interindustry applications at the regional level are still performed using the basic Type II model. While much maligned, the input-output model continues to a substantial workhorse of the regional practitioner, as a basic tool of analysis whose simplicity and transparency, if not its realism, are its major virtue. In fact, the strength and future of input-output probably lies at the small-area level[5], where the effects of the limiting assumptions are minimized and where the user is closer to the action and more familiar with the local economic scene. Here the main contribution would be in terms of community economic analysis (CEA) and the role the table would assume in economic development issues (Shaffer, 1989).

12.3.2 Input-Output/Econometric Models

Input-output econometric models belong to the class of models referred to in the literature as integrated models. Integrated models acknowledge that each model type displays a unique set of characteristics, both good and bad, and attempts to splice the different modeling approaches in such a way so as to enhance the strengths and minimize the weaknesses. Both input-output (IO) and econometric (EC) models have strengths and weaknesses. The strength of input-output lies in the detailed interindustry accounts, the weaknesses are linearity, constant technology, and unlimited capacity. Econometric models, on the other hand, are generally dynamic and non-linear (in an economic sense), but lack industry detail. The perceived advantages of integrating these two methodologies is to construct a model which provides a dynamic, non-linear picture of economic change in a detailed interindustry framework.

The idea of conjoining input-output and econometric models has been around for some time. Glickman (1977) suggested combining the "good qualities" of both approaches, while Klein (1989) also recommends this exercise. National integrated models have been operational for many years, for example the INFORUM family of models (Almon, 1991), but regional integrated models have only recently become popular. Rey (1998) reviewed a number of regional integrated models and suggests a taxonomy of integration strategies: coupling, embedding and linking. The coupling strategy is the most comprehensive requiring the development of a full set of final demand accounts that permits a high degree of model closure and interaction between the IO and EC components. Embedding utilizes prior information from an IO model to achieve parsimony in the specification of the EC model without a full specification of final demand accounts. In the linking strategy, the output from one module provides the input into the other module in a recursive fashion.

How the input-output and econometric models are integrated depends to a large extent on the modeler's objectives. They can range from what can be called input-output / econometric (IO/EC) models, which are dominated by the IO model and use econometrically estimated equations to endogenize the relationships among factor inputs and final demands (the closure), to econometric/input-output (EC/IO) models which use an EC model as a starting point and replace the output component by an input-output block. In practice, the distinction between the two is often blurred, although each method has its own peculiarities and difficulties associated with the integration process (Anselin, *et al.* 1990; Dewhurst and West, 1991).

---

[5] It should be noted that the construction of small-area input-output tables has somewhat different requirements to large-area tables. Building IO tables is a research area in its own right and is not discussed here. See, e.g., Lahr (1993).

In the United States, the most widely implemented framework at the regional level is that established by Conway (1979, 1990), and adopted by the Regional Economic Applications Laboratory (REAL)[6] in the early 1990s, as a means of providing an impacts and forecasting capability with a strong regional flavor (see, e.g., Israilevich *et al.*, 1997). Similar models have been constructed for the States of Washington, Illinois, Iowa and Ohio, and metropolitan areas including Chicago, Cincinnati and Columbus. The IO table does not exist as a separate entity within this framework. Rather, the IO coefficients only exist indirectly in the form of parameters of a subset of econometric equations. These models are therefore similar to more conventional regional EC models, both in terms of overall structure and in terms of individual equation specification. They are identified here as belonging to the EC/IO class of model. Thus, in common with other regional EC models, the EC/IO model has all the features of a forecasting tool.

An alternative, and sharply different, formulation of a coupled integrated model are the Australian models (Dewhurst and West, 1990; West, 1994). In contrast with the Conway-type specification, these models retains the explicit structure of the IO model and its classical output solution as given in equation (12.1), with the econometric relationships integrated into the primary input and final demand components. These models therefore retain the character of a conventional IO model and thus fall into the IO/EC classification. An overview of the two model structures is given in figure 12.3. This distinction is a deliberate act on the part of the model builders, determined partly by data availability and partly by perceived strengths in model design (West and Jackson, 1998).

As a simple demonstration of the IOEC[7] logical structure, compared to CGE-type models, consider the household sector. Many IOEC models identify a *real side* and a *price-income side*, as well as an aggregate or macro component that forms the closure. The real side deals with production and final demands, while the price side deals with industry and commodity prices, as well as wage rates, interest rates, income, etc.

From industry gross outputs we get estimates of employment from labor productivity functions, which combined with wage rate equations generate wages and salary payments by sector. Demographic equations provide estimates of population by various characteristics, including labor force, unemployed, social security recipients, natural population growth and migration, age cohorts and, in some cases, gender cohort. Industry production figures give estimates of value added and profits. Other equations give estimates of other income from sources such as interest payments and dividends. Total income is simply the sum of all the separate income sources. Subtracting income tax payments and other indirect taxes and deductions provides total disposable income. Thus, the model captures all household income, unlike the IO Type II model that only endogenizes wage income.

Household consumption expenditure can then be estimated either by a set of consumption functions by industry or via an aggregate consumption function, which in turn is used to estimate a set of demand functions by major commodity groups. These are transformed into household demands by industry category to provide the private consumption expenditure component of final demand, and thus the closure is complete. Similar processes hold for government and investment. We thus see that the

---

[6] REAL is a cooperative research venture between the University of Illinois and the Federal Reserve Bank of Chicago.

[7] The notation IOEC will be used to represent integrated IO and EC models in general, without differentiating between IO/EC or EC/IO variants.

sequence is logical and intuitive, and all estimates are based on observed data.

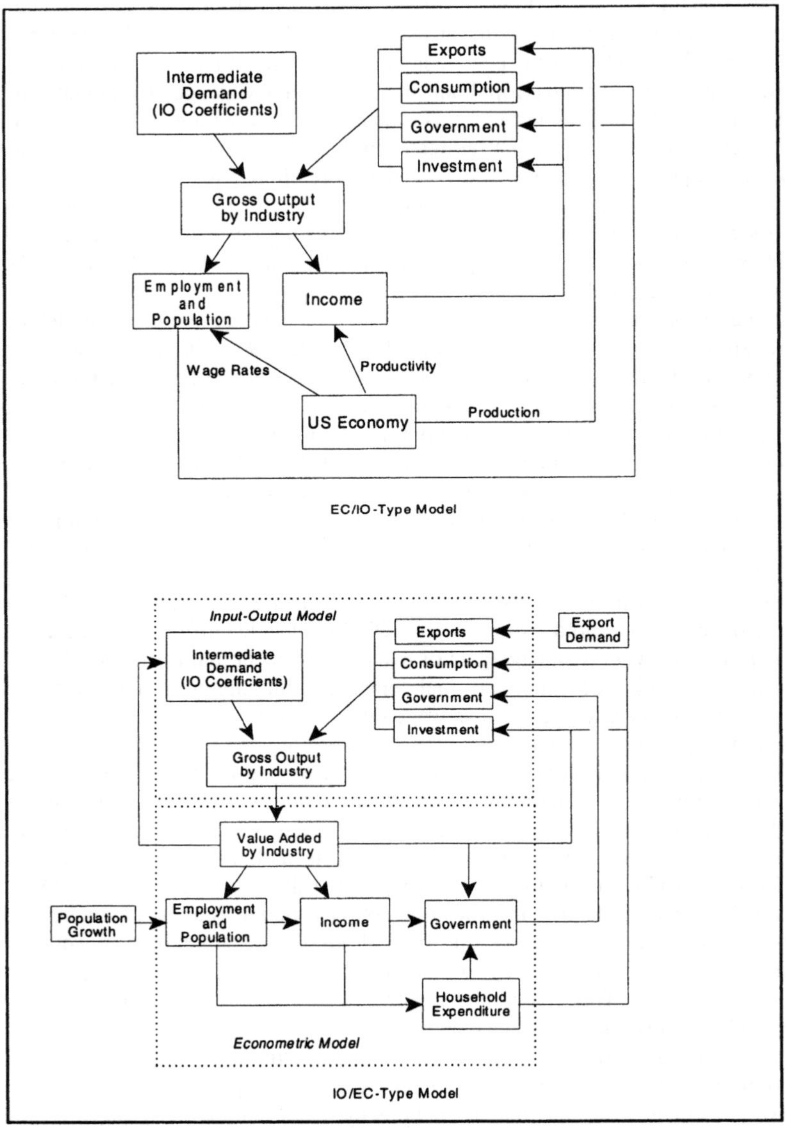

Figure 12.3 Integrated Input-Output Econometric Models

Lack of supply-side specification is an often-quoted criticism of the integrated IO and EC model (Beaumont, 1990). However, this argument is not strictly valid. While some early models were be lacking in this regard, most integrated models now pay attention to this aspect. There is no question that supply constraints need to be imposed on factor inputs otherwise there is no limit to the economic expansion associated with an exogenous stimulus to the economy. Rather, the question is how to implement it.

Empirically, there are several possibilities. Central to the efficient use of scarce resources is the price mechanism. A common method of endogenizing product prices is through the Ghoshian-type supply-driven model (Ghosh, 1958; Dietzenbacher, 1997). Alternatively, one can forecast prices as markups over wages plus intermediate costs (Meade, 1999). Other prices can then be separately determined. Borrowing from macro-economic theory, one possibility is to then link price responses to inflation and interest rates, with the subsequent stimulating/dampening effect on economic activity. A second possibility is to link prices into a micro-economic optimization framework of cost minimization or 'efficiency', either using standard production functions (as in CGE models) or through other integrated systems such as linear programming (single objective optimization) or goal programming (multi-objective optimization). In the eyes of the IOEC fraternity, the macro-economic approach is closer to perceived reality[8], the latter imposes additional 'non-empirical' external constraints into the system. For example, in the optimization route, share parameters and substitution elasticities often need to be imposed and fixed, since the cost minimizing framework of these models generally does not allow for the endogenous estimation of these parameters on real world observations.

To the extent that firms and agents have incomplete information on optimal strategies, it would be desirable for the model to be based on observed revenues and costs to allow for different levels of uncertainty in the decision process. Roy (1997) and West and Roy (1998) suggest such a probabilistic approach based on entropy maximization in an interregional framework. A price adjustment ensures short-run market clearing similar to that adopted in the CGE model but the supply response to changing demands is lagged. In the short-run, capacity is fixed. As actual supply approaches capacity, penalty functions come into force, yielding a lower propensity to supply and forcing demand into adjacent regions, the regional distributions being determined by price differentials, including transport costs, between the regions. As long as total demand does not exceed the total capacity limit over all regions, capacity will never be exceeded in any single region. However, some effort is needed to obtain data on the capacity limits for each factor in each sector and in each region, as well as price levels, since, in Roy's model, these are based on actual data. Long run behavior is determined by estimating the speeds of adjustment of long-run movements to different levels of price differentials between regions.

An important feature of the integrated IO and EC models is the dynamics, as this is what differentiates it from the IO and CGE models. It was realized long ago (e.g. Leontief, 1953; Moore and Petersen, 1955) that a dynamic element is needed if IO or other models are to be used for the analysis of business cycles, industry growth and technological change. As economies develop and become more complex and responsive to internal and external evolutionary pressures, projections of a static model in a dynamic context are clearly inadequate. Static models only measure long-run comparative equilibrium solutions. What is of interest is the time path taken to get to that long-run solution, which is characterized by short-run disequilibrium adjustments. Dynamic models measure these short-run disequilibrium adjustments.

One way of introducing a temporal dimension to a static model is to calculate

[8] This is the view taken by, for example, in the US LIFT model (McCarthy, 1991).

periodic solutions to the model through a system of econometric equations, in a so-called 'recursive dynamic' fashion in which the system of equations is solved for each year before rolling over to the following year. This is the procedure adopted by the integrated IO and EC model. The dynamics of the model obviously follow from the econometric specifications, and as such do not differ to any large extent from any other macro-econometric model.

The dynamics in econometric modeling is well researched and documented.[9] Modern econometric practice postulates both long-run and short-run dynamics within an error correction framework. A long-run relationship is typically expressed in levels form, while short-run disequilibrium fluctuations can be incorporated using partial adjustment mechanisms in which the model needs to be expressed in deviation form. Both the long-run and short-run relationships provide potentially useful information for explaining variations in the variable of interest, and can be combined into a single equation.[10] Such an equation is referred to as an error correction model (ECM) because it not only measures the short-run disequilibrium movements in the variable, but also the forces required to pull it back to a long-run equilibrium value.

Because the models are dynamic, attention must be given to the effects of price changes, technology changes and import substitution on the input coefficients. In the Conway-type EC/IO formulation, coefficient change is generated by means of functions that relate actual sectoral output to predicted output. These functions are then used to adjust predicted sectoral output on the basis of historical trends. The difference between actual and predicted output is a measure of coefficient change from all sources, including relative price changes, technological change and change in import substitution. The separate effects are not identified. This provides for a parsimonious model. For forecasting, this may be adequate, *ceteris paribus*, but in impact modeling is opens the model to possible criticism if the impacts have differential effects on the change components. The IO/EC approach, because it retains the explicit IO structure, facilitates the identification and modeling of these separate effects. Rey (1997) reviews several existing approaches for modeling coefficient change in integrated models.

This raises another advantage of the integrated model in that a natural component of the solution is a consistent series of variable coefficient annual input-output tables. In the IO/EC configuration, this fall directly out of the solution. The input-output coefficients are updated annually for technology, import substitution and relative price effects. This provides a powerful debugging and analysis tool, and an efficient and effective method for updating the input-output table for other purposes. In the Conway-type model, the process is more tedious. Shocking final demand for a single sector by one unit will generate total output impacts over all sectors that corresponds to the column of the Leontief inverse for that sector. Repeating the process for each sector generates the entire Leontief inverse matrix from which the direct coefficients and transactions table can be derived.

It is clear that the integrated model is much more comprehensive than the IO model, in terms of trying the capture a wider subset of reality. The down side is that it is more difficult to build and maintain and, at the small region level in particular, suffers from severe data limitations. This would generally restrict the availability of IOEC models to large regions or states, relegating the IO model to the smaller regions.

---

[9] See, for example, Enders (1995) or Charemza and Deadman (1997) or any of the other numerous texts on econometric time-series modeling.

[10] Provided certain conditions hold, e.g. that the variables are cointegrated.

12.3.3 Computable General Equilibrium

Equilibrium implies a balance between economic variables, such as income and expenditure, or demand and supply. While IO represents a simplified form of equilibrium, computable general equilibrium (CGE) models are intended to capture a wider set of equilibrium relationships than the IO model. In short, they relax the assumptions of linearity and unlimited capacity, and provide an alternative closure mechanism to the IOEC model. This is achieved through endogenizing prices.[11]

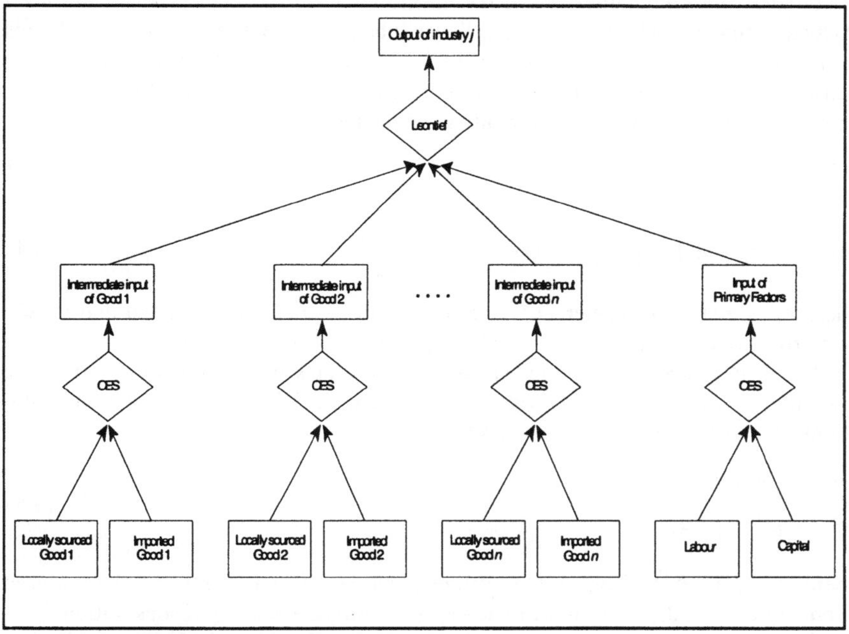

Figure 12.4 CGE Production Technology

The starting point for the GGE model is the IO table. Each transactions flow is disaggregated into two components, price and quantity. One possibility is to assume that the benchmark IO table is a physical quantities table measured in unit prices (on this issue, see Israilevich, 2001, chapter 21 in this volume). Then any exogenous shock will produce price changes measured as relative price changes from unity.

Each producer in a regional industry chooses its inputs so as to minimize its costs of production subject to a multi-layered production function, as shown in figure 12.4. At the first level, there are two broad categories of inputs, intermediate and primary, which are used in fixed proportions to output, using Leontief technology.[12] Thus

[11] See, for example, Dixon, *et al.* (1992), Shoven and Whalley (1992) or Dervis, *et al.* (1982) for a detailed exposition of CGE models.

[12] This is due to the structure of the IO table, which is constructed on the assumption that inputs are homogeneous and non-substitutable; e.g., one does not normally substitute food products for steel products, or vice versa.

industry output is given by

$$X_j = \min\left(\frac{x_{1j}}{a_{1j}},\ldots,\frac{x_{nj}}{a_{nj}},\frac{V_j}{a_{vj}}\right) \tag{12.2}$$

where x_{ij} is the amount of the ith intermediate input used by the jth industry and V_j is the value added or primary factor input. The a_{ij} are the IO technical coefficients that are assumed to be fixed.

The inputs at the first level are composite goods that in turn consist of sub-inputs, *i.e.*, bundles of commodities that make up the broader category. The second level production function allows for the non-linear substitution between sub-inputs. At this level, a CES function is commonly used[13]. For example, intermediate inputs into industry j consist of both locally produced commodities and imported commodities, which can be combined in the cost minimizing manner:

$$\min C_{ij} = p_{ij}^M x_{ij}^M + p_{ij}^D x_{ij}^D \tag{12.3}$$

$$\text{subject to } x_{ij} = A_{ij}\left[\lambda_{ij}\left(x_{ij}^M\right)^{-\rho_{ij}} + \left(1-\lambda_{ij}\right)\left(x_{ij}^D\right)^{-\rho_{ij}}\right]^{-\frac{1}{\rho_{ij}}} \tag{12.4}$$

where A_{ij} is a shift parameter, x_{ij}^M and x_{ij}^D are the amounts of imported and locally used products with prices p_{ij}^M and p_{ij}^D respectively, λ_{ij} is a parameter expressing the benchmark cost share of imported inputs in total inputs of commodity i, and ρ_{ij} the elasticity of substitution between imported and locally produced commodities. Minimizing (12.3) subject to (12.4) gives

$$\frac{x_{ij}^M}{x_{ij}^D} = \left(\frac{p_{ij}^D}{p_{ij}^M}\right)^{\sigma}\left(\frac{\lambda_{ij}}{1-\lambda_{ij}}\right)^{\sigma} \tag{12.5}$$

where $\sigma = 1/\left(1+\rho_{ij}\right)$. That is, the relative quantities of imported to locally produced commodities used depends on the relative prices and the elasticity of substitution.[14]

Similarly, primary inputs consist of labor and capital, which would be combined so as to minimize cost

$$C_{v_j} = w_j L_j + k_j K_j \tag{12.6}$$

according to the relationship

$$V_j = A_j\left[\delta_j L_j^{-\alpha_j} + \left(1-\delta_j\right)K_j^{-\alpha_j}\right]^{-\frac{1}{\alpha_j}} \tag{12.7}$$

where w_j and k_j are prices of labor L_j and capital K_j respectively, A_j is a shift parameter, δ_j is a share parameter and α_j is the elasticity of substitution between labor and capital. Of course, this can be extended further by breaking down capital into imported and

[13] The CES (Constant Elasticity of Substitution) function is a common function used in CGE models because it exhibits certain desirable properties. All functions used in CGE models must have well defined theoretical properties otherwise the model will be unsolvable or become unstable in simulations. One advantage of the CES function is that it is fairly general. For example, the Leontief and Cobb-Douglas functions are both special cases of the CES.

[14] This is often referred to as the Armington (1969) assumption.

local, and labor could be disaggregated into different skill categories in a similar manner.

Household demands for commodity x_{i0} are commonly calculated my maximizing a Stone-Geary or similar utility function subject to a household expenditure constraint:[15]

$$\max u = \ln U = \sum_i \beta_i \ln\left(x_{i0} - \gamma_i\right) \tag{12.8}$$

$$\text{subject to } Y_0 = \sum_i p_i x_{i0} \tag{12.9}$$

where γ_i is the subsistence level for good i and β_i is the marginal budget share allocated to good i. Y_0 is total household expenditure and p_i is the price of consumer good i. Thus the consumer first sets aside the minimum necessary budget given the subsistence levels of each good, and then allocates his remaining budget to good i in proportion to the parameter β_i. At the second level, the consumer chooses between local and imported commodities by maximizing a CES utility function subject to the expenditure allocated to that good.

The closure of a CGE model has both an accounting dimension and a behavioral dimension.[16] Firstly, there are zero pure profit equations that ensure that revenue from the sale of goods and services equals their costs:

$$p_j X_j = \sum_i x_{ij} p_i \tag{12.10}$$

Secondly, there are the market clearing equations in which demand and supply are equated for each commodity produced:

$$\sum_i x_{ij} = X_i \tag{12.11}$$

These equations imply that total income equals total revenue in the region.

The strength of CGE lies in its roots of (neo) classical economic theory, building up from the micro industry level to the macro economy level in a consistent, all encompassing framework. However, it is clear from the above structure that there are a number of points that analysts, contemplating using a CGE model, need to bear in mind.

First, it is an optimization model; optimal in the sense that both producers and consumers optimize their behavior. Producers select the minimum cost factor combination (labor, capital, land) and consumers select the utility maximizing combination of consumer goods and services in a world of perfect information. In practice, producers and consumers simply do not have enough information to practice fully optimal behavior, given the realities of lags in production and other regulatory, geographic and institutional constraints. The best we can hope for is sub-optimal behavior in a limited information situation.

Secondly, critics would argue that a unique static general equilibrium, as distinct from isolated separate or multiple market equilibria, generally does not occur in the

---

[15] Here, again, alternative functional forms can be used. For example, the Leontief function is sometimes used to combine the composite goods derived at the second level.

[16] There are additional accounting equations required to handle interregional and international trade and the balance of payments. These are not addressed specifically here.

real world (Mercenier, 1995). Rather, they would argue that, while the economy may be moving erratically towards such a point, full equilibrium is never reached before it is deflected towards a new equilibrium due to continual unforeseen shocks, both internal and external to the economy, such as interest rate changes, balance of payments and exchange rate effects. This is a function of the real time lagged responses to changes in economic systems. The CGE model, being comparative static just like the IO model, does not recognize 'real time'. Some dynamics can be modeled by specifying different closures and growth functions; for example, capital stocks are normally assumed to be effectively fixed in the short-term but, by selecting an appropriate stock adjustment function, can increase in the longer-term. However, while this type of model exhibits a form of long-run 'dynamic' equilibrium, short-run disequilibria are more difficult to implement.

Thirdly, CGE models generally do not allow the data to 'speak for itself'. CGE models use assumed relationships rather than empirically estimated relationships.[17] Furthermore, the various parameters of these functions need to be quantitified. For example, there are many hundreds or even thousands[18] of elasticities of substitution to be quantified (at least one for each and every cell in the input-output table) before the model can be applied, too many for any meaningful research to be carried out to estimate their values. The model builder has no choice but to use 'imposed values', which are arbitrary values ranging from anywhere between zero and infinity, and use some sensitivity analysis to assess how much the results depend on these imposed values.[19] In large models, the cumulative effect of the many assumed complex mathematical relationships with their arbitrarily imposed parameters can often impose distortions that are beyond the comprehension of the practitioner.[20]

Fourthly, CGE models tend to be very sensitive to the 'closure' rules that are necessary for solving the model. The model will invariably have many more variables than equations, which means that some variables will need to be fixed or given predetermined values. The choice of which variables are allowed to vary (endogenous variables) and which are fixed (exogenous variables) is called the closure. This is by no means an easy decision in a large model. As an example, Skene (1993), in a study of the effects of an increase in international tourist expenditure on GDP in Australia, found that the multiplier can vary between 1.8 to 11.4 depending on the selected closure. For example, tax rates on households and business can be assumed fixed (thus allowing the Government to use the extra revenue to reduce the deficit), or alternatively, the deficit can be assumed to be held constant (with the Government using the extra revenue to reduce taxes).

---

[17] For example, as previously mentioned, the CES production function is assumed to describe the relative demands for local and imported substitutes, or between labour and capital.

[18] The MONASH (formerly known as ORANI) model of the Australian economy contains several million equations (Dixon *et al.*, 1982, 1992).

[19] There are many studies reporting the results of model sensitivity to elasticity values (eg. Boadway and Treddenick, 1978; Dervis *et al*, 1982; Dixon *et al*, 1985). There is sometimes a conflict between econometrically estimated elasticities (Stern *et al*, 1976; Caddy, 1976; Jorgenson, 1984), which generally report low values, and CGE models which use much higher values. Parmenter (1983) illustrates some of the strange results which arise when using export demand elasticities estimated by econometric methods in CGE models.

[20] This raises an interesting question. How can we reconcile the 'conflict of interest' which occurs when a model is used to test or 'prove' an hypothesis when the model builder has selected 'appropriate' functions and parameter values which reflect his or her perception of reality?

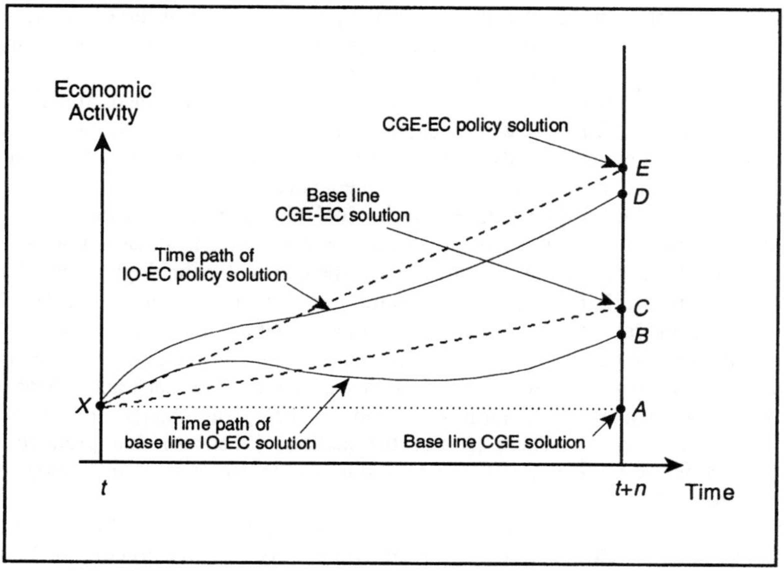

Figure 12.5 IOEC and CGE Solution Paths

Solving the CGE model can be a complex affair. They are highly non-linear which, when combined with the size scale of the models, can result in the need for complex solution techniques. One possibility is to attempt to solve the equations using numerical optimization methods, another is to transform the equations using linear approximation methods into percentage-change form and solve using linear algebra. Either way, the model builder is limited in the choice of functions that can be used in order to ensure solvability and stability of the solution.

12.3.4 Computable General Equilibrium / Econometric

Recent initiatives have centered on the integration of computable general equilibrium with macro-econometric models in an attempt to counter the criticism of lack of empirical dynamics in the CGE model. Current applications appear to be limited to a linking strategy in terms of Rey's (1998) taxonomy, rather than the more common coupled strategy of IO and EC models.

In its basic form, CGE/EC models operate in a two-step procedure. Firstly, the macro-econometric model is run to provide a base-line forecast of macro-economic variables. The CGE model then tries to 'explain' these forecasts by incorporating the macro-forecasts as exogenous variables into the CGE model. This produces a base-line (micro) solution (point *C* in figure 12.5), as distinct from the non-dynamic base-line solution (point *A*). To find the effects of a policy change on the macro-variables, the CGE model closure is then switched around. The micro forecast solution and policy shocks are imposed on the model and macro-variables become endogenous (point *E*). Note the solution is still comparative static; it only compares the equilibrium point *E* with equilibrium point *C*, and not the time paths taken by the economy in reaching those points. This also implies that the long-run equilibrium form of the econometric model and not the short-run non-equilibrium adjustment form is used in the linking process, as lags are not applicable in the CGE framework.

An alternative formulation is to replace some of the assumed functional relationships in the CGE model with econometrically estimated relationships.[21] As above, this requires rewriting the dynamic econometric equations into a form suitable for the CGE system, i.e. as long-run static, annual equations.

As noted in relation to IOEC models, technological change plays a fundamental part in any dynamic model. Unfortunately, technological change is an issue not easily addressed in the CGE model. The norm is to assume constant technology. There has been some recent work on this issue (Beutre and Ahmadi-Esfanhani, 2000) by backcasting the model and incorporating all the available information about the economy into the model. This provides information on the state of technology required to obtain a particular solution. However, currently there does not appear to any way of endogenizing this information on technological change in forward projections of the model. There is also the additional concern that production functions such as the CES may not be appropriate in the presence of technological change (Duchin, 2000).

While these approaches go part of the way in bridging the gap between the theoretical structure of CGE and the empirical dynamics of EC, the structure of CGE currently precludes the integration of fully dynamic, incorporating short-run disequilibrium behavior, econometric relationships.

12.4 Issues of Relevance to Model Builders and Users

So far, we have attempted to provide an appreciation of the properties and characteristics of the alternative modeling approaches. This is only part of the story. This section expands on some issues which were touched briefly and are relevant to builders and users of models, and draws together the more salient similarities and differences of the alternative modeling approaches.

12.4.1 Equilibrium

There are many different views of equilibrium. All IO based models inherit some form of equilibrium behavior. We therefore need to be clear on what form of equilibrium is important. In some sense, all the models represented here rely on the "unnatural view of equilibrium theory that the economy eventually settles at a state of balance" (Morishima, 2000, p.17).

The CGE model relies heavily on neoclassical theory and all that implies; perfect competition where markets operate without friction, full capacity and full market clearing of all goods and services, and perfect or near-perfect knowledge. It does not represent the real economy, for several reasons that have already been discussed.[22]

---

[21] See Fry *et al.* (1999) for an example of this form of integration.

[22] This has implications for model validation. Few economists would claim that actual reality is synonymous

These limitations do not necessarily make general equilibrium analysis invalid. The aim is to provide an insight into the interaction between the micro and macro economic processes under perfect or near-perfect competition, which is a goal of the modern economic rationalist movement. Being comparative static, they provide an indication of the 'optimal' reallocation of resources after the economy is subjected to an exogenous shock.

Advocates of integrated IO and EC models shy away from the neoclassical paradigm in favor of concentrating on the dynamic time path of the economy. While IOEC-type models are, by necessity, generally constrained by some form of long-run equilibrium conditions, the emphasis is on the short-run dynamics. The economy is rarely, at any given point in time, in a steady state situation. They would argue that the market may never reach full-equilibrium; at any point in time it may be moving towards an equilibrium but that point is never reached before it veers off in a different direction due to continual unforeseen shocks, both within and external to the economy. Whether, of course, these unforeseen shocks can be successfully modeled into the future is another question altogether, as we can only be guided by historical data. Nevertheless, they see the actual time path of adjustment processes as being more important and interesting than knowing what the optimal general equilibrium solution could be at some unknown time in the future.

12.4.2 Dynamics

As economies develop and become more complex and responsive to internal and external evolutionary pressures, projections of a static model in a dynamic context are clearly inadequate. Thus dynamics is considered an indispensable part of modern economic analysis.

The CGE model is a static model upon which attempts have been made to add a dynamic element. Integrated IO and EC models, on the other hand, start off by explicitly assuming a dynamic structure. CGE measures impacts in a comparative-static manner by comparing the initial equilibrium solution with the 'counterfactual' policy equilibrium solution. Some dynamics are modeled by specifying different closures and growth functions. Introducing exogenous macro-economic projections enables the base line solution to at least get close to the real solution. While this type of model exhibits a long-run equilibrium, short-run disequilibria are more difficult to implement. Further, the solution to a static equilibrium is timeless. The multiplier rounds resulting from the stimulus are, for all intents and purposes, treated as being instantaneous, even though they may take considerable time to work through the economy.

The objective of the integrated IO and EC model is to track the economy over time as this adjustment process occurs, and to trace the progressive paths of all the variables as they react to each successive multiplier round. This provides for one form for model validation, lacking in IO or CGE, through the comparison of forecasts with ex-post observed values. An additional dimension to the IOEC model is that it is developed within a stochastic framework, unlike CGE that is deterministic. While there is still much research to be done in this area, it does provide a potential structure which,

---

with perfect competition. Rather, advocates of CGE would see it an idealistic goal, and that in itself is sufficient to validate these types of models.

intuitively, should provide for a more robust and reliable set of results.

12.4.3 Production Technology

Production technology is assumed constant in the CGE model based on the benchmark IO table, with intermediate inputs determined by Leontief technology. The integrated IO and EC model, being dynamic, sees structural change in the form of changing technology and trade coefficients as an important feature of economic reality and therefore addresses this issue in some detail.

12.4.4 Substitution

Both CGE and integrated IOEC models recognize the importance of separability and substitutability between factors, i.e., labor and capital. The integrated model estimates industry value added as a non-proportional function of industry output based on historical data while the CGE model retains the Leontief assumption and estimates industry value added as a fixed proportion of industry output. In both cases, labor and capital are split from value added in a non-linear fashion; in the integrated model using econometric estimation and in the CGE model using cost minimization and non-linear production functions. The former requires historical time-series data and the latter relative prices and imposed elasticities of substitution between factors.

Similarly, extra-regional trade is modeled in the CGE model using cost minimization and CES or similar functions based on relative prices and elasticities of substitution between locally produced and foreign goods. The regional IOEC integrated model assumes output is both locally and export oriented, with growth being driven largely by export demand, and is therefore closely tied to national production indices. This is one area where strong national (and international) links and forecasts are deemed important for the operation of the model. Investment plays an important role in determining economic capacity in both models.

12.4.5 Small Region Considerations

How the region of interest interacts with the surrounding regions and nation as a whole effects the model specification. It will impact on the region in two main ways; through prices and through interregional trade. If the region is small, this can greatly simplify the specification.

Generally, the main link with the outside world is prices, i.e., local prices relative to foreign (extra-regional) prices. In the small region assumption, it is assumed that the region on its own is too small to affect the terms of trade; in other words, the region is a price taker so external prices become exogenous. Local supply and demand still interact and determine relative local prices, but these prices will gravitate to the given external prices.[23]

Note the similarity with the IO model. The IO model is an equilibrium model in the sense that demand and supply are forced to equate to each other. From the dual

[23] Subject, of course, to transport and other margins.

Ghoshian model, it is possible to calculate relative prices, but there is no feedback mechanism back to quantities, i.e., local prices are assumed to have no effect on local production. However, local prices will adjust to the external prices if imports are perfect substitutes for local commodities. This is called the 'strong small country assumption', where local prices are set equal to the given (predetermined) world prices.[24] This implies that (a) local demand does not affect the foreign prices for imports, i.e., the extra-regional supply curves are infinitely elastic, and (b) local supply does not affect the world price of exported goods, i.e., demand for exports is infinitely elastic. However, if the region produces a relatively large proportion of the world output for a particular good, then assumption (b) may not be appropriate (at least for that good).

The strong assumption also implies that the region cannot have a trade deficit or surplus, because of the GDP identity. In the standard CGE model, hoarding of money or spending on credit is not permissible. This also applies to labor, with excess demand for labor set to zero. This implies that constructing a CGE model for a small region, while not invalid, may to some extent not be a very efficient use of resources.[25] Given the considerable difficulties associated with parameterizing a large number of coefficients and parameters when there is virtually no local data available, the increased 'fuzziness' may more than offset the increase in model sophistication. In such cases, the principle of Occum's Razor may be worth keeping in mind.[26]

12.4.6 Data Implications

Irrespective of the model category, the core data requirement is a regional input-output table. Many countries, including Australia, are fortunate in that are a number or organizations, both private and government, produce high quality regional IO tables based on extensive region-specific data. There are no government published regional IO tables in the US, but there are some private sources of IO data such as IMPLAN. Most of these are based on top-down estimates. The REAL-type EC/IO models seem to be unique in the US in that they use IO data extracted directly from Census of Manufacturing establishment records.

Apart from the IO table, the integrated IOEC data requirements are mainly time-series. Here again, Australia is fortunate having full sets of annual state accounts on which to base its equations. Data for US states and regions do not exist at the same level of detail and consequently many of the structural parameters are estimated from national data. It is these data characteristics that has, to a large extent, conditioned the formulation of the two integrated models in figure 12.3 and led to their different structural forms.

The CGE model does not use time series data, but in many ways its data requirements are even more demanding. Of particular concern is the pre-specification of numerous elasticities of substitution, between local and imported inputs, labor and capital, local and imported capital, and different skill categories of labor to name but a

[24] This implies that there is a question of aggregation involved. If there is some product differentiation between local and imported commodities, the strong small country assumption may not be suitable.

[25] It has been demonstrated that, particularly under 'small region' assumptions, the CGE solution converges to the IO solution (McGregor and Swales, 1994).

[26] The principle of Occum's Razor states that, if there are two or more theories (models) explaining the same set of observations, the simplest theory (model) is best.

few. These are in addition to various capital and other adjustment coefficient matrices. With an almost complete void of regional empirical data to base these estimates on, 'best guess' values must be used.

It is clear that small regions pose significant data implications on the models. Generally speaking, the smaller the region, the less available and less reliable are the data. Both the CGE and IOEC-type models suffer in this respect, and there is no doubt that a rich region-specific data set clearly opens the door to a wider range of modeling possibilities.

12.5 A Single Model?

The last two sections provide an appreciation of the properties and characteristics of the alternative modeling approaches. All the models have appealing attributes. Thus there are strong arguments for a merging of the more attractive aspects of these attributes to provide a more encompassing model, much as in the same way that input-output and econometric models have merged.

The fundamental hurdle appears to arise from the diametrically opposed philosophies. This comes down to whether we can reconcile optimal behavior in a prefect world with real-time non-optimal behavior. But as the IOEC models have demonstrated, it is possible to build models which are constrained to a long-run steady state equilibrium as well as taking into account short-run real-time dynamics.

Nevertheless, the final product will still be influenced by the model builder's preconceived perceptions of reality. This is not a bad thing. If everyone thought the same, it would be a very boring world. Differences of opinion and perception encourage debate that, together with curiosity, is the driving force of learning and knowledge. In any case, there are strong arguments to KISS (Keep it Simple, Stupid). There is growing evidence to suggest that simple models perform just as well as complex models.

12.6 Conclusion

Returning to the question, can we meaningfully compare models, the answer is clearly 'yes'. This chapter demonstrates that there are substantial differences between models that can be classified by their generic properties. Which model should we use? This is more difficult to answer, but there are some guidelines. For example, if forecasting or dynamics is an important issue, it is relatively clear that a model with an econometric component is preferred.

There is also a question of balance between choosing a simple, easy to understand model versus a more complex, often difficult to understand and apply, but in some ways more theoretically appealing, model. Again, it depends on the application. While many have forecast the end of the simple input-output model due to its inadequacies, it has proved surprisingly resilient. IO still has the advantage over more sophisticated models at the very small region level (e.g. small towns), where it really provides the only option to planners in spite of its known limitations. IOEC and CGE models also occupy their own niches. It is also clear that the integrated IOEC and CGE frameworks are moving closer together, perhaps in a similar manner as the AMOS model (Harrigan *et al.*, 1990). At the same time, it would be advantageous to make the models more flexible and adaptable to local conditions without resorting to making each model 'application specific', although this may be a big ask. It could even mean making the models smaller and more parsimonious rather than bigger and more complex (this is not necessarily a contradiction); large models tend to become a law unto themselves, and complexity is not necessarily a good guide to performance.

Given human nature, it is unavoidable that personal prejudices will play a part. For example, can we really believe that a general equilibrium exists, or that it is a goal worth striving for? Hard-core economists would argue 'yes'; that we are all ultra-rational profit maximizers, out to get as mush as we can with minimal investment of resources. Evolutionary economists, on the other hand, would disagree, citing numerous examples of cooperation for mutual advantage. The social and economic decisions of real-world humans are determined by a constellation of feelings and impulses, rather than cold, analytical, rational calculations. That is the challenge of modeling human behavior and economic systems.

References

Almon, C. 1991. "The INFORUM Approach to Interindustry Modeling." *Economic Systems Research*, 3, 1-7.

Anselin, L., S. Rey, and U. Deichmann. 1990. "The Implementation of Integrated Models in a Multi-regional System." In L. Anselin and M. Madden eds. *New Directions in Regional Analysis*. London, Belhaven.

Armington, P. 1969. "A Theory of Demand for Products Distinguished by Place of Production." *IMF Papers*, 16, 159-178.

Batey, P.W.J., and M. Madden. 1981. "Demographic-Economic Forecasting Within An Activity-commodity Framework: Some Theoretical Considerations and Empirical Results." *Environment and Planning A*, 13, 1067-1083.

Batey, P.W.J., M. Madden, and M.J. Weeks. 1987. "Household Income and Expenditure in Extended Input-Output Models: A Comparative Theoretical and Empirical Analysis." *Journal of Regional Science*, 27, 341-356.

Batey, P.W. and A.Z. Rose. 1990. "Extended Input-Output Models: Progress and Potential." *International Regional Science Review*, 13, 27-49.

Batey, P.W. and M.J. Weeks. 1987. "An Extended Input-Output Model Incorporating Employed, Unemployed and In-migrant Households." *Papers of the Regional Science Association*, 62, 93-115.

Beaumont, P.M. 1990. "Supply and Demand Interactions in Integrated Econometric and Input-Output Models." *International Regional Science Review*, 13, 167-181.

Blackwell, J. 1978. "Disaggregation of the Household Sector in Regional Input-Output Analysis: Some Models Specifying Previous Residence of Workers." *Regional Studies*, 12, 367-377.

Boadway, R. and J. Treddenick. 1978. "A General Equilibrium Computation of the Effects of the Canadian Tariff Structure." *Canadian Journal of Economics*, 11, 424-446.

Bryden, J. 1973. *Tourism and Development: A Case Study of the Commonwealth Caribbean*. Cambridge, Cambridge University Press.

Buetre, B.L. and F.Z. Ahmadi-Esfanhani. 2000. "Updating an Input-output Table for Use in Policy Analysis." *Australian Journal of Agricultural and Resource Economics*, 44, 573-603.

Caddy, V. 1976. "Empirical Estimation of the Elasticity of Substitution: A Review." *Impact Project Preliminary Working Paper No. OP-09*, Industry Commission, Canberra, Australia.
Carrier, H.D. and W.A. Wallace. 1994. "An Epistemological View of Decision Aid Technology with Emphasis on Expert Systems." In W.A. Wallace, ed. *Ethics in Modeling*, Oxford, Pergamon.
Carter, A.P. 1970. *Structural Change in the American Economy*. Cambridge, Harvard University Press.
Charemza, W.W. and D.F. Deadman. 1997. *New Directions in Econometric Practice*. Cheltenham, Edward Elgar.
Conway, R.S. Jr. 1979. "The Simulation Properties of a Regional Interindustry Econometric Model." *Papers of the Regional Science Association*, 43, 45-57.
Conway, R.S. Jr. 1990. "The Washington Projection and Simulation Model: A Regional Interindustry Econometric Model." *International Regional Science Review*, 13, 141-165.
Dervis, K., J. de Melo, and S. Robinson. 1982. *General Equilibrium Models for Development Policy*. Cambridge, Cambridge University Press.
Dewhurst, J.H.L. and G.R. West. 1990. "Closing Interregional Input-Output Models with Econometrically Determined Relationships." In L. Anselin and M. Madden, eds. *New Directions in Regional Analysis*. London, Belhaven.
Dewhurst, J.H.L. and G.R. West. 1991. "Conjoining Regional and Interregional Input-Output Models with Econometric Models." In J.J.Ll. Dewhurst, G.J.D. Hewings and R.C. Jensen, eds. *Regional Input-Output Modeling: New Developments and Interpretations*. Aldershot, Avebury.
Dietzenbacher, E. 1997. "In Vindication of the Ghosh Model: A Reinterpretation of a Price Model." *Journal of Regional Science*, 37, 629-651.
Dixon, P.B., B.R. Parmenter, J. Sutton, and D.P. Vincent. 1982. *ORANI: A Multisectoral Model of the Australian Economy*. Amsterdam, North-Holland.
Dixon, P.B., B.R. Parmenter, A. Powell, and P. Wilcoxen. 1992. *Notes and Problems in Applied General Equilibrium Economics*. Amsterdam, Elsevier.
Dixon, P.B., B.R. Parmenter, and R.J. Rimmer. 1985. "The Sensitivity of ORANI Projections of the Short-Run Effects of Increases in Protection to Variations in the Values Adopted for Export Demand Elasticities." In K. Jungenfelt and D. Hague eds. *Structural Adjustment in Developed Open Economies*. London, Macmillan.
Duchin, F. 2000. "International Trade: Evolution in the Thought and Analysis of Wassily Leontief." Paper presented to the XIII International Conference on Input-Output Techniques, Macerata, Italy.
Enders, W. 1995. *Applied Econometric Time Series*. New York, Wiley.
Evans, W.D. 1954. "Input-Output Computations." In T. Barna ed. *The Structural Interdependence of the Economy*. New York, Wiley.
Friedman, M. 1953. "The Methodology of Positive Economics." In M. Friedman. *Essays in Positive Economics*. Chicago, University of Chicago Press.
Fry, J.M., R.L. Fry, and M.R. Peter. 1999. "Inter-Regional Migration in Australia: An Applied Economic Analysis." *Australasian Journal of Regional Studies*, 5, 111-130.
Gass, S.I. 1983. "Decision-Aiding Models - Validation, Assessment and Related Issues." *Operations Research*, 3, 603-631.
Ghosh, A. 1958. "Input-Output Approach in an Allocation System." *Economica*, 25, 58-64.
Glickman, N.J. 1977. *Econometric Analysis of Regional Systems: Explorations in Model Building and Policy Analysis*. New York, Academic Press.
Hamilton, T.R. and C. Pongtanakorn. 1983. "The Economic Impact of Irrigation Development in Idaho: An Application of Marginal Input-Output Methods." *Annals of Regional Science*, 17, 60-71.
Israilevich, P.R. 2001. "Frame-shifting in regional general equilibrium models." Chapter 21 in this volume.
Israilevich, P.R., G.J.D. Hewings, M. Sonis and C.R. Schindler 1997. "Forecasting Structural Change with a Regional Econometric Input-Output Model." *Journal of Regional Science*, 37, 565-90

Jorgensen, D.W. 1984. "Econometric Methods for Applied General Equilibrium Analysis." In H.E. Scarf and J.B. Shoven, eds. *Applied General Equilibrium Analysis*. New York, Cambridge University Press.

Klein, L.R. 1989. "Econometric Aspects of Input-Output Analysis." In R. Miller, K. Polenske and A. Rose, eds. *Frontiers of Input-Output Analysis*. Oxford, Oxford University Press.

Koopmans, T.C. 1957. *Three Essays on the State of Economics Science*. New York, McGraw-Hill.

Lahiri, S. 1976. "Input-Output Analysis with Scale Dependent Coefficients." *Econometrica*, 55, 947-961.

Lahr, M.L. 1993. "A Review of the Literature Supporting the Hybrid Approach to Constructing Regional Input-Output Models." *Economic Systems Research*, 5, 277-293.

Leontief, W. 1936. "Quantitative Input-Output Relations in the Economic System of the United States." *Review of Economics and Statistics*, 18, 105-125.

Leontief, W. 1951. *The Structure of the American Economy, 1919-1939*. New York, Oxford University Press.

Leontief, W. 1953. *Studies in the Structure of the American Economy*. New York, Oxford University Press.

Madden, M. and A.B. Trigg. 1990. "Interregional Migration in an Extended Input-Output Model." *International Regional Science Review*, 13, 65-85.

McCarthy, M.B. 1991. "LIFT: INFORUM's Model of the U.S. Economy." *Economic Systems Research*, 3, 15-36.

McCarl, B.A. 1984. "Model Validation: An Overview with Some Emphasis on Risk Models." *Review of Marketing and Agricultural Models*, 52, 153-169.

McGregor, P.G. and J.K. Swales. 1994. "An Investigation into a Neo-Classical Interpretation of Regional Input-Output Analysis." *Strathclyde Papers in Economics 94/1*, University of Strathclyde, Glasgow.

Meade, D.S. 1999. "IdLift - Recasting the Inforum Model of the US Economy." Paper to the VII Inforum World Conference, Beijing, China.

Mercenier, J. 1995. "Nonuniqueness of Solutions in Applied General Equilibrium Models with Scale Economies and Imperfect Competition." *Economic Theory*, 6, 161-177.

Miernyk, W.H. 1965. *The Elements of Input-Output Analysis*. New York, Random House.

Miernyk, W.H., E.R. Bonner, J.H. Chapman, Jr, and K. Shellhamer. 1967. *Impact of the Space Program on a Local Economy: An Input-Output Analysis*. Morgantown, West Virginia University Press.

Miller, R.E. and P.D. Blair, P.D. 1985. *Input-Output Analysis: Foundations and Extensions*. Englewood Cliffs, Prentice Hall.

Miyazawa, K. 1976. *Input-Output Analysis and the Structure of Income Distribution*. Berlin, Springer.

Moore, F.T. and J.W. Petersen. 1955. "Regional Analysis: An Interindustry Model of Utah." *The Review of Economics and Statistics*, 37, 368-383.

Morishima, M. 2000. "Economy and Democracy." Keynote presentation to the XIII International Conference on Input-Output Techniques, Macerata, Italy.

Oosterhaven, J. and J.H.Ll. Dewhurst. 1990. "A Prototype Demo-Economic Model With an Application to Queensland." *International Regional Science Review*, 13, 51-64.

Oosterhaven, J. and H. Folmer. 1985. "An Interregional Labor Market Model Incorporating Vacancy Chains and Social Security." *Papers of the Regional Science Association*, 58, 141-155.

Parmenter, B.R. 1983. "The Impact Macro Package and Export Demand Elasticities." *Australian Economic Papers*, 22, 411-417.

Rey, S.J. 1997. "Coefficient Change in Embedded Econometric and Input-Output Models at the Regional Level." *Economic Systems Research*, 9, 307-330.

Rey, S.J. 1998. "The Performance of Alternative Integration Strategies for Combining Regional Econometric and Input-Output Models." *International Regional Science Review*, 21, 1-36.

Richardson, H.W. 1972. *Input-Output and Regional Economics*. London, Weidenfeld and Nicholson.

Roy, J.R. 1997. "A Price-Responsive Framework for Interregional Input-Output." *Annals of Regional Science*, 31, 285-298.

Shaffer, R. 1989. *Community Economics: Economic Structure and Change in Smaller Communities*. Ames, Iowa State University Press.

Shoven, J.B. and J. Whalley. 1992. *Applying General Equilibrium*. Cambridge, Cambridge University Press.

Skene, J. 1993. "The Economic Impact of Growth in Visitor Expenditure: A Quantitative Assessment." *Working Paper No. 92*, Bureau of Industry Economics. Canberra: Australian Government Publishing Service.

Stern, R.M., J. Francis, and B. Schumacher. 1976. *Price Elasticities in International Trade: An Annotated Bibliography*. London, Macmillan.

Tiebout, C.M. 1969. "An Empirical Region Input-Output Projection Model: the State of Washington, 1980." *Review of Economics and Statistics*, 51, 334-340.

Tilanus, C.B. 1967. "Marginal vs Average Input-Output Coefficients in Input-Output Forecasting." *Quarterly Journal of Economics*. 81, 140-145.

van Dijk, J. and J. Oosterhaven. 1986. "Regional Impacts of Migrants' Expenditures: An Input-output Vacancy Chain Approach." In P.W. Batey and M. Madden eds. *Integrated Analysis of Regional Systems*. London, Pion.

Walras, L. 1877. *Elements of Pure Economics*. Translated by W. Jaffe 1954. Homewood, IL., Irwin.

West, G. 1994. "The Queensland Impact and Projection Model: The Household Sector." *Economic Systems Research*, 6, 363-383.

West, G.R. and A. Gamage. 1997. "Differential Multipliers for Tourism in Victoria. *Tourism Economics*, 3, 57-68.

West, G.R. and R.W. Jackson. 1998. "Input-Output+Econometric and Econometric+Input-Output: Model Differences or Different Models?" *Regional Analysis and Policy*, 28, 33-48.

West, G.R. and J.R. Roy. 1998. "Towards an Interregional Framework for Joint Assessment of Tourism and the Environment." *Australasian Journal of Regional Studies*, 4, 161-176.

13 Restrictions in Integrated Econometric+Input-Output Modeling*

James P. LeSage[1] and Sergio J. Rey[2]

[1] Department of Economics, University of Toledo, Toledo, Ohio 43606
e-mail: jpl@jpl.econ.utoledo.edu
[2] Department of Geography, San Diego State University, San Diego, CA 92182
e-mail: rey@typhoon.sdsu.edu

13.1 Introduction

Working with regional time-series on employment at the industry level often results in short time-series containing quarterly observations. Attempts to introduce interindustry and interregional variation into an econometric model produce serious degrees of freedom problems. The problem takes the form of a model containing a large number of parameters relating interregional and interindustry entities in the model relative to the amount of sample data available to estimate these parameters. For this reason researchers have attempted to use restrictions on parameters in these models.

Rey (2000) categorizes three approaches that have been used to integrate input-output relations in the econometric portion of integrated econometric+input-output models. One of these approaches he labels embedding as it attempts to embed input-output model information in a series of econometric equations. Both structural and time-series econometric models have appeared in the literature with a typical employment equation from these models specified as:

$$e_{i,t} = f\left(Z_{ld,t}, Z_{la,t}, Z_{\sup,t}, \beta, \varepsilon\right) \tag{13.1}$$

where $e_{i,t}$ denotes employment for industry i at time t, $Z_{ld,t}$ represent local variables that capture interindustry linkages, $Z_{la,t}$ are local aggregate or macro variables and $Z_{\sup,t}$ reflect supraregional linkages. If one considers a model involving only the 20 manufacturing industries, it becomes clear that there are 20 potentially important local variables that may reflect interindustry influences and 20 candidate national variables as well as possible local aggregate or macro variables. This should make the degrees of freedom problem clear.

A number of non-Bayesian specification approaches have been employed to produce a more parsimonious set of explanatory variables in each of these employment equations in the integrated econometric+input-output model. The earliest approach by Moghadam and Ballard (1988) defined an interindustry demand variable, (*IDV*):

* Development of the database used in this study was funded by a grant from the Ohio Urban Universities Program

$$IDV_{i,t} = \sum_{j \neq i}^{n} \alpha_{i,j} e_{j,t} \tag{13.2}$$

where the *IDV* collapses all possible $n-1$ individual linkages for industry i into a single composite time-series variable using weighting $(\alpha_{i,j})$ information based on input-output table relationships. This linear combination of individual linkages achieves parsimony, but runs a risk of eliminating important information that may be contained in variation associated with individual linkages. Several others have proposed and tested modifications of this approach (Coomes *et al.*, 1991a,b; Israilevich *et al.*, 1996, Rey and Dev, 1997; Rey and Jackson, 1999; Stover, 1994).

One common thread in all of this work is that alternative formulations of the input-output table information is used to produce the linear combination representing the *IDV* variable. These approaches can be viewed as placing exact restrictions on the coefficients in the employment equation. To see this consider the employment equation shown in (13.3), where we replace the local and supraregional interindustry linkages with two *IDV* variables based on local employment $e_{j,t}$ and national employment ne_{jt}:

$$\begin{aligned} e_{i,t} &= \gamma_1 IDV_{ld,t} + \gamma_2 IDV_{\text{sup},t} + Z_{la,t}\beta + \varepsilon_{i,t} \\ e_{i,t} &= \gamma_1 \sum_{j \neq i}^{n} \alpha_{i,j} e_{j,t} + \gamma_2 \sum_{j \neq i}^{n} \Theta_{i,j} ne_{j,t} + Z_{la,t}\beta + \varepsilon_{i,t} \end{aligned} \tag{13.3}$$

where the construction of the input-output-based weights, $\alpha_{i,j}$ for the local *IDV* variable and $\Theta_{i,j}$ for the supraregional *IDV* variable used in specifying the linear combinations differs across the various studies. Despite these specification differences, the weights used in these studies could be viewed as imposing exact restrictions derived from the input-output table information. This eliminates the need to estimate a potentially large number of parameters $\alpha_{i,j}$ and $\Theta_{i,j}$. Only the scalar parameters γ_1 and γ_2 need be estimated and these adjust the input-output-based weights in a proportional fashion to best fit the sample data. Rey (1997) has labeled this approach holistic embedding as potentially all $n-1$ interindustry linkages are reflected in the *IDV*. We will refer to this approach for latter reference as the *IDVH* approach.

A related approach is to use the input-output table coefficients to select a subset of industries that appear as individual components in the variables $Z_{ld,t}$ and/or $Z_{\text{sup},t}$. For example, White and Hewings (1982) proposed using employment from two or three industries with the largest coefficients in the ith row of a regional input-output table to select variables for inclusion in $Z_{ld,t}$. Other approaches can be found in (Glennon and Lane, 1990; Glennon et al., 1986, 1987). This approach can be viewed as achieving parsimony by imposing zero restrictions on some of the input-output-based weights $\alpha_{i,j}$ and $\Theta_{i,j}$ so that the unrestricted weights can be estimated. Rey (1997) classified this as partitive embedding, and we subsequently refer to this approach as *IDVP*. In contrast to the holistic approach (*IDVH*), the partitive embedding may introduce more flexibility in fitting industry-level employment to the sample data because more parameters are estimated.

Bayesian approaches have involved a different use of the input-output information than those discussed above. The Bayesian view of input-output-table information is that it represents non-sample prior knowledge regarding the nature of the interindustry relationships. This information should be combined via Bayes Rule with the time-series sample data on industry-level regional and national employment to produce parameter estimates that reflect a consistent probabilistic framework for treating non-sample information in econometric estimation problems. Examples of the Bayesian approach can be found in (Fawson and Criddle, 1994; LeSage and Magura, 1991; Magura, 1990; Partridge and Rickman, 1998). Note that the *IDVH* approaches are relying on the input-output-table information in various ad-hoc ways to produce weighted composite *IDV* variables and then using estimation to adjust the weights to better fit the sample data. The *IDVP* approach uses the non-sample input-output-table information as a variable selection tool to eliminate variables from the specification via the zero restrictions imposed on the parameters of certain variables.

A key facet of the Bayesian approach is to let all potential interindustry linkage variables appear in the model. The frequent degrees of freedom problems that would arise from doing this are overcome by assigning prior distributions to the parameters in the model. (Note that not all of the Bayesian studies cited above exhibited strict adherence to this principle.) The priors assigned to the parameters for the full set of interindustry variables can be used to downweight variables that should be unimportant, based on the input-output-table coefficients or other sources of non-sample information. This is accomplished by imposing a "stochastic" zero restriction on the parameters associated with variables thought to be unimportant. A major difference between this approach and the *IDVH* or *IDVP* approaches is that when the sample data is combined with the prior information via Bayes Rule the posterior model estimates may reveal that variables thought a priori to be unimportant are indeed important. This is in contrast to the case of *IDVP* where the unimportant variables are a priori eliminated from the model and have no chance of ever entering the final specification.

Why is this an important difference between the *IDVH*, *IDVP* approaches and the Bayesian approach? Given that national input-output tables, or regional tables likely derived from national tables, are used as sources of information, it may be that interindustry relationships in particular regions do not reflect these national patterns. If this is the case, only the Bayesian approach is capable of allowing the input-output-table information to be discounted during estimation. Further, this adjustment takes place automatically during estimation in a consistent probablistic framework. If regional sample information is in dramatic conflict with prior information based on the input-output-tables, the posterior estimates will reflect this, avoiding the costly misspecification that arises in this case when the *IDVH* or *IDVP* approaches are used.

In addition to a relative simple Bayesian regression model with normally distributed prior means and variances that will be described in the next section, we also explore another Bayesian approach based on `Bayesian model averaging' described in Raftery, *et al.*, (1997). Leamer (1983) suggested that a Bayesian solution to model specification uncertainty is to average over all possible models using the posterior probabilities of the models as weights. Raftery, *et al.*, (1997) devise a way to implement this approach using a Metropolis sampling scheme to systematically move through model space, producing a Monte Carlo Markov Chain (hereafter, MCMC) sample from the space of all possible models. A key insight they exploit is that the Bayes factor or posterior odds ratios from two alternative model specifications can be used to construct a Markov chain that traverses model neighborhoods. They argue that this systematic movement of the Markov Chain via a Hastings step generates a stochastic process that moves through model space. Under certain regularity conditions, the average of the parameters from the sampled models converges to the model uncertainty solution proposed by Leamer (1983). We describe the specifics of implementing this approach in the next section. Note that model averaging can be viewed as an estimated *IDVP* approach, where the related industries that will be included in the model are estimated via the MCMC sampling process.

This chapter explores the forecasting accuracy differences between the *IDVH*, *IDVP* and two Bayesian methods in an applied setting using a quarterly time-series sample of twenty manufacturing industries employment for 88 counties in Ohio. Section 13.2 of the chapter describes specifics regarding implementation of the models as well as the data used in a set of forecasting experiments that compare these alternative approaches to incorporating input-output-table information in regional econometric employment relationships. Forecasting accuracy comparisons are set forth in section 13.3 and conclusions are set forth in a final section.

13.2 Data, Models and Methods

A quarterly set of data on employment for the state of Ohio was used to carry out comparative forecasting experiments. Construction of this dataset is described here. Specifics regarding implementation of the two *IDV* models as well as the two Bayesian methods and the forecasting methodology are also described in this section.

13.2.1 Data

The models used in this study involve quarterly time-series covering the period 1989Q1 to 1998Q1 for employment in the twenty 2-digit SIC classifications for manufacturing industries (SIC 20 through SIC 39). Time series were constructed for all 88 counties in Ohio using the ES202 information collected by the Ohio Bureau of Employment Services for unemployment insurance purposes. The initial database contained information on 4-digit SIC employment and zip-code areas for 1,009 Ohio zip-codes. Aggregation to the 2-digit SIC level was carried out. The data required some manipulation to clean up reporting problems involving invalid zip-codes. These employment magnitudes were distributed at the (reported) county level based on the employment distribution for valid zip codes reported in each county. This distribution process was done using 4-digit SIC categories, so the distribution of invalid employment magnitudes was based on a specific distribution for each zip-SIC combination.

Many of the 88 Ohio counties represent rural areas where manufacturing employment is small or non-existent. To overcome this problem and produce a reasonably large sample of cases for our forecasting experiments, a spatial average set of time-series were created. Employment in each county was added to that from all first-order contiguous counties to produce an aggregate time series representing regional industry-level employment centered on each county. This aggregation eliminated zero values in employment allowing a sample of 1,470 industry-county time-series that were used in our forecasting experiment.

Table 13.1 SIC relationship to 1992 use commodities

SIC	Commodity Numbers
20	14
21	15
22	16+17+18
23	19
24	20+21
25	22+23
26	24+25
27	26A+26B
28	27A+27B+28+29A+29B+30
29	31
30	32
31	33+34
32	35+36
33	37+38
34	39+40+41+42+13
35	43+44+45+46+47+48+49+50+51+52
36	53+54+55+56+57+58
37	59A+59B+60+61
38	62+63
39	64

Source: Table 2.1 in Lawson (1997)

In addition to the Ohio data, monthly national data for employment in the twenty 2-digit SIC's was converted to quarterly averages for the same period from 1989Q1 to 1998Q1. As a source of input-output-table information, the 1992 Use of Commodities Table (Table 2.1 from Lawson, 1997) was used to construct a 20 by 20 matrix. Table 13.1 shows the aggregation methodology that was applied.

In the forecasting experiments all employment time-series were transformed to annual growth rates or percentage changes from the same quarter last year. The models were estimated based on data from 1989Q1 to 1995Q4, and these estimates were used to produce a 4-quarter-ahead forecast covering the period 1996Q1 through 1996Q4. Next, an additional sample observation for 1996Q1 was added to the sample data, the model was re-estimated and these new estimates were used to produce another 4-quarter-ahead forecast extending from 1996Q2 through 1997Q1. This iterative process of estimation and forecasting was continued to the end of the sample in 1998Q1. This procedure results in real-time out-of-sample forecast that are comparable to those that would be used in practice over a 6-quarter time period.

13.2.2 The *IDV* Models

The dependent variable in our models is the industry-level employment time-series containing 37 quarterly observations over the period 1989Q1 to 1998Q1. As indicated above, only 1,470 cases of non-zero employment existed. Explanatory variables used in all models were: a constant, a one-period lag of the dependent variable and other 2-digit industry employment at the national level as explanatory variables.

To represent the *IDVH* approach the model shown in (13.4) was used.

$$e_{i,t} = \gamma_0 + \rho e_{i,t-1} + \gamma_1 \sum_{j \neq i}^{n} \Theta_{i,j} ne_{j,t-1} + \varepsilon_{i,t} \tag{13.4}$$

where the weights used for $\Theta_{i,j}$ to create national *IDVH* variables were those from the 20 by 20 national input-output-table. By relying on national series alone and eliminating the local series from the model, we increase the number of cases available for our forecasting model. Attempts to create a model that also used local variables produced only 181 cases where non-zero employment existed for all of the needed input-output-related series. Since our goal is to test the efficacy of alternative approaches to incorporating related industry information, the larger sample of 1,470 cases seemed desirable.

A related issue is our neglect of other local variables in the model represented by $Z_{la,t}$ in (13.1). The experiments carried out here provide a relative comparison of the alternative methods for incorporating non-sample input-output information in employment relations. Since all models used in the forecasting experiments ignore local interindustry relationships and possible local explanatory variables, we should be able to make valid forecast accuracy comparisons of the various methods. Limiting the number of variables in the employment relationship may provide better control, allowing us to more adequately determine the marginal impact of the alternative specification/estimation methodologies we compare.

$$e_{i,t} = \gamma_0 + \rho e_{i,t-1} + Z_{\text{sup},t-1}\gamma + \varepsilon_{i,t} \qquad (13.5)$$

A model to represent the *IDVP* approach is shown in (13.5), where the matrix of national variables, $Z_{\text{sup},t}$ was selected using industries with large input-output-table coefficients. In our case, the input-output-table exhibited a large number of zeros, so industries j supplying more than 1 percent of their output to industry i were used as a selection criterion. This produced a selection of 5.15 related industries on average with no related industries in one case and a maximum of 11 related industries in three cases. The standard deviation for the number of related industries was 3.16. The single case (SIC 21) where there were no related industries was not used in the comparative experiments.

13.2.3 The Bayesian Models

The first Bayesian approach was based on a model that included all variables. This could be depicted as (13.5) with $Z_{\text{sup},t-1}$ containing all 20 national industry series. For later reference we label this model *BAYES*. The degrees of freedom and overparamaterization problems are overcome in the *BAYES* approach by assigning a prior distribution to the parameters in the model. Normal priors were used that involved setting prior means and variances for all parameters in the model. The prior means for related industries were set equal to $1/r$, where r represents the number of related industries. Related industries were defined as in the case of the *IDVP* model – those industries supplying more than 1 percent of their output to industry i. For example, if $r = 3$, we have three related industries and the prior means for the coefficients on these time-series would be 1/3. This suggests that industry i employment in time t should be an average of employment from related industries. Of course, for this to be strictly true, the employment time-series need to be scaled to say growth rates or indices. Growth rates were used here to produce this scaling.

A large prior variance of 0.5 representing uncertainty associated with these prior means was used. This should produce a prior that is centered on $1/r$, but our uncertainty would ascribe a 99 percent confidence that the coefficient values lie between $(1/r)-2.12$ and $(1/r)+2.12$. This allows for a large range of outcomes in the coefficients that will be determined by combining this prior with the sample data information. Note that if the input-output-table information regarding interindustry relationships is incorrect, the posterior coefficient estimate can take on a value of zero reflecting the lack of interindustry relationship indicated by the data.

The prior for unrelated industries involved setting a prior mean of zero for the coefficients on these variables. A prior variance of 0.1 was used to impose these priors fairly tightly. Specifically, one standard deviation would be 0.316, so our 99 percent confidence interval for the prior mean of zero would be around -1 to +1. The motivation for this is that if the sample data indicate that one or more of the industries deemed unrelated by the input-output-table information do in fact play an important role in explaining employment variation for a particular industry, the posterior estimate will take on non-zero values. This is in contrast to the case of *IDVP* where these variables are excluded from the model.

Finally, a diffuse prior was placed on the intercept term in the model and a prior mean of unity was used for the lagged dependent variable consistent with the Minnesota random-walk prior. A prior variance of 0.5 was used for this parameter, allowing for a three standard deviation range of outcomes between -1.21 and 3.12. Implementing these Bayesian priors involves a relatively simple application of Theil and Goldberger (1961) mixed estimation and is computationally competitive with the least-squares estimation method used to implement the *IDVH* and *IDVP* models.

Another Bayesian approach similar in spirit to the *IDVP* model was implemented using Bayesian model averaging. We label this model *BMA* for later reference. Raftery, *et al.*, (1997) rely on an MCMC methodology to generate a stochastic process that moves through model space. They rely on a Markov chain over models $M(i), i=1,2,...$ that has a state space in the set of all possible models and equilibrium distribution equal to the posterior probability of model k, which we might denote by $pr(M_k|D)$, where D represents the data. Leamer (1978) suggested the standard Bayesian solution to a problem involving a set of K models when we are interested in a future value of the dependent variable, y_{t+j}. We should rely on the posterior distribution of y_{t+j} given the data D:

$$pr(y_{t+j}|D)=\sum_{k=1}^{K} pr(y_{t+j}|M_k,D)pr(M_k|D) \tag{13.6}$$

This is an average of the posterior distributions under each model weighted by the corresponding posterior model probabilities. In (13.6), the posterior probability of model M_k is given by:

$$pr(M_k|D)=\frac{pr(D|M_k)pr(M_k)}{\sum_{l=1}^{K} pr(D|M_l)pr(M_l)} \tag{13.7}$$

where $pr(D|M_k)$ represents the marginal likelihood of model M_k and $pr(M_k)$ denotes the prior probability associated with model k.

In constructing the Markov chain, a neighborhood nbd(M) is defined for each model M in the set of all possible models. This neighborhood consists of the model M itself and the set of models with either one variable more or one variable fewer than M . Define a transition matrix q by setting $q(M \rightarrow M')=0$ for all models M' not in nbd(M) and $q(M \rightarrow M')$ equal to a constant for all models M' in nbd(M). The MCMC sampling proceeds in the following fashion. If the chain is currently in state M , a model draw of M' is made from $q(M \rightarrow M')$ and accepted with probability:

$$\min\{1, pr(M'|D)/pr(M|D)\} \tag{13.8}$$

For cases where we do not accept the new model, we stay in state M and proceed to consider another model. This Metropolis sampling scheme systematically moves through model space, producing an MCMC sample from the space of all possible models. A key insight used by Raftery, *et al.*, (1997) is that the Bayes factor or posterior odds ratios from two alternative model specifications shown in (13.8) moves the Markov chain so it traverses model neighborhoods. They argue that this systematic movement of the Markov Chain via a Hastings step set forth in (13.8) generates a stochastic process that moves through model space.

A final point is that uniform prior probabilities were assigned to all models and Bayesian priors suggested by Raftery, *et al.*, (1997) were assigned to the parameters. These priors attempt to place a relatively diffuse but proper prior that allows the sample data to determine the best model. This may not reflect the best available approach in our application where we could draw on the input-output-table information to specify that certain models are a priori more likely than others. This issue needs to be explored in future work.

One possible problem with implementing this approach in a forecasting setting is the computational intensity of the method. For a large model such as ours involving 20 potential explanatory variables there are 2^{20} possible model combinations that need to be explored via the MCMC sampling scheme. To produce a representative sample from the posterior space of all possible models requires a large number of draws. We implemented this approach relying on only 1,000 draws for each of the 1,470 industry-level time-series that we wished to forecast. This number of draws produced samples of between 150 and 500 distinct models.[1] The model selection estimation was carried out only once using data covering the period from 1989Q1 to 1995Q4. The same highest posterior probability model was used in the iterative estimate-forecast loop over all six time periods.

A question arises regarding the adequacy of the 1,000 draws. Do the models from this relatively small number of draws reflect convergence of the MCMC sampling scheme? To explore this issue a single employment series for one county and industry was examined. The MCMC sampler was run twice with 1,000 draws producing two sets of outcomes shown in tables 13.2 and 13.3. In these tables, we present only models with posterior probabilities greater than 1 percent. The tables present the variables associated with each of the 27 models having posterior probability greater than 1 percent. Note that in both runs of the MCMC sampler, 27 models that exhibited posterior probabilities greater than 1 percent existed.

---

[1] Regarding the computational intensity of the MCMC sampling scheme, it took around 40 to 50 seconds to generate a sample of 1,000 draws on a relatively slow Apple Powerbook using a 266 Mhz. PowerPC G3 processor.

Table 13.2 MCMC convergence test run 1

	Models based on 1,000 draws, run 1																				
M_k	V1	V2	V3	V4	V5	V6	V7	V8	V9	V10	V11	V12	V13	V14	V15	V16	V17	V18	V19	V20	Prb
1	0	0	0	0	0	0	0	1	0	0	1	0	1	0	0	0	0	0	1	0	1.03
2	0	0	0	0	0	0	1	1	0	0	0	0	0	0	0	0	0	0	1	0	1.09
3	0	0	0	0	0	0	0	1	0	0	1	0	0	0	0	1	0	0	0	0	1.11
4	0	0	0	0	0	0	0	1	0	1	1	0	0	0	0	0	0	0	0	0	1.13
5	0	0	0	0	0	0	0	1	0	0	1	0	0	1	0	0	0	0	0	0	1.15
6	0	0	0	1	0	0	0	1	0	0	0	0	0	0	0	0	0	0	1	0	1.16
7	0	0	0	0	0	0	0	1	0	0	0	0	0	0	0	0	1	0	1	0	1.29
8	0	0	0	0	0	0	0	1	1	0	1	0	0	0	0	0	0	0	0	0	1.36
9	0	1	0	0	0	0	0	1	0	0	0	0	0	0	0	0	0	0	0	0	1.40
10	0	0	0	0	0	0	0	1	0	0	0	0	0	0	0	1	0	0	1	0	1.14
11	0	0	0	0	0	0	0	1	0	0	1	0	0	0	0	0	1	0	0	0	1.43
12	0	0	0	0	0	0	0	1	0	0	0	1	0	0	0	0	0	0	1	0	1.43
13	0	0	0	0	0	0	0	1	0	0	0	0	0	0	0	0	0	0	1	1	1.43
14	0	0	0	0	0	0	0	1	0	0	0	0	0	0	1	0	0	0	1	0	1.45
15	0	0	0	0	0	1	0	1	0	0	0	0	0	0	0	0	0	0	1	1	1.51
16	1	0	0	0	0	0	0	1	0	0	0	0	0	0	0	0	0	0	1	0	1.53
17	0	0	0	0	0	1	0	1	0	0	0	0	0	0	0	0	0	0	1	0	1.54
18	0	0	0	0	0	0	0	1	0	1	0	0	0	0	0	0	0	0	1	0	1.58
19	0	0	0	0	0	0	0	1	1	0	0	0	0	0	0	0	0	0	1	0	1.68
20	0	0	0	0	0	0	0	1	0	0	1	0	0	0	1	0	0	0	0	0	1.85
21	0	0	0	0	0	0	0	1	0	0	0	0	0	1	0	0	0	0	1	0	1.95
22	0	1	0	0	0	0	0	1	0	0	0	0	0	0	0	0	0	0	1	0	2.27
23	0	0	0	0	0	0	0	1	0	0	0	0	1	0	0	0	0	0	1	0	2.30
24	0	0	0	0	0	0	0	1	0	0	0	0	0	0	0	0	0	1	1	0	2.65
25	0	0	0	0	0	0	0	1	0	0	1	0	0	0	0	0	0	0	1	0	2.80
26	0	0	0	0	0	0	0	1	0	0	1	0	0	0	0	0	0	0	0	0	4.51
27	0	0	0	0	0	0	0	1	0	0	0	0	0	0	0	0	0	0	1	0	11.84

Table 13.3 MCMC convergence test run 2

	Models based on 1,000 draws, run 2																				
M_k	V1	V2	V3	V4	V5	V6	V7	V8	V9	V10	V11	V12	V13	V14	V15	V16	V17	V18	V19	V20	Prob
1	0	0	0	0	0	0	1	1	0	0	0	0	0	0	0	0	0	0	1	0	1.064
2	0	0	0	0	0	0	0	1	0	0	1	0	0	0	0	1	0	0	0	0	1.090
3	0	0	0	0	0	0	0	1	0	1	1	0	0	0	0	0	0	0	0	0	1.108
4	0	0	0	0	0	0	0	1	0	0	1	0	0	1	0	0	0	0	0	0	1.127
5	0	0	0	1	0	0	0	1	0	0	0	0	0	0	0	0	0	0	1	0	1.138
6	0	0	0	0	0	0	1	1	0	0	0	1	0	0	0	0	0	0	1	0	1.158
7	0	0	0	0	0	0	0	1	0	0	0	0	0	0	0	0	1	0	1	0	1.268
8	0	0	0	0	0	0	0	1	1	0	1	0	0	0	0	0	0	0	0	0	1.332
9	0	1	0	0	0	0	0	1	0	0	0	0	0	0	0	0	0	0	0	0	1.369
10	0	0	0	0	0	0	0	1	0	0	0	0	0	0	0	1	0	0	1	0	1.375
11	0	0	0	0	0	0	0	1	0	0	1	0	0	0	0	0	1	0	0	0	1.397
12	0	0	0	0	0	0	0	1	0	0	0	1	0	0	0	0	0	0	1	0	1.401
13	0	0	0	0	0	0	0	1	0	0	0	0	0	0	0	0	0	0	1	1	1.402
14	0	0	0	0	0	0	0	1	0	0	0	0	0	0	1	0	0	0	1	0	1.416
15	1	0	0	0	0	0	0	1	0	0	0	0	0	0	0	0	0	0	1	0	1.500
16	0	0	0	0	0	1	0	1	0	0	0	0	0	0	0	0	0	0	1	0	1.508
17	0	0	0	0	0	0	0	1	0	1	0	0	0	0	0	0	0	0	1	0	1.542
18	0	0	0	0	0	0	0	1	1	0	0	0	0	0	0	0	0	0	1	0	1.639
19	0	0	0	0	0	0	0	1	0	0	1	0	0	0	1	0	0	0	0	0	1.805
20	0	0	0	0	0	0	0	1	0	0	0	0	0	1	0	0	0	0	1	0	1.902
21	0	1	0	0	0	0	0	1	0	0	0	0	0	0	0	0	0	0	1	0	2.222
22	0	0	0	0	0	0	0	1	0	0	0	0	1	0	0	0	0	0	1	0	2.247
23	0	0	0	0	0	0	0	1	0	0	0	0	0	0	0	0	0	1	1	0	2.593
24	0	0	0	0	0	0	0	1	0	0	1	0	0	0	0	0	0	0	1	0	2.738
25	0	0	0	0	0	0	1	1	0	0	0	1	0	0	0	0	0	0	0	0	4.340
26	0	0	0	0	0	0	0	1	0	0	1	0	0	0	0	0	0	0	0	0	4.400
27	0	0	0	0	0	0	0	1	0	0	0	0	0	0	0	0	0	0	1	0	11.552

In addition, in both runs, the same model was identified as the highest posterior probability model and similar posterior probabilities were assigned to this model. This suggests that using more draws would not have changed the resulting models selected for use in the forecasting experiments. From the set of sampled models the variables contained in the model with the highest posterior probability were selected as representing important related industries. Using the example shown in Table 13.3, we would rely on a model with industries 8 (SIC 27) and 19 (SIC 38) as important related industries. The Theil-Goldberger estimation approach used for the *BAYES* model was then used with this set of explanatory variables. Prior means and variances set forth for coefficients associated with related industry variables in the *BAYES* model were used here as well.

One could view this approach as imposing exact zero restrictions on the variables found to be unrelated as a result of the MCMC sampling described above. It should reflect a more parsimonious model than the *BAYES* model since it eliminates unrelated variables. Note that the *IDVP* model and the *BMA* model may differ greatly because the definition of related and unrelated variables in the *BMA* model are determined via the MCMC sampling, not the input-output-table information.

Another point to consider regarding our implementation of Bayesian model averaging is that we do not adhere to Leamer's solution. Rather than average over all models, we simply select the model with the highest posterior probability, and proceed to produce estimates and forecasts based on this model. Future work should explore differences between this approach and the more formal Bayesian model averaging solution of Leamer (1978). An examination of the parameter estimates from the `averaged model' constructed using the Leamer solution showed that unrelated industry coefficients were not statistically significantly different from zero. This motivated the use of the highest posterior probability model with the corresponding exact zero restrictions.

13.3 Performance Comparisons

A series of 4-quarter-ahead out-of-sample forecasts of employment were carried out using: the two *IDV* models; two Bayesian models; a benchmark vector autoregressive (*VAR*) model with a single lag and all 20 national industries; and another benchmark Bayesian vector autoregressive model (*BVAR*) with a single lag, all 20 national industries and the Minnesota prior. It is well-known that short-lag *VAR* and *BVAR* models perform well in cases where the time-series are short and a large number of explanatory variables exist. These two benchmarks allow us to examine the marginal benefits of imposing restrictions using the *IDV* and Bayesian approaches relative to an unrestricted model.

The out-of-sample forecasts covered the period from 1996Q1 to 1998Q1, for a total of six 4-step-ahead quarterly forecasts. Since we are dealing with many industries in many different counties, the state of the business cycle should not influence our comparative results. This is because employment in some industries and counties will be experiencing rapid growth while employment in other industries and counties will be in decline. In other words, our comparative results should be fairly representative of model performance across all phases of the business cycle.

One of the 20 industries, SIC 21 had no interindustry relationships in the input-output table, so only 19 industries were used. Given our sample of 88 counties and 19 industries for which we are producing six 4-step-ahead forecasts, there are a possible 10,032 individual forecasts that might be examined for each model. Of these possible cases, only 8,820 contained non-zero employment time-series, so our experiment involved comparing the forecast accuracy using a series of 8,820 individual 4-step-ahead quarterly forecasts.

To compare models in terms of forecast accuracy we simply recorded the model that produced the most accuracy forecast (based on the absolute forecast error) in each of these 8,820 cases. These results are shown in Table 13.4 for five models, the *VAR* and *BVAR* benchmark models, the two *IDV* models and the Bayes model based on Theil-Goldberger estimation.

Table 13.4 Forecast accuracy comparisons of five models

	Counts of the most accurate model				
Horizon	*VAR*	*BVAR*	*IDVH*	*IDVP*	*BAYES*
1-step-ahead	825	2098	1114	2136	2647
2-step-ahead	826	1985	1096	2137	2776
3-step-ahead	708	1779	1185	2254	2894
4-step-ahead	717	1673	1202	2338	2890
	Counts as a proportion of 8,820 cases				
Horizon	*VAR*	*BVAR*	*IDVH*	*IDVP*	*BAYES*
1-step-ahead	0.094	0.238	0.126	0.242	0.300
2-step-ahead	0.094	0.225	0.124	0.242	0.315
3-step-ahead	0.080	0.202	0.134	0.256	0.328
4-step-ahead	0.081	0.190	0.136	0.265	0.328

From the table we see that the Bayesian prior introduced in the *BAYES* model improves on the forecast accuracy relative to the next best models, the *BVAR* and *IDVP*. The performance of the *BVAR* benchmark model declines as we move to longer forecast horizons, whereas both *IDV* models as well as the *BAYES* model exhibit improved performance at the longer horizons. These results confirm the evidence provided by other studies that restrictions improve forecast accuracy, especially at horizons beyond a single-step-ahead.

The *BAYES* model produced the largest number of winning forecasts, nearly 1/3 of the total 8,820 cases at all four forecast horizons. Our results also point toward the *IDVP* approach as superior to *IDVH*, producing around twice as many winning forecasts. This comparison suggests that the *IDVH* approach where all related industries are collapsed to a single explanatory variable eliminates important variation needed to produce accurate forecasts. At the other extreme, the *VAR* model allows for variation in all 20 industries to enter the model, but this model clearly suffers from degrees of freedom and overparameterization problems.

The *IDVP* approach allows variation in individual related series to enter the model and this proves to be a fairly effective compromise between overparameterization and underparameterization. This is also true of the *BVAR* model that allows all 20 industries to enter the model. However, the *BVAR* model overcomes the degrees of freedom and overparameterization problem by relying on a prior that stresses the first-order autoregressive model, but downplays the importance of related industries. This appears to be effective in one-step-ahead forecasting, but downweighting employment variation in related industries adversely affects longer horizon forecasts. This result confirms previous research comparing *BVAR* models based on the Minnesota random-walk prior to alternative priors that produce less downweighting of related industries (see Magura, 1987 and LeSage and Magura, 1991). The *BAYES* model relies on a prior that appears to effectively capture both the autoregressive nature of the employment time-series as well as information contained in the related industries.

Another experiment was carried out that included the Bayesian model averaging approach (*BMA*) as well as the five models used in the results presented in table 13.4. These results are presented in table 13.5. Given the good performance of the *IDVP* model in the results presented in table 13.4, we might expect that the *BMA* model that attempts to statistically determine a subset of the explanatory variables that constitute important related industries might be quite effective.

Table 13.5 Forecast accuracy comparisons of six models

	Counts of the most accurate model					
Horizon	*VAR*	*BVAR*	*IDVH*	*IDVP*	*BAYES*	*BMA*
1-step-ahead	785	1982	1098	2145	1844	966
2-step-ahead	748	1801	909	1994	1713	1655
3-step-ahead	646	1557	886	2000	1717	2014
4-step-ahead	620	1416	907	1958	1588	2331
	Counts as a proportion of 8,820 cases					
Horizon	*VAR*	*BVAR*	*IDVH*	*IDVP*	*BAYES*	*BMA*
1-step-ahead	0.089	0.225	0.124	0.243	0.209	0.110
2-step-ahead	0.085	0.204	0.103	0.226	0.194	0.188
3-step-ahead	0.073	0.177	0.100	0.227	0.195	0.228
4-step-ahead	0.070	0.161	0.103	0.222	0.180	0.264

Table 13.6 Forecast accuracy combination comparisons

	Counts of the most accurate model		
Horizon	*VAR*+VBAR	*IDVH*+*IDVP*	*BAYES*+*BMA*
1-step-ahead	2767	3243	2810
2-step-ahead	2549	2903	3368
3-step-ahead	2203	2886	3731
4-step-ahead	2036	2865	3919
	Counts as a proportion of 8,820 cases		
Horizon	*VAR*+*BVAR*	*IDVH*+*IDVP*	*BAYES*+*BMA*
1-step-ahead	0.314	0.368	0.319
2-step-ahead	0.289	0.329	0.382
3-step-ahead	0.250	0.327	0.423
4-step-ahead	0.231	0.325	0.444

From the results in Table 13.5, we see that the *BMA* model performed best at the longer horizons involving 3- and 4-step-ahead forecasts. At the shorter horizons involving 1- and 2-step-ahead forecasts this model performed worst than the *IDVP*, *BVAR* and *BAYES* models. Some of the other patterns described for the results in Table 13.3 appear to remain the same in these comparative results. Specifically, the *BVAR* model performance is degraded at longer horizons and the *IDVP* model produces around twice as many winning forecasts as the *IDVH* model. The improved performance of the *BMA* model at the longer horizons appears to take away from winning forecasts produced by the *BAYES* model since we see the greatest decrease in winning cases for the *BAYES* model and a smaller decrease in winning cases for the *IDVP* model.

Table 13.6 combines the counts for the two benchmark models (*VAR+BVAR*), the two sets of counts for the *IDV* models (*IDVH+IDVP*) and those for the Bayesian models (*BAYES+BMA*). This comparison allows us to address the issue of non-Bayesian versus Bayesian approaches to incorporating input-output-table information regarding interindustry relationships.

These results point to decreasing accuracy for the benchmark and *IDV* models at longer forecast horizons and increasing accuracy for the Bayesian models at these horizons. In fact, beginning at the 2-step-ahead horizon, the Bayesian models account for more than 1/3 of the winning forecasts (38.2 percent). This improvement of accuracy with the forecast horizon continues until the Bayesian models account for 44.4 percent of the winning forecasts at the 4-step-ahead horizon. In defense of the *IDV* models, note that most of the additional winning forecasts produced by the Bayesian models come at the expense of the two benchmark models, not the *IDV* models. These two approaches produced a relatively constant share of the winning forecasts around 32 percent for horizons 2- through 4-step-ahead.

13.4 Conclusion

This chapter examined two approaches to incorporating interindustry linkages in regional econometric models of the type employed in econometric+input-output modeling. Both approaches attempt to draw on non-sample information from input-output tables when estimating the interindustry econometric model. The non-Bayesian approaches that have been explored in the literature fall into two categories. Those that use the input-output-table information to form composite variables based on linear combinations of multiple related industry time-series (*IDVH*), and those that rely on the input-output-table information for specification purposes (*IDVP*). Both of these approaches attempt to achieve parsimony in the model that typically suffers from degrees of freedom and overfitting problems. The *IDVH* approach uses a single composite variable to produce parsimony and the *IDVP* approach creates exclusionary restrictions based on input-output-table information about interindustry relationships to achieve parsimony.

These two approaches are compared to alternative Bayesian approaches that rely on less ad-hoc methods. Bayesian approaches formally treat the input-output-table information as non-sample prior information that is incorporated in the interindustry econometric model via Bayes Rule. One of the Bayesian approaches (*BAYES*) involved a relatively straightforward regression that allowed all interindustry variables to enter the model. Prior distributions were assigned to the parameters of the model based on the input-output-table information. It was argued that this has theoretical advantages in cases where the sample data for regional econometric time-series is in disagreement with the information from the national or regional input-output-table. Posterior estimates from the Bayesian approach reflect a formal probabilistic combination of both the sample and non-sample sources of information regarding interindustry relationships. Specific priors that were derived from the input-output-table information were set forth for the means and variances that should be generally applicable in a wide variety of regional interindustry econometric+input-output models.

A second Bayesian approach (*BMA*) was based on Bayesian variable selection methods that work in the spirit of the *IDVP* method. This approach imposes zero restrictions on variables that do not appear in the highest posterior probability model.

A set of forecasting experiments were carried out to compare the performance of the two Bayesian strategies with the two non-Bayesian approaches previously employed in the literature. The results indicate that the Bayesian approach produced more accurate forecasts than the non-Bayesian approaches. However, all approaches appear to have merit relative to two benchmark *VAR* and *BVAR* models. Forecast accuracy of the alternative methods varies over the forecast horizon and the non-Bayesian models produced the most accurate forecast in nearly one third of the time-series used in the experiment. This suggests we cannot ignore these approaches and that they may hold merit.

A formal Bayesian solution to resolving the issue of which model specification/estimation methodology to use was proposed by Leamer (1978). The solution he advocated would require that we combine forecasts from all of these models (*IDVH, IDVP* and *BAYES*). The combination process would rely on posterior model probabilities as weights in producing a single forecast. An operational implementation of this suggestion for the case of econometric+input-output modeling remains a subject for further research. Although the Bayesian model averaging methodology introduced here may provide the means to implement Leamer's suggestion, computational intensity and appropriate specification of prior information hinder the application of this approach.

References

Coomes, P., D. Olson, and D. Glennon. 1991a. "The interindustry employment demand variable: An extension of the I-SAMIS technique for linking input-output and econometric models." *Environment and Planning A*, 23, 1063-1068.

Coomes, P., D. Olson, and J. Merchant. 1991b. "Using a metropolitan-area econometric model to analyze economic development proposals." *Urban Studies*, 28, 369-382.

Fawson, C. and K.R. Criddle. 1994. "A comparative analysis of time series approaches to modeling intersectoral and intercounty employment linkages in rural regional labor markets." *Journal of Regional Science*, 34. 57-74.

Glennon, D. and J. Lane. 1990. "input-output restrictions, regional structural models and econometric forecasts." In L. Anselin and M. Madden, eds. *New Directions in Regional Analysis: Integrated and Multiregional Approaches*. London, Belhaven. pp. 115-132.

Glennon, D., J. Lane, and S. Johnson. 1987. "Regional econometric models that reflect labor market relations." *International Journal of Forecasting*, 3, 299-312.

Glennon, D., 1986. "Incorporating labour market structure in regional econometric models." *Applied Economics*, 18, 545-555.

Israilevich, P.R., G.J.D. Hewings, G.R. Schindler and R. Mahidhara. 1996. "The choice of input-output table embedded in regional econometric input-output models." *Papers in Regional Science*, 75, 103-119.

Lawson, A.M., 1997. "Benchmark Input-Output Accounts for the U.S. Economy, 1992", *Survey of Current Business*, November, 36-82.

Leamer, E.E. 1983. "Model Choice and Specification Analysis." In Z. Griliches and M.D. Intriligator, eds. *Handbook of Econometrics, Volume 1*. Amsterdam, North-Holland.

LeSage, J.P. and M. Magura. 1991. "Using interindustry input-output relations as a Bayesian prior in employment forecast models." *International Journal of Forecasting*, 7, 231-238.

Magura, M. 1987. "The use of input-output tables in specifying interindustry and interregional labor market linkages." *Papers of the Regional Science Association*, 63, 117-123.

Moghadam, K. and K. Ballard. 1988. "Small area modeling of the industry section (SAMIS): An integrated econometric-interindustry approach." *Environment and Planning A*, 20, 665-669.

Partridge, M.D. and D.S. Rickman. 1999. "Generalizing the Bayesian vector autoregression for regional interindustry employment forecasting." *Journal of Business and Economic Statistics*, 16, 62-72.

Raftery, A.E., D.Madigan and J.A. Hoeting. 1997. "Bayesian model averaging for linear regression models." *Journal of the American Statistical Association*, 92, 179-191.

Rey, S.J. 1997. "Integrating regional econometric and input-output models: an evaluation of embedding strategies." *Environment and Planning A*, 29, 1057-1072.

Rey, S.J. 2000. "Integrated regional econometric + input-output modeling: issues and opportunities." *Papers in Regional Science*, 79, 271-292.

Rey, S.J. and B. Dev. 1997. "Integrating econometric and input-output models in a multiregional context." *Growth and Change*, 22, 222-243.

Rey, S.J. and R.W. Jackson. 1999. "Interindustry employment demand and labor productivity in econometric+input-output models." *Environment and Planning A*, 31, 1583-1599.

Stover, M.E. 1994. "A comparison of annual and benchmark input-output tables in regional economic modeling." *Annals of Regional Science*, 28. 223-228.

Theil, H. and A.S. Goldberger. 1961. "On Pure and Mixed Statistical Estimation in Economics." *International Economic Review*, 2, 65-78.

White, E.N. and G.J.D. Hewings. 1982. "Space-time employment modeling: Some results using seemingly unrelated regression estimators." *Journal of Regional Science*, 22, 283-302.

14 Regional Input-Output, Leontief-Strout and Uncertainty

John R. Roy

ETUDES, PO Box 96, Mallacoota, Vic, 3892, Australia
e-mail: johnroy@vicnet.net.au

14.1 Introduction

The multi-regional input-output approach of Leontief-Strout, described in Leontief and Strout (1963), built on the Chenery-Moses model introduced by Chenery (1953). In this model, two key assumptions are embedded (i) the demand pool assumption, whereby the users of intermediate inputs are taken as indifferent to their region of origin and (ii) the supply pool assumption, where producers are taken as indifferent to the region of destination of their outputs. The resulting model turns out to be much more tractable than a full interregional model, and has been widely applied. Leontief and Strout used an independent gravity-type model to estimate the resulting trade flows, as a substitute for the provision of trade coefficients in models from the Chenery-Moses tradition. Wilson (1970) provided a more integrated procedure, setting up a conventional entropy framework to determine the commodity flows enhanced by the Leontief-Strout input-output balance relations introduced as constraints. In other words, the flows were co-determined by the transport cost information together with the technological information embodied in the Leontief-Strout representation of input-output. Another enhancement was to replace the entropy framework by one from information theory based on historical trade patterns (Snickars and Weibull, 1977), yielding models such as those described in Batten (1983).

In Roy (1997), the introduction of uncertainty in the producer profit terms allowed prices to be retained explicitly in a regional input-output framework. Although the retention of prices is desirable from a theoretical viewpoint, such price information at the regional level is often extremely difficult to obtain. In fact, the whole of regional input-output analysis is plagued by a paucity of survey data. Hence, in this chapter, the main emphasis is to base the multi-regional model of interregional flows on just the survey data obtainable without a major effort. In fact, the two key Leontief-Strout assumptions are entirely equivalent to two conditions based on data availability, as follows (i) the input-output coefficients are just defined at the region of production, independently of the mix of the inputs from other regions and (ii) the flows of commodities between regions are only known in terms of the commodity (viz. sector) being shipped, independently of the sector or sectors to which they are being supplied as intermediate inputs. However, the Leontief-Strout input-output balance relations turn out to be logically incorrect, confusing output with the sum of intermediate input flows. New balance relations are derived, compared with the conventional relations and introduced into an entropy maximization framework, which may determine either interregional or multi-regional flows.

In any short run regional supply model, it is desirable to include input capacity constraints. Of course, an obvious way to achieve this is to introduce ≤ inequality constraints on regional capacity for each sector. However, such constraints, when inactive, maintain separability and have no influence whatsoever on the flows - they only factor into the analysis once they become active. Intuitively, this is not very plausible. In most sectors, a 'vintage' distribution over regional capacity exists, and when the capacity limits of a sector are being hard pressed in a certain region, one would expect some spillovers into adjacent regions. In fact, the generic logistic forms of regional supply functions motivated by Hotelling (1932) demonstrate this property. In this chapter, an additional entropy term recognizing heterogeneity within the available capacity is shown to yield a logistic supply function. This generates a further enhancement to the Wilson framework. Of course, if regional price information were available, the transport cost constraint should be replaced by a short run constraint on profits, allowing the result to truly be interpreted as a supply function. In addition, by use of the special information theory method of Roy (1987), the model not only perfectly reproduces the base period flow distribution (as for conventional information theory models), but also is simultaneously responsive to changes in freight prices and the transport network. Technological change can be included by exogenous adjustments to the regional input-output coefficients, with the technological balance relations being imposed anew in the projection time period. Finally, these results are generalized by the introduction of explicit market prices, and compared with the formulation in Roy (1997). Short run profit constraints replace the simple transport cost constraints, and flows are defined in quantity rather than money units. The resulting flow relations then represent logistic supply functions.

14.2 Formulation of Enhanced Models

14.2.1 From Interregional to Multi-regional – Appropriate Balance Relations

In the course of introduction of the new approach, it seems relevant to say something on the respective merits of a 'full' interregional analysis and a multi-regional procedure. Interregional input-output coefficients a_{ij}^{rs} are conventionally defined as:

$$a_{ij}^{rs} = x_{ij}^{rs} / X_j^s \tag{14.1}$$

expressing the quotient of the input x_{ij}^{rs} of sector i from region r into sector j in region s over the total output X_j^s of sector j in region s. Then, the *usage* of the output X_i^r of sector i in region r is expressed as that going to supply intermediate inputs of all sectors into all regions and the amount Y_i^r going to final demand, yielding:

$$X_i^r = \sum_{js} x_{ij}^{rs} + Y_i^r \tag{14.2}$$

We should note that a comparison of the interregional input coefficients a_{ij}^{rs} in region r with a_{ij}^{zs} in another input supply region z yields *no guidance* on the *relative technological effectiveness* of obtaining a unit of output of sector j in region s from a unit of input of sector i from region r *vs.* a unit of the same input from region z. In order to achieve such a comparison, we would need to distinguish the part of the output X_j^{rs} which is produced from inputs of sector i from region r versus those from region z, and have enhanced coefficients $\tilde{a}_{ij}^{rs}$ defined as:

$$\tilde{a}_{ij}^{rs} = x_{ij}^{rs} / X_j^{rs} \qquad (14.3)$$

If it is not feasible in practice to obtain such differentiated output information, it seems to this writer that the gains from interregional analysis may be insubstantial. It appears to yield nothing to enable comparison of the technology embedded in the inputs from different regions regarding their output efficiency in different sectors in the same or other destination regions, which is what a true *interregional production function* should be trying to measure between regions![1] On the other hand, it does allow us to compare the ratios of local inputs vs. the inputs from other regions, specialized for each different producing sector in a region. Thus, although the conventional interregional analysis does not seem capable of identifying the 'transmission' of technology between regions, it can measure the full set of commodity to sector flows between each pair of regions, and try to include the influence of transport costs on these flows. As far as output technology is concerned, it is most appropriately embedded in the multi-regional coefficients a_{ij}^{s}, denoting the number of units $x_{ij}^{s} = \sum_r x_{ij}^{rs}$ of input of sector i going into sector j in region s required to produce a unit of sector j output in the same region s, given as:

$$a_{ij}^{s} = x_{ij}^{s} / X_j^{s} \qquad (14.4)$$

Of course, units of the input x_{ij}^{s} of sector i used for sector j in region s are supplied from region s itself, as well as potentially from all other regions r.

Referring to Leontief and Strout (1963), it is clear that the simplification of the conventional interregional relations (14.1) to the multi-regional relations (14.4) corresponds to their *demand pool* assumption. The total flow $\sum_r x_{ij}^{rs}$ of sector i *into* region s from all regions r (including itself), rather than the output X_i^{r}, is assumed to be distributed to final demand Y_i^{s} and as inputs x_{ij}^{s} to all other sectors j (including i itself), leading to:

$$\sum_s x_i^{sr} = \sum_j x_{ij}^{r} + Y_i^{r} \qquad (14.5)$$

The *supply pool* assumption implies that the outputs of each sector i in each region r are pooled before being allocated to supply regions. Instead of (14.4) with s replaced

[1] Perhaps these points are obvious to the experienced input-output specialist. However, they do not appear to be greatly emphasized in the literature.

by r being substituted for x_{ij}^{r} into (14.5), output is again replaced by a sum of flows (this time by *out*-flows), yielding the final balance relations:

$$\sum_{s} x^{sr} = \sum_{j} a_{ij}^{r} \sum_{s} x_{i}^{rs} + Y_{i}^{r} \qquad (14.6)$$

Upon absorbing the regional index s by denoting the sums over s with '•', we obtain (14.6) in its usual form:

$$x_{i}^{\bullet r} = \sum_{j} a_{ij}^{r} x_{i}^{r\bullet} + Y_{i}^{r} \qquad (14.7)$$

However, these relationships are quite unusual, equating a sum of in-flows to equal the flows to supply intermediate inputs plus final demand. Conditions (14.2), which express *total output* as the sum of flows to supply intermediate inputs plus final demand, are the only relations fully supported by the theory. The challenge is to make them multi-regional rather than interregional, consistent with the availability of technology data just by region of production and flow data between regions just in terms of the commodity (sector) shipped.

If relations (14.1) are transposed, indices r and s interchanged and the whole summed over j and s, we have:

$$\sum_{js} x_{ij}^{rs} = \sum_{js} a_{ij}^{sr} X_{j}^{r} \qquad (14.8)$$

Now making the demand pool assumption, we can set $a_{ij}^{r} = \sum_{s} a_{ij}^{sr}$ in (14.8), yielding:

$$\sum_{js} x_{ij}^{rs} = \sum_{j} a_{ij}^{r} X_{j}^{r} \qquad (14.9)$$

Then, the output term can be removed from (14.9) by substituting for it from (14.2) in terms of the sum of intermediate plus final demands, giving:

$$\sum_{js} x_{ij}^{rs} = \sum_{j} a_{ij}^{r} \left(\sum_{is} x_{ij}^{rs} + Y_{j}^{r} \right) \qquad (14.10)$$

If the commodity flows are just defined as x_{i}^{rs} in terms of the commodity i being shipped, then the extra indices can be removed from (14.10), leading to:

$$\sum_{s} x_{i}^{rs} = \sum_{j} a_{ij}^{r} \left(\sum_{s} x_{j}^{rs} + Y_{j}^{r} \right) \qquad (14.11)$$

The final step, as above, is to denote the s summation by a dot, yielding:

$$x_{i}^{\bullet r} = \sum_{j} a_{ij}^{r} \left(x_{j}^{r\bullet} + Y_{j}^{r} \right) \qquad (14.12)$$

This is clearly seen to be different from the conventional Leontief-Strout condition (14.7), with the final demand included under the summation and scaled by the multi-regional coefficients. As it has eluded this author to find a flaw in the above reasoning, that proceeds directly from the classical conditions (14.1) and (14.2), there seems no other possibility than that the Leontief-Strout result is not correct. As stressed earlier, they abandoned the fundamental relation (14.2) to somehow express total in-flows as the sum of intermediate demands and final demand, without seeming to realize that the outputs must also contribute to *final demands* in the sectors j to which sector i is an intermediate input. However, as multi-regional analysis seems more usually to be carried out via the trade coefficient approach than via the method of Leontief-Strout (Isard, *et. al.*, 1998), the above error may not be of great concern in practice. However, in our quest for a model recognizing the interdependent influences on flows of both technology and transport costs, it is important to have the technology represented by the correct balance relations.

14.2.2 An Integrated Multi-Regional Approach

In this section, a considerable enhancement of Wilson (1970) is made, inserting the correct technological balance relations and including logistic constraints on regional input capacity. Also, a strong distinction is made between the estimation form of the model and a transformed version for projection, building on the formalism introduced by Lesse (1982).

Model estimation. Consider that we have base period data, both on the *capacity*, $\tilde{X}_{ir}^{0}$, of sector i to supply inputs from region r and the total outflow, $\bar{X}^{s0}$, of all sectors into region s. Also, let Y_j^{r0} be the base period final demand for sector j in region r. Finally, let $\bar{X}^0$ be the total value of all inputs in the system, $\bar{c}^0$ be the average transport cost per value unit of commodity shipped and c_i^{rs0} be the transport cost per value unit of sector i between regions r and s.[2] Then, the number of microstates, Z, can be given as the number of ways $\tilde{X}_{ir}^{0}$ distinguishable capacity units may be divided into $\sum_s x_i^{rs}$ which are utilized and $(\tilde{X}_{ir}^{0} - \Sigma_s x_i^{rs})$ which are unutilized, multiplied by the number of ways that the $\sum_s x_i^{rs}$ distinguishable utilized units may be allocated to regions s, yielding:

$$Z = \pi_{ir}\left\{\tilde{X}_{ir}^{0}!/\left[\left(\tilde{X}_{ir}^{0} - \sum_s x_i^{rs}\right)!\left(\sum_s x_i^{rs}\right)!\right]\right\}\pi_{ir}\left\{\left(\sum_s x_i^{rs}\right)!/\left(\pi_s x_i^{rs}!\right)\right\} \tag{14.13}$$

After some cancellation, setting the entropy S as the natural log of Z and applying the Stirling approximation, we obtain as our entropy maximization objective:

$$S = -\sum_{irs} x_i^{rs}\left(\ln x_i^{rs} - 1\right) - \sum_{ir}\left(\tilde{X}_{ir}^{0} - \sum_s x_i^{rs}\right)\left[\ln\left(\tilde{X}_{ir}^{0} - x_i^{rs}\right) - 1\right] \tag{14.14}$$

To the above objective, total destination in-flow constraints are imposed as:

$$\sum_{ir} x_i^{rs} = \bar{X}^{s0} \tag{14.15}$$

The logistic capacity 'constraint' in the second entropy term in (14.14) allows the usual origin constraints to be omitted. Now, apply the average transport cost constraint as:

$$\sum_{irs} x_i^{rs} c_i^{rs0} = \bar{c}^0 \bar{X}^0 \tag{14.16}$$

---

[2] By normalizing with respect to prices, transport costs could be converted into *quantity* units

Finally, for the flow pattern to be consistent with our multi-regional technology, our new input-output balance relations (14.11), not in conflict with (14.15), are applied as:

$$\sum_s x_i^{rs} - \sum_j a_{ij}^{r0} \sum_s x_j^{rs} = \sum_j a_{ij}^{r0} Y_j^{r0} \tag{14.17}$$

With final demand taken as exogenous input, as for the conventional analysis, the right-hand side of (14.17) is a known value, as required. Applying Lagrangian theory, (14.14) is maximized under (14.15) with multipliers λ_s, (14.16) with multiplier β and (14.17) with multipliers α_{ir}. Differentiation with respect to x_i^{rs} and equating to zero gives:

$$x_i^{rs} = \left(\tilde{X}_{ir}^{0} - \sum_s x_i^{rs}\right)\exp-\left[\lambda_s + \beta c_i^{rs0} + \alpha_{is} - \left(\sum_j \alpha_{jr} a_{ji}^{r0}\right)\right] \tag{14.18}$$

Upon transposing, the explicit logistic result emerges:

$$\begin{aligned} x_i^{rs} &= \tilde{X}_{ir}^{0} \exp-\left[\lambda_s + \beta c_i^{rs0} + \alpha_{is} - \left(\sum_j \alpha_{jr} a_{ji}^{r0}\right)\right] / \\ &/\left\{1 + \left(\sum_s \exp-\left[\lambda_s + \beta c_i^{rs0} + \alpha_{is} - \left(\sum_j \alpha_{jr} a_{ji}^{r0}\right)\right]\right)\right\} \end{aligned} \tag{14.19}$$

Setting $A_s = \exp-\lambda_s$; $B_{ir} = \tilde{X}_{ir}^{0} / \left\{1 + \sum_s A_s D_s E_r \exp-\beta c_i^{rs0}\right\}$; $E_{ir} = \pi_r D_{jr}$ and $D_{is} = \exp\text{-}\alpha_{is}$, we can substitute into the constraints. With B_{ir} and E_{ir} already given explicitly above in terms of the other unknowns, we merely need to give expressions for A_s and D_{ir}, which after setting $F_{is} = \left(\sum_r B_{ir} E_{ir} \exp-\beta c_i^{rs0}\right)$, come out as:

$$\begin{aligned} A_s &= \bar{X}^{0} / \sum_i D_{is} F_{is}, D_{ir} = \\ &= \left\{\sum_j a_{ij}^{r0}\left[Y_j^{r0} + B_{jr} E_{jr} \sum_s A_s D_{js} \exp-\beta c_j^{rs0}\right]\right\} / (A_r F_{ir}) \end{aligned} \tag{14.20}$$

Notice that the expression for D_{ir} is a function of itself, requiring an iteration within an iteration. The gravity parameter, β, can be determined simultaneously using linear extrapolation. Alternatively, the non-linear equations for both D_{ir} and β could be solved simultaneously using the Newton-Raphson approach, with those for A_s, B_{ir} and E_{ir} being solved using the conventional successive substitution technique. Convergence is guaranteed (if data are consistent) for this problem with a strictly concave objective function and linear constraints. The flows are then given simply as:

$$x_i^{rs} = A_s B_{ir} D_{is} E_{ir} \exp\left(-\beta c_i^{rs0}\right) \tag{14.21}$$

Although (14.21) may appear to be a *separable* function, connectivity is embedded in the relations (14.20). In fact, the above solution process illustrates the *interdependencies* between transport costs, production technology and logistic capacity constraints in the determination of the flows. After the commodity flows x_i^{rs} are obtained from the above, the regional *outputs* X_i^r can be found from the multi-regional form of (14.2): $X_i^r = \sum_s x_i^{rs} + Y_i^{r0}$. Also, relation (14.4) allows the *intraregional, intersectoral* flows x_{ij}^{s} to be evaluated, consistent with the multi-regional technology. Thus, our model yields intersectoral flows within regions and flows of a given commodity (sector) between regions. At this estimation step, the modeled flows x_{ij}^{s} should be compared with the observed base period flows x_i^{rs0} using a goodness of fit measure, such as Root Mean Square. If the fit is good, the entropy approach will be adequate, especially if the goodness of fit of the model is also accompanied by a significant reduction in the uncertainty of the distribution. Otherwise, one should adopt the information theory procedure to be described later.

Models in the tradition of Chenery (1953) were able to apply trade coefficients to yield *interregional flows*, despite the limitations of a multi-regional technology. The above approach can be modified to do the same if a more disaggregated form of the balance constraints (14.10) is applied, with the summation over j removed, giving

$$\sum_s x_{ij}^{rs} = a_{ij}^{r0}\left(\sum_{is} x_{ij}^{rs} + Y_j^{r0}\right) \tag{14.22}$$

It is easy to show that the multi-regional model (14.19) has the following interregional analogue:

$$\begin{aligned} x_{ij}^{rs} &= \tilde{X}_{ir}^{0}\exp-\left[\lambda_s + \beta c_i^{rs0} + \alpha_{ijs} - \alpha_{ijr} a_{ji}^{r0}\right]/ \\ &/\left\{1+\left(\sum_{js}\exp-\left[\lambda_s + \beta c_i^{rs0} + \alpha_{ijs} - \alpha_{ijr} a_{ji}^{r0}\right]\right)\right\} \end{aligned} \tag{14.23}$$

where the Lagrange multipliers α_{ijs} have one more dimension than those in (14.19). Although no further technological information is provided over (14.19), we can now obtain information on the regional mix of inputs.

Use of model for projection. The main task in transforming the estimation model formulation into a form suitable for projection is to choose the Lagrange multipliers that should be treated as parameters in projection, and those that must be evaluated anew. This clearly relates to which information should reasonably be treated as exogenous input and which treated as endogenous output. In terms of the structure of the model, it is considered that the exogenous input should include any quantity changes, such as changed regional input capacities $\tilde{X}_i^{r0}$ and changed final demand Y_i^r. If transport costs change to c_i^{rs}, the availability as a parameter of the gravity Lagrange multiplier β allows the influence of these changes to be assessed by the model (Lesse, 1982). In addition, any new multi-regional input-output coefficients a_{ij}^{r} must be provided exogenously. Finally, the treatment of the Lagrange multiplier λ_s as a parameter allows the outflows to be endogenous in projection, in response to the changes in input capacities, final demand, transport costs and the multi-regional technology. In this case, the projection form of (14.19) changes to:

$$\begin{aligned} x_i^{rs} &= \tilde{X}_i^{r}\exp-\left[\lambda_s + \beta c_i^{rs} + \alpha_{is}^{l} - \left(\sum_j \alpha_{jr}^{l} a_{ji}^{r}\right)\right]/ \\ &/\left\{1+\left(\sum_s \exp-\left[\lambda_s + \beta c_i^{rs} + \alpha_{is}^{l} - \left(\sum_j \alpha_{jr}^{l} a_{ji}^{r}\right)\right]\right)\right\} \end{aligned} \tag{14.24}$$

with merely the multipliers α_{is}^{l} having to be re-evaluated to satisfy an updated form of the balance relations (14.17). The evaluation of these multipliers would merely entail successive substitution in the relations associated with (14.20), but where A_s and β are now given exogenously. This recursive substitution process retains the non-separable structure of the model. Furthermore, it is clear that our probabilistic approach has bypassed the necessity of matrix inversion, which is routinely required for the deterministic procedure.

An adjustment from information theory. As stressed in Batten (1983), the more general information theory approach may give improved prediction ability for this class of problem. If the goodness of fit of the estimated model is not satisfactory, the projection model is likely to yield improved results if information bias terms are computed and inserted into the model, as demonstrated via an information theory procedure in Roy (1987). We proceed as follows; if the estimated entropy model (14.19) yields $\bar{x}_i^{rs}$ as the modeled flows, we compute ratios z_i^{rs} as the quotient $x_i^{rs0} / \bar{x}_i^{rs}$ of the observed and modeled flows and z_i^r as the quotient $\left(\tilde{X}_i^{r0} - \sum_s x_i^{rs0}\right) / \left(\tilde{X}_i^{r0} - \sum_s \bar{x}_i^{rs}\right)$ of the observed and modeled unutilized capacities. The next step is to normalize the z's as probabilities $q_i^{rs} = z_i^{rs} / \left(\sum_{irs} z_i^{rs}\right)$ and $q_i^r = z_i^r / \left(\sum_{ir} z_i^r\right)$. If the q's are applied as prior probabilities in the denominator of the log terms in the entropy objective (14.14) and this revised estimation problem is solved anew, it is demonstrated in Roy (1987) that (i) all the Lagrange multipliers are *invariant* to this changed objective and (ii) the modeled flows *precisely* correspond to the observed flows x_i^{rs0}. Of course, this is a good basis for projection. In addition, the outflow and gravity parameters are retained, with the latter allowing the model to be sensitive to future transport cost and network changes. The consistency of the flows with the multi-regional technology available at the projection period is assured by applying the technological balance relations anew. The projection relations (14.24) now become:

$$
\begin{aligned}
x_i^{rs} = {} & \tilde{X}_i^r q_i^{rs} \exp-\left[\lambda_s + \beta c_i^{rs} + \alpha_{is}^{//} - \left(\sum_j \alpha_{jr}^{//} a_{ji}^r\right)\right] / \\
& / \left\{ q_i^r + \left(\sum_s q_i^{rs} \exp-\left[\lambda_s + \beta c_i^{rs} + \alpha_{is}^{//} - \left(\sum_j \alpha_{jr}^{//} a_{ji}^r\right)\right]\right)\right\}
\end{aligned}
\qquad (14.25)
$$

where the Lagrange multipliers $\alpha_{is}^{//}$ associated with the new input-output balance constraints will change from those in the pure entropy formulation (14.24). It is suggested that (14.25) be used in place of (14.24) for most applications.

Some comparisons. The approach presented above integrates technology changes and transport network and cost changes in the evaluation of multi-regional flows. As a probabilistic model, it fits parameters to observations, rather than relying on deterministic optimization. The logistic form of the supply relationships promotes spillovers into adjacent regions when there is a high pressure on capacity in a given region. At the same time, the model does not attempt to project changes in technology. It is the user's responsibility to provide any changed input-output coefficients a_{ij}^r. Its primary aim is to estimate the influence on regional flows and output when exogenous changes in input capacities, final demand, transport costs and technical coefficients are introduced. It will need to be tested with conventional multi-regional data to verify its suitability for these tasks. These data will need to be enhanced by capacity data for each sector in each region. Without the technological balance relations, the model would resemble a commodity flow model enhanced by the logistic input capacity constraints. However, we maintain that the flows must be consistent with the multi-regional technology being used, justifying the enforcing of these balance relations. The Leontief-Strout balance relations, that were also used by Wilson (1970), are shown to be not fully grounded in the basic relations expressing the usage of output to be the sum of supplies to intermediate inputs and final demand.

What If We Have No Sector Input Capacity Data ? Data on the sector input capacities $\tilde{X}_i^{r0}$ for each sector in each region may be quite difficult to acquire. In that case, base period constraints are introduced on the total value $\bar{X}^{r0}$ of out-flows from each origin region *r*, in the form

$$\sum\nolimits_{is} x_i^{rs} = \bar{X}^{r0} \tag{14.26}$$

If the capacity entropy is omitted as the second term in (14.14), and (14.26) attached with a multiplier η_r, then the previous solution (14.19) is replaced by:

$$x_i^{rs} = \exp - \left[\lambda_s + \eta_r + \beta c_i^{rs0} + \alpha_{is} - \left(\sum\nolimits_j \alpha_{jr} a_{ji}^{r0} \right) \right] \tag{14.27}$$

With A_s, D_{is} and E_{ir} defined as below (14.19) and B_r defined as *exp* - η_r, we can set up the following set of recursive relations:

$$\begin{aligned} A_s &= \bar{X}^{s0} / \sum\nolimits_{ir} B_r D_{is} E_{is} \exp - \beta c_i^{rs0} \\ B_r &= \bar{X}^{r0} / \sum\nolimits_{is} A_s D_{is} E_{ir} \exp - \beta c_i^{rs0} \\ D_{ir} &= \left\{ \sum\nolimits_j a_{ij}^{r0} \left[Y_j^{r0} + B_r E_{jr} \sum\nolimits_s A_s D_{js} \exp - \beta c_j^{rs0} \right] \right\} / \left\{ \sum\nolimits_s A_s B_s E_{is} \exp - \beta c_i^{sr0} \right\} \end{aligned} \tag{14.28}$$

These three relations, together with that for E_{ir}, can be solved iteratively for the unknown Lagrange multipliers, with β being obtained, as before, via linear extrapolation. The final relations are identical to (14.21) except for B_r replacing B_{ir}. For projection, A_s, B_r and β are treated as parameters, with the recursive relations for D_{is} and E_{ir} providing the interdependencies associated with the inverse in the conventional solution. Clearly, the information theory adjustment should again be used when the fit to the base period flows is not adequate.

14.3 Some Further Developments

In Roy (1997), a probabilistic approach was developed that retained prices in input-output analysis. Although regional prices are not easily obtained, the provision of prices opens the opportunity for input-output models to be developed as short run supply functions, allowing *tâtonnement* with a compatible demand model in a regional CGE framework. The main difference with the foregoing is that the *supply to final demand* is now obtainable as an *output* from our supply model, rather than being inserted as an *input* via our balance relations, which must be omitted here. The first change to the above model is that the flows, x_{ij}^{rs}, are defined as *interregional* in terms of *quantities* shipped, rather than in terms of dollars. Whereas the objective function

(14.14) remains unchanged in form, the outflow constraints (14.15) are summed over *i*, *j*, and *r*. The transport cost constraint (14.16) should now be modified to a constraint on short run profits, reflecting the classical objective of the competitive firm. If $\bar{\pi}^0$ is taken as the base period unit profit per dollar of all commodities produced, then we should replace (14.16) by a profit constraint in terms of revenue minus costs, yielding:

$$\sum_{ijrs} x_{ij}^{rs} p_i^{r0} / \left(m a_{ij}^{s0}\right) - \sum_{ijrs} \left(p_i^{r0} + c_i^{rs0}\right) x_{ij}^{rs} = \bar{\pi}^0 V^0 \tag{14.29}$$

where V^0 are the total dollars of production, *m* the number of row sectors and the *p's* the fob prices in the base period. Also, assuming that the input-output coefficients a_{ij}^{s0} are given (as usual) in value terms, the output prices p_j^{s0} cancel out in the above revenue expression. In this term, the output has been expressed as the *average* over all rows of the quotients of input divided by the regional coefficient, which emerge as constant values in the deterministic theory (Roy, 1997). If the Lagrange multiplier on the profit constraint (14.29) is taken as γ, then constrained maximization of (14.14) yields:

$$\begin{aligned} x_{ij}^{rs} = \tilde{X}_i^{r0} \exp\left[\lambda_{is} - \gamma\left\{\left(p_i^{r0} / m a_{ij}^{s0}\right) - p_i^{r0} - c_i^{rs0}\right\}\right] / \\ / \left\{1 + \sum_{js} \exp\left[\gamma\left\{\left(p_i^{r0} / m a_{ij}^{s0}\right) - p_i^{r0} - c_i^{rs0}\right\}\right]\right\} \end{aligned} \tag{14.30}$$

This truly represents a logistic probabilistic supply function, where the profits are included as a constraint based on observations, rather than as the objective in the deterministic theory. Output can be obtained as an average of the quotients of intermediate inputs and regional coefficients, consistent with their role in the revenue relations. The supply to final demand can then be computed from (14.2). Thus, if regional market prices are available, the relations (14.30) should be used in preference to (14.23), where final demand is exogenous and prices have been 'absorbed', not being capable of modification between the base period and the projection period.

14.4 Conclusions

The overall aim of the chapter has been to extend the conventional deterministic theory to be probabilistic. In addition, we can identify the interdependencies between logistic input capacity constraints, production technology and transport costs, in their influence on the pattern of multi-regional or interregional flows. When regional prices are included, regional supply functions are produced, allowing the supply to final demand to be endogenous. At the same time, an apparent error in the input-output balance relations of the classical multi-regional model has been uncovered. Much empirical work remains to be done to demonstrate the relevance of the proposed alternative model structures.

References

Batten, D.F. 1983. *Spatial Analysis of Interacting Economies.* Boston, Kluwer.

Chenery, H. 1953. "Regional analysis." In H. Chenery, P. Clark, V. Cao Pinna, eds. *The Structure and Growth of the Italian Economy.* Rome, US Mutual Security Agency.

Hotelling, H. 1932. "Edgeworth's taxation paradox and the nature of supply and demand functions." *Journal of Political Economy,* 40, 577-616.

Isard, W. 1998. *Methods of Interregional and Regional Analysis.* Aldershot, Ashgate.

Leontief, W. and A. Strout. 1963. "Multi-regional input-output analysis." In T. Barna, ed. *Structural Interdependence and Economic Development.* London, Macmillan.

Lesse, P.F. 1982. "A phenomenological theory of socioeconomic systems with spatial interactions." *Environment and Planning A,* 14, 869-888.

Roy, J.R. 1987. "An alternative information theory approach for modelling spatial interaction." *Environment and Planning A,* 19, 385-394.

Roy, J.R. 1997. "A price-responsive framework for interregional input-output." *Annals of Regional Science,* 31, 285-298.

Snickars, F. and J. Weibull. 1977. "A minimum information principle: theory and practice." *Regional Science and Urban Economics,* 7, 137-168.

Wilson, A.G. 1970. *Entropy in Urban and Regional Modelling.* London, Pion.

15 Using the REAL Models to Understand Midwest Restructuring

William A. Testa

Federal Reserve Bank of Chicago, P.O. Box 834, Chicago IL 60690-0834
e-mail: wtesta@frbchi.org

15.1 Introduction

The 1980s and early 1990s were a time of profound restructuring in the Midwest. The region had stood as the nation's wealthy and progressive manufacturing center for a long-standing century. But the confluence of shocks that took place during this time shook the region's economy to its foundations—defense spending shocks, farm crisis, foreign competition, and technological change. In turn, these shocks challenged the region's businesses and policymakers to either change course or to wither away. By the mid-1990s, there was very visible evidence – both statistical and otherwise – that the region had been successful in its transition well beyond the hopes and expectations of majority opinion. Indeed, some observed that such a renaissance was probably unique in the annals of those regions experiencing deep manufacturing decline and decay in the industrial age...so much so that the Midwest's experiences merited a deeper analysis and understanding as a guide to policy makers both in the Midwest and elsewhere. In cooperation with many analysts drawn from an array of organizations, the Federal Reserve Bank of Chicago organized a two-year project to bring together the best researchers and their work to address the Midwest turnaround. Over the course of the many topical symposiums, it became apparent that the project was fortunate in its inquiries because crucial tools to understand the Midwest turnaround and to guide its policy decisions were under development by the Regional Economics Applications Laboratory (REAL) and its directors—Philip Israilevich and Geoffrey Hewings. In the following discussion, the contributions of the REAL to understanding the Midwest economy are reviewed the context of the 1996-97 Midwest Assessment project and the important public policy issues and choices that now lie before region.

15.2 Midwest Economy and Assessment Project

A region's economy can be represented by many diverse measures. Unemployment rates are among the most widely recognized indicators of both economic progress and participation of the region's population in the economy. Looking at the aggregate unemployment rate for the Midwest versus the nation from the 1980s to date, two remarkable features can be seen. First, from an average annual unemployment rate that exceeded the nation's by 3 percentage points in 1983, the Midwest's unemployment rate had fallen to a full percentage point below the nation's by 1996 (see figure 15.1). Since then, other U.S. regions have partially closed this gap as the record-breaking national expansion has tightened labor markets in all of the major multi-state U.S. regions. Even so, into the year 2000, the Midwest average workforce enjoyed marginally tighter labor markets than the overall U.S. A second labor market feature is also highly suggestive of a turnabout in structure and/or fortunes of the region. In prior recessions, the highly cyclical nature of the Midwest economy, combined with the region's eroding share of national production, resulted in a more rapid rise in Midwest unemployment relative to the nation. In contrast, during 1990-91, an underlying secular strength of the region's economy allowed its labor market to continue to gain on its national counterpart and, ultimately, to experience a more fully employed work force.

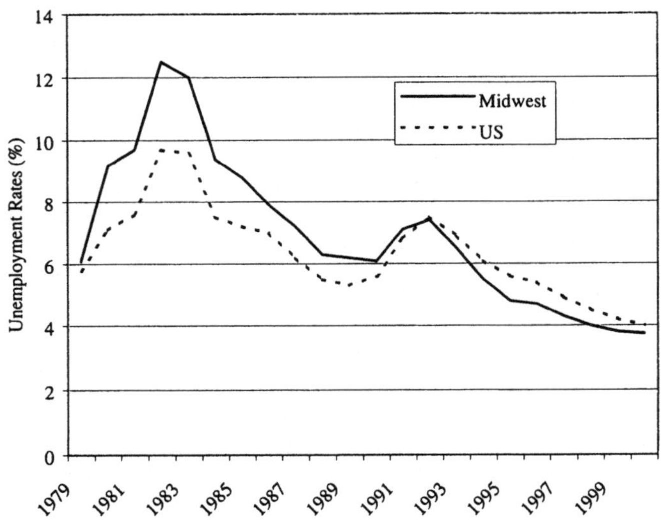

Fig. 15.1. Midwest and US Unemployment Rates, 1979-2000

How to explain these changes? As reported during the past 7-8 years, the dramatic Midwest turnaround has been attributed to both superficial reasons such as timing and depth of national recessions, as well has to substantive reasons such as painful industrial triage and fundamental restructuring. It has also been attributed to agglomeration factors such as reversals of federal domestic spending patterns and foreign exchange rates, but also to internal reasons such as Midwestern public sector and financial thrift, and to shrewd business management. In 1996, the Federal Reserve Bank of Chicago assembled diverse and informed forums with threefold purpose: 1) to accurately document the features of decline and recovery 2) to analyze the underpinnings of the recovery and, most importantly, 3) to identify the most critical policy issues and directions going forward so as to maximize the chances that the Midwest recovery would continue to blossom.[1]

The mode of analysis involved an advisory group of 40 that included directors drawn from academe, labor, public policy, government, and industry. As honorary members, Governors of the 5 states of the Seventh Federal Reserve District—Illinois, Indiana, Iowa, Michigan, and Wisconsin were among them. A series of topical conferences were held at which research papers and roundtable discussion/evidence took place. In crafting a final report, the formal research papers, conference evidence, and published bodies of evidence were drawn upon as source material. Advisory members and other outside experts were consulted in reviewing and synthesizing the conclusions of the final report.

15.3 Models of the REAL

The Regional Economics Applications Laboratory (REAL) is a joint venture of the University of Illinois and the Federal Reserve Bank of Chicago.[2] Its core models have been developed by its founding directors, Geoffrey Hewings of the University of Illinois and Philip Israilevich of the FRB—Chicago, along with various colleagues.[3] These regional models combine detailed inter-industry information constructed from region-specific input–output tables. The industry basis of the tables lie with geographic firm-level data extracted from the U.S. Census (of businesses), and which use highly analytic techniques to estimate regional import/export coefficients. Such information is combined with time-series information and econometric equations to produce forecasts of both economic structure and features. More recently, similar models have been constructed for the states of the Midwest, and these models have been linked using both national transportation data and analytic techniques in arriving at each region's purchase coefficients by industry sector.

The REAL partnership was formed to develop models that would be used to address important policy issues at the subnational level—models that could be applied to practical problems and whose results could be understood by regional policy makers in their deliberations. Especially in U.S. regions, a paucity of regional-specific data has been an impediment to effective decision making. The REAL models draw on previously untapped region-specific data to overcome these impediments, along with advanced analytic models to overcome remaining data difficulties. As we see in the following applications, the REAL models were most timely in the assessment of Midwest change, and in formulating the key policy issues going forward.

[1] See Federal Reserve Bank of Chicago. 1997. *Assessing the Midwest Economy: Looking Back for the Future*. All associated research materials including conference proceedings, working papers, and final report can be located at the web site www.frbchi.org.

[2] See Allardice (1990)

[3] See, for example, Israilevich, *et al.*, (1996, 1997)

15.4 Applications

15.4.1 Structural Change and Globalization Policies

The Midwest had been losing its dominance as the nation's center of manufacturing throughout the latter half of this century. From 1860 to 1947, the Midwest region (as defined by the East North Central Census region) experienced a share of national manufacturing that climbed from 12.7 percent to 30 percent, before falling off to 22.1 percent by 1987—and edging back up since that time (see figure 15.2). Much of this loss reflected a natural dispersion process of population (and manufacturing) deconcentration over the U.S. part of the continent. In this context, it was perhaps inevitable that the Southeast would develop in manufacturing as its work force was released from agriculture, and as air conditioning and highway transportation opened up previously-isolated areas. Timing of population settlement from East to West, along with infrastructure improvements such as large-scale water diversions similarly opened up the east and west coasts to industrial development.

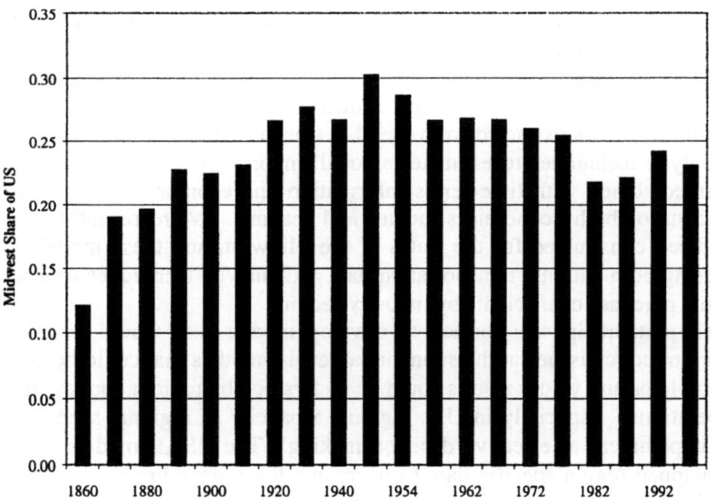

Figure 15.2 Shares of Manufacturing

Even though the Midwest economy remains highly specialized in durable good manufacturing production, its specialization in manufacturing has also eroded sharply during the 20th century according to indexes of specialization constructed by Kim (1995) at the 2-digit SIC level of aggregation.[4] Can this phenomenon lie behind sagging Midwest fortunes? Kim posits that poor transportation infrastructure and

[4] For a more recent analysis of similarity among U.S. states see Bernat and Repice, (2000).

immobile resources—especially energy—led to increasing regional specialization during the 1800s and early 1900s. Such features accord with many prior notions of a Midwest economy built upon the miracle material of its time, e.g. steel, which required heavy immobile inputs of coal, iron ore, and limestone, along with massive burning of coal for energy. Internal scale economies were also achieved on a significant scale, further encouraging centrality in the delivery of inputs and in the production of steel. But as transportation costs fell, internal economies waned, and as energy substitutes were developed, regions became less specialized. The Midwest region, in particular, lost its specialized locational advantage in manufacturing.

Such a view is challenged by the belief in agglomeration economies that are the foundations of regional science, as illustrated by Chinitz (1961) in Pittsburgh, for example, but more recently expounded and formalized by mainstream economist such as Krugman.[5] The answer to the question of the dominant paradigm is far from academic. The absence of specialization would imply that the many "industrial policies" by regions using such tools as selective tax incentives that are practiced by state-local officials are meaningless or wasteful. Subsidies will not be effective in more than a transitory way in determining the location of investment. To the contrary, if agglomerative forces determine the geography of production, then subsidies and development initiatives may be positively effective in creating the initial conditions of what will be a regional cluster.[6]

Evidence and analysis from the REAL models challenges the neoclassical view of regional specialization. In a presentation at the second Midwest Assessment symposium, Hewings cited the joint work with Israilevich in which it was found that a persistent decline was evident in the Chicago MSA's intra-regional linkages. Specifically, the MSA experienced a "hollowing out" characterized by the loss of about 500,000 manufacturing jobs from 1970 to 1990.[7] While a first blush this would appear to support the neoclassical view, further inspection shows that the region was concurrently expanding its linkages with the broader Midwest region. Agglomeration economies are now being realized at a broader geographic scale, which is consistent with the rise of recent transportation (roadway) technologies and delivery/inventory management systems, but highly inconsistent with the featureless plain of Kim's 150 year analysis. More generally, as shown in table 15.1, interstate trade among Midwest states has become highly intense with Illinois, for example, exporting some 32.1 percent of its total commodity outflow to the other 4 states of the East North Central region, and receiving an almost equal proportion in return.[8]

The case for agglomeration economies at the multistate Midwest level of geography is made more compelling by observations from industry case studies. The transportation equipment industry ranks as the top manufacturing industry in terms of interstate commodity flows. And at a more disaggregated level, Klier (1995) and Rubenstein (1992) have documented the recentralization of the auto industry back into the Midwest and into its new southern extension, drawing in plants and investment from coastal regions during the 1980s and 1990s.

[5] See Krugman, (1991).
[6] See Federal Reserve Bank of Chicago, (1996a).
[7] See Hewings, et al. (1998).
[8] See Hewings, *et al.*, (1998).

Table 15.1 Interstate Trade Among the Midwest States, 1993

	Total value of commodity outflows ($1993 billion)	% outflow to other Midwest states
Illinois	228	32.1
Indiana	128	40.7
Michigan	130	37.1
Ohio	196	29.2
Wisconsin	93	34.9
Total	775	34

	Total value of commodity inflows ($1993 billion)	% inflows from other Midwest states
Illinois	185	31.7
Indiana	99	46.8
Michigan	151	44.9
Ohio	171	35.1
Wisconsin	73	41.5
Total	679	38.7

The Midwest policy issues raised by the findings of the REAL models are profound, and they remain both unsettled and yet to be acted on. First, the continued importance of spatial economies of scale suggests that the continued viability of any single sector may be unduly important to broader economic vitality. For that reason, though public subsidies are seldom if ever justified, a close look at remedies and support for beleaguered sectors should merit a detailed analysis and receive some consideration for complementary public infrastructure and other policy instruments. Secondly, the geographic level at which public services are planned and provided should probably be expanded to coincide with the geography of the entire region. The REAL interstate trade flow analyses, which document enormous value and volume of interstate trade among Great Lakes states, add credence to the model of industrial organization that has been purported to characterize the region's manufacturing revival. That model is that key Japanese companies, especially Toyota, pioneered the "pull system" or "just-in-time." Not only were Midwestern companies sufficiently quick to adopt these productivity-enhancing management innovations, but the region's infrastructure has been more suited to adoption of the technology than that of the pioneering country. In particular, the region's dense configuration of interstate and other divided limited access highways facilitates just-in-time across a multi-state landscape. Simple cellular phone communication along with more sophisticated telecommunications such as satellite tracking and global positioning of trucks in transport have raised this multi-state configuration of manufacturers to an unparalleled height.

However, the missing element of perfection may be the complimentary multi-state government planning of highways and other infrastructure. That is, given the region's success based on just-in-time, a greater emphasis on region-wide multi-state policy and government service delivery possibly deserves a greater emphasis in the region. In light of this intense multi-state configuration, it is ironic if not misdirected to see a sharp emphasis on foreign trade policies such as trade missions abroad and export assistance programs in individual states, despite the fact that such overseas trade flows are dwarfed by interstate flows in the region. According to REAL, for example, the Chicago region alone sends out annually $140 billion in shipments, but $120 billion of this represents domestic rather than international shipments. Moreover, much of the remainder is exported to NAFTA partners rather than overseas. There is another irony with respect to public policy. In the 1980s, Midwestern and many other states competed vigorously with tax incentives and other subsidies to lure foreign nameplate car companies to site assembly plants in their states. Critics assailed these subsidies as wasteful. Perhaps so, perhaps not, but owing to the broad agglomeration economies identified above, it may have actually been the case that such subsidies – when successful – benefited the actual *competitor* states against which the winner was bidding. And it remains an open question as to whether the net effect was to solidify the centralization of the automotive industry within the overall region.

A final set of findings relates to the Midwest's linkages to the rest of the world *via* international trade. Significant trading relationships among U.S. regions means that, to the extent that out-region economies are impacted by international trade perturbations, the Midwest economy will also be affected. As it turns out, the Midwest competes with the Rocky Mountain states and the Southwest (see Hewings *et al.*, 1996). That is, rising exports from those states have been associated with a substitution away from exports to the same destination from the Midwest. IN contrast, a complementary relationship is found between the Midwest and far western and Mid-Atlantic states so that the Midwest economy is indirectly tied to Europe and Asia. This points the Midwest toward a more intensive interest in national trade agreements and negotiations. Most accounts suggest that the Midwest has done very well by NAFTA. The indirect ties document by REAL are suggestive that broadened worldwide trade agreements may lift the region's incomes indirectly through coastal channels.

15.4.2 Federal Spending on Defense

In hindsight, the Midwest sailed through the 1990-91 recession. Unemployment rates rose in both the U.S. and the region, but the Midwest gained on the rest of the nation. This Midwest performance is quite remarkable given the region's historic tendency to be whipsawed during downturns by its sharp industrial concentration in the volatile durable goods manufacturing sectors.

Several developments influenced the region's behavioral change in this particular cycle, not the least of which was the pullbacks in the pace of domestic defense spending following the fall of the Berlin wall in 1981. The region experienced short shrift in federal defense spending, which may be expected to have beneficial consequences in times of defense spending pullback. However, there was some significant angst over the phenomenon in the Midwest, because the region had already experienced sufficient trauma from other sources in the 1970s and 1980s. Moreover, there was much uncertainty as to which bases might be closed or curtailed, and what the regional pattern of expenditure reductions might be, as well as their regional impact on jobs and income. Most such changes in federal spending are not easy to cope with in short run transition, but rather demand a shift of resources across sectors.

In this environment, the REAL model for the Chicago metropolitan area was put to work in 1991.[9] Chicago's share of national defense procurement funds amounted to only .8% percent of the national total, significantly lower than its 3 percent share of the national economic aggregates. And so, a lesser impact of reductions was foreshadowed, and this was confirmed by subsequent analytic breakdowns of the specific sectors in which spending was concentrated. Due to the tight interlinkages among Chicago industries, the induced income effects of defense cutbacks were estimated as substantial additions to the direct impacts. However, a scan of the specific industries by REAL revealed that Chicago's specialization in defense spending to be concentrated in products suited to the civilian market, namely electrical machinery, business services, food, and control instruments—representing 73% of the region's procurement funds. Hence, the transition of the Chicago region was not expected to be a difficult one. Nonetheless, a large variation in multiplier effects on the Chicago economy was identified as derived from an incremental change in procurement spending across industry sectors, so that specific impacts on industries and their work forces were not be lightly dismissed.

The expectations that Chicago's transitional adjustment would not be a difficult one proved to be accurate, as demonstrated by the subsequent performance of the second largest category of local defense expenditure sector, personal and business services. The region has been enjoying a literal boom in business service sectors—legal, management consulting, accounting, and business meeting services—during the business cycle expansion of the 1990s. For example, of total job payroll growth in the Chicago metropolitan area over the 1990s, 60 percent can be attributed to business service sectors. In hindsight, then, any public policy actions at that time that would have focussed on defense adjustment would have proven to be a waste of policy resources. In this instance, the analytic tool suggested that Chicago focus on its opportunities and not on any hypothetical problem of defense adjustment.

15.4.3 Workforce Planning Tools

The long-lived and robust recovery of the Midwest economy has meant that there are once again real financial returns to human capital investments on the part of the region's residents. Nationally, for example, average wage premium for a college degree has marched upwards toward 70 percent from the high thirties as recently as 1979. The Midwest recovery has allowed many of its workers to take advantage of such opportunities. The region's workforce participation has soared, and stands above the buoyant national rates of participation. Indeed, the Midwest region's firms have scrambled to acquire workers at wage levels that allow them to compete and achieve returns to investment. In short, the 1980s paradigm of labor glut has become a paradigm of labor shortage, with marked shortage of workers who are trained and skilled.

Despite these opportunities for workers, the rapidly changing nature of the labor market environment has not made planning and investment decisions any easier. The vicissitudes of industrial upheaval have continued to create labor market uncertainty for those who are sometimes categorized as being in blue collar occupations. To this has been added greater turnover in so-called white collar occupations. At root, rapid

[9] See Israilevich and Weiss, (1991), and Federal Reserve Bank of Chicago, (1992).

changes in the information intensity of many industries has shaken up the organizational arrangements within firms. Additional sectoral upheaval can be documented as information industries displace some traditional lines of business, and as individual companies form and dissolve in a world of increasing flexible specialization. Meanwhile, the search for shareholder value has resulted in no small number of mergers and acquisitions in the late 1990s and into 2000, processes that have also contributed to uncertainty in the particular skills and occupations that can be expected to hold promise for students and re-trainees.

To assist educational institutions and their students in making judicious decisions on the direction of their educational offerings and investments, the REAL Chicago model has been linked to detailed occupational structures of industry sectors.[10] In doing so, the goal was to integrate a Chicago-specific labor market forecast into a user friendly software that allows students and schools to examine and predict occupational growth rates, wage information and skill requirements for various careers in the Chicago labor market. Through access to this information system, students would be able to assess what course work needed to work in selected professions. So too, the planning tool would enable a community college system or other educational institution in planning curricula and course offerings.

15.5 Conclusions

The pioneering models available to Chicago and the Midwest, developed by REAL, have proven very useful in framing and shaping policies for the region's decision makers. Their value has derived from providing a factual understanding of the economy's functioning. Where are its market industries, and the region's sources of growth and decline? The identification of defense industry adjustment as a non-issue has been clearly demonstrated on a timely basis. Meanwhile, the region's fortunes and turnabout were effectively delineated. Business services sectors in metropolitan Chicago have proven to be a highly adaptable defense industry, and one that has been a well-spring of growth and rejuvenation for the Chicago region. The broader Midwest region's recovery has stemmed, not from services, but from a re-born manufacturing agglomeration. The spatial proximity, coupled with an infrastructure suited to the new just-in-time technology, have been the source of the well-spring. The REAL models' analysis of this multi-state phenomenon have channeled public policies appropriately toward policies such as transport infrastructure and planning that build on this strength. A final source of regional revival has been the coincidence of a region that is well-endowed with skilled labor and educational institutions along with economic trends that have paid a premium to skills and the ability to move and process information. Models and analytic tools such as those of REAL are attempting to capitalize on these trends by facilitating the educational planning of students, trainees, and the region's schools and workforce training to the skill needs of the coming decades. In a nation characterized by a dearth of regional data and regional modeling tools, the industrial Midwest can be counted as fortunate.

[10] As described and presented by Israilevich at the conference "Work Force Developments: Issues for the Midwest Economy," Federal Reserve Bank of Chicago, May 15, 1996.

References

Allardice, D.R. 1990. "Chicago Fed and University of Illinois form regional research lab." *Economic Perspectives*, Federal Reserve Bank of Chicago, March/April, 13-14.

Bernat, G.A. and E.S. Repice. 2000. "Industrial Composition of State Earnings in 1958-98." *Survey of Current Business*, 80, 70-78.

Chinitz, B. 1961. "Contrasts in Agglomeration: New York and Pittsburgh." *American Economic Review*, 51, 264-285.

Federal Reserve Bank of Chicago. 1991. "Regional Impact Analysis of the Defense Procurement Funds: the Chicago Experience." *Working Paper*, Federal Reserve Bank of Chicago.

Federal Reserve Bank of Chicago. 1996a. "The Midwest Economy: Structure and Performance," *Workshop Proceedings No. 2, Assessing the Midwest Economy*, February.

Federal Reserve Bank of Chicago. 1996b. "Work Force Developments: Issues for the Midwest Economy," *Workshop Proceedings No. 4, Assessing the Midwest Economy*, May.

Hewings, G.J.D., F. Cuello, M. Sonis and F. Mansouri. 1996. "The role of regional interaction in regional growth: Competition and Complementarity in the U. S. Regional System." *Australasian Journal of Regional Studies*, 2, 133-149.

Hewings, G.J.D., M. Sonis, J. Guo, P.R. Israilevich and G.R. Schindler. 1998. "The hollowing out process in the Chicago economy, 1975-2015." *Geographical Analysis*, 30, 217-233.

Hewings, G.J.D., P.R. Israilevich, and G.R. Schindler. 1998. "Interstate Trade Among States." *Chicago Fedletter*, no. 129.

Israilevich P.R. and D.D. Weiss. 1992 "The effect of defense cuts on the Chicago economy." *Chicago Fedletter*, no. 53.

Israilevich, P.R., G.J.D. Hewings, G.R. Schindler and R. Mahidhara. 1996 "The choice of input-output table embedded in regional econometric input-output models." *Papers in Regional Science*, 75, 103-119.

Israilevich, P.R., G.J.D. Hewings, M. Sonis and G.R. Schindler. 1997. "Forecasting Structural Change with a Regional Econometric Input-Output Model." *Journal of Regional Science*, 37, 565-90.

Kim, S. 1995. "Expansion of Markets and the geographic Distribution of Economic Activities: The Trends in U.S. Regional Manufacturing Structure, 1860-1987." *Quarterly Journal of Economics*, 110, 881-908.

Klier, T. 1995. "The Geography of lean manufacturing: Recent Evidence from the U.S. auto industry." *Economic Perspectives*, Federal Reserve Bank of Chicago, 19, 2-17.

Krugman, P. 1991. "Increasing Returns and Economic Geography." *Journal of Political Economy*, 99, 483-99.

Rubenstein, J.M. 1992. *The Changing U.S. Auto Industry—A Geographic Analysis*. London, Routledge.

16 Keystone Sector Identification*

Maureen Kilkenny and Laura Nalbarte

Department of Economics, Iowa State University, Ames, IA
e-mail: kilkenny@iastate.edu; nalbarte@iastate.edu

16.1 Introduction

This chapter presents a new a method for identifying *keystone sectors* in communities, where sectors are broadly defined to include churches, clubs, associations, and public institutions as well as different types of businesses and industries. In an arch, the *keystone* is the one with the unique shape at the top of the arch that is critical for the arch's structural stability. The term *keystone species* was first coined by ecologists in the late 1960s with respect to the species responsibility for the structure and integrity of an ecosystem. We now coin the term for use in community development analysis. In a community, *the keystone sector is one that plays a unique role and without which the community is fundamentally and detrimentally altered.*

There is a long tradition among applied economists seeking useful answers to the question: "What should be given priority for economic development funds or special credit?" Target Industry Analysis (sometimes referred to as critical sector or turnkey industry analysis) is the prevailing method used to respond to this question. This method attempts to match industries with locations for the mutual benefit of the firms and the communities. The method keys off the identification of relatively *dominant industries,* those sectors with relatively high location quotients, that also has a number of input-output linkages with other local industries with high location quotients. The inference is that industries that are already in the area are the best indicators of industries that should be recruited. Two approaches are typically used to estimate the size of the potential market. An industrial 'linkages' approach uses (national) input-output industry×industry intermediate use coefficients times local industry activity. A trade area approach estimates final demand, taking distance, population density, and local income into account using a gravity formula.

Consider the popular linkages approach. In a record of a community's input-output transactions, the strength of the effects of a purchasing sector on the sectors it purchases from, or backward linkages, are given by the column coefficients for the sector in the multiplier matrix.[1] The forward linkages, or the effects of a sector on the

* Financial support in the form of grants from TVA Rural Studies Program 1997-8 is gratefully acknowledged.

[1] A *multiplier matrix* is calculated from an industry *X* industry transactions matrix in three steps as follows. First, divide the transaction cells by the column totals. This gives a matrix of sectoral expenditure shares. Second, subtract this matrix from the Identity matrix. Third, invert the subtrahend. This inverted matrix is the multiplier matrix.

other sectors it sells to, are given by the row coefficients of the multiplier matrix. What economists have been calling critical or key sectors are those sectors whose structure of backward and forward linkages create above-average impacts on the rest of the economy (Sonis *et al.*, 2000; Cella, 1984). These would be the sectors whose column and/or row coefficients are higher than average.

The strengths of input-output based methods are that (i) the biproportional sector-sector transactions table is a popular and useful way to document sectoral interdependencies; (ii) the definition of the system boundary is very operational (i.e., $Y = AY + X \quad => \quad Y = mX$ where $m = [I\text{-}A]^{-1}$); (iii) the input-output methods have proven useful in many other contexts. The weaknesses of input-output based methods include (i) input-output data is prohibitively costly to collect; thus (ii) the most recent national table is for 1992 (too old); and (iii) there is no comprehensive sub-national data; (iv) the input-output approach is limited in scope: only business transactions are considered. There is no consideration of the roles of other entities in a community.

Another way used to determine which industries to target for an area is to survey existing businesses in attempts to identify the regional comparative advantage. In general, a region's comparative advantage activities are those that employ their relatively abundant factors of production most intensively (Hechscher-Ohlin-Samuelson); or those industries in which local producers are more productive (fewer inputs per unit output) than other region producers (Ricardian). The regions with the resources or technology to produce certain items relatively more cheaply should be able to profit most by specializing in those items. Market frictions, however, such as labor or capital immobilities, or, high fixed or transport costs, can undermine these hypothetical gains from specialization and trade in comparative advantage goods. Alternatively, some analysts assume that a region's comparative advantage sectors are revealed by their existing production and trade patterns. The deduction is that if a region is specializing in and exporting something, it must be it's comparative advantage sector.

The results of even the "successful" industrial targeting programs, however, have been criticized for merely crowding-out private activity, or, being an imbalanced use of funds (Jacobs, 1985). If no market failure has been identified, why would public support be needed by any critical or comparative advantage sector that is valued and profitable in a location ? If there are no market failures, public support does only what the market would have done anyway (crowding out), and, at a higher cost. The case of an imbalanced use of funds is one of too much capital investment in one type of industry. Outward signs of "too much" investment in one type of activity include (i) environmental degradation, (ii) stagnation or decline in other sectoral activity, (iii) leakages of capital-related income, and (iv) migration out of the area.

An analogy is that industries induced to locate in an area by subsidies and tax holidays may ultimately behave like predators. In addition to using up tax revenues, the industries may 'feed' on the output of local industries, destroy natural resources, and eclipse existing industries that compete for labor, similar inputs, or similar consumers. When only certain industries are targeted, the diversity of the local economy can be reduced, making it more sensitive to exogenous shocks originating in those sectors. Finally, especially if it is the major employer, an industry designated as "critical" can more effectively threaten to abandon the community if substrate supplies, subsidies, or other attractions diminish (Kilkenny and Wolhgemuth, 1996). If such industries succeed, the predator relationship (analogy) may turn into a parasite/host relationship.

16.2 Keystone Species Concept

The dominant industry and the predator analogy discussed above are a natural point of departure. In this project, we apply the *keystone* concept developed by natural scientists to the social science analysis of economic systems. We do this by formulating a test of 'keystoneness' that uses the techniques of graph theory from mathematics and social network analysis from sociology, and applying it to analyze data about a single local economy.

The concept Keystone Species was first coined by ecologist Robert Paine in the late 1960's, in his identification of a predator as the critical species in an ecosystem. Paine described the effect of removing a species of starfish, the main predator on mussels, from a rocky intertidal zone. Without the starfish, the whole system changed. The mussels proliferated, leading to a significant change (increase) in biodiversity. Paine called the starfish a keystone species:

> The species composition and physical appearance were greatly modified by the activities of a single native species high in the food web [starfish]. These individual populations are the keystone of the community's structure, and the integrity of the community and it's unaltered persistence through time...are determined by their activities and abundances. (Paine, 1969)

Over the decades, the keystone species concept has evolved beyond it's focus on predators, but it remains "poorly defined and non-specific in meaning," (Mills, Soule and Doak, 1993). Natural scientists have tended to proliferate studies arguing the 'keystoneness' of their favorite organism.

In addition, the implied assumption that there will always be one and only one keystone in a system is suspect. Plants, micro-organisms, prey, the physical environment, and other aspects in an ecosystem may all play critical roles. As Princeton University ecologist Simon Levin says, "focusing on particular species often misses a great deal of what's important in an ecosystem" (Stone, 1995). By analogy, in the analysis of community economic systems, the exclusive focus on only one type of species (private sector businesses) may also 'miss a great deal of what is important.'

It is instructive to note that the original 'top-down' keystone species concept in Biology has been fundamentally challenged by a more holistic, 'bottom-up' concept of functional groups, which recognizes that small organisms on the bottom of a food chain can also determine an ecosystem. The functional group concept is exemplified by the work of Robert Stenek, who studied a "curious pattern of continuity in the face of drastic change" among algae clusters floating around the Caribbean island of St. Croix. "Almost none of the dominant species I'd find in one season would I find as dominant in the next," Stone quotes Stenek, but "what was going on in the mats varied little: They consumed nutrients at a fairly constant rate and resisted similar types of predators. Different algae, apparently, were performing the same biological role" (Stone, 1995). It is now widely understood that 'whole suites' of organisms have similar functions in an ecosystem, and their role can be modeled as a single group rather than separately for each species.

The functional group notion in biology corresponds to the economic notion of substitutes: inputs in production, or outputs in supply. Ecologists are now trying to develop methods to identify influential functional groups; i.e., keystone functional groups. By analogy, we (economists) seek to identify keystone sectors, where a 'sector' or group of sectors corresponds to a 'functional group' whose members substitute for one another.

In what follows, we define a community to be the set of businesses and institutions in a single geographic location, such as a town or city. We define the keystone sector to be the type of businesses or institutions, private or public, which play a unique and critical role in achieving the objectives of a community. We use a subset of Graph Theory (Berge, 1962) called network analysis (Wasserman and Faust, 1994) to analyze the interrelationships between varied entities, identify "species," and test for the sensitivity of the system to the absence of each species.

Network analysis has been widely used in transportation system research (Hanson and Huff, 1986, Koppelman and Pas, 1985, Wright, 1979) and anthropology and sociology research (e.g., Granovetter, 1973, Freeman, 1977). Applications of graph theory or network analysis to identifying critical sectors, however, are scarce. The few attempts include the early work of Campbell (1975), and some recent initiatives by Kauffman (1988), Roy (1994, 1995), and Sonis and Hewings (1998).

Statistical models based on graph theory, however, have been used by researchers to study social networks for almost 60 years. The goal of these models was (and remains) the quantitative examination of the stochastic properties of social relations between the actors of a particular network (Wasserman and Pattison, 1996). Applications range from studies of interactions between individuals: interpersonal relations, friendship, leadership, etc; to studies of interactions between groups: global studies of communities, studies of the élite and political behavior, and studies of power-sharing.[2]

16.3 Network Analysis of a Community

In this section, we apply network analysis to study a small community. From our preliminary work (Kilkenny, *et al.*, 1999) and from our review of network analysis and sociomatrices, we learned that we need dyadic data on a variety of entities in one community. We found this type of data in a collection complied by Lauman (1985). In the late 1970's, the sociologists Galaskiewicz and Marsden gathered information on the formal organizations in a small U.S. town. The community was nicknamed, and referred to since, as Towertown. Of the 73 entities they studied, less than a quarter are private businesses (Appendix 1). They assayed three relations among these 73 entities: money, information, and support.

In this section, we apply network analysis techniques to do five things. First, we describe community-wide patterns: Is there a specific structure among agents, or do agents interact randomly with each other? Secondly, we describe the patterns of interactions among the individual agents in the community and compare their various roles. Thirdly, we determine the groups of individual agents whose patterns of interactions are sufficiently similar that

[2] Readers who are not familiar with the lexicon of network analysis, with terms such as relational data, agents, actors, nodes, sociomatrix, dyads, ties, edges, arcs, digraphs, adjacency, and the important basic measures out(in)-degree [row (column) sums in an adjacency matrix] are encouraged to consult Wasserman and Faust (1994), Berge (1962), and/or Robinson and Foulds (1980).

they can be treated as *types* of agent. This step is analogous to classifying numerous individual organisms into less numerous species. If we cannot do this, the number of agents will remain "too large," as illustrated in figure 16.1. Fourthly, we assign ties to the sociomatrix data that we have aggregated according to species. Fifthly, we test for the impact of the excision of each species from the community network. Are there any species that play such important roles that the community structure will be destroyed without them? This final step completes our identification of the "keystone" sector: the entity that is relatively unique and without which the community structure will be fundamentally disrupted.

16.3.1 Towertown Survey

Towertown is the nickname given by to the midwestern community of 32,000 persons studied by Galaskiewicz and Marsden, and documented in Laumann (1985). A total of 109 organizations were identified in Towertown, and 73 were studied. The 73 included all manufacturing firms with more than 20 employees; banks, laws firms, political organizations, associations, health institutions, educational institutions, service clubs, labor unions, city offices and departments, and churches. Galaskiewicz and Marsden interviewed the executive officers of the 73 organizations. Each subject was presented with a list of the other 72 organizations in the community, and was asked the following six questions:

1) To which organizations on this list would your organization be likely to pass an important information concerning community affairs?
2) To which organizations on this list does your organization rely upon for information regarding community affairs?
3) To which organizations on this list does your organization give substantial funds as payments for services rendered or goods received, loans, or donations?
4) From which organizations on this list does your organization get substantial funds as payments for services rendered or goods received, loans, or donations?
5) Which organizations on this list does your organization feel a special duty to stand behind in time of trouble: that is, to which organization would give support?
6) Which organizations on this list would be likely to come to your organization's support in time of trouble?

From the responses to these questions, three dyadic relations were defined: INFORMATION (1,2), MONEY (3,4) and SUPPORT (5,6). An organization was determined to be "in relation to" another organization if the former organization answered yes to the first question in a pair, or the latter organization answered yes to the second question in the pair. Note that if either actor in the dyad reported the existence of a tie, a tie was recorded. In other words, for each relation R a 73×73 adjacency matrix (X^R) was constructed with entries $x_{ij}^R = 1$ if the ith actor has a relational tie with the jth actor and $x_{ij}^R = 0$ if not. (Also, $x_{ii} = 0$.)

16.3.2 Macro/Community Wide Structure

The first step is to study the density and connectivity of the whole network.[3] The *density* measure describes general level of linkage among the actors in the community. This measure compares the number of actual to possible relations, to show how far from *completion* is the graph (the community network). A *complete* graph is one in which all the actors have two-way ties to all other actors. In this case, all nodes are reciprocally adjacent to one another, and all elements of the sociomatrix are equal to one. The more actors that are connected to one another the denser and the more complete is the graph.

The density of a digraph (d) is the actual number of non-reflexive arcs, $a = \sum_{ij} a_{ij}$, in proportion to the maximum possible number of non-reflexive arcs:

$$d = a / \left[N(N-1) \right]$$

Note that *reflexive ties* are ignored ($\alpha_{ii} = 0$ or are not counted). Since all three sociomatrices about Towertown have the same symmetric number of actors (N = 73), the maximum possible number of non-reflexive arcs is 73x72= *5256*. The arcs present in the INFORMATION sociomatrix are *1264*, while the ones present in the MONEY and SUPPORT sociomatrices are *512* and *814* respectively. Consequently, the density measures are 24%, 9.7% and 15.5% for INFORMATION, MONEY and SUPPORT, respectively. INFORMATION linkages are denser, and thus more complete. MONEY relations are the least dense and thus least complete in Towertown.

Next, we measured *connectivity*. An actor is connected when there is at least one arc or set of arcs that relate the actor with another actor (Wasserman and Faust, 1994). While density and completion refer to one-step arcs, connectivity is also based multiple-step arcs. Actors may be directly related (with a one-step arc between them) or indirectly related (more than one one-step apart). An actor can be a transmitter (the arc is away from the node), a receiver (the arc is toward the node), or a carrier (there are at least two arcs, one toward and one away). Consider a digraph of a relation between entities *A, B, C*, and *D*:

$$A \rightarrow B \rightarrow C \quad \text{D}$$

In the above, *A* is a transmitter, *B* is a carrier, and *C* is a receiver; while *D* is isolated. An actor is isolated when there is no arc that relates the actor with any actor in the network. Formally (Wasserman and Faust, 1994), a node is a proper source or transmitter if its indegree is zero and its outdegree is non-zero; that is, if the column sum is zero while the row sum is greater than zero. A node is a proper sink or receiver if its indegree is non-zero and its outdegree is zero. A node is isolated if both indegree and outdegree are zero.

Agents in a network that are all connected to each other can be classified as a subset of the *N* actors as a group (or a sub-graph) called a *component*. A component is the largest subset of connected actors in a network. Components also come in two forms: *strong* and *weak*, depending on the directions of the ties, arcs, or relational links between the members of the component. A strong component is one in which the arcs

---

[3] We used a relatively old-fashioned software package called UCINET IV, and verified calculations using an EXCEL spreadsheet program. UCINET was produced at the University of California, Irvine (UCI). The standard version runs on any XT-compatible with at least 256k of RAM (Scott, 1991).

that make up the paths are aligned in continuous chain without a change of direction. A weak component is made of actors that are linked by non-directional edges (Scott, 1991).[4]

If a sociomatrix is dense, we expect to find a single component. If not, there may be multiple components of various sizes. None of the three Towertown sociomatrices are dense (recall INFORMATION is the most dense, having 24% of the maximum number of ties). So, we expected to find multiple components in the Towertown network; but we did not. A glance at the matrices indicates that every entity has at least one source or sink of INFORMATION, MONEY, and SUPPORT. There are no columns or rows that have all zeros. Furthermore, none of the connected entities are exclusive. UCINET showed the existence of a single (weak) component for each of the three relations. The Towertown community appears to be one big, interconnected group. There are no isolated actors, and there are no cliques.

Now we know that there are no isolated actors in Towertown, but we also know that the links among all the actors are not all mutual. Next we apply the techniques to describe the roles of individual actors by measuring *local centrality* and *prestige* by measuring *prominence*. Which actors are distinguished either because they receive a lot from other actors, or, because they give a lot to other actors? To determine which actors are prominent, we consider all the directed ties (arcs) originating from the actor (outdegree), plus all the received ties (indegree), plus all the indirect ties (carriers or paths) as well.

There are four measures of prominence: local centrality, local prestige (or, rank or popularity), and two versions of global centrality: *closeness* and *betweenness*. Local centrality reflects the number of direct transmissions, and is thus measured simply by the outdegrees (or row sums) of each actor. Local prestige reflects the number of direct receipts, and is thus measured simply by the indegrees (or column sums) of each actor. Since these measures are based on the degrees of the nodes they are also known as degree centrality and degree prestige (Wasserman and Faust, 1994). The global centrality measures are based on the length and the number of carrier and multiple-step path roles.

Tables 16.1, 16.2 and 16.3 present the measures of local centrality and prestige for MONEY, INFORMATION, and SUPPORT. Note that UCINET measures are unstandardized with respect to the maximal number ties in each sociomatrix. In our case with equal dimension sociomatrices, and because we are not comparing across networks in different size communities, standardization is irrelevant. However, if the number of agents surveyed varied from relation to relation, or network-to-network, one would want to standardize each set of degree measures by normalizing with respect to the number of agents.

The first four rows in each of tables 16.1 to 16.3 show the sample statistics for the "degree" measures for agents in Towertown. The mean of local centrality, for example, is the average outdegree among the 73 entities. With respect to MONEY ties (Table 1), on average, a Towertown entity gives money to seven other entities in Towertown. The mean of local prestige is the average indegreee measure across all 73 entities. For example, with respect to INFORMATION ties (table 16.2), on average, a Towertown entity receives INFORMATION from 17 entities in Towertown.

[4] UCINET's algorithm for the analysis of components relies on the weak definition. The algorithm checks for the existence of relations no matter what is the direction of the arcs. That is why we found it preferable to program our own analysis using EXCEL spreadsheets. We prefer that all tests are based on directional ties.

The 5th to 11th rows in each table show the local centrality and prestige measures of the top six most central and prestigious individual entities in Towertown. For example, with respect to MONEY (table 16.1), Towertown Newspaper is the most locally central, giving money to 33 other entities in Towertown. 1st Towertown Bank is the most locally prestigious, receiving money (presumably deposits or interest payments) from 49 entities in Towertown.

Table 16.1 Money

	LOCAL CENTRALITY	LOCAL PRESTIGE
Sample statistics:		
Mean	7.01	7.01
Std. Dev.	6.35	8.97
Minimum	0	0
Maximum	33	49
Top six entities:		
(11) **1st TT Bank**	28	**49**
(12) TT Saving bank	17	38
(13) Bank of TT	23	26
(39) **TT Newspaper**	**33**	17
(69) Family Services	3	36
(71) YMCA	4	24

Table 16.2 Information

	LOCAL CENTRALITY	LOCAL PRESTIGE
Sample statistics:		
Mean	17.29	17.29
Std. Dev.	11.21	11.22
Minimum	1	3
Maximum	63	62
Top six entities:		
(12) TT Savings bank	41	26
(25) City Council	32	43
(26) City Manager's office	43	44
(39) TT Newspaper	42	44
(40) WTWR Radio	**63**	**62**
(69) Family Service	45	36

Table 16.1 shows that four of the top six agents are both locally central and prestigious. These agents are three of the four banks and Towertown Newspaper. Family Services and YMCA, on the other hand, are only locally prestigious (high indegree but low outdegree, and both outdegree measures are below the mean). These measures identify some intuitively logical patterns and relative positions. Banks both give (make loans) and receive (accept deposits) money; and the local centrality and prestige measures document that. Also, Family services and the YMCA both rely on volunteers and donations, so it is logical that they would show up as the major recipients of money. That the newspaper is a source of money for many entities, however, is harder to explain.

In the case of the INFORMATION relation (table 16.2), again the top six agents appear to be both locally central and prestigious. All six agents receive and give information to a significantly (>2 SD) higher number of agents in the community than the rest of the entities. The Radio Station appears to be the most locally central and prestigious in Towertown.

Table 16.3 Support

	LOCAL CENTRALITY	LOCAL PRESTIGE
Sample statistics:		
Mean	11.12	11.12
Std. Dev.	9.42	10.53
Minimum	0	0
Maximum	59	58
Top six entities:		
(12)TT Savings bank	37	14
(20) Small Bus.Assoc.	38	10
(56) **TT Comm.College**	**59**	**58**
(57) State University	20	42
(69) Family Service	12	52
(72) Mental Health	16	36

Table 16.3 shows the results with respect to the SUPPORT relation. The Community College both receives and gives more support than all other entities. "In times of trouble," the Community College is willing to give support to 59 entities, and 58 entities are willing to give support to the Community College.

Towertown Savings Bank appears to be locally central with respect to SUPPORT, but not locally prestigious (has high outdegree but the indegree value is close to the mean). This contrasts with its local centrality being lower than local prestige according to the MONEY relation. Note that Towertown Savings Bank has fewer out- than in-degrees, suggesting that it makes loans to fewer entities in the community than the number from whom it receives deposits. The bundling of many small deposits to make a few larger loans is the main business of financial intermediaries, known as "asset transformation." It is interesting to note, however, that this particular bank does not attract as much SUPPORT as it says it would give. Note also that different actors are prominent in MONEY , INFORMATION and/or SUPPORT flows. Towertown Savings and Loan and Towertown Family Service entities are, however, central and/or prestigious in all three of the relations.

In sum: we have shown how to classify entities with large outdegrees as important sources of INFORMATION, MONEY, or SUPPORT. Actors with low in- or out-degrees are apparently less active, less important, or peripheral to a network. Note, however, the limitations of dichotomous rather than value data. In dichotomous (0/1) data, what counts is the number of ties, not their level. While this may be quite appropriate for the analysis of non-rival types of interactions such as information and support ties, it does not fully describe rival transactions such as money ties. It is likely that agents with a few high-value MONEY ties play more important roles than can be perceived with dichotomous data. For example, a business that buys large amounts of goods and services from just a few other local businesses (who then buy from other local businesses, employ many residents, and provide many donations; and so on) may not have so many ties, but because of their magnitude, their few ties may be critical to the community.

When an actor has a position of strategic significance in the overall network, that actor is considered *globally central.* Globally central actors are detected using both closeness and betweenness measures. Globally central actors are those with the shortest paths relating to all the others actors. The ubiquitousness of an actor's ties makes them global, and the shortness of the paths is measured by closeness. But closeness is not the only factor that makes an actor globally central. The betweenness of an actor is also relevant. Interactions between two non-adjacent actors depend, by definition, on an intermediary. The intermediaries are between the actors, and they can exert some control over the relations. Thus, globally central actors can have widespread effects on a community because they are more closely tied with more of the other agents, and, act as intermediary for more agents; than any others.

Freeman's measure of global centrality relies on the two measures of closeness and betweenness. Both measures rely on a measure of distance called a *geodesic.* Wasserman and Faust (1994) define these measures as follows:

The distance from n_i to n_j is the length of the *geodesic* from n_i to n_j.

The geodesic in a graph is the length of the shortest path between two nodes.

Closeness, $C_c(n_i)$, measures are the inverse of distance measures. As a node grows farther apart in distance from other nodes, its centrality decreases. $C_c(n_i) = \left[\sum^{g} d(n_i, n_j)\right]^{-1}$ where $d(n_i, n_j)$ is the distance (number of steps or ties in the shortest path) between agents n_i and n_j and g is network size.

Betweenness, $C_b(n_i)$, measures the probability that a communication or path from actor j to actor k takes a particular route through agent i. Assume each one-step tie has equal weight, and assume that interactions will occur through the shortest routes. Then,

$C_b = \sum_{j}^{g} \left[g_{jk}(n_i)\right] / g_{jk}$ where $1/g_{jk}$ is the probability that a particular geodesic (path) is chosen, g_{jk} is the number of geodesics linking actors n_j and n_k, and $g_{jk}(n_i)$ is the number of geodesics that go through n_i.

Again, all these measures depend on the size of the network. Thus the measures must be standardized before comparisons are made between networks of different numbers of entities. In degree centrality and closeness measures, the measures are standardized dividing by N-1. For betweeness measures, the standardization factor is $(N-1)(N-2)$, where N is the number of agents.

The summary statistics for global centrality according to both measures, with respect to MONEY, INFORMATION and SUPPORT relations are shown in Table 16.4. The higher is closeness, the more often entities are directly tied. Note that on average there are more direct INFORMATION ties (the mean of closeness is highest) than SUPPORT or MONEY ties. The mean of *betweenness* is the average number of times an actor is articulating (is the intermediary in the shortest path), a relationship between two other actors. With respect to MONEY flows, on average a Towertown entity serves as intermediary in 89 relations between other entities.

Table 16.4 Global Centrality: Sample Statistics

	CLOSENESS			BETWEENESS		
	MONEY	INFO	SUPPORT	MONEY	INFO	SUPPORT
Mean	52.34	59.06	53.42	88.51	57.68	78.73
SD	6.74	7.13	8.38	244.87	131.43	238.37
Minimum	37.50	46.75	32.00	0	0.06	0
Maximum	78.26	88.89	82.76	1762.24	1013.23	1998.32

Table 16.5 shows the measures for the most globally central entities with respect to closeness and betweenness. The higher the value of closeness, the more directly an entity is linked to other entities in the community. For example, 1st Towertown Bank reaches the most other agents with the fewest MONEY steps. 1st Towertown Bank is significantly closer (more than 2 SD's higher than the mean) than other entities in Towertown. Comparing two of the banks, 1st Towertown Bank (closeness value = 78.26) is closer to the rest of the agents in Towertown than the Bank of Towertown (closeness value = 64.86).

Table 16.5 Global Centrality: Entity Values

	CLOSENESS			BETWEENNESS		
	MONEY	INFO	SUPPORT	MONEY	INFO	SUPPORT
1ST TT Bank (11)	78.26			1762.24		
TT Savings (12)	71.29			686.38		
Bank of TT (13)	64.86			409.50		
Ch. Commerce					221.83	
City Council (25)		72.73				
City Mng's office		75.79			307.84	
TT News (39)	70.59	75.00		899.85	343.87	
RADIO (40)	66.67	88.89			1013.23	
CmntyCollege(56)			82.76		253.35	1998.32
State Univ. (57)			69.90			222.42
Family Serv (69)		75.79	76.60			190.60

The higher the values of betweenness, the more potential an actor has to control third-party relationships. Again, 1st Towertown Bank shows the highest betweenness measure, it appears to be in the strongest control position. In both MONEY and SUPPORT flows, the entities that appear to be the most 'close' also appear to be the most 'between' actors. This analysis of the MONEY relation shows that banks and the newspaper are the 'main roads' to other entities. They are closely linked to, and act as intermediaries for, more other agents.

If we consider the flow of SUPPORT, the Community College has a lot of connections with the rest of the community. The global centrality of the Community College is shown both by its closeness to the rest of the agents and because it has a potentially major articulation role as evidenced by its (maximum) betweeness score.

The findings for flow of the INFORMATION relation are consistent with intuition or priors. Our analysis of the INFORMATION network in Towertown shows that the media organizations: the newspaper and radio; and the community's coordinating office: the city manager's office, are globally central.

16.3.3 Cut-Points

This section presents tests for this aspect of "keystoneness". If the single-component structure of the Towertown network is destroyed by the excision of an entity, that entity is considered critical for the maintenance of Towertown's structure.

Entities that are vital for the connectivity of a network are those without which other entities will become isolated. Now we shall test if any individual actors that have been shown to be central are also critical to maintenance of the network structure. The central entities are, one at a time, removed from the data (delete their rows and columns from the three sociomatrices). Then we conduct another analysis of components. If the new network has more subgroups or components, the excised entity is a *cut point*. More formally, a cut-point is the actor whose removal from the system would increase the number of components by dividing the graph into two or more separate subsets (components) between which there are no connections (Scott, 1991).

The results are that some of the entities we identified above as central are also cut-points. In the MONEY relation, isolated actors were produced by removing three entities: 1st Towertown bank, Towertown Savings Bank, and/or Family Services. Removing any one of the two banks and/or Family Services breaks the single Towertown network into 5 components: two isolated actors : 1) the County Medical Society, and 2) the Association of Churches ; two isolated dyads comprised of 3) the Municipal Employees Union I and the Central Labor Union; and 4) University Methodist Church plus the Association of Churches in another dyadic component, with 5) all 64 others in the remaining component.

Similar results were found with respect to the SUPPORT relation. Removing central actors Towertown Savings and Loan, Towertown Community College, and/or State University breaks the single component structure in three components. The three components are: 1) The four Unions in one component, 2) The democratic Committee and the County Housing Authority in another component and, 3) all the 64 others in the remaining component.

With respect to INFORMATION, however, no entity appears to be critical. There is no change to the structure due to the removal of any actor. The single component structure in INFORMATION relation is robust. There is no single agent that does not have a substitute as a vector of information in Towertown.

16.4 Block Modeling

To this point we have treated each entity as unique. There are at least two reasons to group similar entities. One, as the number of entities in a community increases, the patterns of interaction are more complex and detailed. The main patterns (forest) can become obscured by the details (trees). Two, it is also useful to know which entities play similar roles. By 'similar role' is meant that patterns of interaction with all other entities are similar or, that the entities can substitute for each other. In this section we show ways to group or block entities into "sectors" in a network. Then we study the network structure with respect to sectors rather than individual actors. This last step is called *block modeling*.

Block modeling is another form of network structural analysis (Holland and Leinhardt, 1979). It was introduced by White, Boorman and Breiger (1976) for the descriptive algebraic analysis of social roles. A blockmodel is created from an elemental sociomatrix data base by doing two things. First, the entities are partitioned into discrete subsets. This step is called "blocking." Second, 0/1 ties are assigned between each pair of subsets. The following sections explain how this might be done with sociomatrix data on communities.

The blocking procedure consists of partitioning of the population of entities into a set of 'equivalent' subgroups or blocks. The network analysis software UCINET has a procedure called CONCOR (CONvergence of iterated CORrelations). This procedure delineates blocks of stochastically *structurally equivalent* entities. CONCOR is used to identify sets of entities with distinct behavioral patterns. By analogy, we want to group the 73 individual entities in Towertown into a smaller number of "species."

Two entities are strictly *structurally equivalent* if they have identical ties to and from all other entities. Formally, elements i and j are structurally equivalent if, for all other actors $k = 1,2....g$ $(k \neq i, j)$, and all the relations $r = 1,2,.....R$, actor i has a tie to k if and only if j also has a tie to k, and i has a tie from k, if and only if j also has a tie from k (Wasserman and Faust, 1994). For example, if actor 1 relates only with 3 and 4, and actor 2 relates only with 3 and 4, then actor 1 and 2 are structurally equivalent. When there is strict structural equivalence between two of n entities in a network, the sociomatrix will be of rank n-1; one of the rows(columns) contains exactly the same information as another row(column). One of those two can be deleted, or, the two can be collapsed into one, without altering the connectivity of the network.

The first step in the CONCOR procedure is to calculate the correlations between all pairs of cases (ties between dyads) in the sociomatrices. The result of this first step is a square case-by-case correlation matrix. The second step is a clustering procedure to group the cases into (stochastically) structural equivalent sets (Scott, 1991). CONCOR splits the whole set of cases into subsets that have all positive correlation within each subset, and negative correlation between. Using this assignment to groups, the rows (and columns) of the original sociomatrix are permuted (their order is switched) to put the members of the subsets next to each other. The resulting matrix has structural equivalent individuals blocked together.

The structural equivalence criterion is widely used by sociologists to block individuals into groups. We learned from this experience with Towertown data, however, that for economic analysis, one must take particular care interpreting the nature of the composition of the groups that result from its application. The problem is that structural equivalence may group entities that are complements together, while entities that are substitutes may be separated. We propose the following more formal definition of substitutability in a network:

> from the perspective of entity *K*, entities *I* and *J* are perfect substitutes if a slight decrease in the desirability of interacting with *I* leads to interacting with *J* instead.

There is of course an analogy with consumer preferences for a commodity such as brown or white eggs, with the consumer buying whichever is cheapest. In this case, we would observe either a tie between *K* and *I*, or a tie between *K* and *J*, but not both. The dyadic relations of perfect substitutes are mutually exclusive. The CONCOR procedure would treat *I* and *J* as structurally non-equivalent and put them in separate groups. Alternatively, entities *I* and *J* are complements to *K* when *K*'s interaction with *I* is always accompanied by *K*'s interaction with *J*. An example is hot tea and cups: consumers can only drink tea when they use some kind of cup.

We applied CONCOR to each relational sociomatrix separately, and for all three relations together. The CONCOR blockmodeling procedure applied to single relation Towertown data was not satisfactory. It did appear to group complementary but separate substitute entities. Groups were comprised of heterogeneous entities: mixes of businesses, voluntary organizations and government offices. Few groups displayed a clear role division of species. Also, there was a different block structure for each relation.

But the CONCOR group structure based on all three relations simultaneously, shown in Appendix 2, is quite reasonable. Compare the dozen types of entities as listed in Appendix 1 with the fifteen groups determined by CONCOR listed in Appendix 2. Most of the groups in the second list are comprised of what we would consider to be similar types of entities (exceptions are bolded). The only agents that do *not* group in expected ways are the three law firms and the Savings and Loan. These entities appear grouped with otherwise dissimilar entities.

All seven private sector businesses, except banks, (entities 2-8) are in Block 9. Almost all of the health services, boards, centers, and associations in grouped together in Block 2. There are five groups (blocks) that are private voluntary associations, clubs, or churches (Blocks 1,4,5,6,10). All three learning institutions are grouped together in Block 3; with TT Savings and Loan (not intuitive.) All three banks are grouped together (Block 11). Note that the distinct behavior of Towertown Savings and Loan, identified when centrality and prestige were studied, also sets the S&L apart from the commercial banks. Government offices are in two types of groups: public service providers are in Block 8, and the largely administrative offices are grouped with the major information providers in Block 7. The two political party committees are grouped together in Block 13; and there are two groups of unions, Blocks 14 and 15.

Since some of the blocks formed by CONCOR are clearly comprised of substitute entities (the two blocks of unions, the five blocks of private voluntary associations), we decided that further aggregation of the fifteen blocks would be appropriate. The minimum number of groups is three: private businesses, voluntary organizations, and public sector institutions. From all previous analyses, the banking agents displayed significantly more critical network behavior compared to all other private businesses, so we decided to distinguish banks from other businesses. Finally, we decided on four groups 1) banks, 2) other business, 3) government, and 4) voluntary organizations (Appendix 1II).

We proceed to develop the methodology with this very small number of groups for ease of demonstration. Ideally, given the CONCOR results above, and our preference to collapse groups of substitutes into single blocks, we would analyze a nine block structure. Those blocks would be: (1) businesses, (2) banks, (3) health care, (4) schools, (5) associations (including churches and clubs), (6) public service providers, (7) media and public administration, (8) politicals, and (9) the unions.

We also expanded the set of sociomatrices from three to four by calculating a sociomatrix we called "SERVICE," which is the transpose of the MONEY relation. The transpose shows the relation "gives something to" from the row actor to the column actor. The assumption is that all flows of money are reciprocated by something: the provision of a service, delivery of a good, or even a "good feeling" from a charitable act. This is the same convention that records foreign aid given out as an import of the donor country in the current account of the donor's Balance of Payments statistics. The SERVICE relation sociomatrix is qualitatively different from the MONEY relation because arc patterns are not symmetric.

16.4.1 Tie Assignment

After assigning individuals to blocks, ties must be assigned between blocks. We consider three common approaches to defining ties between subsets (blocks). These are 1) Zeroblock, 2) Oneblock, and 3) α density (Wasserman and Faust, 1994). The first assigns a tie if even a single pair of entities between the two blocks have tie, the second assigns a tie only if all pairs across the two blocks have ties, and the third is a convex combination of the first two. We then propose and use a fourth approach based on our own criteria developed to reflect substitutability between sinks (or sources).

First, some notation: individual agents in Towertown are indexed by subscripts $i, j = 1, \ldots\ldots, 73$; while groups in the blockmodel are indexed using subscripted A, B = (banks, BIZ, Vol, and Gov). Let T be any one of the four elemental Towertown sociomatrices of dimension 73 squared, T = { MONEY, INFORMATION, SUPPORT, AND SERVICE}; and B be the corresponding set of four blockmodel (4 by 4) adjacency matrices. The blockmodel adjacency matrices are also called *image matrices* (Wasserman and Faust, 1994). Arcs (and ties) in T are denoted t_{ij}, while arcs (and ties) between blocks in B are denoted b_{AB}.

Zeroblock Criterion The arc, b_{AB}, between two blocks (A,B) for a given relation is 0 only if there are no arcs $(t_{ij} = 0)$ from any actor, i, in the row block to any actor, j, in the column block; otherwise the block arc is 1:

$$b_{AB} = \begin{cases} 0 & \text{if } t_{ij} = 0 \ \forall i \in A, \ \forall j \in B \\ 1 & \text{all other cases} \end{cases}$$

Oneblock Criterion The arc, b_{AB}, between two blocks (A,B) for a given relation is 1 only if all possible arcs (t_{ij}) from all actors in the row block to actors in the column block exist, otherwise the block arc is 0:

$$b_{AB} = \begin{cases} 1 & \text{if } t_{ij} = 1 \ \forall i \in A, \ \forall j \in B \\ 0 & \text{all other cases} \end{cases}$$

α density Criterion The arc, b_{AB}, between two blocks (A,B) for a given relation is 1 if the observed density of arcs between the two blocks (d_{AB}) is at least as large as α, and zero otherwise.

The analyst can choose any value of α; a reasonable reference value is the density of the original sociomatrix. Recall that density, d, is the actual number of non-reflexive arcs, t_{ij}, in proportion to the maximum possible number of non-reflexive arcs:

$$d = \left[\sum\sum \tau_{ij}\right] / \left[N(N-1)\right]$$

Applied to calculate the density of ties between blocks:

$$d_{AB} = \left[\sum\sum \tau_{i\in A, j\in B}\right] / N_A N_B$$

Setting $\alpha = d$: $b_{AB} = \begin{cases} 1 & \text{if } d_{AB} \geq d \\ 0 & \text{for all other cases} \end{cases}$

Sinks Substitute Criterion The arc, b_{AB}, between two blocks (A,B) for a given relation is 1 if there is an arc (t_{ij}) from every actor in the row block to at least one actor in the column block, otherwise the block tie is 0:

$$b_{AB} = \begin{cases} 1 & \text{if } t_{ij} = 1\ \forall i \in A\ \exists j \in B \\ 0 & \text{for all other cases} \end{cases}$$

Sources Substitute Criterion The arc, b_{AB}, between two blocks (A,B) for a given relation is 1 if there is an arc (t_{ij}) to every actor in the column block from at least one actor in the column block, otherwise the block tie is 0:

$$b_{AB} = \begin{cases} 1 & \text{if } t_{ij} = 1\ \forall j \in B\ \exists i \in A \\ 0 & \text{for all other cases} \end{cases}$$

The choice of procedure to use should relate to one's specific objective. Our objective is to represent the relations between types of entities in communities. We have grouped Towertown entities that can substitute for one another, and we know they are not perfect substitutes. The zeroblock procedure is appropriate only for the perfect substitute case. If all entities within blocks are perfect substitutes, a tie by any individual in the block could be made by any other individual in the block, so even a single tie would be recorded as a block tie. But our entities are not perfect substitutes. Nor are they perfect complements. The oneblock procedure may be appropriate when *all* agents within each block are complements for one another. Since each entity is tied in tandem, the whole block should be tied in tandem, or not at all. The first two procedures also lead to image matrices that are either all 1's or all 0's. The α density criterion is somewhere between those unlikely extremes, as are the sink/source substitute criteria. In sum, we developed the substitute criteria for the express use in analyzing blocks of substitutable entities.

In any case, we tried all the criteria to assign ties between our four blocks for the MONEY relation, and we liked our new criteria best. According to the zeroblock criterion, all blocks are reciprocally related (the image matrix, as predicted above, is all 1s.) According to the oneblock criterion, none of the blocks are related (matrix of 0s). According to the α density criterion, the following blockmodel and reduced graph is obtained:

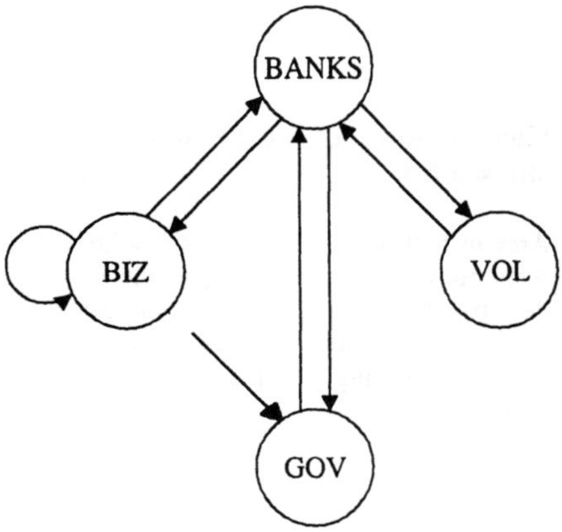

MONEY (α Density)

	Banks	BIZ	Vol.	Gov
Banks	0	1	1	1
BIZ	1	1	1	1
Vol.	1	0	0	0
Gov	1	0	0	0

In contrast, applying the *sinks substitute* criterion resulted in the following blockmodel and reduced graph:

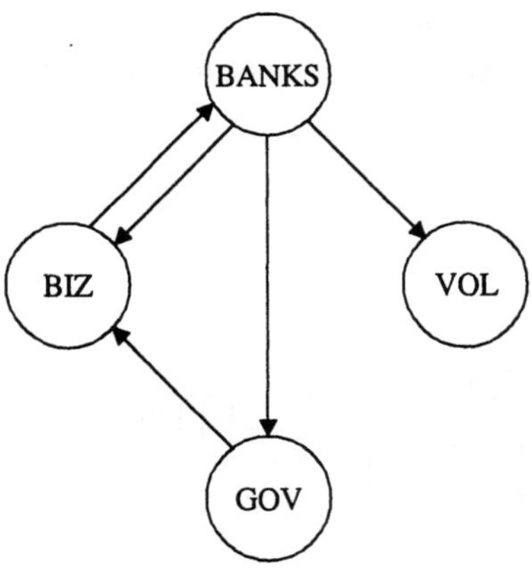

MONEY (Sinks Subst. Criterion)

	Banks	BIZ	Vol.	Gov
Banks	0	1	1	1
BIZ	1	0	0	1
Vol.	0	0	0	0
Gov	0	0	0	0

Both of the *reduced graphs* of the MONEY relation show that banks and business have reciprocated money transactions as lenders, borrowers, depositors, and creditors. Furthermore, businesses and banks give money to government agencies, i.e. pay taxes. Banks give money to voluntary organizations, i.e. donations and/or loans. Note that not enough business supply funds to voluntary associations directly to warrant the recording of a block tie. Businesses, however, are linked indirectly to voluntary associations through banks. Banks are articulating agents.

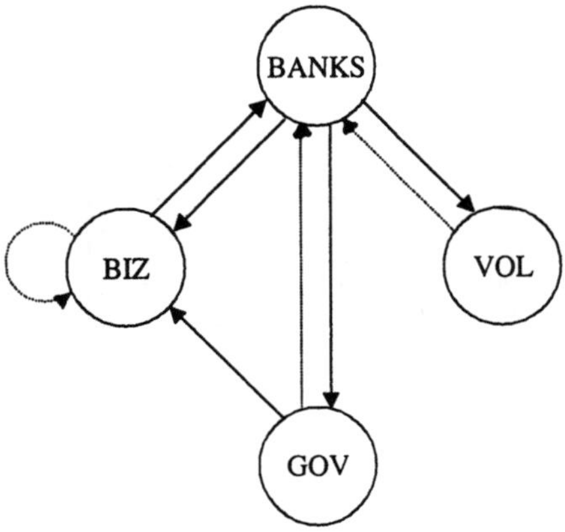

Comparison of α-density to sinks/subst:

Arcs in both reduced graphs are solid. Arcs present only according to the α-density criterion are shown as double lines. There are more ties between blocks according to the α density criterion.

We prefer the *sinks substitute* criterion because it makes it clear that not all businesses have money transactions with other local businesses in the Towertown data, and that not all government entities nor all voluntary associations give money to local banks. We think the tie assignment using the *α-density* criterion is too generous when the groupings are supposed to reflect substitutability.

Applying the sinks-substitute criterion to the other three relations resulted in the following blockmodels and reduced graphs:

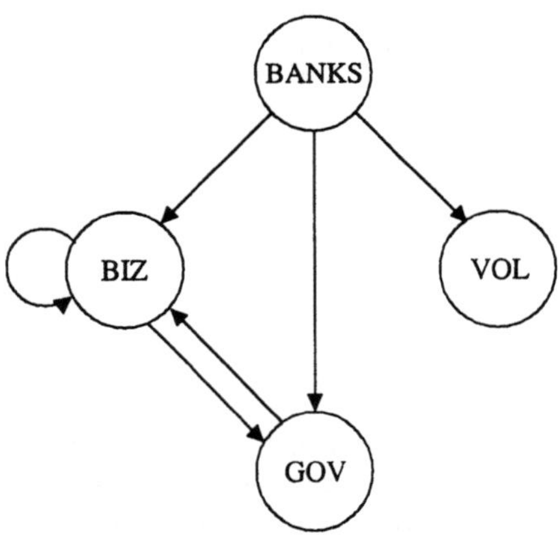

SERVICE (Sinks Subst.)

	Banks	BIZ	Vol.	Gov
Banks	0	1	1	1
BIZ	0	1	0	1
Vol.	0	0	0	0
Gov	0	1	0	0

The reduced digraph of SERVICE, the transpose of the MONEY relation, clearly shows that SERVICE is not simply a reverse or mirror image of the MONEY relation. In contrast with MONEY, we observe no SERVICE reciprocity between business and banks. This digraph makes it clear that local banks provide services (manage savings, provide credit) to local businesses. The MONEY relation showed that Businesses pay for those services, and that if local Banks buy from businesses, not all are local businesses. This digraph also shows a reciprocal relationship between local businesses and government agencies. The assumptions behind this transpose are that businesses provide services paid for by the public sector which provide services back to businesses. Interindustry transactions are also documented in this image matrix; there is a reflexive tie (arrow from/to businesses) showing that (according to our sinks substitute criterion) all local businesses in Towertown serve at least one other business in Towertown. Note that banks are (again) a critical proper source or transmitter in the system.

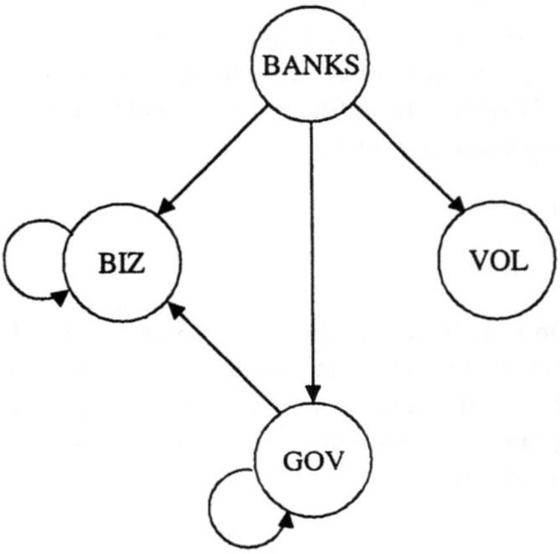

INFORMATION (Sinks Subst. Criterion)

	Banks	BIZ	Vol.	Gov
Banks	0	1	1	1
BIZ	0	1	0	1
Vol.	0	0	0	0
Gov	0	1	0	1

The reduced graph for INFORMATION shows that information flows parallel money or service flows. Banks are again the key suppliers of information. All local businesses supply information to at least some other local businesses. And all government agencies provide information to at least some local business, as well as to at least one other public agency.

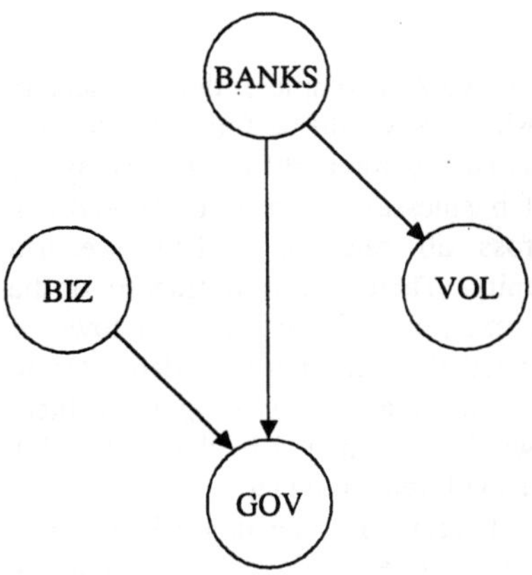

SUPPORT (Sinks Subst. Criterion)

	Banks	BIZ	Vol.	Gov
Banks	0	0	1	1
BIZ	0	0	0	1
Vol.	0	0	0	0
Gov	0	0	0	0

associations (or banks). Again, banks are significant as sources in the Towertown community.

16.5 The Keystone Test

In the introduction we posed the following definition: in a community, the keystone sector is one that plays a unique role and without which the community is fundamentally and detrimentally altered. To this point we have identified the roles of individual entities, assigned individuals that play similar roles to groups (sectors), and identified the roles of sectors. From the image matrices and the reduced graphs it is clear that all of the sectors play unique roles. Now it is time for the test of sufficiency: which sectors are critical to the network? We present two tests.

16.5.1 Fracture Test

The first test is non-directional: if the excision of a sector fractures the connectivity of the network, (breaks up the component structure) that sector is a *keystone*. There can be more than one keystone sector according to this criterion. The results of this application of the test for cut-points in the image matrix or the reduced graph, which we call the "fracture test" are summarized in table 16.6.

Table 16.6 Fracture Test

	MONEY	SERVICE	INFO	SUPPORT
Excised	number of components			
None	1	1	1	1
BIZ	1	1	1	1
Vol	1	1	1	1
Gov	1	1	1	**2**
BANKS	**2**	**2**	**2**	**2**

When all sectors are present, the Towertown network is complete: the four sectors are an intact single component. The polar opposite case would be four components: each sector being a singleton. A completely dissociated community would display the maximum number of components, that is N. If businesses are excised, Towertown remains associated into one component, across all relations. This scenario corresponds, for example, to a retirement community. There is also no fracture of the remaining network if voluntary associations are excised. For example, a town of individualistic or self-sufficient atheists could nonetheless be interdependent, due to the intermediation of banks with respect to money, information, *and* support. If there are no government entities, not all businesses would remain tied in the SUPPORT network; but banks' ties with voluntary associations will remain intact.

If there were no local banks, however, across ALL relations, the single Towertown network would be fractured into two. With respect to money, SERVICE, information, and support, without local banks, the voluntary associations would be cut off, breaking Towertown into two components. One component would be the business - government dyad, the other would be the voluntary organization sector singleton.

With respect to the first three of the four relations, the network is comprised of two sub-components, with banks being the common element in both sub-components. This documents that banks provide connectivity to the community. The removal of banks leads to two disconnected components. In the case of the SUPPORT relation, initially there are three sub-components. Both banks and the government sector play articulating roles.

16.5.2 Efficient Path Test

The fracture test is easy to apply graphically. But it is based on ties rather than directional relations (arcs). We think the source-sink directional information is relevant, so we propose an analytical alternative to the simple fracture test, which we call the "efficient path" test.

Recall that a path is the set of arcs between any two nodes in a relational network. If establishing and maintaining a dyadic relation is at all costly, the fewer the arcs used for a given number of components, the more efficient the network. For example, N entities could each connect with each other unilaterally, requiring $N(N-1)$ arcs (or one-step paths). If any one entity is excised, the network remains fully-connected. But it is an inefficient network. Alternatively, each of the N entities could all belong to an $N+1$st entity, such as an association based on shared values and principles. In that case, the single component (of $N+1$ entities) would require only N arcs (or N one-step paths). Again, the network remains fully connected despite the excision of any one (or even any number of) the original N entities. But if the $N+1^{st}$ association is excised; the network would fracture into N singletons, which clearly indicates the key role the association plays in the efficient network.

In the example we give above, the $N+1$ association is by far the most central actor, and it is also the only articulating actor. Thus, we showed that articulating sectors not only provide coherence, they also enhance efficiency. We designed the "efficient path" test to highlight a sector's contribution to efficiency. It documents any reduction of efficiency following the excision of a sector. First, document the shortest paths (also called geodesics) between sectors in the original network. Then, excise a sector and recompute the lengths of the shortest paths between the remaining sectors. If the excision increases any of the other shortest paths, the excised sector had an efficiency-enhancing role, and is a candidate for keystone sector. Again, there may be more than one keystone sector according to this criterion.

Finding the shortest path between any two sectors requires simple matrix multiplication. Obviously, the image matrix shows all the dyads connected by one-step paths. There may also be multi-step paths between dyads for which the image matrix element is 0 (i.e., for which $b_{AB} = 0$). To find the multi-step paths, simply square, cube, and so on, the image matrix. The squared matrix will show all the dyads connected by two-step paths, as well as how many two-step paths there are between each dyad; all other possible connections will be 0. The cubed matrix shows only the numbers of three-step path dyads, and so on. Continue raising the image matrix to higher powers until a zero matrix is obtained or the pattern stabilizes. At that point, you will have gone one step farther than the longest geodesic in the network. The geodesic for each dyad is the power to which the matrix must be raised to get the first non-zero arc. Formally, for any digraph D with adjacency matrix $A(D)$, each entry a_{ij}^{p} of $A(D)^{p}$ equals the number of paths of length p from node i to j in D, for any positive integer p (Robinson and Foulds, 1980).

The procedure was applied directly to the digraphs (without symmetrizing them into adjacency matrices) for each of the four relations. The results are the same as shown by the "fraction test." In all four relations, the removal of banks destroys any path to voluntary associations. Also, with respect to SUPPORT, the excision of government leaves businesses isolated.

16.6 Summary

This chapter has presented a new a method for identifying keystone sectors in communities, where sectors are broadly defined to include churches, clubs, associations, and public institutions as well as different types of businesses and industries. In an arch, the keystone is the one with the unique shape at the top of the arch that is critical for the arch's structural stability. The term keystone species was first coined by ecologists in the late 1960s with respect to the species responsibility for the structure and integrity of an ecosystem. In this chapter, we developed a new method for identifying a keystone entity in any kind of system, but explicitly for community development analysis. We propose that a keystone sector in a community plays a unique role, without which the community is fundamentally and detrimentally altered.

This chapter has described and applied new ways to (1) quantify the structure, (2) describe the variety of roles, and (3) identify the keystone sectors; in a community. We adapted existing methods of graph theory and social network analysis to the analysis of a local economic system. We do not know of any precedents for community-level economic analysis.

We have also raised many caveats. Dichotomous data implies that all interactions are of equal significance. This assumption is acceptable for non-rival interactions, but it is less appropriate for rival transactions, such as those concerning money(!) It is possible that a sector with a few large links may be much more critical than the sectors with many (smaller) links; and this methodology will fail to identify those sectors as key.

Also, the articulation roles of some entities are exaggerated when analyses are based on measures for which symmetry is imposed. When we ignore the direction of a relation, we incorrectly assume that an exchange is reciprocated, when it may not be. Other potential pitfalls may arise from blocking and tie assignment procedures. The patterns of ties to and from a block depend on the entities in the block, so the blocking procedure matters. We also showed that different criteria for tie assignment give a different block model. In the Towertown application, we are just lucky that the results of our tests for 'keystoneness' are the same regardless of the procedure used for tie assignment. The α-density network is just as sensitive to the excision of banks as our sinks/substitute networks are. However, with other data, the results of the fracture and efficient path tests for keystone-ness may be different across blockmodels developed using different criteria.

By replicating these methods and analyzing the network structure of other communities we may learn how sensitive the approach is to these potential pitfalls. Meanwhile, it is clear that the approach can offer significantly new types of insight. Our finding that financial intermediators play a critical role in a community is an example of one of those insights. Previous studies in the critical sector tradition, based on material input-output relationships, have ignored the banking sector (along with government entities and voluntary associations). This is because input-output data concerns only current account transactions. We believe that in some communities, public service providers, private voluntary associations, or other non-business entities may also be key. One lesson is that many types of interactions and many types of entities may be very important, not just business interactions. Here we have demonstrated a method that can be used to quantify and analyze almost any kind of interaction information between any kinds of entities.

References

Berge, C. 1962. *The Theory of Graphs and Its Applications*. New York, Wiley.

Campbell, J. 1975. "Application of graph theoretic analysis to interindustry relationships: The example of Washington state." *Regional Science and Urban Economics*, 5, 91-106.

Cella, G. 1984. "The input-output measurement of interindustry linkages." *Oxford Bulletin of Economics and Statistics*, 46, 73-84.

Fienberg, S.E., M.M. Meyer, and S. Wasserman. 1981. "Analyzing data from multivariate directed graphs: an application to social networks." In V. Barnett, ed. *Interpreting Multivariate Data*. London, John Wiley. Pp. 289-306.

Fienberg, S.E., M.M. Meyer, and S. Wasserman. 1985. "Statistical Analysis of multiple sociometric relations." *Journal of American Statistician Association*, 80. 51-67.

Freeman, L. 1977. "A set of Measures of Centrality Based on Betweenness." *Sociometry*, 1, 35-41.

Galaskiewicz, J. and P.V. Mardsen. 1978. "Interorganizational resource networks: formal patterns of overlap." *Social Science Research*, 7, 89-107.

Goode, F., and S. Hastings. 1988. Northeast Industrial Targeting (NIT) and Economic Development Data Base (EDD) System *User's Manual* version 1, Dept. of Agricultural Economics and Rural Sociology, The Pennsylvania State University, University Park, PA 16802; March.

Granovetter, M. 1973. "The Strength of Weak Ties." *American Journal of Sociology*, 78, 1360-1380.

Hanson, S. and J. Huff. 1986. "Classification Issues in the Analysis of Complex Travel Behavior." *Transportation* 13, 271-293.

Holland, P.W., and S. Leinhardt, S. 1979. "Perspectives on Social Network Analysis." *Mathematical Social Science Board's Advanced Research Symposium on Social Networks*. New York, Academic Press.

Jacobs, J. 1984. *Cities and the Wealth of Nations*. New York, Random House.

Kauffman, S.A. 1988. "The evolution of economics webs." In P.W.Anderson, K.J. Arrow and D.Pines, eds. *The Economy as a Complex Evolving System*. New York, Addison-Wesley. Pp. 125-146.

Kilkenny, M., L. Nalbarte, and T. Besser. 1999. "Reciprocated Community Support and Small-Town, Small-Business Success." *Entrepreneurship and Regional Development*, 11, 231-246.

Paine, R. 1969. "A Note on Trophic Complexity and Community Stability." *American Naturalist* 103, 91-93. Cited in S. Mills, M. Soule, and D. Doak. 1993. "The Keystone Species Concept in Ecology and Conservation." *BioScience* 43, 219-224.

Robinson, D.F. and L.R. Foulds. 1980. *Digraphs: Theory and Techniques*. London, Gordon and Breach.

Roy, J.R. 1994. "Trade with and without intermediaries: some alternative model formulations." *Annals of Regional Science*, 28, 329-344.

Roy, J. R. 1995 "Dispersed spatial input demand functions." *Annals of Regional Science*, 29, 329-334.

Scott, J. 1991. *Social Network Analysis*. London, Sage Publications Ltd.

Sonis, M. and G.J.D. Hewings. 1998. "Economic complexity as network complication: multiregional input-output structural path analysis." *Annals of Regional* Science, 32, 407-436.

Sonis, M., G.J.D. Hewings, and J. Guo. 2000. "A new image of classical key sector analysis: minimum information decomposition of the Leontief inverse." *Economic Systems Research* 12, 401-423

Stone, R. 1995. "Taking a New Look at Life through a Functional Lens." *Science* 269, 316-317.

Wasserman, S. and K. Faust. 1994. *Social Network Analysis*. Cambridge, Cambridge University Press.

Wasserman, S. and P. Pattison. 1996. "Logit models and logistic regressions for social networks." *Psychometrika*, 61, 401-425.

Wright, C.C. 1979. "Arcs and Cars: An Approach to Road Traffic Management based on Graph Theory. In R.J. Wilson, ed. *Graph Theory and Combinatorics*. London, Pitman.

Appendix 1 Entities in "Towertown"

1-Farm Bureau
2-Farm Equip. Co.
3-Clothing Mfg. Co.
4-Farm Supply Co.
5-Mechanical Co.
6-Electric Equip. Co.
7-Metal Products Co.
8-Music Equip. Co.
9-Chamber of Commerce
10-Banker's Association
11-1st Towertown Bank
12-Towertown Savings and Loan
13-Bank of Towertown
14-2nd Towertown Bank
15-Brinkman Law Firm
16- Cater Law Firm
17-Lenhart Law Firm
18-County Bar Association
19-Towertown Board of Realtors
20-Towertown small Bs. Association
21-Municipal Employees Union 1
22-Municiapal Employees Union 2
23-Teacher's Union
24-Central Labor Union
25-City Council
26-City Manager's Office
27-County Board
28-Fire Department
29-Human Relations Commission
30-Mayor's Office
31-Police Department
32-Sanitary District
33-Streets and Sanitation
34- Park District
35- Zoning Board
36-Democratic Committee
37 Republican Committee
38-League of Women Voters
39-The Towertown Newspaper
40-WTWR Radio Station
41-Towertown Public Hospital Board
42-Towertown Public Hospital
43-County Medical Society
44-County Board of Mental Health
45-County Board of Health
46-County Health Service Center
47-State Highway Authority
48-Kiwanis Club 1
49-Kiwanis Club 2
50-Rotary Club
51-Lions Club
52-United Fund
53-School Board
54-Towertown High School
55-Towertown Parent-Teacher Assoc.
56-Towertown Community College
57-State University
58-Association of Churches 1

59-Association of Churches 2
60-St. Hilary's Catholic Church
61-1st Baptist Church
62-1st Church of the Light
63-1st Congregational Church
64- 1st Methodist Church
65- Unity Lutheran
66- University Methodist Church
67-State Department of Public Aid
68-County Housing Authority
69-Family Services
70-State Employment Services
71-YMCA
72-Mental Health Center
73-Towertown Youth Services Bureau

Appendix 2 CONCOR Results

Block1: Farm Bureau, St. Hilary's Catholic Church, University Methodist Church, Association of Churches 1, 1st Congregational Church and 1st Methodist Church

Block 2: County Medical Society, County Board of Mental Health, TT Public Hospital Board, County Housing Authority, TT Public Hospital, State Employment Services, State Department of Public Aid, Mental Health Center, and County Board of health.

Block 3: TT Community College, State University, TT High School, and **TT Savings and Loan**

Block 4: YMCA, United Fund, County Health Service Center, Family Services, and **Brinkman Law Firm**

Block 5: 1ST Church of the Light, League of Women Voters, 1st Baptist Church, School Board, TT Small Business Association, Bankers Association, and Chamber of Commerce

Block 6: Kiwanis Club 1, Kiwanis Club 2, Rotary Club, Lions Club, TT Parent Teacher Association, and **Park District**

Block 7: WTWR Radio Station, Association of Churches 2, City Manager's Office, TT Newspaper, City Council, County Bar Association and **Cater Law Firm**

Block 8: Human Relations Commission, Fire Department, Police Department, Sanitary District, Mayor's Office, County Board, and Zoning Board

Block 9: Farm Equip Co., Clothing Mfg. Co, Farm Supply Co, Mechanical Co, Electric Equip Co, Metal Products Co and Music Equip Co

Block 10: Unity Lutheran Church

Block 11: 1ST TT Bank, 2ND TT Bank , and Bank of TT

Block 12: Streets and Sanitation, State Highway Authority, TT Board of Realtors, and **Lenhart Law Firm**

Block 13: Democratic and Republican Committees

Block 14: Municipal Employees Union 1 and Teachers' Union

Block 15: Municipal Employees Union 2 and Central Labor Union

Appendix 3 BLOCKMODEL Sectors

Sector 1: **BANKS**:
Block 11: 1ST TT Bank, 2ND TT Bank , and Bank of TT and TT Savings and loan

Sector 2: **BUS**inesses:
Block 9: Farm Equip Co., Clothing Mfg. Co, Farm Supply Co, Mechanical Co, Electric Equip Co, Metal Products Co and Music Equip Co
not from intact CONCOR blocks: Lenhart Law Firm, Brinkman Law Firm, Cater Law Firm, WTWR Radio Station, TT Newspaper

Sector 3: **GOV**ernment agencies
Block 2: County Medical Society, County Board of Mental Health, TT Public Hospital Board, County Housing Authority, TT Public Hospital, State Employment Services, State Department of Public Aid, Mental Health Center, and County Board of health.
Block 3: TT Community College, State University, TT High School
Block 8: Human Relations Commission, Fire Department, Police Department, Sanitary District, Mayor's Office, County Board, and Zoning Board
Not from intact CONCOR blocks: County Health Service Center, Family Services, Streets and Sanitation, State Highway Authority, City Manager's Office, City Council, and Park District

Sector 4: **VOL**untary associations:
Block1: Farm Bureau, St. Hilary's Catholic Church, University Methodist Church, Association of Churches 1, 1st Congregational Church and 1st Methodist Church
Block 5: 1ST Church of the Light, League of Women Voters, 1st Baptist Church, School Board, TT Small Business Association, Bankers Association, and Chamber of Commerce
Block 6: Kiwanis Club 1, Kiwanis Club 2, Rotary Club, Lions Club, TT Parent Teacher Association
Block 10: Unity Lutheran Church
Block 13: Democratic and Republican Committees
Block 14: Municipal Employees Union 1 and Teachers' Union
Block 15: Municipal Employees Union 2 and Central Labor Union
Not in an intact CONCOR block: YMCA, United Fund, Association of Churches 2, County Bar Association, TT Board of Realtors

CONCOR groups that were split: Blocks 4, 7, and 12

17 A Spatial Output Decomposition Method for Assessing Regional Economic Structure

Randall W. Jackson[1] and David A. Dzikowski[2]

[1]Regional Research Institute, West Virginia University, Morgantown, WV, USA
e-mail: randall.jackson@mail.wvu.edu
[2]ESRI, 380 New York Street, Redlands, CA, 92373-8100
e-mail: ddzikowski@esri.com

17.1 Prologue

This chapter is dedicated to the memory of Philip Israilevich, a close friend and valued colleague, whose enthusiasm, intellectual curiosity and good nature were inspirational to all who knew him. These pages present a method for measuring and comparing economic structure, using the input-output framework as a foundation, and demonstrated using data for the Midwest economy. These topics are among the many that captured Phil's interest and imagination throughout his career.

17.2 Introduction

An input-output table provides a rich and detailed static picture of a region's economic structure. Numerous approaches have been developed to characterize and summarize economic structure using these collections of industrial interdependence data. Comparisons overtime provide a means for assessing structural change, while comparisons across space enable an assessment of the differences in economic structure across regions.

This chapter reports on the development and implementation of a method for assessing regional economic structure that is derived from the structural change method introduced by Feldman *et al.*, (1987) and later examined by Sonis *et al.*, (1996). The work reported here is a piece of a larger research project reported more comprehensively in (Dzikowski 1999).

The Midwest economy, comprised of Illinois, Indiana, Michigan, Ohio, and Wisconsin, presents an ideal workshop for assessing structural change and interregional structural differences. This region has historical significance as a major manufacturing center of the US, and has undergone substantial economic restructuring over the past four decades. Insights into the nature of these state economies enhance our understanding of the position and role of the region in the larger US economy. The current status and trends in these state economies is more fully elaborated in Dzikowski (1999), and two more traditional analytical approaches to the assessment of economic structure are implemented. Readers primarily interested in the Midwest economy are encouraged to consult that work, along with Testa's excellent Federal Reserve Bank report on that region (Testa *et al.*, 1997).[1] In this chapter, however, we focus on the methodological extension presented in Dzikowski (1999). Our goal is to use the Midwest economic data as a vehicle to demonstrate the utility of the approach we present.

The method we introduce uses the input-output framework to decompose differences in gross output into two distinct categories. It partitions gross output differences into those that are a function of the technical structure of production and those that are attributable to final demand characteristics. Our method adds to the understanding of interindustry structure gained from using traditional cross-sectional methods, such as the Hirschman-Rasmussen (Hirschman 1958, Rasmussen 1956) key sector approaches, as well as from more recently introduced methods such as the multiplier product matrix (MPM) of Hewings *et al.* (1998) and Sonis *et al.* (2000).[2] First, it provides a measure of the differences in interindustry structure among regions. Secondly, it provides a measure of the way in which differences in interindustry structure and final demand distributions differentiate production across.

17.3 Justification

The Midwest is an integral part of the U.S. economy. Its population of 62.6 million comprises 23.4% of the total U.S. population (U.S. Department of the Census, 1998). The region employees 25.1 million full and part-time workers which represent 16% of the total U.S. labor force. Manufacturing workers in the Midwest account for 2.7 million, or 13.8% of the total manufacturing employees in the U.S. The Midwest generates 19.3% of total U.S. personal income, while the service industry in the Midwest accounts for 21% of this total (Regional Economic Information System, 1997).[3]

The Midwest has experienced significant economic restructuring over the past two decades (Kim, 1996). These changes have led to the continued hearty growth of its economy in the late 1990s (Testa *et al.*, 1997). The economic structural characteristics of the Midwest have tended toward a more homogenous region over this same period (Israilevich and Hewings, 1998), contributing substantially to a more resilient economy that is better prepared to deal with future macroeconomic change (Melcher *et al.*, 1998). Israilevich and Hewings (1998) also note that while output is increasing, there is evidence to suggest that the degree of intersectoral interdependence within the region is decreasing. While some might attribute these changes only to increases in international trade (see, for example, The Economist, 1997), Israilevich and Hewings (1998) believe international trade to be only a small part of the answer. Changes in interindustry trade within each state as a result of industrial specialization have also played a substantial role in the changing nature of these economies. Hewings *et al.* (1998) suggest that a 'hollowing out' process is occurring within these states.

[1] Some of these issues are also raised by Testa in chapter 15 of this volume.
[2] For a critique of other recent extensions of structural decomposition analysis see Rose and Casler, (1996). For a critique and extension of the Feldman *et al.*, method, see Sonis *et al.*, (1996).
[3] All data in this paragraph are based upon 1997 figures.

'Hollowing out' is a process whereby increases in sectoral output in the majority of sectors are accompanied by decreasing intersectoral interdependence. Firms in economies that are 'hollowing out' are buying and selling fewer goods intraregionally (see, for example, Jackson *et al.* (1989) and Hewings *et al.* (1998)). A combination of changes in the production structure of the region and changes in the orientation of trading relationships provides the backdrop for this research.

17.4 Data

The Regional Economics Applications Laboratory (REAL), a collaborative organization sponsored by the University of Illinois and The Federal Reserve Bank of Chicago, generated the data for this analysis. The data are comprised of interindustry purchase values for Illinois, Indiana, Michigan, Ohio, Wisconsin, and the rest of the U.S., import and export coefficients, final demands, and gross outputs. These data were created using a procedure developed by REAL and discussed by Israilevich *et al.* (1993). The data are derived from establishment level Census of Manufacturing forms, organized in a traditional input-output framework. The 53 sectors used in this analysis are listed in Appendix 1.

17.5 The Model and Method

Many traditional measures of regional economic structure focus entirely on interindustry structure, despite the recognition that final demand structures also differ significantly from place to place and time to time. Feldman et al. (1987) describe a method for investigating change in gross industry output based upon the portion attributable to change in final demand and the portion attributable to change in interindustry structure as reflected by regional input-output coefficients. Their derivation of change begins with the traditional input-output model solution:

$$X = (I - A)^{-1} f \tag{17.1}$$

where X is a vector of industry output, A is a matrix of technical coefficients, and f is a vector of final demands. Letting C represent the standard Leontief inverse matrix, (17.1) becomes:

$$X = Cf \tag{17.2}$$

Equation (17.2) is time subscripted to represent the initial and terminal period for analysis, yielding:

$$X_{t-1} = C_{t-1} f_{t-1} \tag{17.3}$$

$$X_t = C_t f_t \tag{17.4}$$

Interperiod gross output changes can be expressed in one of two ways. Subtracting (17.3) from (17.4), then both adding and subtracting $C_t f_{t-1}$ to the right hand side of the difference equation provides:

$$X_t - X_{t-1} = C_t f_t - C_{t-1} f_{t-1} + C_t f_{t-1} - C_t f_{t-1} \tag{17.5}$$

Collecting terms in (17.5) produces the analytical form shown in (17.6):

$$X_t - X_{t-1} = C_t (f_t - f_{t-1}) + (C_t - C_{t-1}) f_{t-1} \tag{17.6}$$

Feldman *et al.* (1987) note that the first term on the right of (17.6) captures the change in industry output in the two time periods attributable to changing final demands, weighted by the interindustry structure of the terminal period, C_t. The second term represents the portion of output change attributable to changing interindustry structure weighted by the initial period final demand, f_{t-1}.

The alternative expression for gross output change is derived in a similar fashion but adding and subtracting $C_{t-1} f_t$ on the right hand side of the inter-period difference equation, yielding:

$$X_t - X_{t-1} = C_t f_t - C_{t-1} f_{t-1} + C_{t-1} f_t - C_{t-1} f_t \tag{17.7}$$

that, once its terms have been collected, results in (17.8):

$$X_t - X_{t-1} = C_{t-1} (f_t - f_{t-1}) + (C_t - C_{t-1}) f_t \tag{17.8}$$

In this expression, the first term on the right of (17.8) captures the change in industry output in the two time periods attributable to changing final demands, weighted by the initial period interindustry structure, C_{t-1}. The second term represents the portion of output change attributable to changing interindustry coefficients weighted by the terminal period final demand, f_t.

The final demand changes and coefficient change weightings differ in the two equations. Further, the two decomposition forms above are not unique. Elsewhere in this volume, Dietzenbacher and Hoekstra (2002) present two alternative decomposition forms that include multiplicative interaction terms, and note that the average of the decompositions in equation 17.6 and equation 17.8 approximates the average of all the decomposition forms considered by Dietzenbacher and Los (1997, 1998). Equation 17.9 includes the final demand difference right-hand-side terms of that average, and measures the portion of change in gross output for industry i attributable to inter-period changes in final demand:

$$\frac{1}{2}\left[\sum_{j=1}^{n} c_{ij}^{t}(f_j^{t-1} - f_j^{t}) + \sum_{j=1}^{n} c_{ij}^{t-1}(f_j^{t-1} - f_j^{t})\right] \tag{17.9}$$

where c_{ij}^{t-1} is an element of the Leontief inverse matrix for the initial time period and c_{ij}^{t} is an element of the Leontief inverse matrix for the terminal period. The element f_j^{t-1} denotes an element in the final demand vector at the initial period and f_j^{t} is an element in the final demand vector for the terminal period. A 53 x 1 vector is thus obtained, providing for each industry a measure of the contribution of changes in final demand to changes in gross industry output (Feldman *et al.*, 1987).

Equation (17.10) is the interindustry, structural change counterpart to (17.9), and measures the portion of changes in gross industry output attributable to changes in interindustry structure, for each industry *i*,:

$$\frac{1}{2}\left[\sum_{j=1}^{n}(c_{ij}^{t-1}-c_{ij}^{t})f_j^{t-1}+\sum_{j=1}^{n}(c_{ij}^{t-1}-c_{ij}^{t})f_j^{t}\right] \tag{17.10}$$

This vector provides industry-specific measures of the contribution of change in interindustry coefficients to change in gross industry output between the two time periods under investigation.

Our analysis departs from temporal output decomposition method of Feldman *et al.* (1987) in that it approaches the decomposition of output from a spatial rather than temporal perspective. We modify the temporal measure and use the modified framework to obtain a spatial output decomposition (SOD). The SOD can be used to explore output differences between each state in the Midwest and an "average" Midwest state. For each state we use two different computational methods. The first method (SODL) compares a state to an average Midwest interindustry coefficient table and an average vector of final demand levels. The second method uses, instead, a standardized final demand vector for each state and for the average Midwest state (SODS).[4] The first method, SODL, emphasizes differences in the sizes of the state economies, while the second, SODS, emphasizes final demand distributions.

Our derivation of spatial output differences follows the temporal formulation, using (17.1) and (17.2) as a point of departure. Adding regional subscripts to represent each state and our average Midwest economy provides the following equations,

$$X_s = C_s f_s \tag{17.11}$$

$$X_m = C_m f_m \tag{17.12}$$

for state *s* and "average state" *m*. The average state is represented by the inverse table derived from averages of the elements in the five coefficients tables and an average of the elements in the five final demand vectors.

Analogous to the temporal model, the differences in spatial economic structure can be represented in two ways. We obtain the first by subtracting (17.11) from (17.12, then both adding and subtracting $C_m f_s$ on the right hand side:

$$X_m - X_s = C_m f_m - C_s f_s + C_m f_s - C_m f_s \tag{17.13}$$

or

$$X_m - X_s = C_m (f_m - f_s) + (C_m - C_s) f_s \tag{17.14}$$

The first term on the right of (17.14) captures the difference in industry outputs attributable to differences in regional final demand distributions, weighted by the average Midwest interindustry structure, C_m. The second term measures the portion of output differences attributable to differences in interindustry coefficients, weighted by the final demand structure of the study region (state, in the present study), f_s. The alternate decomposition of differences across regions is

[4] The interindustry relationships for each state and the coefficient table for the average Midwest state are already standardized since we use the Leontief inverse matrix.

$$X_m - X_s = C_m f_m - C_s f_m + C_s f_m - C_s f_s \tag{17.15}$$

or

$$X_m - X_s = C_s(f_m - f_s) + (C_m - C_s) f_m \tag{17.16}$$

The first term on the right of (17.16) measures the difference in industry output in the two regions attributable to differences in final demands, weighted by the state-specific interindustry distribution, C_s. The second term measures the portion of industry output difference attributable to differences in interindustry coefficients weighted by the final demands, either levels or standardized, for the f_m. Equation (17.17) is a combination of (17.14) and (17.16) and measures, for each industry *i*, the difference in gross industry output as a result of differences in final demand:

$$\frac{1}{2}\left[\sum_{j=1}^{n} c_{ij}^{M}(f_j^S - f_j^M) + \sum_{j=1}^{n} c_{ij}^{S}(f_j^S - f_j^M)\right] \tag{17.17}$$

where c_{ij}^M and c_{ij}^S are elements in the Leontief inverse matrix for the average Midwest state and the state under investigation, respectively. The 53 x 1 vector obtained provides a measure of the contribution of differences in final demand to differences in gross industry output between the average Midwest state and the particular Midwest state under investigation. Equation (17.18) is a combination of (17.14) and (17.16) and measures, for each industry *i*, the difference in gross industry output as a result of differences in interindustry coefficients:

$$\frac{1}{2}\left[\sum_{j=1}^{n} (c_{ij}^{S} - c_{ij}^{M}) f_j^S + \sum_{j=1}^{n} (c_{ij}^{S} - c_{ij}^{M}) f_j^M\right] \tag{17.18}$$

This vector measures the contribution of differences in interindustry structure to differences in gross industry output between the average Midwest state and the Midwest state under investigation.

17.6 Results and Discussion

The spatial output decomposition measure provides a way of differentiating state production structures on the basis of coefficient and final demand characteristics. As suggested above, the results of (17.17) using final demand levels (SODL) and standardized (SODS) final demands provide a measure of the contribution of final demand differences to regional output differences. In the SODL final demand analysis, a large positive value for an industry sector in a given Midwest state identify, primarily greater than average final demands for that industry. For such a sector, output differences can be attributed to high levels of final demand. Conversely, small values for a given industry sector indicate that any differences in output between the states cannot be attributed to differences in final demand levels. In the SODS analysis, a large value for an industry sector in a given Midwest state identifies a substantial role for that sector with respect to the overall regional final demand distribution. Likewise, small values for such a sector in a given state indicate a role for the sector that is more in line with the other Midwest states. The SODL method places greater emphasis on the scale of a state economy than on its distribution of activities, while the SODS methods emphasize the distributions of industry activity.

Equation (17.18) measures the extent to which interindustry structure distinguishes a given state from our average Midwest state economy. Using levels or standardized final demands, this measure indicates the strength of spatial variation in interindustry interaction. A large positive value for a sector indicates a larger than average intermediate industry output orientation. The results from equation 18 will be virtually identical whether we use the raw or standardized final demands, at least in relative terms. The range of values across states for a given sector will expand or contract, but the relative positions of the values for each state will be identical.

The gross output decompositions for all states can be effectively assessed as a group. Displaying the components of the output decomposition for all industries and states on a single graph makes it possible to quickly identify which sectors have the largest range of structural variation, and which states differ most strongly from the average region. Figures 17.1 and 17.2 illustrate final demand differences by state in the Midwest. Figure 17.1 displays the results using final demand levels (SODL), while figure 17.2 displays the results from the standardized final demand analysis (SODS). These charts provide an indication of how final demand by economic sector differentiates each state's production structure.[5]

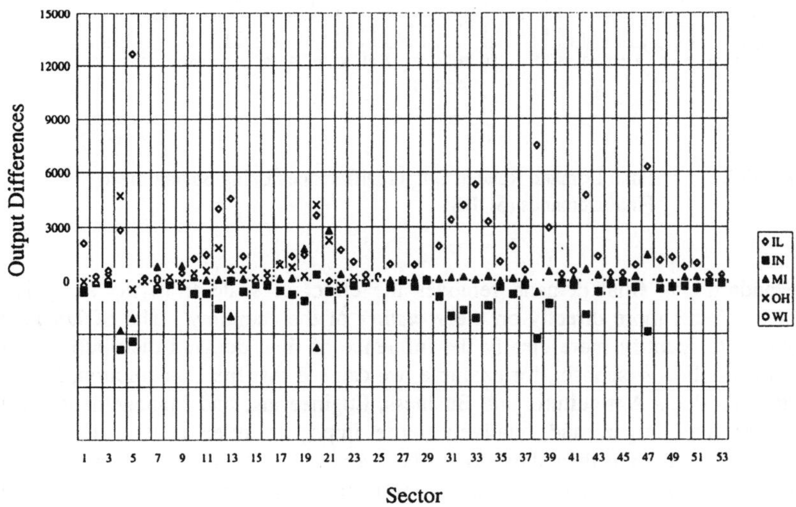

Figure 17.1 Final Demand Related Output Differences Using Final Demand Levels (SODL)

---

[5] In interpreting the graphs, arbitrary cut-off values were employed in identifying significance. Since these measures are not statistically derived, analysts should select values that correspond to more or less natural cutoffs. The visual display of the measure values facilitates this process.

The most prominent feature of figure 17.1 is the dominance of Illinois in terms of final demand levels. Because of its size, Illinois' final demand levels are consistently larger than average. Likewise, output differences for Wisconsin can be uniformly attributed to its lower final demand levels. Since we would almost always expect a high correlation between final demand and output, these results are not especially surprising. In all five states it is interesting to note that the nature of production in the secondary sector appears to be most dissimilar. There is a great deal of similarity in the transportation sectors.

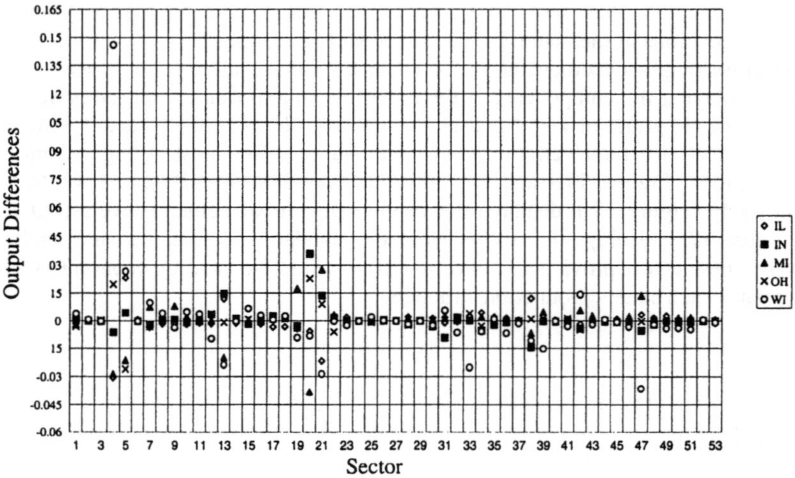

Figure 17.2 Final Demand Related Output Differences Using Standardized Final Demands (SODS)

Standardizing final demand removes the effect of scale from the analysis and enables a focus more directly on the *structure* of the economy. The SODS method allows us to identify more clearly the influence of final demand distributions rather than levels. For Wisconsin, for example, we can see that the Construction, Food and Kindred Products Agriculture, and Business, Engineering, and Management Services industries play larger, and relatively more important roles relative to the other industries in the state than they do in the average Midwest state. Conversely, the relative roles of Petroleum and Coal Products, Transportation Equipment, Retail Trade, Eating and Drinking Places, and Health Services industries in Wisconsin are much smaller than the average Midwest state. Likewise, Petroleum and Coal Products and Electric and other Electric Equipment are the two final demand sectors that distinguish most strongly the Indiana economy from the rest of the Midwest. In contrast to the dominance of Illinois in figure 17.1, we observe from figure 17.2 an Illinois economy that is much more representative of the Midwest in its final demand distribution, with only Food and Kindred Products playing a relatively important role in distinguishing Illinois from the rest of the Midwest, in a positive sense. The most important Michigan industries in their role in final demand structure are Industrial

Machinery and, as expected, Transportation Equipment. As in the SODL analysis, there appears to be somewhat more dissimilarity in final demand structures among the secondary sectors than among the others. The industry sector with the greatest variation in its role in final demand distributions is Construction.

Figure 17.3 shifts attention to the interindustry structure of the Midwest states. The interpretation of this chart is much more straightforward. Industries with large positive values are more strongly oriented to interindustry, intrastate sales than their average Midwest counterpart. There are several implications. Industries that are more heavily interdependent play an important role in regional economies in much the same sense as the Hirschman-Rasmussen key sectors. Regions that are characterized by high levels of interindustry interaction are more complex, in the sense that more interaction is required, including information exchange (Jackson, *et al.* 1989, Hewings *et al.* 1989, Hewings 1998). Finally, regions whose industries are tightly interconnected through sales and purchases typically will have large multipliers. Hence, the fortunes of the regions industries are closely tied to one another. Bear in mind, however, that the key sectors interpretation using this measure is relative to the average Midwest state.

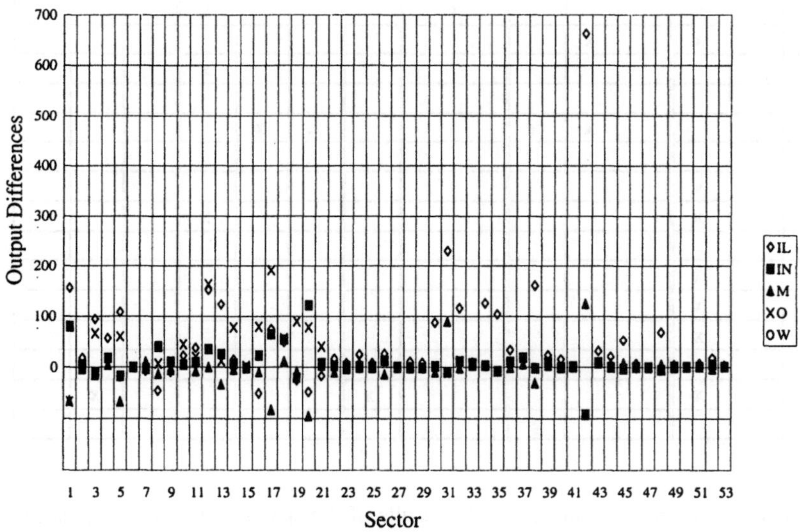

Figure 17.3 Output Differences Due to Interindustry Structure

The two largest positive values for obtain for Electric, Gas, and Sanitary and Business, Engineering, and Management Services industries in Illinois. Other key Illinois sectors in terms of intermediate interindustry structure include Agriculture, Food and Kindred Products, Chemicals and Allied Products, Petroleum and Coal Products, Wholesale Trade, Banking and Other Credit Agencies, Securities and

Commodity Brokers, and Real Estate. Illinois has by far the greatest number of key sectors relative to the rest of the Midwest.

In terms of interindustry structure, Ohio has the next largest number of key industries. Industries with the largest values for Ohio include Chemicals and Allied Products, Primary Metals, and Wholesale Trade. Indiana has only one sector with comparably high values, Electric and Other Electric Equipment. Michigan's Business, Engineering & Management Services industry also has similarly high values, while none of Wisconsin's industries score as highly as those already named. It is also notable that there is very little variation in the values obtained for nearly half of the sectors, including a large number of the transportation and tertiary sectors.

Table 17.1 Spatial Output Decomposition Summary

	Illinois			Indiana			Michigan			Ohio			Wisconsin		
IND	SODI	SODS	Coeffs	SODI	SODS	Coeffs	SODI	SODS	Coeffs	SODI	SODS	Coeffs	SODI	SODS	Coeffs
1			x												
4										x	x			x	
5	x	x	x											x	
12	x		x									x			
13	x		x		x										
17												x			
19								x							
20	x				x	x				x	x				
21								x							
31	x		x												
32	x		x									x			
33	x														
34	x		x												
35			x												
38	x		x												
39	x														
42	x		x						x					x	
47	x														

Table 17.1 presents a summary of the results of the spatial output decomposition. Industry rows are omitted where no decomposition score is notably high. Illinois stands out as the economy that is most strongly differentiated from the rest of the Midwest. The Agriculture Products industry scores highly on all three dimensions of the spatial output decomposition. This sector is obviously quite important to the Illinois economy. Had this been a policy analysis, this sector, along with seven others that scored high on two of the three measures, would be prime candidates for further scrutiny. Indiana has only one industry that scores highly on two or more dimensions. Ohio has two sectors that score highly on two final demand dimensions, both of which are final demand indicators. Neither Wisconsin nor Michigan has any industries that score highly on two or more dimensions. Michigan and Indiana are, by and large, nearer the to average Midwest state than the rest on the combination of dimensions.

17.7 Conclusions

Input-output analysis provides a powerful framework for exploring the similarities and differences between economic regions. This study applied a new method, based upon the input-output framework, to five Midwest states. The spatial output decomposition is an approach that separates change in gross output into one component attributed to differences in final demand and another attributed to differences in interindustry structure, and provides a quick and effective way of comparing regional economic structure. Applying this method to state interindustry data can enhances understanding of the structural economic characteristics inherent in these economies.

Like any analytical method based on regional industrial categories, the spatial output decomposition approach is subject to issues of both spatial and sectoral aggregation. Future researchers may wish to explore the effects of aggregation on the results. Another direction for further research might be found in a combination of the temporal and spatial output decomposition methods. Such an approach would yield important insights into the dynamics of regional economic structure.

The spatial output decomposition method has been shown to be a useful technique for identifying similarities and differences among states. It provides a clear and interpretable indication of similarities and differences among regional economies in terms of final demand and interindustry structure. The health of a state economy is reflected in each of the three measures presented. Industries with high scores on both the coefficient decomposition and either of the two final demand decompositions are important components of their state's economies. The SODL approach places appropriate emphasis on industrial scale in regional economies, while the SODS approach identifies a subtler structure of economy based upon relative final demand distributions. Combined with the SOD component based on input-output coefficient change, the spatial output decomposition is a useful addition to the regional analysis toolkit.

References

"A Test of Midwest Mettle." *The Economist*, April 19, 1997: 27.

Feldman, S.J., D. McClain, and K. Palmer K. 1987. "Sources of Structural Change in the United States, 1963 - 78: An Input-Output Perspective." *The Review Of Economics and Statistics* 69, 503 - 510.

Dietzenbacher, E, and B. Los. 1997. "Analyzing Decomposition Analyses." In A. Simonovits and A.E. Steenge (eds). *Prices, Growth and Cycles*. London, MacMillan, 108-131.

Dietzenbacher, E. and B. Los. 1998. "Structural Decomposition Techniques: Sense and Sensitivity." *Economic Systems Research*, 10, 307-323.

Dietzenbacher, E. and R. Hoekstra. 2002. "The RAS Structural Decomposition Approach." This volume, chapter 10.

Dzikowski, D.A. 1999. "Production Structure in the American Midwest: A Comparative State Analysis." Unpublished Masters Thesis, The Ohio State University.

Hewings, G. J. D., M. Sonis, J. Guo, P.R. Israilevich, and G.R. Schindler. 1998. "The Hollowing-Out Process in the Chicago Economy, 1975 - 2011." *Geographical Analysis* 30, 217-233.

Hirschman, A. 1958. *The Strategy of Economic Development*. New Haven, Yale University Press.

Israilevich, P.R., G.J.D. Hewings, and E.B. Martins. 1993 "A New Alternative to the BEA Method of Constructing Input-Output Tables." *Discussion Paper* 93-T-9, Regional Economics Applications Laboratory, University of Illinois.

Israilevich, P.R., and G.J.D. Hewings. 1998. "Interstate Trade Among Midwest Economies." *Chicago Federal Reserve Letter* 129, 1-4.

Jackson R.W., G.J.D. Hewings, and M. Sonis. "Decomposition Approaches to the Identification of Change in Regional Economies." *Economic Geography* 65, 216-231.

Kim, S. 1996. "Changing Structure of U.S. Regions: A Historical Perspective." *The Midwest Economy: Structure and Performance*, Federal Reserve Bank of Chicago, Chicago Ill.

Melcher, R.A., D. Weimer, and P. Galuszka. 1998. "This Isn't Your Father's Rust Belt." *Business Week*, 41.

Rasmussen, P. 1956. *Studies in Inter-Sectoral Relations*. Copenhagen, Einar Harks.

Rose, A. and S. Casler. 1996. "Input-Output Structural Decomposition Analysis: A Critical Appraisal." *Economic System Research* 8, 33-62.

Sonis, M., G.J.D. Hewings, and J. Guo. 1996. "Sources of Structural Change in Input-Output Systems: A Field of Influence Approach." *Economic Systems Research* 8, 15-32.

Sonis, M., G.J.D. Hewings, and J. Guo. 2000. "A New Image of Classical Key Sector Analysis: Minimum Information Decomposition of the Leontief Inverse." *Economic Systems Research* 12, 401-423.

Testa, W.A., T.A. Klier, and R.A. Mattoon. 1997. "Reversal of Fortune: Understanding the Midwest Recovery." *Economic Perspectives*, [Federal Reserve Bank of Chicago] 21,2-17 .

Appendix 17.1 Industry Sectors

	Title	SIC
1	Livestock, Livestock Products, and Agricultural Products	01, 02
2	Agriculture, Forestry, and Fisheries	07, 08, 09
3	Mining	10, 12, 13, 14
4	Construction	15, 16, 17
5	Food and Kindred Products	20
6	Tobacco	21
7	Apparel and Textile Products	22, 23
8	Lumber and Wood Products	24
9	Furniture and Fixtures	25
10	Printing and Publishing	27
12	Chemicals and Allied Products	28
13	Petroleum and Coal Products	29
14	Rubber and Misc. Plastics Products	30
15	Leather and Leather Products	31
16	Stone, Clay, and Glass Products	32
17	Primary Metals Industries	33
18	Fabricated Metal Products	34
19	Industrial Machinery and Equipment	35
20	Electronic and Electric Equipment	36
21	Transportation Equipment	37
22	Instruments and Related Products	38
23	Miscellaneous Manufacturing Industries	39
24	Railroad Transportation and Transportation	40, 47
25	Local and Interurban Passenger Transit	41
26	Trucking and Warehousing	42
27	Water Transportation	44
28	Transportation by Air	45
29	Pipelines, Except Natural Gas	46
30	Communications	48
31	Electric, Gas, and Sanitary Services	49
32	Wholesale Trade	50, 51
33	Retail Trade	52-57, 59
34	Banking and Other Credit Agencies	60, 61, 67
35	Security and Commodity Brokers	68
36	Insurance Carriers	63
37	Insurance Agents, Brokers, and Service	64
38	Real Estate	65
39	Eating and Drinking Places	58
40	Hotels and Other Lodging Places	70
41	Personal Services	72
42	Business, Engineering, and Management Services	73, 87, 89
43	Auto Repair, Services, and Parking	75
44	Miscellaneous Repair Services	76
45	Motion Pictures	78
46	Amusement and Recreation Services	79
47	Health Services	80
48	Legal Services	81
49	Educational Services	82
50	Social Services	83
51	Membership Organizations and Households	84, 86, 88
52	Federal Government Enterprises	
53	State and Local Government Enterprises	

18 New Explanatory Models for Analyzing Spatial Innovation: A Comparative Investigation*

A. Reggiani,[1] P. Nijkamp,[2] and E. Sabella[1]

[1] Department of Economics, Faculty of Statistics, University of Bologna, Piazza Scaravilli 2, 40126 Bologna, Italy
e-mail: reggiani@economia.unibo.it; sabel00@economia.unibo.it

[2] Department of Spatial Economics, Free University, De Boelelaan 1105, 1085 HV Amsterdam, The Netherlands
e-mail: pnijkamp@econ.vu.nl

18.1 The Scope of Spatial Innovation

The period of the 1980s and 1990s has witnessed a profound interest in innovation research. At first, we have seen much attention for technological innovations as part of a long-term cycle based on Schumpeterian views (see e.g. Kleinknecht, 1988). Later on, the interest shifted from macro-economic analyses to regional and urban economic investigations into the success conditions for new innovations (e.g. incubation theory; see e.g. Davelaar, 1991) as well as to the spatio-temporal diffusion and acceptance patterns of innovations (see e.g. Bertuglia *et al.*, 1997).

The spatial component has thus increasingly gained importance in innovation research. In this context, also territorial openness, spatial factor mobility and outsourcing are playing an important role. Thus, the urban region (or the urban area in a broader setting) is increasingly regarded as the main territorial focus for creative economic development. An urban region has a knowledge base, a tight socio-economic network and a cultural support mechanism that renders it suitable as a source of Schumpeterian entrepreneurs (Amin and Thrift, 1994; Sonis, 1992). This also means that the urban region offers an effective framework for spatial competition, mainly as a result of the social embeddedness of socio-economic connectivity in the city (see Simmie, 1997).

In recent years we have also seen an overwhelming interest in the spatial organizational and managerial conditions of urban regions for successful innovative behavior. The linkages with socio-cultural processes, institutional ramifications and public-private undertakings are increasingly coming to the fore. Against this background we have to consider also the recently emerged concepts of learning regions or self-organizing regions (see also van Geenhuizen and Nijkamp, 1999, and Bertuglia *et al.*, 1998).

* This chapter has been carried out in the framework of the SOEIS (The Self-Organization of the European Information Society) project. The authors wish to thank Dr. Giovanni Russo (University of Utrecht) for his helpful methodological suggestions as well as the SOEIS group for the interesting comments. The third author is also grateful to the Faculty of Statistics (University of Bologna) for the grant assigned to him.

The aim of the present chapter is to identify the critical success factors of spatial innovations, based on an extensive database on entrepreneurial innovations in a series of European cities. Particular attention will be paid to spatial innovative behavior from the viewpoint of city size, degree of centrality and sector orientation. In this context, the potential of self-organization of regions and cities will also be addressed.

The chapter is organized as follows. The next section will offer some background reflections on self-organizing strategies of cities and regions from the viewpoint of innovative behavior. Then we address in section 18.3 the methodology of an empirical analysis (in particular, regression analysis and NN analysis). In this section also the database for our comparative analysis will be described. The results of the statistical analysis of our data are then described in section 18.4, while the results of the empirical experiments related to (non) linear regression analysis and NNs are illustrated in sections 18.5 and 18.6, respectively. Section 18.7 offers some concluding remarks.

18.2 The Self-Organizing Core Competence of Urban Regions

Modern urban regions incorporate a body of entrepreneurial and managerial skills, which gives them a competitive advantage. Examples are research institutes, laboratories, universities, consultancy firms and so forth. This productivity augmenting structure is reinforced by the synergy created by communication, information and education networks in the city. As a result, we observe that such learning regions have the ability to organize themselves in a way that provides them also a competitive advantage in a global market.

Thus, it seems plausible that modern urban regions derive their strong innovative position largely from exploiting their core competence, viz. the efficient organization of all relevant input, processing, production and marketing activities. The core competence has two knowledge components, viz. certified knowledge incorporated in hardware and tacit knowledge incorporated in 'humanware' (using e.g. learning – by – doing principles). Especially the 'humanware' component is responsible for the articulation of the need for spatial proximity in innovation and creates the spatial framework for organizational and learning behavior of urban regions (see also Morgan, 1997).

It should be noticed that 'humanware' might also lead to inert and routine behavior caused by past successes. Such a danger is, for instance, reflected in path dependency of decisions, when it is almost impossible to abandon established technologies due to an accumulation of expenses, routines or capital from previous periods. Path dependency can essentially only be coped with by so-called de-learning.

The innovative success of urban regions depends thus on a variety of creating seedbed conditions in a particular area. An important additional factor is also the dissemination potential present in an urban area. In other words, how fast and to which groups are new findings or new knowledge distributed? Again urban areas have a great potential in this respect due to their self-organizing power regarding networking, transformation of knowledge, human capital management, identification of knowledge needs or consensus building using stakeholders in the region.

Knowledge, managerial and organizational networks are usually regarded as a sine qua non for effective and innovative learning strategies. Such networks may be formal or informal in nature and serve to reduce uncertainty in a business environment (see Storper, 1996).

In the light of the previous remarks, it is clear that an urban area offers a complex and dynamic array of core competences that may position these areas at a highly competitive edge. On the other hand, local cultures, geographical conditions, the urban economic composition, local management styles and local governance conditions are site-specific and may hence lead to a great variation in empirical findings (see also Nijkamp and Kangasharju, 1998). Therefore, in the sequel of this paper we will try to set up a framework for comparative analysis of innovative behavior of firms in different sectors and in different urban regions in different European countries. By using such a contrast analysis we hope to be able to identify commonalities and contrasts in innovative behaviors of firms.

18.3 Methodology and Database for the Case Study on European Cities

18.3.1 Introduction

The spatial and temporal aspects of innovations are a typical example of a complex evolutionary phenomenon. Spatial and economic sciences, in recent years have shown an increasing tendency to promote new 'universal' concepts, such as network evolution, complexity and non-linear dynamics (see Nijkamp and Reggiani, 1998). In parallel, new models and tools originating mainly from the field of artificial intelligence, like the neuro-computing approaches, are popular for their ability to map out complex patterns with uncertain or fuzzy information. Applications of neuro-computing tools, such as neural networks (NNs) and genetic algorithms (GAs) to transport analysis have also demonstrated the promising potential of these instruments in comparison with conventional analytical models, like the well-known logit model (see, e.g., Himanen *et al.*, 1998; Reggiani *et al.*, 1998, 2000, 2001).

Scientific researchers are nowadays successfully using logit models – and the analogous spatial interaction models – as well as regression analysis (which may – analytically – be considered to be its logarithmic form). Logit models belong to the class of discrete choice models (see, e.g., McFadden, 1974) and are playing a prominent role in spatial-economic analysis due to their underlying foundation in micro-economic theory.

However, when applying a logit or spatial interaction model, the inherent *IIA assumption* (independence of irrelevant alternatives) is often disregarded or overlooked. On the other hand, probit models, which are able to overcome the IIA limitation, are more complicated and rarely used.

In this context it is certainly useful to adopt new tools such as NNs, which, because they are based on data/image processing, apparently do not suffer from any theoretically restrictive hypothesizing process. NNs also show an 'easy' manageability in their use and application.

Beginning with the above considerations, it seems thus worthwhile to explore the NN tool, to compare it to conventional approaches like regression and logit models, and to apply it in fields of analysis other than the transportation sector. The industrial and innovation sector, where data are often uncertain and incomplete, is therefore employed – in this chapter – for an empirical analysis. The subsequent subsection 18.3.2 will provide a concise overview of the methodology used (regression analysis and NN analysis); Subsection 18.3.3 will then present the available database. Section 18.4 will next be devoted to an empirical analysis using the concept of a so-called local environment score for innovation. Section 18.5 and section 18.6 will offer the results from a regression analysis and an NN analysis, respectively. Finally, we will conclude with some methodological considerations as well as suggestions for future research.

18.3.2 The Methodology Adopted

Preface. A methodology serves to develop analytical tools that are also applicable outside the domain of the actual case study, e.g. generalization or forecasting. "*The application of a model in a context other than that in which it was originally estimated is described as model transfer*" (Koppelman and Pas, 1986, p.321). The debate on model transferability has instigated numerous empirical studies, especially on spatial behavior in the transport sector. It is evident that the analysis of transferability measures has also become a central issue in general research areas such as spatial economics. The uncertainty on future spatial-economic events has prompted many questions on the validity of scientific references, especially since the advent of the globalization process and within the new European economic-geographical setting.

It has also increasingly become common and necessary – in adopting new techniques and models of analysis – to focus on the joint use of different tools in order to evaluate their ability to describe the observed behavior in the application context of a changing space-economy. To this end, we have adopted – in our case study concerned with spatial innovation analysis – two *theoretically* different techniques, regression analysis and neural network analysis. These two techniques will be briefly described in the following subsections.

Regression analysis. Regression analysis may be regarded as the conventional 'centerpiece' of quantitative spatial economic analysis. From a methodological viewpoint, regression analysis is also closely connected with spatial interaction modeling from both a static and dynamic perspective (see Nijkamp and Reggiani, 1992). The limitation inherent in the use of the regression model is mostly its inability to map *complex* patterns of the performance/behavior of actors regarding the variables at hand. In general and briefly stated, regression analysis aims to correlate variables in a (non)linear, causal way as follows:

$$Z_j = f(\alpha_i, X_i) \quad i=1...n; \quad j=1...m \tag{18.1}$$

where Z_j are dependent variables, X_i independent variables, α_i the parameters/coefficients to be estimated, and $f(\bullet)$ the causal or explanatory relationship (which may be linear or non-linear). It should be noted that the non-linearity incorporated in (1) may be of any form, e.g. quadratic or cubic.

The neural network approach. NNs belong to the methodological class of biocomputing (as do genetic algorithms, fuzzy logic, cellular automata, etc.). "*Biocomputing refers to biologically inspired approaches to creating software*" (see Valdes, 1991). The idea behind biocomputing is to explain complex phenomena by means of simple rules, according to the principle that intricate structures such as living systems are comprised of simpler components (cells). Progressing both from the need to emulate the human learning process – which is based on experience – and from the concept of biocomputing, neural networks represent a new technology for information processing based on current theories concerning the way the human brain works. In a human brain, nerve cells called neurons are the fundamental elements of the central nervous system. The central nervous system has about five billion neurons; their simple cooperation generates complex behavior. The basic features of a neuron may be summarized as follows (see Davalo and Naim, 1991):

- it receives signals coming from other neurons;
- it integrates these signals;
- it propagates the resulting signal to other neurons (with different intensities) by means of electrochemical connections.

Thus by analogy, the structure of NNs is comparable to the architecture of the human brain and is generally represented by logical units ('neurons') connected by channels of communication which interact independently, since each unit cooperates in the transmission of information by means of a different weight[1]. By changing the values of the weights to obtain the desired output, the learning process occurs; NNs are trained to output the desired results. The back-propagation algorithm is especially able to 'assign back' the mean-squared error signal from the output to the input units. In this way NNs can learn from experience; this is the key advantage of NNs over conventional algorithms.

The application areas of NNs are wide-ranging, although their main task is pattern recognition. In recent years, NNs have been adopted for image processing, speech synthesis, noise filtering, robotic control, financial modeling, and so on.

The term 'neural networks' is used nowadays to describe a number of different models which are usually categorized into two classes; NNs *without* and NNs *with* supervisor. This difference is based on the difference in the learning process. In fact, the networks with *unsupervised training* do not require the target outputs; they modify the weights by means of competitive learning algorithms in response to the input data. On the other hand, *supervised training* indicates the knowledge of input/output data in order to find, during the learning phase, the weights[2] of the network that minimize the error function of the target outputs and the network outputs. Although various training algorithms[3] exist, the one most often used is the back-propagation algorithm, where in the case of a two-layer feed-forward NN, at least one 'hidden' layer is defined between the input and output layers to map internal representations necessary for associating input and output configurations (see figure 18.1 and, for details on NNs, Chapter 7 in Nijkamp and Reggiani, 1998).

---

[1] Here a weight is a real number assigned to a connection between two units.

[2] The weights are the values (adaptive coefficients) assigned to the links between the units of the network. The goal of the training phase is to find the values of the weights that will produce a reasonable output in response to the input.

[3] The aim of the training algorithm is to minimize the error function by adjusting the value of the weights.

Following the majority of applications on NNs, in this study we adopt a two-layer feed-forward, totally connected NN application (see figure 18.1). The methodological structure of the primary steps in the application of a feed-forward NN is described in Reggiani and Tritapepe (1997). It consists of three subsequent stages: a) definition of network architecture; b) a learning phase; and c) a forecasting phase. It is necessary to define the correct architecture of the network, i.e. the number of units on the relevant levels. The input and output units usually depend on the number of input and output variables defining the problem.

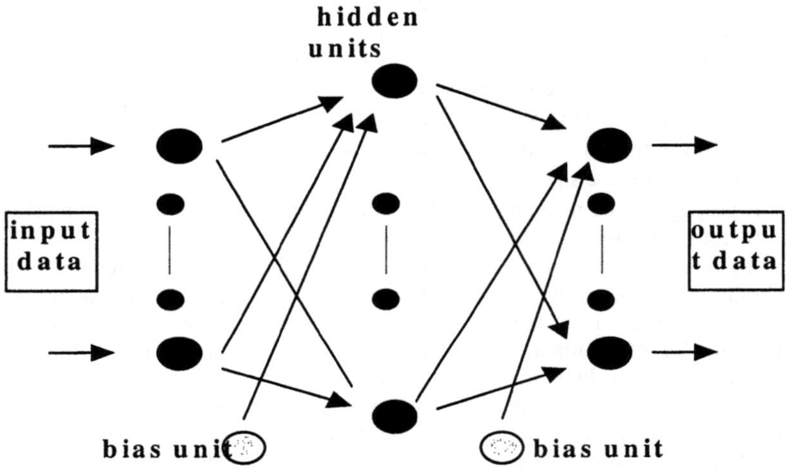

Figure 18.1. A feed-forward (back-propagation) neural network architecture

Section 18.5 will offer empirical results obtained by applying a NN model to innovation data. It should be noted that the use of the NN model in the context of industrial innovation dynamics is rather rare and still in an experimental stage.

18.3.3 The Data Set

The data set used in our empirical applications contains detailed information on entrepreneurial innovation based on interviews – from the URBINNO[4] study (see, for details, Damman, 1994) – of different manufacturing industries (273) in various cities in three European countries: the Netherlands (33), Italy (32) and the United Kingdom (208) (see table 18.1). In addition, the cities in our survey have been divided into core, intermediate and peripheral regions on – the basis of geographical location and size – in order to study the innovation adoption phenomena, not only according to their national average patterns, but also according to additional characteristics such as the size of the cities (see table 18.2).

[4] The URBINNO (Urban Innovation) study was a project originally financed by Volkswagen Foundation (between 1987 and 1989) for studying innovations in several urban areas under various categories such as population, urban economy, institution and infrastructure, and urban firm (see, for details, Damman, 1994).

Table 18.1 The geographical location of the firms under analysis

Country	The Netherlands (NL)	Italy (IT)	United Kingdom (UK)
City	Rotterdam, Eindhoven and Tilburg	Milan and Como	Sheffield, Bristol, Coventry, Newcastle Nottingham, Blackburn, Peterborough and Reading
Number of firms	33	32	208

Table 18.2 The characteristics of the cities under consideration

	Intermediate Region	Core Region	Peripheral Region
Population	300,000-386,000	426,000-2,000,000	50,000-141,000
City	Eindhoven, Coventry, Newcastle, Nottingham	Milan, Rotterdam, Sheffield and Bristol	Blackburn, Como, Peterborough, Reading and Tilburg
Number of firms	99	93	81

According to Kangasharju and Nijkamp (1997), this implies that we expect that the spatial diffusion to emerge not only according to physical distance to central regions, but rather according to their ability and willingness to adopt innovations (approximated here by size of a city). The extensive questionnaire submitted to the companies refers to retrospective (past) and prospective (future) views of managers on various local factors (see table 18.3 as well as Nijkamp *et al.*, 1997).

The next sections will depict the statistical results emerging from our empirical analysis of the interviews. These empirical experiments have been primarily based on the modeling techniques and methodologies described in section 18.3.2.

18.4 Attitudinal Preferences of Firms Towards Their Local Environment

For each firm a simple statistical indicator, coined the local environment score (LES[5]), has been computed in order to create a measure concerning the perception (by the firm) of the importance of the relevant local factors. Table 18.3 lists the twenty-one local factors considered in our survey.

[5] According to Nijkamp *et al.* (1997), the local environment score (LES) is computed as follows: $LES = \left[\left(\beta_i X_i + \beta_j X_j\right) / \sum Y\right] 100$, where β_i ='major importance', β_j ='some importance', X_i = the frequency of the answers offering the score 'major importance', X_j = the frequency of the answers offering the score 'importance' and ΣY= the total number of possible attributes/ alternatives y. In our specific case β_i=1, β_j=2, ΣY=21.

Table 18.3 The twenty-one factors important to the success of the company in business, product innovation, market innovation, process innovation, and management structure (based on Kangasharju and Nijkamp, 1997)

Agglomeration	**A1** Local suppliers **A2** Local subcontractors Quality of local business services: **A3** Supporting technology **A4** Supporting marketing **A5** Supporting management
Population Structure	**B1** Skills in labour market **B2** Skills in training support **B3** Local customers
Information Network Infrastructure	**C1** Science & technology links with local university or college **C2** Management links with local university or college **C3** Chambers of commerce and industry **C4** Trade association **C5** Clubs and societies **C6** Conferences services
Physical Network Infrastructure	**D1** Quality of telecommunications services **D2** Quality of local transport facilities **D3** Quality of international transport links
Institutional Network Infrastructure	**E1** Local investment subsidies **E2** Local financial institution **E3** Favourable attitude of local politicians **E4** Available land and building

More specifically, the importance of the local factors under analysis – perceived by each firm – has been evaluated for the following five objectives: (1) *commercial success of the company* in the recent past as well as in the mid-1990s (future); (2) *product innovation* in the recent past and product innovation in the next decade (future); (3) *market innovation* in the recent past and market innovation in the next decade (future); (4) *production process innovation* in the recent past and production process changes in the next decade (future); (5) *management structure or procedural innovation* in the recent past and managerial changes in the next decade (future).

The LES indicators at the firm level have then been aggregated at the country level (see table 18.4). The aggregate value, computed as the average of the LES scores located in each country under analysis (NL, IT, UK), offers a standard measure of the perceptions – of the firms – on the importance of the local factors, seen from their national perspective. Table 18.4 shows that the Italian firms in particular are more 'sensitive' to the importance of these local factors in comparison with the firms located in the Netherlands and the United Kingdom, which appear to be more homogeneous in their behavioral patterns. This result will most likely have a significant impact on the sensitivity analysis concerning the 'space-transferability' of the firms (see section 18.6.3)

Table 18.4 The LES indicators in the past for the firms under analysis (country level)

Country	Success in business Past	Product innovation Past	Market innovation Past	Process innovation Past	Management structure Past
NL	61.76	24.24	13.71	14.86	4.47
IT	**101.34**	**60.71**	**56.10**	**43.00**	**43.45**
UK	76.90	20.40	23.83	17.76	17.81

Table 18.5 The LES indicators in the future for the firms under analysis (country level)

Country	Success in business Future	Product innovation Future	Market innovation Future	Process innovation Future	Management innovation Future
NL	66.67	25.97	15.44	20.78	5.19
IT	**120.98**	**83.93**	**65.62**	**59.97**	**59.67**
UK	83.13	23.26	25.75	19.73	19.60

The above LES indicators have also been computed for the future (see table 18.5) wherein one finds the result that the perceptions about the importance of the twenty-one local factors of the Italian firms for objectives *a, b, c, d* and *e* (in table 18.3) are higher compared to the other countries in the future context. In order to better illustrate this, we have also extrapolated the difference between the LES indicators in the future and in the past to offer a 'dynamic' perspective of the changes of the firms' opinions (see table 18.6). The positive 'dynamic' perception – towards the local factors – of the Italian firms compared to the Dutch and English firms, is again evident here. However, it should be noted that in general each country perceives the twenty-one local factors more important in the near future than in the past.

Table 18.6 The differences - between future and past - in the attitudinal preferences of the firms towards the adopted local factors (country level)

Country	Success in business Future-Past	Product innovation Future-Past	Market innovation Future-Past	Process innovation Future-Past	Management innovation Future-Past
NL	4.90	1.73	1.73	0.92	0.72
IT	**19.64**	**23.21**	**9.52**	**16.96**	**16.22**
UK	6.23	2.86	1.92	1.97	1.79

Our analysis will now attempt to further explore – through using the statistical-methodological tools of regression and NN analysis – the 'behavioral attitude' of these different clusters of firms (NL, IT, UK), in order to provide proper insight into their 'space- transferability' pattern.

18.5 An Explanatory Regression Analysis for the Local Environment Score

In this section, the analysis will investigate the possibility of explaining the LES indicators relevant to the commercial *success of the company* as a (non)linear combination of the LES indicators related to *product innovation*, *market innovation*, *process innovation* and *management structure*. The methodology adopted in this section based on a simple regression model. A linear regression model will first be carried out to assess whether the variables under analysis are combined in a 'linear' form or are otherwise of a non-linear form, e.g., of a quadratic or cubic type. In the next section, an NN approach will be used to explore the possibility of a more complex non-linear relationship. Moreover, the NN model is also adopted as a specific tool for analyzing the (micro) behavior of the firms.

The statistical indicators ARV (Average Relative Variance), MSE (Mean Square Error), MPE (Mean Percentage Error) and MAPE (Mean Absolute Percentage Error) (see footnote 8 for their mathematical definition) are considered in this chapter for the comparison and evaluation of the results for each adopted model. For this purpose the data set has been randomly subdivided into three sub-sets[6]:

- *training set* containing 218 observations, about 80% of the data set;
- *cross-validation set* containing 44 observations, about 20% of the training set;
- *test set* containing 55 observations, about 20% of the data set.

Finally, a sensitivity analysis will be carried out to analyze the 'transferability' potential (see, for details, section 18.6.3), as specified at the end of section 18.4. The regression analysis concerning the LES indicators that we use here considers as a

[6] The training set has been used for the learning/calibration phase. The cross-validation has been used for solving the overfitting problem of a NN in the learning phase (see for details, Fischer and Gopal, 1994). The test set is used for comparing the results of the models adopted after the introduction of the data not used in the learning/calibration phase.

dependent variable the **LES** indicator related to the **commercial success** of the company. The independent explanatory variables are defined as follows:

Product (LES) = Local environment score related to product innovation;
Market (LES) = Local environment score related to market innovation;
Process (LES) = Local environment score related to production process innovation;
Management (LES) = Local environment score related to management performance;
Dum1_NL = Dummy variable related to a location in the Netherlands;
Dum2_IT = Dummy variable related to a location in Italy;
Dum3_UK = Dummy variable related to a location in United Kingdom;
Dum4_Peri = Dummy variable related to a location in a peripheral region;
Dum5_Cent = Dummy variable related to a location in a core region;
Dum6_Iter = Dummy variable related to a location in an intermediate region.

The data on these variables stem from the survey among the firms concerned.

Table 18.7 displays the results of the estimated coefficients for the case of a linear regression model as well as the values of the statistical confidence indicators (*t*-values).

Table 18.7 The results of the linear regression model

Variable[7]	Coefficients	t-Value
(Constant)	98.876	14.519
Product (LES)	6.8E-02	.901
Market (LES)	.159	2.222
Process (LES)	3.8E-03	0.047
Management (LES)	-5.1E-04	-.007
Dum1_NL	-37.702	-4.407
Dum3_UK	-20.773	-3.132
Dum4_Peri	-18.014	-3.506
Dum6_Iter	-3.783	-.785

Next, we have also calculated other statistical indicators in order to allow for a comparison of the results with those stemming from NN experiments. Table 18.8 shows the values of these statistical indicators[8], viz. *ARV*, *MSE*, *MPE* and *MAPE*, for the above linear regression model. However, these results highlight also a possible situation of a 'hybrid solution'. In other words, we cannot confirm, from the value of

[7] The dummies related to Italy and to a central location have been excluded, since they are redundant. It means that they can be expressed as a combination of the others.

[8] The Average Relative Variance (ARV) is defined as: $ARV = \sum (y-\hat{y})^2 / \sum (y-\overline{y})^2$; the Mean Squared Error (MSE) is defined as: $MSE = (1/n)\sum (y-\hat{y})^2$; the Mean Percentage Error (MPE) is defined as: $MPE = (1/n)\sum\left[(\hat{y}-y)/y\right]*100$ and the Mean Absolute Percentage Error (MAPE) is defined as: $MAPE = (1/n)\sum\left[|\hat{y}-y|/y\right]*100$.

where y is the observed/target value, $\hat{y}$ = the predicted value by the adopted model, $\overline{y}$ = the average of the observed/target values and n = the number of the patterns. These indicators imply a good performance of the calibrated model, when their values approach zero.

the statistical indicators expressed in table 18.8, whether the adopted relationship among the LES indicators has a linear or non-linear specification.

Table 18.8 The values of the statistical indicators for the linear regression model

Indicator	ARV	MSE	MPE	MAPE
Calibration set	0.788	769.59	24.49 %	45.03 %
Test set	0.801	694.45	11.93 %	30.26 %
Data set	0.799	614.55	21.96 %	42.05 %

A possible next step in our analysis would be to switch to a non-linear regression by adding, for example, quadratic and cubic terms for the independent variables in the previous regression. The results of the estimation of both these two non-linear models show better results (see tables 18.9 and 18.10, respectively), as they exhibit a clear non-linear pattern among the variables under scrutiny.

Table 18.9 The values of the statistical indicators for a non-linear regression model (quadratic terms for the independent variables)

Indicator	ARV	MSE	MPE	MAPE
Calibration set	0.775	766.34	23.76 %	44.07 %
Test set	**0.798**	**679.49**	**10.79 %**	**29.55 %**
Data set	0.778	611.94	21.14 %	41.15 %

Table 18.10 The values of the statistical indicators for a non-linear regression model (quadratic and cubic terms for the independent variables)

Indicator	ARV	MSE	MPE	MAPE
Calibration set	0.734	736.01	22.14 %	41.93 %
Test set	**0.737**	**672.03**	**11.37 %**	**30.42 %**
Data set	0.733	587.73	19.97 %	39.61%

We notice here that because a linear regression model is a logarithmic expression of a spatial interaction model, the independent variables listed in table 18.7 can also be interpreted as utility or cost functions for the dependent variable. Seen from this perspective, our results suggest that the product innovation and market innovation indicators are more significant than the production process innovation and the management performance of the company. This finding also confirms the outcomes of a previous analysis of these data (see Kangasharju and Nijkamp, 1997).

In order to explore more thoroughly this (non-linear) explanatory relationship, we will also utilize the NN approach, which can in principle incorporate a more 'complex' relationships among our variables. We will describe the results emerging from the NN approach in the next section.

18.6 The Neural Network Approach

18.6.1 Neural Network Results

For the experiments conducted by means of the NN approach, we have concentrated on the most popular class of NN, the two-layer feed-forward totally connected, a back-propagation (BP) algorithm in order to identify the 'optimal' connection of the weights in the learning phase (see, for details, section 18.3.2).

In our application the NN architecture contains ten inputs that correspond to the independent variables (see the previous subsection), one output unit corresponding to the LES indicators related to the commercial success of the company (dependent variable) and nine hidden units[9]. Figure 18.2 shows the structure of the NN model adopted in our application, while table 18.11 displays the results after the learning phase of the NN model.

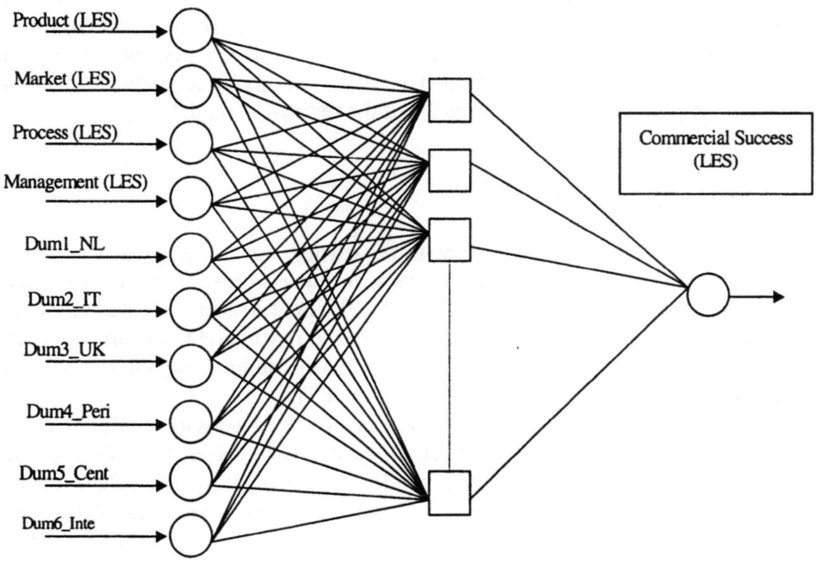

Figure 18.2 The structure of the adopted NN model

Table 18.11 The values of statistical indicators for the Neural Network model

Indicator	ARV	MSE	MPE	MAPE
Calibration set	0.684	685.25	20.41 %	40.33 %
Test set	**0.714**	**656.96**	**4.63 %**	**27.63 %**
Data set	0.689	547.20	17.23 %	37.77 %

[9] The number of hidden units has been defined by a trial and error procedure.

18.6.2 Comparison of Results

The NN results show clearly a better performance of NNs compared to the previous regression models. We will now compare in more detail the NN results with those from linear, quadratic and cubic regression. The results of the test phase through the use of the regression and NN models are illustrated more specifically in table 18.12.

Table 18.12 The results of the test phase for the adopted models

MODEL	ARV	MSE	MPE	MAPE
Linear Regression	0.801	694.45	11.93 %	30.26 %
Quadratic Regression	0.798	679.49	10.79 %	29.55 %
Quadratic + Cubic Regression	0.737	672.03	11.37 %	30.42 %
Neural Network	0.714	656.96	4.63 %	27.63 %

By examining the tables shown above we can infer that for all test statistics NN model performs much better than the three types of regression models. Consequently, we may argue that the NN analysis is able to encapsulate more complex relationships, compared to non-linear quadratic and cubic forms, among the explanatory variables at hand. Clearly, some caution is warranted here, as the statistical indicator values suggest still some potential good performance of the regression models.

18.6.3 Sensitivity Analysis

In this section, a sensitivity analysis will be carried out to analyze the space transferability issue for the firms under analysis. In other words, we will investigate the impact of the geographical allocation (NL, IT, UK) on the success of the individual firms. For this purpose, the linear and cubic regression model and the neural network model will again be utilized by varying the values of the dummy variables related to the country location (Dum1_NL, Dum2_IT and Dum3_UK).

Tables 18.13 and 18.14 illustrate the results of the sensitivity analysis as an average of the results at a micro (firm) level. More precisely, table 18.13 displays the results concerning the regression approach, while table 18.14 shows the values for the NN approach. The micro level results for the NN model are extrapolated and illustrated in Appendix A (see tables A.1-A.3). It should be noted that, given results of the sensitivity analysis, the behavior of the firms is comparable among all three models utilized, although the values emerging from the linear regression seem to be closer to those emerging from the NN model than the results obtained from the cubic regression. It should be note that the NN model offers the possibility of analyzing the behavior of the firm at the micro level (cf. tables A1-A3).

In substantive terms, the information in these tables indicates that the 'Italian attitudinal preference' has apparently a positive impact, when we also include in the Italian analysis the relative position of industries from other countries, as these results show increasing positive values of LES variations. This is a plausible result, because the Italian firms revealed relatively high LES values (see tables 18.4 to 18.6).

Table 18.13 The results of the sensitivity analysis related to the LES variations for the variable 'commercial success' for the regression model[10]

Country	The Netherlands	Italy	United Kingdom
The Netherlands	*****	37.702 (28.125)	16.929 (9.748)
Italy	-37.702 (-28.125)	*****	-20.773 (-18.377)
United Kingdom	-16.929 (-9.748)	20.773 (18.377)	*****

Table 18.14 The results of the sensitivity analysis for the NN model

Country	The Netherlands	Italy	United Kingdom
The Netherlands	*****	49.93	13.71
Italy	-31.97	*****	-20.13
United Kingdom	-16.68	32.87	*****

On the contrary, The Netherlands demonstrates a negative variation of the LES values, in the 'hypothetical case' the Dutch/English industries would virtually 'move' to Holland. It should be noted that the UK 'behaves' in a way similar to the Netherlands. We may thus conclude this part by emphasizing that the emerging behavioral pattern for the industries analyzed might also offer new insights into the plausible allocation of 'new' industries.

18.7 Summary and Conclusions

The primary objective of this study was to analyze the self-organizing mechanism of industrial innovation processes in the light of the 'new' economic and information society. Based on European data obtained from the 'URBINNO' project, our approach has followed two related sub-objectives: (1) to depict trends and dynamics of the innovation process at hand (time transferability) and (2) to draw lessons from the spatial 'forecasting' of innovative industries (space transferability). For the above purposes this study has developed a new modeling framework consisting of the joint use of a (non)linear regression model and a neural network approach. The estimation results provide a solid argument in favor of the use of the NN model; however, both the regression and NN approach do not yet provide a sufficiently strong enough basis for choosing either model structure.

Further research should be undertaken to offer a proper methodological and practical interpretation of the available data. Within this context one research direction is surely oriented towards a further exploration of neurocomputing approaches (e.g., by investigating and employing the genetic algorithm tool in conjunction with the NN approach). Another research direction could be the use of a probit model (instead of a regression analysis), as this model is able to overcome the limitations caused by the IIA assumption.

[10] The values in parentheses denote the results for the cubic regression.

References

Amin A., and N.J. Thrift. eds. 1994. *Globalization, Distributions and Regional Development in Europe*. Oxford, Oxford University Press.

Bertuglia, C.S., S. Lombardo and P. Nijkamp. eds. 1997. *Innovative Behavior in Space and Time*. Heidelberg, Springer-Verlag.

Bertuglia, C.S., G. Bianchi and A. Mela. eds. 1998. *The City and its Sciences*. Heidelberg, Springer-Verlag.

Fischer M.M. and S. Gopal. 1994 "Artificial Neural Networks: a New Approach to Modeling Interregional Telecommunications Flows." *Journal of Regional Science*, 34, 503-527.

Geenhuizen M.S. van, and P. Nijkamp. 1999 "The Learning Capability of Regions: Patterns and Policies." *Research Memorandum*, Dept. of Economics, Free University, Amsterdam.

Damman M. 1994. *Individual and Spatial Success Factors of Innovative Firms*, Unpublished M.A. Thesis, Department of Economics, Free University, Amsterdam.

Davalo E. and P. Naim. 1991. *Neural Networks*, London, Macmillan Education Ltd.

Davelaar E.J. 1991. *Regional Economic Analysis of Innovation and Incubation*. Aldershot, Avebury.

Himanen V., P. Nijkamp and A. Reggiani. Eds. 1998. *Neural Networks in Transport Application*. Aldershot, Ashgate.

Kangasharju A. and P. Nijkamp. 1997. "Innovation Dynamics in Space." *Discussion Paper* TI 97-062/3, Tinbergen Institute, Amsterdam, 1997.

Kleinknecht A. 1988. *Innovation Patterns in Crisis and Prosperity*. London, MacMillan.

Koppelman F. and E.I. Pas. 1986. "Multidimensional Choice Model Transferability." *Transport Research B*, 20, 321-330.

Morgan K. 1997. "The Learning Regions." *Regional Studies*, 31, 491-503.

Nijkamp P. and A. Kangasharju. 1998. "Innovation Dynamics in Space: Local Actors and Local Factors." *Research Memorandum*, Dept. of Economics, University, Amsterdam, 1998.

Nijkamp P. and A. Reggiani. 1992. *Interaction, Evolution and Chaos in Space*. Heidelberg, Springer-Verlag.

Nijkamp P. and A. Reggiani. 1998. *The Economics of Complex Spatial Systems*. Amsterdam, Elsevier.

Nijkamp P., M. Damman and M. Van Geenhuizen. 1997. "Innovative Behavior in European Cities: the Relevance of Knowledge Networks." *Applied Geographic Studies*, 1, 13-30.

McFadden D. 1974. "Conditional Logit Analysis of Qualitative Choice Behavior." In P. Zarembka, ed. *Frontiers in Econometrics*. New York, Academic Press.105-142.

Reggiani A., P. Nijkamp and E. Sabella. 1998. "Evolutionary Algorithms for Modeling Interregional Transport Flows." *Discussion Paper* TI 98-077/3, Tinbergen Institute, Amsterdam.

Reggiani A., P. Nijkamp and E. Sabella, 2000. "A Comparative Analysis of the Performance of Evolutionary Algorithms and Logit Models in Spatial networks." In A. Reggiani, ed. *Spatial Economic Science*. Berlin, Springer-Verlag.

Reggiani A., P. Nijkamp and E. Sabella. 2001. "New Advances in Spatial Network Modeling: Towards Evolutionary Algorithms." *European Journal of Operational Research*, 128, 385-401.

Simmie J. ed. 1997. *Innovation Networks and Learning Regions*. Jessica Kingsley, London.

Sonis M. 1992. "Innovation Diffusion and Schumpeterian Competition." *Journal of Scientific and Industrial Research*, 51, 172-186.

Storper M. 1996. "Innovation as Collective Action." *Industrial and Corporate Change*, 5, 761-790.

Valdes R. 1991. "What Is BioComputing?" *Dr. Dobb's Journal*, 46, 108-109.

Appendix 18.A

In this Appendix an extrapolation of the results concerning the sensitivity analysis illustrated in section 18.6.3 is displayed (see tables 18.A.1-A.3). In particular, the variable *Old Output* refers to the local environment score (LES) related to the commercial success (by the firm) predicted by the NN model, while the variables *New1* and *New2* indicate the results - for the NN model - of the sensitivity analysis in order to study the 'transferability factor'. In more detail, the variable *New1* (see table A.1) indicates the output (Business (LES)) of the NN after the 'virtual movement' of the Dutch firms in Italy.

Table 18.A.1 The results of the sensitivity analysis - for the NN model - for Dutch firms (micro level)

Dutch firms Firm code	Old Output	New1 NL → IT	New2 NL → UK	New1-Old	New2-Old
1	67.48	132.40	76.60	64.92	9.12
2	67.89	130.33	76.28	62.44	8.39
3	80.66	132.14	76.91	51.47	-3.75
4	70.58	138.61	80.61	68.03	10.02
5	69.76	95.60	82.81	25.83	13.04
6	61.12	140.88	76.49	79.76	15.38
7	80.07	127.18	78.69	47.10	-1.37
8	88.22	134.61	85.64	46.38	-2.58
9	47.38	90.24	74.97	42.85	27.58
30	65.48	99.87	75.66	34.38	10.18
31	51.33	91.92	75.84	40.58	24.50
32	75.42	96.43	84.98	21.01	9.56
33	69.22	96.63	84.09	27.40	14.87
Average				49.93	13.71

Note: These tables are only an extrapolation of the 273 firms, viz. 33 (Dutch), 32 (Italian) and 208 (English) firms. For the sake of space not all the 273 results are presented. The dots indicate that the tables are not complete*.

Table 18.A.2 The results of the sensitivity analysis - for the NN model - for Italian firms (micro level)

Italian firms Firm code	Old Output	New1 IT → NL	New2 IT → UK	New1-Old	New2-Old
34	96.78	107.80	96.37	11.02	-0.41
35	100.22	79.82	84.11	-20.40	-16.11
36	130.85	89.34	65.48	-41.51	-65.37
37	115.88	112.71	97.78	-3.17	-18.09
38	132.47	82.47	95.08	-50.01	-37.39
39	108.33	108.66	96.55	0.32	-11.78
40	105.98	110.99	98.67	5.01	-7.31
41	149.40	124.68	94.11	-24.71	-55.29
42	111.84	100.42	101.86	-11.41	-9.97
62	85.17	26.31	70.03	-58.85	-15.13
63	123.01	40.40	85.83	-82.60	-37.18
64	83.38	25.33	67.44	-58.05	-15.94
65	87.62	28.95	69.80	-58.67	-17.82
Average				-31.97	-20.13

* The full details are available from the authors.

Table 18.A.3 The results of the sensitivity analysis - for the NN model - for English firms (micro level)

English firms	Old	New1	New2	New1-Old	New2-Old
Firm Code	Output	UK → NL	UK → IT		
66	72.20	38.97	87.35	-33.20	15.15
67	72.60	43.90	88.94	-28.70	16.34
68	72.04	42.56	88.09	-29.42	16.04
69	72.20	38.99	87.35	-33.21	15.15
70	72.20	38.99	87.35	-33.21	15.15
71	91.91	81.63	103.65	-10.28	11.74
72	72.20	38.99	87.35	-33.21	15.15
73	72.20	38.99	87.35	-33.21	15.15
74	72.20	38.99	87.35	-33.21	15.15
270	59.53	18.32	71.37	-41.21	11.84
271	47.85	13.88	64.35	-33.97	16.50
272	84.08	72.78	121.89	-11.30	37.81
273	81.13	64.50	98.60	-16.63	17.46
Average				-16.6768	32.87

19 Vertical Specialization and Interregional Trade: Hierarchy of Spatial Production Cycles and Feedback Loop Analysis in the Midwest Economy*

Michael Sonis,[1] Geoffrey J. D. Hewings,[2] and Yasuhide Okuyama[3]

[1] Regional Economics Applications Laboratory, University of Illinois, USA and Bar Ilan University, Israel
e-mail: sonism@mail.biu.ac.il
[2] Regional Economics Applications Laboratory, University of Illinois, USA
e-mail: hewings@uiuc.edu
[3] Department of Planning, State University of New York at Buffalo
e-mail: yokuyama@ap.buffalo.edu

19.1 Introduction

The renewed interest in international trade has drawn attention to the phenomenon of vertical specialization, the use of imported inputs for producing goods that are exported (see Bruelhart and Hine, 1999). Balassa (1967, p.97) coined the term, vertical specialization; in a recent paper, Hummels *et al*, (1998) introduced and discussed the following definition of vertical specialization:

> (1) a good must be produced in multiple sequential stages, (2) two or more countries must specialize in producing some, but not all, stages, and (3) at least one stage must cross an international border more then once... Thus, countries link sequentially to produce a final good.

This definition speaks to the role of sequential production or spatial production cycles and bears an important relationship with the notion of an hierarchy of feedback loops of inter-industry flows elaborated in a series of papers by Sonis and Hewings (1993, 1995a,b; 1997). The further elaboration and visualization of this approach, which is a purpose of this chapter, may be shown to be connected with an analogy between the behavior of flows of goods and hydrodynamic turbulence (*cf.* Ghasghale *et al.,* 1996). A flow of energy from large to small scales is one of the main characteristics of fully developed homogeneous isotropic turbulence in three-dimensional space. Energy is pumping into the system at large scales, transferred to smaller scales through a hierarchy of eddies of decreasing sizes, and dissipates at the smallest scale. (This cascade of kinetic energy generates the scaling behavior of eddies; see Richardson, 1922). The turbulence analogy is provided through the way in which large, aggregate interregional feedback loops (spatial production cycles) of intermediate input flows are decomposed into feedback loops between economic

* An earlier, abbreviated version of this chapter appeared as Sonis *et al.*, 2000.

activities (such as resources, manufacturing and services) and then further decomposed into the loops of flows on the scale of individual industries (interindustry production cycles). Moreover, the scaling of eddies, analogous to the hierarchy of economic subsystems, is presented with the help of so-called "Matrioshka" principle (see Sonis and Hewings, 1990). Thus, the ideas rank-size hierarchy of spatial production cycles (hierarchical feedback loop analysis) can be used for structural economic analysis.

19.2 Interregional Trade: Expectations and Structure

The new trade theory associated with Krugman (1990) and others has turned attention to factors other than endowments as a source of explanation for trade. To be sure, initial factor endowments will still allow for specialization to occur with cost advantages leading to a cumulative process of product differentiation. However, at the interregional level, this process could occur simultaneously in two or more regions, leading to the exploitation of increasing returns and thus to increasing trade between regions. However, this trade will be more heavily concentrated in intraindustry trade for many of the reasons provided by Krugman. It so happens these are reasons that find their fullest expression in the state economies of the Midwest of the US. For example, if the economies in question are large, of similar size and with few differences in factor endowments then something other than comparative advantage has to be proposed to explain trade. Per capita income is high - thus providing opportunities for product differentiation to serve the demand for higher quality products and a greater variety of products. Scale economies exist and capital/labor ratios and high and similar (no comparative advantage here); however, it is the lower transportation costs, the region-wide agglomeration effects, the effectiveness and ease of information flows that all combine to facilitate intraindustry specialization. At the level of trade between regions that is focused on intermediate goods and services, it is unlikely that much of the apparent cross-hauling can be explained by product differentiation. The development of niche products and markets probably accounts for the vast majority of this intraindustry trade.

Complementary evidence for this process may be found in Martins (1993) and Hewings *et al.* (1998). In the former analysis, it was observed that establishments at the regional level produced a smaller array of secondary products than similar establishments drawn from throughout the nation. In the latter analysis, it was found that average purchases of locally-sourced inputs declined over the period 1970-1990 in the Chicago region while production did not decline. Taken together, one might infer that the average establishment is focusing production on a narrow range of products and purchasing more of the inputs needed for this production from outside the region. The greater variety of products sought by consumers is being realized in production processes that are extended over many establishments that may be located in different regions; intermediate inputs formerly sourced locally are now imported and a smaller variety of products is being produced at any given establishment. Taken together, the demand for trade has increased.

The next issue addresses methods for analyzing the spatial structure of this trade. The analysis of the hierarchy of spatial production cycles (feedback loop analysis) is employed since it lends itself readily to the identification of the spatial geographic structure of these flows. Furthermore, a spatial hierarchy of trade flows can be extracted from the flow data, providing additional insights into the nature and strengths of interregional connectivities. In addition, feedback loop analysis operates at a level that is more detailed than traditional macro analysis yet does not provide the potential myriad paths of interaction that can be extracted from structural path analysis (see Defourny and Thorbecke, 1984). It does, however, share the property that each path in a structural path is part of a global feedback loop that includes the transactions between all sectors (see Sonis *et al*, 1997).

In the next section, a brief introduction to feedback loop analysis is provided; further details may be found in Sonis *et al.*, (1993, 1995a, 1995b, 1997).

19.3 The Spatial Production Cycles Analysis as a Multiregional Feedback Loop Approach

19.3.1 Closed Feedback Loops and Block-Permutation Matrices

Consider a multi-regional, multi-countries, inter-industry system described with the help of a square block-matrix, F, of interregional inputs of the following form:

$$F = \begin{pmatrix} F_{11} & F_{12} & \cdots & F_{1n} \\ F_{21} & F_{22} & \cdots & F_{2n} \\ \vdots & \vdots & \ddots & \vdots \\ F_{n1} & F_{n2} & \cdots & F_{nn} \end{pmatrix} \tag{19.1}$$

It is assumed that there are n regions in which there exist m divisions of the economy, organized into activities and there is the subdivision of activities in the different sub-categories. The central point of the feedback loops decomposition analysis is the use of spatial /functional feedback loops represented by block-permutation matrices. By definition, a block-permutation matrix includes in each block-row and block-column only one non-zero block.

In the two-region case:

$$F = \begin{pmatrix} F_{11} & F_{12} \\ F_{21} & F_{22} \end{pmatrix} \tag{19.2}$$

there are only two block-permutation sub-matrices:

$$F_1 = \begin{pmatrix} F_{11} & 0 \\ 0 & F_{22} \end{pmatrix}, \quad F_2 = \begin{pmatrix} 0 & F_{12} \\ F_{21} & 0 \end{pmatrix} \tag{19.3}$$

and

$$F = F_1 + F_2 \tag{19.4}$$

The matrix $F_1 = \begin{pmatrix} F_{11} & 0 \\ 0 & F_{22} \end{pmatrix}$ represents the circulation of intermediate goods in the same geographical region, and the matrix $F_2 = \begin{pmatrix} 0 & F_{12} \\ F_{21} & 0 \end{pmatrix}$ represents the spatial production cycle mirroring the bilateral connections between the two regions.

Within a three-region system:

$$F = \begin{pmatrix} F_{11} & F_{12} & F_{13} \\ F_{21} & F_{22} & F_{23} \\ F_{31} & F_{32} & F_{33} \end{pmatrix} \tag{19.5}$$

there are six block-permutation sub-matrices:

$$F_1 = \begin{pmatrix} F_{11} & 0 & 0 \\ 0 & F_{22} & 0 \\ 0 & 0 & F_{33} \end{pmatrix} \quad F_2 = \begin{pmatrix} 0 & 0 & F_{13} \\ F_{21} & 0 & 0 \\ 0 & F_{32} & 0 \end{pmatrix} \quad F_3 = \begin{pmatrix} 0 & F_{12} & 0 \\ 0 & 0 & F_{23} \\ F_{31} & 0 & 0 \end{pmatrix} \tag{19.6}$$

$$F_4 = \begin{pmatrix} F_{11} & 0 & 0 \\ 0 & 0 & F_{13} \\ 0 & F_{32} & 0 \end{pmatrix} \quad F_5 = \begin{pmatrix} 0 & F_{12} & 0 \\ F_{21} & 0 & 0 \\ 0 & 0 & F_{33} \end{pmatrix} \quad F_6 = \begin{pmatrix} 0 & 0 & F_{13} \\ 0 & F_{22} & 0 \\ F_{31} & 0 & 0 \end{pmatrix} \tag{19.7}$$

and

$$F = F_1 + F_2 + F_3 = F_4 + F_5 + F_6 \tag{19.8}$$

Here, the block-permutation matrices F_2, F_3, F_4, F_5 represent the different spatial production cycles reflecting the three-lateral trade connections between three regions, the block-diagonal matrix F_1 represent the "circulation" of intermediate flows within the same region and the block-permutation F_6 represents the spatial production cycle reflecting the bilateral trade between first and third regions and the "circulation" within the second region.

In the case of *n* regions, there exists *n!* different block-permutation matrices and it is possible to prove that the number of possible additive decompositions of the type (19.8) is equal to *(n-1)!(n-2)!...2!*. Thus, the problem focuses on the appropriate choices from this very large set of possible decompositions, namely, the decompositions with the sound spatial economic meaning. This problem can be solved through the adoption of a hierarchical stepwise approach; the procedure operates at successive levels in the system, but the approach at each stage is similar. This top-down decomposition may be considered analogously to an exfoliation process in the removal of the layers of an onion or, using the turbulence analogy to the construction of an hierarchy of feedback loops (whirlpools) ordered with the help of aggregated cumulative flows within the blocks belonging to the loop. The feedback loops on the inner hierarchical level of economic activities should be placed into the loops of the higher levels in the same manner as a set of *Matrioshka* dolls in which successively smaller dolls of exactly the same shape and style are nested within the larger dolls. Hence, the Matrioshka approach examines the intra- and inter-regional transactions in terms of the hierarchical structure of feedback effects drawing upon the superposition principle conceptual framework (see Sonis, 1982). The superposition principle considers the economic system as a decentralized system that is comprised of a set of subsystems acting according to different and often conflicting and non-commensurable objectives. These objectives may be presented in the form of extreme tendencies or trends; the hierarchical viewpoint enables the analyst to extract the tendencies from the most to the least important. In this fashion, the procedure is not unlike that used in principal component analysis. A brief summary of the methodology for extracting the system of closed feedback loops may be found in Sonis *et al.*, (1997).

One natural method for dealing with such a large amount of complete feedback loops is of course the derivation of some hierarchical structure. Essentially, the hierarchical feedback loop approach attempts to extract complete feedback loops that successively account for the most "explanation" in each stage of the selection process. The procedure continues until all transaction flows have been included. It is important to note that each block matrix F of the type (19.1) can be replaced by the numerical matrix T_F whose components are the sum of all economic flows in the corresponding block - the aggregated block-flows. Such a sub-matrix T_F represents a complete feedback loop if it includes in each row and in each column only one non-zero entry from the matrix F and zeros elsewhere. One can define the *flow intensity* of a complete feedback loop (the *flow intensity* of a spatial production cycle) as the sum of all flows of the corresponding sub-matrix T_F.

If all non-zero entries of T_F are replaced by ones, the result is a so-called *permutation matrix* P_F. This zero-one matrix corresponds to some permutation of the sequence of numbers $1,2,\ldots,n$. Such a permutation (of regions) represents the spatial structure of the corresponding complete feedback loop. The corresponding sub-matrices T_F are referred to as *quasi-permutation matrices.*

It is important to note that for each permutation matrix P_F there is an integer k such that P_F^k is the unit matrix I. For that k, the corresponding quasi-permutation matrix T_F has the property that T_F^k is a diagonal matrix, implying that the corresponding feedback loop indeed represents the notion of *self-influence.*

The hierarchy of all complete feedback loops is defined as the sequence of quasi-permutation sub-matrices T_F chosen according to the rank-size of their flow intensities. This means that on the top of the hierarchy, one finds the complete feedback loop with the maximal flow intensity.

The problem of the determination of the quasi-permutation sub-matrix with the maximal flow intensity is mathematically equivalent to the solution of the optimal personnel assignment of n persons (here rows) between n jobs (here columns) in such a way that one person will have one job while profit is maximized (see Dantzig, 1963). Here profit is defined by the size of the flows in matrix T. The procedure is summarized in Sonis *et al.*, (1997).

19.3.2 Matrioshka Principle for the Description of the Nested Hierarchy of Spatial Production Cycles

It is necessary and possible to combine the interregional and interactivity interdependencies. To this aim, the aggregated table needs to be replaced by the detailed table describing the interplay between the interactivity and international interdependencies. Further, it is important to stress that the flexible form of the spatio-economic feedback loop analysis employed in this analysis allows an easy extension to the spatio-sectional level. In such an extension, the analysis will relate to activities per region. Thus, the hierarchy of the feedback loops will reflect the interactivity interdependencies intertwined spatially, enabling one to distinguish the spatial extent of multi-regional industrial complexes.

Consider, as an example, the three-region/two-activity table of the following form:

$F =$ 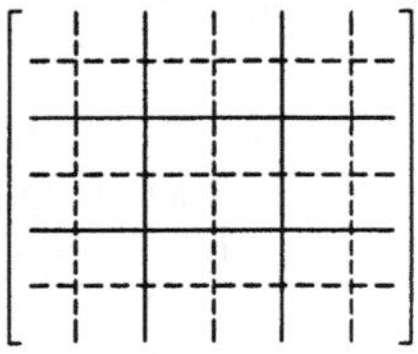

At the regional spatial scale (i.e., where interest is merely focused on the aggregate flows rather than the interactivity flows), the following hierarchical feedback loop structure can be identified:

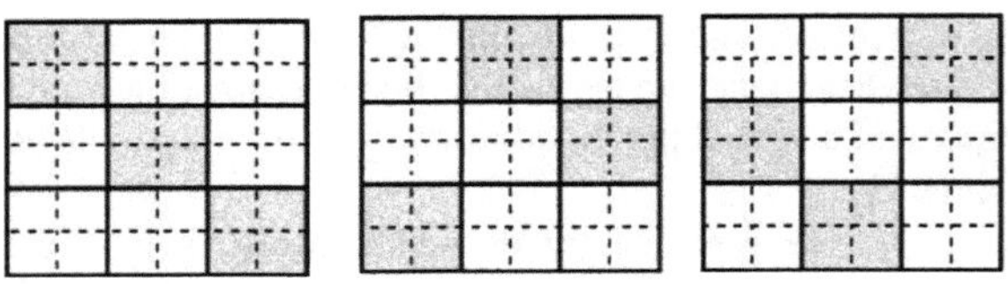

At the activity level, the simple decomposition holds:

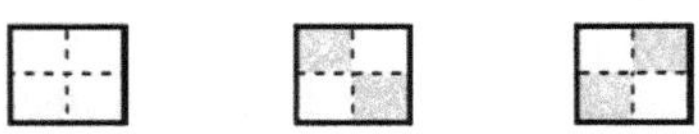

Therefore, the following nested hierarchical decomposition satisfies the rules of the Matrioshka principle:

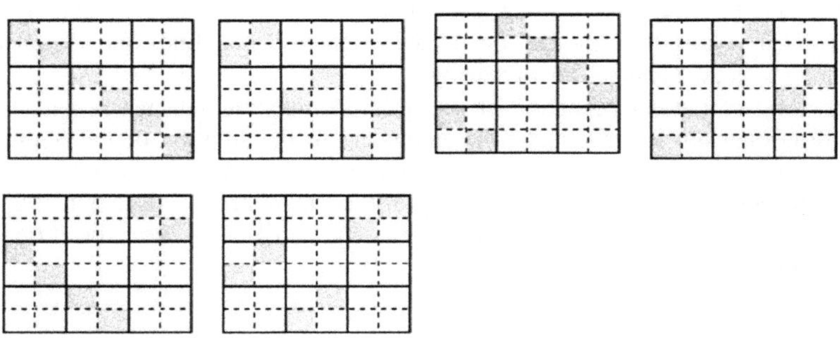

A similar structure of nested feedback loop hierarchies could be extracted for the general case of an n-region/m-activities input-output system. Of course, the Matrioshka principle is applicable to the disaggregation of regions into sub-regions and further successive spatial and activities disaggregation.

19.4 The Midwest Interregional Flows, 1992

The methodology used to estimate the interstate trade flows is described more formally in Hewings *et al.* (1997). Essentially, several sets of data were used; first, for each of the five Midwest states, an input-output table was constructed primarily from the establishment-level data base at the US Bureau of the Census. From this calculation process, estimates were made of vectors of regional imports and exports at the 53-sector level of aggregation (approximately all two-digit SIC). An input-output table was also constructed for the Rest of the US by subtraction of the aggregated Midwest transactions from the US national table. International exports and imports were subtracted using state and MISER estimates. What remained were vectors of interstate inflows and outflows but without any specificity as to their geography. The Commodity Flow Statistics (CFS) were used for sectors 1 through 26, except sectors 4 and 11 (see table A1 in the appendix for a description of the sectors). Information was provided for flows for sector specific origins in one state to destination state (but without sector specificity); assumptions underlying the allocation to sector within destination state relied on the column coefficient model (see Polenske, 1970a, 1970b), namely that the use of imports from another state was proportional to the inflow from that state in comparison to all inflows.

For the remaining sectors, a gravity model was employed with the distances adjusted so that the resulting flows were consistent with the import/export vector for each state. Some further adjustments were made to handle inconsistencies and to ensure that the system of flows was balanced. Note that the flows that are the focus of this chapter represent interindustry transactions and exclude flows to final demand sectors.

19.5 Hierarchical Spatial Production Cycles Analysis of Midwest Interregional Trade Flows, 1992

The analysis was conducted at three levels – at an aggregated level in which all sectors were collapsed into one; at the level of three sectors – primary, secondary and tertiary and finally, at a six-sector level into which the previous three sectors were each divided into two.

Table 19.1 Midwest Interregional Flows (1992 million US dollars)

	Illinois	Indiana	Michigan	Ohio	Wisconsin	RUS
Illinois	154,926	5,042	7,262	3,550	8,828	111,398
Indiana	5,798	61,858	9,220	5,271	2,240	44,317
Michigan	6,190	5,910	104,122	11,158	4,520	90,265
Ohio	3,746	4,647	20,334	139,912	2,172	77,815
Wisconsin	13,688	2,768	9,492	3,819	30,951	90,257
RUS	76,202	34,994	83,228	60,998	69,836	2,581,622

Note: RUS refers to the Rest of the US

19.5.1 Interregional Level of Spatial Production Cycles Analysis.

Table 19.1 shows the geographical division of the trade between the Midwest States in 1992. From this table, it is easy to calculate that the global intensity of trade in the Midwest in 1992 reached $3.9 trillion, while the interregional trade was $894.9 million, which is 22.2% of all US trade. 85.5% of Midwest interregional trade includes export and import with the Rest of US; the remaining 15% that flows among the Midwest states amounts to $135 billion.[1] Without a detailed analysis of this table, it would be difficult to identify and interpret the dominant interregional and inter-activities linkages. This is accomplished in the following tables. On the most aggregated regional level of analysis, there is the decomposition of the Midwest trade flows into five feedback loops hierarchically ordered according to the intensity (sum of flows) of trade through this loop. Table 19.2 presents the two largest feedback loops connecting all the states of Midwest and the Rest of US. The larger of the two includes 25.9% of all interregional trade and has the following spatial structure:

(Rest of US, Michigan, Ohio, Indiana, Wisconsin, Illinois)

This loop includes the largest export flow, from Illinois to the Rest of US, and the largest import flow, from the Rest of US to Michigan. The second of these two feedback loops accounts for 23.3% of all interregional trade and has this structure:

(Rest of US, Illinois, Wisconsin, Indiana, Ohio, Michigan).

This feedback loop includes the largest inner Midwest trade flow, from Ohio to Michigan. It is important to note that the spatial structure of these two loops is topologically identical; they differ only in the direction of flows. This means that the Midwest economy is well developed and bilaterally balanced: to each flow, there corresponds the equivalent counter-flow.

Table 19.2 Two Largest Spatial Production Cycles

	Illinois	Indiana	Michigan	Ohio	Wisconsin	RUS
Illinois					2	1
Indiana				2	1	
Michigan				1		2
Ohio		1	2			
Wisconsin	1	2				
RUS	2		1			

1 First Production Cycle: (RUS, Michigan, Ohio, Indiana, Wisconsin, Illinois) 25.9%

2 Second Production Cycle: (RUS, Illinois, Wisconsin, Indiana, Ohio, Michigan) 23.3%

Note: RUS refers to the Rest of the US

These two feedback loops together account for 49.2% of all Midwest interregional trade. They characterize the multilateral trade connections between all Midwest states.

[1] If flows to final demand accounts were included, the total Midwest interstate flow would be of the order of $350-400 billion, of which $262 billion represented physical commodities

Some further amplification can be provided; the two previously defined multilateral feedback loops together can be presented with the help of another pair of feedback loops including only bilateral trade connections. Table 19.3 presents the spatial structure of these loops and their intensity. This decomposition of multilateral connections into sets of bilateral flows may help reveal the structure of the process whereby shifts occur from bilateral to multilateral trade connections; however, with only one observation, little can be ventured about the structural changes in the flows over the past several decades.

Table 19.3 Largest Bilateral Trade Connections

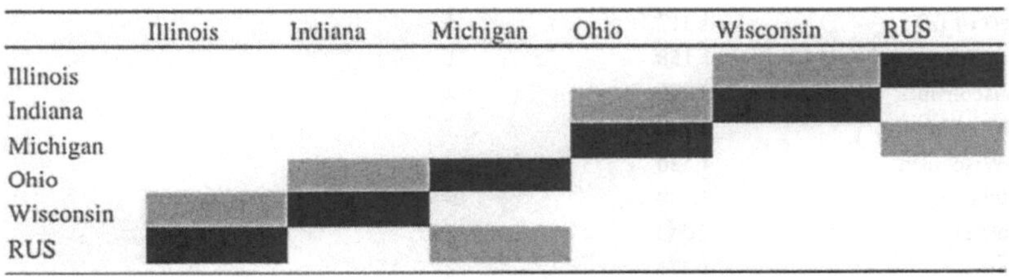

Table 19.4 Interregional Production Cycles of Midwest Trade Flows

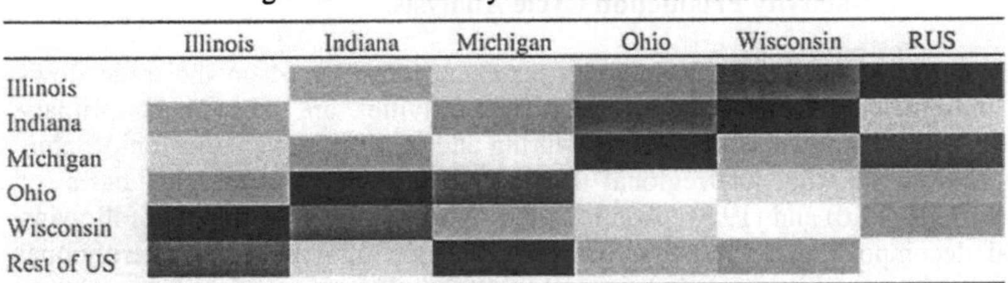

	First Production Cycle: (Rest US, Michigan, Ohio, Indiana, Wisconsin, Illinois)	25.9%
	Second Production Cycle: (Rest US, Illinois, Wisconsin, Indiana, Ohio, Michigan)	23.3%
	Third Production Cycle: (Rest of US, Wisconsin)(Ohio, Illinois)(Michigan, Indiana)	20.9%
	Fourth Production Cycle: (Rest of US, Ohio)(Michigan, Wisconsin)(Indiana, Illinois)	18.7%
	Fifth Production Cycle: (Rest of US, Indiana)(Michigan, Illinois)(Wisconsin, Ohio)	11.3%

Further analysis reveals three more feedback loops with the bilateral spatial structure (see table 19.4). Thus, five feedback loops taken together describe the turbulent picture of the interregional Midwest trade. It is important to note that the hierarchy of feedback loops is defined (see table 19.5) by the intensity of bilateral connection with the Rest of US and, after that, by the intensity of bilateral connections between individual Midwest states. Note that, on interindustry account, each state has a positive trade balance with the Rest of the US, with Illinois' positive balance being the largest in absolute terms.

Table 19.5 Rank-Size* Hierarchy of Bilateral Connections

Bilateral Connections	Aggregated Flows	*Feedback Loop Number*
Illinois-Rest of US	111,398	1
Michigan-Rest of US	90,265	2
Wisconsin-Rest of US	90,257	3
Ohio-Rest of US	77,815	4
Indiana-Rest of US	44,317	5
Michigan-Ohio	11,158	1
Illlinois-Wisconsin	8,828	2
Indiana-Michigan	9,220	3
Michigan-Wisconsin	4,520	4
Illinois-Michigan	7,262	5
Illinois-Indiana	5,042	4
Indiana-Ohio	5,271	2
Illlinois-Ohio	3,550	3
Ohio-Wisconsin	2,182	5
Indiana-Wisconsin	2,240	1

Note: Flows are ranked according to their magnitude within each loop

19.5.2 Inter-activity Production Cycle Analysis.

The analysis of interregional inter-activity feedback loops based on the trade flows data is presented in table 19.6. Here, three activities are considered: primary (agriculture, forestry and fishing), manufacturing and services. The inclusion of inter-activity loops into the interregional loop can be achieved on the basis of decompositions (19.6) and (19.8). Adopting the "Matrioshka" principle, the following structural decomposition of the first interregional loop into the inner interregional inter-activity loops can be revealed (see table 19.7). The meaning and the relative intensity of these three production loops are presented in table 19.8.

It is important to stress that *each* inter-regional loop can be decomposed into three inter-activity loops in which the most intensive loop has a block-diagonal form presenting the main tendency of the inter-regional trade to concentrate within the same activity (i.e., intra-industry trade dominates over interindustry trade) This tendency also underlines the "hollowing out" process occurring within the Midwest economy (*cf.* Hewings *et al.*, 1998) and further reinforces the propositions of the new trade theory that suggests that intraindustry trade will be a feature of economies that share similar characteristics. Clearly, greater levels of disaggregation would need to be adopted to examine the structure of flows; in the next sub-section, a further, initial disaggregation is explored.

Table 19.6 Midwest Interregional Inter/Intra Activities Flows (1992 million US dollars)

		Illinois			Indiana			Michigan			Ohio			Wisconsin			Rest of US		
		P	M	S	P	M	S	P	M	S	P	M	S	P	M	S	P	M	S
Illinois	Primary	1,500	3,945	3,664	147	339	346	1	14	27	23	61	21	26	44	203	1,375	3,846	10,306
	Manufacturing	5,633	30,665	11,621	179	1,745	895	331	4,260	1,309	225	1,980	829	308	3,146	885	3,066	12,240	6,456
	Services	6,348	22,761	68,789	73	1,002	315	97	784	439	33	220	158	305	2,359	1,552	10,381	25,690	38,038
Indiana	Primary	76	409	131	670	987	1,717	34	115	33	63	170	68	0	1	6	574	1,467	3,157
	Manufacturing	501	3,494	612	3,394	24,555	4,584	427	6,845	1,285	301	2,855	880	131	1,503	268	2,210	10,090	4,127
	Services	66	339	170	2,303	9,836	13,812	35	252	195	85	524	325	22	123	185	3,571	7,401	11,719
Michigan	Primary	51	371	104	66	246	63	373	1,474	1,658	194	534	159	4	7	26	645	1,438	5,028
	Manufacturing	336	3,037	1,648	254	3,084	1,605	2,933	40,224	6,998	496	6,415	3,042	205	2,955	864	2,310	21,755	16,615
	Services	69	371	203	31	424	137	3,178	16,416	30,870	30	130	158	28	201	230	6,979	14,116	21,378
Ohio	Primary	18	135	36	57	231	69	90	305	86	935	2,487	3,550	3	13	3	894	2,401	3,390
	Manufacturing	365	1,997	907	203	2,434	1,113	561	13,675	2,826	3,976	55,013	8,336	117	1,314	403	3,337	16,631	10,283
	Services	29	141	117	33	270	237	250	1,880	661	4,265	24,131	37,219	18	89	211	6,079	9,921	24,880
Wisconsin	Primary	364	1,508	82	0	1	3	0	1	1	14	34	2	471	1,594	1,234	218	502	706
	Manufacturing	1,224	5,509	2,522	175	1,624	778	663	6,479	2,176	275	2,326	1,096	972	12,132	2,317	5,002	19,233	9,985
	Services	265	1,137	1,076	9	118	59	14	80	76	6	30	37	911	4,908	6,412	6,984	15,088	32,539
Rest of US	Primary	1,026	3,611	4,963	359	954	2,238	890	4,671	5,205	749	1,848	4,326	495	1,776	3,419	77,356	161,916	98,250
	Manufacturing	1,718	5,611	2,327	505	3,616	1,216	1,298	13,455	3,317	1,133	7,320	2,570	719	4,906	1,239	109,206	435,366	216,561
	Services	6,757	22,014	28,174	1,470	12,215	12,423	4,940	18,034	31,419	3,641	13,420	25,992	4,795	22,624	29,862	140,536	262,268	1,080,160

Table 19.7 Three Interregional/Interactivities Production Loops within the First Interregional Feedback Loop

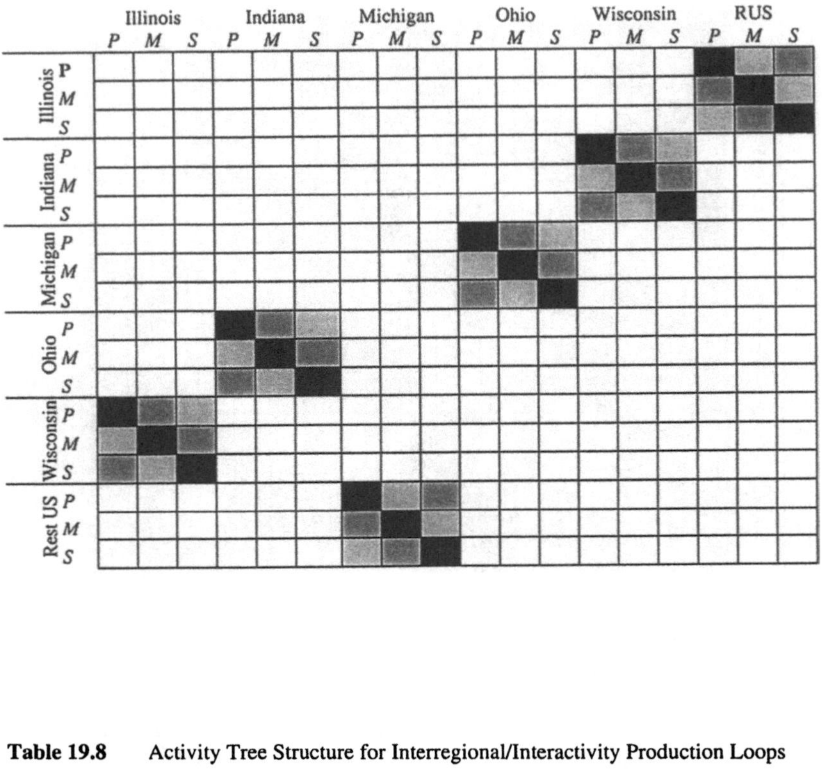

Table 19.8 Activity Tree Structure for Interregional/Interactivity Production Loops

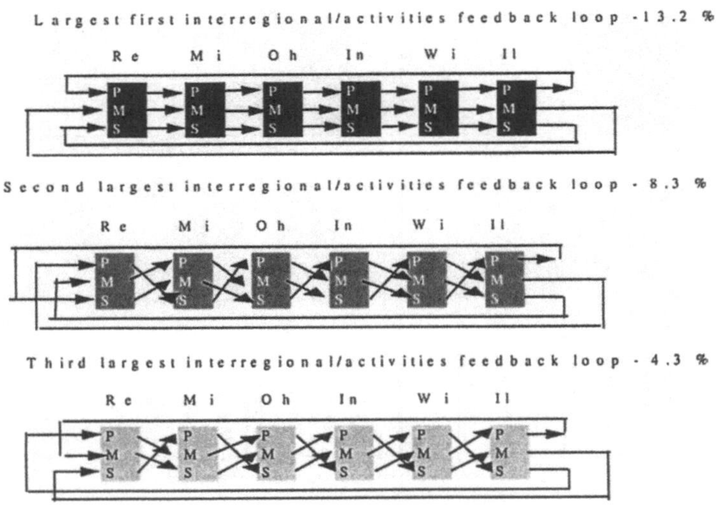

Table 19.9 Two Interregional /Inter-subactivities Production Loops within the First Interregional Loop

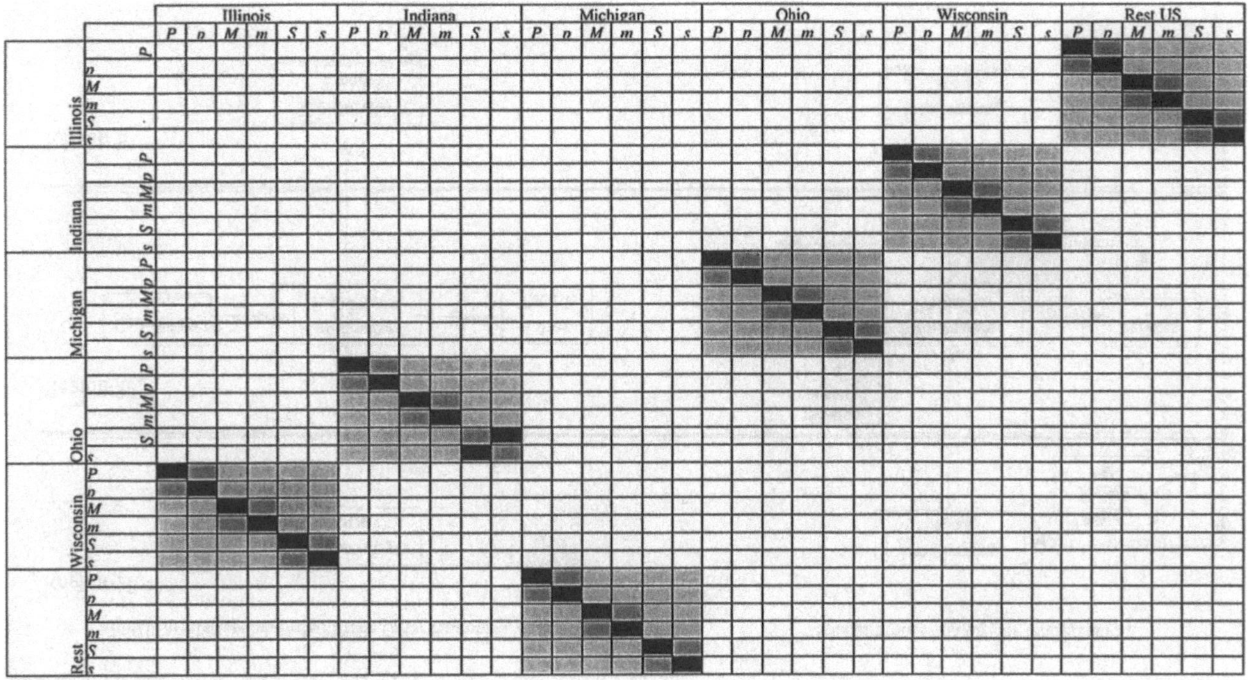

First Interregional inter sub-activities production cycle - 9.8%

Second Interregional inter sub-activities production cycle - 3.4%

Table 19.10 Vertical Trade: Two Interpretations

Vertical-Specialization-Based Trade (after Hummels, *et al.*, 1998)

Spatial Production Cycles Interpretation

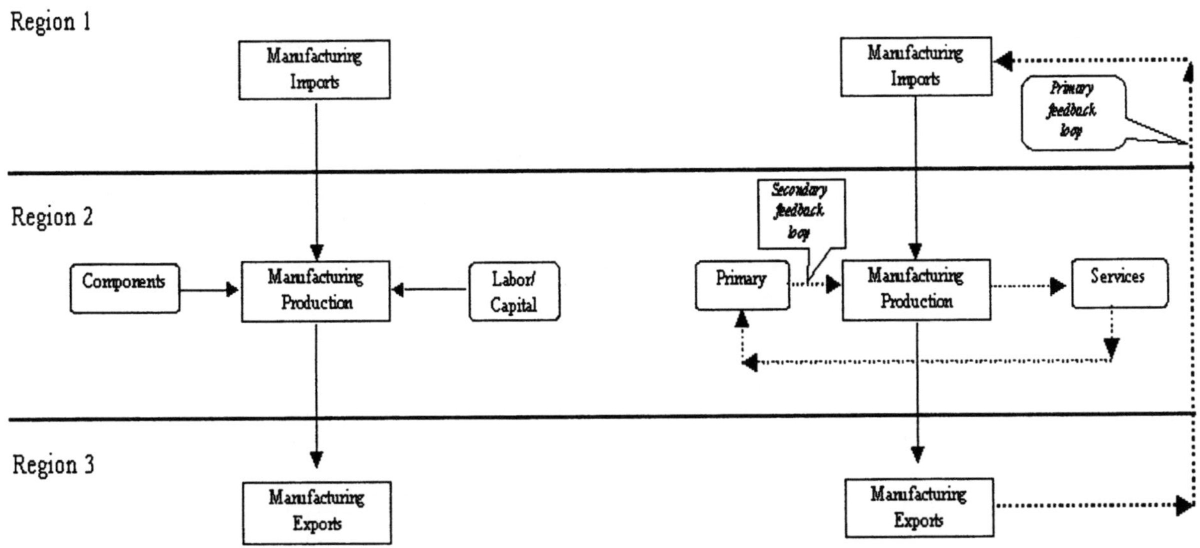

19.5.3 Inner Sub-Activities Production Loop Analysis

The Primary, Manufacturing and Services activities can be sub-divided into the following groups: Primary: P (agricultural activities), p (non-agricultural) Manufacturing: M (non-durable goods), m (durable goods); Services: S (Business services) and s (personal services). The application of the "Matrioshka" principle will be based on the decompositions (19.2), (19.3), and (19.4) (see table 19.9).

Table 19.9 presents two interregional inter-sub-activities feedback loops which are included in the following proportions, 9.8% to 3.2%, within the largest interregional interactivities feedback loop that, in turn, are derived from the three interregional interactivities feedback loops, which are included into the first interregional feedback loop.

19.6 Discussion and Conclusions

The method of hierarchical spatial production cycle analysis used in this chapter excluded more complex numerical manipulations with flows and allows the consideration of the non-homogeneous flows of different streams (goods) and the use of turbulence analogy. The need of the feedback loops analysis is justified by the economic phenomenon of vertical specialization of international trade.

In what way is this approach different from that adopted by Hummels *et al.* (1998)? Table 19.10 provides a comparative perspective for the two approaches; essentially, the non-feedback loop approach may be considered to be an *open loop* in the sense that flows enter the system as exports from one country to a second, circulate and then exit as exports to a third country. However, there is no connection between the first and third region. Spatial Production Cycle analysis, on the other hand, explores the degree to which the pattern of flows just described is completed with the addition of a final flow from the third region back to the first.

In this fashion, feedback loop analysis focuses on self-influence –the journey through the system of economies may be complex or very simple; it may involve all or part of the system and the intensity of interaction may vary significantly. The Midwest case study reveals a set of economies that are interacting very intensively; there are only relatively small differences between the magnitudes of the flows accounted for by each of the first three feedback loops. With the possibility of a regular US interregional commodity flow survey, the evolution of this trading regime can be monitored to see whether the expectations of increased interregional at the expense of intraregional flows continues. Early evidence from the European Union (Sonis *et al.*, 1993) found such a spatial pattern to be evolving at the level of nation-states. Spatial production cycle analysis offers insights into this evolving complexity and geographical transformation, thus complementing and enhancing understanding of trade and spatial economic development.

References

Balassa, B. 1967. *Trade Liberalization among Industrial Countries*. New York, McGraw Hill.

Bruelhart, M. and R.C. Hine, eds. 1999. *Intra-industry Trade and Adjustment*. New York, St. Martins Press.

Christofides, W. 1975. *Graph Theory: An algorithmic Approach*. New York, Academic Press.

Dantzig, G.B. 1963. *Linear Programming and Extensions*. Princeton University Press.

Defourny J. and E. Thorbecke. 1984. "Structural Path Analysis and Multiplier Decomposition within a Social Accounting Matrix Framework." *Economic Journal*, 94, 111-136.

Gower, J.C. 1977. "The analysis of symmetry and orthogonality.". In J.R. Barra, ed. *Recent Developments in Statistics*. Amsterdam, North Holland. pp. 109-123.

Feinberg, S. 1970. "An Iterative Process for Estimation of Contingency Tables." *Annals of Mathematical Statistics*, 41, 907-917.

Hewings, G.J.D., P.R. Israilevich, Y. Okuyama, D.K. Anderson, G.R. Schindler, M. Foulkes and M. Sonis. 1997. "Returns to scope, returns to trade and the structure of spatial interaction in the US Midwest," *Discussion Paper* 97-P-3, Regional Economics Applications Laboratory, University of Illinois, Urbana.

Hewings, G.J.D. M. Sonis, J. Guo, P.R. Israilevich and G.R. Schindler. 1998. "The Hollowing-out Process in the Chicago Economy, 1975-2011." *Geographical Analysis*, 30, 217-223.

Hummels, D., D. Rappoport and K-M. Yi. 1998. "Vertical Specialization and the Changing Nature of Word Trade." *Federal Reserve Bank of New York, Economic Policy Review*, June 1998.

Jurcat W.D. and H.J. Ryser. 1967. "Term Ranks and Permanents of Nonnegative Matrices." *Journal of Algebra*, **5**, 342-357.

Krugman, P. 1991. "Is Bilateralism bad?" In E. Helpman and A. Razin, eds. *International Trade and Trade Policy*. Cambridge, MIT Press. pp. 9-23.

Krugman P. 1993. "Regionalism versus multilateralism: analytical notes." In J. De Melo and A. Panagaria, eds. *New Directions in Regional Integration*. Cambridge University Press. pp.58-79.

Polenske, K.R. 1970a. "Empirical estimation of interregional input-output models: estimation of 1963 Japanese production." *American Economic Review*, 60, 76-82.

Polenske, K.R. 1970b. "Empirical implementation of a multiregional input-output gravity trade model." In A.P. Carter and A. Bródy, eds. *Contributions to Input-Output Analysis*. Amsterdam, North Holland.

Martins, E.B. 1993. "Notes on the construction of the 1992 Illinois input-output table." *Discussion Paper* 93-T-2, Regional Economics Applications Laboratory, University of Illinois, Urbana.

Richardson, L.F. 1922. *Weather Prediction by Numerical Process*. Cambridge University. Press.

Slater, D.B. 1981. "Combinatorial Procedures for Structuring Internal Migration and other Transaction Flows." *Quality and Quantity*, 15, 179-202.

Sonis, M. 1980. "Location Push-Pull Analysis of Migration Streams." *Geographical Analysis*, 12, 80-97.

Sonis, M. 1982. "The Decomposition Principle versus Optimization in Regional Analysis – the Inverted problem of Multiobjective Programming." In G.P. Chiotis, D.A. Tsoukalas, H.D. Louri, eds. *The Regions and Enlargement of European Economic Community*. School of Economics and Business Science, Athens.

Sonis, M. and G.J.D. Hewings. 1990. "The 'Matrioshka Principle' in the hierarchical decomposition of multiregional social accounting systems." In L. Anselin and M. Madden, (eds. *New Directions in Regional Analysis: Integrated and Multiregional Approaches*. London, Pinter.

Sonis, M., J. Oosterhaven and G.J.D. Hewings. 1993. "Spatial Economic Structure and Structural Changes in the European Common Market: Feedback Loop Input-Output Analysis." *Economic Systems Research*, 5, 173-184.

Sonis, M., G.J.D. Hewings and R. Gazel. 1995a. "The structure of multi-regional trade flows: Hierarchy, Feedbacks and Spatial Linkages." *The Annals of Regional Science*, 29, 409-430.

Sonis, M., J.J.M. Guilhoto and G.J.D. Hewings. 1995b. "The Asian Economy: Trade Structure interpreted by Feedback Loop Analysis." *Journal of Applied Input-Output Analysis,* 2, 24-40.

Sonis, M., G.J.D. Hewings, J. Guo and E. Hulu. 1997. "Interpreting Spatial Economic Structure: Feedback Loops in the Indonesian Economy, 1980-1985." *Regional Science and Urban Economics*, 27, 325-342.

Sonis, M., G.J.D. Hewings, and S. Sulistyowati. 1997. "The Structure of the Indonesian Economy: A Generalized Structural Path Analysis." *Economic Systems Research* 9, 265-280.

Sonis, M., G.J.D. Hewings, and Y. Okuyama. 2000. "Vertical Specialization and Interregional Trade: Turbulence Analogy and Feedback Loops Analysis of the Midwest Economy." In H. Herrmann and J. Bröcker, eds. *Spatial Change and Interregional Flows in the Integrating Europe*. Heidelberg, Physica-Verlag.

Appendix 19.A

Table 19.A.1 Sectoring Scheme in the Midwest Trade Model

No.	*Description*	*SIC*	*6-sector number*
1	Livestock; Livestock and Agricultural Products	01, 02	P
2	Agriculture, Forestry, and Fisheries	07, 08, 09	P
3	Mining	10, 12, 13, 14	p
4	Construction	15, 16, 17	M
5	Food and Kindred Products	20	M
6	Tobacco	21	M
7	Apparel and Textile Products	22, 23	M
8	Lumber and Wood Products	24	M
9	Furniture and Fixtures	25	M
10	Printing and Publishing	27	M
12	Chemicals and Allied Products	28	M
13	Petroleum and Coal Products	29	M
14	Rubber and Misc. Plastics Products	30	M
15	Leather and Leather Products	31	M
16	Stone, Clay, and Glass Products	32	M
17	Primary Metals Industries	33	m
18	Fabricated Metal Products	34	m
19	Industrial Machinery and Equipment	35	m
20	Electronic and Electric Equipment	36	m
21	Transportation Equipment	37	m
22	Instruments and Related Products	38	m
23	Miscellaneous Manufacturing Industries	39	m
24	Railroad Transportation and Transportation	40, 47	S
25	Local and Interurban Passenger Transit	41	S
26	Trucking and Warehousing	42	S
27	Water Transportation	44	S
28	Transportation by Air	45	S
29	Pipelines, Except Natural Gas	46	S
30	Communications	48	S
31	Electric, Gas, and Sanitary Services	49	S
32	Wholesale Trade	50, 51	S
33	Retail Trade	52-57, 59	S
34	Banking and Other Credit Agencies	60, 61, 67	S
35	Security and Commodity Brokers	68	S
36	Insurance Carriers	63	S
37	Insurance Agents, Brokers, and Service	64	S
38	Real Estate	65	s
39	Eating and Drinking Places	58	s
40	Hotels and Other Lodging Places	70	s
41	Personal Services	72	s
42	Business, Engineering, and Management Services	73, 87, 89	s
43	Auto Repair, Services, and Parking	75	s
44	Miscellaneous Repair Services	76	s
45	Motion Pictures	78	s
46	Amusement and Recreation Services	79	s
47	Health Services	80	s
48	Legal Services	81	s
49	Educational Services	82	s
50	Social Services	83	s
51	Membership Organizations and Households	84, 86, 88	s
52	Federal Government Enterprises		
53	State and Local Government Enterprises		

20 Miyazawa-Sraffa-Leontief Income Distribution Models

Yoshio Kimura,[1] Michael Sonis[2] and Geoffrey J.D. Hewings[3]

[1] Faculty of Economics and Information, Gifu Shoutoku Gakuen University, 1-38 Nakauzura, Gifu, Japan 500-8288
e-mail: kimura@gifu.shotoku.ac.jp
[2] Department of Geography, Bar Ilan University, 52900, Ramat-Gan, Israel and Regional Economics Applications Laboratory, University of Illinois, 607 South Mathews, #220, Urbana, Illinois, 61801-3671, USA
e-mail: sonism@mail.biu.ac.il
[3] Regional Economics Applications Laboratory, University of Illinois, 607 South Mathews, #220, Urbana, Illinois, 61801-3671, USA
email: hewings@uiuc.edu

20.1 Introduction

This chapter extends several of the contributions in Hewings *et al.*, (1999) that attempted to explore intersections between the work of Miyazawa and several other familiar theoretical and modeling paradigms. In the present case, the extensions link the work of Sraffa, Leontief and Miyazawa to explore the ways in which a more extensive framework can yield new insights into economic structure. The contributions of Sraffa (1960) to the understanding of economic structure have been significantly advanced in recent years by the interpretative assessments of Steenge (1995, 1997). In section 20.2, the standard Sraffian model is presented and some of the initial modifications are outlined. Following this exposition, section 20.3 provides a complement with some additional modifications that attempt to simplify the presentation of the new Sraffa-Leontief system (Sonis and Hewings, 2000), focusing on two alternative matrix decompositions. The conditions of solvability of this model are elaborated in detail in section 20.4. Section 20.5 revisits the Miyazawa income distribution model and establishes the foundation for the presentation of the Miyazawa-Sraffa-Leontief income distribution model in section 20.6. Attention is also directed here to solvability. The penultimate section addresses the role of profits, wages and consumption in this integrated system. The chapter concludes with some brief summary remarks and suggestions for further extensions.

20.2 The Sraffian Model

Drawing on Sraffa (1960), Pasinetti (1977), Kurz and Salvadori (1995) and Sonis and Hewings, (2000), the classical model of income distribution which is conventionally attributed to the name of Sraffa has the following form (see formula (6.1) in Kurz and Salvadori, 1995):

$$p = (1+r)pA + w^*l \tag{20.1}$$

where, p is a vector of prices, l is a vector of direct labor coefficients, r is the uniform rate of profits and w^* is the wage, hence, $0 \leq w^* \leq 1$.

Consider a non-negative matrix, A, of direct input coefficients. From the theory of non-negative matrices (see, for example, Horn and Johnson, 1985, p. 503), it follows that there are non-negative eigenvectors (left hand and right hand) p and x of A corresponding to a non-negative eigenvalue μ :

$$pA = \mu p, \quad Ax = \mu x \tag{20.2}$$

Sraffa found the linear relation between the rate of profits r and the wage rate w^* (see Sraffa, 1960, p.22; and Pasinetti, 1977, p. 115):

$$r = (1-w^*)\left[(1-\mu)/\mu\right] \tag{20.3}$$

Obviously, the maximal rate of profits, corresponding to the case $w^* = 0$ is equal to

$$r_{\max} = (1-\mu)/\mu \tag{20.4}$$

provided that $\mu \neq 0$

The simplicity of μ means that the eigenspaces of all left hand and right hand eigenvectors, corresponding to μ , are one-dimensional spaces; i.e., each left hand eigenvector is proportional to some vector p^*, and each right hand eigenvector is proportional to some vector x^*.

Let us chose (following Steenge, 1995, p. 57) vectors p^* and x^* such that:

$$p^*x^* = 1 \tag{20.5}$$

and consider the matrix

$$S = x^*p^* \tag{20.6}$$

This matrix assumes a major role in the subsequent analysis and it will be referred to as the *Sraffian matrix* with the vector x^*, the vector of standard commodities, and the vector p^*, the vector of standard prices.

Condition (20.5) implies that these vectors are fixed points of the transformation S:

$$p^*S = p^*, \quad Sx^* = x^* \tag{20.7}$$

The conditions (20.2) imply that:

$$AS = SA = \mu S \tag{20.8}$$

Consider further $C = I - S$. Obviously:

$$S^2 = S, C^2 = C, \quad CS = SC = 0,$$
$$AS = SA = \mu S, \; AC = CA \tag{20.9}$$

i.e.,

$$A = A(S + C) = \mu S + CA \tag{20.10}$$

The minimum information properties of the Sraffian matrix and the associated artificial economic landscapes are described in Sonis and Hewings, (2000).

20.3 Sraffa-Leontief Prices Decomposition Primary Model and Commodities Decomposition Dual Model

The simplest and most obvious way to construct the Sraffa-Leontief income distribution model is as follows (see Steenge, 1995; Sonis and Hewings, 2000): the input-output model is defined in the usual manner:

$$x = Ax + f \tag{20.11}$$

where x is gross output, A the matrix of input coefficients, and f is final demand. Multiplying (20.11) by the vector of prices p, we obtain:

$$px = pAx + pf \tag{20.12}$$

Multiplying the Sraffa income distribution model (20.1) by the vector of gross output x we have:

$$px = (1 + r)\, pAx + w^* lx \tag{20.13}$$

Now let us introduce the fundamental assumption:

$$lx = pf \tag{20.14}$$

which means that the price of final demand is defined by the amount of labor embedded in gross output.

Substituting (20.12) and (20.14) into (20.13), the Sraffa-Leontief income distribution model may be obtained:

$$px = (1 + r) pAx + w^* p(I - A)x \tag{20.15}$$

In matrix form, this model can be presented in the form of a prices decomposition matrix primal model (the Primary Sraffa-Leontief matrix model):

$$p = (1 + r) pA + w^* p(I - A) \tag{20.16}$$

and in the form of the commodities decomposition matrix dual model (the Dual Sraffa-Leontief matrix model):

$$x = (1 + r) Ax + w^* (I - A)x \tag{20.17}$$

Post-multiplication of (20.16) on x and pre-multiplication of (20.17) on p, together with $AS=SA$ obtained from (20.9) yield:

$$S\left[(1-w^*)I-(1+r-w^*)A\right]=\left[(1-w^*)I-(1+r-w^*)A\right]S=[0]$$

From the above equations and (20.7), theorems (20.1) and (20.2) and proposition 20.1 that Sonis and Hewings (2000)established, follow at once.

Theorem 20.1 *If in the Primary Sraffa-Leontief matrix model* (20.16) $w^*\neq 1$, *then in this model it is equivalent to*:

$$\begin{cases}1-w^*=\mu(1+r-w^*)\\ \mu p=pA\end{cases}\qquad (20.18)$$

□

The following proposition is the reformulation and clarification of the considerations of Steenge, (1995, pp.63-66). Steenge proved that in Propositions 20.1 and 20.2, both conditions in (20.18) and (20.20) are equivalent in the Sraffa-Leontief model.

Proposition 20.1 *If in the Primary Sraffa-Leontief matrix model* (20.11) $w^*\neq 1$, *then this model is equivalent to*

$$\begin{cases}1-w^*=\mu(1+r-w^*)\\ p=pS\end{cases}\qquad (20.19)$$

Theorem 20.2 *If in the Dual Sraffa-Leontief matrix model* (20.17) $w^*\neq 1$, *then in this model it is equivalent to*:

$$\begin{cases}1-w^*=\mu(1+r-w^*)\\ \mu x=Ax\end{cases}\qquad (20.20)$$

□

Proposition 20.2 (Steenge, 1995). *If in the Dual Sraffa-Leontief matrix model* (20.17) $w^*\neq 1$, *then this model is equivalent to*:

$$\begin{cases}1-w^*=\mu(1+r-w^*)\\ x=Sx\end{cases}\qquad (20.21)$$

This price vector, p, and commodity vector, x, are the right and left fixed points of the Sraffa matrix, S.

20.4 Solvability of the Sraffa-Leontief Model

In what follows, we examine the solvability of Sraffa-Leontief model (20.16 to 20.17), starting from the Primary Sraffa-Leontief model (20.16). Rearranging the terms of (20.16), we have:

$$p(1-w^*)I-\left[(1-w^*+r)A\right]=0. \tag{20.22}$$

If $1-w^*+r=0$ then in both cases when $1\neq w^*$ or $1=w^*$, equation (20.22) has a unique solution 0 or infinitely many solutions. If $1-w^*+r\neq 0$, then (20.22) further reduces to the eigenvalue problem:

$$\left[(1-w^*)/(1-w^*+r)\right]p=pA \tag{20.23}$$

Based on this view, the following theorem is immediate.

Theorem 20.3 Assume that $1-w^*+r\neq 0$. Then (20.16) has a semi-positive solution if and only if $(1-w^*)/(1-w^*+r)$ lies in the set QFR of quasi Frobenius eigenvalues (for the definition, see mathematical appendix) to each of which there corresponds a semi-positive row eigenvector of A. □

Proof. Let p be any semi-positive solution of (20.16). Then, it satisfies (20.23), because $1-w^*+r\neq 0$. Accordingly, $1-w^*+r$ surely belongs to QFR. Conversely, if $(1-w^*)/(1-w^*+r)$ is in QFR, then there exists a semi-positive vector p for which (20.23) holds. Since $1-w^*+r$ is nonvanishing, (20.23) implies (20.16).

Remark 1: Theorem 20.3 is an extended version of Theorem 20.1 (section 20.2) since Theorem 20.3 reduces to Theorem 20.1 when QFR is a singleton consisting solely of the Frobenius eigenvalue of the matrix A.

Remark 2: Rewrite $(1-w^*)/(1-w^*+r)$ as $h(r,w^*)$. Then, $h(r,1)=0$ and (20.16) or (20.23) is consistent for $h(r,1)$ if and only if $0\left[=h(r,1)\right]$ is in QFR. However, if QFR is thought to consist of the Frobenius eigenvalue alone, as in Theorem 20.1 or in Steenge (1995, pp. 63-66), then $h(r,1)$ can scarcely be in QFR consisting solely of the Frobenius eigenvalue of A which is known to varnish if and only if $A^n=0$ (see Nikaido 1968; Theorem 7.2, p. 103) or Kemp and Kimura 1978; Corollary 1, p. 85). This clarifies the reason why the Theorem 20.1 and Steenge (1995) assumed that $w^*\neq 1$, while Theorem 20.3 does not.

From the economic point of view, to suppose that 0 belongs to QFR implies that every commodity can be produced without paying any cost of intermediate inputs ($pA=0$ for some semi-positive eigenvector p associated with 0). However, this is inappropriate in Leontief models that emphasize the interdependence of industries via intermediate inputs. Therefore, it seems rather reasonable to exclude zero from QFR. Evidently, the exclusion of zero from QFR is equivalent to the supposition that $w^*\neq 1$, so far as the solvability of equation (20.16) is concerned.

The essence of propositions such as Theorem 20.3, Theorem 20.1 and Steenge (1995; pp. 63-66) can be found in that they offer us an apparatus to find the pairs of r and w^* which make equation (20.16) consistent with all possible pairs that can be given exogenously. For illustration, let QFR be $\{\beta_1,\beta_2,\beta_3\}$ and suppose that $1>\beta_1>\beta_2>\beta_3>0$ (thus, β_1 is the Frobenius eigenvalue). Then, all pairs of r and w^* that yield the vectors of equilibrium prices are depicted in figure 20.1.

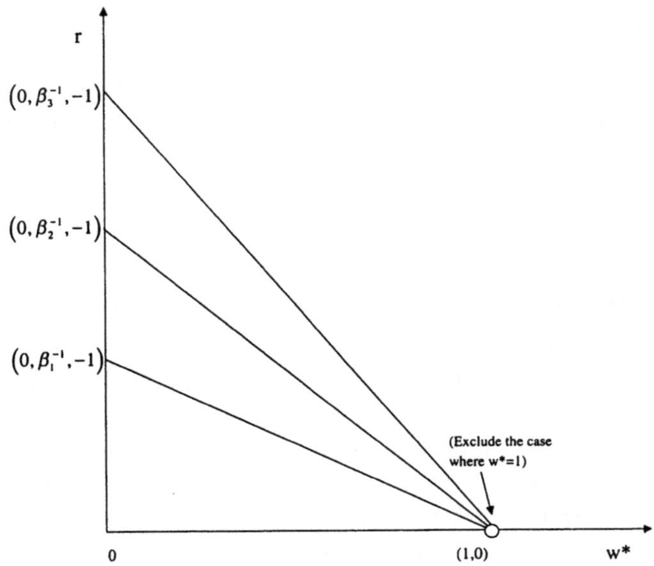

Figure 20.1 Loci of r and w^* Yielding Equilibrium Prices

Turning to the dual system, equation (20.17) is equivalent to:

$$[(1-w^*)/(1-w^*+r)](I-A)x = 0, \tag{20.24}$$

provided that the assumption $1-w^*+r \neq 0$ holds. Therefore, a necessary and sufficient condition for (20.17) to possess semi-positive solutions is established at once.

Theorem 20.4 Keeping the assumption $1-w^*+r \neq 0$ intact, the dual system (20.17) has semi-positive solutions if and only if $(1-w^*)/(1-w^*+r)$ is in QFC, the set of quasi-Frobenius eigenvalues of *A*, with each of which there are associated semi-positive column eigenvectors. □

Theorems 20.3 and 20.4 generate a corollary that incorporates the results of Steenge (1995; pp. 63-66):

Corollary 20.1 Suppose that there exists a quasi-Frobenius eigenvalue μ^* of *A* satisfying the condition:

(a) μ^* is in the intersection of QFR and QFC.

Denote further a row (column) eigenvector corresponding to μ^* by $p^*(x^*)$, and define $S = p^*x^*$. Then, we have:

(i) a semi-positive vector *p* for which $p = pS$ solves the equation (20.16), and

(ii) if, in addition, μ^* is a simple root of the characteristic equation of A, with the property that $p^*x^*=1$, a solution p of (20.16) obtained for the pair (r, w^*) such that $\mu^*=(1-w^*)/(1-w^*+r)$ satisfies $p=pS$.

Proof (i) Postmultiplying the both sides of $p=pS$ by A and making use of the definition of S, we at once see that

$$pA = pSA = px^*p^*A = \mu^* pS = \mu^* p$$

which means that $pS=p$.

(ii) Since μ^* is a simple root of the characteristic equation of A and since $\mu^* p = pA$, there exists a scalar t such that $p=tp^*$. Hence, in view of condition $p^*x^*=1$, it is easily seen that:

$$pS = tp^*S = tp^*x^*p^* = tp^* = p.$$

Remarks about Corollary 20.1

(i) Since the Frobenius eigenvalue undoubtedly meets condition (a), it is by no means an empty assumption (an assumption that never holds true) and if attention is paid exclusively to the Frobenius eigenvalue, as in the Theorem 20.1, we can dispense condition (a). Furthermore, as is implied by Theorem 20.3, some non-negative square matrices do have quasi-Frobenius eigenvalues other than their respective Frobenius eigenvalue and at the same time satisfy condition $p^*x^*=1$ and (a).

(ii) Corollary 20.1 is valid for the dual system (20.17) *mutatis mutandis*. More specifically, it suffices to replace p and pS in the corollary by x and Sx respectively.

So far, the focus has been on equation (20.16); however, the Leontief-like flavor of the equation induces us to examine whether equation (20.16) is compatible with one employed to determine the equilibrium prices in usual Leontief models. To this end, we need the condition:

(C.1) The Frobenius eigenvalue μ^* of A is less than unity.

By the Frobenius theorem on non-negative matrices, $\left[I-(1+r)A\right]^{-1}$ is non-negative if and only if $(1+r)^{-1} > \mu^*$. However, if μ^* is not less than unity, then condition that $(1+r)^{-1}$ exceeds μ^* holds only when r is nonpositive. This is the reason why (C.1) is introduced here. Proceeding in the usual manner, the equilibrium price of any commodity should cover just the unit production cost. The equilibrium prices are to be determined so that:

$$p = (1+r)pA + wa_0 \tag{20.25}$$

where a_0 is the vector of labor input coefficients and w signifies the wage-rate given exogenously.

Let S_{sp} and S_L be the set of solutions of (20.16) and (20.25) respectively. Then, the following theorem elucidates that the compatibility of equations (20.16) and (20.25) hinges heavily on the relationship between the quasi-Frobenius eigenvalues of A and the vector labor input coefficients.

Theorem 20.5 To ensure that (20.25) has a meaningful solution, assume that r is chosen so that $\mu^* < (1+r)^{-1}$ and consider the case $1-w^*+r \neq 0$. Then, under assumption (C.1), it is asserted that:
(i) if a semi-positive vector $\tilde{p}$ lies in both S_{sp} and S_L, there exists a quasi-Frobenius eigenvalue $\tilde{\mu}$ for which $\tilde{\mu}a_0 = a_0 A$ and that:
(ii) if $\tilde{\mu}a_0 = a_0 A$ for some $\tilde{\mu}$ from QFR, then any one of the triplet (r, w^*, w) can be specified in such a way that the remaining two of the triplet make it possible for S_{sp} and S_L to have a semi-positive vector in common. □

Proof (i) First, it should be noted that $w \neq 0$, for otherwise (20.25) has a unique solution 0. Nevertheless, this obviously violates the hypothesis. From the definition of $\tilde{p}$, it follows that

$$\tilde{p}\left[I-(1+r)A\right]=wa_0 \tag{20.26}$$

and that

$$\tilde{p}\left\{\left(1-w^*\right)I-\left(1-w^*+r\right)A\right\}=0. \tag{20.27}$$

Subtraction of (20.27) from (20.26) yields:

$$wa_0 = w^*\tilde{p}\left(I-A\right). \tag{20.28}$$

Drawing on Theorem 20.3, there can be found a $\tilde{\mu}$ from QFR such that $\tilde{\mu}\tilde{p}=\tilde{p}A$. Hence:

$$\tilde{p}\left(I-A\right)=\tilde{p}-\tilde{p}A=\left(1-\tilde{\mu}\right)\tilde{p}. \tag{20.29}$$

Notation: $w^*(r)$ and $w(r)$ are the solutions of 20.10 and 20.11 where r is exogenously specified

$$\underline{w}^* = \left(\mu^*-\tilde{\mu}\right)/\mu^*\left(1-\tilde{\mu}\right)$$
$$w = \left(1-\tilde{\mu}\right)w^* = \left(\mu^*-\tilde{\mu}\right)/\mu^*$$

Range of parameter values:

$$0 \le r \le \left[\left(1-\mu^*\right)/\mu^*\right]$$
$$\underline{w}^* \le w^* \le 1$$
$$0 \le w \le \underline{w}$$

Postmultiplying the both sides of (20.28) by $\left(\tilde{\mu}I-A\right)$, and making use of (20.29), we obtain that:

$$wa_0\left(\tilde{\mu}I-A\right)=w^*\tilde{\mu}\left(I-A\right)\left(\tilde{\mu}I-A\right)=0.$$

Since w is nonzero, a_0 is surely the row eigenvector corresponding to $\tilde{\mu}$ from QFR.
(ii) Consider the triplet (r, w^*, w) satisfying:

$$\tilde{\mu}=\left(1-w^*\right)\left(1-w^*+r\right)^{-1} \tag{20.30}$$

and

$\tilde{\mu}(1+r)+w=1$.

Then, Theorem 20.3, together with the assumption $\tilde{\mu}a_0 = a_0 A$, guarantees that a_0 solves (20.16) for any pair satisfying (20.30) and a direct calculation yields:

$$a_0\left[I-(1+r)A\right]-wa_0 = a_0\left[I-(1+r)A\right]-w(1/\tilde{\mu})a_0 A = \\ (1/\tilde{\mu})a_0\left\{\tilde{\mu}I-\left[\tilde{\mu}(1+r)+w\right]A\right\}=(1/\tilde{\mu})a_0(\tilde{\mu}I-A)=0 \qquad (20.31)$$

Figure 20.2 visualizes the relationship among *r*, *w**, and *w* for which equations (20.30) and (20.31) hold.

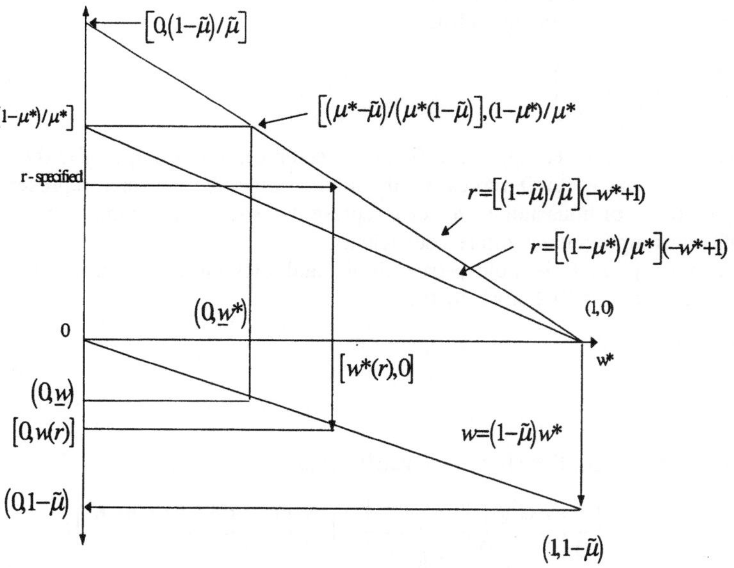

Figure 20.2 Relationships between *r*, *w** and *w*

Remark In this chapter, we have examined the Sraffa-Leontief type of income distribution theory without relying on the assumption of the indecomposability of Leontief matrix and studied an extended Leontief model into which the Sraffian income distribution theory is incorporated.

Theorems 20.3 and 20.4 and Corollary 20.1 are small generalizations of the related results of Theorems 20.1 and 20.2 so far attained and exhibit features resulting from extending the analysis to the decomposable case. Theorem 20.5, on the other hand, seems to deserve further attention, because equation (20.25) is substantially identical with one that played a central role in the so-called reswitching controversy in capital theory. Further, the condition that a_0 is the row eigenvector associated with a quasi-Frobenius eigenvalue of A is quite similar to the condition that a_0 is the Frobenius row eigenvector of A, a necessary and sufficient condition for the prices to be independent of the rate of profit (Ara, 1975; p. 130).

20.5 Miyazawa Income Distribution Model

Drawing on Miyazawa (1976) and Hewings *et al.* (1999), the link with the Miyazawa income distribution model will be explored. In two seminal publications (Miyazawa, 1960, 1968), and summarized in Miyazawa (1976), Miyazawa developed the generalization of the Keynesian income multiplier in the form of a matrix referred to as the inter-relational income multiplier.
The matrix Miyazawa model has a form:

$$\begin{pmatrix} x \\ Y \end{pmatrix} = \begin{pmatrix} A & C \\ V & 0 \end{pmatrix} \begin{pmatrix} x \\ Y \end{pmatrix} + \begin{pmatrix} f \\ g \end{pmatrix} \tag{20.32}$$

Here A is a matrix of direct input coefficients; vector x is gross output, f is the vector of final demand, the vector Y represents the total income, the matrix V represents the value-added ratios of households, vector g represents exogenous income, the matrix C represents consumption expenditure coefficients.

The following analysis holds, (see Sonis and Hewings, 1999a,b): Miyazawa considers the following 2x2 block-matrix:

$$M = \begin{pmatrix} A & C \\ V & 0 \end{pmatrix} \tag{20.33}$$

The Leontief inverse for the Miyazawa matrix (20.33) has a form:

$$\begin{aligned} B(M) = (I - M)^{-1} &= \left(\begin{array}{c|c} I & BC \\ \hline 0 & I \end{array}\right)\left(\begin{array}{c|c} I & 0 \\ \hline 0 & K \end{array}\right)\left(\begin{array}{c|c} B & 0 \\ \hline VB & I \end{array}\right) = \left(\begin{array}{c|c} B(I + CKVB) & BCK \\ \hline KVB & K \end{array}\right) \\ &= \left(\begin{array}{c|c} I & 0 \\ \hline V & I \end{array}\right)\left(\begin{array}{c|c} \Delta & 0 \\ \hline 0 & I \end{array}\right)\left(\begin{array}{c|c} I & C \\ \hline 0 & I \end{array}\right) = \left(\begin{array}{c|c} \Delta & \Delta C \\ \hline VB & I + V\Delta C \end{array}\right) \end{aligned} \tag{20.34}$$

where $B = (I - A)^{-1}$ is the Leontief inter-industry inverse matrix, $L=VBC$ is the matrix of inter-income group coefficients,

$$K = (I - L)^{-1} = (I - VBC)^{-1} = I + V\Delta C \tag{20.35}$$

is the Miyazawa inter-relational income multiplier or generalized Keynesian multiplier:

$$\Delta = (I - A - CV)^{-1} = B(I + CKVB) \tag{20.36}$$

is an enlarged Leontief inverse.
Also, the Miyazawa fundamental equations of income formation:

$$\begin{cases} V\Delta = KVB \\ \Delta C = BCK \end{cases} \tag{20.37}$$

20.6 Miyazawa-Sraffa-Leontief Income Distribution Model and Its Solvability

The factor rewards attributed to factor-owners according to Sraffian income distribution theory are naturally thought to affect the final demands in particular consumption expenditures. Consequently, the next task is to incorporate the income-consumption relationship into the Sraffa-Leontief model .

Miyazawa (1976) has extended Leontief model so as to include the final demands recognized as the functions of various factor income. Thus, following Miyazawa (1976), it is assumed that the consumption function of each commodity is given by

$$c_i = c_{iK}\left(rpAx\right) + c_{iL}w^* p\left(I - A\right)x + f_i \qquad i = 1,\ldots,n \tag{20.38}$$

where c_{iK} and c_{iL} are assumed to be positive constant, f_i represents the consumption of commodity *i* at the subsistence level and *x* denotes the column vector of outputs.

Equilibrium of every market requires that:

$$x = Ax + C_K\left(rpAx\right) + w^* C_L p\left(I - A\right)x + f$$

or

$$\left\{I - \left[A + rC_K pA + w^* C_L p\left(I - A\right)\right]\right\}x = f \tag{20.39}$$

where $C_K = \left(c_{1K}, c_{2K}, \ldots, c_{nK}\right)^T$; $C_L = \left(c_{1L}, c_{2L}, \ldots, c_{nL}\right)^T$ and f is the vector of final demand.

Recalling Theorem 20.3, the vector p of equilibrium prices, if it exists, satisfies $\tilde{\mu}p = pA$ and . $\tilde{\mu} = \left(1 - w^*\right)\left(1 - w^* + r\right)^{-1}$. Hence, (20.39) reduces to:

$$\left\{I - \left[A + C_K\left(r\tilde{\mu}p\right) + C_L w^*\left(1 - \tilde{\mu}\right)p\right]\right\}x = f \tag{20.40}$$

Define the block-matrix of consumption C as

$$C = \left(C_K, C_L\right) \tag{20.41}$$

Further, capital income V_K can be defined as:

$$V_K = rpA = r\tilde{\mu}p \tag{20.42}$$

and labor income V_L can be defined as:

$$V_L = w^* p\left(I - A\right) = w^*\left(1 - \tilde{\mu}\right)p \tag{20.43}$$

The block-matrix of income, *V*, is thus:

$$V = \begin{pmatrix} V_K \\ V_L \end{pmatrix} = \begin{pmatrix} r\tilde{\mu}p \\ w^*(1-\tilde{\mu})p \end{pmatrix} = (1-\tilde{\mu})\begin{pmatrix} (1-w^*)p \\ w^*p \end{pmatrix} \tag{20.44}$$

Then, (20.40) can be rewritten as:

$$[I-(A+CV)]x = f \tag{20.45}$$

which reveals a complete formal analogy of the present model to 3 x 3 block expansion of the Miyazawa 2 x 2 block model (20.32) and (20.33):

$$\begin{pmatrix} x \\ y_K \\ y_L \end{pmatrix} = \begin{pmatrix} A & C_K & C_L \\ V_K & 0 & 0 \\ V_L & 0 & 0 \end{pmatrix}\begin{pmatrix} x \\ y_K \\ y_L \end{pmatrix} + \begin{pmatrix} f \\ g_K \\ g_L \end{pmatrix} \tag{20.46}$$

Here, we introduced in the Miyazawa 2x2 block model (20.32) and (20.33), the division of total income *Y* into income from employment and profits of capital with the help of block-column and block-row vectors. The first block-column vector $Y = \begin{pmatrix} y_K \\ y_L \end{pmatrix}$ represents total income, the second, $V = \begin{pmatrix} V_K \\ V_L \end{pmatrix}$ with the components, V_K, V_L, representing the income from capital profits and employment respectively, the block-column vector $g = \begin{pmatrix} g_K \\ g_L \end{pmatrix}$ representing the exogenous income from capital and labor, and the block-row vector $C = (C_K, C_L)$ representing consumption expenditures from income from employment and profits.

To proceed further, we need two further conditions:

$$\text{(C.2)} \begin{cases} eA < e & \text{(C.2.1)} \\ (eC_K \quad eC_L) < (1,1) & \text{(C.2.2)} \end{cases}$$

where $e = (1,1,\ldots,1)$ is the row vector consisting of finitely many ones (whose number is unambiguously understood from the context).

Bearing in mind that $\tilde{\mu} = (1-w^*)/(1-w^*+r)$, it follows that:

$$r\tilde{\mu} + w^*(1-\tilde{\mu}) = 1-\tilde{\mu}, \tag{20.47}$$

This, in conjunction with the definition of *V*, implies that

$$eV = [r\tilde{\mu} + w^*(1-\tilde{\mu})]p = (1-\tilde{\mu})p. \tag{20.48}$$

Therefore, a direct computation gives:

$$e(A+V) = eA + (1-\tilde{\mu})p, \tag{20.49}$$

and

$$e(A+CV) = eA + eC_K\tilde{\mu}rp + eC_L w^*(1-\tilde{\mu})p \tag{20.50}$$

In view of (C.2.1), $\tilde{\mu}<1$ and the nonnegativity of w^* (see figure 20.1) and $r\left[1>\tilde{\mu}>(1+r)^{-1}\right]$ is obvious. Hence, from (20.47), (20.50) and (A.2) it follows that:

$$e(A+CV)\leq eA+(1-\tilde{\mu})p \tag{20.51}$$

If $p_j=0$, then (C.2.1) and (51) ensure that:

$$\left[e(A+CV)\right]_j\leq(eA)_j<1, \tag{20.52}$$

where $\left[e(A+CV)\right]_j$ denotes the jth element of $e(A+CV)$.

On the other hand, when $p_j>0$, it is safely assumed that

$$\left[e(A+CV)\right]_j\leq(eA)_j+(1-\tilde{\mu})p_j<1 \tag{20.53}$$

since, in addition to (C.2.1), it does not harm the generality that p is thought to be normalized so that $ep^T=1$. Thus, we have argued that there is enough ground to assume that $e(A+CV)<e$ and under this assumption, the Sraffa-Leontief-Miyazawa model so far constructed can produce non-negative outputs for any given bill of goods f.

Noting that inequalities (20.52) and (20.53), together with the nonnegativity of $B=(I-A)^{-1}$ and (C.2.2), guarantee that $e(VBC)<e$, it can be seen immediately that the power series of VBC converges to $(I-VBC)^{-1}$, the interrelational income multiplier matrix (Miyazawa (1976; p. 25)). Consequently,:

$$(I-CVB)^{-1}=I+C\left[I+VBC+(VBC)^2+....\right]V=I+C(I-VBC)^{-1}VB \tag{20.54}$$

Directly from (20.54), it follows that:

$$\left[I-(A+CV)\right]^{-1}-(I-A)^{-1}=B\left[I-(CVB)^{-1}-I\right]=BC(I-VBC)^{-1}VB \tag{20.55}$$

Equation (20.55) combined with the equation $\tilde{\mu}=(1-w^*)/(1-w^*+r)$ provides us with the information about how the matrix multiplier $\left[I-(A+CV)\right]^{-1}$ reacts to the changes in r and/or w^*.

20.7 Role of the Rate of Profits, Wages and Consumption in the Miyazawa-Sraffa-Leontief Model

The model (20.46) includes two building blocks representing separately the income generation from capital and labor:

$$\begin{pmatrix} x \\ y_K \end{pmatrix} = \begin{pmatrix} A & C_K \\ V_K & 0 \end{pmatrix} \begin{pmatrix} x \\ y_K \end{pmatrix} + \begin{pmatrix} f \\ g_K \end{pmatrix} \tag{20.56}$$

$$\begin{pmatrix} x \\ y_L \end{pmatrix} = \begin{pmatrix} A & C_L \\ V_L & 0 \end{pmatrix} \begin{pmatrix} x \\ y_L \end{pmatrix} + \begin{pmatrix} f \\ g_L \end{pmatrix} \tag{20.57}$$

These building blocks have the original Miyazawa 2x2 blocks form of income generation. Therefore, the following analysis holds (see Sonis and Hewings, 1999a).

Consider first the Miyazawa model (20.56) for income generation connected with capital. Miyazawa evaluated the following block matrix:

$$M_K = \begin{pmatrix} A & C_K \\ V_K & 0 \end{pmatrix} = \begin{pmatrix} A & C_K \\ r\mu p & 0 \end{pmatrix} \tag{20.58}$$

The Leontief inverse for the Miyazawa matrix (20.58) has the form:

$$\begin{aligned} B(M_K) &= (I - M_K)^{-1} = \\ &= \begin{pmatrix} I & BC_K \\ 0 & I \end{pmatrix} \begin{pmatrix} I & 0 \\ 0 & K_K \end{pmatrix} \begin{pmatrix} B & 0 \\ V_K B & I \end{pmatrix} = \begin{pmatrix} B + BC_K K_K V_K B & BC_K K_K \\ K_K V_K B & K_K \end{pmatrix} = \\ &= \begin{pmatrix} I & 0 \\ V_K & I \end{pmatrix} \begin{pmatrix} \Delta_K & 0 \\ 0 & I \end{pmatrix} \begin{pmatrix} I & C_K \\ 0 & I \end{pmatrix} = \begin{pmatrix} \Delta_K & \Delta_K C_K \\ V_K B & I + V_K \Delta_K C_K \end{pmatrix} \end{aligned} \tag{20.59}$$

where $B = (I - A)^{-1}$ is the Leontief inter-industrial inverse matrix, and:

$$K_K = (I - V_K B C_K)^{-1} = I + V_K \Delta_K C_K = I + r\mu p \Delta_K C_K \tag{20.60}$$

is the Miyazawa capital inter-relational income multiplier or generalized Keynesian multiplier:

$$\Delta_K = (I - A - C_K V_K)^{-1} = B + BC_K K_K V_K B \tag{20.61}$$

is an enlarged Leontief inverse.

Also the Miyazawa fundamental equations of income formation from capital hold:

$$\begin{cases} V_K \Delta_K = K_K V_K B \\ \Delta_K C_K = BC_K K_K \end{cases} \tag{20.62}$$

Analogously, it is possible to obtain similar results for the Miyazawa model (20.57) for income generation connected with labor, replacing the index K by the index L in formulae (20.61) and (20.62).

Returning to the Miyazawa 3x3 block model (20.46), we will obtain the Leontief inverse:

$$B(M)=(I-M)^{-1}=$$
$$=\begin{pmatrix} I & 0 & 0 \\ V_K & I & 0 \\ V_L & 0 & I \end{pmatrix}\begin{pmatrix} \Delta & 0 & 0 \\ 0 & I & 0 \\ 0 & 0 & I \end{pmatrix}\begin{pmatrix} I & C_K & C_L \\ 0 & I & 0 \\ 0 & 0 & I \end{pmatrix}= \tag{20.63}$$
$$=\begin{pmatrix} \Delta & \Delta C_K & \Delta C_L \\ V_K\Delta & I+V_K\Delta C_K & V_K\Delta C_L \\ V_L\Delta & V_L\Delta C_K & I+V_L\Delta C_L \end{pmatrix}$$

where:

$$\Delta=(I-A-CV)^{-1}=\left[I-A-\begin{pmatrix} C_K & C_L \end{pmatrix}\begin{pmatrix} V_K \\ V_L \end{pmatrix}\right]^{-1}= \tag{20.64}$$
$$=(I-A-C_KV_K-C_LV_L)^{-1}$$

is the enlarged Leontief inverse for the model (20.56), and:

$$K=(I-VBC)^{-1}=\left[I-\begin{pmatrix} V_K \\ V_L \end{pmatrix}B\begin{pmatrix} C_K & C_L \end{pmatrix}\right]^{-1}=$$
$$=\left[I-\begin{pmatrix} V_KBC_K & V_KBC_L \\ V_LBC_K & V_KBC_L \end{pmatrix}\right]^{-1} \tag{20.65}$$
$$I+V\Delta C=\begin{pmatrix} I+V_K\Delta C_K & V_K\Delta C_L \\ V_L\Delta C_K & I+V_L\Delta C_L \end{pmatrix}$$

is the Miyazawa labor-capital inter-relational income multiplier or generalized Keynesian multiplier for labor-capital.

The fine structure of the Miyazawa labor-capital inter-relational income multiplier K can be presented with the help of the interlaced inter-relational income multipliers:

$$\Delta_{KLK}=(I-V_K\Delta_LC_K)^{-1}=I+V_K\Delta_LC_K$$
$$\Delta_{LKL}=(I-V_L\Delta_LKC_L)^{-1}=I+V_L\Delta_KC_L \tag{20.66}$$

This fine structure of the Miyazawa labor-capital inter-relational income multiplier K has the following form:

$$K=\begin{pmatrix} \Delta_{KLK} & K_KV_KBC_L\Delta_{LKL} \\ K_LV_LBC_K\Delta_{KLK} & \Delta_{LKL} \end{pmatrix} \tag{20.67}$$

where the Miyazawa fundamental equations of income formation appear as:

$$\Delta C_K=\Delta_LC_K\Delta_{KLK};\quad V_K\Delta C_K=\Delta_{KLK}C_KV_K$$
$$\Delta C_L=\Delta_KC_L\Delta_{LKL};\quad V_K\Delta=\Delta_{LKL}C_LK_L \tag{20.68}$$

Hence, the Leontief inverse (20.63) can be presented in the form:

$$B(M)=\begin{pmatrix} \Delta & \Delta_L C_K \Delta_{KLK} & \Delta_K C_L \Delta_{LKL} \\ \Delta_{KLK} V_K \Delta_K & \Delta_{KLK} & K_K V_K B C_L \Delta_{LKL} \\ \Delta_{LKL} V_L \Delta_L & K_L V_L B C_K \Delta_{KLK} & \Delta_{LKL} \end{pmatrix} \tag{20.69}$$

20.8 Conclusions and Further Explorations

This chapter has revealed an important connection between the classical Sraffa model and some new interpretations afforded by its expansion to the Sraffa-Leontief models and further expansion by considering the closed system of a Miyazawa type in which profits and wages are distributed and their impacts on the economy are traced. Thus, this provides motivation for the potentially new and innovative insights that can be gained by exploring connections between different modeling systems. One of these insights would involve consideration of the relationship between changes in the rate of profit (or any other parameter) and the impact on income distribution. There now exists a set of methodology, drawing on the field of influence notion, to examine the economy-wide impact of changes in one parameter or sets of parameters in Leontief-related systems (see Sonis and Hewings, 1992; Sonis *et al.*, 1997). However, to date, this methodology has only been applied to Leontief and Miyazawa systems but not the integrated Miyazawa-Sraffa-Leontief model developed in this chapter.

References

Ara, K. 1975. "Parable and Realism in the Theory of Capital: A Generalization of Prof. Samuelson's Theory of Surrogate Production Function." *The Economic Studies Quarterly* (presently, *The Japanese Economic Review*), 26, 1-13.

Hewings, G.J.D., M. Sonis, M. Madden and Y. Kimura, eds. 1999. *Understanding and Interpreting Economic Structure.* Advances in Spatial Sciences, Heidelberg, Springer-Verlag.

Horn, R.A. and C.A. Johnson. 1985. *Matrix Analysis.* Cambridge, Cambridge University Press.

Israilevich, P.R., G.J.D Hewings, M. Sonis and G. R. Schindler. 1997. "Forecasting structural change with a regional econometric input-output model." *Journal of Regional Science,* 37, 565-590.

Kurz, H.D. and N. Salvadori. 1995. *Theory of Production: A Long Period Analysis.* Cambridge, University Press.

McKenzie, L.W. 1960. "Matrix with Dominant Diagonals and Economic Theory." In K.J. Arrow, S.Karlin, and P. Suppe, eds. *Mathematical Methods in the Social Sciences.* Palo Alto, CA., Stanford University Press.

Miyazawa, K. 1960. "Foreign trade multiplier, input-output analysis and the consumption function." *Quarterly Journal of Economics*, 74, 53-64.

Miyazawa, K. 1968. "Input-output analysis and interrelational multiplier as a matrix." *Hitotsubashi Journal of Economics*, **7**, 39-58.

Miyazawa, K. 1976. *Input-Output Analysis and the Structure of Income Distribution.* Heidelberg, Springer-Verlag.

Murray, K.C. and Y. Kimura. 1978. *Introduction to Mathematical Economics.* Heidelberg, Springer-Verlag.

Pasinetti, L.L. 1977. *Lectures on the Theory of Production.* New York, Columbia University Press.

Sonis, M. and G.J.D. Hewings. 1992. "Coefficient change in input-output models: theory and applications." *Economic Systems Research,* 4, 143-157.

Sonis, M., G.J.D. Hewings and K. Miyazawa. 1997. "Synergetic interactions within pair-wise hierarchy of economic linkages sub-systems." *Hitotsubashi Journal of Economics* 38, 183-199.

Sonis, M. and G.J.D. Hewings. 1999a. "Miyazawa's Contributions to Understanding Economic Structure: Interpretation, Evaluation and Extensions." In G.J.D. Hewings, M. Sonis, M. Madden and Y. Kimura, eds. *Understanding and Interpreting Economic Structure.* Advances in Spatial Sciences, Heidelberg, Springer-Verlag.

Sonis, M. and G.J.D. Hewings. 1999b. "Economic landscapes: multiplier product matrix analysis for multiregional input-output systems." *Hitotsubashi Journal of Economics,* 40, 59-74.

Sonis, M. and G.J.D. Hewings. 2000. "On the Sraffa-Leontief Model." *Discussion Paper 00-T-2.* Regional Economics Applications Laboratory, University of Illinois, Urbana.

Sraffa, P. 1960. *Production of Commodities by Means of Commodities.* Cambridge, Cambridge University Press.

Steenge, A.E. (1995) "Sraffa and Goodwin: a unifying framework for standards of value in the income distribution problem." *Journal of Economics,* 62, 55-75.

Steenge, A.E. 1997. "The elusive standard commodity: eigenvectors as standards of value." In A. Simonovits and A. E. Steenge, eds. *Prices, Growth and Cycles: Essays in Honor of Andreas Brody.* London, Macmillan Press.

Appendix

In this appendix, we are mainly concerned with an extended notion of the Frobenius eigenvalue of a real square matrix with every non-negative, off-diagonal element, henceforth referred to as a Metzlerian matrix. To this end, let us introduce:

Definition A.1 By A denote an n x n Metzlerian matrix. Then, a real eigenvalue μ of A to which there corresponds a semi-positive row eigenvector or a semi-positive column eigenvector, is said to be the quasi-Frobenius eigenvalue of A. Moreover, the set of quasi-Frobenius eigenvalues to each of which a semi-positive row (column) eigenvector corresponds is signified by QFR_A (QFC_A) and if the context allows us to expect no confusions to arise, we drop the suffix A.

Evidently, the Frobenius eigenvalue of any Metzlerian matrix belongs to QFR as well as QFC. Hence, QFR and QFC are necessarily non-empty for any Metzlerian matrix. Furthermore, the Frobenius theorem on Metzlerian matrices (McKenzie, 1960; Kemp and Kimura, 1978, pp. 80-82) ensures QFR and QFC coincide with a singleton consisting of the Frobenius eigenvalue alone, if the Metzlerian matrix under consideration is indecomposable. However, some decomposable Metzlerian matrices possess the quasi-Frobenius eigenvalues different from their respective Frobenius eigenvalue. In fact, we have:

Lemma 1 Let A be a decomposable Metzlerian matrix of order n. Then, without loss of generality, A is supposed to be decomposed into submatrices A_{ij} $(i, j = 1,...,m)$ with the property:

(L.1) $A_{ij} = [0]$ $(i = j+1,...,m; j = 1,...,m)$

and that each A_{ij} is indecomposable, where [0] is a zero matrix with suitably many rows and columns. (The number of rows and columns are unambiguously understood from the context.) Assume further that there exists a diagonal block A_{kk} for which the following two conditions hold:

(i) $\tilde{\mu}_k < \max_{1 \le i \le m} \tilde{\mu}_k^* = \tilde{\mu}$ and

(ii) $A_{kj} = [0]$ for $j = k+1,...m$

where $\tilde{\mu}_i$ is the Frobenius eigenvalue of each diagonal block A_{ii} $(i = 1,...,m)$.
Then, $\tilde{\mu}_k$ is a quasi-Frobenius eigenvalue of *A*, which is different from the Frobenius eigenvalue of *A* and with $\tilde{\mu}_k$ there are associated a semi-positive row eigenvector p^* and a semi-positive column eigenvector x^* such that $p^* x^* = 1$.
Proof Denoting the Frobenius row (column) eigenvector of A_{kk} by $\tilde{p}_k$ $(\tilde{x}_k)$, the Frobenius theorem aforementioned asserts that both $\tilde{p}_k$ and $\tilde{x}_k$ are positive. Define

$$\tilde{p} = (0_1,...,0_{k-1}, \tilde{p}_k, 0_{k+1},...,0_m)$$
$$(\tilde{x})^T = (0_1,...,0_{k-1}, (\tilde{x}_k)^T, 0_{k+1},...,0_m)^T$$

It is obvious that $\tilde{p}\tilde{x} > 0$, where 0_i is a row zero vector of the same order as that of A_{ii} $(i = 1,...,m)$. Let $p^* = \tilde{p}/(\tilde{p}\tilde{x})^{1/2}$; $x^* = \tilde{x}/(\tilde{p}\tilde{x})^{1/2}$. Then, a direct calculation yields $p^* A = \tilde{\mu}_k p^*$, $Ax^* = \tilde{\mu}_k x^*$ and $p^* x^* = 1$. Thus, the lemma follows from noticing that $\tilde{\mu}$ is the Frobenius eigenvalue of *A*, by virtue of condition (*i*).

Remark If, instead of **(L.1),** the decomposition of the matrix *A* is characterized by

(L2) $A_{ij} = [0]$ $(j = i+1,...,m; i = 1,...,m)$

The lemma is easily seen to remain valid by replacing condition (ii) with

(iii) $A_{jk} = [0]$ for $j = k+1,...m$

Since conditions (i) and (ii) are fairly loose, a number of Metzlerian matrices satisfy these conditions. This, in turn, implies that Corollary 20.1 holds true for a wide range of Leontief matrices of direct input coefficients.

A theoretical feature of this appendix is in considering the case where QFR or QFC contains a quasi-Frobenius eigenvalue different from the Frobenius eigenvalue. Therefore, the next lemma plays an important role to strengthen the logical foundation of this appendix.

Lemma 2 Let *A* be as in Lemma 1. If there exists $\tilde{\mu}_k$ other than $\tilde{\mu}$ such that

(L.3) $\tilde{\mu}_i < \tilde{\mu}_k$, $i = k+1,...,m$,

then to $\tilde{\mu}_k$ there corresponds a semi-positive row eigenvector of *A*. Similarly, if (L.3) is replaced by

(L.4) $\tilde{\mu}_i < \tilde{\mu}_k$, $i = 1,\dots,k-1$,

then there exists a semi-positive column eigenvector of A associated with $\tilde{\mu}_k$.

Proof It suffices to verify the first half of the lemma. Bearing in mind that A_{kk} has a positive row Frobenius eigenvector $p_k{*}$ and that $\tilde{\mu}_k I - A_{k+1,k+1}$ is nonnegatively invertible, define $p*_i$ $(i \neq k)$ by $p*_i = 0$, $i = 1,\dots,k-1$ and

$$p*_{k+1} = \left(\sum_{j=k}^{i} p*_j A_{ji} \right) \left(\tilde{\mu}_k I - A_{k+i,k+i} \right)^{-1}, \; i = 1,\dots,m-k$$

Then, $p* = \left(0_1,\dots,0_{k-1}, p*_k, 0_{k+1},\dots,0_m\right)$ is the desired semi-positive eigenvector of A, associated with $\tilde{\mu}_k$.

Part III Methodological Issues

21 Frame-Shifting in Regional General Equilibrium Models*

Philip R. Israilevich

Deceased: formerly, Regional Economics Applications Laboratory, Federal Reserve Bank of Chicago, 230 S LaSalle, Chicago, IL 60604-1413, USA and the University of Illinois.

21.1 Introduction

In CGE (Computable General Equilibrium) models, input-output coefficients are balanced row-wise through a supply-demand interaction for a physical commodity. Input-output columns consist of physical flows that require a unique set of prices to balance income and sales of intermediate goods and services. Another type of model, developed originally by Conway (1990, 1991) and further developed by Israilevich *et al.* (1997), termed the Regional Econometric Input-Output Model [REIM] approach, balances the input-output table rows in value terms. This approach has no physical flows of inputs nor does it have prices. It utilizes Marshallian (see Takayama, 1985) output equilibrium that requires no explicit price values. Since REIM has no prices, it is impossible to impose column-wise constraints. As a result, value-added rows can be considered a residual that creates a potential problem in that the value added may be too small, or even negative, as a result of simulation exercises, impact analyses or forecasts.

CGE models assume fixed input-output coefficients, simplifying model construction because no attention has to be directed to the mechanism for determining coefficient changes. REIM solves this problem by allowing value-termed input-output coefficients to be endogenous, i.e., to be a function of other variables. This mechanism allows for changes in input-output coefficient values as a result of a number of interactions between a set of nonlinear equations. Therefore, there is no explicit relationship between the input-output coefficients and other variables in the model. In a recent effort, we numerically determined how changes in input-output coefficients related to changes in other variables via a simulation of the model (see Israilevich *et al.* 1997).

In CGE models, values of transaction flows are balanced and, as a result, prices are determined. There is, however, no corresponding column-sum constraint on physical coefficients. One might object to the use of physical coefficients on the basis of the fact that these coefficients are not observed. Instead, input-output tables are constructed based on information related to expenditure shares, and such shares must

* The first draft of this paper was prepared by Israilevich for presentation at the Regional Science Association Meetings in Buffalo, November, 1997; the paper was completed after his death, using drafts, notes, and prior conversations, by Geoffrey J.D. Hewings, Graham Schindler, Michael Sonis, and John J.Y. Seo. Michael Kouparitsas provided valued assistance in interpretations.

sum to unity (i.e., the column constraints). However a unity column constraint implies unity prices, which eliminates the possibility of estimating prices using input-output relationships.

We overcome this shortcoming by constructing price equations using Shephard's Lemma. In this approach, input-output coefficients are used as expenditures shares, similar to the approach of Hudson and Jorgenson, (1974) and Nakamura (1984). As a result, we derive prices using the input-output structure, but avoid the CGE requirement of having to observe physical coefficients. However, with our methodology, input-output imbalances will be generated with price changes. We develop procedures that allow variations in prices (and other variables) and still allow us to balance the input-output system. This approach also allows us to introduce structural changes within an input-output framework that functionally relates to changes in output and other variables of the model.

Lately, there has been renewed interest in input-output cluster analysis. This suggests that economists believe the structural relationship within the input-output system is important. In this light, we have incorporated changes in the sub-blocks of input-output into our model.

21.2 Methodology

Inclusion of capital stock into the system will enable column constraints to be included into the modified input-output system. In the Chicago REIM, there are row constraints, which transform the input-output row constraint from a linear into a nonlinear constraint. In the Leontief system, value added is in constant proportion to output; since we made the row relationship nonlinear then value added will have a nonlinear relationship to output as well. This presents a potential shortcoming that given certain shocks to the system, value added as a residual could be negative, which would make no economic sense. Therefore, column constraints are necessary to preserve not only the non-negativity of value of value added but also to prevent the values being squeezed to unreasonably small values. In other words, a functional relationship between output and value added should be introduced.

CGE establishes relations between output and intermediate inputs and value added in many forms, most often using a Cobb-Douglas function. Thus, input-output has fixed technology relative to value added (value added is a vector and cannot be disaggregated into a matrix, which is another short coming). REIM has nonlinear relations between output and value added but these relations are implicit in the system (value added is fully disaggregated) and CGE has nonlinear and explicit relations between output and value added (value added is fully disaggregated).

21.2.1 CGE Models

Prices are generated in part by the demand from the final and intermediate markets of goods and services. Input-output coefficients change over time, particularly the regional purchase coefficients in response not only to technological and price changes but also changes in the competitive position of a region vis a vis the rest of the world. However, in the CGE models these coefficients are fixed; hence, the demand equation can lead to some improper price changes. In addition there is a serious aggregation problem since the price for intermediates are different on the industry-by-industry basis, and different from the prices for the final demand components. As a result, price formation can be a serious problem at the regional level. The prices line that is a tangent to the production frontier forms the optimal choice; if the slope of the price line is affected by changes in input-output coefficients, then its slope may be modeled incorrectly. Secondly, prices are influenced by corresponding values at the national level; often, however, only import prices enter competition in the form of the choice of the source of the intermediate good. At the regional level, this competition would involve specification of import prices from extra-regional sources.

The choice process for the intermediate goods is inadequate as well since it focuses on total intermediate goods and value added components. There is no substitution between individual intermediate components and this neglect may mask the true substitution process between intermediates and value added. In CGE models, primary factor prices are observed and prices for goods and services are derived form the model (see Hoffman *et al.*, 1996; McGregor *et al.*, 1996). Is it possible to construct an export vector that will do the following - increase some exports, that will decrease some value added? This can be done by taking into consideration substitution between total intermediates and total value added. These relationships are usually modeled as Cobb-Douglas as shown in equation (21.1):

$$X_j = \left(\sum_i a_{ij} X_j \right)^{\alpha} \left(VA_j \right)^{\beta} \tag{21.1}$$

An increase in exports will induce output changes leading to price changes. As a result, the optimal combination on the intermediate-value added isoquant would shift towards the cheaper item. Assume that intermediates lower their price, then there will be a decrease in the consumption of value added. However, this lowering of price on the intermediates can be due to the low primary factor cost of one good. For example, if this is an agricultural commodity, then by lowering an agricultural price, we lower an intermediate price and shift along the isoquant toward intermediates. Within intermediates, there is no substitution, yet changes in agriculture will shift the whole intermediate vector. Realistically agriculture may substitute either commodity or value added but in this setting it is erroneously assumed that agriculture will shift the whole intermediate vector and will lower value added. Thus, while in input-output the value added proportion is fixed, in CGE models, the value added proportion may have an unreasonable shift due to the incorrect substitutability assumption. Alternatively, one can specify CES technology but the estimation of substitution coefficients may be too difficult. Consider this example with a nondecomposable input-output matrix; the changes just described would result in the building of bottlenecks in the intermediate purchases. For another case, consider a diagonal matrix for input-output to see the results of simulation. To simplify, further assume that there are no imports, i.e. instead of regional purchase coefficients, substitute technical coefficients.[1] In this case we will avoid competition between intermediate consumption locally and import by assuming that the import price is infinity.

[1] In this case, the economy is assumed to be entirely closed to the rest of the world.

In GCE production function, it is usually written as shown in equation (21.2):

$$q_j = \min\left(q_{1j}/a_{1j}, q_{2j}/a_{2j}, \ldots, q_{nj}/a_{nj}, \beta_j k_j^{\alpha_j} l_j^{1-\alpha_j}\right) \tag{21.2}$$

However, under the assumption that producers minimize costs and earn zero after-tax profits, the implication is that producers never waste inputs and therefore (see Kehoe and Kehoe, 1994):

$$q_j = q_{1j}/a_{1j} = q_{2j}/a_{2j}, = \ldots = q_{nj}/a_{nj} = \beta_j k_j^{\alpha_j} l_j^{1-\alpha_j} \tag{21.3}$$

This equation is easier for analysis with CGE models in large part because in this form it is similar to input-output.

21.2.2 Interpretation of Input-Output

Data reported by the US Bureau of the Census on industry expenditure patterns provides the cornerstone for the construction of input-output tables. Viewing the column of input-output table, the following identity is derived:

$$X^T = V^T \hat{P}_V + 1^T A\hat{X} \tag{21.4}$$

In other words, identity (21.4) is a share distribution of revenue, x_i. If we denote $x_i = p_i q_i$ revenue as a product of output and price then identity (21.4) can be rewritten as:

$$P^T = V^T \hat{P}_V \hat{Q}^{-1} + 1^T A\hat{X}\hat{Q}^{-1} = V^T \hat{P}_V \hat{Q}^{-1} + 1^T A\hat{P} \tag{21.5}$$

In the expression (21.5), the price of a unit of a good is represented by the expenditure shares normalized (divided) by output. In the CGE literature, equation (21.5) is interpreted as a physical representation of inputs that add up to a physical output, for example, $A\hat{Q}^{-1}$ are computers plus food items etc. For presentation purposes, we will consider unit production, i.e. Q=1, then (21.5) becomes:

$$P^T = V^T \hat{P}_V + P^T A \tag{21.6}$$

where $a_{ij} = \left(p_{ij} q_{ij}\right)/p_j$ represents an expenditure share for a unit production. In CGE models, A is assumed fixed over time; obviously, except for the base year (a year when the input-output was observed) the identity will not hold. In CGE models, equation (21.6) is imposed, therefore assuming that input-output is never balanced. This equation represents column-constraints or demand constraints:

$$P^T (I - A) = V^T \hat{P}_V$$

However, in the balanced input-output:

$$(I - A) = V^T \hat{P}_V \tag{21.7}$$

therefore P=1 for the balanced input-output. For the imbalanced disturbances, the change in value added will pass-through to prices. Let A=0, then, $\Delta P^T = \Delta V^T \hat{P}_V$, since there are no interindustry purchases price change will be equal to the change in the primary resources. Consider another simple example, the case when A is diagonal then $\Delta P^T > \Delta V^T \hat{P}_V$ because each industry will consume its own good which will increase in price by more than the change in value added. Thus in (21.7), there is a linear transformation of value added into prices; in other words, there is no substitution between inputs (in the form of weights for prices represented by a_{ij}). For example, if value added for gas declines, no industry will substitute gas for electricity. Gas prices will decline and electricity prices will decline and, as a result, all other prices will decline. However, if gas for electricity substitution could take place, then the price decline for manufacturers (as consumers of these inputs) would be greater.

Considering row constraints or supply-constraints we have:

$$X = AX + F1 \tag{21.8}$$

where F is a *matrix* of final demand. Revenues, X, are equal to the total sales of good i for intermediate and final uses. In CGE models, X is assumed to be physical output; as a result, there is a problem interpreting equation (21.8).

$$p_i q_i = \sum_j a_{ij} p_j q_j + f_i p_i^f \tag{21.9}$$

In CGE models, there is physical balance across the row; using (21.9), we may derive:

$$q_i = \sum_j a_{ij} q_j + f_i \tag{21.10}$$

Since (21.9) holds by input-output construction, this equation can be true only for all prices equal to unity whereas CGE models assume that (21.10) is true for any price. Indeed (21.10) would hold if input-output coefficient normalization would be row-wise (as in some versions of the supply-driven input-output model). In CGE models, input-output coefficients are derived column-wise, therefore their row constraint (21.10) is violated.

Good i output is not homogenous across the row; for instance, chemical producers provide fertilizers for agricultural producers, paint for the construction industry and plastic dishes for personal consumption. Our physical output therefore is $Q = \hat{P}^{-1} X$.

21.2.3 Deflated Input-Output

Deflating input and output, one can assume that physical input-output is derived: $H = P^{-1} AP$ where H is a deflated input-output coefficient matrix. Another equation that has to be satisfied is $P^T = V^T (I - H)^{-1}$. In both equations, P has to be the same. For that purpose, V can be derived from the double deflation method, as a residual $P^T - P^T H = V^T$, therefore for a given price vector we can derive deflated value added (see Israilevich, 1991). However, if primary resources are deflated and they sum to value added, then the above equation most likely will not be satisfied. Thus, to establish the relationship between prices and deflated V we need input-output information. Then V is related to primary resources. In CGE models, the relation between prices and deflated V is $P^T = V^T (I - H)^{-1}$. This is based on the *cost-push* assumption, however there is no explicit economic reasoning for the relation between prices and deflated V. Observed input-output establishes current V to current P relations, where V is the value sum of primary resources. If one uses fixed (over time) physical input-output, H, then it is unclear how the deflator for V should be determined if prices are unknown. Due to double deflation, V can be nonlinearly related to prices via a cost-push formula. In the observed input-output, V is a sum of the value of primary resources, therefore V can be determined without prices P. However, prices in this case are all unity. Thus, value termed input-output yields trivial prices and deflated input-output cannot determine deflated value added from the primary resources and therefore cannot determine prices. CGE models assume cost-push relations and a constant deflation *correction* coefficient for primary resources. For example $v = \gamma k^{\alpha} l^{\beta}$ for a specific sector then γ reflects a correction for deflation. This correction is fixed over time.

21.2.4 REIM Approach

In CGE models, prices and output represent supply and demand that helps to determine equilibrium but for practical purposes one can forgo prices and replace dynamic equilibrium with output relations only (see Israilevich *et al.* 1997). This approach was first suggested by Conway (1990) and later implemented in the development of forecasts for the input-output coefficients in the Chicago REIM. Such an approach is theoretically less tractable but empirically it is easier to implement and results in forecasts that are most likely to be superior, because the time series relations in the REIM provide estimates for coefficients while in the CGE model, only a single year calibration process determines coefficients.

In the REIM approach, row constraints are similar to the Cobb-Douglas model of output (21.1), (see Israilevich *et al.* 1996 for specific formulation). Although, it has only a row that includes final demand, one could separate intermediate supply from the final demand to make it similar to (21.1). To add column-constraints to the REIM system, we would have to model value added explicitly and link value added to the intermediate components. This would serve as a column-wise constraint, whereas in the original formulation only a row constraint was imposed. In the next section, we will suggest several approaches for inclusion of column constraints into REIM models.

21.2.5 Approach 1. Relate Output to Value Added Components

$$X_j = K_j^{\alpha} L_j^{\beta} \tag{21.11}$$

In this case output, X_j, will be determined from the row constraint, labor and capital are determined from (21.11). Later on, we link capital in the dynamic system and determine derived demand for investment. This approach does not balance intermediate expenditures with value added; this is similar to the approach adopted by Kehoe and Kehoe (1994) that uses an assumption of optimality on the input side.

21.2.6 Approach 2. Pseudo RAS

Price as a unit cost production (output block). To avoid confusion related to the intermediate prices, we will employ a cost function approach. For a given industry, cost is assumed to be equal to revenue *X*. Now consider a column-demand equation that can be expressed as a unit-cost production. Assuming a competitive system, unit-price is equal to unit-cost, $\left(p_i = x_i / q_i\right)$ then:

$$\ln P = \text{translog}\left(P_{Int}, P_k, P_l, P_m\right) \tag{21.12}$$

Using Shephard's Lemma, we can derive shares of expenditure for total intermediate (*Int*), capital (*k*) and labor (*l*) outlays and imports (*m*). Import expenditures are derived by assuming a constant coefficients approach:

$$P_m = \sum_i 0.5\left(p_i + p_{f_i}\right)\left(a_{ij}^T - a_{ij}^{RPC}\right) \tag{21.13}$$

and

$$P_{Int} = \sum p_i a_{ij}^{RPC} \tag{21.14}$$

where p_i are national prices, p_{f_i} regionally weighted foreign prices and a_{ij}^T, a_{ij}^{RPC} represent the total technology and regional purchase coefficients respectively. P_m and P_{Int} are proxies for estimating the share equations derived from (21.12):

$$S_{Int}^T = \Phi^T + \Gamma^T \ln\left(P_{Int}, P_k, P_l, P_m\right) \tag{21.15}$$

Equations (21.12 to 21.15) endogenously determine output prices, p_i ,, import prices, p_{m_i} , the weighted price of aggregated intermediate goods and services, p_{Int} , and the total share of expenditures, S_{Int_i} . Foreign prices, p_{f_i} , are exogenous. Now, we can estimate the intermediate share expenditures, local and/or import, which are exogenous to (21.12 to 21.15). We will refer only to the regional purchase coefficients (RPC) expenditure shares as S_{Int} . It is important to note that while national prices were used as a substitute for regional prices, these prices were used only to determine regression coefficients; in the simulation exercises, we do not need national prices.

Using the REIM equation for the expected outputs (see Israilevich *et al.* 1996) and equation (21.15) for calculating the column constraints, we can express the modification to the input-output table as an RAS procedure:

$$S_{Int}^T = 1^T \hat{R} A \hat{S}$$
$$X = \hat{R}\left(A\hat{S}X + F1\right) \tag{21.16}$$
$$R = f\left(X, \text{ other variables}\right)$$

In the system, (21.16), the input-output modification block, we have three equations with three endogenous variables, *X*, *R*, *S*, assuming S_{Int}^T is exogenous. In actuality, S_{Int}^T is endogenously determined in (21.15) but it is exogenous for the (21.16) block, this may be referred to as the *output formation block* since (21.16) together with (21.12 to 21.15) endogenously determine outputs, input-output coefficients and prices.

From the output block, we can determine demand for the primary resources (note $x = pq$):

$$q_i = \frac{\left(\beta_i k_i^{\alpha_i} l_i^{1-\alpha_i}\right)}{p_i} \tag{21.17}$$

This equation relates primary inputs and industry output. From this equation, derived demand for capital or labor can be determined. This is the first equation in the *primary block* formation. It relates physical output (price of good is in the denominator) to physical capital and labor

21.3 Frame Shifting and Future Developments

An economic interpretation of the input-output block (21.16) will now be provided. In CGE models, it seems that all expenditures in the economy are balanced across columns and rows. This is achieved through the adoption of two restrictive assumptions. As was noted earlier, the column constraints require input-output to be determined as a physical flow of quantities, even though these are rarely observed; in addition, it requires homogeneity of inputs across row, which is violated due to aggregation. Our output block, (21.16), balances input-output in value terms and thereby eliminates the above concerns. Secondly, CGE models assume fixed input-output coefficients over time. We overcome this restriction by using block (21.16). This equation system not only facilitates biproportional changes among input-output coefficients, it also allows even greater flexibility in determining structural input-output changes. Using Israilevich *et. al.* (1997), one can illustrate the expansion of block (21.15) into subblocks, where a slight modification of block (21.15) would allow changes in the subblocks along with the whole input-output system. These subblocks can be modified to represent economic or technological clusters.

We assume that clusters of relationships within input-output are changing over time. For example, in Chicago in the 1950's there were prominent relationships between metal producers and related metal processors, auto-parts and tools manufacturers. In the 1990's, this block had diminished in prominence but the financial block linking exchanges between banks, real estate and insurance companies began to dominate the input-output landscape. The output block can potentially capture the movements of clusters and relate them to changes in output and final demand components (for more details, see Hewings *et al.*, 1997). Since the output block will constantly modify the input-output structure in relation to exogenous changes to these block variables, we refer to changes in input-output structure as *frame shifting*. The implication here is that changes are taking place across a wide array of interconnected sectors, rather than in one or two coefficients - hence the appeal to the notion of a *frame* of changes. Ignoring frame shifting would imply incorrect estimates of the effects of exogenous changes on the region's variables (impact analysis) and incorrect forecasts. For example, persistent changes over time in exports would modify the economic structure of purchases and sales within the region; in other words, there would be changes in the nature and strength of intermediation between export and primary resources of the region. This intermediation is determined by the input-output system. By ignoring the changes in the input-output structure, we assume that there is no link between intraregional purchases and sales and exogenous factors like export, labor migration, national wages and other macroeconomic variables. Such an assumption makes little sense.

Given this perspective, some options for the development of the system that might enhance the way in which the frame shifting of changes in the input-output could be accomplished.

21.3.1 Price Formation Block

This price formation is an alternative to output block price formation, and may offer a better approach. Viewing input-output coefficients as shares of cost (see Jorgenson *et al.*, 1987, Nakamura, 1984; Israilevich, 1991) we can determine a *price block*. In CGE models, prices are a linear function of the value added prices as in (21.6):

$$P = (I - A)^{-1} P_V V \tag{21.18}$$

on the assumption that the input-output system is represented in physical values and the value added entries do not add up to unity, otherwise all prices will be unity. For the value-termed input-output coefficients (i.e. the observed values), this approach would always yield unit prices, therefore not reflecting any regional price movements. To enable the usage of a value termed input-output table in the derivation of prices, we propose to use a translog form for the price relations. Using (21.12), and assuming that revenue is equal to cost, unit price can be expressed as:

$$\ln p_i = \text{translog}(P, P_k P_l) \qquad \forall i \tag{21.19}$$

then using Shephard's Lemma, we derive shares for an industry i as:

$$S_i = \Psi + \Gamma \ln P + \Phi \ln P_V \tag{21.20}$$

where Ψ is a vector of intercepts, Γ is a matrix of coefficients that relates shares to prices and Φ is an (n x 2) matrix relating capital and labor prices to each share. The capital and labor shares are assumed to be independent of prices for simplification (although we could form capital and labor shares as part of equation 21.20). Then intermediate purchase prices for industry i can be determined as:

$$\ln P = \Gamma^{-1}\left(S - \Psi - \Phi \ln P_V\right) \tag{21.21}$$

where Γ is a symmetric positive definite matrix and homogeneity constraints on coefficients should be imposed. Obviously, there are *n* set of vectors *P* derived for each industry *i*. The reason derives from the fact that value-based input-output assumes n^2 prices; hence, in (21.19), instead of industry prices *P*, we should have a vector of input prices for that industry. Equation (21.19) uses *P* as a proxy for industry-specific input prices. To resolve the problem of conversion of input prices to industry prices, we can substitute $\ln P$ as defined in (21.21) into the industry price, p_i, in (21.21):

$$\ln p_i = \text{translog}\left[\left(\exp\left\{\Gamma^{-1}\left(S_i, -\Psi - \Phi \ln P_V\right)\right\}\right), P_V\right] \quad \forall i \tag{21.22}$$

In this price block, (21.22), the value for each industry price, p_i, is determined by value added component prices and fixed coefficients. This represents a similar set of variables to those used in CGE equations of the kind shown in (21.18), however, here the relations between industry prices and value added prices are nonlinear as a result of the substitution allowed between inputs. Secondly, each individual price for value added is entered into the price definition (21.22), while in CGE models, value added component prices are usually aggregated into one indicator, $P_V V$ in the competition between intermediate inputs and value added.

The estimation procedure for the price block, (21.22), proceeds as follows. We will assume that prices across regions vary only due to differences in product mix, i.e., there is national arbitrage where prices are determined for all regions. In reality, they differ at least due to the transportation margin, differences in the age of capital and so forth. However, since we use prices to relate to regional input-output systems, we assume that the coefficients in (21.22) will adjust to reflect regional price differentials. Hence, prices, *P*, are national prices, and these will be used to estimate the input-output coefficients in the output block for all historical years. Then we estimate equation (21.20). In equation (21.19), we need to estimate only the intercept since all other coefficients will be determined from the share equations (21.20). Unfortunately, because of degree of freedom limitations, we will not be able to use SUR estimation procedures. The input-output coefficients are assumed to be RPCs.

21.3.2 Import Generation Block

To determine the *import block* we will use the Armington (1969) specification. In this specification, we assume that goods are distinguished by region of origin. This may be justified on the basis of aggregation and cross hauling (see Hewings *et al.* 1997 for some recent empirical evidence of significant intra-industry trade for the Midwest). Thus, the same sector may contain different product mixes; therefore, analyzing the origin of a given product may actually reveal the existence of a different product. The procedure adopted here provides a creative way of accounting for differences in product mix. Unfortunately, there is virtually no information on price differentials for a given sector across regions. We propose the following estimate of import shares among input-output coefficients (i.e., 1-RPC coefficients). We will use the shares estimation from (21.20) for determination of import share assuming that the price of primary resources from importing regions are imbedded in import prices, P^M . Then, the share of import in the input-output cell is:

$$\Psi_i^M = \frac{S_i^M}{S_i} \tag{21.23}$$

where the import coefficients are:
$S_i^M = C_i\left(\Psi_i + \Gamma \ln P^M\right)$ and C_i is a calibration vector for industry i that adjusts national prices to fit the observed import shares derived for the base year. Obviously, the RPC's are $\left(1 - \Psi_i^M\right)$.

For the import block coefficients derivation, we first derive technological coefficients (shares) as in (21.20), then we implement the model and derive regional prices P from (21.22). Secondly, using national prices, P^M , and technological coefficients derived from the model, we use (21.23) to derive an import share for each technological coefficient. Finally, we express the model in its final form where the A matrix represents RPCs. This is a nested procedure: first we derive technological coefficients then, via prices, we derive the RPC matrix. This procedure represents an alternative to equation (21.13).

21.3.3 Capital Formation Block

Denote value added in value terms as $P_V V = V^P$. For sector i, value added is an ith component of the vector V^P:

$$v_i^P = r_i k_i + w_i l_i \tag{21.24}$$

then, using an assumption of price ratio equal to the ratio of marginal products from (21.17):

$$\frac{w_i}{r_i} = \frac{\left(1 - \alpha_i\right) k_i}{\alpha_i k_i} \tag{21.25}$$

In addition, we assume that the industry regional wage is related to the previous year's regional wage and to the national industry wage, w_i^N :

$$w_{it} = f\left(w_{it-1}, w_i^N\right) \tag{21.26}$$

Vector V^P will be determined as $\left(1 - \hat{S}_{Int}^T\right) X = V^P$. Using equation (21.17) and equations (21.24 to 21.26) we can solve for k, l, w and r for each sector.

To determine a demand for investment for each sector, the following expression can be used:

$$i_t = k_t - k_{t-1} \delta \tag{21.27}$$

where δ is a depreciation rate. Now attention needs to be directed to the capital speed of adjustment. Some industries may have limits to the rates of change; for example, a semiconductor producer considering production of a good in year 2 will have to expand its capacity in year 1, therefore relating k_1 capital in year 1 to output x_2 in year 2. If different producers are aggregated in the regional economy, then relations between k_1 and x_2 can be different than those for a single producer. In the latter case, this relationship would differ relative to the stage of their development, i.e. if a plant operates at less than capacity, then it does require extra capital to produce additional output. If the plant is at capacity, then additional output would require new capital. However, aggregation would tend to *smooth* such differences. Therefore, we can present output to capital relations as a continuous function (following Shapiro, 1986, and Glick and Rogoff, 1995) and our production function (21.17) will change to:

$$q_{i,t} = \frac{\left(\beta_{i,t} k_{i,t}^{\alpha_i} l_{i,t}^{1-\alpha_i}\right)}{p_{i,t}} \exp\left[-.5\varphi_t \left(\frac{i_{i,t}}{k_{i,t-1}}\right)^2\right] \qquad \varphi \geq 0 \tag{21.28}$$

Then, the marginal products ratios (21.25) will change; dropping subscript i and t, and recalling that $i_t = k_t - \delta k_{t-1}$, which we will rewrite as $i = k - \delta k_{t-1}$, we have:

$$\frac{r}{w} = \frac{\partial q / \partial k}{\partial q / \partial l} =$$

$$= \frac{\beta \alpha k^{\alpha-1} l^{1-\alpha} \exp\left[-.5\phi\left(\frac{i}{k_{t-1}}\right)^2\right] + \beta k \alpha l^{1-\alpha} \exp\left[-.5\phi\left(\frac{k_t}{k_{t-1}} - 1\right)^2\right] \phi\left(\frac{1}{k_{t-1}}\right)}{(1-\alpha)\beta k \alpha l^{-\alpha} \exp\left[-.5\phi\left(\frac{i}{k_{t-1}}\right)^2\right]} = \tag{21.29}$$

$$= \frac{\alpha l}{(1-\alpha)k} - \frac{l\left(\phi \frac{1}{\delta k_{t-1}}\right)}{(1-\alpha)} = \frac{l\left(\alpha - \phi \delta k_{t-1}^{-1}\right)}{(1-\alpha)k}$$

This equation assumes that the production function has a quadratic capital adjustment cost and that the typical producer maximizes output in year t subject to capital and labor cost but with no consideration of the dynamics of future capital accumulation. In other words, this is a static presentation of the capital adjustment model.

In the dynamic formulation, a producer would maximize cash flow as a difference between the cost of production and labor and capital expenses over time. The expected cash flow will be:

$$E_t \sum_{i=0}^{\infty} R_{t+1} \left\{ f\left(z_{t+1}, \Delta z_{t+1}, \beta_{t+i}\right) - p_{t+i}^k \left(k_{t+1} - \delta k_{t+i-1}\right) - w_{t+i} l_{t+1} \right\} = 0 \tag{21.30}$$

where E_t denotes expectations conditional on the information available at time t. $R_{t+i} = \prod_{j=t+1}^{t+i} r_{j-1}$ are the returns and $r_t = 1/(1+\rho_t)$ where ρ is the required rate of return from periods t to t+1. Distortions in productivity are revealed by β_{t+i}. The first part of (21.30) provides the cost of producing goods that is equal to defined revenue x_i. The second part of the expression represents expenditures on capital and labor. Labor cost in particular has been simplified so that there is no adjustment for education within the firm or other expenses due to a change in the firm's size (such as provisions for compensation for firing etc.). To determine the first order conditions for (21.30), we will use *Euler's equation*:

$$f_x - \frac{d}{dt} f_{x'} = 0$$

then the first-order conditions for equation (21.30) are (in this derivation, the production function has been converted into log form with $\frac{\partial \ln y}{\partial \ln k} = z$ and $\frac{\partial y}{\partial k} = z\frac{y}{k}$ and dropping the subscript i:) for capital:

$$E\left[\left(\frac{\alpha}{k_t} - \phi\frac{i_t}{k_t}\right)x_t + \left(\phi\frac{i_{t+1}}{k_{t+1}}\right)x_{t+1}dr_t - p_t^k + dr_t p_{t+1}^k\right] = 0 \tag{21.31}$$

where two arguments are considered: k_t and $\frac{i_t}{k_t}$. In addition, we assume that

$$\frac{\partial k_t}{\partial t} = 0 \text{ but } \frac{\partial}{\partial t}\left(\frac{i_t}{k_t}\right) = \frac{i_{t+1}}{k_{t+1}}.$$

For labor, the first-order condition is:

$$\frac{1-\alpha}{l_t}x_t - w_t + r_t w_{t+1} = 0 \tag{21.32}$$

If we assume that producers maximize expected cash flow, then the equations (21.31) and (21.32) should replace equation (21.25).

Investment i is a scalar that has to be disaggregated for the purpose of defining the final demand portion of investment demand as a final good. For this purpose, we consider three types of investment: (1) investment in residential structures, (2) investment in nonresidential structures, and (3) investment in equipment. Furthermore, each group of investments is disaggregated into an individual commodity; this is accomplished by proration using the national input-output structures. Each of these three investment categories is represented in a way that is based, in part on the national variables.

In the REIM models, the vector of investment is entered as a part of final demand, assuming that investment is generated by the demand side. There are three types of investments - in residential structures, in nonresidential structures and investment in equipment. Investment in residential structures, (21.33), is a function of AAA bond rates (*Ar*), GNP and is related to the residential investments through an autoregressive process. Similarly, investment in nonresidential structures, (21.34), is a function of AAA bond rates, prime interest rate (*Pr*), Chicago estimates of GRP and nonresidential investments as an autoregressive process. Investment in equipment,

(21.35), is a function of GNP, U.S. labor force (l^{US}) and investment in equipment as an autoregressive process. Each of these three investment categories is decomposed to a 2-digit sector for goods and services; the decomposition is based on the U.S. vector for the corresponding category.

$$i_{RES} = g_R(Ar, GNP), AR \tag{21.33}$$

$$i_{NRES} = g_{NR}(Ar, Pr, GRP), AR \tag{21.34}$$

$$i_E = g_E(GNP, l^{US}), AR \tag{21.35}$$

Finally, the individual investment categories have to balance the total investment demanded by all sectors of the region:

$$i = i_E + i_{NRES} + i_{RES} \tag{21.36}$$

This completes the capital block that defines investment as derived demand from the production function specification and then disaggregates this demand to three categories of investment that are necessary to relate this demand for outputs through the final demand vector of investments. Some additional considerations that involve the development of regional capital stock estimates are discussed in an appendix.

21.3.4 Labor Supply

In the REIM systems, labor supply is determined as a function of unemployment and the participation rate. The regional labor force, l, is defined as:

$$l = \frac{n}{1-u} \tag{21.37}$$

where n is employment by place of residence, and u is unemployment rate. Employment by place of residence is determined as a function of total employment by place of work, n_{tot}, and employment in the previous period:

$$n = f(n_{tot}), AR1 \tag{21.38}$$

The unemployment rate is assumed to be a function of national unemployment and the previous year's regional unemployment:

$$u = f(u_{US}), AR1 \tag{21.39}$$

Finally, total employment is the sum of demand for employment by individual industries.

In these systems, total employment is constrained by the growth in population block. The block within the REIM systems links the demographic characteristics of a region with their underlying economic determinants. This block is added to the feedback system to predict growth in total population along with eight age and sex cohort groups, and also birth, death, and net-migration totals. Among them, only two variables, total population and population of driving age, are directly related to the economic system. In the model structure, total population partially bounds the linkage of employment, labor-force participation, and unemployment information. Changes in total population due to changes in employment demand will be met by an adjustment of migration flows (for details, see Israilevich *et al.*, 1997). Meanwhile, the driving population is linked to the set of final demand, via an estimation of expenditure on auto and auto parts.

21.3.5 Household Sector and Government Expenditure

We determine two sources of income, namely wage and nonwage income. Wages are the sum of each sector's labor payment, *inc;* the time subscript, *t,* is omitted to simplify presentation:

$$inc = \sum_i w_i l_i \qquad \forall i \tag{21.40}$$

In addition to the industrial payrolls, there are four nonwage income series used in the REIM models. The first series is property income (RYPROP), the income received from personal assets, i.e. dividends, interest, and rent. Next are transfer payments (RYTR), total payments received from government, and contributions to social insurance (RYCSI). Lastly, the residential adjustment to income (RYRESAD) is an adjustment that accounts for those people who work and earn wages within the region but do not reside there. Thus, besides the wage income, we can obtain the nonwage income (*tr*) of the region using the accounting identity:

$$tr = \text{ RYPRO} + \text{PRYTR RYRESAD} + \text{RYRESAD} \tag{21.41}$$

Disposable household income therefore is:

$$y_d = (inc + tr)(1 - tx) \tag{21.42}$$

where *tx* is the personal income tax rate.

Consumption expenditures estimation follows along similar lines to the procedures adopted by West (1994) using the permanent income hypothesis with error corrections. Long-run consumption is assumed to be a linear function of income: $c = k * y_d$,, with short-run non-equilibrium relations defined as follows:

$$\ln c_t = \beta_0 + \beta_1 \ln c_{t-1} + \beta_2 \ln y_{d_t} + \beta_3 \ln y_{d_{t-1}} \tag{21.43}$$

subject to: $(\beta_2 + \beta_3)/(1 - \beta_1) = 1$.

In building the REIMs, we consider 4 categories of personal expenditures, instead of constructing a consumption function for each product, i.e. one for each sector in the model. These four consumption variables are non-auto durable goods, non-durable goods, services, and autos and auto parts. In principle, it would be optimal to have a consumption function for each sector in the model but in practice the data are simply too sparse to allow for such detail. Even in deriving the aggregated consumption series, regional tallies of consumption by commodity or class are in general not available, although comparable series for the nation do exist. Assuming that consumption patterns are not substantively different locally than they are nationally, we can then use the national data to synthesize similar series for the region in correspondence to the relationship between national and local income series.

We will now use an alternative way of modeling expenditures using West's (1994) approach. In this approach, West emphasizes that intermediate prices and consumer goods are different (an assumption that is consistent with the Armington procedure discussed earlier). Next, West assumes that consumer goods' prices are not endogenous to the system. Based on these assumptions, we can estimate the long-run expenditure shares and then the short-run disequilibrium coefficients. The long-run set of equations are estimated for each consumption category, *i* as:

$$c_i = \alpha + \beta_i c \tag{21.44}$$

where c is a disposable income derived from equation (21.42). The short-run disequilibrium equation may be presented as:

$$c_{it} = \beta_{i0} + \beta_{i1} \ln c_{it-1} + \beta_{i2} c_t + \beta_{i3} c_{t-1} \tag{21.45}$$

subject to the following constraints on the coefficients:

$$\beta_{i0} = 0, \qquad \frac{\beta_{i2} + \beta_{i3}}{1 - \beta_{i1}} = \beta_i, \qquad \sum_i \beta_i = 1$$

For estimation purposes, we estimate both equations, (21.44) and (21.45), but in simulation exercises, we need only equation (21.45).

Finally, government activities also need to be defined in an appropriate manner in the final demand category, because consumer spending accounts for the bulk of domestic demand, with the rest made up of capital spending and, to a lesser degree, government purchases. In the REIMs, we generally separate government expenditures into two main categories: federal government expenditures made within the region and state and local government expenditures within the region. Federal government expenditures are further divided into civilian and military expenditures with civilian expenditures divided again into construction and non-construction expenditures. Likewise, state and local government expenditures are divided into construction and non-construction expenditures.

21.4 Conclusion

In this chapter, we have shown that the CGE approach is consistent with input-output tables if coefficients are expressed as physical quantities. However, such tables are rarely presented. For an actual input-output table, the CGE approach would be inconsistent, and prices derived from such a system would be uniformly unity, which would not satisfy one of the major features of CGE systems, namely the representation of prices that are arbitraged to ensure market clearing in both commodity and factor markets. West (1994) offers a different, intermediate approach in which he assumes that the input-output table is used to define only price changes, $\Delta P = (I - A)^{-1} \Delta V$. However, utilizing the above price definition described earlier, West balances the input-output table at each time period, *t*. However, this introduces another inconsistency -- if for each *t*, the input-output table is balanced, then prices are all unity; yet in his approach, $P = P + \Delta P$. In other words, prices in *t* are not necessarily unity. Thus both CGE models and West's approaches fail to incorporate a price mechanism that is consistent with the input-output framework.

In the REIM approach modifications suggested here, we linked prices to input-output coefficients using Shephard's Lemma; this allows us to balance the input-output table in value terms (using observed input-output data). Since physical quantities are not defined explicitly, prices do not interfere with the balancing of the input-output table. In addition, we have assumed that the input-output structure is sensitive to changes in output and other variables. This was accomplished via the frame shifting procedure. We consider frame shifting an important relaxation of the CGE assumption of the fixed input-output coefficients. Further work on projecting subblocks of input-output as a function of different variables will be an important extension, some work in this direction was undertaken by Israilevich (1991), but this latter paper did not consider a full CGE framework.

References

Armington, P.S. 1965. "A Theory of Demand for Products Distinguished by Place of Production." *International Monetary Fund Staff Papers.*

Conway, R.S. 1990. "The Washington projection and simulation model: a regional interindustry econometric model." *International Regional Science Review*, 13, 141-166.

Conway, R.S. 1991. "An empirical comparison of regional multipliers." In J.J.Ll. Dewhurst, G.J.D. Hewings and R.C. Jensen, eds. *Regional Input-Output Modelling: New Developments and Interpretations.* Aldershot: Avebury, pp. 178-195.

Glick R., and K. Rogoff. 1995. "Global versus country-specific productivity shocks and the current account." *Journal of Monetary Economics*, 35, 159-192.

Hewings, G.J.D., P.R. Israilevich, M. Sonis and G.R. Schindler. 1997. "Structural change in a metropolitan economy: the Chicago region, 1975-2010." In S. Bertuglia, S. Lombardo and P. Nijkamp, eds. *Spatial Effects of Innovative Behaviour*. Heidelberg: Springer-Verlag.

Hewings, G.J.D., P.R. Israilevich, Y. Okuyama, D.K. Anderson, G.R. Schindler, M. Foulkes and M. Sonis. 1997. "Returns to Scope, Returns to Trade and the Structure of Spatial Interaction in the US Midwest." *Discussion Paper* 97-P-3, Regional Economics Applications Laboratory, University of Illinois, Urbana.

Hoffman, S., S. Robinson and S. Subramanian. 1996. "The role of defense cuts in the California recession: computable general equilibrium models and interstate factor mobility." *Journal of Regional Science*, 36, 571-595

Hudson, E. and D.W. Jorgenson. 1974. "US energy policy and economic growth, 1975-2000." *Bell Journal of Economics,* 5, 461-514

Hulten, C.L. 1990. "The Measurement of Capital." In E.R. Berndt and J.E. Triplett (eds), *Fifty Years of Economic Measurement*. New York: NBER

Israilevich, P.R. 1991. "The construction of input-output coefficients with flexible functional forms." In J.J.Ll. Dewhurst, G.J.D. Hewings and R.C. Jensen, eds. *Regional Input-Output Modelling: New Developments and Interpretations.* Aldershot: Avebury.

Israilevich, P.R., G.J.D. Hewings, G.R. Schindler and R. Mahidhara. 1996. "The choice of input-output table embedded in regional econometric input-output models." *Papers in Regional Science*, 75, 103-119.

Israilevich, P.R., G.J.D. Hewings, M. Sonis and G.R. Schindler. 1997. "Forecasting Structural Change with a Regional Econometric Input-Output Model." *Journal of Regional Science*,37, 565-90.

Jorgenson, D.W. F.M. Gollop, and B. M. Fraumeni. 1987. *Productivity and U.S. Economic Growth*. Cambridge, Mass: Harvard University Press.
Kehoe, P.J. and T.J. Kehoe. 1994. Capturing NAFTA's impact with applied general equilibrium models. *Quarterly Review, Federal Reserve Bank of Minneapolis*, 18, 17-22.
McGregor, P.G., J.K. Swales and Y.P. Yin. 1996. "A long-run interpretation of regional input-output analysis." *Journal of Regional Science*, 36, 479-500
Nakamura, S. 1984. *An Inter-Industry Translog Model of Prices and Technical Change for the West German Economy*. Berlin: Springer-Verlag.
Shapiro, M., 1986. "The Dynamic Demand for Capital and Labor." *Quarterly Journal of Economics*, 101, 513-542.
Takayama, Akira. 1985. *Mathematical Economics*. Cambridge, U.K.: University Press.
West, G.R. 1994. "The Queensland Impact and Projection Model: The Household Sector." *Economic Systems Research*, 6, 363-383.

Appendix 21 Derivation of Regional Capital Stock - a Possible Approach

In general, the demand for capital along with the supply of funds in the open market will determine the price of capital. Price of the capital stock depends on this equilibrium process together with considerations related to the vintage of the stock and rates of depreciation. In the region, the market price of funds is not determined by regional conditions but by the national market. For this reason, we adopt the general statement that the national not regional market determines the price of capital. Jorgenson *et al.* (1987) have developed a set of prices of capital services at the two-digits SIC level.

In our research, we will adopt these national series for the price of capital. To reproduce Jorgenson *et al.*'s (1987) calculation of the price of capital services at the regional level would be extremely time-consuming if not impossible. We will collect the value of capital services for each industry from which the flow of capital services will be determined. Next, we will again *borrow* national figures on the quality of capital stock from the Jorgenson study. Thereafter, we can estimate regional capital stock for each industry and this will facilitate the estimation of the investment flow by industry. The combined investment figure for all industries has to align with the figure we have generated in the model; recall that this investment series represents final demand in the model and should be equal to the combined investment in all sectors that is part of the supply of the primary resources. This identity between supply and demand will force some re-alignment that will enable the estimation of the equilibrium quantity of capital stock and thus provide a better reflection of the regional aspect of capital stock. This process is detailed below.

Derivation of the regional capital stock. First, derive the value of capital services $P_k K$ as a residual from value added (after subtraction of the value of labor services). Then:

$$K = (P_k K) / P_k \tag{A1}$$

where P_k can be determined from the Jorgenson national study for each industry on an annual basis. This estimation will provide a flow capital services. Next we determine capital stock:

$$K(t) = Q_K(t)A(t) \tag{A2}$$

where Q is the quality of capital stock and **A** is capital stock. Again, we can determine Q from Jorgenson's study. Then:

$$A(t) = A(t-1) - d\left[A(t-1)\right] + I(t) \tag{A3}$$

and from equation (A3), we can determine $I(t)$.

Next we have to align all $I_i(t)$, where i is an industry sector, so that $\sum_i I_i(t) = I(t)$ where $I(t)$ is determined in the REIM. After the adjustments, $I_i(t)$, will change; therefore we can assume that $A_i(t)$ will change, as will $Q_{k_i}(t)$. All these values can be recalculated.

Now we have capital services and investment flows for the historical period. Next, we estimate the production function of the form shown in (21.17) and from this function we determine K. Then we can determine stock, and finally investment. Thus, the remaining problem will be the projections of capital quality $Q_k(t)$. One approach to this problem might be to use the formulation of the perpetual inventory method in which it is assumed that investment from all surviving vintages is weighted by a number $0 \le \phi_{t-v} \le 1$ to allow for a declining contribution from older capital. Capital then is defined as:

$$K = \phi_0 I_t + \phi_1 I_{t-1} + \ldots + \phi_T I_{t-T} \tag{A4}$$

where $\phi_0 = 1$ and $\phi_{0+k} < 1$ for $k > 0$. Alternative approaches might adopt a straight-line efficiency assumption, or geometric decay.

22 Input-Output Systems in Regional and Interregional CGE Modeling

Eduardo A. Haddad,[1] Geoffrey J. D. Hewings[2] and Matthew Peter[3]

[1] FIPE, Universidade de São Paulo, Brazil and Regional Economics Applications Laboratory, University of Illinois, USA
e-mail: ehaddad@usp.br

[2] Regional Economics Applications Laboratory, University of Illinois, USA
e-mail: hewings@uiuc.edu

[3] Centre of Policy Studies and Impact Project, Monash University, Australia
e-mail: peter@tgm.com.au

22.1 Introduction

As models used in economic analysis become more and more complex, issues of reliability, tractability and analytical importance take on a greater role in the allocation of resources for model construction and updating. In this chapter, attention is directed to the role of input-output tables in broader, economy-wide models; while a number of papers have addressed this issue, the approaches have varied, in large part due to different motivations in the use or applications of the economy-wide models. Essentially, there are two types of issues that need to be addressed. The first is related to the source of the input-output data; how important is the quality of the input-output data that are to be incorporated into the economy-wide model? The second issue refers to the way the input-output structure is specified in the model, i.e., the functional form for the production system.

The scope of this chapter is as follows. In the next section, a general review of approaches to incorporating input-output models in Walrasian computable general equilibrium models will be provided. Section three will provide a complementary review of a less common approach, using a Marshallian general equilibrium formulation. The fourth section will illustrate some experimentation that has been conducted with examples of these models but with a particular focus on problems of coefficient change, market clearing and closure rule, consistency, and analytical importance and behavioral specifications. The chapter concludes with some summary perspectives.

22.2 Input-Output in Walrasian CGE Models

In this section, we investigate the role of input-output tables in Walrasian-type CGE (hereafter WCGE) models, in which the determination of equilibrium quantities and prices is achieved in a system of perfectly competitive markets and maximizing behavior by the agents. We used a common theoretical structure presented in the MONASH-MRF Model (Naqvi and Peter, 1996) which is an interregional multisectoral model of the Australian economy. The model was calibrated with Australian and Brazilian data, using the respective interregional input-output tables and parameters files available from Peter *et al.* (1996) and Haddad (1999).[1] By calibrating a common theoretical CGE specification with different sets of data, we intend to isolate the role of data sources in the functioning mechanisms of the model.

The equations of the CGE core module of the model are defined following the same structure of the ORANI Model (Dixon *et al.*, 1982), with a regional subscript added, when appropriate. While a model built in the Walrasian foundation, it may be considered a Johansen-type model, in that the solutions are obtained by solving the *linearized* equations of the model. A typical result shows the percentage change in the set of endogenous variables, after a policy is carried out, compared to their values in the absence of such policy, in a given environment. The schematic presentation of Johansen solutions together with the assumptions used in the model specification may be found in Haddad (1999).

Input-output data play a major role in the functioning mechanisms of WCGE models in different ways: a) providing the basis for calibrating cost, revenue and sales coefficients; b) defining the production technology in the economy; and c) enabling theoretical innovation in the specification of the models. The calibration of regional CGE models, i.e., the assignment of values to the relevant parameters and coefficients of the model, is a very demanding process. It consists of fitting the model specification to a consistently adjusted basic data set for the economy for a single year. This procedure determines the parameters' values of the model for a benchmark equilibrium. [Shoven and Whalley (1992), and Koh *et al.* (1993) discuss the calibration procedure of CGE models.]

For interregional WCGE models, an interregional input-output data base is required, with full specification of interregional flows. Data should also include interregional trade elasticities and other regional variables, for which econometric estimates are rarely available in the literature. Input-output tables provide the various production and consumption estimates. Interregional commodity flows data are seldom available. It has been common practice in interregional CGE modeling to use nonsurvey techniques to estimate them, and this practice might incorporate bias in the model estimates. Gravity type models (Leontief and Strout, 1963), contingency table method (Batten, 1982), and a combination of Round's method (Round, 1978, 1983) and *ad hoc* splits of rows and columns of national tables based on exogenous regional shares (Hulu and Hewings, 1993) are examples of techniques utilized. In Gazel *et al.* (1996), considerable attention was given to the estimation of the interregional trade matrix. The method developed by Hulu and Hewings (1993) was adopted, and sensitivity analysis for the interregional trade flows data was carried out in which a 10% increase in imports was assumed. Remarkable differences were noted for labor and capital incomes, but not for aggregated income.

Even though consistent non-survey techniques for the estimation of interregional trade flows are available, the quality of regional data has always been a problem. A

---

[1] The Brazilian data come from the Brazilian Multisectoral And Regional/Interregional Analysis Model (B-MARIA), presented in Haddad and Hewings (1997) and Haddad (1997), which is based on MONASH-MRF. However, in this paper, the theoretical structure of MMRF is adopted requiring some modifications in the Brazilian data set.

validation test was carried out in Ko (1985), showing that results for the national aggregates are far better than those for regional variables. Improving the regional results would involve not only the availability of better data but also the type of data collected.

Bias in the estimates of the interregional CGE models is frequently compromised by the estimation procedure of the interregional input-output components. It is not uncommon to find models in which the spatial disaggregation of the national input-output table relies on *ad hoc* column and row splits based on regional shares. The use of other non-survey techniques that carry the theoretical background essential to a more reliable construction of regional input-output tables under limited information, widely available in the literature, should be considered more often (see Round, 1978, 1983; Hulu and Hewings, 1993; Haddad, 1999).

Another data-related problem that modelers frequently face is the absence of trade elasticities at the regional level. The rule-of-thumb has been to use international trade elasticities as benchmarks for "best guess" procedures. Other elasticities are commonly borrowed from econometric studies; in this case, more reliable estimates are available. Sensitivity analysis for key parameters is sometimes performed, providing a more reliable range of model results.

To better understand the results of the model, a thorough analysis of the structure of the economy is needed. A close inspection of the benchmark data base is necessary, conducted not only on the relationships in the input-output data base, but also on the other relevant parameters of the model. Back-of-the-envelope calculations, which extensively employ the input-output estimates, help to trace out in some detail the mechanisms of large models, providing convincing evidence that the computations have been performed correctly and a better understanding of the model (see Dixon *et al.*, 1982).

Figure 22.1 illustrates the basic variations of production technology encountered in most interregional CGE models. Dotted-lined boxes represent standard functional forms used at each stage. Two broad categories of inputs are usually recognized: intermediate inputs and primary factors. Producers in each regional industry choose inputs requirements per unit of output through optimizing behavior (e.g. cost minimization). Constraints are given by the nested production technology. In the first level, primary factors and an intermediate-input bundle are combined, either assuming fixed proportions (Leontief) or some degree of substitution between them (Cobb-Douglas or CES). The use of CES production functions at the top level of the production structure dominates modeling procedures. Fixed proportion combinations of intermediate inputs are assumed in the second level, on one side, and substitution between capital and labor, on the other side. The third level involves substitution between domestically produced and imported intermediate inputs. At the fourth level, bundles of domestically produced inputs are formed as combinations of inputs from different regional sources.

Standard modeling procedures use either Cobb-Douglas or constant elasticity of substitution (CES) functions in the lower levels to combine goods from different sources. More flexible functional forms have been rarely attempted in regional models, due to data availability. One exception in regional CGE modeling is the model developed by Despotakis and Fisher (1988) for California. In that model, a generalized Leontief specification is adopted. Dixon *et al.* (1982) propose the use of constant ratios of elasticities of substitution, homothetic (CRESH) functions, a generalization of CES which allows for the elasticities of substitution between different pairs of inputs to differ. However, the estimation procedure was not satisfactory, leading the authors to adopt CES estimates.

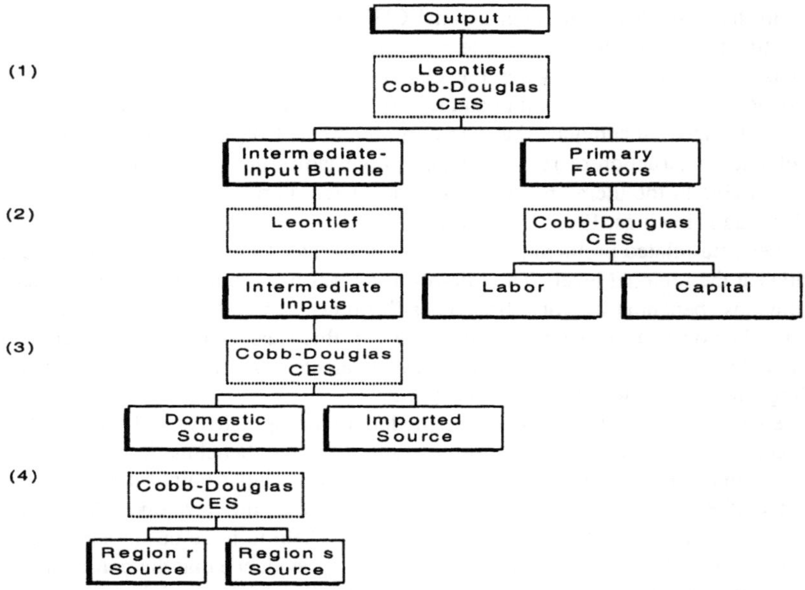

Figure 22.1 Standard Nesting Structures of Regional Production Technology in Interregional CGE Models

The generalized use of the Leontief specification at the top levels of the nesting structure of the production technology in CGE models has strong implications for the model results. It constrains the changes in sectoral results to the available technology even though substitution effects allow for structural changes at the regional level. The procedure also makes it possible to mimic input-output-model results when appropriate closures for the model are defined (see McGregor *et al.*, 1999).

In many instances, the way the input-output data are compiled enables theoretical innovations in the specification of the models. The availability of key information for the calibration of specific coefficients motivates experiments with the structure of the model. For instance, the nature of the input-output data base used to calibrate B-MARIA enabled the isolation of the consumption of public goods by both the federal and regional governments, which encouraged the experimental specification of the government demand for public goods. Another instance in which data availability induced theoretical experimentation in B-MARIA relates to the explicit modeling of the transportation services and the costs of moving products based on origin-destination pairs. The model is calibrated taking into account the specific transportation structure cost of each commodity flow, made available from the use of regional input-output tables and interregional transportation cost indices, providing spatial price differentiation, which indirectly addresses the issue related to regional transportation infrastructure efficiency.

22.3 Input-Output in Marshallian CGE Models[2]

Less well known are computable general equilibrium models of the Marshallian kind (hereafter MCGE); they have been adopted at the regional level, where price information is much more difficult to obtain, and thus, alternative approaches to economy-wide modeling have to be adopted. The role of the input-output tables assumes greater importance here, since changes in the input-output coefficients serve as the mechanism by which markets clear. However, the issues of choice of input-output tables and the way in which the system is specified in a functional sense remain critical.

Earlier work (see Drake 1976; Coomes *et al.*, 1991; Harrigan, 1992; Harrigan *et al.*, 1991; Hewings, 1977, 1984; Israilevich, 1991; Jensen, 1980; Round, 1983) has explored the role of input-output coefficient estimation (primarily focusing on the role of nonsurvey techniques) in the determination of model accuracy. However, with the exception of the Harrigan *et al.*, 1991 paper, this work has been exclusively oriented to analysis that explores the implications on the input-output system alone. In this section, that concern will be extended to economy-wide models. As such, attention will be directed to the issues of input-output coefficient estimation and adjustment.

Input-output tables are used in MCGE models as a deterministic linear predictor of output:

$$z_i^t = \sum_j a_{ij}x_j^t + \sum_j f_{ij}y_j^t + e_i n_i^t \qquad \forall i = 1,\dots,n \, , \tag{22.1}$$

where f_{ij} is a normalized regional purchase coefficient in the final demand matrix,

$Y = \left[y_j\right]$ is the final demand vector consisting of the following components: personal consumption elements, investment, government expenditures, and net exports,

$N = [n_i]$ is a vector of variables exogenous to the regional economy (such as GNP, national industrial production indices and other national data),

$E = [e_i]$ is a vector of normalized regional gross export coefficients,

$Z = [z_i]$ are predicted output values (as opposed to x_i which are observed values of output) and t indicates year.

For brevity we omit this superscript in the rest of this chapter. Exports, derived as a residual in the base year, are assumed to be proportional to the corresponding national variable (equation 22.1). The crucial difference between traditional input-output approaches and equation (22.1) is the weights assigned by (22.1) to each of the input coefficients. These weights are expressed as *observed* outputs, X, for each time period. In order to formalize the difference between the traditional input-output approach and equation (22.1), we can rewrite (22.1) in matrix form:

$$Z_{REIM} = AX + Y \tag{22.2}$$

where A is the input-output matrix and Y is a vector of aggregated final demand; all variables change in time, but we omit the time parameter to simplify exposition.

---

[2] This section draws heavily on Israilevich *et al.* (1996, 1997) and Israilevich (1998)

Denote the difference between the observed and estimated outputs as $\Delta = Z_{REIM} - X$. Then equation (22.2) can be presented as:

$$Z_{REIM} = \Delta + X = AX + Y. \tag{22.3}$$

If the usual input-output approach is used then:

$$Z_{IM} = (I - A)^{-1} Y. \tag{22.4}$$

From (22.4), we have:

$$\Delta + X - AX = \Delta + (I - A)X = Y. \tag{22.5}$$

Expression (22.5) then can be rewritten as:

$$Z_{IM} = (I - A)^{-1} Y = (I - A)^{-1} \Delta + X. \tag{22.6}$$

The difference between the IM and REIM estimation of outputs are as follows:

$$Z_{IM} - Z_{REIM} = \left[(I - A)^{-1} \Delta + X\right] - (\Delta + X) = \left[(I - A)^{-1} - I\right]\Delta, \tag{22.7}$$

and, by using the power series decomposition of the Leontief inverse, we have:

$$Z_{IM} - Z_{REIM} = \left(A + A^2 + \ldots + A^\infty\right)\Delta. \tag{22.8}$$

From this expression, it is clear that the difference between the traditional input-output estimates (IO) and those generated by equation (22.1) (these being the output estimates from MCGE), will be amplified by the structure of the *A* matrix. Hence, the differences between the two estimates will be directly related to the nature of the linkages between industries, measured by the indirect multiplier effects. It is not unreasonable to expect that the use of the input-output system in (22.1) as opposed to the traditional input-output formulation may amplify the effect of differently constructed input-output tables on the prediction of total output, *Z*.

22.3.1 Stochastic Equations for the Input-Output Components

To turn this model into an econometric forecasting model, vector *Z* has to be stochastically related to the observed vector, *X*. In the MCGE, this is accomplished through a set of regression equations:[3]

$$\log\left(\frac{x_{it}}{z_{it}}\right) = \alpha_0 + \alpha_z\left(\frac{z_{i,t-1}}{x_{i,t-1}}\right) + \alpha_g g_{it} + \varepsilon_{it} \qquad \forall i = 1,\ldots,N;\ \forall t = 1,\ldots,T \tag{22.9}$$

where $z_{i,t-1}$ is a lagged input-output-generated predicted output, and g_i is the set of exogenous variables selected by the modeler (there are $(T \times N)$ equations in 22.9). The lag structure shown in (22.9) varies by sector; in some cases, the lag will be zero, while in other cases a first-order or even second-order nonlinear difference equation

[3] This specification was adopted from Conway (1990).

will be appropriate. Equation (22.9) is estimated separately for each industry i with the vector of random errors, ε_i. Equations are estimated using EGLS, assuming autocorrelation, otherwise an OLS procedure is adopted.

Equation (22.9) assigns a set of regression coefficients to each row of the input-output table, weighted by annually observed outputs, in a nonlinear fashion. This means that the input-output column sums would not provide enough information for the system (22.9) and, hence, Drake's (1976) short-cut method could not be employed in a MCGE model.

In a fully specified MCGE system, the final demand matrix is itself endogenous within the whole model. However, for the presentation in this section, we break the link with the rest of the MCGE by assuming that vector Y is exogenously determined. As a result, system (22.9) can be represented in the following fashion to illustrate the relationship to traditional input-output computations. First, denote the right-hand side of (22.9) as:

$$\beta_{it} = \exp\left(\alpha_0 + \alpha_z \log\left(\frac{z_{i,t-1}}{x_{i,t-1}}\right) + \alpha_g g_{it}\right) \qquad \forall i = 1,\ldots,N;\ \forall t = 1,\ldots,T\,. \tag{22.10}$$

Then (22.9) can be rewritten (dropping the time subscript) as:

$$x_i = \beta_i z_i \qquad \forall i = 1,\ldots N;\ \forall t = 1,\ldots,T\,. \tag{22.11}$$

By diagonalizing β_i as a diagonal matrix, $\hat{\beta}_i$, and utilizing (22.3), the system (22.9) can be presented as:

$$X = \hat{\beta}AX + \hat{\beta}Y \qquad \forall t = 1,\ldots,T\,, \tag{22.12}$$

or, finally, as:

$$X = \left[\left(I - \hat{\beta}A\right)^{-1}\hat{\beta}\right]Y \qquad \forall t = 1,\ldots,T\,. \tag{22.13}$$

It is important to stress that the matrix, $\hat{\beta}$ is a nonlinear first-difference operator that modifies the static Leontief inverse into a dynamic one. This modified inverse, $L = \left[\left(I - \hat{\beta}A\right)^{-1}\hat{\beta}\right]$ changes with the choice of the input-output table in two respects. First, if A is modified, then the estimates in (22.9) will change (i.e., β is a function of A) and secondly, the matrix A itself will be different.

The system of equations (22.13) provides a forecasting or impact capability, assuming that Y is determined exogenously. However, in MCGE, only the vector of exports within final demand Y is a function of exogenous variables (such as national indices of industrial production, GDP etc.). All other components of final demand are linked to other submodules within REIM. Hence, (22.13) does not represent a full MCGE-based solution but provides insight into how the input-output component plays a different role from standard input-output analysis.

22.3.2 Shock Specification in MCGE Models

In the standard IO system, a shock is usually introduced through a change in an element of the final demand vector. Similarly, the system (22.13) can be shocked exogenously by adding a vector of change to the output, *X*. Therefore, the impact on all outputs, *X*, is measured as:

$$X = \hat{\beta} AX + \hat{\beta} Y + s \qquad \forall t = 1,...,T , \tag{22.14}$$

where s is a vector with positive (negative) shock, s_i, and zeroes elsewhere, and thus represents a positive (negative) shock to sector *i*.[4] The closed form solution for the impact analysis is:

$$X = \left(I - \hat{\beta} A\right)^{-1} \left(\hat{\beta} Y + s\right) \qquad \forall t = 1,...,T . \tag{22.15}$$

However, recall that *Y* is part of a larger system within MCGE and therefore the closed form solution would involve interactions with other equations from other modules within REIM. In both forecasting and impact analysis (equations 22.13 and 22.15), the differences in A can be compensated by the estimated $\hat{\beta}$. In other words, $\hat{\beta}$ compensates for differences in input-output tables so that the final fit to the observed output is achieved by minimizing random error. As a result, one may argue that survey-based input-output tables within MCGE would yield the same results for impact analyses and forecasts as those generated with nonsurvey tables. If this is the case, then the efforts expended on estimating the input-output coefficients should be minimized. The implications from this assertion are that the debates initiated by Drake (1976) may have applicability in REIM systems.

In the next section, a variety of experiments with WCGE and MCGE models are performed; since the modeling systems are different in terms of underlying assumptions, no direct comparisons can be made. However, the role of the experiments is to explore the role the input-output system plays in the model – in short and long-run impact analysis and forecasting.

22.4 Experiments

22.4.1 WCGE Models

The calibration of the WCGE model used in the simulations is based on two subsets of data. First, an absorption matrix containing the information presented in figure 22.2 needs to be generated from input-output data sources. By working with percentage changes rather than absolute changes, the coefficients of the model are often readily interpretable cost and sales shares, and they can be derived from input-output tables.

---

4 In Conway (1990), the shock was entered through equation (22.11), which is identical to (22.15). In Conway, by substituting $X = \hat{\beta} Z + s$ for *Z* in (22.4), one may derive (22.16).

Together with some supplementary data on values of capital stocks, depreciation rates, demographic variables, and some other variables, which should be consistent with the absorption matrix estimates, the first piece of data is complete. Because of their nature – these estimates are based on snapshot observations for a single year revealing the economic structure of the economic system – this subset of data is denoted "structural coefficients". The second piece of data necessary to calibrate the model is represented by the parameter files defining the various elasticities and long-term strucutural behavior of agents; these are called "behavioral parameters". These two subsets of information provide an initial solution for the model, highlighting two different aspects of the economic system, which could also be interpreted as short-term and long-term structural information.

In the following analysis, the results from four different models were considered. As already mentioned, the system of equations of MMRF was used as the common WCGE structure, and calibrated with four different data sets derived from the combination of the short-term and long-term structural information for the economies of Australia and Brazil. The results reported involve a common 10% tariff cut imposed in the four different models (one representing the Brazilian economy, one representing the Australian economy, and the two others combining structural coefficients and behavioral parameters from the two economies). We concentrate our analysis on some expenditure components of national GDP and sectoral aggregate output. Table 22.1 gives the data sources for each model.

Table 22.1 Data Sources for Simulation Models

	Structural	*Behavioral*
Model 1	Brazil	Brazil
Model 2	Brazil	Australia
Model 3	Australia	Australia
Model 4	Australia	Brazil

The strategy for testing the role of different data sources is based on the principles of qualitative sensitivity analysis, as suggested in Haddad (1999) as a way to overcome the scarcity of estimates of regional trade elasticities (and any other key parameter). The idea is to estimate policy results based on different *qualitative* sets of values for the parameters. Through the judgment of the modeler, a range of alternative combinations reflecting differential structural hypotheses for the regional economies can be used to achieve a range of results for a policy simulation. This method, called *qualitative or structural sensitivity analysis*[5], provides a "confidence interval" to policy makers, and incorporates an extra component to the model's results that contributes to increased robustness through the use of possible structural scenarios. As data deficiency has always been a big concern in regional modeling, one that will not be overcome in the near future, this method tries to adjust the model for possible

[5] The term "qualitative sensitivity analysis" is used as opposed to "quantitative sensitivity analysis", which is the common practice adopted by modelers to define confidence intervals for the simulations' results. Usually, the parameters are allowed to deviate over a range centered in the initial assigned values, or to present small increases/decrease in one direction, which does not address the likely cases of structural mispecifications, as reported previously.

parameter mispecification. Qualitative sensitivity analysis should be used on a regular basis in regional CGE modeling in order to avoid, paradoxically, speculative conclusions over policy outcomes. If the modeler knows enough about the functioning of the particular national and regional economies, the model achieves a greater degree of accuracy when such procedure is adopted.

By using the qualitative approach to carry out sensitivity analysis in the simulations, the role of the input-output data files can be investigated in a consistent way. Because of the interdependence of the coefficients in the model (i.e. cost shares must add up to unity), consistency of the data set is required to carry on the testing procedure. In this case, we will be checking how the use of different data sets affect the model results when a shock is imposed in the system in equilibrium, and not how exogenous changes in the data set affect model results. The latter type of analysis has been performed elsewhere (Gazel *et al.*, 1996). By departing from a balanced system rather than disturbing some of its structural elements, consistency is assured and the role of the data source can be evaluated.

Two standard closures for alternative time frames of analysis in single-period simulations are adopted. A distinction between the two closures relates to the treatment of capital stocks encountered in the standard microeconomic approach to policy adjustments. In the short-run closure, capital stocks are held fixed, while, in the long-run, policy changes are allowed to affect capital stocks.

Short-run. In addition to the assumption of interindustry and interregional immobility of capital, the short-run closure would include fixed regional population and labor supply, fixed regional wage differentials, and fixed national real wage. Regional employment is driven by the assumptions on wage rates, which indirectly determine regional unemployment rates; these assumptions describe the functioning of the regional labor markets. First, changes in the demand for labor are met by changes in the unemployment rate, rather than by changes in the real wage; second, interregional immobility of labor in the short-run suggests that migration is not a short-term decision; finally, nominal wage differentials reflect the geographical segmentation of the workforce. On the demand side, investment expenditures are fixed exogenously – firms cannot reevaluate their investment decisions in the short-run. Household consumption follows household disposable income, and government consumption, at both regional and federal levels, is fixed. Finally, since the model does not present any endogenous-growth-theory-type specification, technology variables are exogenous (Peter, 1997).

Long-run. A standard long-run (steady-state) equilibrium closure is also used in which capital is mobile across regions and industries. Capital and investment are generally assumed to grow at the same rate. The main differences from the short-run are encountered in the labor market and the capital formation settings. In the first case, aggregate employment is determined by population growth, labor force participation rates, and the natural rate of unemployment. The distribution of the labor force across regions and sectors is fully determined endogenously. Labor is attracted to more competitive industries in more favored geographical areas; in the same way, capital is oriented towards more attractive industries. This movement keeps rates of return at their initial levels.

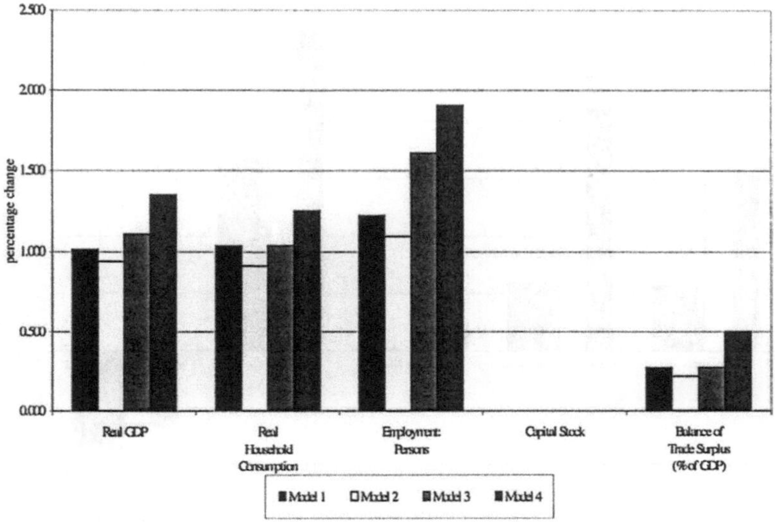

Figure 22.2 Short-Run Effect of a 10% Across-the-board Tariff Cut: Selected Macro Variables

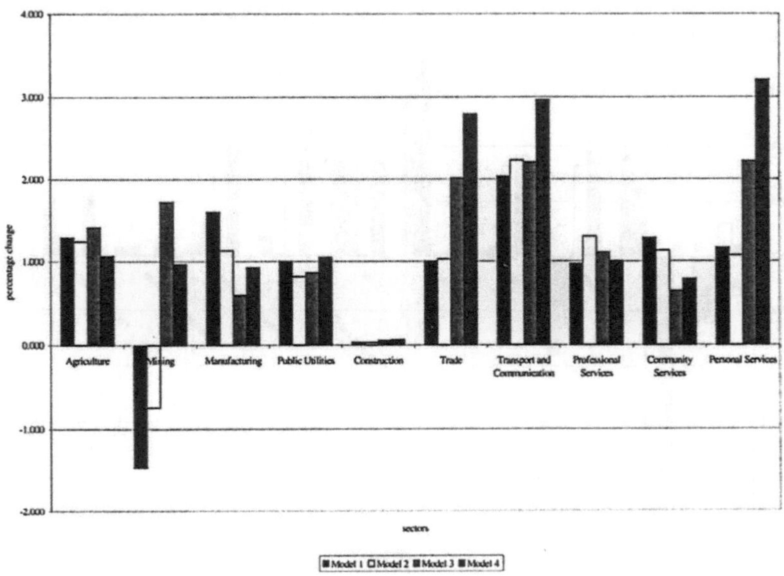

Figure 22.3 Short-Run Output Effects of a 10% Across-the-board Tariff Cut: Selected Sectors

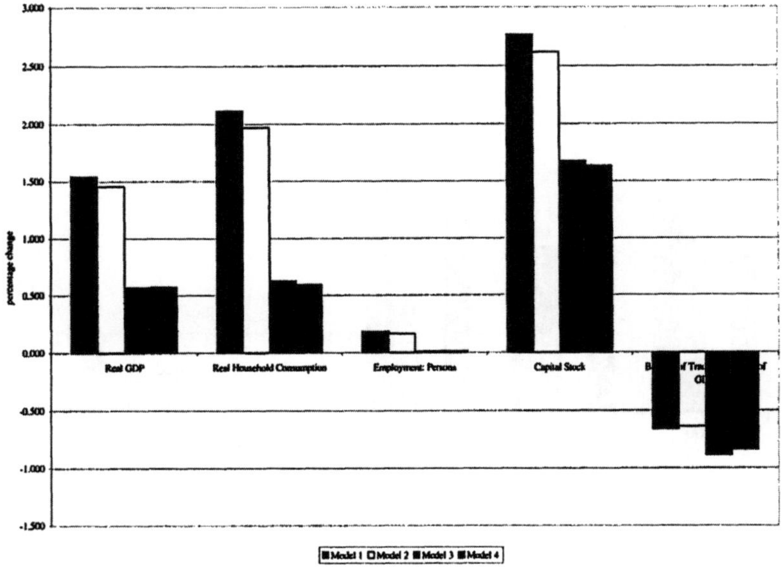

Figure 22.4 Long-Run Effect of a 10% Across-the-board Tariff Cut: Selected Macro Variables

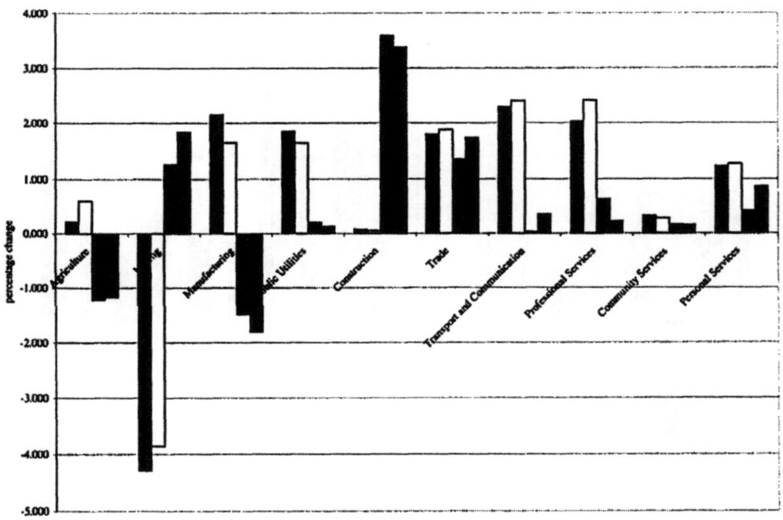

Figure 22.5 Long-Run Output Effects of a 10% Across-the-board Tariff Cut: Selected Sectors

Table 22.2 Short-Run and Long-Run Impact of a 10% Across-the-Board Tariff Cut on Selected Variables

	Short-Run				Long-Run			
	Model 1	Model 2	Model 3	Model 4	Model 1	Model 2	Model 3	Model 4
Macro Variables								
Real GDP	1.015	0.941	1.107	1.352	1.543	1.457	0.571	0.574
Real Household Consumption	1.038	0.910	1.041	1.251	2.117	1.970	0.630	0.598
Employment: Persons	1.222	1.093	1.609	1.906	0.185	0.164	0.012	0.015
Capital Stock	0.000	0.000	0.000	0.000	2.771	2.621	1.675	1.635
Balance of Trade Surplus (% of GDP)	0.277	0.220	0.277	0.502	-0.660	-0.637	-0.888	-0.841
Sectoral Output*								
1. Agriculture	1.295	1.245	1.416	1.073	0.214	0.605	-1.218	-1.168
2. Mining	-1.468	-0.747	1.725	0.966	-4.289	-3.858	1.262	1.838
3. Manufacturing	1.605	1.137	0.601	0.925	2.158	1.651	-1.488	-1.809
4. Public Utilities	1.003	0.818	0.867	1.057	1.854	1.644	0.206	0.130
5. Construction	0.032	0.029	0.056	0.064	0.077	0.049	3.598	3.387
6. Trade	1.004	1.028	2.014	2.792	1.800	1.878	1.359	1.730
7. Transport and Communication	2.036	2.229	2.204	2.966	2.305	2.414	0.029	0.355
8. Professional Services	0.968	1.305	1.116	1.003	2.035	2.425	0.639	0.224
9. Housing**	0.165	0.158	0.000	0.000	1.846	1.816	1.049	0.896
10. Public Services**	0.000	0.000	0.208	0.280	1.958	1.821	0.569	0.572
11. Community Services	1.293	1.137	0.647	0.786	0.328	0.281	0.167	0.154
12. Personal Services	1.170	1.078	2.219	3.212	1.232	1.269	0.424	0.874

Notes: * A non-competitive imports sector is also defined for models 3 and 4 but the results are not shown here.
** These results are not comparable as a result of aggregation and classification differences.

Table 22.2 presents the simulations results for selected variables. The results are reported for each model using both the short-run and long-run closures. A comparison of the results achieved by the different models gives an idea of the extent of the role played by the absorption matrix estimates in the two different contexts. If models 1 and 2 present a common pattern differentiated from a similar pattern found in models 3 and 4, one can infer that, in this case, structural coefficients are relatively more relevant than behavioral parameters to drive model results.

The results for the short-run (figures 22.2 and 22.3) are not conclusive, when analyzed in isolation. Even though inspection of the macro variables suggest a pattern in which the use of the Brazilian input-output tables produce slightly lower estimates, assertion from sectoral output estimates cannot be made in this way. However, one should note that the signs of the effects conform to the respective input-output data sources – despite sign differences be perceived in only one sector.

When the restrictions on capital movements and labor mobility are relaxed, it is evident from the models results that the role played by the input-output data set in the functioning mechanisms of the model achieves greater distinction. The results generated have shown that, when the model is calibrated with the same absorption matrix (models 1-2 and 3-4), its data source dictates not only the direction but also the size of the effects. This point is clearly perceived by inspecting figures 22.4 and 22.5, which show the long-run effects of the tariff cut for selected macro variables and sectoral output.

These results are in accordance with the findings reported in McGregor *et al.* (1999), which revealed that one can mimic interregional input-output results for demand disturbances by adopting appropriate closures for an interregional CGE system. A reinterpretation of these results, together with the findings presented here, would suggest that the less restrictive the constraints in factor flows in CGE models, the more relevant the input-output coefficients are in the driving of the model results.

22.4.2 MCGE Models

For the MCGE models, two sets of experiments were performed. One focused on the short-run impacts (impact analysis) using the model calibrated with input-output tables that were generated from different sources. The second experiment used the same alternative sets of input-output coefficients in the model under forecasting conditions. While not directly comparable, the latter experiment could be considered as an analogy to a long-run simulation with a WCGE model.

In contrast to standard input-output models, MCGE models utilize all the information present in the detailed final demand matrix, including national variables; therefore, the MCGE multipliers will change with different values of national forecasts. However, it should be noted that the inverse matrix is calculated analytically (in large part because of the autoregressive time lags in many of the equations; see Israilevich *et al.*, 1997 for more details)

In MCGE, there is only one input-output table on which all historical estimates and forecasting values are based. For the year (base year) corresponding to the input-output table:

$Z \equiv X$,

but for all other years, this identity does not hold. The base year identity is achieved by either assuming exports as a residual or by allowing some adjustment procedure to balance rows only of the input-output table. For all other periods, $\hat{\beta}$ adjusts the rows of the input-output table through equation (22.15). Since (22.15) is derived from (22.9), in which there is a random error term, X on the left-hand side of (22.9) is estimated, not observed. This balancing procedure is different from the *columns and rows* adjustment approaches used in more traditional input-output and social accounting systems. Although this is a potential limitation, in our experience the procedure did not produce coefficients that violate the Hawkins-Simon conditions. In macro national models, such as the one developed by Hudson and Jorgenson (1974), the input coefficients are estimated through a derivation using Shepard's Lemma. In this type of approach, analysts balance derived input coefficients with column-constrained adjustments. As shown by Israilevich (1991, 1998), this procedure may cause imbalances.

While the forecasting ability of input-output is not of great interest in itself, we investigate it as it is a building block in MCGE-type models. We thus analyze how differently constructed input-output tables affect its forecasting ability. A second aspect of MCGE is in its role in impact analysis; in this respect, MCGE is similar to input-output. Both models lack an observed figure against which the performance of the model can be judged, since no one knows what the "true" impact is.

For the tests, we consider the input-output portion of the Chicago MCGE (CREIM). We consider three tables, which are balanced for 1982 according to equation (22.3). The Chicago-observed input-output table (CIO) is constructed from observed (Manufacturing Census) data combined with regionalized data from the national input-output table and other sources.[6] The second table is referred to as the Chicago-national input-output table (NIO) and is constructed directly from the national input-output table using location quotients for the regionalization procedure. Finally, in the spirit of earlier work by Hewings (1977), a third table is constructed; the Chicago-random input-output (RIO) table consists of randomly generated input-output coefficients. All three tables have the same normalized final demand matrix f_{ij}; some variations in this final demand matrix are the result of construction procedures explained in the Haddad (1999). All three tables are balanced to the same total outputs. The export vector is determined as a residual and, therefore, varies for each of the input-output tables. Since the purpose of this study is to explore the effects of changes in the input-output table on the output vector specified in (22.15), all changes due to simulations with different input-output tables will be recorded as changes in X.

Forecast Experiments In order to estimate the Z variables of equation (22.3), we allow vectors X, Y, and N to vary over the historical period (1983-92) using three different sets of input-output coefficients: CIO, NIO, and RIO. Afterwards, we

[6] A description of the CIO construction is provided in the Israilevich *et al.*, (1996). The manufacturing output series are constructed using data from various sources. Wages from BEA and output deflators from the BLS are used, value added, cost of materials, and payroll data from the Census of Manufactures and Annual Survey of Manufactures are also included. We then take Census Product, cost of materials plus value added, multiplied by the ratio of BEA wages to Census payroll. This is then deflated using the BLS deflator.

reestimate β coefficients for each of the three versions of Z. This completes the estimation of coefficients necessary for the simulation of the system (22.12). The other REIM modules are unchanged since the estimation of these modules is unaffected by the changes in the input-output table. (The system 22.12 is endogenized within REIM by making the final demand vector F endogenous. For example, changes in personal income will affect personal consumption, part of F). Accordingly, we derive three versions of REIM that we simulate over the historical period.

Table 22.3 Average Absolute Percent Difference

Number of occasions $\lvert\varepsilon_{NIO}\rvert > \lvert\varepsilon_{CIO}\rvert$	Average Percent Difference [NIO-CIO]	Number of occasions $\lvert\varepsilon_{RIO}\rvert > \lvert\varepsilon_{CIO}\rvert$	Average Percent Difference [RIO-CIO]
Resources		*Resources*	
3 out of 4	2.4	2 out of 4	11.1
Manufacturing		*Manufacturing*	
16 out of 19	42.1	13 out of 19	73.0
Services		*Services*	
10 out of 13	13.1	9 out of 13	12.4

In order to gauge the differences among the three simulations, we compare estimated outputs with observed outputs in the following manner:

- First, we accumulated absolute percent errors, over the simulation period (1983-92). The results are presented in figure 22.6. In this figure, errors are averaged over time and accumulated over industries. The best results were obtained with the Chicago input-output model (CIO) while the national table adjusted to Chicago totals produced forecasts that were superior to those obtained from the randomly generated input-output table.
- Secondly, we accumulated absolute percent errors for each individual industry over the simulated period (see figure 22.7). In this figure, we compare the results from NIO and CIO.[7] It is clear that, for most industries, CIO provides better estimates. The comparisons are summarized in table 22.3.

The first column of Table 22.3 records the number of industries for which the forecasting error derived with NIO exceeds the forecasting error with CIO. Similar information is recorded in the third column for the comparison between CIO and the randomly generated coefficients. In the second and fourth columns, the averaged absolute percent differences are recorded for both sets of paired comparisons.

These results suggest that the differences in the construction of input-output tables translate into differences over the forecast period. Within the sectors, the manufacturing sector exhibits the greatest difference; here the survey-based input-output table predicts better by 42 percent over the table constructed using the national coefficients and over 73 percent in comparison to the randomly generated tables. This is not surprising since the manufacturing component of CIO was derived from

7 A similar figure for RIO was omitted because it does not convey new information; a summary of the comparisons is provided in table 1.

aggregations of individual establishment-level data. On the other hand, the differences in the nonmanufacturing sectors are smaller than those observed in manufacturing.

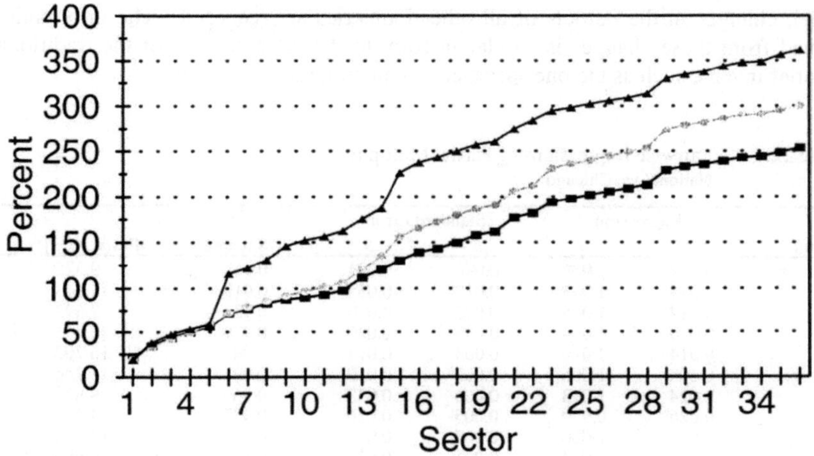

Figure 22.6 Forecasted Output Average Absolute Cumulative Error, 1983-1992

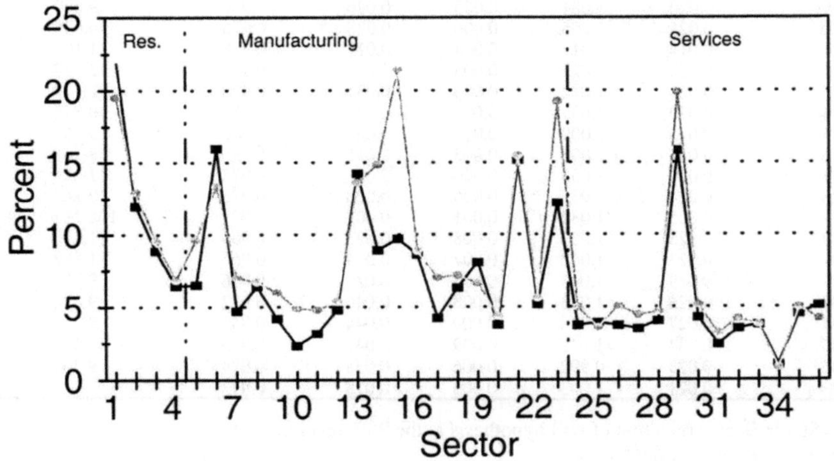

Figure 22.7 Cumulative Absolute Percent Error by Sector, 1983-1992

Impact Analysis The second set of experiments is devoted to impact analysis. In the forecast analysis, we allowed the entire set of exogenous variables to vary over time. In the impact analysis, we fix all exogenous variables for the year in which the shock is implemented. Then, we change one exogenous variable, in this case, the export of a given industry, to represent a shock to that sector. Once this shock is entered in the model, changes in the outputs of all other industries are recorded. The information derived from these changes is similar in form to that of a column of the traditional Leontief inverse such as the one specified in equation (22.1).

Table 22.4 Pairwise Regressions of Partial Multipliers
National vs. Chicago

	Regression		Standard Errors			
Sector	*a*	*b*	*a*	*b*	R-Squared	F-Stat [0, 1]*
1	0.022	1.031	0.006	0.034	0.964	9.325
2	0.035	1.093	0.012	0.055	0.919	11.543
3	0.012	1.005	0.003	0.020	0.987	7.593
4	0.020	1.034	0.005	0.026	0.979	12.663
5	0.014	1.020	0.003	0.013	0.995	16.702
6	0.008	1.006	0.002	0.010	0.997	11.786
7	0.024	1.018	0.006	0.033	0.966	9.834
8	0.026	0.979	0.005	0.026	0.976	14.603
9	0.026	1.006	0.005	0.031	0.968	13.240
10	0.019	1.094	0.005	0.023	0.986	26.668
11	0.021	1.094	0.006	0.033	0.970	16.290
12	0.023	1.097	0.006	0.026	0.982	24.296
13	0.006	1.053	0.001	0.008	0.998	41.680
14	0.021	1.017	0.005	0.024	0.982	11.495
15	0.019	1.044	0.005	0.028	0.976	10.665
16	0.024	1.021	0.005	0.030	0.972	12.891
17	0.023	1.209	0.005	0.028	0.982	56.023
18	0.034	1.049	0.008	0.048	0.934	11.332
19	0.020	1.081	0.005	0.026	0.980	19.662
20	0.025	1.055	0.006	0.028	0.976	16.646
21	0.014	1.017	0.004	0.019	0.988	11.102
22	0.023	1.021	0.005	0.029	0.974	12.929
23	0.024	1.022	0.006	0.031	0.970	12.112
24	0.020	1.031	0.005	0.023	0.983	10.835
25	0.015	1.009	0.004	0.021	0.986	9.157
26	0.011	1.008	0.003	0.015	0.993	8.706
27	0.020	1.055	0.006	0.028	0.977	11.674
28	0.024	1.031	0.006	0.028	0.975	10.142
29	0.005	1.082	0.001	0.007	0.999	108.387
30	0.025	1.059	0.008	0.035	0.964	11.440
31	0.023	1.062	0.007	0.034	0.966	11.862
32	0.019	1.015	0.005	0.027	0.976	9.785
33	0.025	1.033	0.008	0.040	0.952	9.026
34	0.027	1.048	0.009	0.044	0.943	9.359
35	0.034	1.045	0.009	0.047	0.935	11.517
36	0.023	0.992	0.006	0.028	0.974	9.364
Ave	0.021	1.043	0.005	0.028	0.973	

*F-Stat indicates rejection of null hypothesis at the 95% level in all cases.
Note: Nation = $a + b$*Chicago.

Each of the 36 sectors was shocked for 1990, representing a 10 percent change over the base case output (see Israilevich *et al.* 1997 for details), and the average impact on all other sectors was recorded. While the choice of 1990 was arbitrary, other benchmark years would have yielded the same qualitative ordering in the pattern of results. Since REIM has a recursive structure of equations, we had to simulate the model for several years; a shock to the model would eventually lose its effect but there is a minimum number of years that should be considered for tracking the effects. In this case, it was decided to use 6 years, but for any greater number of years, the derived multipliers would be practically the same (see Israilevich *et al.* 1997). In essence, the impact from a shock is largely independent of a chosen number of years beyond some minimum value. Of course, with a REIM, the impact is considered to be more diffused in time in contrast to the comparative static nature of the usual Leontief system in which the time path of the shock through the system is not considered (for modifications, see Romanoff and Levine, 1986; McGregor *et al.* 1995).

Table 22.5 Pairwise Regressions of Partial Multipliers
Random vs. Chicago

	Regression		Standard Errors			
Sector	*a*	*b*	*a*	*b*	R-Squared	F-Stat [0, 1]**
1	0.004	0.919	0.005	0.030	0.966	3.838*
2	0.002	0.878	0.010	0.045	0.918	4.884
3	0.015	1.252	0.005	0.027	0.984	63.664
4	-0.001	0.950	0.006	0.033	0.960	1.507*
5	0.010	0.841	0.003	0.013	0.992	80.322
6	0.019	0.973	0.003	0.017	0.989	19.746
7	0.013	0.745	0.003	0.017	0.982	108.565
8	0.011	0.910	0.004	0.019	0.985	11.970
9	0.007	1.382	0.006	0.035	0.979	74.008
10	0.009	0.854	0.004	0.022	0.978	22.575
11	-0.001	0.958	0.006	0.033	0.961	1.078*
12	0.006	0.467	0.002	0.010	0.984	1449.599
13	0.016	0.974	0.003	0.017	0.990	14.231
14	0.006	1.483	0.017	0.079	0.911	22.268
15	0.006	0.886	0.006	0.032	0.957	6.375
16	0.007	0.940	0.005	0.028	0.970	2.363*
17	0.016	1.419	0.006	0.031	0.984	124.116
18	0.009	0.988	0.004	0.022	0.983	2.681*
19	0.010	0.957	0.004	0.019	0.986	4.775
20	0.008	0.899	0.004	0.021	0.982	11.770
21	0.010	0.944	0.004	0.020	0.984	5.569
22	0.001	0.991	0.005	0.026	0.977	0.060*
23	0.003	0.991	0.006	0.035	0.960	0.105*
24	0.006	0.806	0.005	0.021	0.978	46.249
25	0.009	0.977	0.004	0.022	0.984	2.700*
26	0.012	0.851	0.004	0.020	0.981	26.926
27	0.010	0.917	0.005	0.024	0.977	6.267
28	0.011	0.796	0.005	0.022	0.975	44.103
29	0.013	0.983	0.004	0.020	0.986	5.684
30	0.013	0.883	0.004	0.019	0.985	19.618
31	0.001	0.878	0.010	0.049	0.905	3.715*
32	0.003	2.106	0.014	0.076	0.957	125.953
33	0.004	0.881	0.006	0.031	0.960	8.389
34	0.007	0.941	0.006	0.029	0.969	2.156*
35	0.008	0.978	0.006	0.031	0.966	0.971*
36	-0.005	0.785	0.014	0.065	0.809	7.540
Ave	0.008	0.983	0.006	0.029	0.967	

* Failed to reject the null hypothesis at the 95% level.
** F-Stat indicates rejection of null hypothesis in 25 of 36 cases.
Note: Random = $a + b$*Chicago.

In this part of the analysis, there is no observed forecast against which we can compare derived results (as it was the case in the forecasting section). Hence, our analysis compares results derived from each of the three tables. For comparison, we form two pairs: the first pair is NIO and CIO, and the second pair is RIO and CIO.

To enable a concise comparison among the three models, we regress the changes in all sectors induced by a shock in one experiment on the comparable changes found in the other experiments. For example, in comparing the simulation results from NIO and CIO, we form the regression:

$$\Delta X_{NIO} = a + b\Delta X_{RIO} \tag{22.16}$$

The results are recorded in tables 22.4 and 22.5.

The maintained hypothesis, H_0, namely that $a=0$ and $b=1$, implies that there are no differences between the partial multipliers derived from both experiments; a similar hypothesis is formed for the comparisons between RIO and CIO. To test the null hypothesis of $B_0 = [0,1]$, we use an F-statistic, calculated as:

$$F = \frac{\left[\left(B^{OLS} - B_0\right)' X'X \left(B^{OLS} - B_0\right)\right]}{2} / \frac{SSE_u}{d.f.},$$

where SSE_u is the sum of squared errors from the pairwise regression and *d.f.* are the degrees of freedom. For both experiments, H_0 was strongly rejected. In essence, the choice of tables provides significantly different results; however, unlike the case of the forecast experiment, no preference ordering can be provided in terms of which set of tables provides the better fit. All we are able to state is that the observed differences are not due to chance.

Finally, we should note that Coomes *et. al.* (1991) show that employment adjusted by input-output coefficients have significant regression coefficients for 10 out of 28 industries. We show, similarly, that input-output coefficients matter for forecasting purposes. Coomes *et al.* (1991) show that the substitution of national coefficients instead of regional coefficients changes regression coefficients for input-output adjusted employment figures in small increments, which, however, "... result in rather large differences in impact multipliers between models." Again, these results are similar to our impact analysis differences. In the present study, the majority of industries have significant intercept but insignificant slope; this result may be due to the deficiencies of the location quotient methodology. The results indicate that the overall level of output prediction by NIO is higher (lower) than the corresponding value predicted by CIO (table 22.4). Obviously, alternative methodologies, such as the estimation of input coefficients using regional purchase coefficients, could have different results. The sensitivity of the model for impact analysis to changes in input-output coefficients is clearly demonstrated by tables 22.4 and 22.5.

22.5 Evaluation

The original formulation of the MPSM system (Conway, 1990, 1991) equilibrates outputs demanded by both intermediate and final sectors with the supply of output. Hence, to draw on Takayama (1985), the dynamic output adjustment equation for this system of markets can be presented as:

$$\dot{q} = \tilde{k}\left[D(q) - S(q)\right] \tag{22.17}$$

where both demand, *D(q)* and supply *S(q)* are expressed as functions of output and k is the speed of adjustment of the market. The process described above may be referred to as an adjustment along the lines of a Marshallian output adjustment process (see Takayama, 1985 p. 295ff).[8] Takayama (1985) noted that there has been some confusion about the differences between Walrasian and Marshallian adjustment processes; he notes that
"... the Marshallian adjustment is better suited (for the case in which) the adjustment of output is explicitly considered. It is important to note that the Marshallian output adjustment process is ... perfectly relevant for a competitive market."

In CREIM, there is an underlying (though not observed) price adjustment process but the operation of the model focuses on the market clearing quantity adjustment mechanisms. Hence, the system shares more of a Marshallian character in the terms defined by Takayama (1985). Since regional price differentials for goods and services are generally unavailable, Marshallian equilibrium adjustment is easier to model than a Walrasian process.

The degree of what may be referred to as *Leontief closure* determines the degree to which the input-output multipliers fully capture the interactions in the economy. It is well known that input-output multipliers derived only from the *n x n* interindustry transactions table will yield lower multipliers than those derived from an *(n+1) x (n+1)* system such as would be the case in which households were made endogenous. In the latter case, the feedback effects derived from increases in wages and salaries and their expenditures are accounted for in this expanded system. In the MCGE case, where the coefficients are derived, the completeness of information is judged by the *A* matrix not the Leontief inverse; the derived matrix is a static (annual) representation of the interactions that is based on all the interactions modeled in CREIM. The derived input coefficient matrix corresponds to the output of *n* sectors of the economy while the number of variables in CREIM is about five times the number of sectors. Hence, the derived input coefficients may be considered to be analogous to those associated with a Type I multiplier. We recognize that the derived system is, in this sense, incomplete but our main interest is in the properties of the derived tables within the context of MCGE and not the precision of these tables. The correspondence between the derived tables and observed tables is beyond the scope of this chapter.

Hence, the derivation of the input-output coefficients in this chapter is derived from a non-traditional approach and this represents the most unusual and innovative aspects of the work. In this chapter, we derive the matrix B_n, associated with the

[8] As Takayama (1985) notes, the Walrasian equilibrium system would solve $\dot{p} = k\left[D(p) - S(p)\right]$ where demand and supply are functions of prices, *p*.

output of n sectors; by deriving numeric derivatives with respect to other variables, we could potentially form a B_{n+k} matrix where $(n+k)$ is the total number of variables in CREIM. Hence, A_n is derived (from B_n) by assuming that the derivatives represented by $B_{k,\bullet}$ rows and $B_{\bullet,k}$ columns are all zero. However, the process is not easily tractable and it is often unclear how to include this system of numeric derivatives into the form of the traditional Leontief inverse. For example, changes in demographic variables, in respect to an output shock, would not easily place itself in the form of the traditional Leontief matrix.

The results indicate that when the system is used in a forecast mode, the differences appear to be pronounced. Since only the set of coefficients for the manufacturing sectors are fully observed in Chicago, the corresponding input-output coefficients are more independent of those derived from adjustments of the corresponding national coefficients. As a result, the forecasts for these sectors were shown to be particularly sensitive to the choice of input-output tables. In essence, the results provide a different perspective to the one advanced by Drake (1976) and Katz and Burford (1985). However, a word of caution should be interjected here.

The differences in the partial, static multipliers associated with impact analysis reveal significant variations as well. In this regard, the results parallel most strongly the earlier experiments by Hewings (1977). The next step would be to promote a similar inquiry in a full forecasting context and to link this work with some of the new developments proposed by Sonis and Hewings (1989, 1992) in the context of the specification of a field of influence of change. Here attention would be focused on the sources of error or change generated by individual coefficients rather than on the source of differences generated by differently constructed tables *in toto*.

Finally, the analysis needs to be extended to test the sensitivity to alternative closures and alternative national variable forecasts. In both model formulations, the input-output system plays an important role that affects the quality and reliability of the model results. However, the degree to which the results are affected by variations in input-output data cannot be divorced from the quality of data and model assumptions that are associated with the rest of the system. The recent issues raised by Israilevich (1998) point to the need to articulate more thoroughly the assumptions implicit in the use of input-output formulations in general equilibrium models, especially under shocked conditions. The difference in focus of the two approaches, WCGE and MCGE, suggest the need for some careful evaluation of the potential mapping between the two systems in an analytical sense. With the advent of dynamic WCGE models and more complete specification of MCGE models (especially with reference to capital markets), one might anticipate a greater convergence in form over the next decade; it is unlikely that this will evolve towards a common modeling base but rather a greater ability to move between the two systems.

References

Batten, D. 1982. "The International Linkages Between National And Regional Input-Output Models." *International Regional Science Review*, 7, 53-68.

Conway, R.S. 1990. "The Washington Projection and Simulation Model: ten years of experience with a regional interindustry econometric model." *International Regional Science Review*, 13, 141-165.

Coomes, P., D. Olson, and D. Glennon. 1991. "The interindustry employment demand variable: an extension of the I-SAMIS technique for linking input-output and econometric models." *Environment and Planning A*, 23, 1063-1068.

Despotakis, K. A. and A.C. Fisher. 1988. "Energy In A Regional Economy: A Computable General Equilibrium Model For California." *Journal of Environmental Economics and Management*, 15, 313-330.

Dixon, P. B., B.R. Parmenter, J. Sutton, and D.P. Vincent. 1982. *ORANI: A Multisectoral Model Of The Australian Economy*. Amsterdam, North-Holland.

Drake, R.L. 1976. "A short-cut to estimates of regional input-output multipliers: methodology and evaluation." *International Regional Science Review* 1, 1-17.

Gazel, R. C. 1994. *Regional and Interregional Economic Effects of the Free Trade Agreement Between the US and Canada*. Unpublished doctoral dissertation. University of Illinois at Urbana-Champaign.

Gazel, R.C., G.J.D. Hewings and M. Sonis. 1996 "Trade, sensitivity and feedbacks: interregional impacts of the US-Canada Free Trade Agreement." In J.C.J.M. van den Bergh, P. Nijkamp and P. Rietveld, eds. *Recent Advances in Spatial Equilibrium Modeling*. Heidelberg, Springer-Verlag.

Guccione, A., W.J. Gillen, P.D. Blair, and R.E. Miller. 1988. "Interregional feedbacks in input-output models: the least upper bound." *Journal of Regional Science* 28, 397-404.

Haddad, E.A. 1999. *Regional Inequality and Structural Changes: lessons from the Brazilian Experience*. Brookfield, VT, Ashgate.

Haddad, E. A. and G.J.D. Hewings. 1997. "The Theoretical Specification of B-MARIA." *Discussion Paper 97-T-5*. Regional Economics Applications Laboratory, University of Illinois at Urbana-Champaign.

Harrigan, F., P. McGregor, N. Dourmashkin, K. Swales and Y.P. Yin. 1991. "The sensitivity of output multipliers to alternative technology and factor market assumptions: a computable general equilibrium analysis." In J.H.Ll. Dewhurst, G.J.D. Hewings, R.C. Jensen, eds. *Regional Input-Output Modeling: New Developments and Interpretations*. Aldershot, Avebury. pp. 210-228.

Harrigan, F.J. 1982. "The estimation of input-output type output multipliers when no input-output model exists: a comment." *Journal of Regional Science* 22, 375-381.

Hewings, G.J.D. 1977. "Evaluating the possibilities for exchanging regional input-output coefficients." *Environment and Planning A*, 9, 927-944.

Hewings, G.J.D. 1984. "The role of prior information in updating regional input-output models." *Socio-Economic Planning Sciences*, 18, 319-336.

Hewings, G.J.D., and R.C. Jensen. 1986. "Regional, interregional and multiregional input-output analysis." In P. Nijkamp and E.S. Mills, eds. *Handbook of Regional and Urban Economics*. Amsterdam, North-Holland. pp. 295-355.

Hudson, E.A., and D.W. Jorgenson. 1974. "US energy policy and economic growth: 1975-2000." *Bell Journal of Economics*, 5, 461-514.

Hulu, E. and G.J.D. Hewings. 1993. "The development and use of interregional input-output models for Indonesia under conditions of limited information." *Review of Urban and Regional Development Studies*, 5, 135-153

Israilevich, P.R. 1991. "The construction of input-output coefficients with flexible functional forms." In J.H.Ll. Dewhurst, G.J.D. Hewings, R.C. Jensen, eds. *Regional Input-Output Modeling: New Developments and Interpretations*. Aldershot, Avebury. pp. 98-117.

Israilevich, P.R. (1998) "Frame Shifting in Regional General Equilibrium Models," *Discussion Paper* 98-T-6, Regional Economics Applications Laboratory, University of Illinois, Urbana. [Chapter 21 in this volume is a modified version of this paper].

Israilevich P.R., and R. Mahidhara. 1991. "Hog butchers no longer: 20 years of employment change in metropolitan Chicago." *Economic Perspectives* (Federal Reserve Bank of Chicago) 15, 2-13.

Israilevich, P.R., G.J.D. Hewings, G.R. Schindler and R. Mahidhara. 1996. "The choice of input-output table embedded in regional econometric input-output models." *Papers in Regional Science*, 75, 103-119.

Israilevich, P.R., G.J.D. Hewings, M. Sonis, and G.R. Schindler. 1997. "Forecasting Structural Change with a Regional Econometric Input-Output Model." *Journal of Regional Science*, 37, 565-90

Jensen, R.C. 1980. "The concept of accuracy in input-output." *International Regional Science Review*, 5, 139-154.

Katz J.L., and R.L. Burford. 1985. "Shortcut formulas for output, income and employment multipliers." *The Annals of Regional Science*, 19, 61-76.

Ko, S. 1985. *A Regional Computable General Equilibrium Model For Korea*. Unpublished doctoral dissertation. University of Illinois at Urbana-Champaign.

Koh, Y., D.F. Schreiner and H. Shin, H. 1993. "Comparisons Of Regional Fixed Price And General Equilibrium Models." *Regional Science Perspectives*, 23, 33-80.

Kraybill, D.S. 1991. "Multiregional computable general equilibrium models: an introduction and survey." Unpublished paper, Department of Agricultural and Applied Economics, University of Georgia.

Leontief, W. and A. Strout. 1963. "Multiregional Input-Output Analysis." In T. Barna, ed. *Structural Interdependence and Economic Development*. London, MacMillan.

McGregor, P.G., J.K. Swales, and Y.P. Yin. 1995. "Input-output analysis, labour scarcity and relative price endogeneity: aggregate demand disturbances in a *flex-price* Leontief system." *Economic Systems Research*, 7, 189-208.

McGregor, P.G., J.K. Swales, and Y.P. Yin. 1999. "Spillover and Feedback Effects in General Equilibrium Interregional Models of the National Economy: A Requiem for Interregional Input-Output?" In G.J.D. Hewings, M. Sonis, M. Madden and Y. Kimura eds. *Understanding and Interpreting Economic Structure* Heidelberg, Springer-Verlag.

Miller, R.E. 1986. Upper bounds on the sizes of interregional feedbacks in multiregional input-output models. *Journal of Regional Science* 26, 285-306.

Naqvi, F. and M.W. Peter. 1996. "A Multiregional, Multisectoral Model of The Australian Economy With An Illustrative Application." *Australian Economic Papers*, 35, 94-113.

Peter, M.W. 1997. "Notes on comparative Static closures for MONASH-MRF." Unpublished paper, Monash University, Victoria, Australia.

Peter, M.W., S.H. Han, G.A. Meagher, and F. Naqvi. 1996a. "The Database Of MONASH-MRF. Mimeo, IMPACT Project, Monash University, Victoria, Australia.

Phibbs P.J., and A.J. Holsman. 1981. "An evaluation of the Burford and Katz short cut technique for deriving input-output multipliers." *The Annals of Regional Science*, 15, 11-19.

Romanoff, E., and S.H. Levine. 1986. "Capacity limitations, inventory and time-phased production in the sequential interindustry model." *Papers of the Regional Science* Association, 59, 73-91.

Round, J.I. 1978. "An interregional input-output approach to the evaluation of nonsurvey methods." *Journal of Regional Science*, 18, 179-194.

Round, J.I. 1983. "Nonsurvey techniques: a critical review of the theory and the evidence." *International Regional Science Review*, 8, 189-212.

Shoven, J. B. and J. Whalley. 1984. "Applied General-Equilibrium Models Of Taxation And International Trade: An Introduction And Survey" *Journal of Economic Literature*, 22, 1007-1051.

Sonis, M., and G.J.D. Hewings. 1989. "Error and sensitivity input-output analysis: a new approach." In R.E. Miller, K.R. Polenske, A.Z. Rose, eds. *Frontiers of Input-Output Analysis*. New York, Oxford University Press. pp. 232-244.

Sonis, M., and G.J.D. Hewings. 1992. "Coefficient change in input-output models: theory and applications." *Economic Systems Research*, 4, 110-121.

Stevens, B.H., and G.A. Trainer. 1976. "The generation of errors in regional input-output impact models." *Working Paper*. Regional Science Research Institute, Peace Dale, Rhode Island.

Takayama, A. 1985. *Mathematical Economics*. Cambridge, University Press.

Treyz, G.I. 1993. *Regional Economic Modeling*. Boston, Kluwer.

Treyz, G.I., and B.H. Stevens. 1985. "The TFS Modeling Methodology." *Regional Studies*, 19, 547-562.

23 Direct and Indirect Industrial Pollution Generation: A Field of Influence Approach

Oliver Fritz,[1] Michael Sonis[2] and Geoffrey J.D. Hewings[3]

[1] Austrian Institute of Economic Research, P.O. Box 91, A-1103 Vienna, Austria
e-mail: ofritz@wifo.ac.at

[2] Regional Economics Applications Laboratory, University of Illinois and Bar Ilan University, Ramat Gan, Israel
e-mail: sonism@mail.biu.ac.il

[3] Regional Economics Applications Laboratory, University of Illinois, Urbana, Illinois 61801, USA
e-mail: hewings@uiuc.edu

23.1 Introduction

Economic change within regional economies can create significant impacts on a variety of indicators; while attention has been focused on the role that structural change has played in transforming many Midwestern metropolitan and state economies over the last two decades, far too much attention has been directed to one indicator, employment, with the result that some important dimensions of change have been ignored. In the case of the Chicago region, while employment declined by almost 500,000 jobs in manufacturing between 1970 and the early 1990s, this dramatic change was not accompanied by a concomitant decrease in output levels (see Israilevich and Mahidhara, 1990, 1991). In fact, subsequent analysis has revealed that the pattern of transformation is even more complicated, with manufacturing employment declining, manufacturing output increasing slightly and the levels of intermediate transactions declining (see Hewings *et al.* 1998). In this context, it is important that environmental regulations be tailored to address past and projected future structural changes so as to avoid reducing activity levels beyond those necessary to meet air quality targets.

The present chapter offers a new perspective to address some of the problems posed by structural change by focusing on what has happened and is likely to happen in the Chicago region in terms of pollution generation. In any economy, only a small number of the interactions tend to dominate changes in this system over time. In this chapter, the field of influence approach is adopted to identify the changes in the direct coefficients table of an input-output model that created the largest impact on sectoral pollution multipliers. The field of influence approach follows a line of analysis that may be traced to the work of Sherman and Morrison (1949, 1950) with subsequent elaboration by Bullard and Sebald (1977, 1988), Hewings and Romanos (1981), Jackson (1991), Xu and Madden (1991) and West (1981). The formal presentation was revealed in Sonis and Hewings (1989, 1992).

The chapter is organized as follows; in the next section, the field of influence methodology is introduced. Following this exposition, the pollution analysis framework is described prior to an application to the Chicago region. Some summary remarks conclude the chapter.

23.2 The Field of Influence[1]

The condensed form of the solution of the coefficient change problem can be presented in the following manner: let $A=(a_{ij})$ be an *nxn* matrix of direct input coefficients; let $E=(e_{ij})$ be a matrix of incremental changes in the direct input coefficients; let $B=(I-A)^{-1}=(b_{ij})$, $B(E)=(I-A-E)^{-1}$ be the Leontief inverses before and after changes and let *detB*, *detB(E)* be the determinants of the corresponding inverses. Then the following propositions hold:

Proposition 1. The ratio of determinants of the Leontief inverses before and after changes is the polynomial of the incremental changes, e_{ij}, expressed in the following form:

$$Q(E)=\frac{\det B}{\det B(E)}=1-\sum_{i_1 j_1} b_{j_1 i_1} e_{i_1 j_1}+ \\ +\sum_{k=2}^{n}(-1)^k \sum_{\substack{i_r<i_{r+1} \\ j_r \neq j_s}}^{\prime} B_{or}\left[(j_1,i_1),(j_2,i_2),\ldots,(j_k,i_k)\right] e_{i_1 j_1} e_{i_2 j_2} \ldots e_{i_k j_k} \tag{23.1}$$

where:

$B_{or}\left[(j_1,i_1),(j_2,i_2),\ldots,(j_k,i_k)\right]$ is a determinant of order k that includes the components of the Leontief inverse B from the ordered[2] set of columns $i_1,i_2,\ldots,i_k$, and rows $j_1,j_2,\ldots,j_k$. Further, in the sum $\sum^{\prime}$, the products of the changes $e_{i_1 j_1} e_{i_2 j_2} \ldots e_{i_k j_k}$ that differ only by the order of multiplication, are counted only once.

Proposition 2. This provides a fundamental formula between the Leontief matrices in matrix form:

$$B(E)=B+\frac{1}{Q(E)}\left[\sum_{k=1}^{n} \sum_{\substack{i_r \neq i_s \\ j_r<j_{r+1}}} F\left[(j_1,i_1),(j_2,i_2),\ldots,(j_k,i_k)\right] e_{j_1 i_1} \ldots e_{j_k i_k}\right] \tag{23.2}$$

[1] This section draws heavily from Sonis and Hewings (1992)

[2] It should be emphasized that the order of columns and rows in B_{or} is essential.

where the matrix field of influence of order k, $F[(j_1,i_1),(j_2,i_2),...,(j_k,i_k)]$ of the incremental changes $e_{j_1i_1}...e_{j_ki_k}$ includes the components:

$$f_{ij}[(j_1,i_1),(j_2,i_2),...,(j_k,i_k)] = \\ = (-1)^k \begin{vmatrix} b_{i_1j_1} & b_{i_1j_2} & \cdots & b_{i_1j_k} & b_{i_1j} \\ b_{i_2j_1} & b_{i_2j_2} & \cdots & b_{i_2j_k} & b_{i_2j} \\ \vdots & \vdots & \cdots & \vdots & \vdots \\ b_{i_kj_1} & b_{i_kj_2} & \cdots & b_{i_kj_k} & b_{i_kj} \\ b_{ij_1} & b_{ij_2} & \cdots & b_{ij_k} & 0 \end{vmatrix} \qquad i,j=1,...,n \quad . \tag{23.3}$$

Proposition 3. This proposition provides the fine structure of the fields of influence. Initially, two types may be identified, the first order being confined to changes in only one element in the matrix while the second order examines the field of influence associated with changes in two elements. Further, higher order fields can be defined.
(1) The first order field of influence $F[(i,j)]$ of the increment e_{ji} is the matrix generated by a multiplication of the jth column of the Leontief inverse B with its rth row:

$$F[(i,j)] = \begin{pmatrix} b_{1j} \\ b_{2j} \\ \vdots \\ b_{nj} \end{pmatrix} .(b_{i1}b_{i2}...b_{in}) \tag{23.4}$$

Moreover, the first order field of influence includes the components of the gradient of the function, b_{ij} , considered as a scalar function of all components of the matrix, A:

$$F[(i,j)] = \text{grad } b_{ij}(A) \tag{23.5}$$

(here, the pq^{th} component of the gradient is placed in the intersection of the qth row and p^{th} column).
(2) The second order field of influence created from the synergetic interaction between two incremental changes $e_{j_1i_1}$ and $e_{j_2i_2}$ is reduced to the following linear combination of four first order fields of influence:

$$\begin{aligned} F[(i_1,j_1),(i_2,j_2)] = & -b_{i_1j_1}F[(i_2,j_2)] + b_{i_1j_2}F[(i_2,j_1)] \\ & + b_{i_2j_1}F[(i_1,j_2)] - b_{i_2j_2}F[(i_1,j_1)] \end{aligned} \tag{23.6}$$

Obviously, if $i_1 = i_2$ or $j_1 = j_2$, then $F[(i_1,j_1),(i_2,j_2)]$ is a null matrix.
(3) For each $k = 2,3,...,n-1$, the following recurrent formula is true:

$$F\left[\left(i_1,j_1\right),\ldots,\left(i_k,j_k\right)\right]=$$
$$=\frac{1}{k-1}\sum_{s=1}^{k}\sum_{r=1}^{k}(-1)^{s+r+1}b_{j_s i_r}F\left[\left(i_1,j_1\right),\ldots,\left(i_{s-1},j_{r-1}\right),\left(i_{s+1},j_{r+1}\right),\ldots,\left(i_k,j_k\right)\right] \tag{23.7}$$

This formula also provides for the possibility of presenting the field of influence of order k through the use of fields of influence of lesser order, *1,2,...,k-1*. Further, the implication of the above theory provides the basis for the consideration of different, combinations of changes derived from empirical observations about the nature of changes.

These developments will now be related to the notion of inverse importance. The specific applications begin with the initial scheme of Sherman and Morrison (1950); assume the change occurs only in one place, $\left(i_1,j_1\right)$, i.e.,

$$e_{ij}=\begin{cases}e & i=i_1,\ j=j_1\\ 0 & \text{otherwise}\end{cases} \tag{23.8}$$

For each component $b_{ij}\left(e\right)$ of the Leontief inverse *B(E)*, the following Sherman-Morrison formula holds:

$$b_{ij}(e)=b_{ij}+\frac{b_{ii_1}b_{j_1j}e}{1-b_{j_1i_1}e} \tag{23.9}$$

This formula serves as the basis for the direct first-order field of influence $F\left[\left(i_1,j_1\right)\right]$ for the change in location $\left(i_1,j_1\right)$:

$$F\left[\left(i_1,j_1\right)\right]=\begin{pmatrix}b_{1i_1}\\ b_{2i_1}\\ \vdots\\ b_{ni_1}\end{pmatrix}\left(b_{j_11}b_{j_12}\ldots b_{j_1n}\right) \tag{23.10}$$

or in coordinate form:

$$\left\|f_{ij}\left[\left(i_1,j_1\right)\right]\right\|=\left\|b_{ii_1}b_{j_1j}\right\| \tag{23.11}$$

In matrix notation, the Leontief inverse *B(E)* has the following form:

$$B(E)=B+\frac{1}{1-b_{j_1i_1}e}F\left[\left(i_1,j_1\right)\right]e \tag{23.12}$$

Expression (23.9) provides the analytical basis for the notion of inverse important coefficients, namely, the direct input coefficients whose change will create the greatest impact on the rest of the economy (Hewings and Romanos, 1981). In the context of industrial pollution, the interest is not so much on the economy-wide effects of changes in direct input coefficients, but on the effects that these changes will have in terms of pollution generation. The decision rules that identify inverse importance have to be modified to accommodate this purpose.

23.3 The Pollution Analysis Framework

Assume that the economy can be divided into two types of sectors, referred to as polluting and non-polluting; let B_c and B_p denote the Leontief inverses for the non-polluting and polluting sectors respectively, and let B_{cp} and B_{pc} be the Leontief inverses for the interactions between the two sectors such that:

$$B = \left(\begin{array}{c|c} B_c & B_{cp} \\ \hline B_{pc} & B_p \end{array} \right) \tag{23.13}$$

The field of influence, $F(j_1, i_1)$, describing the impact of a change in the element, $a_{i_1 j_1}$ on all elements of the Leontief inverse, can be partitioned in a similar way:

$$F(j_1, i_1) = \left(\begin{array}{c|c} F_c(j_1, i_1) & F_{cp}(j_1, i_1) \\ \hline F_{pc}(j_1, i_1) & F_p(j_1, i_1) \end{array} \right) \tag{23.14}$$

The effects of changes in the element, $a_{i_1 j_1}$, on the elements of the Leontief inverse related to the polluting sector, including B_p and B_{pc} may then be assessed according to the following decision rule:

$$\left|F_{p,pc}\right| = \sum_{i_p j_c} \left|f_{i_p j_c}\right| + \sum_{i_p j_p} \left|f_{i_p j_p}\right| \tag{23.15}$$

where $i_p, j_p = 1, \ldots, n_p$ and $j_c = 1, \ldots, n_c$ are the rows and columns of polluting industries and the columns of the non-polluting industries, respectively. In order to evaluate the impacts in pollution units, F_p and F_{pc} will be premultiplied by a diagonal matrix of direct pollution coefficients. Let F^p be the field of influence in pollution units, then:

$$\left|F^p\right| = \left|\hat{R}F_{p,pc}\right| = \sum_{i_p j_c} \left|r_{i_p} f_{i_p j_c}\right| + \sum_{i_p j_p} \left|r_{i_p} f_{i_p j_p}\right| \tag{23.16}$$

is employed as a decision rule to identify coefficients that are said to be inverse important.

23.4 Application to the Chicago Region

The field of influence approach can be applied to matrices in various units, such as output, employment, income or energy. Two types of fields of influence, based on the 1987 input-output table are computed here; one is based on (23.15) and evaluates the inverse importance of coefficients with respect to the polluting sectors in monetary output terms, while the other field is based on (23.16) and helps to identify pollution inverse important coefficients, i.e., it evaluates potential changes in direct coefficients in pollution units.

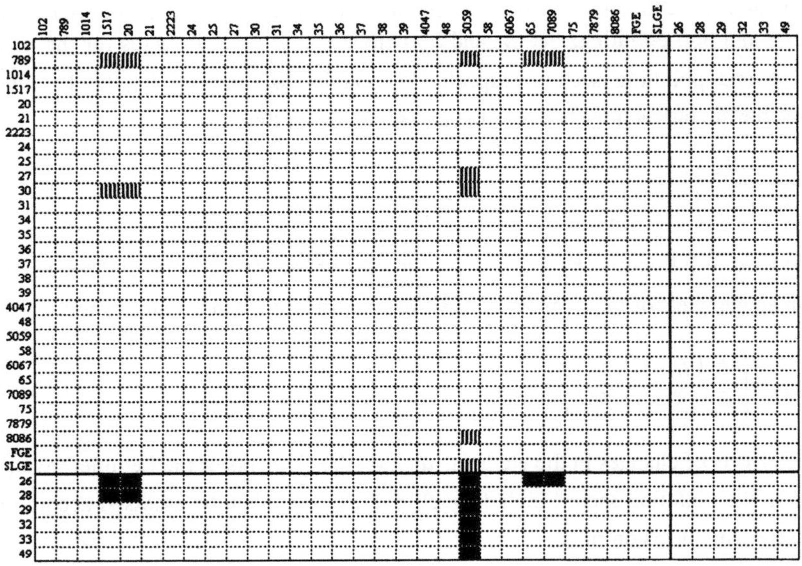

Figure 23.1 Chicago Field of Influence with Respect to Polluting Sectors, *1988*

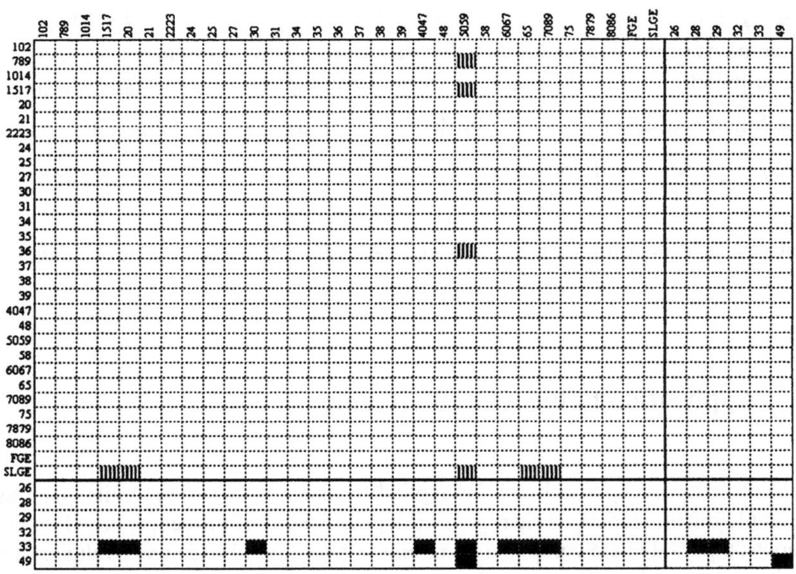

Figure 23.2 Chicago Field of Influence with Respect to Polluting Sectors, *1988* *[pollution units]*

The results appear not to have changed dramatically from earlier periods when similar analysis was conducted; hence, these findings will not be reviewed here. However, since the method of deriving the input-output tables from the regional econometric-input-output model allows for construction of tables for each year in both the historical period and forecast horizon, estimates of changes in direct input coefficients over time can be calculated (for further discussion on the methodology for extracting the coefficients, see Israilevich *et al.*, 1996, 1997). These changes can be evaluated in terms of their impacts on pollution multipliers. In the following section, two issues will be addressed:

in which cells did changes, positive or negative, have the most significant effect on the polluting sector's part of the Leontief inverse (i.e., the sum of all sectoral pollution multipliers?)

which structural changes in A_c were responsible for the increase in shares of indirect pollution multipliers that took place for some non-polluting industries?

The inverse important coefficients of these fields can be seen in figures 23.1 and 23.2; the following characteristics are evident from these results. First, the cells in the submatrices, A_{pc} and A_{pp} are far more important than the cells in other parts of the table. The same result is maintained no matter in which units the fields are evaluated although the dominance is more striking when pollution units are used. Secondly, the field of influence evaluated in monetary terms shows that the wholesale and retail trade sector (SIC 50-59) is the most important in terms of coefficient sensitivity (see Appendix for sector definitions). In addition, a large number of important cells are also located in the paper row (SIC 26). Thirdly, the field evaluated in pollution units reveals the importance of the primary metals sector (SIC 33) as a supplier of inputs to non-polluting industries. This result occurs because of the high direct pollution coefficient in that industry. Compared to other non-polluting industries, wholesale and retail trade contain a larger number of important cells.

The changes in direct coefficients for the period 1975-1988 were assessed based on (23.12) and the derived input-output table for 1975-80. This is acceptable since the trends discussed in the previous section concerning the change of shares in total sectoral pollution multipliers over the period 1975-2010 hold for the period 1975-1988 as well. Figure 23.3 shows the cells with the most important positive changes; these cells are located, for the most part, in section A_c of the table, supporting the earlier findings that some non-polluting sectors experienced an increase in their share of indirect (internal) pollution generation. Most notably, the hotels, personal and business services sectors recorded three cells with important changes. With respect to polluting inputs, only two significant positive changes are identified - self-consumption of chemicals and the use of chemicals in the rubber and plastics sector.

It appears that additional inputs from rubber & plastic, one of the fastest growing sectors in the Chicago economy, are the single most important cause for changes in direct input coefficients that have the tendency to lead to higher emissions. It should be noted, though, that the interpretation of derived regional input-output tables is different from conventional input-output tables. For example, the direct coefficients are essentially regional purchase coefficients whose change depends on both technological changes and changes in the demand for local intermediate goods.

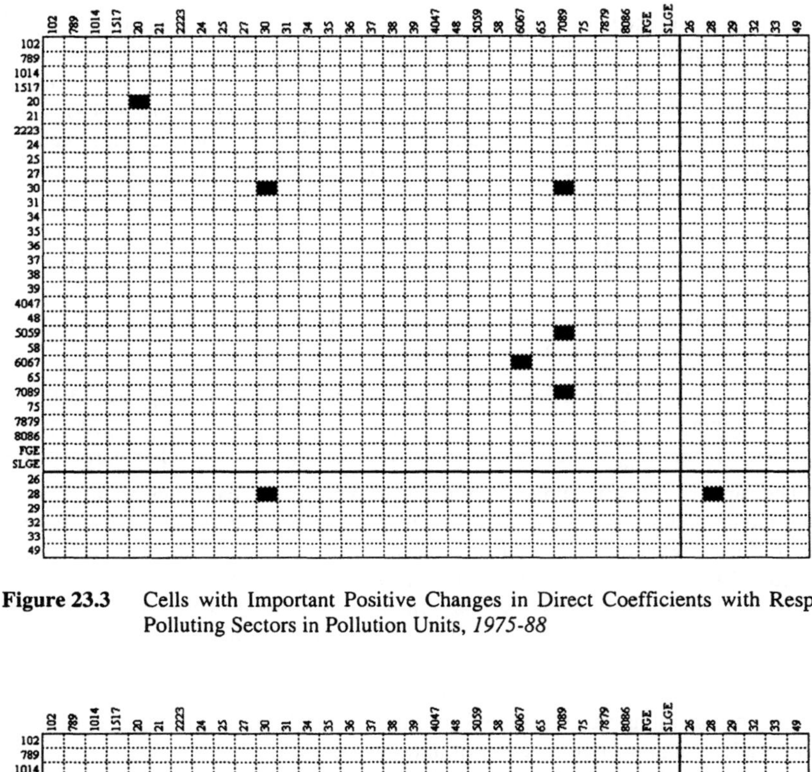

Figure 23.3 Cells with Important Positive Changes in Direct Coefficients with Respect to Polluting Sectors in Pollution Units, *1975-88*

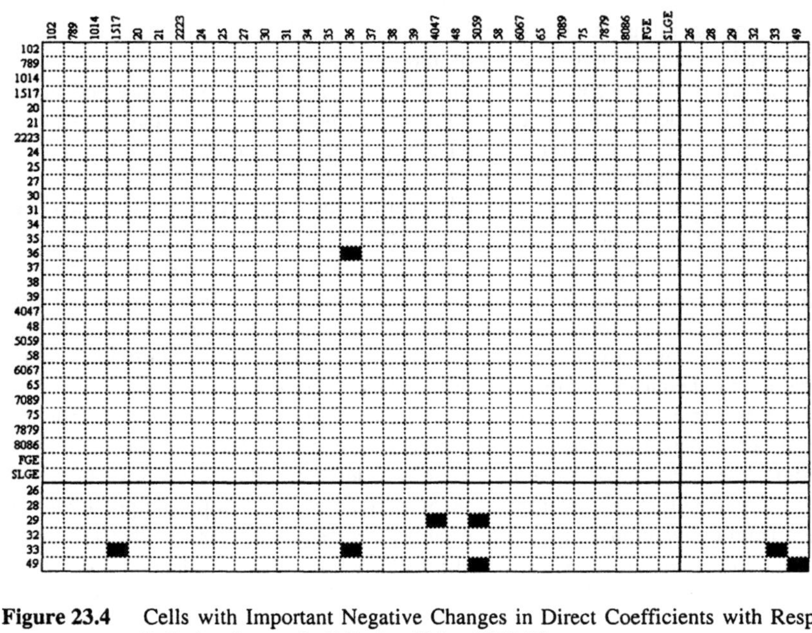

Figure 23.4 Cells with Important Negative Changes in Direct Coefficients with Respect to Polluting Sectors in Pollution Units, *1975-88*

Table 23.1 Positive Changes with Significant Pollution Consequences

Sector	*Nature of Change*
Food & Kindred Products	increase in self inputs
Apparel & Textiles	increase in self inputs
Leather	increase in inputs from rubber & plastic and food & kindred products
Fabricated Metals	increase in inputs from trade and rubber & plastic
Communications	increase in self inputs
Eating and Drinking	increase in self inputs and from food & kindred products
Finance & Insurance	increase in own inputs and from rubber & plastic
Real Estate	increase in own inputs and from finance & insurance, and hotels, personal & business services
Hotels, Personal & Business Services	increase in own inputs, and from rubber & plastic, trade and food & kindred products
Amusements	increase from rubber & plastic and trade
Federal Government Enterprises	increase from rubber & plastic

Turning to structural changes in columns of the sectors that revealed an increase in indirect internal pollution generation, table 23.1 lists the positive changes (increased inputs per unit of output) and the consequences for pollution.

The matrix of negative inverse important changes (figure 23.4) reveals that many of the key cells are located in A_{pc}. This supports the hypothesis that significant changes occurred in direct input coefficients from pollution sectors, lowering the pollution multipliers. Two of the pollution inverse important changes were found in cells in the trade sector, a sector in which many of the pollution inverse important coefficients were found. Only one cell is located in A_c while the remaining cells are distributed in A_{pc} and A_p.

23.5 Conclusions

Even though direct pollution coefficients decline, the share of direct inputs in total pollution multipliers increases, while the share of indirect pollution generation increases for some industries and declines for others. This finding indicates that while reducing their inputs from polluting industries, at least some non-polluting industries in Chicago demand less from other non-polluting industries with relatively large shares of polluting inputs, thus leading to a decrease in the share of indirect pollution generation. In addition, the polluting industries are themselves becoming cleaner with respect to the composition of their intermediate demand. The major impact of structural changes will move the economy along a path that will continue a process of hollowing out (a decrease in internal dependence and a concomitant increase in external trade); this trend, begun in the early 1970s, is forecast to continue over the next two decades (see Hewings *et al.*, 1998)

Nevertheless, total emissions are predicted to increase, unless abatement efforts and technological change reduce direct pollution generation. These changes may be traced to the ongoing and predicted changes in Chicago's sectoral mix of activities; industries with high pollution multipliers, in particular some of the service-oriented sectors, are growing faster than other industries. It should be noted, however, that the change in emissions varies by pollutant, with SO_2 and NO_2 emissions increasing, PM10 and VOC discharges decreasing slightly and CO emissions rather significantly (see Fritz *et al.*, 1996). The findings in the present chapter complement earlier work that noted that the services industries, particularly the trade sectors and hotels, personal and business services, were important indirect sources of air pollution. It is also somewhat ironic that one of the few manufacturing sectors to record both positive output and employment growth in the recent past, rubber and plastic, is one of the major sources of increase in indirect pollution generation in the non-polluting industries.

One of the most important issues could not be addressed, that relating a change in a firm's/sector's input composition in response to environmental regulation vis a vis technological change independent of regulatory restrictions. The interplay between these two actions has important consequences since one option might be to relocate activity without changing environmental emissions (relocating to a region that has spare capacity to absorb pollutants). In this case, the Chicago region moves towards a cleaner structure at the expense of other regions. Whether this relocation may be viewed as welfare enhancing will depend on whether the additional emissions in other regions cause any significant deterioration in air quality in those regions. It is clear that in considering future air quality standards, attention must be paid to the dynamics of structural change so that regions do not end up over-regulating when market forces (independent of environmental regulation) may serve to generate changes that move the region's economy closer to a cleaner frontier.

References

Bullard, C.W., and A.V. Sebald. 1977. "Effects of parametric uncertainty and technological change in input-output models." *Review of Economics and Statistics*, 59, 75-81.

Bullard, C.W., and A.V. Sebald. 1988. "Monte Carlo sensitivity analysis of input-output models." *Review of Economics and Statistics*, 70, 705-12.

Fritz, O.M., M. Sonis, and G.J.D. Hewings. 1996. "Forecasting industrial residual pollution generation in the Chicago region, 1992-2006." *Discussion Paper* 96-T-8, Regional Economics Applications Laboratory, University of Illinois, Urbana.

Hewings, G.J.D. and M.C. Romanos. 1981 "Simulating less developed regional economies under conditions of limited information." *Geographical Analysis*, 13:373-390

Hewings, G.J.D., M. Sonis, J. Guo, P.R. Israilevich, and G.R. Schindler, G.R. (1998) "The hollowing out process in the Chicago economy, 1975-2010." *Geographical Analysis*, 30, 217-233.

Israilevich, P.R. and R. Mahidhara. 1990. "Chicago's economy: twenty years of structural change." *Economic Perspectives*, Federal Reserve Bank of Chicago, 14, 15-23.

Israilevich, P.R. and R. Mahidhara. 1991. "Hog butchers no longer: 20 years of employment change in metropolitan Chicago." *Economic Perspectives* 15, 2-13

Israilevich, P.R., G.J.D. Hewings, G.R. Schindler, and R. Mahidhara. 1996. "The choice of input-output table embedded in regional econometric input-output models." *Papers in Regional Science*, 75, 103-119.

Israilevich, P.R., G.J.D. Hewings, M. Sonis, and G.R. Schindler. 1997. "Forecasting Structural Change with a Regional Econometric Input-Output Model." *Journal of Regional Science*, 37, 565-590.

Jackson, R.W. 1991. "The relative importance of input coefficients and transactions in input-output structure." In J.H.Ll. Dewhurst, G.J.D. Hewings and R.C. Jensen, eds. *Regional Input-Output Modelling*. Aldershot, Avebury. pp. 51-65.

Sherman, J., and W.J. Morrison. 1949. "Adjustment of an inverse matrix corresponding to changes in the elements of a given column or a given row of the original matrix." *Annals of Mathematical Statistics*, 20, 621.

Sherman, J. and W.J. Morrison. 1950. "Adjustment of an inverse matrix corresponding to a change in an element of a given matrix." *Annals of Mathematical Statistics*, 21, 124-127.

Sonis, M., and G.J.D. Hewings. 1989. "Error and sensitivity input-output analysis: a new approach." In R.E. Miller, K.R. Polenske, and A.Z. Rose, eds. *Frontiers of Input-Output Analysis*. New York, Oxford University Press. pp. 232-244

Sonis, M., and G.J.D. Hewings. 1992. "Coefficient change in input-output models: theory and applications." *Economic Systems Research*, 4, 143-57.

West, G.R. 1981. "An efficient approach to the estimation of input-output multipliers." *Environment and Planning A*, 13, 857-67.

Xu, Songling and M. Madden. 1991. "The concept of important coefficient in input-output models." In J.H.Ll. Dewhurst, G.J.D. Hewings and R.C. Jensen, eds. *Regional Input-Output Modelling*. Aldershot, Avebury. pp. 66-97.

Appendix 23

Table 23.A.1 Sector Definitions in the Chicago Model

0102	Agriculture	35	Machinery
0789	Forestry and Fishing	36	Electrical Machinery
1014	Mining	37	Transportation Equipment
1517	Construction	38	Instruments
20	Food & Kindred Products	39	Miscellaneous Manufacturing
21	Tobacco	4047	Transportation
2223	Apparel & Textile	48	Communications
24	Lumber & Wood	49	Utilities
25	Furniture & Fixtures	5059	Wholesale & Retail
26	Paper	58	Finance & Insurance
27	Printing & Publishing	6067	Real Estate
28	Chemicals	65	Hotels, Personal & Business Services
29	Petroleum	7089	Eating & Drinking Establishments
30	Rubber & Plastic	75	Auto Repair
31	Leather	7879	Amusements
32	Stone, Clay & Glass	8086	Health, Educational & Nonprofit
33	Primary Metals	FGE	Federal Government Enterprises
34	Fabricated Metals	SLGE	State & Local Government Enterprises

24 Regional Economic Modeling in Denmark: Construction of an Interregional SAM with Data at High Levels of Disaggregation, Subject to National Constraints

Bjarne Madsen[1] and Chris Jensen-Butler[2]
[1]Local Government Research Institute (AKF), Nyropsgade 37, DK 1602 Copenhagen
e-mail: bm@akf.dk
[2]Department of Economics, University of St. Andrews, Fife KY16 9AL, Scotland, UK
e-mail: cnj@st-and.ac.uk

24.1 Introduction

Philip Israilevich made significant contributions to regional economics and regional science in a number of fields. He is particularly well known for his work on structural change in regional economies (Hewings, *et al.*, 1998, Israilevich, *et al.*, 1997) and for his work on regional economic performance in a decision-making context (Schindler, *et al.*, 1997). He had scientific interests in a related set of issues concerning estimation of regional input-output coefficients, embedded in an accounting framework (Israilevich, *et al.*, 1996), and in the broader context of CGE models (Israilevich 2001). Issues related to the use of survey data and non-survey methods in the determination of input-output coefficients were important themes in his work (Jackson, *et al.*, 1992) and in a 1991 paper (Israilevich and Hewings, 1991) he combines individual establishment-level data with non-survey based regional purchase coefficients to examine the assumption of identity between national and regional technologies underlying use of non-survey methods.

In an unpublished paper (Israilevich and Martins, 1994), he approached the question of product mix and secondary production in the construction of regional input-output tables, an issue largely ignored in regional modeling. In the traditional approach to the question of product mix and secondary production, firms are at the first step allocated to the sector that produces its primary product. On the basis of this sectoral assignment, commodity output mix (the Make matrix) and the commodity input mix (the Use matrix) for all firms belonging to the given sector can be determined. At the second step, the sector-by-sector matrix is derived as the product of the Make and Use coefficient matrices. In a similar manner commodity by commodity input-output matrices can be derived. Israilevich criticized this approach for mixing the input structure for other commodities than the primary product with that of the primary product. He outlined the consequences for multiplier analyses, which become biased because of non-relevant inputs for secondary production.

The solution that he proposed was to establish *pure technology* assumptions (Israilevich and Martins, 1998). In this approach there are two key elements. The first is the use of detailed survey based data, at high levels of disaggregation, for firms that produce only one commodity, in order to estimate commodity inputs for other firms that produce that commodity in addition to others. The second is the construction of aggregate Make and Use tables on the basis of firm level data. The pure technology assumption approach was demonstrated to provide significantly different results from using the traditional approach when applied to regional input-output (commodity by commodity) coefficients for Illinois.

This important contribution raises a central question, namely that of reaching the correct specification of the relationship between production of a given commodity and the demand for intermediate consumption by commodity. In the traditional and pure technology approaches the analytical problem has been divided into two: i) a Make relation (sector by commodity) and ii) a Use relation (commodity by sector). This distinction is also to be found in much regional accounting literature, as the problem of finding the correct distribution of costs of inputs to joint production. A number of different theoretical solutions to the problem can be considered. The practical choice between these models should be based on empirical study, for example an econometric analysis, where firm data on output by commodity are explained by commodity inputs. Israilevich made an important contribution with the pure technology approach, a theoretical model that he subjected to empirical test.

The present contribution continues in the spirit and line of investigation developed by Israilevich. In recent years we have been heavily involved in the construction of an interregional general equilibrium model for Denmark, involving data at a high level of spatial disaggregation. This model builds upon the construction of an interregional SAM where the principle of disaggregation, both in terms of region, sector and commodity is central. Whilst disaggregation to the level of the individual firm has not been undertaken, the analysis comes very close, as the level of disaggregation is very high and Denmark is a small country.

24.2 The Basis of Interregional Modeling for Denmark: A Disaggregated Interregional SAM for Danish Municipalities

24.2.1 Introduction

Since 1996 an expanded set of National Accounts has been developed for each of the 275 municipalities in Denmark, using Social Accounting Matrix (SAM) principles, entitled SAM-K. This work is being undertaken in close co-operation with Statistics Denmark and a number of studies have already employed the social accounting principles involved (for example Jensen-Butler, Madsen and Caspersen, 1998).

The regional accounts in Denmark are conventional national accounts at regional level. The SAM-K represents extensions and improvements to the conventional national accounts at regional level in a number of respects. First, the SAM-K is set up for 275 municipalities instead of 16 counties (regions). Secondly, economic activities in SAM-K are not only accounted for by sectors as in the regional accounts, but also for factors of production (labor force by sex, age and qualification group), institutions (types of families, level of public sector, companies), wants and commodities. One further consequence is that the institutional input-output tables (sector by sector tables) have been replaced by Make matrices (sector by commodity matrix or output matrix) and Use matrices (commodity by sector/component of final demand matrix or input matrix). Thirdly, economic activities and interaction are systematically assigned to their geographical origin and function. Economic activities are assigned either to the place of production, the place of residence or to the place of demand. Economic interactions such as trade, commuting and shopping, are assigned to both origin and destination for interaction, where origin and destination in the case of trade is the place of production and the place of demand. In the regional accounts, activities and interaction were not assigned to geographical origin and destination in a systematic way. Fourthly, relevant activities are accounted for using different price concepts (e.g. basic prices, market prices) and fixed/current prices. Production and trade are accounted for in basic prices whist demand (intermediate consumption private consumption, etc.) is in market/buyers prices. Production activities, commodity and trade balance and demand have been deflated to real terms. In existing regional accounts deflation was more ad hoc and was used to meet the needs of Danish regional models. In SAM-K all variables, for which deflation is relevant, have been deflated.

24.2.2 The One-Region SAM

To illustrate the basic structure of the interregional SAM for Denmark the structure of a one-region SAM without a foreign sector is presented in table 24.1. The SAM is built on principles similar to an input-output table, where revenue flows are to be found on rows and expenditures are to be found in the columns. By definition, the sum of revenues is equal to the sum of expenditures. An example illustrates these accounting principles. The row for Activities (8) shows that production activities gain revenues from sale of commodities ($T_{8,7}$). Total revenue (y_8) is shown in the right hand column. The column for Activities (8) shows total expenditure on factors ($T_{2,8}$), on commodities (Intermediate consumption) ($T_{1,8}$) and on other taxes and subsidies on production ($T_{5,8}$). Total expenditure (y_8') is to be found in the last row. It is by definition true that $y_8 = y_8'$. There is a built-in causal structure in the SAM: considering only flows inside region 1, there is a relation from Activities (8) to Factors (2), $T_{2,8}$, which shows the payment of production activities to factors of production. Next, there is a flow from factors to institutions: to households, $T_{3,2}$ and to companies,$T_{4,2}$. There are also links from households to other institutional sectors (households $T_{3,3}$, government $T_{5,3}$). Thirdly, households satisfy wants ($T_{1,3}$) and flows to capital in the form of financial savings ($T_{6,3}$). Wants are linked to commodities ($T_{7,8}$), which in turn are linked to Activities ($T_{8,7}$), which completes the demand circle. Inside the structure of the SAM for region 1, other causal circuits can also be described.

The elements of the one region SAM can be interpreted in different ways: these are described next.

Government expenditure and revenue in SAM In the SAM there is a representation of transfers between government and different actors: public consumption is included in public sector wants ($T_{1,5}$). Transfers to households and companies are accounted for in $T_{3,5}$ and $T_{4,5}$. On the revenue side, taxes on households and companies are registered in $T_{5,3}$ and $T_{5,4}$. Taxes less subsidies on products is part of the wants account ($T_{5,1}$), whereas other taxes less subsidies on production is part of the activity account ($T_{5,8}$)

Price concepts in SAM As indicated above different price concepts are included in different accounts: In the account for wants, total wants are measured in market prices. Supply of commodities entering the wants account is accounted for in basic prices. Going from market/buyers prices to basic prices involves subtraction of commodity taxes and trade margins, where trade margins also are a part of the commodity account.

Table 24.1 A One-Region SAM for a Closed Economy

				Institutions						
		Wants	Factors	Households	Companies	Governments	Capital	Commodities	Activities	Total
	Wants			$T_{1,3}$		$T_{1,5}$	$T_{1,6}$		$T_{1,8}$	y_1
	Factors								$T_{2,8}$	y_2
Institutions	Households		$T_{3,2}$	$T_{3,3}$	$T_{3,4}$	$T_{3,5}$	$T_{3,6}$			y_3
	Companies		$T_{4,2}$	$T_{4,3}$	$T_{4,4}$	$T_{4,5}$	$T_{4,6}$			y_4
	Governments	$T_{5,1}$	$T_{5,2}$	$T_{5,3}$	$T_{5,4}$	$T_{5,5}$	$T_{5,6}$		$T_{5,8}$	y_5
	Capital			$T_{6,3}$	$T_{6,4}$	$T_{6,5}$				y_6
	Commodities	$T_{7,1}$								y_7
	Activities							$T_{8,7}$		y_8
	Total	y'_1	y'_2	y'_3	y'_4	y'_5	y'_6	y'_7	y'_8	

24.2.3 SAM-K - A Disaggregated, Interregional SAM for Denmark

An interregional SAM is a comprehensive accounting system for transactions between different actors and regions in an economy. Many different categories of actors can be used, but in relation to data construction for the Danish interregional SAM, the following groups are used:

Activities (sectors - 133)
Factors (labor qualification - 7)
Institutions (household types - 12)
Wants (intermediate consumption, 133; private consumption,72; governmental individual consumption 17; governmental collective consumption, 8; gross fixed capital formation,10; and changes in inventories, 7)
Commodities (131)

Each of these actors has an account, showing expenditures (columns) and revenue (rows). The Danish SAM is interregional: in principle, the interregional transactions of each actor are accounted for, as for example, interregional trade. Some 277 local areas are included, 275 municipalities, 1 extra non-existent municipality (used to account for special activities, such as crude oil production) and the island Christiansø, which is a state district outside the municipalities. The foreign sector, representing international trade, commuting, shopping and tourism, consists of one region, the Rest of the World.

The structure of the interregional SAM for Danish municipalities is presented in table 24.2 and those parts of the SAM that have already been constructed and those which will be constructed in near future are indicated. Table 24.2 shows the basic structure of the interregional SAM, but only for the two-region case and with a foreign sector.

In this illustrative interregional SAM consists of two intraregional SAMs (see table 24.1), two interregional matrices showing interactions between region 1 and region 2, and two import and two export matrices. For each actor, there are interregional and international links. Factor income flows from region 1 going to households and companies in region 2 are transferred to region 2 in two steps. First, factor income in region 1 is transferred to the factor account in region 2, before it is distributed to the household sector in region 2. Therefore, commuting is represented as an intermediate calculation that transfers revenues to factor accounts in region 2 ($T_{10,2}$). Examining international interaction, some of the factor income is transferred to institutions (households or companies) abroad ($T_{17,2}$) and some factor income is received from abroad ($T_{2,17}$). For other actors, similar transfers from one account to the same account in another region or to abroad occur.

Table 24.2 An Interregional SAM with Two Regions and a Foreign Sector

		Region 1								Region 2								ROW	TOTAL
		1	2	3	4	5	6	7	8	9	10	11	12	13	14	15	16	17	
Region 1																			
Wants	1			$T_{1,3}$		$T_{1,5}$	$T_{1,6}$		$T_{1,8}$	$T_{1,9}$								$T_{1,17}$	y_1
Factors	2								$T_{2,8}$		$T_{2,10}$							$T_{2,17}$	y_2
Institutions HH	3		$T_{3,2}$	$T_{3,4}$	$T_{3,4}$	$T_{3,5}$	$T_{3,6}$					$T_{3,11}$						$T_{3,17}$	y_3
Institutions CO	4		$T_{4,2}$	$T_{4,3}$	$T_{3,4}$	$T_{4,5}$	$T_{4,6}$						$T_{4,12}$					$T_{4,17}$	y_4
Institutions GOV	5	$T_{5,1}$	$T_{5,2}$	$T_{5,3}$	$T_{5,4}$	$T_{5,5}$	$T_{5,6}$		$T_{5,8}$					$T_{5,13}$				$T_{5,17}$	y_5
Capital	6			$T_{6,3}$	$T_{6,4}$	$T_{6,5}$									$T_{6,14}$			$T_{6,17}$	y_6
Commodities	7	$T_{7,1}$														$T_{7,15}$		$T_{7,17}$	y_7
Activities	8							$T_{8,7}$									$T_{8,16}$	$T_{8,17}$	y_8
Region 2																			
Wants	9	$T_{9,1}$										$T_{9,11}$		$T_{9,13}$	$T_{9,14}$		$T_{9,16}$	$T_{9,17}$	y_9
Factors	10		$T_{10,2}$														$T_{10,16}$	$T_{10,17}$	y_{10}
Institutions HH	11			$T_{11,3}$							$T_{11,10}$	$T_{11,11}$	$T_{11,12}$	$T_{11,13}$				$T_{11,17}$	y_{11}
Institutions CO	12				$T_{12,4}$						$T_{12,10}$	$T_{12,11}$	$T_{12,13}$	$T_{12,13}$	$T_{12,14}$			$T_{12,17}$	y_{12}
Institutions GOV	13					$T_{13,5}$				$T_{13,9}$	$T_{13,10}$	$T_{13,11}$	$T_{13,12}$	$T_{13,13}$	$T_{13,14}$		$T_{13,16}$	$T_{13,17}$	y_{13}
Capital	14						$T_{14,6}$					$T_{14,11}$	$T_{14,12}$	$T_{14,13}$				$T_{14,17}$	y_{14}
Commodities	15							$T_{15,7}$		$T_{15,9}$								$T_{15,17}$	y_{15}
Activities	16								$T_{16,8}$							$T_{16,15}$		$T_{16,17}$	y_{16}
Rest of World	17	$T_{17,1}$	$T_{17,2}$	$T_{17,3}$	$T_{17,4}$	$T_{17,5}$	$T_{17,6}$	$T_{17,7}$	$T_{17,8}$	$T_{17,9}$	$T_{17,10}$	$T_{17,11}$	$T_{17,12}$	$T_{17,13}$	$T_{17,14}$	$T_{17,15}$	$T_{17,16}$		y_{17}
TOTAL		y'_1	y'_2	y'_3	y'_4	y'_5	y'_6	y'_7	y'_8	y'_9	y'_{10}	y'_{11}	y'_{12}	y'_{13}	y'_{14}	y'_{15}	y'_{16}	y'_{17}	

Note: Data in shaded cells are not included in the interregional SAM for Denmark.

Examining the interregional SAM in detail, the elements can be given different interpretations. First taking the interaction part of the SAM, including both the interregional and international interaction, Wants transferred from region 2 ($T_{1,9}$) and from abroad ($T_{1,17}$) to region 1 are shopping activities in region 1, where demand originates from region 2 and abroad. Wants originating from region 1 and going to region 2 ($T_{9,1}$) and abroad ($T_{17,1}$) are shopping going out of region 1. The matrix that can be put together from these eight sub matrices forms an interregional/international shopping matrix ($T_{1,1}$,$T_{9,1}$,$T_{1,9}$,$T_{9,9}$,$T_{17,1}$,$T_{17,9}$,$T_{1,17}$,$T_{9,17}$).

In this context, shopping is broadly defined and includes intermediate consumption (origin: place of production, destination: place of demand) private consumption (divided into local private consumption and tourist expenditure with origin: place of residence, destination: place of demand) public consumption (origin: place of residence, destination: place of demand) investment (origin: place of residence/production, destination: place of demand). Wants are measured in market/buyers prices.

The commodity account shows interregional and international trade: Commodities transferring revenue from region 2 ($T_{7,15}$) and from abroad ($T_{7,17}$) to region 1 are interpreted as export to other regions and foreign export. Import of commodities from region 2 ($T_{15,7}$) and from abroad ($T_{17,7}$) are shown in the commodity account column. The commodity account is measured in basic prices.

The activity account also shows interregional and international transfer of activities: If an activity is divided into units, then the interaction shows how production tasks are transferred from one region to another. Activities are measured in basic prices.

Factor income for mobile factors are transferred from one region to another: For production inward commuting gives jobs/income to the labor force in other regions (T10,2) and countries (T17,2), whereas outward commuting to other regions (T2,10) and abroad (T2,17) gives jobs/income to the labor force in the residence region. Putting the matrices for intra-regional commuting (T2,2 and T10,10) together with the 6 external matrices forms the total commuting matrix. Factor income is defined in factor prices.

Examining the institutional sectors (households, companies and government), interaction between other regions and abroad also occurs. Interregional (T11,3,T12,4 and T13,5) and international (T17,3, T17,4 and T17,5) transfers of institutional income not used in the region (other current transfers and capital transfers) are made to institutional sectors in other regions or abroad. Finally, savings are also transferred to other regions and abroad.

Not all the elements in the ideal interregional SAM presented above are included in the Danish SAM. First, only the household and the government columns and rows are fully included in the Danish SAM, whereas the interaction between companies and other actors is only partly represented. Secondly, the capital account only includes investment, whereas capital accumulation, profit etc. will eventually be included later. Thirdly, interregional and international interaction in activities is non-existent. In the Danish case all production activities are assigned directly to the place of production. Fourthly due to lack of data, interregional and international links for certain actors are excluded (institutional sectors and capital) or they will be included later (international commuting with factor income and shopping with wants). The elements that are not or will not be represented in the Danish SAM either today or in the future are shown as shaded cells in table 24.2.

In addition to lacking elements, there are some important deviations from the interregional SAM as presented by Round (1988). Only a part of the Danish interregional SAM is consistent with the National Accounts for Denmark. The commodity balance system adds up to the commodity balance for Denmark both in fixed and current prices and using different price concepts. However, for the household account, some inconsistency can be identified: The regional household account does not add up to the account for households in the National Accounts for Denmark. The reason for this discrepancy is that the data sources for the institutional account in the National Accounts and for the institutional account in the local SAM are not completely consistent. The government accounts are fully consistent with National Accounts. The supraregional account only includes the Rest of the World - and not central government and indirect taxes. This forced regionalization of the government account makes it possible to evaluate the local economic effects of central government activities.

24.3 The Commodity Balance

24.3.1 Introduction

Commodity balances for Danish municipalities have been constructed at a very disaggregated level. The point of departure for local commodity balances is on the one hand data on local supply (production) and local demand (intermediate consumption, private consumption, investments) and on the other hand, the national commodity balances as represented in the national Make and Use tables.

The earlier Regional-National Accounts were constructed on sector-by-sector principles where the accounting balance between demand and supply was determined by sector. The sectoral supply was the sum of local production, interregional imports and foreign imports. This supply was equated with demand by sector, comprising regional demand, interregional exports and foreign exports, all by sector. Calculation of these regional balances by sector was based upon national sector by sector input-output data. This procedure posed a number of problems. For example, it was unclear which assumptions were actually involved, because assumptions concerning technology in the national input-output table are intertwined with the regional structure of production.

As in the case of other countries, for example Holland, Canada and Finland, the point of departure in Denmark has now become the commodity balance rather than the sector balance, described above. The advantages of this approach are that the information content of local data is better exploited and that to the extent that national data are employed, these data are in pure form and do not involve technology assumptions, as is the case for the sector by sector input-output tables (Madsen and Jensen-Butler, 1999). Finally, the construction of interregional trade data is outlined.

24.3.2 Constructing the Commodity Balance

The commodity balance is determined for the 277 local areas, a system set up in basic prices where supply equals demand in basic prices. The commodity balance also contains information on components of demand and demand in both basic prices and market prices, including data on trade margins and commodity taxes. Therefore the demand side is estimated in two steps: first, demand is converted from components to commodities and, in the second step, from market prices to basic prices. The commodity balance is estimated in both fixed and current prices, as both supply and demand are in both fixed and current prices. The core of the commodity balance in SAM-K is the commodity balance equation for each municipality and each commodity:

Local production + interregional imports + international imports = Supply

Local demand (intermediate consumption + final demand) + interregional exports + international exports = Demand

and

Supply = Demand

The difference between the local and the national commodity balance is that interregional imports and exports enter. In the construction of the local commodity balance, the national commodity balance is used, as the sum of each component over all municipalities is equal to the component at the national level. In the discussion below, initially, interregional export and import are not dealt with. Once the commodity balance has been established, interregional trade is dealt with in a special step. Here a number of issues are addressed, including the difference between mobile and immobile commodities, and the problem of cross hauling. These procedures operate under the constraint that for each commodity the sum of interregional imports must equal the sum of interregional exports.

24.3.3 The Supply Side

Different estimation techniques for the elements in the commodity balance are used. For the local production of commodities, the local supply commodities is estimated using local sectoral values for gross output combined with sector-specific information on the composition of gross output by commodity (the Make matrix).

Gross output by commodity, by sector and by municipality = Gross output by sector and by municipality **x** *national commodity share in the sector*

The data on gross output by sector and by municipality are obtained from Statistics Denmark. Gross output is in basic prices (by definition) and is also in both fixed and current prices. Most data have their origin in register-based data, where the unit of measurement is the individual firm.

Data on the composition of gross output by commodity originate from the national make matrices. Use of the national commodity composition by sector is a somewhat restrictive assumption and work to test the validity of this assumption is on going. Estimation of gross output is undertaken again at very high level of sectoral and commodity disaggregation (133 sectors and 131 commodities).

The basic approach to estimation of international imports at the local level is to multiply local demand for a commodity by a (national) import share (of the aggregated local demand):

International import by commodity by municipality = Local demand by commodity by municipality **x** *national import share by commodity*

Local demand is calculated as the sum of local intermediate and local final demand in basic prices. Again, it is assumed that there is no major deviation between national and local import shares, though obviously, proximity to a national border may have some effect. Work is also in progress to assess the validity of this assumption and again, a high level of disaggregation is used in the estimation (131 commodities).

24.3.4 The Demand Side

Local demand, by municipality, by commodity and in total, is by definition:

Local demand = intermediate consumption+ private consumption expenditure
+ private consumption in membership organization
+ governmental individual consumption expenditure
+ governmental collective consumption expenditure+ gross fixed capital formation
+ changes in inventories

First, demand is estimated in market prices and by sector (intermediate consumption) and by component (private and public consumption and investment). Demand is then converted into demand by commodity in market prices. Finally, market prices are converted to basic prices.

Demand by sector/components These elements of demand have been estimated using a range of techniques combined with national and regional statistics from Statistics Denmark. Intermediate consumption by sector has been estimated by Statistics Denmark as a part of the regional production statistics. These statistics build mainly on register based information at the level of the individual firm.

Private consumption has been estimated using two data sources, one being data on disposable income by municipality and by type of household, which has its origins in register based data at individual level. The other is a household expenditure survey, which has been regionalized. For specific components production statistics have been used (for example housing services). Private consumption has further been divided into local private consumption and tourist consumption. All elements of private consumption have been estimated using highly disaggregated data.

Governmental individual and collective consumption have been estimated using production data for service commodities. It is assumed that demand is immobile, that is, gross output is by definition equal to demand. This also relies on the assumption that demand in basic prices is distributed in same way as demand in market prices.

Gross fixed capital formation is distributed partly using data on gross output and partly using data on intermediate consumption for selected commodities. Construction has been distributed with data on production of the *construction commodity*. Changes in inventories have been regionalized using data on gross output by commodity.

From demand by sector/components to demand by commodities Demand by sector (intermediate consumption) and component (final demand) is transformed into demand by commodity by multiplying demand by national Use tables in market prices.

From demand in market prices to demand in basic prices Demand for commodities in market prices is transformed into demand in basic prices by subtracting retail and wholesaling margins, value-added taxes and commodity taxes. Again, these elements, which are subtracted from market prices, are derived from national level data.

Export to Rest of the World Export to Rest of the World is distributed according to gross output by commodity and by place of production. The basic approach to estimation of international export is to multiply gross output by a national export share:

International export by commodity by municipality = gross output by commodity by municipality **x** *national export share by commodity.*

The national approach in this field also relies on there being no border effect. In addition, special treatment is given to non-mobile commodities (such as dentists and hairdressers), where local demand and supply are, by definition, equal. Adjustments are made for cross-hauling.

24.3.5 Inter- and Intraregional Trade

The point of departure for estimating inter- and intraregional trade is either excess demand or excess supply in relation to the regional commodity balance. By definition, the sum of regional excess demand is equal to the sum of regional excess supply.

Interregional trade balances The elimination of regional excess supply or demand is undertaken in two steps: First, a technical accounting problem must be addressed. This is the problem of immobile commodities - like hairdressing or dentistry. Here, regional demand (at place of demand) must by definition be equal to regional supply (at place of production). This problem is solved by assuming that production data are more dependable than estimated demand, and various techniques are used to bring regional demand into line.

Secondly, excess demand and supply for mobile commodities is an indicator that the region is participating in interregional trade. Different strategies for estimation of trade flows can be adopted. One extreme solution is to assume that a region is exclusively an exporter or an importer of a commodity. Alternatively, assumptions about cross hauling or two-way trade in a commodity can be built in. In the Danish case, an assumption that 10% of regional demand is always imported has been adopted as a working hypothesis on the basis derived from a number of studies. Work is in progress to check the validity of this assumption for individual commodities.

Interregional trade flows Interregional trade flows are estimated using the calculated totals for interregional export (*eloav*) and imports (*mlodv*) by municipality and by commodity. There are alternative approaches. One is to employ entropy maximizing procedures, including as a special case the linear programming solution:

$$emadv = A_a \cdot B_d \cdot eloav \cdot mlodv \cdot e^{-\beta_v c_{v,a,d}}$$

where

emadv is inter- and intramunicipality trade by place of production, *a*, and place of demand, *d*, by commodity, *v*;

$c_{v,a,d}$ are transport costs for commodity *v* from region *a* (supply) to region *d*; (demand)

A_a, B_d are balancing factors defined as:

$$A_a = \left[\sum_d B_d \cdot mlodv \cdot e^{-\beta_v \cdot c_{v,a,d}} \right]^{-1}$$

$$B_d = \left[\sum_a A_a \cdot eloav \cdot e^{-\beta_v \cdot c_{v,a,d}} \right]^{-1}$$

Another alternative is to employ a solution based on a model of monopolistic competition. Work to test the validity of the entropy maximizing procedure and alternative approaches is ongoing.

24.4 Employment, Income, Taxes and Transfers for Factors and Households

In addition to establishing data on commodity balances at regional level, a central part of SAM-K is the data for income, taxes, transfers etc. for activities (sectors), for production factors (labor) and for institutions (households). Even though the bottom-up procedure for creation of these data is more straightforward, it is nevertheless of central importance for the SAM-K, and is described briefly in the following. These data, as with Israilevich's data at firm level, are register-based data at individual level, based on social security system numbers. In the SAM-K data on income comes from the income statistics of Statistics Denmark and enters as part of the factor accounts (both the revenue row and the expenditure column) and institutional accounts (revenue row and expenditure row). Adding to this data at the individual level on employment and unemployment, SAM-K forms a comprehensive database for modeling income and employment in an interregional general equilibrium model (LINE) being developed at the Local Government Research Institute in Copenhagen (Madsen *et al.*, 2001). Information on gross value added by sector is included in the activity accounts or the production statistics. From the income and employment statistics of Statistics Denmark, information on primary income by sector is available. This information enters the factor and institutional accounts and is the source of the data in the factor account on the expenditure side, as well as data for the revenue part of the institutional (household) account. The factor account is by definition related to place of production, whereas the institutional account refers to place of residence. Commuting in income terms is accounted for in the interregional cells in the SAM-K. Adding to this data on employment, commuting, the labor force etc. the income and employment statistics generate a database for modeling income, employment and unemployment in local economies.

24.5 The Links to Israilevich's Work[1]

In his approach to the problem of secondary production and product mix, Israilevich made an important contribution in the combination of data at the level of the individual firm with regional and national macroeconomic aggregate data. His original and stimulating ideas have provided a valuable input to our own work on the same problems. We have approached these problems using the principles of high levels of disaggregation, by sector, by commodity and by region, where the limiting case is the individual firm, coupled together with national level data, used primarily as a consistency constraint. As with

[1] See citations to his work in the Reference list.

Israilevich's work, our approach builds upon the commodity technology assumption, which is made explicit through the application of a Make step and a Use step - both in data construction and in modeling. The advantage of this is that the commodity technology assumption is made explicit, no longer being concealed in sector-by-sector or a commodity-by-commodity input-output model.

Establishing true relationships between inputs and outputs at the commodity level are an important issues in regional economic modeling and Israilevich's ideas, involving the concept of pure technology, is an important contribution. However, in the final analysis what is probably required is econometric analysis of commodity input and output relations based either on firm level data or even aggregate data. Given the practical problems associated with estimation of intermediate demand functions, there is considerable scope for innovation with respect to methodology in order to solve these problems.

References

Hewings, G.J.D., M. Sonis, J. Guo, P.R. Israilevich, and G.R. Schindler. 1998. "The hollowing-out process in the Chicago economy." *Geographical Analysis* 30, 217-233.

Israilevich, P.R. 2001. "Frame shifting in Regional General Equilibrium models." Chapter 21 in this volume.

Israilevich P.R., Hewings G.J.D. 1991. "Regional trade and regional structure: Implications for the construction of regional input-output models." Unpublished manuscript, Regional Economics Applications Laboratory, Urbana, Illinois.

Israilevich P.R., G.J.D. Hewings, G.R. Schindler and R. Mahidhara. 1996. "The choice of an input-output table embedded in regional econometric input-output models." *Papers in Regional Science,* 75, 103-119.

Israilevich P.R., G.J.D. Hewings, M. Sonis and G.R. Schindler. 1997. "Forecasting structural change with a regional econometric input-output model." *Journal of Regional Science* 37, 565-590.

Israilevich P.R. and E.B. Martins. 1994. "Solving the product mix problem in Input-Output: An alternative framework." *Discussion Paper 94-T-4*, Regional Economics Applications Laboratory, Urbana, Illinois.

Jackson R.W., P.R. Israilevich and J.C. Comer. 1992. "A note on the role of survey data and expert opinion in constructing input-output tables." *Papers in Regional Science* 71, 87-93.

Jensen-Butler C.N., B. Madsen and S. Caspersen. 1998. "Rural areas in crisis? The role of the welfare state in income creation, the case of Denmark.". Paper presented to the 45th Annual Meeting of the Regional Science Association International, Santa Fe, New Mexico, November 1998.

Madsen B, and C.N. Jensen-Butler. 1999. "Commodity balance and regional trade: Make and use approaches to interregional modeling." *Economic Systems Research* 11, 277-299.

Madsen, B., C.N. Jensen-Butler, D. Pu and M. Johnson. 2001. "The Line Model." Copenhagen, AKF Forlag.

Round J.L. 1988. "Incorporating the international, regional and spatial dimension into a SAM: Some methods and applications." In: F.J. Harrigan and P.G. McGregor, eds. *Recent Advances in Regional Economic Modeling*. Pion, London.

Schindler G.R., P.R. Israilevich and G.J.D. Hewings. 1997. "Regional economic performance: An integrated approach." *Regional Studies* 31, 131-137.

Subject Index

Note: Page numbers in **bold type** refer to tables.

MIX
Papier aus verantwortungsvollen Quellen
Paper from responsible sources
FSC® C105338

If you have any concerns about our products,
you can contact us on
ProductSafety@springernature.com

In case Publisher is established outside the EU,
the EU authorized representative is:
Springer Nature Customer Service Center GmbH
Europaplatz 3, 69115 Heidelberg, Germany

Printed by Libri Plureos GmbH
in Hamburg, Germany